PENNSYLVANIA COLLEGE OF TECHNOLOGY LIBRARY

5 0608 01154981 2

Doing Business 2011

DATE DUE

Making a Difference for Entrepreneurs

D1384504

A COPUBLICATION OF THE WORLD BANK AND THE INTERNATIONAL FINANCE CORPORATION

Madigan Library
Pennsylvania College
of Technology

One College Avenue
Williamsport, PA 17701-5799

MAR 0 0 2011

MAR 2 2 2011

© 2010 The International Bank for Reconstruction and Development / The World Bank
1818 H Street NW
Washington, DC 20433
Telephone 202-473-1000
Internet www.worldbank.org

All rights reserved.

1 2 3 4 08 07 06 05

A copublication of The World Bank and the International Finance Corporation.

This volume is a product of the staff of the World Bank Group. The findings, interpretations and conclusions expressed in this volume do not necessarily reflect the views of the Executive Directors of the World Bank or the governments they represent. The World Bank does not guarantee the accuracy of the data included in this work.

Rights and Permissions

The material in this publication is copyrighted. Copying and/or transmitting portions or all of this work without permission may be a violation of applicable law. The World Bank encourages dissemination of its work and will normally grant permission to reproduce portions of the work promptly.

For permission to photocopy or reprint any part of this work, please send a request with complete information to the Copyright Clearance Center, Inc., 222 Rosewood Drive, Danvers, MA 01923, USA; telephone 978-750-8400; fax 978-750-4470; Internet www.copyright.com.

All other queries on rights and licenses, including subsidiary rights, should be addressed to the Office of the Publisher, The World Bank, 1818 H Street NW, Washington, DC 20433, USA; fax 202-522-2422; e-mail pubrights@worldbank.org.

Additional copies of *Doing Business 2011: Making a Difference for Entrepreneurs, Doing Business 2010: Reforming through Difficult Times, Doing Business 2009, Doing Business 2008, Doing Business 2007: How to Reform, Doing Business in 2006: Creating Jobs, Doing Business in 2005: Removing Obstacles to Growth* and *Doing Business in 2004: Understanding Regulations* may be purchased at www.doingbusiness.org.

ISBN: 978-0-8213-7960-8
E-ISBN: 978-0-8213-8630-9
DOI: 10.1596/978-0-8213-7960-8
ISSN: 1729-2638

Library of Congress Cataloging-in-Publication data has been applied for.
Printed in the United States

Contents

Doing Business 2011 is the eighth in a series of annual reports investigating the regulations that enhance business activity and those that constrain it. *Doing Business* presents quantitative indicators on business regulations and the protection of property rights that can be compared across 183 economies—from Afghanistan to Zimbabwe—and over time.

Regulations affecting 11 areas of the life of a business are covered: starting a business, dealing with construction permits, registering property, getting credit, protecting investors, paying taxes, trading across borders, enforcing contracts, closing a business, getting electricity and employing workers. The getting electricity and employing workers data are not included in the ranking on the ease of doing business in *Doing Business 2011*.

Data in *Doing Business 2011* are current as of June 1, 2010. The indicators are used to analyze economic outcomes and identify what reforms have worked, where and why.

The methodology for the employing workers indicators changed for *Doing Business 2011*. See Data notes for details.

THE DOING BUSINESS WEBSITE

Current features
News on the *Doing Business* project
http://www.doingbusiness.org

Rankings
How economies rank—from 1 to 183
http://www.doingbusiness.org/Rankings

Doing Business reforms
Short summaries of DB2011 reforms, lists of reformers since DB2004
http://www.doingbusiness.org/Reforms

Historical data
Customized data sets since DB2004
http://www.doingbusiness.org/Custom-Query

Methodology and research
The methodology and research papers underlying *Doing Business*
http://www.doingbusiness.org/Methodology
http://www.doingbusiness.org/Research

Download reports
Access to *Doing Business* reports as well as subnational and regional reports, reform case studies and customized country and regional profiles
http://www.doingbusiness.org/Reports

Subnational and regional projects
Differences in business regulations at the subnational and regional level
http://www.doingbusiness.org/Subnational-Reports

Law library
Online collection of laws and regulations relating to business and gender issues
http://www.doingbusiness.org/Law-library
http://wbl.worldbank.org

Local partners
More than 8,200 specialists in 183 economies who participate in *Doing Business*
http://www.doingbusiness.org/Local-Partners/Doing-Business

Business Planet
Interactive map on the ease of doing business
http://rru.worldbank.org/businessplanet

Preface

A vibrant private sector—with firms making investments, creating jobs and improving productivity—promotes growth and expands opportunities for the poor. In the words of an 18-year-old Ecuadoran in *Voices of the Poor,* a World Bank survey capturing the perspectives of poor people around the world, "First, I would like to have work of any kind." Enabling private sector growth—and ensuring that poor people can participate in its benefits—requires a regulatory environment where new entrants with drive and good ideas, regardless of their gender or ethnic origin, can get started in business and where firms can invest and grow, generating more jobs.

Doing Business 2011 is the eighth in a series of annual reports benchmarking the regulations that enhance business activity and those that constrain it. The report presents quantitative indicators on business regulation and the protection of property rights for 183 economies—from Afghanistan to Zimbabwe. The data are current as of June 2010.

A fundamental premise of *Doing Business* is that economic activity requires good rules—rules that establish and clarify property rights and reduce the cost of resolving disputes; rules that increase the predictability of economic interactions and provide contractual partners with certainty and protection against abuse. The objective is regulations designed to be efficient, accessible to all and simple in their implementation. *Doing Business* gives higher scores in some areas for stronger property rights and investor protections, such as stricter disclosure requirements in related-party transactions.

Doing Business takes the perspective of domestic, primarily smaller companies and measures the regulations applying to them through their life cycle. Economies are ranked on the basis of 9 areas of regulation—for starting a business, dealing with construction permits, registering property, getting credit, protecting investors, paying taxes, trading across borders, enforcing contracts and closing a business. In addition, data are presented for regulations on employing workers and for a set of pilot indicators on getting electricity.

Doing Business is limited in scope. It does not consider the costs and benefits of regulation from the perspective of society as a whole. Nor does it measure all aspects of the business environment that matter to firms and investors or affect the competitiveness of an economy. Its aim is simply to supply business leaders and policy makers with a fact base for informing policy making and to provide open data for research on how business regulations and institutions affect such economic outcomes as productivity, investment, informality, corruption, unemployment and poverty.

Through its indicators, *Doing Business* has tracked changes to business regulation around the world, recording more than 1,500 important improvements since 2004. Against the backdrop of the global financial and economic crisis, policy makers around the world continue to reform business regulation at the level of the firm, in some areas at an even faster pace than before.

These continued efforts prompt questions: What has been the impact? How has business regulation changed around the world—and how have the changes affected firms and economies? *Doing Business 2011* presents new data and findings toward answering these questions. Drawing on a now longer time series, the report introduces a new measure to illustrate how the regulatory environment for business has changed in absolute terms in each economy over the 5 years since *Doing Business 2006* was published. This measure complements the aggregate ranking on the ease of doing business, which benchmarks each economy's current performance on the indicators against that of all other economies in the *Doing Business* sample. Research is also taking advantage of the longer time series, and studies on business regulation reforms in Latin America and Eastern Europe and Central Asia show some promising results. But this is only the beginning. The coming years will be exciting as this growing time series and other emerging data sets allow researchers and policy makers to find out more about what works in business regulation—and how and why.

Since its launch in 2003, *Doing Business* has stimulated debate about policy through its data and benchmarks, both by exposing potential challenges and by identifying where policy makers might look for lessons and good practices. Governments have reported more than 270 business regulation reforms inspired or informed by *Doing Business* since 2003. Most were nested in broader programs of investment climate reform aimed at enhancing economic competitiveness, as in Colombia, Kenya and Liberia. In structuring their reform programs for the business environment, governments use multiple data sources and indicators. And reformers respond to many stakeholders and interest groups, all of whom bring important issues and concerns to the debate. World Bank Group dialogue with governments on the investment climate is designed to encourage critical use of the data, sharpening judgment, avoiding a narrow focus on improving *Doing Business* rankings and encouraging broad-based reforms that enhance the investment climate.

Doing Business would not be possible without the expertise and generous input of a network of more than 8,200 local experts, including lawyers, business consultants, accountants, freight forwarders, government officials and other professionals routinely administering or advising on the relevant legal and regulatory requirements in the 183 economies covered. In particular, the *Doing Business* team would like to thank its global contributors: Allen & Overy LLP; Baker & McKenzie; Cleary Gottlieb Steen & Hamilton LLP; Ius Laboris, Alliance of Labor, Employment, Benefits and Pensions Law Firms; KPMG; the Law Society of England and Wales; Lex Mundi, Association of Independent Law Firms; Noronha Advogados; Panalpina; PricewaterhouseCoopers; PricewaterhouseCoopers Legal Services; Russell Bedford International; SDV International Logistics; and Toboc Inc.

The project also benefited throughout the past year from advice and input from governments and policy makers around the world. In particular, the team would like to thank the governments of Burkina Faso, Colombia, the Arab Republic of Egypt, the Republic of Korea, the former Yugoslav Republic of Macedonia, Mexico, Portugal and Rwanda for providing statistical information on the impact of business regulation reforms as well as the more than 60 governments that contributed detailed information on business regulation reforms in 2009/10.

This volume is a product of the staff of the World Bank Group. The team would like to thank all World Bank Group colleagues from the regional departments and networks for their contributions to this effort.

Janamitra Devan
Vice President and Head of Network
Financial & Private Sector Development
The World Bank–International Finance
Corporation

Executive summary

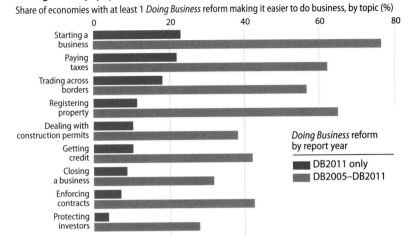

FIGURE 1.1

Easing start-up, payment of taxes and trade most popular in 2009/10

Share of economies with at least 1 *Doing Business* reform making it easier to do business, by topic (%)

Doing Business reform by report year

DB2011 only
DB2005–DB2011

Note: Not all indicators are covered for the full period. Paying taxes, trading across borders, dealing with construction permits and protecting investors were introduced in *Doing Business 2006*.
Source: Doing Business database.

Against the backdrop of the global financial and economic crisis, policy makers around the world took steps in the past year to make it easier for local firms to start up and operate. This is important. Throughout 2009/10 firms around the world felt the repercussions of what began as a financial crisis in mostly high-income economies and then spread as an economic crisis to many more. While some economies have been hit harder than others, how easy or difficult it is to start and run a business, and how efficient courts and insolvency proceedings are, can influence how firms cope with crises and how quickly they can seize new opportunities.

Between June 2009 and May 2010 governments in 117 economies implemented 216 business regulation reforms making it easier to start and operate a business, strengthening transparency and property rights and improving the efficiency of commercial dispute resolution and bankruptcy procedures. More than half those policy changes eased start-up, trade and the payment of taxes (figure 1.1).

Through indicators benchmarking 183 economies, *Doing Business* sheds light on how easy or difficult it is for a local entrepreneur to open and run a small to medium-size business when complying with relevant regulations. It measures and tracks changes in the regulations applying to domestic, primarily smaller companies through their life cycle, from

start-up to closing (box 1.1). The results have stimulated policy debates in more than 80 economies and enabled a growing body of research on how firm-level regulation relates to economic outcomes across economies.[1] A fundamental premise of *Doing Business* is that economic activity requires good rules that are transparent and accessible to all.

Doing Business does not cover all

factors relevant for business. For example, it does not evaluate macroeconomic conditions, infrastructure, workforce skills or security. Nor does it assess market regulation or the strength of financial systems, both key factors in understanding some of the underlying causes of the financial crisis. But where business regulation is transparent and efficient, opportunities are less likely to be based on per-

BOX 1.1

Measuring regulation throughout the life cycle of a local business

This year's aggregate ranking on the ease of doing business is based on indicator sets that measure and benchmark regulations affecting 9 areas in the life cycle of a business: starting a business, dealing with construction permits, registering property, getting credit, protecting investors, paying taxes, trading across borders, enforcing contracts and closing a business. *Doing Business* also looks at regulations on employing workers and, as a new initiative, getting electricity (neither of which is included in this year's aggregate ranking).[1]

Doing Business encompasses 2 types of data and indicators. "Legal scoring indicators," such as those on investor protections and legal rights for borrowers and lenders, provide a measure of legal provisions in the laws and regulations on the books. *Doing Business* gives higher scores in some areas for stronger property rights and investor protections, such as stricter disclosure requirements in related-party transactions. "Time and motion indicators," such as those on starting a business, registering property and dealing with construction permits, measure the efficiency and complexity in achieving a regulatory goal by recording the procedures, time and cost to complete a transaction in accordance with all relevant regulations from the point of view of the entrepreneur. Any interaction of the company with external parties such as government agencies counts as one procedure. Cost estimates are recorded from official fee schedules where these apply. For a detailed explanation of the *Doing Business* methodology, see Data notes.

1. The methodology underlying the employing workers indicators is being refined in consultation with relevant experts and stakeholders. The getting electricity indicators are a pilot data set. (For more detail, see the annexes on these indicator sets.) Aggregate rankings published in *Doing Business 2010* were based on 10 indicator sets and are therefore not comparable. Comparable rankings based on 9 topics for last year along with this year are presented in table 1.2 and on the *Doing Business* website (http://www.doingbusiness.org).

FIGURE 1.2

Seventy-five percent of economies in East Asia and the Pacific reformed business regulation in 2009/10

Share of economies with at least 1 *Doing Business* reform making it easier to do business (%)

Eastern Europe & Central Asia	84
East Asia & Pacific	75
OECD high income	67
South Asia	63
Middle East & North Africa	61
Sub-Saharan Africa	59
Latin America & Caribbean	47

Source: Doing Business database.

sonal connections or special privileges, and more economic activity is likely to take place in the formal economy, where it can be subject to beneficial regulations and taxation. Since 2003, when the *Doing Business* project started, policy makers in more than 75% of the world's economies have made it easier to start a business in the formal sector. A recent study using data collected from company registries in 100 economies over 8 years found that economies with efficient business registration systems have a higher firm entry rate and greater business density on average.[2]

Ultimately this is about people. The economic crisis has made it more important than ever to create new jobs and preserve existing ones. As the number of unemployed people reached 212 million in 2009, 34 million more than at the onset of the crisis in 2007,[3] job creation became a top priority for policy makers around the world. With public budgets tighter as a result of stimulus packages and contracting fiscal revenues, governments must now do more with less. Unleashing the job creation potential of small private enterprises is therefore vital.

Small and medium-size businesses indeed have great potential to create jobs. They account for an estimated 95% of firms and 60–70% of employment in OECD high-income economies and 60–80% of employment in such economies as Chile, China, South Africa and Thai-

land.[4] It makes sense for policy makers to help such businesses grow. Improving their regulatory environment is one way of supporting them.

Consider the story of Bedi Limited, a garment producer in Nakuru, Kenya.[5] After spending 18 months pursuing a trial order for school items from Tesco, one of the largest retail chains in the United Kingdom, Bedi lost out on the chance to become part of its global supply chain. Bedi had everything well planned to meet a delivery date set for July. But the goods were delayed at the port. When they arrived in the United Kingdom in August, it was too late. The back-to-school promotion was over. Changes to regulations and procedures can help improve the overall trade logistics environment, enabling companies like Bedi to capture such growth opportunities.

WHAT WERE THE TRENDS IN 2009/10?

For policy makers seeking to improve the regulatory environment for business, priorities varied across regions this past year.

QUICK RESPONSE TO CRISIS

The global crisis triggered major legal and institutional reforms in 2009/10. Facing rising numbers of insolvencies and debt disputes, 16 economies, mostly in Eastern Europe and Central

Asia and the OECD high-income group, reformed their insolvency regimes, including Belgium, the Czech Republic, Hungary, Japan, the Republic of Korea, Romania, Spain, the United Kingdom and the Baltic states (table 1.1).[6] Particularly in times of economic distress, efficient court and bankruptcy procedures are needed to ensure that assets can be reallocated quickly and do not get stuck in court. Most of the reforms in this area focused on improving or introducing reorganization procedures to ensure that viable firms can continue operating. Before, it was common for insolvent firms in many economies of Eastern Europe and Central Asia to be liquidated even if they were still viable. Not surprisingly, the average recovery rate in the region as calculated by *Doing Business* is 33 cents on the dollar. In OECD high-income economies the average is 69 cents.

Swift action has been the name of the game in Eastern Europe and Central Asia. The region's policy makers have been the most active in implementing business regulation reforms as measured by *Doing Business* since 2004. This past year was no different, with 21 of 25 economies (84%) reforming business regulation. Besides improving insolvency procedures, making it easier for firms to start up and to pay taxes were popular measures—more than a third of the region's economies introduced changes in each of these areas. Less happened in some of the other areas, such as credit information systems. But thanks to 36 reforms in this area since 2004, such

TABLE 1.1

Economies improving the most in each *Doing Business* topic in 2009/10

Starting a business	Peru
Dealing with construction permits	Congo, Dem. Rep.
Registering property	Samoa
Getting credit	Ghana
Protecting investors	Swaziland
Paying taxes	Tunisia
Trading across borders	Peru
Enforcing contracts	Malawi
Closing a business	Czech Republic

Source: Doing Business database.

systems are already better developed. Average coverage is up from 3% of the adult population to 30%.

ECONOMIES IN EAST ASIA AND THE PACIFIC HIT THEIR STRIDE

For the first time in the 8 years of *Doing Business* reports, economies in East Asia and the Pacific were among the most active in making it easier for local firms to do business. Eighteen of 24 economies reformed business regulations and institutions—more than in any other year. The pace of *Doing Business* reforms had been steadily picking up since 2006, when only a third of the region's economies implemented such reforms. In the past year 75% did (figure 1.2).

Emerging-market economies such as Indonesia, Malaysia and Vietnam took the lead, easing start-up, permitting and property registration for small and medium-size firms and improving credit information sharing. Hong Kong SAR (China), after seeing the number of bankruptcy petitions rise from 10,918 in 2007 to 15,784 in 2009, is working on a new reorganization procedure.

The momentum in the region may continue. Recently leaders of the Asia-Pacific Economic Cooperation (APEC) organization launched an initiative aimed at making it easier for small and medium-size companies to do business through systematic peer learning and assistance across economies. The idea is that economies in the region that have benefited from making it easier to do business can now share their experience with others. The Korea Customs Service, for example, estimates that predictable cargo processing times and rapid turnover by ports provide a benefit of some $2 billion annually. Singapore's online registration system for new firms saves businesses an estimated $42 million annually.[7] Using firm surveys, planners identified 5 priority areas for the APEC initiative—starting a business, getting credit, trading across borders, enforcing contracts and dealing with permits. The goal is to improve regulatory performance in those areas as measured by

Doing Business by 25% by 2015. Small Pacific island states, which face special challenges, have also been active, getting key support from donors.

TRADE FACILITATION POPULAR IN AFRICA AND THE MIDDLE EAST

About half of all trade facilitation reforms in 2009/10 took place in Sub-Saharan Africa (with 9) and the Middle East and North Africa (6). Several were motivated by regional integration. Some of these efforts built on existing initiatives such as the Southern African Customs Union. In East Africa single border controls speeded up crossings between Rwanda and Uganda. Different electronic data systems are still used by customs authorities in Kenya, Tanzania and Uganda. But efforts are under way to create a single interface between these systems. Overall, 27 of 46 Sub-Saharan African economies implemented *Doing Business* reforms, 49 in all.

In the Middle East and North Africa 11 of 18 economies implemented business regulation reforms, 22 in all. Six modernized customs procedures and port infrastructure to facilitate trade and align with international standards. These include Bahrain, the Arab Republic of Egypt and the United Arab Emirates.

ELECTRONIC SYSTEMS ON THE RISE AROUND THE GLOBE

In economies around the world, regardless of location and income level, policy makers adopted technology to make it easier to do business, lower transactions costs and increase transparency. In Latin America and the Caribbean, where 47% of economies implemented business regulation reforms in the past year, 23 of the 25 reforms simplified administrative processes. Many did so by introducing online procedures or synchronizing the operations of different agencies through electronic systems. In this way Brazil, Chile, Ecuador and Mexico simplified start-up, Colombia eased construction permitting, and Nicaragua made it easier to trade across borders.

In South Asia, where 5 of 8 econo-

mies introduced changes (7 in all), India continued improvements to its electronic registration system for new firms by allowing online payment of stamp fees. Across Eastern Europe the implementation of European Union regulations encouraging electronic systems triggered such changes as the implementation of electronic customs systems in Latvia and Lithuania.

WHERE IS IT EASIEST TO DO BUSINESS?

Globally, doing business remains easiest in OECD high-income economies. In Sub-Saharan Africa and South Asia entrepreneurs have it hardest and property protections are weakest across the 9 areas of business regulation included in this year's ranking on the ease of doing business (figure 1.3).

Singapore retains the top ranking on the ease of doing business this year, followed by Hong Kong SAR (China), New Zealand, the United Kingdom, the United States, Denmark, Canada, Norway, Ireland and Australia (table 1.2). Change continued at the top. Among the top 25 economies, 18 made it even easier to do business this past year. Within the

FIGURE 1.3

Which regions have the most business-friendly environment in *Doing Business*?

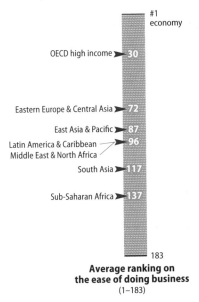

Average ranking on the ease of doing business
(1–183)

Source: Doing Business database.

TABLE 1.2
Rankings on the ease of doing business

DB2011 RANK	DB2010 RANK	ECONOMY	DB2011 REFORMS
1	1	Singapore	0
2	2	Hong Kong SAR, China	2
3	3	New Zealand	1
4	4	United Kingdom	2
5	5	United States	0
6	6	Denmark	2
7	9	Canada	2
8	7	Norway	0
9	8	Ireland	0
10	10	Australia	0
11	12	Saudi Arabia	4
12	13	Georgia	4
13	11	Finland	0
14	18	Sweden	3
15	14	Iceland	0
16	15	Korea, Rep.	1
17	17	Estonia	3
18	19	Japan	1
19	16	Thailand	1
20	20	Mauritius	1
21	23	Malaysia	3
22	21	Germany	1
23	26	Lithuania	5
24	27	Latvia	2
25	22	Belgium	1
26	28	France	0
27	24	Switzerland	0
28	25	Bahrain	1
29	30	Israel	1
30	29	Netherlands	1
31	33	Portugal	2
32	31	Austria	1
33	34	Taiwan, China	2
34	32	South Africa	0
35	41	Mexico	2
36	46	Peru	4
37	35	Cyprus	0
38	36	Macedonia, FYR	2
39	38	Colombia	1
40	37	United Arab Emirates	2
41	40	Slovak Republic	0
42	43	Slovenia	3
43	53	Chile	2
44	47	Kyrgyz Republic	1
45	42	Luxembourg	1
46	52	Hungary	4
47	49	Puerto Rico	0
48	44	Armenia	1
49	48	Spain	3
50	39	Qatar	0
51	51	Bulgaria	2
52	50	Botswana	0
53	45	St. Lucia	0
54	55	Azerbaijan	2
55	58	Tunisia	2
56	54	Romania	2
57	57	Oman	0
58	70	Rwanda	3
59	74	Kazakhstan	4
60	59	Vanuatu	0
61	67	Samoa	1
62	61	Fiji	1
63	82	Czech Republic	2
64	56	Antigua and Barbuda	0
65	60	Turkey	0
66	65	Montenegro	3
67	77	Ghana	2
68	64	Belarus	4
69	68	Namibia	0
70	73	Poland	1
71	66	Tonga	1
72	62	Panama	2
73	63	Mongolia	0
74	69	Kuwait	0
75	72	St. Vincent and the Grenadines	0
76	84	Zambia	3
77	71	Bahamas, The	0
78	88	Vietnam	3
79	78	China	1
80	76	Italy	1
81	79	Jamaica	1
82	81	Albania	1
83	75	Pakistan	1
84	89	Croatia	2
85	96	Maldives	1
86	80	El Salvador	0
87	83	St. Kitts and Nevis	0
88	85	Dominica	0
89	90	Serbia	1
90	87	Moldova	1
91	86	Dominican Republic	0
92	98	Grenada	3
93	91	Kiribati	0
94	99	Egypt, Arab Rep.	2
95	92	Seychelles	1
96	106	Solomon Islands	1
97	95	Trinidad and Tobago	0
98	94	Kenya	2
99	93	Belize	0
100	101	Guyana	3
101	100	Guatemala	0
102	102	Sri Lanka	0
103	108	Papua New Guinea	1
104	103	Ethiopia	1
105	104	Yemen, Rep.	0
106	105	Paraguay	1
107	111	Bangladesh	2
108	123	Marshall Islands	1
109	97	Greece	0
110	110	Bosnia and Herzegovina	2
111	107	Jordan	2
112	117	Brunei Darussalam	3
113	109	Lebanon	1
114	114	Morocco	1
115	113	Argentina	0
116	112	Nepal	0
117	119	Nicaragua	1
118	126	Swaziland	2
119	118	Kosovo	0
120	120	Palau	0
121	115	Indonesia	3
122	129	Uganda	2
123	116	Russian Federation	2
124	122	Uruguay	1
125	121	Costa Rica	0
126	130	Mozambique	1
127	124	Brazil	1
128	125	Tanzania	0
129	131	Iran, Islamic Rep.	3
130	127	Ecuador	1
131	128	Honduras	0
132	142	Cape Verde	3
133	132	Malawi	2
134	135	India	2
135	133	West Bank and Gaza	1
136	136	Algeria	0
137	134	Nigeria	0
138	137	Lesotho	0
139	149	Tajikistan	3
140	138	Madagascar	2
141	139	Micronesia, Fed. Sts.	0
142	140	Bhutan	1
143	143	Sierra Leone	3
144	144	Syrian Arab Republic	3
145	147	Ukraine	3
146	141	Gambia, The	0
147	145	Cambodia	1
148	146	Philippines	2
149	148	Bolivia	0
150	150	Uzbekistan	0
151	154	Burkina Faso	4
152	151	Senegal	0
153	155	Mali	3
154	153	Sudan	0
155	152	Liberia	0
156	158	Gabon	0
157	156	Zimbabwe	3
158	157	Djibouti	0
159	159	Comoros	0
160	162	Togo	0
161	160	Suriname	0
162	163	Haiti	1
163	164	Angola	0
164	161	Equatorial Guinea	0
165	167	Mauritania	0
166	166	Iraq	0
167	165	Afghanistan	0
168	173	Cameroon	1
169	168	Côte d'Ivoire	1
170	172	Benin	1
171	169	Lao PDR	1
172	170	Venezuela, RB	1
173	171	Niger	1
174	174	Timor-Leste	1
175	179	Congo, Dem. Rep.	3
176	175	Guinea-Bissau	1
177	177	Congo, Rep.	1
178	176	São Tomé and Principe	1
179	178	Guinea	0
180	180	Eritrea	0
181	181	Burundi	1
182	182	Central African Republic	0
183	183	Chad	0

Note: The rankings for all economies are benchmarked to June 2010 and reported in the country tables. This year's rankings on the ease of doing business are the average of the economy's rankings on 9 topics (see box 1.1). Last year's rankings, shown in italics, are adjusted: they are based on the same 9 topics and reflect data corrections. The number of business regulation reforms includes all measures making it easier to do business.

Source: Doing Business database.

group of top 25, Sweden improved the most in the ease of doing business, rising from 18 to 14 in the rankings. It reduced the minimum capital requirement for business start-up, streamlined property registration and strengthened investor protections by increasing requirements for corporate disclosure and regulating the approval of transactions between interested parties.

Economies where it is easy for firms to do business often have advanced e-government initiatives. E-government kicked off in the 1980s, and economies with well-developed systems continue to improve them. Hong Kong SAR (China) and Singapore turned their one-stop shops for building permits into online systems in 2008. Denmark just introduced a new computerized land registration system. The United Kingdom recently introduced online filing at commercial courts.

Top-ranking economies also often use risk-based systems to focus their resources where they matter most, such as the supervision of complex building projects. Germany and Singapore are among the 85 economies that have fast-track permit application processes for small commercial buildings.

Finally, these economies tend to hold public servants accountable through performance-based systems. Australia, Singapore and the United States have used performance measures in the judiciary since the late 1990s. Malaysia introduced a performance index for judges in 2009. Case disposal rates are already improving.

MORE WAYS OF TRACKING CHANGE IN BUSINESS REGULATION

Every year *Doing Business* recognizes the 10 economies that improved the most in the ease of doing business in the previous year and introduced policy changes in 3 or more areas. This past year Kazakhstan took the lead (table 1.3). Kazakhstan amended its company law and introduced regulations to streamline business start-up and reduce the minimum capital requirement to 100 tenge ($0.70). It made dealing with construction permits less cumbersome by introducing several new building regulations in 2009, a new one-stop shop for construction-related formalities and a risk-based approach for permit approvals. Traders benefit from improvements to the automated customs information system and risk-based systems. Several trade-related documents, such as the bill of lading, can now be submitted online, and customs declarations can be sent in before the cargo arrives. Modernization efforts, already under way for several years, also include a risk management system to control goods crossing the national border and a modern inspection system (TC-SCAN) at the border crossing point shared with China. As a result, the time to export fell by 8 days, the time to import by 9 days and the number of documents required for trade by 1. Kazakhstan also increased the legal requirements for disclosure in related-party transactions. Thanks to the amendments to its company law, companies must describe transactions involving conflicts of interest in their annual report.

The runner-up this year was Rwanda, followed by Peru, Vietnam, Cape Verde, Tajikistan, Zambia, Hungary, Grenada and Brunei Darussalam.

Yearly movements in rankings can provide some indication of changes in an economy's regulatory environment for firms, but they are always relative. An economy's ranking might change because of developments in other economies. Moreover, year-to-year changes in rankings do not reflect how the business regulatory environment in an economy has changed over time.

To illustrate how the regulatory environment as measured by *Doing Business* has changed within economies over time, this year's report introduces a new measure. The DB change score provides a 5-year measure of how business regulations have changed in 174 economies.[8] It reflects all changes in an economy's

TABLE 1.3

The 10 economies improving the most in the ease of doing business in 2009/10

Economy	Starting a business	Dealing with construction permits	Registering property	Getting credit	Protecting investors	Paying taxes	Trading across borders	Enforcing contracts	Closing a business
Kazakhstan	✔	✔			✔		✔		
Rwanda		✔		✔			✔		
Peru	✔	✔	✔				✔		
Vietnam	✔	✔		✔					
Cape Verde	✔		✔			✔			
Tajikistan	✔				✔	✔			
Zambia	✔						✔	✔	
Hungary		✔	✔			✔			✔
Grenada	✔		✔				✔		
Brunei Darussalam	✔					✔	✔		

Note: Economies are ranked on the number and impact of reforms. First, *Doing Business* selects the economies that implemented reforms making it easier to do business in 3 or more of the 9 topics included in this year's aggregate ranking (see box 1.1). Second, it ranks these economies on the increase in their ranking on the ease of doing business from the previous year using comparable rankings. The larger the improvement, the higher the ranking as a reformer.

Source: Doing Business database.

FIGURE 1.4

In the past 5 years about 85% of economies made it easier to do business

Five-year measure of cumulative change in *Doing Business* indicators between DB2006 and DB2011

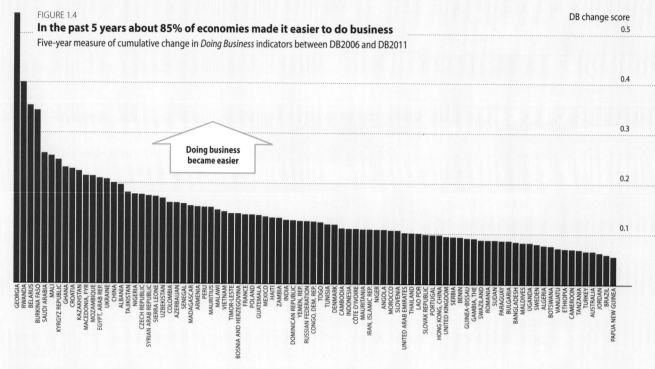

Note: The DB change score illustrates the level of change in the regulatory environment for local entrepreneurs as measured by 9 *Doing Business* indicator sets over a period of 5 years. This year's DB change score ranges from –0.1 to 0.54. More details on how the DB change score is constructed can be found in the Data notes.
Source: Doing Business database.

business regulation as measured by the *Doing Business* indicators—such as a reduction in the time to start a business thanks to a one-stop shop or an increase in the strength of investor protection index thanks to new stock exchange rules that tighten disclosure requirements for related-party transactions. The findings are encouraging: in about 85% of the 174 economies, doing business is now easier for local firms (figure 1.4).

The 10 economies that made the largest strides in making their regulatory environment more favorable to business are Georgia, Rwanda, Belarus, Burkina Faso, Saudi Arabia, Mali, the Kyrgyz Republic, Ghana, Croatia and Kazakhstan. All implemented more than a dozen *Doing Business* reforms over the 5 years. Several—including Georgia, Rwanda, Belarus, Burkina Faso, the Kyrgyz Republic, Croatia and Kazakhstan—have also been recognized as top 10 *Doing Business* reformers in previous years.

Rwanda, for example, was recognized last year. The cumulative improvement over the past 5 years as measured by the DB change score shows that this was

not a one-time effort and that the changes introduced were substantial. Since 2005 Rwanda has implemented 22 business regulation reforms in the areas measured by *Doing Business*. Results show on the ground. In 2005 starting a business in Rwanda took 9 procedures and cost 223% of income per capita. Today entrepreneurs can register a new business in 3 days, paying official fees that amount to 8.9% of income per capita. More than 3,000 entrepreneurs took advantage of the efficient process in 2008, up from an average of 700 annually in previous years. Registering property in 2005 took more than a year (371 days), and the transfer fees amounted to 9.8% of the property value. Today the process takes 2 months and costs 0.4% of the value. A new company law adopted in 2009 strengthened investor protections by requiring greater corporate disclosure, increasing the liability of directors and improving shareholders' access to information.

Others, such as Ghana and Mali, took a steady approach, improving the business environment over several years. Ghana implemented measures in 6 areas.

It created its first credit bureau, computerized the company registry and overhauled its property registration system, moving from a deed to a title registration system. The multiyear reform reduced the time to transfer property from 24 weeks to 5. The state now guarantees the title and its authenticity. Regulatory reforms in Mali picked up in recent years. Key achievements include customs reforms, a new one-stop shop for business start-up and amendments to the civil procedure code in 2009 that strengthened protections for minority shareholders and improved the (still lengthy) court procedures to resolve commercial disputes.

Some large emerging-market economies also made significant changes at a steady pace. China is one. Over several years China introduced 14 policy changes making it easier to do business, affecting 9 areas covered by *Doing Business*. In 2005 a new company law reduced what had been one of the world's highest minimum capital requirements from 1,236% of income per capita to 118%. In 2006 a new credit registry started operating. Today 64% of adults have a

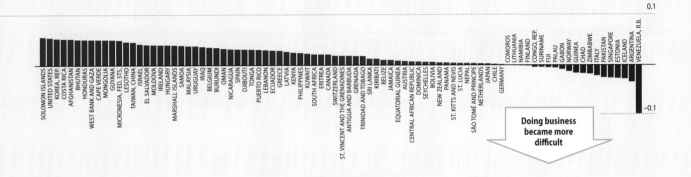

DB change score

0.5

0.4

0.3

0.2

0.1

Doing business became more difficult

-0.1

credit history. In 2007, after 14 years of consultation, a new property rights law came into effect, offering equal protection to public and private property and expanding the range of assets that can be used as collateral.

India implemented 18 business regulation reforms in 7 areas. Many focused on technology—implementing electronic business registration, electronic filing for taxes, an electronic collateral registry and online submission of customs forms and payments. Changes also occurred at the subnational level. In India, as in other large nations, business regulations can vary among states and cities. While *Doing Business* focuses on the largest business city in an economy, it complements its national indicators with subnational studies, recognizing the interest of governments in these variations. According to *Doing Business in India*, 14 of the 17 Indian cities covered in the study implemented changes to ease business start-up, construction permitting and property registration between 2006 and 2009.[9]

The level of change depends not only on the pace of business regulation reform but also on the starting point. For example, Finland or Singapore, with efficient e-government systems in place and strong property rights protections by law, has less room for improvement. Others, such as Italy, implemented several regulatory reforms in areas where results might be seen only in the longer term, such as judiciary or insolvency reforms.

WHAT IS THE EFFECT ON FIRMS, JOBS AND GROWTH?

Rankings and the 5-year measure of cumulative change (DB change score) are still only indicative. Few would doubt the benefit of reducing red tape for business, particularly for small and medium-size businesses. But how do business regulation reforms affect the performance of firms and contribute to jobs and growth? A growing body of empirical research has established a link between the regulatory environment for firms and such outcomes as the level of informality, employment and growth across economies.[10] The broader economic impact of lowering barriers to entry has been especially well researched. But correlation does not mean causality. Other country-specific factors or other changes taking place simultaneously—such as macroeconomic reforms—may also have played a part.

How do we know whether things would have been any different without the regulatory reform? Some studies have been able to test this by investigating variations within a country over time, as when Colombia implemented a bankruptcy reform that streamlined reorganization procedures. Following the reform, viable firms were more likely to be reorganized than liquidated, and firms' recoveries improved.[11] Other studies investigated policy changes that affected only certain firms or groups. Using the unaffected group as a control, they found that reforms easing formal business entry in Colombia, India and Mexico led to an increase in new firm entry and competition.[12] Thanks to simplified municipal registration formalities for firms in Mexico, the number of registered businesses increased by 5%, and employment by 2.8%, in affected industries.

FIGURE 1.5
Eastern Europe and Central Asia setting a strong pace

Share of economies with at least 1 *Doing Business* reform making it easier to do business by *Doing Business* report year (%)

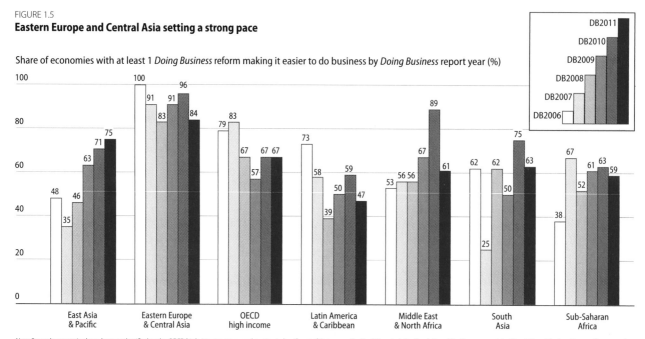

Note: Several economies have been reclassified to the OECD high-income group and are treated as if part of that group for the full period: the Czech Republic, Hungary and the Slovak Republic from Eastern Europe and Central Asia in 2008, and Poland and Slovenia in 2010; and Israel from the Middle East and North Africa in 2010. In addition, 15 additional economies were added to the sample between *Doing Business 2006* and *Doing Business 2011*.

Source: Doing Business database.

Other promising results are emerging. Using panel data from enterprise surveys, new research associates business regulation reforms in Eastern Europe and Central Asia with improved firm performance.[13] While such factors as macroeconomic reforms, technological improvements and firm characteristics may also influence productivity, the results are encouraging.

The region's economies were the most active in improving business regulation over the past 6 years, often in response to new circumstances such as the prospect of joining the European Union or, more recently, the financial crisis (figure 1.5). Some 93% of its economies eased business start-up, and 20 economies established one-stop shops. Starting a business in the region is now almost as easy as it is in OECD high-income economies. Immediate benefits for firms are often cost and time savings. In Georgia a 2009 survey found that the new start-up service center helped businesses save an average of 3.25% of profits—and this is just for registration services. For all businesses served, the direct and indirect savings amounted to $7.2 million.[14]

WHERE ARE THE OPPORTUNITIES IN DEVELOPING ECONOMIES?

More than 1,500 improvements to business regulations have been recorded by *Doing Business* in 183 economies since 2004. Increasingly, firms in developing economies are benefiting. In the past year about 66% of these economies made it easier to do business, up from only 34% of this group 6 years before. Compelling results are starting to show, as illustrated by Rwanda and Ghana, and these results have inspired others.

This is good news, because opportunities for regulatory reform remain. Entrepreneurs and investors in low- and lower-middle-income economies continue to face more bureaucratic formalities and weaker protections of property rights than their counterparts in high-income economies. Exporting, for example, requires 11 documents in the Republic of Congo but only 2 in France. Starting a business still costs 18 times as much in Sub-Saharan Africa as in OECD high-income economies (relative to income per capita). Many businesses in developing economies might simply opt out and remain in the informal sector.

There they lack access to formal business credit and markets, and their employees receive fewer benefits and no protections. Globally, 1.8 billion people are estimated to be employed in the informal sector, more than the 1.2 billion in the formal sector.[15]

While overly complicated procedures can hinder business activity, so can the lack of institutions or regulations that protect property rights, increase transparency and enable entrepreneurs to make effective use of their assets. When institutions such as courts, collateral registries and credit information bureaus are inefficient or missing, the talented poor and entrepreneurs who lack connections, collateral and credit histories are most at risk of losing out.[16] So are women, because institutions and regulations such as credit bureaus and laws on movable collateral support the types of businesses that women typically run—small firms in low-capital-intensive industries in both the formal and the informal sector (box 1.2).[17]

Today only 1.3% of adults in low-income economies are covered by a credit bureau. Many micro, small and medium-size enterprises, which typically have

BOX 1.2
Encouraging women in business

Women make up more than 50% of the world's population but less than 30% of the labor force in some economies. This represents untapped potential. For policy makers seeking to increase women's participation in the economy, a good place to start is to ensure that institutions and laws are accessible to the types of businesses and jobs women currently hold.

Take credit bureaus. With the advent of microfinance institutions in the 1970s, poor women in some parts of the world were able to access credit for the first time. By 2006 more than 3,330 microfinance institutions had reached 133 million clients. Among these clients, 93 million had been in the poorest groups when they took their first loans, and 85% of the poorest were women. But only 42 of 128 credit bureaus in the world cover microfinance institutions, limiting the ability of their borrowers to build a credit history. A new World Bank Group project, *Women, Business and the Law,* looks into discrepancies such as these as well as regulations that explicitly differentiate on the basis of gender.[1]

A recent analysis of existing literature concludes that aspects of the business regulatory environment are estimated to disproportionately affect women in their decision to become an entrepreneur and their performance in running a formal business. Barriers to women's access to finance might drive their concentration in low-capital-intensive industries, which require less funding but also have less potential for growth and development. One possible barrier is that women may have less physical and "reputational" collateral than men.[2]

Women can benefit from laws facilitating the use of movable assets such as equipment or accounts receivable as security for loans. While women often lack legal title to land or buildings that could serve as collateral, they are more likely to have movable assets. In Sri Lanka women commonly hold wealth in the form of gold jewelry. Thankfully, this is accepted by banks as security for loans.[3]

Women often resort to informal credit, which involves high transactions costs. A recent study in Ghana reports that women, to ensure access to credit, invest considerable time in maintaining complex networks of informal credit providers.[4]

Improving firms' access to formal finance has been shown to pay off, by promoting entrepreneurship, innovation, better asset allocation and firm growth.[5] Everyone should be able to benefit, regardless of gender.

1. http://wbl.worldbank.org/.
2. Klapper and Parker (2010).
3. Pal (1997).
4. Schindler (2010).
5. World Bank (2008).

95% of their assets in movable property rather than real estate, cannot use those assets to raise funds to expand their business. But this is not so everywhere. While only 35% of Sub-Saharan African economies have laws encouraging the use of all types of assets as collateral, 71% of East Asian and Pacific and 68% of OECD high-income economies do. Seventy low- and lower-middle-income economies lack centralized collateral registries that tell creditors whether assets are already subject to the security right of another creditor. All this presents an opportunity for changes that can promote the growth of firms and employment.

WHAT'S NEXT?

Doing Business has been measuring business regulation from the perspective of local firms and tracking changes over time since 2003. Since its initiation, the project has introduced 5 new topics and added 50 economies to the sample. In the past year *Doing Business* has been working on 2 indicator sets—a new set on getting electricity and a refined one on employing workers.[18]

IDENTIFYING REGULATORY REFORM POSSIBILITIES IN GETTING ELECTRICITY

According to World Bank surveys of businesses, managers in 108 economies consider the availability and reliability of electricity to be the second most important constraint to their business activity, after access to finance. Studies have shown that poor electricity supply adversely affects the productivity of firms and the investments they make in their productive capacity.[19] But electricity services not only matter to businesses; they also are among the most regulated areas of economic activity. *Doing Business* measures how such regulations affect businesses when getting a new connection. The indicators complement data on access levels that exist outside the *Doing Business* report as well as other data on the availability and reliability of electricity supply and consumption prices. The new data allow objective comparison of the procedures, time and cost to obtain a new electricity connection across a wide range of economies. Some, such as Germany, Iceland and Thailand, perform well: a business with moderate electricity demand can get a connection in 40 days or less. But in the Czech Republic it can take 279 days, in Ukraine 309 and in the Kyrgyz Republic 337.

Analysis of the data presented in the annex on getting electricity sheds some light on both bottlenecks and possible starting points for dialogue on regulatory reform. In 100 of 176 economies connection costs are insufficiently transparent.[20] Utilities present customers with individual budgets rather than clearly regulated capital contribution formulas. This reduces the accountability of

BOX 1.3
Other World Bank indicator sets on business regulations

Women, Business and the Law (http://wbl.worldbank.org/)
Data on legal differentiation on the basis of gender in 128 economies, covering 6 areas

Investing Across Borders (http://iab.worldbank.org/)
Data on laws and regulations affecting foreign direct investment in 87 economies, covering 4 areas

Subnational Doing Business (http://www.doingbusiness.org/Subnational/)
Doing Business data comparing states and cities within economies (41 studies covering 299 cities)

World Bank Enterprise Surveys (http://www.enterprisesurveys.org/)
Business data on more than 100,000 firms in 125 economies, covering a broad range of business environment topics

utilities that provide a critical economic service, exposes customers to potential abuse and might mask excessively high utility cost structures. In many economies it is customers, not the utility, that must take on the complex process of coordinating clearances across multiple government agencies, because opportunities to streamline the coordination between the utility and other agencies are missed. In many middle-income economies customers also face unnecessarily complex procedural steps for fire and wiring safety checks, while some governments in Sub-Saharan Africa and the Middle East and North Africa omit requirements for such checks entirely.

These and other findings suggest that many governments and regulators could ease a critical bottleneck for businesses by encouraging reforms around the electricity connection process. Requiring more transparency in utility connection pricing and encouraging better interagency coordination could be a start.

REFINING THE EMPLOYING WORKERS INDICATORS

Maintaining and creating productive jobs and businesses is a priority for policy makers around the world, particularly in these times. Good labor regulation is flexible enough to help those currently unemployed or working in the informal sector to obtain new jobs in the formal sector. At the same time, it provides adequate protections for those already holding a job, so that their productivity is not stifled. Finding the right balance is no easy task.

To inform policy makers and researchers, *Doing Business* is working to refine the methodology for its employing workers indicators and expand the data set. Based on input from a consultative group of experts and stakeholders, new thresholds are being introduced to recognize minimum levels of protection in line with relevant conventions of the International Labour Organization—those for minimum wage, paid annual leave and the maximum number of working days per week. This provides a framework for balancing worker protection against employment restrictions in the areas covered by the indicators. In addition, new data are being collected on regulations according to length of job tenure (9 months, 1 year, 5 years and 10 years). The annex on employing workers presents initial findings from this work.

INITIATIVES COMPLEMENTING *DOING BUSINESS*

The World Bank Group has introduced additional benchmarking indicator sets that complement the perspectives of *Doing Business* (box 1.3). The *Women, Business and the Law* database, launched in March 2010, for the first time provides objective measures of differential treatment based on gender. *Investing Across Borders,* launched in July 2010, provides measures of business regulations from the perspective of foreign investors. Subnational *Doing Business* reports, introduced in 2004, provide insights into variations within large economies. Other

World Bank Group initiatives provide valuable complementary data based on a different approach. These include the World Bank Enterprise Surveys.

As *Doing Business* continues to measure and track changes to business regulation around the world from the perspective of local firms, these and other data sets provide a rich base for policy makers and researchers alike to continually test and improve their understanding of what works and what does not—and why.

1. Some 656 articles have been published in peer-reviewed academic journals, and about 2,060 working papers are available through Google Scholar (http://scholar.google.com).

2. Klapper, Lewin and Quesada Delgado (2009). *Entry rate* refers to newly registered firms as a percentage of total registered firms. *Business density* is defined as the number of businesses as a percentage of the working-age population (ages 18–65).

3. International Labour Organization (ILO) data.

4. OECD (2004b); ILO and SERCOTEC (2010, p. 12); South Africa, Department of Trade and Industry (2004, p. 18); China, State Administration for Industry and Commerce, http://www.saic.gov.cn/english/; and Ayyagari, Beck and Demirgüç-Kunt (2007).

5. Bedi (2009).

6. In the United Kingdom, for example, 19,077 companies were liquidated in 2009, 22.8% more than in the previous year.

7. World Bank conference, "The Singapore Experience: Ingredients for Successful Nation-Wide eTransformation," Singapore, September 30, 2009.

8. *Doing Business* has tracked regulatory reforms affecting businesses throughout their life cycle—from start-up to closing—in 174 or more economies since 2005. Between 2003 and 2005 *Doing Business* added 5 topics and increased the number of economies covered from 133 to 174. For more information on the motivation for the 5-year measure of cumulative change (DB change score), see About *Doing Business*. For more on how the measure is constructed, see Data notes.

9. World Bank (2009a).

10. For a comprehensive literature review on business start-up regulation as it relates to such economic outcomes as productivity and employment, see Djankov (2009b) and Motta, Oviedo and Santini (2010). See also Djankov, McLiesh and Ramalho (2006). More research can be found on the *Doing Business* website (http://www.doingbusiness.org/).

11. Giné and Love (2006).

12. Aghion and others (2008), Bruhn (2008), Kaplan, Piedra and Seira (2007) and Cardenas and Rozo (2009).

13. Amin and Ramalho (forthcoming). Using data on a panel of about 2,100 firms in 28 economies in Eastern Europe and Central Asia, the authors compare changes in labor productivity over time in reforming and nonreforming economies. The difference in the change in labor productivity between the 2 groups of economies is statistically significant at less than the 5% level. Differences in time-invariant factors such as firm composition or GDP per capita do not affect the results.

14. International Finance Corporation, "IFC Helps Simplify Procedures for Georgian Businesses to Save Time and Resources," accessed September 20, 2010, http://www.ifc.org/.

15. ILO data.

16. World Bank (2008).

17. Chhabra (2003) and Amin (2010).

18. Neither is included in this year's aggregate ranking on the ease of doing business.

19. See, for example, Calderon and Servén (2003), Dollar, Hallward-Driemeier and Mengistae (2005), Reinikka and Svensson (1999) and Eifert (2007). Using firm-level data, Iimi (2008) finds that in Eastern Europe and Central Asia eliminating electricity outages could increase GDP by 0.5–6%.

20. In these economies the fixed connection fee based on publicly available fee schedules represents less than 1% of the total cost of connection.

About *Doing Business*: measuring for impact

Governments committed to the economic health of their country and opportunities for its citizens focus on more than macroeconomic conditions. They also pay attention to the laws, regulations and institutional arrangements that shape daily economic activity.

The global financial crisis has renewed interest in good rules and regulation. In times of recession, effective business regulation and institutions can support economic adjustment. Easy entry and exit of firms, and flexibility in redeploying resources, make it easier to stop doing things for which demand has weakened and to start doing new things. Clarification of property rights and strengthening of market infrastructure (such as credit information and collateral systems) can contribute to confidence as investors and entrepreneurs look to rebuild.

Until recently, however, there were no globally available indicator sets for monitoring such microeconomic factors and analyzing their relevance. The first efforts, in the 1980s, drew on perceptions data from expert or business surveys. Such surveys are useful gauges of economic and policy conditions. But their reliance on perceptions and their incomplete coverage of poor countries constrain their usefulness for analysis.

The *Doing Business* project, initiated 9 years ago, goes one step further. It looks at domestic small and medium-size companies and measures the regulations applying to them through their life cycle. *Doing Business* and the standard cost model initially developed and applied in the Netherlands are, for the present, the only standard tools used across a broad range of jurisdictions to measure the impact of government rule-making on the cost of doing business.[1]

The first *Doing Business* report, published in 2003, covered 5 indicator sets and 133 economies. This year's report covers 11 indicator sets and 183 economies. Nine topics are included in the aggregate ranking on the ease of doing business. The project has benefited from feedback from governments, academics, practitioners and reviewers.[2] The initial goal remains: to provide an objective basis for understanding and improving the regulatory environment for business.

WHAT *DOING BUSINESS* COVERS

Doing Business provides a quantitative measure of regulations for starting a business, dealing with construction permits, registering property, getting credit, protecting investors, paying taxes, trading across borders, enforcing contracts and closing a business—as they apply to domestic small and medium-size enterprises. It also looks at regulations on employing workers as well as a new measure on getting electricity.

A fundamental premise of *Doing Business* is that economic activity requires good rules. These include rules that establish and clarify property rights and reduce the cost of resolving disputes, rules that increase the predictability of economic interactions and rules that provide contractual partners with core protections against abuse. The objective: regulations designed to be efficient in their implementation, to be accessible to all who need to use them and to be simple in their implementation. Accordingly, some *Doing Business* indicators give a higher score for more regulation, such as stricter disclosure requirements in related-party transactions. Some give a higher score for a simplified way of implementing existing regulation, such as completing business start-up formalities in a one-stop shop.

The *Doing Business* project encompasses 2 types of data. The first come from readings of laws and regulations. The second are time and motion indicators that measure the efficiency and complexity in achieving a regulatory goal (such as granting the legal identity of a business). Within the time and motion indicators, cost estimates are recorded from official fee schedules where applicable.[3] Here, *Doing Business* builds on Hernando de Soto's pioneering work in applying the time and motion approach first used by Frederick Taylor to revolutionize the production of the Model T Ford. De Soto used the approach in the 1980s to show the obstacles to setting up a garment factory on the outskirts of Lima.[4]

WHAT *DOING BUSINESS* DOES NOT COVER

Just as important as knowing what *Doing Business* does is to know what it does not do—to understand what limitations must be kept in mind in interpreting the data.

LIMITED IN SCOPE

Doing Business focuses on 11 topics, with the specific aim of measuring the regulation and red tape relevant to the life cycle of a domestic small to medium-size firm. Accordingly:

- *Doing Business* does not measure all aspects of the business environment that matter to firms or investors—or all factors that affect competitiveness. It does not, for example, measure security, macroeconomic stability, corruption, the labor skills of the population, the underlying strength of institutions or the quality of infrastructure.[5] Nor does it focus on regulations specific to foreign investment.
- *Doing Business* does not assess the strength of the financial system or market regulations, both important factors in understanding some of the underlying causes of the global financial crisis.
- *Doing Business* does not cover all regulations, or all regulatory goals, in any economy. As economies and technology advance, more areas of economic activity are being regulated. For example, the European Union's body of laws (*acquis*) has now grown to no fewer than 14,500 rule sets. *Doing Business* covers 11 areas of a company's life cycle, through 11 specific sets of indicators. These indicator sets do not cover all aspects of regulation in the area of focus. For example, the indicators on starting a business or protecting investors do not cover all aspects of commercial legislation. The employing workers indicators do not cover all areas of labor regulation. The current indicator set does not include, for example, measures of regulations addressing safety at work or the right of collective bargaining.

BASED ON STANDARDIZED CASE SCENARIOS

Doing Business indicators are built on the basis of standardized case scenarios with specific assumptions, such as the business being located in the largest business city of the economy. Economic indicators commonly make limiting assumptions of this kind. Inflation statistics, for example, are often based on prices of consumer goods in a few urban areas.

Such assumptions allow global coverage and enhance comparability. But they come at the expense of generality. *Doing Business* recognizes the limitations of including data on only the largest business city. Business regulation and its enforcement, particularly in federal states and large economies, differ across the country. And of course the challenges and opportunities of the largest business city—whether Mumbai or São Paulo, Nuku'alofa or Nassau—vary greatly across countries. Recognizing governments' interest in such variation, *Doing Business* has complemented its global indicators with subnational studies in such countries as Brazil, China, Colombia, the Arab Republic of Egypt, India, Indonesia, Kenya, Mexico, Morocco, Nigeria, Pakistan and the Philippines.[6]

In areas where regulation is complex and highly differentiated, the standardized case used to construct the *Doing Business* indicator needs to be carefully defined. Where relevant, the standardized case assumes a limited liability company. This choice is in part empirical: private, limited liability companies are the most prevalent business form in most economies around the world. The choice also reflects one focus of *Doing Business*: expanding opportunities for entrepreneurship. Investors are encouraged to venture into business when potential losses are limited to their capital participation.

FOCUSED ON THE FORMAL SECTOR

In constructing the indicators, *Doing Business* assumes that entrepreneurs are knowledgeable about all regulations in place and comply with them. In practice, entrepreneurs may spend considerable time finding out where to go and what documents to submit. Or they may avoid legally required procedures altogether—by not registering for social security, for example.

Where regulation is particularly onerous, levels of informality are higher. Informality comes at a cost: firms in the informal sector typically grow more slowly, have poorer access to credit and employ fewer workers—and their workers remain outside the protections of labor law.[7] *Doing Business* measures one set of factors that help explain the occurrence of informality and give policy makers insights into potential areas of reform. Gaining a fuller understanding of the broader business environment, and a broader perspective on policy challenges, requires combining insights from *Doing Business* with data from other sources, such as the World Bank Enterprise Surveys.[8]

WHY THIS FOCUS

Doing Business functions as a kind of cholesterol test for the regulatory environment for domestic businesses. A cholesterol test does not tell us everything about the state of our health. But it does measure something important for our health. And it puts us on watch to change behaviors in ways that will improve not only our cholesterol rating but also our overall health.

One way to test whether *Doing Business* serves as a proxy for the broader business environment and for competitiveness is to look at correlations between the *Doing Business* rankings and other major economic benchmarks. The indicator set closest to *Doing Business* in what it measures is the OECD indicators of product market regulation;[9] the correlation here is 0.72. The World Economic Forum's Global Competitiveness Index and IMD's World Competitiveness Yearbook are broader in scope, but these too are strongly correlated with *Doing Business* (0.79 and 0.64, respectively).[10]

A bigger question is whether the issues on which *Doing Business* focuses matter for development and poverty reduction. The World Bank study *Voices of the Poor* asked 60,000 poor people around the world how they thought they might escape poverty.[11] The answers were unequivocal: women and men alike pin their hopes above all on income from their own business or wages earned in employment. Enabling growth—and ensuring that poor people can participate in its benefits—requires an environment where new entrants with drive and good ideas, regardless of their gender or ethnic origin, can get started in business and where good firms can invest and grow, generating more jobs.

Small and medium-size enterprises are key drivers of competition, growth and job creation, particularly in developing countries. But in these economies up to 80% of economic activity takes place in the informal sector. Firms may be prevented from entering the formal sector by excessive bureaucracy and regulation.

Where regulation is burdensome and competition limited, success tends to depend more on whom you know than on what you can do. But where regulation is transparent, efficient and implemented in a simple way, it becomes easier for any aspiring entrepreneurs, regardless of their connections, to operate within the rule of law and to benefit from the opportunities and protections that the law provides.

In this sense *Doing Business* values good rules as a key to social inclusion. It also provides a basis for studying effects of regulations and their application. For example, *Doing Business 2004* found that faster contract enforcement was associated with perceptions of greater judicial fairness—suggesting that justice delayed is justice denied.[12]

In the context of the global crisis policy makers continue to face particular challenges. Both developed and developing economies have been seeing the impact of the financial crisis flowing through to the real economy, with rising unemployment and income loss. The foremost challenge for many governments is to create new jobs and economic op-

portunities. But many have limited fiscal space for publicly funded activities such as infrastructure investment or for the provision of publicly funded safety nets and social services. Reforms aimed at creating a better investment climate, including reforms of business regulation, can be beneficial for several reasons. Flexible regulation and effective institutions, including efficient processes for starting a business and efficient insolvency or bankruptcy systems, can facilitate reallocation of labor and capital. As businesses rebuild and start to create new jobs, this helps to lay the groundwork for countries' economic recovery. And regulatory institutions and processes that are streamlined and accessible can help ensure that as businesses rebuild, barriers between the informal and formal sectors are lowered, creating more opportunities for the poor.

BENCHMARKING EXERCISE

Doing Business, in capturing some key dimensions of regulatory regimes, has been found useful for benchmarking. Any benchmarking—for individuals, firms or economies—is necessarily partial: it is valid and useful if it helps sharpen judgment, less so if it substitutes for judgment.

Doing Business provides 2 takes on the data it collects: it presents "absolute" indicators for each economy for each of the 11 regulatory topics it addresses, and it provides rankings of economies for 9 topics, both by indicator and in aggregate.[13] Judgment is required in interpreting these measures for any economy and in determining a sensible and politically feasible path for reform.

Reviewing the *Doing Business* rankings in isolation may show unexpected results. Some economies may rank unexpectedly high on some indicators. And some economies that have had rapid growth or attracted a great deal of investment may rank lower than others that appear to be less dynamic.

For reform-minded governments, how much the regulatory environment for

local entrepreneurs improves matters more than their relative ranking. To aid in assessing such improvements, this year's report presents a new metric (DB change score) that allows economies to compare where they are today with where they were 5 years ago. The 5-year measure of cumulative change shows how much economies have reformed business regulations over time (for more details, see Data notes). This complements the yearly ease of doing business rankings that compare economies with one another at a point in time.

As economies develop, they strengthen and add to regulations to protect investor and property rights. Meanwhile, they find more efficient ways to implement existing regulations and cut outdated ones. One finding of *Doing Business*: dynamic and growing economies continually reform and update their regulations and their way of implementing them, while many poor economies still work with regulatory systems dating to the late 1800s.

DOING BUSINESS— A USER'S GUIDE

Quantitative data and benchmarking can be useful in stimulating debate about policy, both by exposing potential challenges and by identifying where policy makers might look for lessons and good practices. These data also provide a basis for analyzing how different policy approaches—and different policy reforms—contribute to desired outcomes such as competitiveness, growth and greater employment and incomes.

Eight years of *Doing Business* data have enabled a growing body of research on how performance on *Doing Business* indicators—and reforms relevant to those indicators—relate to desired social and economic outcomes. Some 656 articles have been published in peer-reviewed academic journals, and about 2,060 working papers are available through Google Scholar.[14] Among the findings:

- Lower barriers to start-up are associated with a smaller informal sector.[15]
- Lower costs of entry encourage entrepreneurship, enhance firm productivity and reduce corruption.[16]
- Simpler start-up translates into greater employment opportunities.[17]
- The quality of a country's contracting environment is a source of comparative advantage in trade patterns. Countries with good contract enforcement specialize in industries where relationship-specific investments are most important.[18]
- Greater information sharing through credit bureaus is associated with higher bank profitability and lower bank risk.[19]

How do governments use *Doing Business*? A common first reaction is to ask questions about the quality and relevance of the *Doing Business* data and on how the results are calculated. Yet the debate typically proceeds to a deeper discussion exploring the relevance of the data to the economy and areas where business regulation reform might make sense.

Most reformers start out by seeking examples, and *Doing Business* helps in this (box 2.1). For example, Saudi Arabia used the company law of France as a model for revising its own. Many countries in Africa look to Mauritius—the region's strongest performer on *Doing Business* indicators—as a source of good practices for reform. In the words of Luis Guillermo Plata, the former minister of commerce, industry and tourism of Colombia,

It's not like baking a cake where you follow the recipe. No. We are all different. But we can take certain things, certain key lessons, and apply those lessons and see how they work in our environment.

Over the past 8 years there has been much activity by governments in reforming the regulatory environment for domestic businesses. Most reforms relating to *Doing Business* topics were nested in broader programs of reform aimed at enhancing economic competitiveness, as in Colombia, Kenya and Liberia, for example. In structuring their reform programs for the business environment, governments use multiple data sources and indicators. And reformers respond to many stakeholders and interest groups, all of whom bring important issues and concerns to the reform debate. World Bank Group dialogue with governments on the investment climate is designed to encourage critical use of the data, sharpening judgment, avoiding a narrow focus on improving *Doing Business* rankings and encouraging broad-based reforms that enhance the investment climate.

METHODOLOGY AND DATA

Doing Business covers 183 economies—including small economies and some of the poorest countries, for which little or no data are available in other data sets.

The *Doing Business* data are based on domestic laws and regulations as well as administrative requirements. (For a detailed explanation of the *Doing Business* methodology, see Data notes.)

INFORMATION SOURCES FOR THE DATA

Most of the indicators are based on laws and regulations. In addition, most of the cost indicators are backed by official fee schedules. *Doing Business* respondents both fill out written surveys and provide references to the relevant laws, regulations and fee schedules, aiding data checking and quality assurance.

For some indicators—for example, the indicators on dealing with construction permits, enforcing contracts and closing a business—part of the cost component (where fee schedules are lacking) and the time component are based on actual practice rather than the law on the books. This introduces a de-

---

BOX 2.1

How economies have used *Doing Business* in regulatory reform programs

To ensure coordination of efforts across agencies, such economies as Colombia, Rwanda and Sierra Leone have formed regulatory reform committees reporting directly to the president that use the *Doing Business* indicators as one input to inform their programs for improving the business environment. More than 20 other economies have formed such committees at the interministerial level. These include India, Malaysia, Taiwan (China) and Vietnam in East and South Asia; the Arab Republic of Egypt, Morocco, Saudi Arabia, the Syrian Arab Republic, the United Arab Emirates and the Republic of Yemen in the Middle East and North Africa; Georgia, Kazakhstan, the Kyrgyz Republic, Moldova and Tajikistan in Eastern Europe and Central Asia; Kenya, Liberia, Malawi and Zambia in Sub-Saharan Africa; and Guatemala, Mexico and Peru in Latin America.

Beyond the level of the economy, the Asia-Pacific Economic Cooperation (APEC) organization uses *Doing Business* to identify potential areas of regulatory reform, to champion economies that can help others improve and to set measurable targets. In 2009 APEC launched the Ease of Doing Business Action Plan with the goal of making it 25% cheaper, faster and easier to do business in the region by 2015. Drawing on a firm survey, planners identified 5 priority areas: starting a business, getting credit, enforcing contracts, trading across borders and dealing with permits. The next 2 steps: the APEC economies setting targets to measure results, and the champion economies selected, such as Japan, New Zealand and the United States, developing programs to build capacity to carry out regulatory reform in these areas.[1]

1. Muhamad Noor (executive director of APEC), speech delivered at ASEAN-NZ Combined Business Council breakfast meeting, Auckland, New Zealand, March 25, 2010, http://www.apec.org.

gree of subjectivity. The *Doing Business* approach has therefore been to work with legal practitioners or professionals who regularly undertake the transactions involved. Following the standard methodological approach for time and motion studies, *Doing Business* breaks down each process or transaction, such as starting and legally operating a business, into separate steps to ensure a better estimate of time. The time estimate for each step is given by practitioners with significant and routine experience in the transaction.

Over the past 8 years more than 11,000 professionals in 183 economies have assisted in providing the data that inform the *Doing Business* indicators. This year's report draws on the inputs of more than 8,200 professionals. Table 14.1 lists the number of respondents for each indicator set. The *Doing Business* website indicates the number of respondents for each economy and each indicator. Respondents are professionals or government officials who routinely administer or advise on the legal and regulatory requirements covered in each *Doing Business* topic. Because of the focus on legal and regulatory arrangements, most of the respondents are lawyers. The credit information survey is answered by officials of the credit registry or bureau. Freight forwarders, accountants, architects and other professionals answer the surveys related to trading across borders, taxes and construction permits.

The *Doing Business* approach to data collection contrasts with that of enterprise or firm surveys, which capture often one-time perceptions and experiences of businesses. A corporate lawyer registering 100–150 businesses a year will be more familiar with the process than an entrepreneur, who will register a business only once or maybe twice. A bankruptcy judge deciding dozens of cases a year will have more insight into bankruptcy than a company that may undergo the process.

DEVELOPMENT OF THE METHODOLOGY

The methodology for calculating each indicator is transparent, objective and easily replicable. Leading academics collaborate in the development of the indicators, ensuring academic rigor. Eight of the background papers underlying the indicators have been published in leading economic journals.

Doing Business uses a simple averaging approach for weighting component indicators and calculating rankings. Other approaches were explored, including using principal components and unobserved components. They turn out to yield results nearly identical to those of simple averaging. The 9 sets of indicators included in this year's aggregate ranking on the ease of doing business provide sufficiently broad coverage across topics. Therefore, the simple averaging approach is used.

IMPROVEMENTS TO THE METHODOLOGY AND DATA REVISIONS

The methodology has undergone continual improvement over the years. Changes have been made mainly in response to country suggestions. For enforcing contracts, for example, the amount of the disputed claim in the case study was increased from 50% to 200% of income per capita after the first year of data collection, as it became clear that smaller claims were unlikely to go to court.

Another change relates to starting a business. The minimum capital requirement can be an obstacle for potential entrepreneurs. Initially *Doing Business* measured the required minimum capital regardless of whether it had to be paid up front or not. In many economies only part of the minimum capital has to be paid up front. To reflect the actual potential barrier to entry, the paid-in minimum capital has been used since 2004.

This year's report includes changes in the core methodology for one set of indicators, those on employing workers. With the aim of measuring the balance between worker protection and efficient employment regulation that favors job

creation, *Doing Business* has made a series of amendments to the methodology for the employing workers indicators over the past 3 years, including in this year's report. While this process has been under way, the World Bank has removed the employing workers indicators as a guidepost from its Country Policy and Institutional Assessment questionnaire and instructed staff not to use the indicators as a basis for providing policy advice or evaluating country development programs or assistance strategies. A note to staff issued in October 2009 outlines the guidelines for using the indicators.[20]

In addition, the World Bank Group has been working with a consultative group—including labor lawyers, employer and employee representatives and experts from the International Labour Organization (ILO), the Organisation for Economic Co-operation and Development (OECD), civil society and the private sector—to review the methodology and explore future areas of research.[21] The consultative group has met several times over the past year, and its guidance has provided the basis for several changes in methodology, some of which have been implemented in this year's report. Because the consultative process and consequent changes to the methodology are not yet complete, this year's report does not present rankings of economies on the employing workers indicators or include the topic in the aggregate ranking on the ease of doing business. But it does present the data collected for the indicators. Additional data collected on labor regulations are available on the *Doing Business* website.[22]

The changes so far in the methodology for the employing workers indicators recognize minimum levels of protection in line with relevant ILO conventions as well as excessive levels of regulation that may stifle job creation. Floors and ceilings in such areas as paid annual leave, working days per week and the minimum wage provide a framework for balancing worker protection against excessive restrictiveness in employment regulations (see Data notes).

Doing Business also continues to benefit from discussions with external stakeholders, including participants in the International Tax Dialogue, on the survey instrument and methodology.

All changes in methodology are explained in the Data notes as well as on the *Doing Business* website. In addition, data time series for each indicator and economy are available on the website, beginning with the first year the indicator or economy was included in the report. To provide a comparable time series for research, the data set is back-calculated to adjust for changes in methodology and any revisions in data due to corrections. The website also makes available all original data sets used for background papers.

Information on data corrections is provided in the Data notes and on the website. A transparent complaint procedure allows anyone to challenge the data. If errors are confirmed after a data verification process, they are expeditiously corrected.

1. The standard cost model is a quantitative methodology for determining the administrative burdens that regulation imposes on businesses. The method can be used to measure the effect of a single law or of selected areas of legislation or to perform a baseline measurement of all legislation in a country.

2. This has included a review by the World Bank Independent Evaluation Group (2008) as well as ongoing input from the International Tax Dialogue.

3. Local experts in 183 economies are surveyed annually to collect and update the data. The local experts for each economy are listed on the *Doing Business* website (http://www.doingbusiness.org).

4. De Soto (2000).

5. The indicators related to trading across borders and dealing with construction permits and the pilot indicators on getting electricity take into account limited aspects of an economy's infrastructure, including the inland transport of goods and utility connections for businesses.

6. http://www.doingbusiness.org/Subnational/.

7. Schneider (2005).

8. http://www.enterprisesurveys.org.

9. OECD, "Indicators of Product Market Regulation Homepage," http://www.oecd.org/.

10. The World Economic Forum's *Global Competitiveness Report* uses part of the *Doing Business* data sets on starting a business, employing workers, protecting investors and getting credit (legal rights).

11. Narayan and others (2000).

12. World Bank (2003).

13. This year's report does not present rankings of economies on the pilot getting electricity indicators or the employing workers indicators. Nor does it include these topics in the aggregate ranking on the ease of doing business.

14. http://scholar.google.com.

15. For example, Masatlioglu and Rigolini (2008), Kaplan, Piedra and Seira (2007), Ardagna and Lusardi (2009) and Djankov (2009b).

16. For example, Alesina and others (2005), Perotti and Volpin (2004), Klapper, Laeven and Rajan (2006), Fisman and Sarria-Allende (2004), Antunes and Cavalcanti (2007), Barseghyan (2008), Djankov and others (2010) and Klapper, Lewin and Quesada Delgado (2009).

17. For example, Freund and Bolaky (2008), Chang, Kaltani and Loayza (2009) and Helpman, Melitz and Rubinstein (2008).

18. Nunn (2007).

19. Houston and others (2010).

20. World Bank (2009e).

21. For the terms of reference and composition of the consultative group, see World Bank, "Doing Business Employing Workers Indicator Consultative Group," http://www.doingbusiness.org.

22. http://www.doingbusiness.org.

Starting a business

FIGURE 3.1

Peru cut the time and procedures to start a business by a third

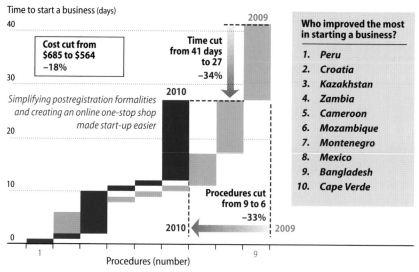

Time to start a business (days)

Cost cut from $685 to $564 −18%

Time cut from 41 days to 27 −34%

2009

2010

Simplifying postregistration formalities and creating an online one-stop shop made start-up easier

Procedures cut from 9 to 6 −33%

2010   2009

Procedures (number)

Who improved the most in starting a business?
1. **Peru**
2. **Croatia**
3. **Kazakhstan**
4. **Zambia**
5. **Cameroon**
6. **Mozambique**
7. **Montenegro**
8. **Mexico**
9. **Bangladesh**
10. **Cape Verde**

Source: Doing Business database.

Kainaz Messman, a successful young entrepreneur in Mumbai, says that she "grew up in a sweet-smelling home." Her mother ran a small confectionery business there. Her father also worked for himself. So it was no surprise when Kainaz started her own business. But it was not easy. "When I started my business I knew how to bake cakes and little else. Suddenly I was thrown into the deep end without a float and had no option but to swim."[1]

Starting a business always takes a leap of faith. And governments increasingly are encouraging the daring. Since 2004 policy makers in more than 75% of the world's economies have made it easier for entrepreneurs to start a business in the formal sector. Formal incorporation has many benefits. Legal entities outlive their founders. Resources can be pooled as several shareholders join together. Limited liability companies limit the financial liability of company owners to their investments, so personal assets are not put at risk. And companies have access to services and institutions from courts to banks as well as to new markets.

Many economies have simplified business registration. In India women like Kainaz can now complete many registration formalities online, including filing incorporation documents, paying stamp fees and registering for value added tax. They no longer have to stand in line.

This is a good thing, because burdensome procedures can affect women more than men. A study in India found that women had to wait 37% longer than men on average to see the same local government official. Another, in Bangladesh, found that government clerks seeking "speed payments" to process applications were more likely to target women.[2] In the worst case, additional barriers such as long, complex registration and licensing procedures can make it impossible for women to formalize a business. Indeed, women typically make up a minority of the owners of registered businesses—less than 10% in the Democratic Republic of Congo and about 40% in Rwanda, for example.

Research finds that business regulations affect women's decision to become an entrepreneur.[3] Many other factors also determine whether women (and men) become entrepreneurs, including education level and cultural norms and traditions. But governments can help ensure a level playing field for all through

TABLE 3.1

Where is starting a business easy— and where not?

Easiest	RANK	Most difficult	RANK
New Zealand	1	Iraq	174
Australia	2	Djibouti	175
Canada	3	Congo, Rep.	176
Singapore	4	São Tomé and Principe	177
Macedonia, FYR	5		
Hong Kong SAR, China	6	Haiti	178
		Equatorial Guinea	179
Belarus	7	Eritrea	180
Georgia	8	Guinea	181
United States	9	Chad	182
Rwanda	10	Guinea-Bissau	183

Note: Rankings are the average of the economy's rankings on the procedures, time, cost and paid-in minimum capital for starting a business. See Data notes for details.
Source: Doing Business database.

FIGURE 3.2

What are the time, cost, paid-in minimum capital and number of procedures to get a local, limited liability company up and running?

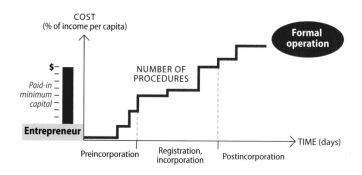

COST (% of income per capita)

Formal operation

$

Paid-in minimum capital

NUMBER OF PROCEDURES

Entrepreneur

Preincorporation   Registration, incorporation   Postincorporation

TIME (days)

TABLE 3.2
Who made starting a business easier in 2009/10—and what did they do?

Feature	*Economies*	*Some highlights*
Simplified registration formalities (seal, publication, notarization, inspection, other requirements)	Bangladesh, Brunei Darussalam, Chile, Democratic Republic of Congo, Croatia, Grenada, Guyana, Haiti, India, Kazakhstan, Kenya, Kyrgyz Republic, Lithuania, Luxembourg, Panama, Syrian Arab Republic, Tajikistan, Zimbabwe	Haiti, before the earthquake, eliminated the requirement that the office of the president or prime minister authorize publication of company statutes in the official gazette. Entrepreneurs can now publish them directly in the gazette. This cut start-up time by 90 days. Bangladesh replaced the requirement for buying a physical stamp with payment of stamp fees at a designated bank. It also enhanced its electronic registration system. Start-up time fell by 25 days.
Introduced or improved online procedures	Brazil, Brunei Darussalam, Chile, Croatia, Ecuador, Germany, India, Indonesia, Islamic Republic of Iran, Italy, Malaysia, Mexico, Peru	Croatia made it possible for limited liability companies to file registration applications electronically through the notary public. This cut 1 procedure and 15 days from the start-up process.
Cut or simplified postregistration procedures (tax registration, social security registration, licensing)	Brazil, Cape Verde, Arab Republic of Egypt, Montenegro, Mozambique, Peru, Philippines, Taiwan (China)	The Philippines introduced a one-stop shop for the municipal license and cut the inspection by the mayor's office, reducing start-up time by 15 days.
Created or improved one-stop shop	Cameroon, FYR Macedonia, Mexico, Peru, Slovenia, Tajikistan, Vietnam	Peru created an online one-stop shop allowing an entrepreneur to receive confirmation of business registration and the tax registration number at the same time. This cut 3 procedures and 14 days from start-up.
Abolished or reduced minimum capital requirement	Bulgaria, Denmark, Kazakhstan, Sweden, Syrian Arab Republic, Ukraine, Zambia	Zambia eliminated its minimum capital requirement. Syria reduced its requirement by two-thirds.

Source: Doing Business database.

transparent and easily accessible regulatory processes.

Rich or poor, men and women around the world seek to run and profit from their own business. A 2007 survey among young people in the United States showed that 4 in 10 have started a business or would like to someday.[4] With some 550,000 small businesses created across the country every month,[5] entrepreneurs are a powerful economic force, contributing half the GDP and 64% of net new jobs over the past 15 years.[6] Such impacts are possible where business registration is efficient and affordable. A recent study using data collected from company registries in 100 economies over 8 years found that simple business start-up is critical for fostering formal entrepreneurship. Economies with smart business registration have a higher entry rate as well as greater business density.[7]

Doing Business measures the procedures, time and cost for a small to medium-size enterprise to start up and operate formally (figure 3.2). The number of procedures shows how many separate interactions an entrepreneur is required to have with government agencies. Business entry requirements go beyond simple incorporation to include the registration of a business name; tax registration; registration with statistical, social security and pension administrations; and registration with local authorities.[8]

In 2009/10, 42 economies made it easier to start a business, with streamlining registration formalities the most popular feature of business registration reforms (table 3.2). Peru improved the ease of starting a business the most, establishing a one-stop shop and simplifying postregistration formalities at the district council level. This reduced the number of procedures to start a business by 33%, the time by 34% and the cost by 18%.

WHAT ARE THE TRENDS?

Starting a business has become easier across all regions of the world. In the past 7 years *Doing Business* recorded 296 business registration reforms in 140 economies (figure 3.3). As a result of these reforms, the average time to start a company fell from 49 days to 34, and the average cost from 86% of income per capita to 41%.

STREAMLINED PROCEDURES

Seventy-one economies streamlined the procedures to start a business. Of these, some established or improved a one-stop shop by consolidating procedures into a single access point. But simplifying procedures does not necessarily require creating new institutions: 19 economies simply merged procedural requirements or delegated them to one agency. Georgia merged tax registration with company registration in 2007. Kazakhstan did the same in 2009. Ghana, Hungary, Montenegro, Samoa and Singapore allow firms to check and reserve the company name at the time of company registration. In Portugal, Serbia and Ukraine the registry can now publish information about the company registration, so companies no longer have to arrange with a newspaper to advertise it.

Other economies merged postregis-

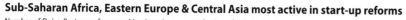

FIGURE 3.3

Sub-Saharan Africa, Eastern Europe & Central Asia most active in start-up reforms

Number of *Doing Business* reforms making it easier to start a business by *Doing Business* report year

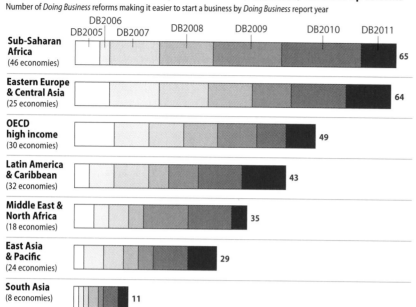

Note: A *Doing Business* reform is counted as 1 reform per reforming economy per year. The data sample for DB2005 (2004) includes 155 economies. Twenty-eight more were added in subsequent years.
Source: Doing Business database.

tration procedures. This makes particular sense for tax registrations. In 2006 Armenia unified tax and social security registrations, and Liberia merged value added and income tax registrations. In the past year Montenegro introduced a single form for registering with the employment bureau, health fund, pension fund and tax administration.

PERSISTENT GAPS

Despite business entry reforms, discrepancies remain among regions and income groups. Entrepreneurs in OECD high-income economies still benefit from the fastest and least costly processes to start a business, taking 14 days and costing 5.34% of income per capita on average. And OECD high-income economies continue to improve, with 9 introducing or upgrading online procedures in the past 7 years.

Compared with OECD high-income economies, starting a business takes 4 times as long on average in Latin America and the Caribbean—and costs 18 times as much (relative to income per capita) in Sub-Saharan Africa. Entrepreneurs in Sub-Saharan Africa also continue to

face the highest paid-in minimum capital requirements, 146% of income per capita on average. By contrast, entrepreneurs in two-thirds of economies in Latin America and the Caribbean face no such requirements.

MANY ONE-STOP SHOPS IN EASTERN EUROPE AND CENTRAL ASIA

Economies in Eastern Europe and Central Asia were the most active in easing business start-up over the past 7 years, with 93% introducing improvements. More one-stop shops have been established in this region than in any other. In 2002 the Russian Federation integrated several registers under one function,[9] freeing entrepreneurs from having to visit separate agencies involved in business start-up. Since then 19 other economies in the region, including Azerbaijan, Belarus, the former Yugoslav Republic of Macedonia, Serbia and Ukraine, have adopted similar approaches. The changes in the region since 2005 reduced the average number of procedures by 4, the time by 21 days and the cost by 8.8% of income per capita.

BIG CUTS IN PAID-IN MINIMUM CAPITAL

Thirty-nine economies around the world reduced or abolished their minimum capital requirement in the past 7 years. Local entrepreneurs in the Middle East and North Africa benefited the most. The average paid-in minimum capital requirement in the region dropped from a record 847% of income per capita in 2005 to 104% in 2010 (figure 3.4).

Economies in the region also streamlined processes by introducing new technologies, particularly since 2008. Compared with other regions, however, the use of e-services is still low.

WHAT HAS WORKED?

Policy makers can encourage entrepreneurs to "take the plunge" by making start-up fast, easy and inexpensive. Among the most common measures have been creating a single interface, reducing or abolishing minimum capital requirements and adopting technology.

MAKING IT SIMPLE: ONE INTERFACE

Businesses created what might have been one of the world's first one-stop shops 150 years ago, when the first department store, Le Bon Marché, opened its doors in Paris. The public loved the convenience of one-stop shopping. Achieving this kind of convenience has been among the main motivations for governments that have adopted this concept for businesses since the 1980s.

Today 72 economies around the world have some kind of one-stop shop for business registration, including the 50 that established or enhanced one in the past 7 years (table 3.3). It is not surprising that such setups are popular. They do not necessarily require legal changes. And entrepreneurs and governments alike often see immediate benefits. The coordination among government agencies eliminates the need for entrepreneurs to visit each agency separately, often to file similar or even identical information—yet maintains regulatory checks. In 2006 FYR Macedonia established a central registry allowing entre-

FIGURE 3.4
Minimum capital reduced the most in the Middle East and North Africa
Regional averages in starting a business

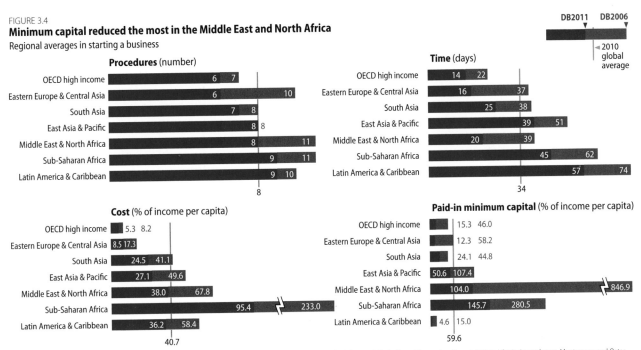

Note: The data sample for DB2006 (2005) includes 174 economies. The sample for DB2011 (2010) also includes The Bahamas, Bahrain, Brunei Darussalam, Cyprus, Kosovo, Liberia, Luxembourg, Montenegro and Qatar, for a total of 183 economies.
Source: Doing Business database.

preneurs to complete company, tax and statistics registrations; open a company bank account; and publish the notice of the company's formation on the registry's website. In the past year it streamlined the process even more by adding registration with the social fund. One-stop shops in economies as diverse as El Salvador and Mali offer similar services.

Single interfaces not only save time and money; they also increase transparency. In Indonesia a new one-stop shop for business permits opened recently in Solo (formally known as Surakarta).[10] Civil servants sit in full view behind open counters. There is no opportunity to seek "speed money." A flat fee of 5,000 rupiah replaced a fee schedule ranging from

25,000 to 100,000 rupiah, further reducing discretion. In Jakarta work is under way to set up a one-stop shop that will include business registration and licensing for small and medium-size enterprises. Zambia implemented a one-stop shop like the one Jakarta is setting up.

While some one-stop shops are solely for business registration, others carry out many integrated functions, such as postregistration formalities. Some of these are virtual; others are physical, with one or more windows. In the 72 economies that have one-stop shops offering at least one service besides business registration, start-up is more than twice as fast as in those without such services (figure 3.5).

One-stop shops are starting to expand beyond business registration formalities. In Tbilisi, Georgia, a public service center assists entrepreneurs not only with business licenses and permits but also with investment, privatization procedures, tourism-related issues and state-owned property management. According to a firm survey in 2008, senior managers in Georgia spend only 2% of their time dealing with regulatory requirements—and 92% of firms report spending less than 10% of their time on such requirements.[11] By saving time, Georgian entrepreneurs save money too. Another survey, in 2009, found that the service center's simplified procedures helped businesses save an average of 3.25% of profits that year. For all businesses served, this amounted to direct and indirect savings of $7.2 million.[12]

Economies with established one-stop shops are inspiring others to follow their lead. Portugal's one-stop shop, *Empresa no dia* (company in a day), was the inspiration for Uruguay's similarly named *Empresa en el dia.*

TABLE 3.3
Good practices around the world in making it easy to start a business

Practice	Economies[a]	Examples
Putting procedures online	105	Cape Verde, FYR Macedonia, Maldives, New Zealand, Puerto Rico, Saudi Arabia, Singapore
Having no minimum capital requirement	80	Bangladesh, Belarus, Canada, Colombia, Mauritius, Tunisia, Vietnam
Having a one-stop shop	72	Afghanistan, Azerbaijan, Italy, Jordan, Peru, Philippines, Rwanda

a. Among 183 economies surveyed.
Source: Doing Business database; World Bank (2009f).

FIGURE 3.5
Economies with a one-stop shop make starting a business easier
Procedures and time by type of one-stop shop

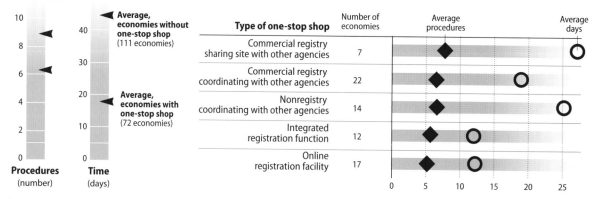

Source: Doing Business database.

REDUCING OR ELIMINATING MINIMUM CAPITAL

The minimum capital requirement dates to the 18th century. Yet today 103 economies still require entrepreneurs to put up a set amount of capital before even starting registration formalities. Such requirements are intended to protect investors and creditors. But they have not proved to be effective. In 71% of the economies requiring paid-in capital, the capital can be withdrawn immediately after incorporation. So entrepreneurs often simply borrow the money. "It even created a new market," explains an official from the United Arab Emirates. "Entrepreneurs would pay $20 just to borrow the required money for one day. A much higher interest rate than anyone would ever receive from a bank." Moreover, fixed requirements do not account for differences in firms' credit and investment risk.

Minimum capital requirements can also have counterproductive effects. Recent research suggests that they lower entrepreneurship rates across the 39 economies studied.[13] Not surprisingly, the economies that originally introduced the requirement have long since removed it.

Some economies have found other ways to protect investors and creditors, particularly in the case of limited liability companies. Hong Kong SAR (China) outlines provisions on solvency safeguards in its company act. Mauritius conducts solvency tests. Taiwan (China) requires an audit report showing that the amount

a company has invested is enough to cover its establishment cost.

The reduction or elimination of minimum capital requirements in several economies was followed by a jump in initial registrations. In the year after Jordan reduced its requirement from 30,000 Jordanian dinars to 1,000, the number of newly registered companies in the country increased by 18%. In Morocco a reduction from 30,000 to 1,000 dirham led to a 40% increase in the following year. Morocco is now considering abolishing the requirement altogether. In many of the economies that did so, such as the Arab Republic of Egypt and the Republic of Yemen, companies are more likely to declare their actual capital.

USING TECHNOLOGY TO BOOST EFFICIENCY

Governments around the world are increasingly using technology to improve the efficiency of services and the accountability of public officials. E-government initiatives range from data centers and shared networks to government-wide information infrastructure and unified service centers for the public. Fifty-four economies introduced information and communication technology in their business start-up processes in the past 7 years, saving time and effort for businesses and governments alike. When Mauritius introduced a computerized system for all types of business registrations in 2006,

total registration time fell by 80%. Singapore's online registration system saves businesses an estimated $42 million annually.[14] Electronic services are also more accessible, saving entrepreneurs the time and cost of traveling to government agencies and waiting in line.[15]

Today 105 economies use information and communication technology for services ranging from name search to entirely online business registration. New Zealand, the easiest place to start a business, was the first to launch an online company registration system, in 1996 (table 3.4). The online option has been mandatory since July 1, 2008. Canada, the third easiest place to start a business, followed suit in 1999. Its system has been entirely paperless since May 2006. India, Italy and Singapore also made online filing mandatory. Egypt recently launched a new system to establish companies electronically. The first phase of the system, allowing online submission of the registration application, is in place.

To encourage use, some economies set lower fees for online registration. In Belgium online registration costs €140 and paper registration €2,004. In Canada the costs are Can$200 and Can$350. In Estonia documents filed online no longer have to be notarized.

TABLE 3.4
Who makes starting a business easy—and who does not?

Procedures *(number)*

Fewest		Most	
Canada	1	China	14
New Zealand	1	Bolivia	15
Australia	2	Brazil	15
Kyrgyz Republic	2	Brunei Darussalam	15
Madagascar	2	Greece	15
Rwanda	2	Philippines	15
Slovenia	2	Guinea-Bissau	17
Belgium	3	Venezuela, RB	17
Finland	3	Uganda	18
Hong Kong SAR, China	3	Equatorial Guinea	20

Time *(days)*

Fastest		Slowest	
New Zealand	1	Lao PDR	100
Australia	2	Brunei Darussalam	105
Georgia	3	Haiti	105
Macedonia, FYR	3	Brazil	120
Rwanda	3	Equatorial Guinea	136
Singapore	3	Venezuela, RB	141
Belgium	4	São Tomé and Principe	144
Hungary	4	Congo, Rep.	160
Albania	5	Guinea-Bissau	216
Canada	5	Suriname	694

Cost *(% of income per capita)*

Least		Most	
Denmark	0.0	Djibouti	169.9
Slovenia	0.0	Comoros	176.5
Ireland	0.4	Togo	178.1
New Zealand	0.4	Zimbabwe	182.8
Canada	0.4	Guinea-Bissau	183.3
Sweden	0.6	Gambia, The	199.6
Puerto Rico	0.7	Haiti	212.0
United Kingdom	0.7	Chad	226.9
Australia	0.7	Central African Republic	228.4
Singapore	0.7	Congo, Dem. Rep.	735.1

Paid-in minimum capital

Most	% of income per capita	US$
Chad	387	2,397
Mauritania	412	3,956
Guinea-Bissau	415	2,117
Burkina Faso	416	2,122
Djibouti	434	5,556
Central African Republic	469	2,109
Togo	487	2,142
Guinea	519	1,922
Niger	613	2,084
Timor-Leste	921	5,000

Note: Eighty economies have no paid-in minimum capital requirement.
Source: Doing Business database.

WHAT ARE SOME RESULTS?

Making business entry easier has been popular around the world. Many economies have undertaken business registration reforms in stages—and often as part of a larger regulatory reform program (figure 3.6). Among the benefits have been greater firm satisfaction and savings and more registered businesses, financial resources and job opportunities.

BIG JUMPS IN REGISTRATIONS

Egypt introduced a one-stop shop in 2005. Further reforms included incorporating more agencies in the one-stop shop, introducing a flat fee structure and reducing and then abolishing the paid-in minimum capital requirement. The time and cost of incorporation were reduced in both 2005 and 2006, and by 2007 the number of registered companies had increased by more than 60%. Reductions of the minimum capital requirement in 2007 and 2008 led to an increase of more than 30% in the number of limited liability companies.

Business registration reforms in FYR Macedonia made it one of the easiest places to start a business today. In 2006 company registration was changed from a judicial process to an administrative one, and a one-stop shop combined company, tax and statistics registrations. The publication requirement in the official gazette was replaced with automatic registration on the registrar's website. In the year following these first changes, new firm registrations increased by about 20%.

Portugal eased business start-up in 2006 and 2007, reducing the time to start a business from 54 days to 5. In 2007 and 2008 new business registrations were up by 60% compared with 2006. In Belarus, which reformed business entry in 2006, the number of new businesses registered almost tripled in 2007 and 2008. In 2008 Colombia introduced online company registration. In 2009 new company registrations increased by 20%, twice the increase experienced in previous years. In 2006 Rwanda simplified its registra-

FIGURE 3.6

One-stop shops popular in Eastern Europe and Central Asia and Sub-Saharan Africa

Number of economies implementing change by region and feature, DB2005–DB2011

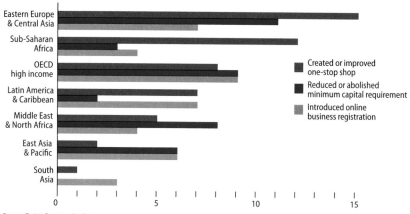

Source: Doing Business database.

tion formalities. The following year 77% more firms registered. Malaysia reduced registration fees in 2008, in response to the economic crisis. New business registrations increased by 15.8% in 2009.

Entrepreneurs open new businesses even in times of economic crisis. In 2008 Germany introduced a new legal form of limited liability company (*Unternehmergesellschaft*, or UG) with no minimum capital requirement while maintaining the €25,000 requirement for the standard form (GmbH). While many still opt for the traditional form, the number of registered UGs increased by 12,000 between November 2008 and January 2010.[16] Colombia also introduced a new type of limited liability company (*sociedad por acciones simplificadas*, or SAS) in 2008. This type is incorporated by the shareholders through a private document, with no need for a public deed. Over the next year almost 18,000 such companies were created, representing a big shift from the traditional type to the new one.

BETTER ECONOMIC AND SOCIAL OUTCOMES

These experiences in easing start-up illustrate some of the more immediate results in cost savings and increased registrations. Empirical research is increasingly focusing on economic and social outcomes such as entrepreneurship, competition, corruption and productivity. One study shows that economies

where it takes less time to register new businesses have seen higher rates of entry in industries with a potential for expansion.[17] Another finds that regulations affect the decision to start a new business, particularly for individuals who engage in an entrepreneurial activity to pursue a business opportunity.[18] Yet another study finds that regulatory costs remain more burdensome for small firms than for large ones.[19]

A recent study finds that higher entry costs are associated with a larger informal sector and a smaller number of legally registered firms.[20] Informal firms are typically less productive or efficient, adversely affecting overall productivity and growth.[21] The same study also finds that variations in regulatory costs across countries lead to differences in total productivity and output. When regulation is too heavy handed, compliance and start-up costs increase, cutting into firms' profits. This discourages entrepreneurs and increases the share of the population choosing to become employees instead. Job creation suffers.[22] These costs also deter entrepreneurship driven by opportunity but have no impact on that driven by necessity.[23] Another recent study among 95 economies concluded that more dynamic formal business creation occurs in economies that provide entrepreuners with a stable legal and regulatory regime, fast and inexpensive registration process, more

flexible employment regulations and low corporate taxes.[24]

In evaluating impact, researchers often face the dilemma of the counterfactual: how to determine what would have happened if there had been no action? Luckily, some measures affect only a specific group, allowing researchers to compare that group with those unaffected. When Mexico implemented a business registration reform across municipalities in stages, researchers took advantage of the opportunity. One study found that the reform increased the number of registered businesses by 5% and employment by 2.8%. Moreover, consumers benefited. Competition from new entrants lowered prices by 0.6%[25].Another study, using a different approach, found similar results: a 5% increase in new registrations. It also found that the program was more effective in municipalities with less corruption and cheaper additional postregistration procedures.[26]

Other recent studies investigate whether reforms of business registration have different effects on economic outcomes depending on the local institutional setting. One such study looked at India's gradual elimination of the bureaucratic industrial licensing system known as the "license raj." It shows that the effect on manufacturing output, employment, entry and investment varied across Indian states, depending on the institutional environment.[27]

Another study finds that in economies with a favorable regulatory environment for firms, particularly for firm entry, trade is more likely to improve living standards. If the structure for business entry is flexible, trade openness can have a stronger impact on the allocation of resources across and within industries. The authors show that a 1% increase in trade is associated with a more than 0.5% rise in income per capita in economies that facilitate firm entry and has no positive income effects in more rigid economies.[28] Lower entry costs combined with better credit information sharing are also associated with a larger small and medium-size enterprise sector.[29]

1. Speech by Kainaz Messman at a May 5, 2010, ceremony held by the Federation of Indian Chambers of Commerce and Industry (FICCI) Ladies Organization in Mumbai, where she was honored as a "young entrepreneur."

2. Simavi, Manuel and Blackden (2010) citing Corbridge (2007) and Government of Bangladesh (2007).

3. Ardagna and Lusardi (2010).

4. Kauffman Foundation (n.d.).

5. "The United States of Entrepreneurs: America Still Leads the World," *The Economist,* March 12, 2009.

6. U.S. Small Business Administration, "Frequently Asked Questions: Advocacy Small Business Statistics and Research," accessed July 28, 2010, http://web.sba.gov/faqs/faqindex.cfm?areaID=24.

7. Klapper, Lewin and Quesada Delgado (2009). *Entry rate* refers to newly registered firms as a percentage of total registered firms. *Business density* is defined as the number of businesses as a percentage of the working-age population (ages 18–65).

8. International Finance Corporation, FIAS, "Business Entry," accessed September 23, 2010, http://www.fias.net/.

9. World Bank (2009f).

10. World Bank (2009b).

11. World Bank (2009h).

12. International Finance Corporation, "IFC Helps Simplify Procedures for Georgian Businesses to Save Time and Resources," accessed September 20, 2010, http://www.ifc.org/.

13. Van Stel, Storey and Thurik (2007).

14. World Bank conference, "The Singapore Experience: Ingredients for Successful Nation-Wide eTransformation," Singapore, September 30, 2009.

15. World Bank (2009g).

16. Common Register Portal of the German Federal States, https://www.handelsregister.de/rp_web.

17. Ciccone and Papaioannou (2007).

18. Ardagna and Lusardi (2008).

19. Crain (2005).

20. Barseghyan and DiCecio (2009).

21. Dabla-Norris and Inchauste (2008).

22. Fonseca, Lopez-Garcia and Pissarides (2001).

23. Ho and Wong (2006).

24. Klapper and Love(2010).

25. Bruhn (2008).

26. Kaplan, Piedra and Seira (2007).

27. Aghion and others (2008).

28. Freund and Bolaky (2008).

29. Ayyagari, Beck and Demirgüç-Kunt (2007).

Dealing with construction permits

FIGURE 4.1

The Democratic Republic of Congo made dealing with construction permits faster and cheaper

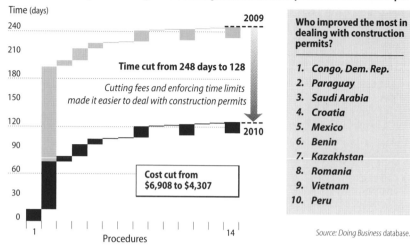

Time cut from 248 days to 128

Cutting fees and enforcing time limits made it easier to deal with construction permits

Cost cut from $6,908 to $4,307

Who improved the most in dealing with construction permits?

1. **Congo, Dem. Rep.**
2. **Paraguay**
3. **Saudi Arabia**
4. **Croatia**
5. **Mexico**
6. **Benin**
7. **Kazakhstan**
8. **Romania**
9. **Vietnam**
10. **Peru**

Source: Doing Business database.

The devastating earthquake in Port-au-Prince in January 2010 left more than 1.3 million Haitians homeless. Virtually every building in the capital was damaged or destroyed. Haiti lacks a comprehensive national building law and seismic design code, and construction in Port-au-Prince had followed inadequate standards and building practices. Just a month later Chile was rocked by an earthquake 500 times as powerful as the one in Haiti. The earthquake damaged 750,000 homes. Many believe the outcome could have been worse. Chile's building codes and risk-based building rules have been regularly updated since their adoption in 1931.

Regulation of construction is critical to protect the public. But it needs to be efficient, to avoid excessive constraints on a sector that plays an important part in every economy (table 4.1). According to a recent OECD study, the construction industry accounts on average for 6.5% of GDP.[1] The building sector is Europe's largest industrial employer, accounting for about 7% of employment. In the European Union, the United States and Japan combined, more than 40 million people work in construction. It is estimated that for every 10 jobs directly related to a construction project, another 8 jobs may be created in the local economy.[2] Small domestic firms account for most of the sector's output and most of its jobs.

Some of the jobs have been lost as a result of the global economic crisis. Between December 2007 and January 2010, 1.9 million construction workers in the United States lost their jobs.[3] According to the ILO, 5 million jobs in the global construction industry disappeared in 2008 alone.[4]

In 2009/10, 19 economies made it easier to deal with construction permits (table 4.2). Sub-Saharan Africa accounted for the most reforms of the construction permitting process, followed by Eastern Europe and Central Asia. For the first time a conflict-affected economy, the Democratic Republic of Congo, improved the ease of dealing with construction permits the most (figure 4.1). A regulatory reform program streamlined construction permitting in Kinshasa, reducing the time to deal with construction permits from 248 days to 128 and the average cost from $6,908 to $4,307.

Doing Business measures the procedures, time and cost for a small to medium-size business to obtain all the necessary approvals to build a simple commercial warehouse and connect it to basic utility services (figure 4.2). Such in-

TABLE 4.1

Where is dealing with construction permits easy—and where not?

Easiest	RANK	Most difficult	RANK
Hong Kong SAR, China	1	Malawi	174
		Burundi	175
Singapore	2	Serbia	176
St. Vincent and the Grenadines	3	India	177
		Tajikistan	178
Belize	4	Ukraine	179
New Zealand	5	Tanzania	180
Marshall Islands	6	China	181
Georgia	7	Russian Federation	182
St. Kitts and Nevis	8	Eritrea[a]	183
Maldives	9		
Denmark	10		

Note: Rankings are the average of the economy's rankings on the procedures, time and cost to comply with formalities to build a warehouse. See Data notes for details.

a. No practice.

Source: Doing Business database.

FIGURE 4.2

What are the time, cost and number of procedures to comply with formalities to build a warehouse?

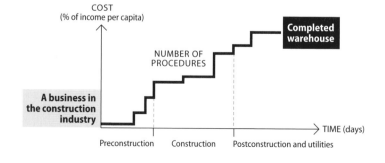

COST (% of income per capita)

NUMBER OF PROCEDURES

Completed warehouse

A business in the construction industry

Preconstruction   Construction   Postconstruction and utilities

TIME (days)

FIGURE 4.3
Eastern Europe and Central Asia leads in number of reforms in construction permitting
Number of *Doing Business* reforms making it easier to deal with construction permits by *Doing Business* report year

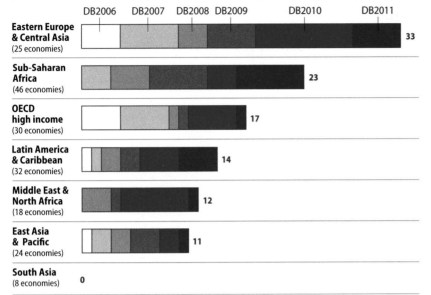

Note: A *Doing Business* reform is counted as 1 reform per reforming economy per year. The data sample for DB2006 (2005) includes 174 economies. The sample for DB2011 (2010) also includes The Bahamas, Bahrain, Brunei Darussalam, Cyprus, Kosovo, Liberia, Luxembourg, Montenegro and Qatar, for a total of 183 economies.
Source: *Doing Business* database.

683% of income per capita to complete all required procedures, down from 220 days and 839% of income per capita in 2005. OECD high-income economies have streamlined their systems the most. Obtaining approvals for building a simple warehouse now takes on average 16 procedures, 166 days and 62.1% of income per capita.

A large gap remains for much of the rest of the world. Authorities in Eastern Europe and Central Asia require the most procedures to obtain construction approvals, 22 on average. Delays are common in Sub-Saharan Africa. To comply with formalities takes longer than 2 months there than in OECD high-income economies. And in South Asia an entrepreneur has to pay on average 2,039% of income per capita in permitting fees.

MORE REFORMS IN EASTERN EUROPE AND CENTRAL ASIA

Eastern Europe and Central Asia was the region with the most reforms of construction permitting in the past 6 years (figure 4.3). Twenty economies implemented 33 new regulations, mainly to revamp outdated construction formalities from the communist era. And the region that used to have the longest average

dicators can be telling. A recent competitiveness report by KPMG indicated that construction costs and the permitting process were among the top 20 factors determining the location of a start-up in the United States.[5]

WHAT ARE THE TRENDS?

In an effort to ensure building safety while keeping compliance costs reasonable, governments around the world have worked on consolidating permitting requirements. Today an entrepreneur spends on average 202 days and

TABLE 4.2
Who made dealing with construction permits easier in 2009/10—and what did they do?

Feature	Economies	Some highlights
Reduced time for processing permit applications	Benin, Burkina Faso, Democratic Republic of Congo, Croatia, Hungary, Kazakhstan, Mexico, Peru, Romania, Rwanda, Sierra Leone	In Benin a new commission to process building permit applications reduced the average time for dealing with construction permits from 410 days to 320.
Streamlined procedures	Côte d'Ivoire, Croatia, Kazakhstan, Mali, Mexico, Saudi Arabia, Ukraine	Ukraine cut 9 of 31 procedures, reducing time by a third and cost by 6%.
Adopted new building regulations	Croatia, Hungary, Kazakhstan, Romania	Amendments to Romania's construction law and building regulations cut time by 15 days and cost by 12.9%.
Reduced fees	Burkina Faso, Democratic Republic of Congo, Rwanda, Vietnam	Vietnam's new registration fee for completed buildings cut total cost by 43%.
Introduced or improved one-stop shop	Kazakhstan, Paraguay, Russian Federation, Saudi Arabia	In Paraguay a new single-window approach in the municipality cut time from 291 days to 179.
Introduced risk-based approvals	Kazakhstan, Mali	Mali's new simplified environmental impact assessment for noncomplex commercial buildings cut time by 9% and cost by 32.7%.
Improved electronic platforms or online services	Colombia	Colombia improved its electronic verification of prebuilding certificates, which cut 1 procedure.

Source: *Doing Business* database.

TABLE 4.3
Good practices around the world in making it easy to deal with construction permits

Practice	Economies[a]	Examples
Using risk-based building approvals	84	Colombia, Germany, Mauritius, Singapore
Having an approved building code	43	Croatia, Kenya, New Zealand, Republic of Yemen
Having a one-stop shop	22	Bahrain, Chile, Georgia, Hong Kong SAR (China)

a. Among 183 economies surveyed.
Source: Doing Business database.

delays achieved significant time savings. These changes reduced the average time for dealing with construction formalities by 30 days, from 280 to 250 (figure 4.4). Performance varies within the region. Georgia, after 6 years of steady improvements, has the most efficient permitting system. To comply with formalities in Tbilisi takes 98 days, far fewer than the regional average of 250 days or the Albanian one of 331.

COST STILL HIGH IN AFRICA

In Sub-Saharan Africa 23 reforms making it easier to deal with construction permits were implemented in the past 6 years. Burkina Faso set up a new one-stop shop, Kenya introduced risk-based approvals, Liberia reduced fees, and Benin, the Democratic Republic of Congo, Mali and Rwanda streamlined permitting procedures. These improvements have reduced permitting delays in the region by 16 days. More can be done.

The cost remains the second highest globally, at 1,631% of income per capita on average. The high cost largely reflects high fees to connect to water, telephone and electricity service.

ONLINE IN THE MIDDLE EAST AND NORTH AFRICA…

Economies in the Middle East and North Africa that made dealing with construction permits easier focused on introducing online services and electronic platforms. This trend was initiated in the early 1990s by some Gulf Cooperation Council countries (Bahrain, Qatar, Saudi Arabia and the United Arab Emirates). In Bahrain, where complying with building formalities takes the least time in the region, applicants can download forms, submit applications and building plans, track the status of their applications and pay bills—all online.[6] The changes in the region reduced the average permitting time by 41 days, making the Middle East and North Africa the fastest globally.

…AND IN EAST ASIA

The Middle East and North Africa was not the only region where technology was used to make construction permitting more efficient. In East Asia and the Pacific, Singapore and Hong Kong SAR (China) converted their one-stop shops for building permits to online systems in 2008. In Singapore the Building and Construction Authority provides easy access to relevant information and allows online submission of all paperwork. In Hong Kong SAR (China), while the application process still has to be completed in person, all application forms and zoning maps are now online.

WHAT HAS WORKED?

Smart regulation ensures that standards are met while making compliance easy and accessible to all. Coherent and transparent rules, efficient processes and adequate allocation of resources are especially important in sectors where safety is at stake (table 4.3). Construction is one of them.

FIGURE 4.4
Biggest time savings in the Middle East and North Africa
Regional averages in dealing with construction permits

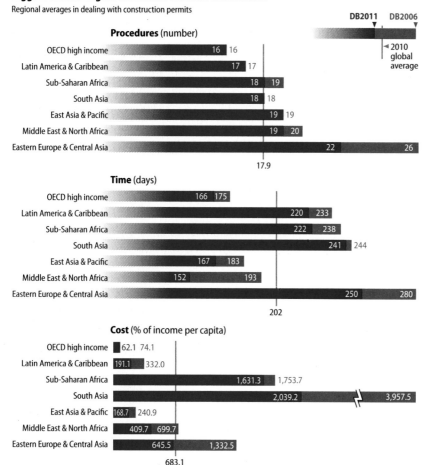

Note: The data sample for DB2006 (2005) includes 174 economies. The sample for DB2011 (2010) also includes The Bahamas, Bahrain, Brunei Darussalam, Cyprus, Kosovo, Liberia, Luxembourg, Montenegro and Qatar, for a total of 183 economies. Zimbabwe is not included in the samples due to the impact of inflation on the average cost estimates.

Source: Doing Business database.

TABLE 4.4
Who makes dealing with construction permits easy—and who does not?

Procedures (number)			
Fewest		**Most**	
Denmark	6	Azerbaijan	31
Hong Kong SAR, China	7	Brunei Darussalam	32
New Zealand	7	Guinea	32
Vanuatu	7	Poland	32
Sweden	8	El Salvador	34
Maldives	9	Kazakhstan	34
St. Lucia	9	Czech Republic	36
Georgia	10	China	37
Grenada	10	India	37
Marshall Islands	10	Russian Federation	53

Time (days)			
Fastest		**Slowest**	
Singapore	25	Brazil	411
Korea, Rep.	34	Nepal	424
United States	40	Suriname	431
Bahrain	43	Russian Federation	540
Colombia	50	Côte d'Ivoire	592
Vanuatu	51	Lesotho	601
Marshall Islands	55	Cyprus	677
Solomon Islands	62	Cambodia	709
United Arab Emirates	64	Zimbabwe	1,012
New Zealand	65	Haiti	1,179

Cost (% of income per capita)			
Least		**Most**	
Qatar	0.8	Niger	2,352
St. Kitts and Nevis	4.8	Zambia	2,454
Palau	5.1	Congo, Dem. Rep.	2,692
Trinidad and Tobago	5.1	Tanzania	2,756
Brunei Darussalam	6.7	Russian Federation	4,141
St. Vincent and the Grenadines	7.0	Chad	6,684
Malaysia	7.9	Burundi	7,048
Thailand	9.5	Zimbabwe	8,021
Hungary	9.8	Afghanistan	11,355
Dominica	11.0	Liberia	29,574

Source: Doing Business database.

FOCUSING ON RESULTS

Efficient regulation starts with a uniform building code—and its uniform implementation. Forty-three economies globally have adopted uniform construction rules. Most commonly, a central authority outlines the rules and local authorities implement them. When regulations are not organized and applied coherently, builders and authorities can become confused about how to proceed. This often leads to delays, uncertainty and disputes.

In Nigeria a new national building code was drafted in 2006, but it has yet to be enforced. Some Nigerian states have started implementing several provisions of the code, such as by amending local urban and regional planning laws to require new inspections and certificates. Others have not. The result is wide variation across states—confusing for builders with projects in more than one.[7]

Building rules also have to be adaptable so that they can keep up with economic and technological change—particularly important in the light of growing environmental concerns. New Zealand chose an effective approach: performance-focused building codes set targets and overall technical standards but do not regulate how to achieve those standards. This allows room for innovation in building techniques.

If provisions are too precise, this creates a challenge for keeping regulation up to date. Some building codes specify what materials can be used in construction. This seems to make sense. The materials are tested for safety, and their technical parameters mandated in the code. But this approach works only when codes are up to date. And they rarely are in the transition economies of Eastern Europe and Central Asia, where such rules are most common. Construction norms in Ukraine still refer to materials that used to be produced in the Soviet Union. Today these materials are no longer available, so no one can fully comply with the regulations.

USING ONE-STOP SHOPS TO IMPROVE COORDINATION

Before a building plan is approved, appropriate clearances are needed to ensure quality and safety. Often several agencies are involved. To prevent overlap and ensure efficiency, many economies have opted to put the agencies in one location. These one-stop shops improve the organization of the review process—not by reducing the number of checks needed but by better coordinating the efforts of different agencies. That way, more resources can be devoted to safety checks rather than to paperwork.

There are different ways to organize a one-stop shop. In Paraguay authorities moved professionals from 7 municipal departments into 1. Since early 2010 Burkina Faso has held periodic meetings of all approving bodies to speed up clearances. In 2009 the local government in Hong Kong SAR (China), as part of its "Be the Smart Regulator" program, merged 8 procedures involving 6 different agencies and 2 private utilities through a one-stop center. A single window facilitates interaction for customers. Globally, 22 economies

FIGURE 4.5
Taking advantage of one-stop shops and streamlined procedures in construction permits

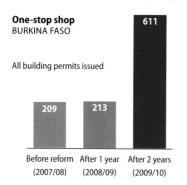

One-stop shop
BURKINA FASO

All building permits issued

209	213	611
Before reform (2007/08)	After 1 year (2008/09)	After 2 years (2009/10)

Streamlined procedures
CANADA

Commercial building permits issued

7,899	9,375	9,757
Before reform (2005)	After 1 year (2006)	After 2 years (2007)

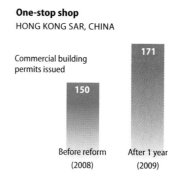

One-stop shop
HONG KONG SAR, CHINA

Commercial building permits issued

150	171
Before reform (2008)	After 1 year (2009)

Source: Burkina Faso, Centre de Facilitation des Actes de Construire (CEFAC); Toronto City Building Department; Hong Kong SAR Government, Hong Kong Economic and Trade Office, Washington, D.C.

coordinate agencies involved in approving construction permits through some form of one-stop shop.

DIFFERENTIATING PROJECTS BY RISK

Not all buildings involve the same social, cultural, economic or environmental impacts. A hospital or skyscraper cannot be compared with a 2-story commercial warehouse. Efficient governments have implemented rigorous yet differentiated construction permitting processes to treat buildings according to their risk level and location.

Simple or low-risk buildings require less documentation than more complex structures and can be approved faster. This saves time for both entrepreneurs and authorities and allows them to direct their efforts and resources more efficiently. Kazakhstan recently implemented differentiated approval procedures for complex and noncomplex projects, allowing a fast-track procedure for projects under 1,000 square meters. Belarus, Canada, Colombia and Germany are among the 84 economies that have functioning fast-track application processes for small commercial buildings. After Bavaria implemented differentiated permitting approaches for low- and high-risk projects, builders saved an estimated €154 million in building permit fees in a year, while building authorities needed 270 fewer employees on their payroll.[8]

WHAT ARE SOME RESULTS?

Over the past 6 years *Doing Business* recorded 110 reforms streamlining construction permitting procedures worldwide. Governments, the private sector and citizens alike are starting to see benefits.

GREATER CAPACITY

More efficient systems can prepare governments to take advantage of a pickup in construction activity. Look at Colombia. In 1995 obtaining building authorizations in Bogotá took 3 years on average. Today it takes about a month. This is thanks to a broad program of reforms targeting the construction permitting process. The government transferred the administration of building permits to the private sector, created a risk-based approval process and introduced electronic verification of the ownership status of buildings and land. The changes were timely, because construction activity took off. In 1996 the approved building construction area was 11.3 million square meters. In 2007 it was 19.2 million—70% more. Meanwhile, the construction sector grew from 6% of GDP to 7%.[9]

Georgia's story is similar. The government overhauled the construction permitting system between 2005 and 2009. Among other things, it created a one-stop shop and gradually consolidated 25 procedures into 10, reducing the time to comply with formalities from 195 days to 98. Today construction is among

the most dynamic and rapidly growing sectors of the economy. The construction area in the capital tripled between 2004 and 2007, from 463,000 square meters to 1.5 million. During the same period the construction sector expanded from 6.3% of GDP to 11%.[10]

In other economies too, more efficient approval procedures allowed agencies to process greater volumes of permit approvals and increased client satisfaction. In 2006 Burkina Faso was among the 10 economies with the most complex requirements in the world. Not surprisingly, a survey that year found that more than 23% of local companies identified licenses and permits as a major constraint to doing business in the country.[11] To address this concern, a one-stop shop for construction permits, the Centre de Facilitation des Actes de Construire, was opened in May 2008. A new regulation merged 32 procedures into 15, reduced the time required from 226 days to 122 and cut the cost by 40%. Entrepreneurs took note. From May 2009 to May 2010 611 building permits were granted in Ouagadougou, up from an average of about 150 a year in 2002–06 (figure 4.5).[12] Another firm survey, conducted in 2009, showed that the share of entrepreneurs considering the construction permitting process to be problematic had dropped by 6 percentage points in the previous 3 years.[13]

Hong Kong SAR (China), after finishing 2 years of regulatory changes to reengineer its construction permitting system, also saw an increase in volume. The number of commercial building permits grew by 14%, from 150 in 2008 to 171 in 2009—despite the global economic downturn.

The Canadian city of Toronto revamped its construction permitting process in 2005 by introducing time limits for different stages of the process and presenting a unique basic list of requirements for each project. Later it provided for electronic information and risk-based approvals with fast-track procedures ("Commercial Xpress" for commercial buildings and "Residential Fast Track" for residential buildings). Between 2005 and 2007 the number of commercial building permits increased by 24% and between 2005 and 2008 the construction value of new commercial buildings rose by 84%.[14]

LOWER COST—FOR BUILDERS AND REGULATORS

Effective and efficient use of information technology can reduce the regulatory cost of construction. Jurisdictions across the United States are using information technology to increase efficiency. More than 500 now use an advanced e-permit processing system. Introduced since 2003, the system has reduced the time that professionals in the construction industry spend on permits by 30–40%. Interactive voice response systems enable customers to use a touch-tone telephone to connect with a jurisdiction's database of building code and land management applications, reducing the time to schedule and conduct inspections from 2–3 days to less than 24 hours. Mobile field inspection technology has increased the number of inspections per day by 25% and reduced contractors' downtime while waiting for inspections and their results by 20%. More than 20 U.S. cities use e-plan review. This system of online submission of building plans has shortened the review period by 40%, eliminated the risk of lost plans and re-

duced by 80% the number of in-person visits made to building authorities by out-of-state owners and architects.[15]

Reducing delays benefits more than just builders and owners. A study in the United States estimates that accelerating permit approvals by 3 months in a 22-month project cycle could increase construction spending by 5.7% and property tax revenue for local governments by 16%.[16]

GREATER SAFETY AND TRANSPARENCY

By some estimates 60–80% of building projects in developing economies are undertaken without the proper permits and approvals.[17] In the Philippines 57% of new construction is considered illegal. In Egypt this share might reach 90%.[18] In Georgia before the new permitting process that was initiated in 2005, fewer than 45% of construction projects had legal permits. If procedures are overly complicated or costly, builders tend to proceed without a permit. This leads to revenue losses for local authorities, limitations on access to credit for the builders and owners and the loss of formal jobs in the construction sector.[19]

Overly complicated construction rules also can increase opportunities for corruption. World Bank Enterprise Survey data show that the share of firms expecting to give gifts in exchange for construction approvals is correlated with the level of complexity and cost of dealing with construction permits.[20] According to a 2005 survey conducted in 15 countries by Transparency International, entrepreneurs perceive construction as one of the most corrupt industries, surpassing arms and defense, oil and gas, real estate and mining.[21]

Good regulation ensures compliance with the standards and protects the public while making the permitting process transparent and affordable for construction companies. Where informal construction is rampant, the public can suffer. Nigeria, like Haiti, lacks a uniform building code that sets the standards for construction. Many of the

buildings erected do not comply with proper safety standards. Without clear rules, enforcing even basic standards is a daunting task. Structural incidents have multiplied. According to the Nigerian Institute of Building, 84 buildings collapsed in the past 20 years, killing more than 400 people.[22]

1. OECD (2010).
2. PricewaterhouseCoopers (2005).
3. U.S. Bureau of Labor Statistics, "Employment Situation," January 2010, http://www.bls.gov/.
4. ILO (2009).
5. KPMG (2009).
6. Bahrain, Ministry of Municipalities and Agricultural Affairs, http://websrv.municipality.gov.bh/.
7. World Bank (2010a).
8. Bayerisches Staatsministerium des Innern (2002).
9. Espinosa-Wang (forthcoming).
10. IFC (2008a).
11. World Bank Enterprise Surveys (http://www.enterprisesurveys.org/).
12. Information provided by Burkina Faso's Centre de Facilitation des Actes de Construire.
13. World Bank Enterprise Surveys (http://www.enterprisesurveys.org/).
14. According to information provided by the City of Toronto's Office of the Chief Building Official, the construction value of commercial buildings (excluding industrial and institutional buildings) rose from Can$1.56 billion in 2005 to Can$2.87 billion in 2008.
15. Information available at http://www.natlpartnerstreamline.org/.
16. PricewaterhouseCoopers (2005).
17. De Soto (2000).
18. De Soto (2000).
19. Moullier (2009).
20. World Bank (2009d).
21. Kenny (2007).
22. Agence France Presse, "Nigeria Approves Building Code," News24.com, August 3, 2006, http://www.news24.com/. Because many cases go unreported, the actual figure is probably higher.

FIGURE 5.1

Samoa increased the efficiency of property registration

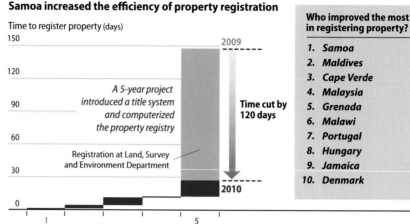

Time to register property (days)

A 5-year project introduced a title system and computerized the property registry

Registration at Land, Survey and Environment Department

Time cut by 120 days

Procedures

Who improved the most in registering property?

1. **Samoa**
2. **Maldives**
3. **Cape Verde**
4. **Malaysia**
5. **Grenada**
6. **Malawi**
7. **Portugal**
8. **Hungary**
9. **Jamaica**
10. **Denmark**

Source: Doing Business database.

In the early 1990s people wanting to register property in Minsk needed to arrive outside the land registry by 5 a.m. and, if it was winter, keep a fire going to stay warm during the long wait.[1] Newly independent Belarus had a complicated registration process with many layers of duplication, leading to delays of up to 231 days. The system could not keep up with the growing real estate market. That changed after 2004 (table 5.1). A new one-stop shop cut unnecessary procedures by centralizing the registration process and hired 10 times as many registrars. Today registering property takes 15 days, and the system covers 5 million property units and manages 760,000 sales and first-time registrations a year.

Property is often requested by banks as collateral for loans. But where property is informal or poorly administered, it has little chance of being used as a guarantee. Hernando de Soto calls such assets "dead capital."[2] The result is limited access to finance, which can limit economic growth.[3] Women can be particularly affected. "I tried many times to apply for a loan but didn't get even a quarter. They tell me to bring collateral that I can't provide… One time they asked for land and I don't even have land. Sometimes they ask for buildings as collateral as well," says Antonia, a detergent manufacturer in Ghana. Her experience is not uncommon. In 9 of 128 economies, including Cameroon and Chile, women's ownership rights over movable and immovable property are not equal to men's, and in even more economies women have less right than men to mortgage it.[4]

Ensuring formal property rights is fundamental. Effective administration of land is part of that. If formal property transfer is too costly or complicated,

formal titles might go informal again. Even if titles remain formal, property markets will not function effectively if regulations keep investment from being channeled to its most productive use. And titles won't lead to more credit if collateral laws make mortgaging property expensive and inefficient courts prevent banks from enforcing collateral when a debtor defaults. Some studies report cases where titling failed to bring significant increases in credit or income.[5]

Doing Business records the full sequence of procedures necessary for a business to purchase a property from another business and transfer the property title to the buyer's name. The transaction is considered complete when it is opposable to third parties and the purchasing company can use the property, use it as collateral in taking new loans or, if necessary, sell it to another business (figure 5.2).

In 2009/10, 21 economies made it

TABLE 5.1

Where is registering property easy—and where not?

Easiest	RANK	Most difficult	RANK
Saudi Arabia	1	Angola	174
Georgia	2	Guinea-Bissau	175
New Zealand	3	Liberia	176
United Arab Emirates	4	Belgium	177
		Eritrea	178
Armenia	5	Nigeria	179
Belarus	6	Timor-Leste	180
Lithuania	7	Micronesia, Fed. Sts.	181
Norway	8	Marshall Islands	182
Slovak Republic	9	Brunei Darussalam	183
Azerbaijan	10		

Note: Rankings are the average of the economy's rankings on the procedures, time and cost to register property. See Data notes for details.
Source: Doing Business database.

FIGURE 5.2

What are the time, cost and number of procedures required to transfer a property between 2 local companies?

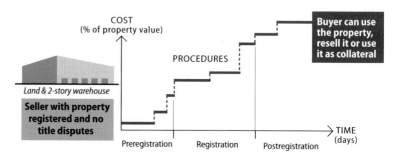

COST (% of property value)

PROCEDURES

Buyer can use the property, resell it or use it as collateral

Land & 2-story warehouse

Seller with property registered and no title disputes

Preregistration — Registration — Postregistration

TIME (days)

TABLE 5.2
Who made registering property easier in 2009/10—and what did they do?

Feature	Economies	Some highlights
Reduced taxes or fees	Bangladesh, Cape Verde, Democratic Republic of Congo, Hungary, Jamaica, Mali	*Average cost reduction: 3.6% of the property value* Changes ranged from 2% of the property value in Jamaica to 6% in Hungary (which halved the transfer tax). Cape Verde introduced a fixed registration fee, going from 2% of the property value to $256.
Increased administrative efficiency	Bosnia and Herzegovina, Grenada, Malawi, Maldives, Samoa, Sierra Leone	*Average time saved: 66 days* Sierra Leone cut 150 days by removing restrictions on private land transfers. Grenada's registrar now focuses only on property matters. Malawi decentralized government consents for property transfers, saving 39 days.
Computerized procedures	Denmark, Malaysia, Poland, Samoa, Slovenia	*Average time saved: 4 months* Time savings were greatest in Slovenia (9 months) and Samoa (4 months). Malaysia digitized property registration, saving more than 2 months.
Introduced online procedures	Austria, Denmark, Jamaica, Malaysia, Poland	*Average time saved: 4 days* Malaysia introduced online procedures to assess and pay stamp duties, cutting 6 days. Jamaica provided online access to the company registry. Austria introduced electronic communication between notaries and the registry.
Combined and streamlined procedures	Denmark, Portugal, Sweden, Uruguay	*Average reduction: 4 days and 2 procedures* New one-stop shops merged 3 procedures in Denmark and 4 in Portugal. Municipalities in Sweden and Uruguay abolished the requirement for clearance of preemption rights.
Introduced fast-track procedures	Jamaica, Peru	Registration for simple property sales is possible in 2 days in Jamaica (down from 7) and Peru (down from 9).

Source: Doing Business database.

easier to register property, 7 of them in the OECD high-income group and 4 in Latin America and the Caribbean. Samoa improved the ease of registering property the most. It completed a 5-year project to move to a title system and computerized the property registry, saving 4 months from the time to register property. Six economies lowered the cost, and 6 (including Samoa) increased administrative efficiency at their registries (table 5.2). Five others raised the cost to transfer property (compared with 2 on average in previous years). Bahrain, Greece, Pakistan, Panama and Thailand raised the transfer tax by an average of 4.2% of the property value—with Greece reversing previous cuts and Thailand reversing a temporary cut. Antigua and Barbuda and Belgium added new procedures.

WHAT ARE THE TRENDS?

In the past 6 years 105 economies undertook 146 reforms making it easier to transfer property (figure 5.3). Globally, the time to transfer property fell by 38% and the cost by 10%.

GLOBAL TRENDS

The most popular feature of property registration reform in those 6 years, implemented in 52 economies, was lowering transfer taxes and government fees. This reduced the cost by 3.1% of the property value on average. Sub-Saharan Africa was the most active, with 22 economies lowering costs. Two gradually reduced high transfer costs, Burundi by 10% of the property value and Burkina Faso by 7%. Two others made big cuts all at once, Rwanda by 8.8% of the property value and Mozambique by 7.5%.

The second most popular feature, implemented in 32 economies, was streamlining procedures and linking or improving agencies' systems to simplify registration. These measures reduced interactions between entrepreneurs and agencies—saving 2 procedures on average—while maintaining security and controls.

Thirteen such reforms took place in Eastern Europe and Central Asia. Besides Belarus, Azerbaijan and Kazakhstan also created one-stop shops for property transfers. In Latvia the land registry can now check municipal tax databases directly, saving entrepreneurs a step. FYR Macedonia centralized property encumbrance and cadastre information. The 2 certificates are now issued together.

Eight economies in Sub-Saharan Africa undertook similar measures. Ethiopia and Rwanda decentralized their land registries to eliminate bottlenecks, creating new branches responsible for properties in their jurisdiction. Ethiopia's 10 new branches and Rwanda's 5 coordinate the work with municipalities and tax agencies. And Ethiopia's registry now assesses property's market value using predetermined tables, eliminating the need for physical inspections.

Twenty-eight economies, 9 in Sub-Saharan Africa, increased administrative efficiency. Botswana and Madagascar reorganized their land registries, hired more staff and added more computers and branches. Botswana also linked staff salary increases to the achievement of targets set by the land department's 3-year plan. Mali and Niger reorganized their land registries by reassigning workloads and enhancing supervision.

With 7 similar reforms, Latin America and the Caribbean was also active. Grenada recently nominated 2 new registrars, 1 dedicated to property transactions. This reduced the court registrar's

FIGURE 5.3

Fast pace in property registration reforms in Sub-Saharan Africa over the years

Number of *Doing Business* reforms making it easier to register property by *Doing Business* report year

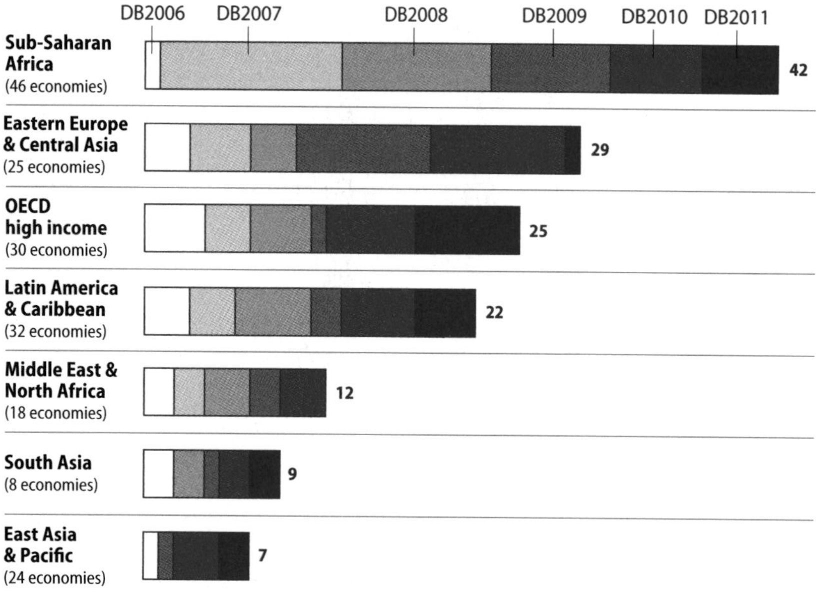

Note: A *Doing Business* reform is counted as 1 reform per reforming economy per year. The data sample for DB2006 (2005) includes 174 economies. The sample for DB2011 (2010) also includes The Bahamas, Bahrain, Brunei Darussalam, Cyprus, Kosovo, Liberia, Luxembourg, Montenegro and Qatar, for a total of 183 economies.
Source: Doing Business database.

workload, cutting the time to register property by half. Guatemala's registry improved customer service by installing delegates in major banks, providing text message notifications and offering a special service for frequent users such as notaries. Another new service blocks sales as extra security for customers not expecting to sell property for a while. Employees benefit from an incentive system that accounts for the speed and quality of their work. Combined with computerization, these efforts halved the time to transfer property in Guatemala.

COMPUTERIZATION IN OECD HIGH-INCOME ECONOMIES...

OECD high-income economies, along with the Middle East and North Africa, have the fastest property registration, taking 33 days on average (figure 5.4). Compare that with the slowest—around 3 months on average in South Asia and East Asia and the Pacific.

Twenty-nine of 30 OECD high-income economies have electronic registries, and 85% allow online access to information on encumbrances, either for all or for such professionals as notaries.

Eleven, including France, the Netherlands and New Zealand, offer electronic registration. Portugal's new customer service center, Casa pronto, has processed 109,000 transactions since its 2007 launch and now covers 30% of sales. It allows users not only to register property transfers but also to complete all due diligence—including checking tax payments, ownership and encumbrances—in one step.

...AND IN EASTERN EUROPE AND CENTRAL ASIA

In Eastern Europe and Central Asia most property registration systems have undergone a complete overhaul. Land and building databases have been unified, then computerized. Today the region accounts for 5 of the top 10 economies on the ease of registering property. Transferring property takes on average 6 procedures and costs 2.4% of the property value, less than in any other region.

COST HIGHEST IN AFRICA

In Sub-Saharan Africa, despite improvements, transferring property still costs the most, 9.6% of the property value on

average. The reason? High transfer taxes (averaging 7% of the property value) and high professional fees, such as for lawyers and notaries. In Brazzaville, in the Republic of Congo, notary fees amount to 4% of the property value. The transfer process is also complicated, requiring 7 procedures on average. Nineteen economies require an assessment of taxes to be paid. This can add up to 3 procedures in such economies as Kenya and Uganda, where physical inspections are required.

A cumbersome system can create opportunities for corruption. In Kenya in 2010 a raid uncovered thousands of land files blocked in the drawers of public officials hoping to collect bribes.[6] The need for ministerial consents can also add delays, up to 60–75 days in such economies as The Gambia, Lesotho, Malawi and Nigeria. The good news: Ghana eliminated this consent in 2006. In 2005 Côte d'Ivoire limited its use to properties not included in the zoning plan, and property sales doubled. Across the region, land registries are still mostly paper based. This partly explains registration delays such as the 113 days in Benin and 270 in Togo. The average time to transfer property in the region is 68 days; the world average, 58.

But efforts to improve property registration have been picking up. Economies such as Botswana, Burkina Faso, Madagascar, Mali and Mauritius have made agencies and systems more efficient through incentives, reorganization and better management tools. Despite being paper based, the land registry in Bamako, Mali, can complete registration in 2–3 weeks. Through broad property reforms implemented since 2007, Mauritius has reduced the transfer tax by 5% of the property value, eliminated separate clearances by utilities and set strict time limits for notaries and the land registry. Like most African economies, Mauritius lacks a cadastre, and it still requires a physical valuation for each property sale. But a new computerized property registry linking the valuation office with a new cadastre that will use aerial maps is expected to change this.

FIGURE 5.4
Property registration a third faster around the world since 2005
Regional averages in registering property

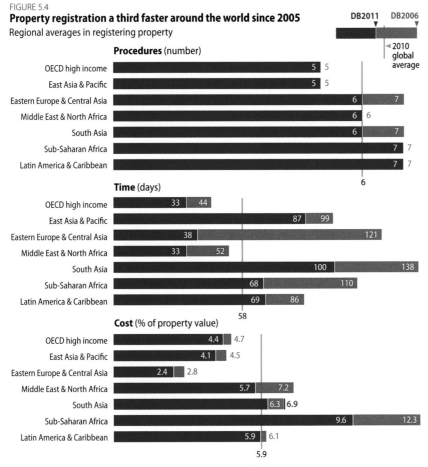

Note: The data sample for DB2006 (2005) includes 174 economies. The sample for DB2011 (2010) also includes The Bahamas, Bahrain, Brunei Darussalam, Cyprus, Kosovo, Liberia, Luxembourg, Montenegro and Qatar, for a total of 183 economies.
Source: Doing Business database.

COMPLEXITY IN LATIN AMERICA

Registering property in Latin America and the Caribbean tends to be complex, taking 7 procedures and 69 days on average. Numerous visits to different agencies are often the reason. Seven economies require a separate certificate from the commercial registry. Seven others mandate registrations beyond the land registry, such as with the municipality, the tax agency or the cadastre. Sixteen of 32 economies require a tax clearance. While this generally takes 1 or 2 days, it can take up to 20 in Paraguay and 42 in Trinidad and Tobago. Linking all agencies through a common database could help.

Remarkably, 20 of the region's economies have an electronic database for encumbrances and ownership. But only 6 of them make their electronic database available online for all. So paper certificates are still widely used, increasing delays. Checking for encumbrances still takes 5 days on average, compared with only 1 in OECD high-income economies.

SPEEDY PROCESS IN THE MIDDLE EAST AND NORTH AFRICA

Transferring property in the Middle East and North Africa is as fast as in OECD high-income economies at 33 days on average. In the United Arab Emirates it is just 2 days. Eleven of 18 economies have electronic databases for encumbrances and ownership verification, though Bahrain is the only one offering online registration. The average cost in the region remains fairly high, at 5.7% of the property value. But in 5 economies, including Kuwait and Qatar, the cost is less than 1% of the property value. In 9 others the cost exceeds 5%—and it ranges up to 28% in the Syrian Arab Republic, with the world's highest transfer taxes.

SOME LONG DELAYS IN SOUTH AND EAST ASIA

Transferring property can take time in South Asia, 100 days on average. The cost is also high, averaging 6.9% of the property value and ranging from almost 0 in Bhutan to 17% in Maldives. The process takes 6 procedures on average.

East Asia and the Pacific has the second lowest average transfer cost, 4.1% of the property value. While the average time to transfer property is 87 days, several economies, mostly small island states, stand out for the longest delays globally. In Kiribati transferring property takes 513 days, mostly for court verification. In the Solomon Islands, where one registry handles property, companies, movable property and intellectual property rights, registration takes 240 days. And as in Sub-Saharan Africa, transferring property can require high-level government consents. These take time, ranging from 25 days in the Solomon Islands to 105 in Tonga.

Some economies are moving forward with online services. In Hong Kong SAR (China) and Malaysia taxes can be paid online. In Singapore all due diligence can be done online, through one portal.

TABLE 5.3
Good practices around the world in making it easy to register property

Practice	Economies[a]	Examples
Using an electronic database for encumbrances	108	Jamaica, Sweden, United Kingdom
Setting time limits for registration	49	Botswana, Guatemala, Indonesia
Setting fixed transfer costs	17	Arab Republic of Egypt, Estonia, New Zealand
Offering expedited procedures	16	Azerbaijan, Bulgaria, Georgia

a. Among 177 economies surveyed.
Source: Doing Business database.

FIGURE 5.5
Most economies in Eastern Europe and Central Asia have time limits for property registration
Share of economies in region (%)

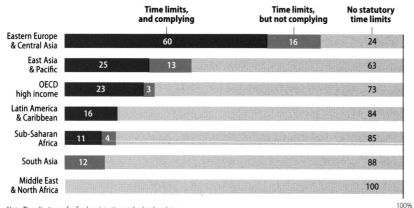

Note: Time limits are for final registration at the land registry.
Source: Doing Business database.

WHAT HAS WORKED?

Governments worldwide have been making it easier for entrepreneurs to register and transfer property. Some good practices can help in achieving that goal (table 5.3).

GOING ELECTRONIC

Worldwide, 61% of economies have an electronic database for encumbrances, including almost all OECD high-income and Eastern European and Central Asian economies. But in Sub-Saharan Africa and South Asia more than 80% still have paper-based systems. This makes a difference. In economies with computerized registries, transferring property takes about half as much time. Properly backed up, electronic databases can also help ensure property security. In Haiti after the 2010 earthquake, damaged records in the paper-based land registry make reconstruction even harder.[7]

Twenty-four economies as diverse as Belarus, Portugal and Zambia computerized their registries in the past 6 years. Full implementation can take time, ranging from 3 to 10 years. Gradual implementation or a pilot approach can facilitate the process. The cost can reach $2 million or more if surveying and cadastre work is involved. But the impact is substantial. These 24 economies cut their average time to transfer a property in half, by about 3 months on average.

COMPLYING WITH TIME LIMITS

Forty-nine economies worldwide have legal time limits for registration procedures, and 13 of them have expedited procedures. Globally, 77% of economies comply with statutory time limits. Eastern Europe and Central Asia, OECD high-income economies and Latin America and the Caribbean stand out for the highest compliance (figure 5.5).

In Eastern Europe and Central Asia 19 of 25 economies have time limits. Most are a success. In only 4 economies—Bulgaria, FYR Macedonia, Serbia and Ukraine—is compliance a problem. In Latin America and the Caribbean only 5 of 32 economies have statutory time limits, ranging from 2 days in Peru to 30 in Brazil. All 5 have good compliance. Spain has an innovative way to ensure compliance: the registry's fees are cut by 30% if registration takes more than 15 days.

In the past 6 years 14 economies introduced time limits. But most went further. Twelve, including Belarus, Burkina Faso, Egypt, FYR Macedonia, Mauritius and Rwanda, did so as part of broader reforms that included merging procedures through computerization, reorganization of the land registry or creation of one-stop shops.

OFFERING FAST-TRACK PROCEDURES

Sixteen economies offer expedited registration procedures at a premium of 2–5 times the basic fee. Time savings range

from 1 day to 32 and fees from $14 to $450. "I often get calls from friends who need to expedite a transfer," says a land registrar in Central America. But if expedited service is available to all, it doesn't matter whom you know in the registry.

Expedited procedures are most popular in Eastern Europe and Central Asia, where 9 economies offer them. In Moldova property can be registered in 10 days (for $38), 3 days ($111) or 1 day ($185). In Georgia in 2009 nearly 13% of transactions at the registry were expedited. Azerbaijan, Bulgaria and Romania all introduced this option in the past 6 years. Expedited procedures can also apply to certificates. They save 6 days for nonencumbrance certificates in Argentina and 4 days for tax clearance by Asmara Municipality in Eritrea.

SETTING LOW FIXED FEES

Seventeen economies have low fixed taxes and fees for property transfer, ranging from around $20 to $300, regardless of the property value. Nine economies in Eastern Europe and Central Asia apply fixed transfer taxes and fees, including Estonia, the Kyrgyz Republic and Russia. Egypt and New Zealand also do so. Twelve others, including Finland, the Republic of Korea and Malawi, have fixed fees for registration but charge other taxes and stamp duties in proportion to the property value.

Governments' administrative cost for registration is independent of the property value, so registration fees can be fixed and low. Combined with low transfer taxes, this may encourage formal registration and prevent underreporting of property values. Four economies switched to fixed registration fees in the past 6 years: Egypt and Poland in 2006, Rwanda in 2008 and Cape Verde in 2009. Rwanda made a radical change, reducing fees from 6% of the property value to $33.

Among the 154 economies with transfer costs that vary with the property value, at least 21 have sliding scales for fees or taxes. In 16 economies tax rates increase with the property value. In Angola

TABLE 5.4
Who makes registering property easy—and who does not?

Procedures (number)			
Fewest		**Most**	
Georgia	1	Ethiopia	10
Norway	1	Liberia	10
Portugal	1	Qatar	10
Sweden	1	Algeria	11
United Arab Emirates	1	Eritrea	11
Bahrain	2	Greece	11
New Zealand	2	Uzbekistan	12
Oman	2	Nigeria	13
Saudi Arabia	2	Uganda	13
Thailand	2	Brazil	14

Time (days)			
Fastest		**Slowest**	
Portugal	1	Vanuatu	188
Georgia	2	Puerto Rico	194
New Zealand	2	Suriname	197
Saudi Arabia	2	Guinea-Bissau	211
Thailand	2	Bangladesh	245
United Arab Emirates	2	Afghanistan	250
Lithuania	3	Togo	295
Norway	3	Solomon Islands	297
Iceland	4	Haiti	405
Australia	5	Kiribati	513

Cost (% of property value)			
Least		**Most**	
Bhutan	0.00	Côte d'Ivoire	13.9
Saudi Arabia	0.00	Guinea	14.0
Belarus	0.03	Maldives	16.9
Kiribati	0.04	Chad	18.2
Slovak Republic	0.05	Central African Republic	18.5
Kazakhstan	0.06	Cameroon	19.3
New Zealand	0.08	Senegal	20.6
Georgia	0.10	Comoros	20.8
Russian Federation	0.14	Nigeria	20.9
Azerbaijan	0.23	Syrian Arab Republic	27.9

Source: Doing Business database.

and Lithuania rates initially increase and then decrease as the property value rises.

WHAT ARE SOME RESULTS?

Formal titles can help facilitate access to credit. A study in Peru, where a large land titling program was implemented, suggests that when requested by lenders, property titles are associated with approval rates on public sector loans as much as 12% higher. And regardless of whether collateral is requested, interest rates are significantly lower for applicants with title.[8] A study in Nicaragua found that receipt of a title increased land values by 30% as well as the propensity to invest.[9] In Argentina property owners with formal title invested up to 47% more in their property.[10] Security in property ownership can also reduce the need to defend land rights: a study in Peru showed that property titles allowed people to work more away from the home.[11]

In surveys in 99 economies, an average of 21% of firms considered access to land a major constraint to business.[12] For some, formalizing title might simply be too costly. When Egypt reduced the cost of registration from 5.9% of the property value to 1% in 2006, new property registrations jumped by 39% in the following year. After Burkina Faso halved registration taxes to 8%, the stock of properties registered increased by 63% in the country as a whole—and by 93% in the capital city, Ouagadougou. But with less than 10% of properties formally registered, there is still a long way to go.

Increasing the efficiency of property registration systems benefits users as well as administrators. FYR Macedonia cut the time to register property by 40 days. For the 177,000 people buying property in 2009, that meant being able to use or mortgage their property 40 days earlier. Many benefited: twice as many properties were sold in 2009 as in 2007, despite the financial crisis. New delays to register property sales cut the other way. In Denmark in 2009 practitioners reported losing thousands of kroner in interest because transaction money was blocked in escrow accounts for more than a month while the new online registry was being implemented.[13] But new systems may be worth the wait. Electronic interactions are more transparent. A survey in India found that fewer users paid bribes to accelerate e-government services.[14]

Guatemala halved the time to transfer property, saving 45 days for each of the about 100,000 people selling property each year.[15] The land registry, digitized over the past 5 years, offers cadastral certificates as well as electronic access to data on encumbrances and ownership. People choose to use electronic services: in 2005, 66% of certificates were requested electronically; now 80% are. Buyers save the time and cost of going to the registry, standing in line and waiting 3 days for the paper certificate. And they can get instant information about encumbrances just before closing a property sale, increasing security.

Georgia now allows property transfers to be completed through 500 authorized users, notably banks. This saves time for entrepreneurs. A third of people transferring property in 2009 chose authorized users, up from 7% in 2007.

Efficient systems also prepare economies for the development of vibrant property markets. Belarus's unified and computerized registry was able to cope with the addition of 1.2 million new units over 3 years. The registry issued 1 million electronic property certificates in 2009. Georgia's new electronic registry managed 68,000 sales in 2007, twice as many as in 2003. FYR Macedonia's electronic registry now covers almost all the country, twice as much as in 2006.

1. Interview with Andrei A. Gayev, State Property Committee, Minsk, Belarus, September 2008.

2. De Soto (2000).

3. World Bank (2008).

4. World Bank, *Women, Business and the Law* database (http://wbl.worldbank.org/).

5. Pande and Udry (2005).

6. "Lands Ministry Officers on the Spot," *Daily Nation* (Nairobi), March 1, 2010, http://www.nation.co.ke/; "Missing Titles, Logbooks Starve Small Firms of Credit," *Financial Post* (Nairobi), March 22, 2010.

7. Anastasia Moloney, "Unclear Land Rights Hinder Haiti's Reconstruction," Reuters, *AlertNet*, July 5, 2010, http://alertnet.org/.

8. Field and Torero (2006).

9. Deininger and Chamorro (2002).

10. Galiani and Schargrodsky (2006).

11. Field (2007).

12. World Bank Enterprise Surveys, 2006–09 (http://www.enterprisesurveys.org).

13. Conference call with contributor.

14. Bhatia, Bhatnagar and Tominaga (2009).

15. Information provided by Guatemala's land registry and *Doing Business* database.

Getting credit

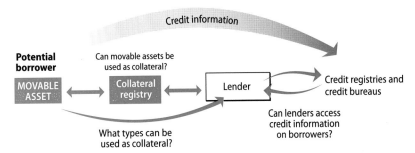

FIGURE 6.1

Do lenders have credit information on entrepreneurs seeking credit?
Is the law favorable to borrowers and lenders using movable assets as collateral?

Maria produces soybeans for export. She registered her small business after obtaining her first microfinance loan. For the past 5 years she has consistently repaid her loans, each time qualifying for a larger amount. Now she wants to obtain a commercial loan to diversify production. Maria's several years as a diligent microfinance borrower will not go unnoticed. In Bolivia, as in 45 other economies, private credit bureaus obtain data on the repayment patterns of microfinance borrowers.

Ideally, Maria's willingness to give her next soybean harvest as collateral would also help her loan application. But Bolivia's legal framework for secured transactions makes it extremely difficult for banks to accept movable assets

such as future crops and inventory as collateral. It requires a specific description of collateral in the loan agreement. Yet how can Maria know at the beginning of the season how many pounds of soybeans she will harvest? Where the secured transactions system has been improved—as it has in such economies as Bosnia and Herzegovina, Cambodia and Vanuatu—farmers, retailers and other small businesses do not face this problem (table 6.1).

Around the world movable assets, not land or buildings, often account for most of the capital stock of private firms and an especially large share for micro, small and medium-size enterprises. In the United States movable property makes up about 60% of the capital stock of enterprises.[1] Unlike in Bolivia and other economies that do not allow a general description of assets granted as collateral, in the United States most of this movable property could serve as collateral for a loan. Research shows that in developed economies borrowers with collateral get 9 times as much credit as those without it. They also benefit from repayment periods 11 times as long and interest rates up to 50% lower.[2]

In 2009, however, the global financial crisis adversely affected access to credit globally. According to recent research, the volume of loans around the world declined from 74% of global GDP to 65%, while the volume at the national level declined as a share of GDP in more

than 80% of countries.[3] Supporting the use of collateral to lower the risks associated with lending therefore matters in the current economic context.

Doing Business measures 2 types of institutions and systems that can facilitate access to finance and improve its allocation: credit information registries or bureaus and the legal rights of borrowers and lenders in secured transactions and bankruptcy laws. These institutions and systems work best together. Information sharing helps creditors assess the creditworthiness of clients, while legal rights can facilitate the use of collateral and the ability to enforce claims in the event of default.

Credit histories are no substitute for risk analysis, whose importance has been underscored by the global financial crisis. But when banks share information, loan officers can assess borrowers' creditworthiness using objective criteria. For regulators, credit information systems provide a powerful tool for supervising and monitoring credit risk in the economy. And greater information sharing can support competition. A recent study in the Middle East and North Africa found that lack of credit information systems may curtail competition in the banking sector.[4]

The 2 types of institutions are measured by 2 sets of indicators. One describes how well collateral and bankruptcy laws facilitate lending. The other measures the scope and accessibility of

TABLE 6.1

Where is getting credit easy— and where not?

Easiest	RANK	Most difficult	RANK
Malaysia	1	Syrian Arab Republic	174
Hong Kong SAR, China	2	Tajikistan	175
New Zealand	3	Bhutan	176
South Africa	4	Djibouti	177
United Kingdom	5	Eritrea	178
Australia	6	Madagascar	179
Bulgaria	7	São Tomé and Principe	180
Israel	8		
Singapore	9	Venezuela, RB	181
United States	10	Timor-Leste	182
		Palau	183

Note: Rankings are based on the sum of the strength of legal rights index and the depth of credit information index. See Data notes for details.
Source: Doing Business database.

FIGURE 6.2

Eastern Europe and Central Asia still leading in credit reforms

Number of *Doing Business* reforms making it easier to get credit by *Doing Business* report year

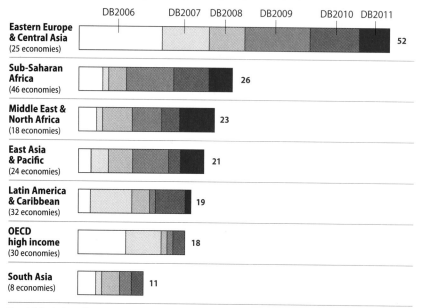

Note: A *Doing Business* reform is counted as 1 reform per reforming economy per year. The data sample for DB2006 (2005) includes 174 economies. The sample for DB2011 (2010) also includes The Bahamas, Bahrain, Brunei Darussalam, Cyprus, Kosovo, Liberia, Luxembourg, Montenegro and Qatar, for a total of 183 economies.
Source: Doing Business database.

credit information available through public credit registries and private credit bureaus and provides information on coverage (figure 6.1).

Nineteen economies made it easier to get credit in 2009/10. Ghana improved the most in both credit information and legal rights.

WHAT ARE THE TRENDS?

Doing Business data since 2005 show that credit information and secured transactions systems continue to vary across regions, as do their strengths and weaknesses. A brief snapshot of trends over the past 6 years follows (figure 6.2).

LEADING THE WAY IN LEGAL RIGHTS

Economies in the OECD high-income group, Eastern Europe and Central Asia and East Asia and the Pacific stand out globally for their regulations facilitating the use of movable collateral and modern secured transactions systems (figure 6.3). Economies in these 3 regions also had the most reforms strengthening their legal frameworks as recorded by *Doing Business* over the past 6 years. Some created

relevant institutions, such as the registries for movable assets in Serbia (established in 2005)[5] and Cambodia (2007).

Doing Business recorded 13 changes in laws to improve the legal rights of

borrowers and lenders in Eastern Europe and Central Asia. In East Asia and the Pacific 10 economies strengthened the legal rights of borrowers and lenders. These include Cambodia, China, the Solomon Islands and Vanuatu, all of which have introduced laws since 2007 allowing small and medium-size companies to use inventory and accounts receivable as collateral. In Tonga, in August 2010 the parliament adopted the Personal Property Securities Bill, which is about to come into force. Some OECD high-income economies, such as Denmark, also improved their collateral laws. And Australia will soon implement its 2009 Personal Property Securities Act establishing a national system for the registration of security interests in personal property.[6]

Still, secured transactions systems differ substantially among the 3 regions. Most economies encourage the use of all types of assets as collateral through laws allowing a general description of assets in the loan contract. In East Asia and the Pacific almost 71% of economies have such laws, and in the OECD high-income group 67% do—though in

FIGURE 6.3

Better regulations and institutions easing access to credit

Regional averages in getting credit indicators

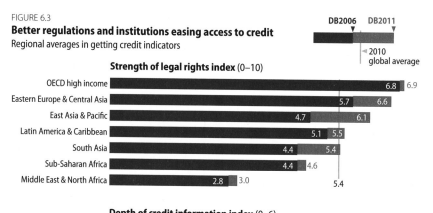

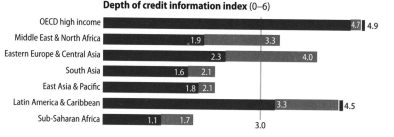

Note: The data sample for DB2006 (2005) includes 174 economies. The sample for DB2011 (2010) also includes The Bahamas, Bahrain, Brunei Darussalam, Cyprus, Kosovo, Liberia, Luxembourg, Montenegro and Qatar, for a total of 183 economies.
Source: Doing Business database.

TABLE 6.2
Who made getting credit easier in 2009/10—and what did they do?

Feature	Economies	Some highlights
Created a unified registry for movable property	Georgia, Ghana, Marshall Islands, Solomon Islands	The Marshall Islands and the Solomon Islands outsourced collateral registration to virtual registries (accessible at http://www.stformi.com and http://www.stfosi.com). Ghana now requires any secured credit agreement covering an amount of 500 cedi (about $350) or above to be registered with the collateral registry.
Allowed out-of-court enforcement of collateral	Belarus, Estonia, Saudi Arabia, Solomon Islands	Estonia amended its code of enforcement procedure to allow out-of-court enforcement after notarization of an agreement providing for this.
Expanded range of revolving movable assets that can be used as collateral	Marshall Islands, Saudi Arabia, Solomon Islands	The Solomon Islands passed Secured Transactions Act No. 5 of 2008. Since the filing office started operating in 2009, 6,439 new registrations of movable collateral have been entered.
Allowed a general description of debts and obligations	Marshall Islands, Solomon Islands	In both the Marshall Islands and the Solomon Islands the secured transactions act permits security interests to secure obligations described specifically or generally.
Gave priority to secured creditors' claims outside bankruptcy procedures	Marshall Islands	The Marshall Islands' secured transactions act provides that parties secured by a security interest or lien have priority over all other claims except those associated with expenses relating to the disposition of the collateral.
Improved regulatory framework related to sharing credit information	Guyana, Jordan, Rwanda, United Arab Emirates, Vietnam	Rwanda reformed its regulatory framework, and a new private credit bureau is starting operations.
Created a new credit registry or bureau	Ghana, Islamic Republic of Iran, Papua New Guinea, Uganda	Uganda's first private credit bureau covers more than 200,000 individuals. A new biometric data system allows each new loan applicant to be identified and issued a financial identity card. Papua New Guinea's credit bureau was set up at the initiative of a group of financial institutions with the goal of sharing credit information about their customers.
Expanded set of information collected in credit registry or bureau	Lithuania, Syrian Arab Republic	Syria's public credit registry removed the minimum threshold for loans to be reported to the central bank.
Provided online access to data at credit registry or bureau	Azerbaijan, Lebanon	Azerbaijan improved its infrastructure and communications systems. Commercial banks can now provide and receive information using an online platform. In Lebanon banks and financial institutions can now access the public credit registry online.

Source: Doing Business database.

Eastern Europe and Central Asia only 54% do. Where a general description of assets is not allowed, the use of certain types of movable collateral—such as inventory and accounts receivable—is less appealing. Imagine a computer sales company wanting to use its inventory as collateral where the law requires that each computer be identified by serial number, color, weight and value. Using the inventory as collateral would be almost impossible—because any changes to it would have to be recorded at the registry or in the loan agreement.

In Eastern Europe and Central Asia 69% of economies give the highest priority possible in bankruptcy to secured creditors (including, in several cases, priority over labor and tax claims). Only 16% of economies in the Middle East and North Africa and 9% of those in Latin America and the Caribbean do so. First priority for secured creditors

is not enough, though. Clear priority rules to resolve conflicting claims between secured creditors when a debtor defaults can influence lending decisions too. Strong creditor rights expand the availability of loans because where lenders have better legal protection during bankruptcy and reorganization, they are more willing to extend credit on favorable terms.[7] A recent study finds that where secured creditors have priority over unsecured claims, the recovery rate for loans tends to be higher and the risks for creditors lower.[8]

CATCHING UP IN CREDIT INFORMATION

Credit information systems are well developed in most OECD high-income economies, and economies in Eastern Europe and Central Asia are catching up. In the past 6 years the region implemented 36 improvements to credit in-

formation systems, more than any other region (figure 6.4). The average coverage by public credit registries and private credit bureaus increased from 4% of the adult population to 30%, while in OECD high-income economies it rose from 54% to 67%. While coverage remains uneven, and a reliable credit information system is only one element of stable financial markets, some economies benefited from such systems during the global financial crisis. A recent study suggests that in Serbia the credit bureau helped preserve liquidity in the banking sector and ensure its stability during the crisis.[9] A study in transition economies suggests that in economies with poor creditor rights, information sharing can improve both access to credit and the terms of loan contracts.[10]

In East Asia and the Pacific half the economies have no credit bureau or registry, scoring 0 on the depth of credit

FIGURE 6.4

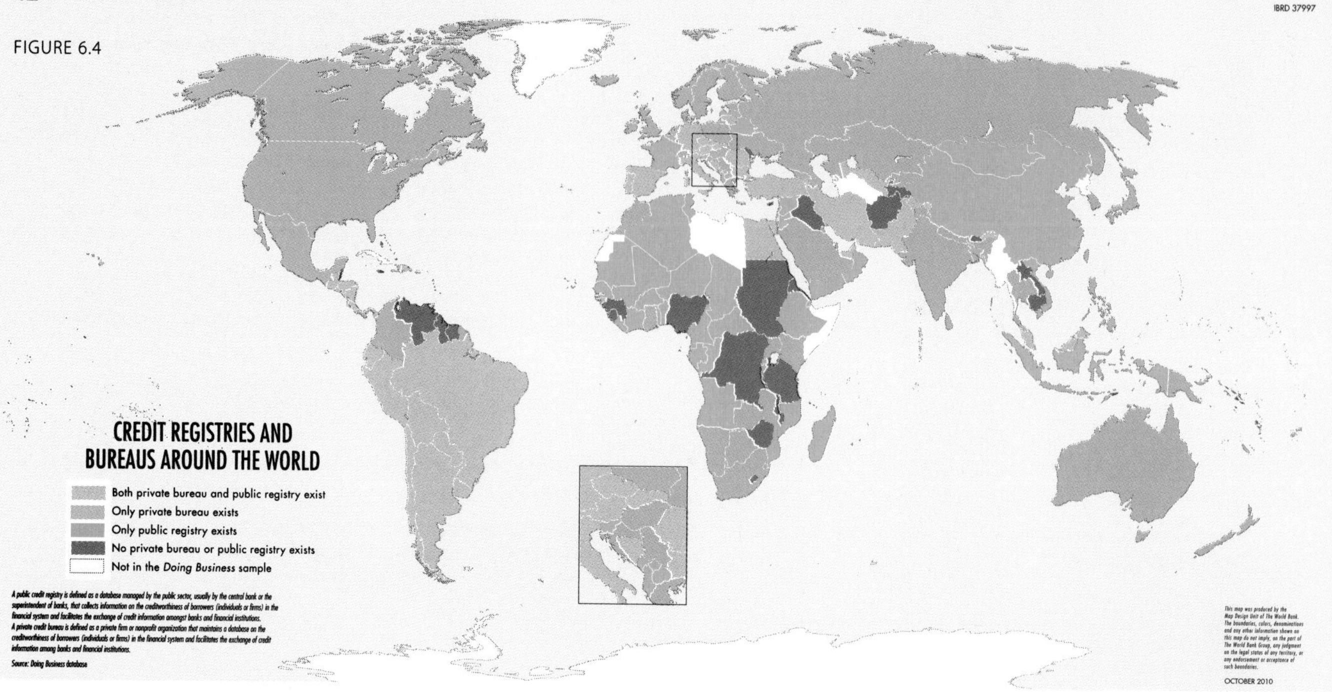

CREDIT REGISTRIES AND
BUREAUS AROUND THE WORLD

Both private bureau and public registry exist
Only private bureau exists
Only public registry exists
No private bureau or public registry exists
Not in the *Doing Business* sample

A public credit registry is defined as a database managed by the public sector, usually by the central bank or the superintendent of banks, that collects information on the creditworthiness of borrowers (individuals or firms) in the financial system and facilitates the exchange of credit information amongst banks and financial institutions.
A private credit bureau is defined as a private firm or nonprofit organization that maintains a database on the creditworthiness of borrowers (individuals or firms) in the financial system and facilitates the exchange of credit information among banks and financial institutions.
Source: *Doing Business* database

OCTOBER 2010

information index. But things are improving. Timor-Leste is working to make its new public credit registry fully operational. In the Pacific a regional credit bureau project is under way. The aim is to provide credit information across the islands using a "hub and spoke" system. Such a system is generally built around a central hub that serves as the host for the data and the main information technology infrastructure. Participating economies are linked into the hub as "spokes," benefiting from economies of scale.

CREDIT INFORMATION GAINS IN THE MIDDLE EAST AND NORTH AFRICA

In the Middle East and North Africa banks cite lack of transparency among small and medium-size enterprises and the weak financial infrastructure (credit information, creditor rights and collateral infrastructure) as the main obstacles to lending more to such enterprises.[11] Legal frameworks do little to encourage the use of movable collateral. Only 11% of economies in the region allow a general description of encumbered assets. And until recently few had attempted to modify their legal structure. Saudi Arabia amended its commercial lien law in 2010 to expand the range of assets that can be used as collateral (table 6.2). It also plans to implement an electronic

collateral registry. West Bank and Gaza is in the process of adopting a new secured transactions law.

In contrast, about three-fourths of the region's economies have reformed their credit information systems since 2005. Indeed, the region ranks second in the number of such reforms, with 22. In 2005 only 3 economies in the region had private credit bureaus; today 7 do. Yet the credit bureaus differ greatly in scope. Nearly half the economies in the region have a score of 3 or less on the depth of credit information index, while half have a score of 4 or more. Among the best performers are Egypt, Lebanon, Morocco, Saudi Arabia, Tunisia and the United Arab Emirates.

GROWING MOMENTUM IN AFRICA

In Sub-Saharan Africa only 35% of economies allow a general description of encumbered assets. And only 13% give priority to secured creditors. A major effort is under way in the 16 member countries of the Organization for the Harmonization of Business Law in Africa to amend the Uniform Act Organizing Securities, first implemented in 1998. In the meantime Ghana introduced a new collateral registry, in February 2010.

Credit information is hardly shared in Sub-Saharan Africa, even though South Africa is thought to have the world's oldest private credit bureau, established in 1901. But efforts to develop much-needed credit information systems started picking up in 2008, when Zambia established a private credit bureau. Its database initially covered about 25,000 borrowers. Thanks to a strong communications campaign and a central bank directive, coverage has grown almost 10-fold, to more than 200,000 by the beginning of 2010. A new private credit bureau started operating in Ghana in 2010, and one in Uganda in 2009. Another, in Rwanda, is getting ready to begin operating. Kenya and Nigeria have started issuing licenses for private credit bureaus.

CONTINUED LEGAL CONSTRAINTS IN LATIN AMERICA

The coverage provided by credit information systems in Latin America and the Caribbean is among the highest in the world. But legal frameworks do not necessarily encourage lending. Less than 9% of the region's economies give priority to secured creditors. Of the 32 economies in the region, only 14 permit out-of-court enforcement and 15 allow a general description of assets. Only 3 economies—Guatemala, Haiti and

Peru—have updated their secured transactions legislation since 2005. But Chile, Honduras, Mexico and Nicaragua are expected to adopt new laws and regulations in the near future.[12] They will join the growing number of countries that are adopting the Inter-American Model Law on Secured Transactions developed under the umbrella of the Organization of American States in 2002.

Initiatives are also under way to further improve credit information sharing. Eighteen economies already have good systems, with a score of 5 or higher on the depth of credit information index. And Latin America has the largest percentage of economies with systems that include data from utilities, retailers and trade creditors. But 12 economies, most of them small economies or Caribbean island states, lack any kind of credit bureau.

For small economies, the high fixed costs of private credit bureaus can be prohibitive. One alternative, if allowed by law, is to transfer the data to a neighboring economy.[13] Another is to create a regional credit bureau. Credit bureaus covering Costa Rica, El Salvador and Honduras work out of a hub in Guatemala. Such a system makes services efficient while reducing the initial investment for each participating economy.

Now a project is under way to set up a regional credit bureau in the Caribbean. Guyana recently passed the first credit bureau law in Latin America to allow the transfer of data to a regional credit bureau, the Credit Reporting Act 2010.

MORE OPPORTUNITY IN SOUTH ASIA

South Asia has opportunity for further improvement. So far only India has a registry that is unified geographically and by asset type and that covers security interests in companies' movable property. But the registry is limited because it registers only security interests over the assets of incorporated companies, excluding such entities as sole proprietorships. Afghanistan adopted a new secured transactions law in 2009 but has not yet implemented its registry. Nepal also adopted such a law, in 2006, but its registry too is not yet operating. And Sri Lanka passed a new secured transactions law in 2009 but has not yet implemented it.

South Asia has had the fewest improvements to credit information systems, limited mainly to India and Sri Lanka. But Afghanistan is now undertaking a groundbreaking effort to establish a modern credit registry.

WHAT HAS WORKED IN SECURED TRANSACTIONS?

A sound secured transactions system has 3 main pillars. The first, already addressed, relates to creation of the security interest, covering how and what kind of movable property can be used as collateral. The second consists of the methods of publicizing the security interest, usually through registration. The third deals with priority rules and enforcement of the security interest, determining how easily creditors can recover their investment after default by the debtor. Over the years economies have focused on a number of features of these 3 pillars (table 6.3).

UNIFYING REGISTRIES

A centralized collateral registry protects secured creditors' rights by providing objective information on whether assets are already subject to the security right of another creditor. It also helps clarify priority among creditors.

Sixty-seven of the 183 economies covered by *Doing Business* have an efficient institution for registering security interests in business assets over their entire geographic area.[14] Thirteen economies, most of them in Eastern Europe and Central Asia and East Asia and the Pacific, have collateral registries that follow good practice standards (figure 6.5). These feature online access for registration and searches; register almost all types of assets as collateral, regardless of the nature of the parties involved; establish clear parameters for priority; and maintain a central database searchable by the debtor's name or a "unique identifier." Once registered, security interests immediately have effect against third parties.

Electronic systems can increase efficiency, but they are no magic wand. Spain created an electronic registration system in 2002. But since the law still requires registrants to have their deed notarized before completing registration, most people still submit a paper-based registration form. As a result, there have

TABLE 6.3
Good practices around the world supporting access to credit

Practice	Economies[a]	Examples
Allowing out-of-court enforcement	105	Australia, India, Nepal, Peru, Russian Federation, Serbia, Sri Lanka, United States
Allowing a general description of collateral	87	Cambodia, Canada, Nigeria, Romania, Rwanda, Singapore, Vanuatu, Vietnam
Maintaining a unified registry	67	Bosnia and Herzegovina, Ghana, Guatemala, Marshall Islands, Federated States of Micronesia, Montenegro, New Zealand, Romania, Solomon Islands
Distributing data on loans below 1% of income per capita	110	Albania, Bolivia, Bulgaria, France, Republic of Korea, Mexico, Saudi Arabia
Distributing both positive and negative credit information	96	Argentina, Brazil, China, Ecuador, Lithuania, Morocco, Portugal, Rwanda, United Kingdom
Distributing credit information from retailers, trade creditors or utilities as well as financial institutions	51	Australia, Canada, Denmark, Japan, Kenya, Kuwait, Netherlands, South Africa, United States, Uruguay

a. Among 183 economies surveyed.
Source: Doing Business database.

TABLE 6.4

Who has the most credit information and the most legal rights for borrowers and lenders—and who the least?

Legal rights for borrowers and lenders *(strength of legal rights index, 0–10)*			
Most		**Least**	
Hong Kong SAR, China	10	Bhutan	2
Kenya	10	Burundi	2
Kyrgyz Republic	10	Eritrea	2
Malaysia	10	Madagascar	2
Montenegro	10	Bolivia	1
New Zealand	10	Djibouti	1
Singapore	10	Syrian Arab Republic	1
Australia	9	Timor-Leste	1
Denmark	9	Palau	0
United Kingdom	9	West Bank and Gaza	0

Borrowers covered by credit registries *(% of adults)*			
Most		**Least**	
Argentina	100	Burundi	0.21
Australia	100	Djibouti	0.20
Canada	100	Côte d'Ivoire	0.19
Iceland	100	Burkina Faso	0.18
Ireland	100	Ethiopia	0.13
New Zealand	100	Niger	0.13
Norway	100	Qatar	0.10
Sweden	100	Mauritania	0.10
United Kingdom	100	Mali	0.10
United States	100	Madagascar	0.05

Note: The rankings reflected in the table on legal rights for borrowers and lenders consider solely the law. Problems may occur in the implementation of legal provisions and are not reflected in the scoring. Those on borrower coverage include only economies with a public credit registry or private credit bureau (139 in total). Another 44 economies have no credit registry or bureau and therefore no coverage. See Data notes for details.

Source: Doing Business database.

been fewer online registrations than expected. In 2007 there were 10,472 online registrations but 24,941 paper-based ones. And in 2009, while 20,586 online registrations were recorded, there were 32,739 paper-based registrations.[15]

Cost matters for the use of collateral registries. A survey of 31 registries suggests that the higher the fees to register or amend a security interest or to search the registry, the lower the volume of transactions recorded. The 2 economies with the lowest registration fees, New Zealand ($2) and Romania ($10), have the most registrations. New Zealand's peak was 649,188 registrations, in 2005, while Romania's was 531,205, in 2007. Malaysia, with one of the highest registration fees ($90), had a peak of only 25,066, in 2008.

UNIFYING THE LAWS

To function properly, collateral registries must be supported by an adequate legal framework. Some economies, such as New Zealand and Romania, have a secured transactions law that treats all security interests in movable property equally with respect to publicity, priority and enforcement, regardless of the form in which the security interest is given (whether a pledge, a financial lease or a loan and trust agreement, for example). Such laws are in line with internationally accepted practices. New Zealand adopted its law in 1999. Called the Personal Property Securities Act, it includes all types of collateral. New Zealand also has a modern, online collateral registry for all types of movable assets. Not surprisingly, the filings to register collateral far outnumber those in similar economies. And searches in the registry rose from 661,944 in 2002 to close to 2.5 million in 2009.[16]

Although movable property is widely used as collateral, many economies still have fragmented collateral laws, with separate laws dealing with different subsets of lenders or types of collateral.[17] Hong Kong SAR (China), Ireland, Malaysia and Singapore are all examples. This fragmentation increases the risk of conflict between laws, such as when determining the priority rules for secured creditors. It also increases the risk of the same security being registered in different places, and that means greater risk for lenders. Such systems are not only less transparent but also more costly to operate.

ALLOWING OUT-OF-COURT ENFORCEMENT

For security interests to be cost-effective requires quick and inexpensive enforcement in case of default.[18] Efficient enforcement procedures are particularly important for movable property, which generally depreciates over time. The efficiency of enforcement can influence the accessibility and terms of credit. Most economies recognize this: 105 of the 183 economies covered by *Doing Business* have legal provisions allowing the parties to a security agreement to agree to some form of out-of-court enforcement.

WHAT HAS WORKED IN CREDIT INFORMATION?

Forty-four economies around the world still lack any kind of credit information system. But not just any credit bureau will do; many continue to cover only a tiny fraction of the adult population (table 6.4). Specific practices help increase coverage, encourage use and protect borrowers.

CASTING A WIDE NET

An ongoing study in Italy has looked at the effect of providing a credit bureau with repayment information from a water supply company. The findings show that more than 83% of water customers who previously lacked a credit history now have a positive one thanks to paying their utility bills.[19] This makes it easier for them to obtain credit.

Including such data in credit bu-

FIGURE 6.5

PUBLICIZING THE SECURITY INTEREST:
COLLATERAL REGISTRIES AROUND THE WORLD

- Registries with centralized database for secured claims over companies' assets
- Collateral registries likely to become operational in the near future
- Collateral registries per province or state
- ⊘ Good practice notice-based collateral registries

Source: Doing Business database

IBRD 37998
This map was produced by the Map Design Unit of The World Bank. The boundaries, colors, denominations and any other information shown on this map do not imply, on the part of The World Bank Group, any judgment on the legal status of any territory, or any endorsement or acceptance of such boundaries.

OCTOBER 2010

reaus can also benefit the utility companies. According to a recent study surveying 70 utility companies in the United States, 72% reported that the benefits of credit reporting amounted to at least 2–5 times the costs. Half of all customers indicated that they would be more likely to pay their bills on time if those payments were fully reported to credit bureaus and could affect their credit score.[20]

In emerging markets, where the working poor make up more than 60% of the labor force,[21] allowing the distribution of payment information from sources other than banks could make a big difference. China has close to 750 million mobile phone subscribers. Only a fraction have taken out a commercial loan in the past. For all others, the ability to unlock credit through a history of reliably paying mobile phone bills could open new opportunities.

REPORTING GOOD AS WELL AS BAD

A credit information system that reports only negative information penalizes borrowers who default on payments—but fails to reward diligent borrowers who pay on time. Sharing information on reliable repayment allows customers to establish a positive credit history, useful information

for financial institutions seeking proven good customers. A study of Latin American economies suggests that private credit bureaus that distribute both positive and negative information and have 100% participation from banks help increase lending to the private sector.[22]

STEERING CLEAR OF HIGH THRESHOLDS

Coverage can also be affected by minimum thresholds for the loans reported. High thresholds hurt groups that could benefit most from credit information systems—such as small and medium-size enterprises and female entrepreneurs, whose loans are typically smaller. Private credit bureaus tend to have lower minimum loan thresholds, with a global average of $459. For public credit registries the average exceeds $30,000.

When smaller loans are reported to credit bureaus, more borrowers can establish credit histories. When Belarus eliminated its $10,000 threshold in 2008, more than 1 million women and men benefited from having their loans—no matter the size—reported to the credit registry. Coverage of individuals rose from around 113,000 to 1,920,000 in a single year.[23]

WHAT ARE SOME RESULTS?

In a world with asymmetric information, banks are more likely to lend to larger firms, which typically are more transparent and use international accounting standards. But supported by information sharing systems, banks can sensibly extend credit to smaller and less transparent firms by basing their credit decisions on past borrower behavior.[24] This can increase entrepreneurs' opportunities for success, regardless of personal connections. One study found that an increase of 10 percentage points in the population share covered by a private credit bureau is associated with a 6% increase in private sector lending.[25]

Lending officers tend to have substantial discretion in offering loans, including in the interest rates they set and even in the types of collateral they require from a borrower. This can open the door to bribery. By reducing the discretion in evaluating loan applicants, credit information systems can help reduce corruption in bank lending.[26]

Access to credit remains particularly sparse in developing economies. In developed economies adults have an estimated 3.2 bank accounts on average, and 81%

FIGURE 6.6
Users take advantage of electronic registries for movable property as collateral
Percentage increase in registrations indexed to the first year of the registry's existence

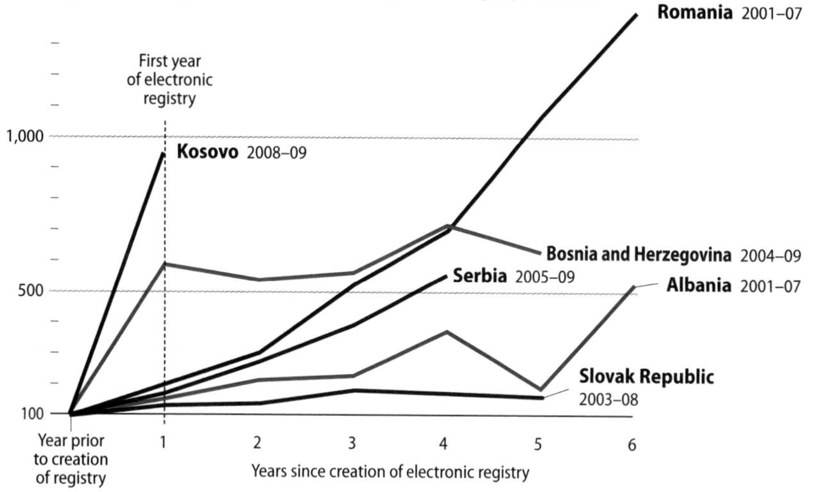

Source: Doing Business database.

have accounts. In developing economies adults have 0.9 accounts on average, and 28% have accounts.[27] But the outlook is improving. In the past 6 years 71 economies implemented more than 121 reforms to improve credit information systems. Low-income economies increased the coverage of private or public credit registries from 0.6% of the adult population to 2.3%.[28] And 20 more economies gained a private credit bureau.

Institutions are of no benefit if they go unused. But a recent survey of collateral registries is encouraging: 20 of 27 registries that provided information on the volume of registrations showed a substantial increase since 2000 or since the year they were created. In 4 economies that improved their secured transactions

system in the past 10 years—Albania, Bosnia and Herzegovina, New Zealand and Serbia—registrations of movable collateral increased sharply (figure 6.6). Serbia's volume of registrations jumped from 4,346 in 2005 to 24,059 in 2009, while Albania's rose from 1,874 in 2001 to 4,105 in 2009, peaking at 9,860 in 2007.

Romania also improved its secured transactions system, in 1999. In the next 4 years 600,000 new security interests were registered, generating at least $60 million in sustainable credit.[29] Vietnam is another good example. It passed Decree 163 in 2006. Although its registry is still being computerized, the number of registrations increased from 43,000 in 2005 to 120,000 by the end of 2008.[30]

1. Fleisig, Safavian and de la Peña (2006).
2. Alvarez de la Campa and others (2010).
3. CGAP and World Bank (2010).
4. Anzoategui, Martinez Pería and Rocha (2010).
5. Simpson and Menze (2000).
6. The Australian law was still awaiting implementation on June 1, 2010.
7. Qian and Strahan (2007).
8. Djankov, Hart, McLiesh and Shleifer (2008).
9. Simovic, Vaskovic and Poznanovic (2009).
10. Brown, Jappelli and Pagano (2009).
11. Rocha and others (2010).
12. Kozolchyk (2009).
13. The Czech Republic, with a population of around 10 million, decided to outsource its credit information services in 2002 to a private firm already set up in Italy. The bureau has already reached almost 100% penetration in retail banking. The banking register contains more than 13 million records, covering 6.5 million individuals.
14. These may include company registries, deed registries, filing offices and any other institution with a central electronic database that records security interests over companies' assets.
15. Data provided by the Spanish registry, Colegio de Registradores de la Propiedad, Mercantiles y Bienes Muebles de España.
16. *Doing Business* database.
17. Fleisig and de la Peña (2003).
18. Kozolchyk and Furnish (2006).
19. Preliminary findings of ongoing internal study at CRIF SpA, Italy (credit information services firm).
20. Turner and others (2009).
21. Stein (2010).
22. Turner and Varghese (2007).
23. *Doing Business* database.
24. Brown, Jappelli and Pagano (2009).
25. Turner, Varghese and Walker (2007).
26. Barth and others (2009).
27. Kendall, Mylenko and Ponce (2010).
28. *Doing Business* database.
29. Fleisig, Safavian and de la Peña (2006).
30. Alvarez de la Campa and others (2010).

Protecting investors

FIGURE 7.1

Swaziland's new company act strengthened investor protections

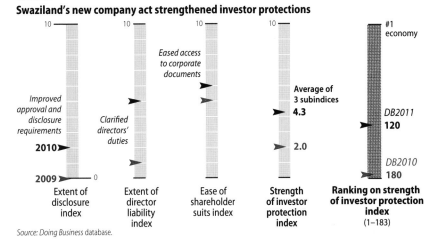

Source: Doing Business database.

In 2007 the directors of CNOOC Ltd., a Chinese oil company incorporated in Hong Kong SAR (China) and listed on the Hong Kong Stock Exchange, wanted to deposit funds in its sister company CNOOC Finance Ltd. for 3 years.[1] The transaction represented more than 10% of CNOOC's net assets. Shareholders were concerned because the transaction was unsecured. If CNOOC Finance were to default or file for bankruptcy, CNOOC would be unable to recover the money. A shareholders meeting was called to approve the transaction. More than 52% of independent shareholders voted against it, forcing the company to recover the money already deposited with CNOOC Finance. Potential damage was prevented—thanks to the disclosure and approval requirements of the securities and company laws in Hong Kong SAR (China).

Legal provisions requiring disclosure and access to information allow minority investors to monitor the activities of companies and preserve firm value. These provisions matter for the ability of companies to raise the capital needed to grow, innovate, diversify and compete. One common way to raise capital is to obtain credit from banks—but with the global financial crisis, this has become increasingly challenging. Another way is to issue or sell company shares to equity investors. In return, investors ask for transparency and accountability from the company's directors and the ability to take part in major decisions of the company. If the laws do not provide such protections, investors may be reluctant to invest unless they become the controlling shareholders.[2]

One of the most important issues in corporate governance, and a particular concern for minority investors, is self-dealing, the use of corporate assets by company insiders for personal gain. Related-party transactions are the most common example. High ownership concentration and informal business relations can create the perfect environment for such transactions, which allow controlling shareholders to profit at the expense of the company's financial health—whether because company assets are sold at an excessively low price, assets are purchased at an inflated price or loans are given by the company to controlling shareholders on terms far better than the market offers.

To ensure transparency and prevent abuse, policy makers regulate related-party transactions. Research has found that companies can independently improve investor protections by adopting internal corporate governance codes. But these are no substitute for a good legal framework.[3] Strong regulations clearly define related-party transactions, promote clear and efficient disclosure re-

TABLE 7.1

Where are investors protected—and where not?

Most protected	RANK	Least protected	RANK
New Zealand	1	Guinea	174
Singapore	2	Gambia, The	175
Hong Kong SAR, China	3	Micronesia, Fed. Sts.	176
Malaysia	4	Palau	177
Canada	5	Vietnam	178
Colombia	6	Venezuela, RB	179
Ireland	7	Djibouti	180
Israel	8	Suriname	181
United States	9	Lao PDR	182
United Kingdom	10	Afghanistan	183

Note: Rankings are based on the strength of investor protection index. See Data notes for details.

Source: Doing Business database.

FIGURE 7.2

How well are minority shareholders protected against self-dealing in related-party transactions?

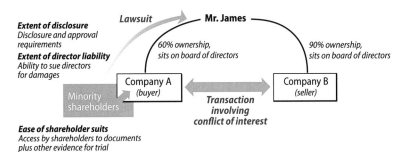

TABLE 7.2

Who strengthened investor protections in 2009/10—and what did they do?

Economy	Area	Some highlights
Chile	Approval of related-party transactions	An October 2009 amendment to the securities law requires stricter corporate disclosure and approval of transactions between interested parties. *Improved score on the extent of disclosure index by 1 point.*
Georgia	Access to internal corporate information	A November 2009 amendment to the civil procedure code allows parties to question their opponents during trial. The judge can interfere when the questions are inappropriate or irrelevant. *Improved score on the ease of shareholder suits index by 2 points.*
Kazakhstan	Disclosure of information	Amendments to the Joint Stock Company Law and the Law on Accounting and Financial Reports adopted in July 2009 require greater corporate disclosure in company annual reports. *Improved score on the extent of disclosure index by 1 point.*
Morocco	Disclosure of information	A decree was issued clarifying the interpretation of the company law with respect to the type of information in the report of the independent auditor who reviews related-party transactions. *Improved score on the extent of disclosure index by 1 point.*
Swaziland	Approval of related-party transactions	A new company act enacted in April 2010 requires approval by the board of directors for related-party transactions. The director with a conflict is allowed to participate in the voting. *Improved score on the extent of disclosure index by 1 point.*
	Disclosure of information	Directors are now required to immediately disclose their conflict of interest to the board of directors. *Improved score on the extent of disclosure index by 1 point.*
	Directors' liability	Directors found liable must now compensate the company for damages caused and disgorge profits made from prejudicial related-party transactions. *Improved score on the extent of director liability index by 4 points.*
	Access to internal corporate information	Minority investors holding 5% of company shares can now request the appointment of a government inspector if they suspect mismanagement of the company's affairs. *Improved score on the ease of shareholder suits index by 1 point.*
Sweden	Approval of related-party transactions	The NASDAQ Stockholm Stock Exchange adopted a new rulebook in January 2010 requiring approval of transactions between interested parties by a shareholders meeting. *Improved score on the extent of disclosure index by 1 point.*
	External review of related-party transactions	The rulebook also mandates an independent review of the terms of related-party transactions before approval by the shareholders. *Improved score on the extent of disclosure index by 1 point.*
Tajikistan	Disclosure of information	A January 2010 amendment to the Joint Stock Company Law requires detailed disclosure of transactions between interested parties in the annual report. *Improved score on the extent of disclosure index by 2 points.*
	Access to internal corporate information	The amended law grants minority shareholders access to all corporate documents. *Improved score on the ease of shareholder suits index by 1 point.*

Source: Doing Business database.

quirements, require shareholder participation in major decisions of the company and set clear standards of accountability for company insiders.

Doing Business measures the transparency of related-party transactions, the liability of company directors for self-dealing and the ability of shareholders to sue directors for misconduct. A higher ranking on the strength of investor protection index indicates that an economy's regulations offer stronger investor protections against self-dealing in the areas measured. The indicator does not measure all aspects related to the protection of minority investors, such as dilution of share value or insider trading. Nor does it measure the dynamism of capital markets or protections specific to foreign investors.

This year's ranking shows that New Zealand protects minority investors the most (table 7.1). Since 2005, 51 economies have strengthened investor protections as measured by *Doing Business*, through 68 legal changes. Seven did so in 2009/10 (table 7.2), slightly fewer than in previous years. Swaziland strengthened investor protections the most (figure 7.1). It adopted a new company act that requires greater corporate disclosure, higher standards of accountability for company directors and greater access to corporate information. After about 10 years of discussion and drafting, the new law came into force at the end of April 2010.

WHAT ARE THE TRENDS?

Over the past 6 years the most reforms to strengthen investor protections took place in OECD high-income economies and the fewest in South Asia. Eastern Europe and Central Asia was the second most active region. Progress was mixed in East Asia and the Pacific and in the Middle East and North Africa. Investor protection reforms started to pick up in Sub-Saharan Africa and in Latin America and the Caribbean (figure 7.3).

STRONGEST PROTECTIONS IN OECD HIGH-INCOME ECONOMIES

OECD high-income economies have on average the strongest protections of minority shareholder rights in the areas measured. Four economies stand out for their strict regulations on the transparency of related-party transactions, liability of company directors for self-dealing and ability of shareholders to sue directors for misconduct: Canada, New Zealand, the United Kingdom and the United States.

Others offer strong protections in some areas but not all. Fifteen of 30 economies, including Australia, France and Italy, clearly regulate approval and disclosure of related-party transactions. Seventeen economies, including Belgium, Japan and the United Kingdom, have clear provisions on director liability, allowing minority investors to sue directors for misuse of corporate assets. Only 4 economies, including France and Korea, limit the liability of directors to fraudulent transactions. Five economies offer easy access to corporate documents, both

FIGURE 7.3

Steady strengthening of investor protections in Eastern Europe and Central Asia

Number of *Doing Business* reforms strengthening investor protections by *Doing Business* report year

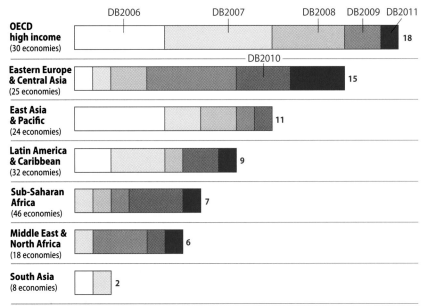

Note: A *Doing Business* reform is counted as 1 reform per reforming economy per year. The data sample for DB2006 (2005) includes 174 economies. The sample for DB2011 (2010) also includes The Bahamas, Bahrain, Brunei Darussalam, Cyprus, Kosovo, Liberia, Luxembourg, Montenegro and Qatar, for a total of 183 economies.

Source: Doing Business database.

directly and through a government inspector, including Hungary and Sweden.

In the past 6 years *Doing Business* recorded 18 reforms in investor protections in 14 of the 30 OECD high-income economies. These economies, including Iceland, Italy and Sweden, focused mainly on improving disclosure requirements for related-party transactions.

ACCELERATING CHANGE IN EASTERN EUROPE AND CENTRAL ASIA

In Eastern Europe and Central Asia *Doing Business* recorded 14 reforms in investor protections in 11 of the 25 economies. Most adopted new legislation. Examples are Albania and Tajikistan.[4] Policy makers emphasized stricter disclosure requirements and better standards for company directors. The region's average score on the extent of disclosure index rose from 4.9 to 6.3 between 2005 and 2010 (figure 7.4).

Thanks in part to these changes, approval requirements for related-party transactions are now well defined. Only 4 economies—Azerbaijan, Croatia, Cyprus and Lithuania—still allow directors with a conflict of interest to vote. Economies

in the region have also moved toward defining clear standards and duties for directors. Only Bulgaria and Moldova still allow directors to waive their liability for misconduct.

MANY NEW LAWS IN SUB-SAHARAN AFRICA

Sub-Saharan Africa has had some of the most comprehensive investor protection reforms. Such economies as Botswana, Mozambique, Rwanda, Sierra Leone, Swaziland and Tanzania updated their company laws following global good practices (figure 7.5). Rather than modifying a few provisions, policy makers adopted entirely new laws. And more is expected. The 16 member countries of the Organization for the Harmonization of Business Law in Africa have started reviewing the Uniform Commercial Act. Burundi, Kenya, Malawi and Uganda are developing new commercial laws to improve corporate governance. Once these are adopted, almost half the region's economies will have adopted a new commercial law since 2005.

Doing Business recorded 7 reforms in investor protections in 7 of the region's

46 economies. Such efforts are worthwhile. More than half the region's economies still have poor provisions or none at all on disclosure and approval of related-party transactions, and regulations on the liability of company directors for mismanagement are often outdated.

MIXED PROGRESS IN EAST ASIA

Six of the 24 economies in East Asia and the Pacific implemented 11 investor protection reforms, aimed mostly at strengthening disclosure requirements and directors' duties. Regional competition for investment spurred legal changes in Indonesia and Thailand, inspired by neighboring Hong Kong SAR (China) and Singapore. These economies as well as Malaysia now offer strict protections for minority investors: regulated approval of related-party transactions, a high level of disclosure, clear duties for directors and easy access to corporate information.

Others can still improve. The Lao People's Democratic Republic and the Federated States of Micronesia lack clear rules on disclosure and approval of related-party transactions. Holding directors liable can be difficult in some countries, including Vietnam. And Cambodia permits only limited access to corporate documents for minority investors.

MANY OUTDATED LAWS IN LATIN AMERICA

Investor protection reforms were sparse in Latin America and the Caribbean in the past 6 years, with a few exceptions. Colombia consistently improved its legislation in the past 4 years. The Dominican Republic adopted a new company law in 2009. Mexico adopted a new securities law in 2006.[5] Chile amended its securities law in December 2009. *Doing Business* recorded 9 reforms in investor protections in 7 of the region's 32 economies.

Rules governing self-dealing remain weak across the region. Clear provisions are often missing, particularly on disclosure and approval. Only Colombia and El Salvador require shareholder approval for related-party transactions. Bolivia, Hon-

FIGURE 7.4
Strongest investor protections in OECD high-income economies
Regional averages in protecting investors indicators

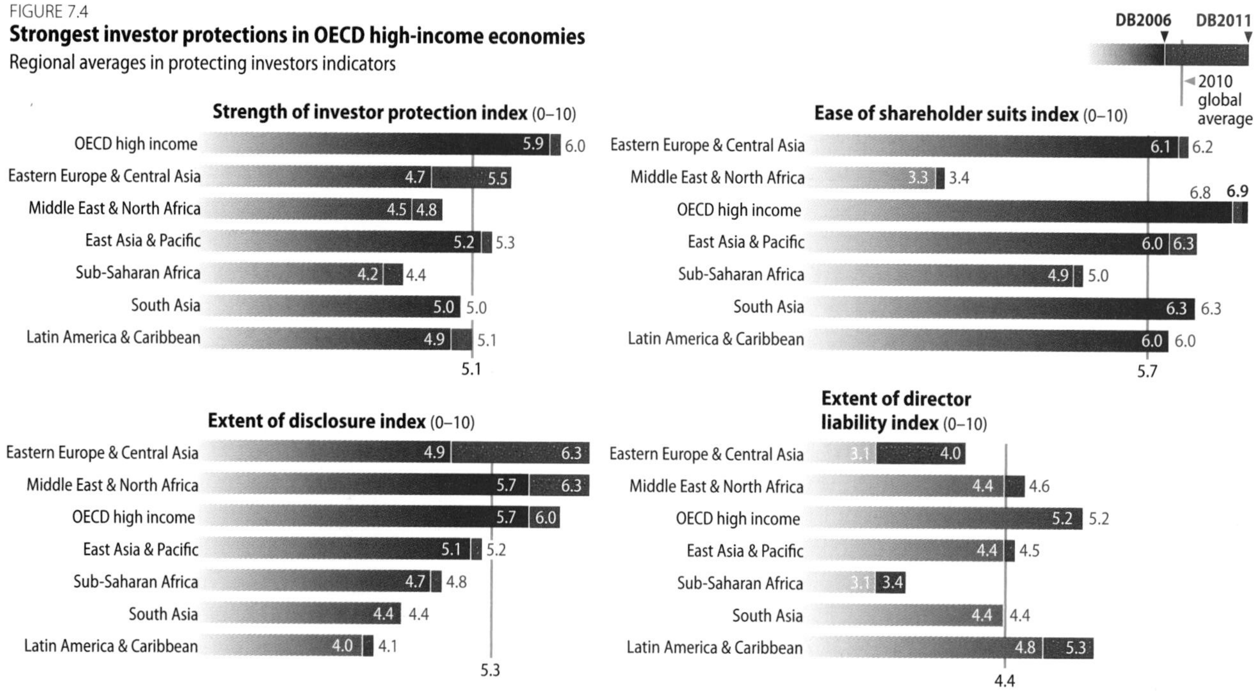

DB2006   DB2011

◄ 2010
global
average

Strength of investor protection index (0–10)

OECD high income	5.9 / 6.0
Eastern Europe & Central Asia	4.7 / 5.5
Middle East & North Africa	4.5 / 4.8
East Asia & Pacific	5.2 / 5.3
Sub-Saharan Africa	4.2 / 4.4
South Asia	5.0 / 5.0
Latin America & Caribbean	4.9 / 5.1

5.1

Ease of shareholder suits index (0–10)

Eastern Europe & Central Asia	6.1 / 6.2
Middle East & North Africa	3.3 / 3.4
OECD high income	6.8 / 6.9
East Asia & Pacific	6.0 / 6.3
Sub-Saharan Africa	4.9 / 5.0
South Asia	6.3 / 6.3
Latin America & Caribbean	6.0 / 6.0

5.7

Extent of disclosure index (0–10)

Eastern Europe & Central Asia	4.9 / 6.3
Middle East & North Africa	5.7 / 6.3
OECD high income	5.7 / 6.0
East Asia & Pacific	5.1 / 5.2
Sub-Saharan Africa	4.7 / 4.8
South Asia	4.4 / 4.4
Latin America & Caribbean	4.0 / 4.1

5.3

Extent of director liability index (0–10)

Eastern Europe & Central Asia	3.1 / 4.0
Middle East & North Africa	4.4 / 4.6
OECD high income	5.2 / 5.2
East Asia & Pacific	4.4 / 4.5
Sub-Saharan Africa	3.1 / 3.4
South Asia	4.4 / 4.4
Latin America & Caribbean	4.8 / 5.3

4.4

Note: The data sample for DB2006 (2005) includes 174 economies. The sample for DB2011 (2010) also includes The Bahamas, Bahrain, Brunei Darussalam, Cyprus, Kosovo, Liberia, Luxembourg, Montenegro and Qatar, for a total of 183 economies.
Source: Doing Business database.

duras and Panama require no disclosure.

Part of the reason might be outdated legislation. Most company laws in continental Latin America were adopted in the early 1970s. Nicaragua's dates to 1914, and Honduras's to 1948. The Caribbean islands updated their legislation in the 1990s and more strictly regulate conflicts of interest. One exception is Haiti, which still uses commercial legislation from the 19th century. The countries that brought their legal traditions to the region periodically update their laws, with Portugal last updating its securities regulations in 2008, France its commercial code in 2005 and Spain its civil procedure code in 2004.

PROTECTIONS OFTEN WEAK IN THE MIDDLE EAST AND NORTH AFRICA

In the Middle East and North Africa 6 investor protection reforms in 4 of the 18 economies have been recorded since 2005. When corporate governance reforms started in 2001, the first challenge was to find an Arabic equivalent for *corporate governance*. The reforms would not have been possible without an agreement about the meaning of the

term in the local language and context. Thanks to a committee of linguists from across the region, *hawkamat al-sharikat,* meaning "the governance of companies," was agreed on after about a year.[6]

Despite recent improvements, legal protections in the region are often weak. Access to corporate information during a trial to establish director liability is often limited. Such access helps minority investors who suspect that the company has been run improperly to gather the evidence needed to prove their case. Four economies—Egypt, Morocco, Saudi Arabia and Tunisia—have started to focus more on regulating corporate disclosure and related-party transactions.

FEWEST INVESTOR PROTECTION REFORMS IN SOUTH ASIA

South Asia has been the least active in strengthening investor protections against self-dealing. *Doing Business* recorded 2 reforms in investor protections in 2 of the region's 8 economies—India and Pakistan. These 2, along with Bangladesh, have the strongest investor protections in the region.

WHAT HAS WORKED?

Economies with the strongest protections of minority investors from self-dealing require more disclosure and define clear duties for directors. They also have well-functioning courts and up-to-date procedural rules that give minority investors the means to prove their case and obtain a judgment within a reasonable time.

SETTING STRICT RULES OF DISCLOSURE

Thirty-seven of the 183 economies covered by *Doing Business* stand out for the strictest rules on disclosure of related-party transactions. These include New Zealand, Singapore, Albania and, thanks to investor protection reforms in 2009, Rwanda (table 7.3). The global financial crisis as well as earlier corporate scandals prompted governments around the world to strengthen disclosure requirements. This has been the most popular feature in investor protection reforms since 2005, accounting for 33 of the total.

Eight economies, including Croatia, Maldives and Panama, require no disclosure of related-party transactions. Austria and Switzerland have strict dis-

FIGURE 7.5

FIGURE 7.5
Stronger investor protections in Sub-Saharan African economies since 2005
Strength of investor protection index (0–10)

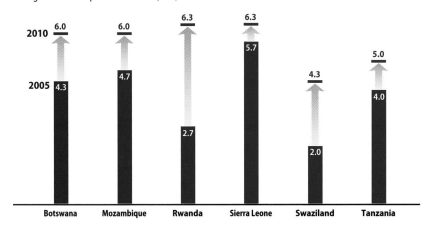

Source: Doing Business database.

closure provisions—but only for "material" transactions not carried out "in the ordinary course of business." Since Austrian and Swiss law does not define "material" transactions outside the "ordinary course of business," even a related-party transaction representing 10% of the company's assets could be considered to be in the "ordinary course of business." This contrasts with Belgian and French law, which defines "ordinary course of business" as excluding transactions representing 10% or more of assets.

REGULATING APPROVAL OF RELATED-PARTY TRANSACTIONS

The more participation by shareholders—and the less by interested directors—in the approval of related-party transactions, the greater the protections. Fifty-seven economies require shareholder approval of large related-party transactions. Albania and Tajikistan adopted such rules in the past 5 years.

Such approval mechanisms work well only if the law does not allow many exceptions and if the approval is required at the time of the transaction. In Cameroon and Lebanon shareholders can vote on the transaction only at the annual meeting, after the transaction has already occurred. Greece and the Slovak Republic require shareholder approval only if the transaction does not take place "in the ordinary course of business"—

without defining that concept.

In 21 economies, including Costa Rica, the Philippines and Spain, related-party transactions can be approved by the manager, director, chief executive officer or whoever is specified in the company statutes. In 44 economies, including the Czech Republic, Israel and the United States, these transactions are approved by the board of directors and interested parties are allowed to vote. Allowing interested parties to vote can open the door to abuse.

MAKING DIRECTORS LIABLE

Economies with the strongest protections regulate not only disclosure and approval of related-party transactions but also the liability of directors when such transactions turn out to be prejudicial. This can be done by adopting a clear catalogue of the rights and duties of directors or a special regime of liability for directors in the event of an abusive related-party transaction. The board of directors is responsible for monitoring managerial performance and achieving an adequate return for shareholders while preventing conflicts of interest and balancing competing demands on the corporation.[7] To fulfill their responsibilities effectively, directors need clear rules and independent judgment.

Forty-three economies have clear rules on the liability of company di-

rectors in case of abusive related-party transactions. These include Canada, Mexico and the United Arab Emirates, which have rules encouraging directors to be prudent in the company's day-to-day management. Thirty-seven economies, including Bulgaria, China and Kazakhstan, do not clearly regulate the liability of directors for abusive related-party transactions. There, as long as the interested parties comply with requirements for disclosure and approval of related-party transactions, they are not liable for any harm that results. The other 103 economies have rules on the liability of directors, but often with loopholes.

ALLOWING ACCESS TO EVIDENCE

Once a potentially prejudicial related-party transaction has occurred, what recourse do minority shareholders have in court? This depends in part on their access to documentary evidence before and during the trial. Without access to evidence, it is more difficult for minority investors to prove that directors have been managing the company's affairs improperly. Economies can have good laws, but if access to corporate information is limited and courts are inefficient, investors are unlikely to resort to the courts.

Only 15 of the 183 economies covered by Doing Business, including Israel and Japan, permit full access to documentary evidence both before and during the trial. More than 30, including Canada, the Dominican Republic and Hong Kong SAR (China), allow shareholders access to any corporate document before the trial. Cyprus, France and the United Kingdom allow shareholders to request the appointment of a government inspector with full powers to verify and obtain copies of any corporate document. Kazakhstan, New Zealand, Peru and South Africa require that all company documents related to the case be open for inspection during the trial. Mauritania, Syria and the Republic of Yemen permit limited or no access to evidence during the trial, making it virtually impossible for minority investors to prove their case.

TABLE 7.3
Who provides strong minority investor protections—and who does not?

Extent of disclosure index (0–10)

Most		Least	
Bulgaria	10	Afghanistan	1
China	10	Bolivia	1
France	10	Cape Verde	1
Hong Kong SAR, China	10	Croatia	1
Indonesia	10	Honduras	0
Ireland	10	Maldives	0
Malaysia	10	Micronesia, Fed. Sts.	0
New Zealand	10	Palau	0
Singapore	10	Sudan	0
Thailand	10	Switzerland	0

Extent of director liability index (0–10)

Most		Least	
Albania	9	Afghanistan	1
Cambodia	9	Belarus	1
Canada	9	Benin	1
Israel	9	Bulgaria	1
Malaysia	9	Zimbabwe	1
New Zealand	9	Marshall Islands	0
Rwanda	9	Micronesia, Fed. Sts.	0
Singapore	9	Palau	0
Slovenia	9	Suriname	0
United States	9	Vietnam	0

Ease of shareholder suits index (0–10)

Easiest		Most difficult	
Kenya	10	Lao PDR	2
New Zealand	10	Senegal	2
Colombia	9	Syrian Arab Republic	2
Hong Kong SAR, China	9	United Arab Emirates	2
Ireland	9	Venezuela, RB	2
Israel	9	Yemen, Rep.	2
Mauritius	9	Guinea	1
Poland	9	Morocco	1
Singapore	9	Djibouti	0
United States	9	Iran, Islamic Rep.	0

Source: Doing Business database.

WHAT ARE SOME RESULTS?

Corporate scandals have shown the consequences of inadequate transparency and weak investor protections. Investors take note. A study analyzing the effects of related-party transactions on companies listed on the Hong Kong Stock Exchange during 1998–2000 finds that they led to significant losses in value for minority shareholders. Indeed, the mere announcement of a related-party transaction led to abnormal negative stock returns. The study concludes that investors considered companies with a history of such transactions (even if not prejudicial) to be riskier investments than those with no such history.[8]

PAYOFFS IN PERFORMANCE

Empirical research shows that stricter regulation of self-dealing is associated with greater equity investment and lower concentration of ownership.[9] This is in line with the view that stronger legal protections make minority investors more confident about their investments, reducing the need for concentrated own-

ership to mitigate weaknesses in corporate governance. Both ex ante protections (extensive disclosure and approval requirements) and ex post measures against self-dealing (rights of action for minority shareholders) seem important. The 2 combined are associated with larger and more active stock markets, lower block premiums, more listed firms, higher market capitalization and higher rates of initial public offerings.

Most economies that strengthened investor protections did so as part of wider corporate governance programs—including Albania, Colombia, the Dominican Republic, FYR Macedonia, Mexico, Mozambique, Rwanda, Sierra Leone and Thailand. This is a good thing. Most research suggests a positive relationship between sound corporate governance systems and firms' performance as measured by valuation, operating performance or stock returns.[10] A Deutsche Bank study of the Standard & Poor's 500 shows that companies with strong or improved corporate governance structures outperformed those with poor or deteriorating governance practices by about 19% over a 2-year period.[11] There is room for more research to fully understand which corporate governance provisions are important for different types of firms and environments.[12]

BENEFITS FOR MORE INVESTORS

For legal protections to be effective, they must be applied. But pinning down the precise effect of specific legislative changes in an economy is difficult. Such changes generally apply to all firms at the same time, leaving no counterfactual to assess what would have occurred without them. But the experiences of several economies show how increased protections are benefiting greater numbers of investors thanks to growth in both the number of listed firms and the number of enforcement cases uncovering prejudicial transactions.

Thailand amended its laws in 2006 and in 2008. Since 2005 more than 30 new companies have joined its stock exchange, bringing the number of listed companies

TABLE 7.4

Good practices around the world in protecting investors

Practice	Economies[a]	Examples
Allowing rescission of prejudicial related-party transactions	69	Brazil, Mauritius, Rwanda, United States
Regulating approval of related-party transactions	57	Albania, France, United Kingdom
Requiring detailed disclosure	48	Hong Kong SAR (China), New Zealand, Singapore
Allowing access to all corporate documents during the trial	43	Chile, Ireland, Israel
Requiring external review of related-party transactions	38	Australia, Arab Republic of Egypt, Sweden
Allowing access to all corporate documents before the trial	30	Japan, Sweden, Tajikistan
Defining clear duties for directors	27	Colombia, Malaysia, Mexico, United States

a. Among 183 economies surveyed.
Source: Doing Business database.

to 523. Since 2005 more than 85 transactions that failed to comply with the disclosure standards have been suspended while the Thai regulator requests clarification. Thirteen of these were deemed to be prejudicial and were therefore canceled, in each case preventing damage to the company and preserving its value.[13]

In Indonesia, another economy that consistently improved its laws regulating investor protections, the number of firms listed on the Indonesia Stock Exchange increased from 331 to 396 between 2004 and 2009. Meanwhile, market capitalization grew from 680 trillion rupiah ($75 billion) to 1,077 trillion rupiah ($119 billion).[14] Malaysia and Singapore, both regional leaders in investor protections, have seen the number of listed firms rise by more than 100 since 2005. In that same period the Malaysian securities commission has sanctioned more than 100 companies for noncompliance with disclosure requirements and more than 20 for noncompliance with approval requirements for related-party transactions.[15]

Brazil's experience shows the value that investors place on strong corporate governance rules. For firms seeking equity funding in Brazil, 2002 and 2003 were tough years. The São Paulo Stock Exchange (BOVESPA) Index had fallen by 14% in U.S. dollar terms. But the market showed that it could recognize value in solid businesses that offered good governance.[16] In 2001 a special segment of the exchange, Novo Mercado, had been created for trading shares in companies that voluntarily adopted corporate governance practices that went beyond what was required under Brazilian law.[17] The assumption was that an investor perception of better corporate governance would boost share values.

Initially people had little faith in this possibility. But by 2004, for the first time in more than a decade, several leading companies decided to go public. Their initial public offerings, the first in Brazil since January 2002, signaled the beginning of a renaissance for the stock market. Toward the end of 2004 Novo Mercado had 7 new listings. By the end of 2007 it had 156 companies listed, representing 57% of BOVESPA's market capitalization, 66% of its trading value and 74% of the number of trades in the cash market.[18] By the end of 2009 Novo Mercado had 3 more new listings.[19] Imagine the benefits if its corporate governance rules applied to all companies.

1. OECD (2009).
2. Dahya, Dimitrov and McConnell (2008).
3. Klapper and Love (2004).
4. Lobet (2009).
5. Johns and Lobet (2007).
6. Anna Nadgrodkiewicz and Aleksandr Sckolnikov, "What's in a Word? Corporate Governance, Language and Institutional Change," *Development Blog,* March 2, 2010, http://www.cipe.org.
7. OECD (2004a).
8. Cheung, Rau and Stouraitis (2006).
9. Djankov, La Porta, López-de-Silanes and Shleifer (2008).
10. Cross-country studies include Klapper and Love (2004), Durnev and Kim (2005), Bauer, Guenster and Otten (2004) and Baker and others (2007).
11. Grandmont, Grant and Silva (2004).
12. Love (2010).
13. Information provided by the Securities and Exchange Commission of Thailand.
14. Indonesia Stock Exchange (2009).
15. Information provided by Securities Commission Malaysia.
16. IFC (2006).
17. *Doing Business* does not take into account the rules that apply in Novo Mercado because they are voluntary.
18. IFC (2008b).
19. BOVESPA (2010).

Paying taxes

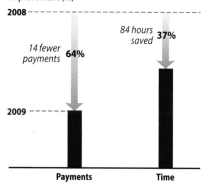

FIGURE 8.1

Entrepreneurs in Tunisia benefit from e-system for paying taxes

Improvement (%)

2008

14 fewer payments **64%**

84 hours saved **37%**

2009

Payments   **Time**

Who improved the most in paying taxes?

1. *Tunisia*
2. *Cape Verde*
3. *São Tomé and Principe*
4. *Canada*
5. *Macedonia, FYR*
6. *Bulgaria*
7. *China*
8. *Hungary*
9. *Taiwan, China*
10. *Netherlands*

Source: Doing Business database.

For Carolina, who owns and manages a Colombian-based retail business, paying taxes has become easier in the past few years. In 2004 she had to make 69 payments of 13 different types of taxes and spend 57 days (456 hours), almost 3 months, to comply with tax regulations.[1] Today, thanks to new electronic systems to pay social security contributions, she needs to make only 20 payments and spend 26 days (208 hours) a year on the same task. But high tax rates mean that her firm still has to pay about 78.7% of profit in taxes. Juliana, the owner of a juice processing factory in Uganda, faces a different environment. She makes 32 payments cutting across 16 tax regimes and spends about 20 days (161 hours) a year on compliance. She has to pay only

35.7% of her profit in taxes. But that's not all. Recent evidence suggests that in dealing with government authorities, female-owned businesses in Uganda are forced to pay significantly more bribes and are at greater risk of harassment than male-owned businesses.[2]

Some economies treat women differently by law. Côte d'Ivoire is an example. There, married women can pay 5 times as much personal income tax as their husbands do on the same amount of income. Three other economies also impose higher taxes on women—Burkina Faso, Indonesia and Lebanon. But Israel, Korea and Singapore impose lower taxes on women, to encourage them to enter the workforce. Explicit gender bias in the tax law can affect women's decision to work in the formal sector and report their income for tax purposes.[3] Reforms that simplify tax administration and make it easier for everyone—individuals and firms—to pay taxes can also remove gender biases.

Taxes are essential. In most economies the tax system is the primary source of funding for a wide range of social and economic programs. How much revenue these economies need to raise through taxes will depend on several factors, including the government's capacity to raise revenue in other ways, such as rents on natural resources. Besides paying for public goods and services, taxes also provide a means of redistributing income, including to children, the aged and the unemployed. But the level of tax rates needs to be carefully chosen. Recent firm surveys in 123 economies show that companies consider tax rates to be among the top 4 constraints to their business.[4] The economic and financial crisis has caused fiscal constraints for many economies, yet many are still choosing to lower tax rates on businesses. Seventeen reduced profit tax rates in 2009/10. Canada, Germany and Singapore implemented tax cuts in 2009 to help businesses cope with economic slowdown.[5]

TABLE 8.1

Where is paying taxes easy—and where not?

Easiest	RANK	Most difficult	RANK
Maldives	1	Jamaica	174
Qatar	2	Panama	175
Hong Kong SAR, China	3	Gambia, The	176
		Bolivia	177
Singapore	4	Venezuela, RB	178
United Arab Emirates	5	Chad	179
		Congo, Rep.	180
Saudi Arabia	6	Ukraine	181
Ireland	7	Central African Republic	182
Oman	8		
Kuwait	9	Belarus	183
Canada	10		

Note: Rankings are the average of the economy's rankings on the number of payments, time and total tax rate. See Data notes for details.
Source: Doing Business database.

FIGURE 8.2

What are the time, total tax rate and number of payments necessary for a local medium-sized company to pay all taxes?

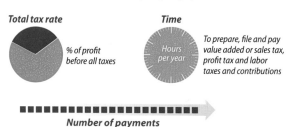

Total tax rate — % of profit before all taxes

Time — Hours per year — To prepare, file and pay value added or sales tax, profit tax and labor taxes and contributions

Number of payments (per year)

BOX 8.1
Does an economy's size or resource wealth matter for the ease of paying taxes?

Some economies, especially small ones, rely on 1 or 2 sectors to generate most government revenue. This enables them to function with a narrower tax base than would be possible in larger, more diverse economies. Maldives and Kiribati, for example, choose to tax mainly hotels and tourism, sectors not captured by the *Doing Business* indicators, which focus on manufacturing. Other economies, such as Qatar, the United Arab Emirates, Saudi Arabia and Oman, are resource-rich economies that raise most public revenue through means other than taxation.

Among both resource-rich economies and small island developing states there is great variation in rankings on the ease of paying taxes (see figure).[1] Differences in applicable tax rates account for some of the variation. But so do differences in the administrative burden. Among resource-rich economies the total tax rate ranges from as low as 11% of profit in Qatar to as high as 72% in Algeria. Among small economies the total tax rate averages around 38%. The administrative burden of paying taxes varies just as dramatically—being small or obtaining revenue from resources does not always make taxation administratively easy. To comply with profit, consumption and labor taxes can take as little as 12 hours a year in the United Arab Emirates and 58 in The Bahamas—and as much as 424 hours in São Tomé and Principe and 938 in Nigeria.

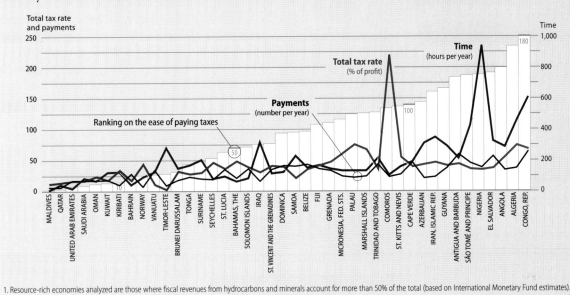

1. Resource-rich economies analyzed are those where fiscal revenues from hydrocarbons and minerals account for more than 50% of the total (based on International Monetary Fund estimates).

Keeping tax rates at a reasonable level can be important for encouraging the development of the private sector and the formalization of businesses. This is particularly relevant for small and medium-size enterprises, which contribute to job creation and growth but do not add significantly to tax revenue.[6] Taxation largely bypasses the informal sector, and overtaxing a shrinking formal sector leads to resentment and greater tax avoidance. Decisions on whom to tax and at what part of the business cycle can be influenced by many different factors that go beyond the scope of this study.

Tax revenue also depends on governments' administrative capacity to collect taxes and firms' willingness to comply. Compliance with tax laws is important to keep the system working for all and to support the programs and ser-

vices that improve lives. Keeping rules as simple and clear as possible is undoubtedly helpful to taxpayers. Overly complicated tax systems risk high evasion. High tax compliance costs are associated with larger informal sectors, more corruption and less investment. Economies with well-designed tax systems are able to help the growth of businesses and, ultimately, the growth of overall investment and employment.[7]

Doing Business addresses these concerns with 3 indicators: payments, time and the total tax rate borne by a standard firm with 60 employees in a given year. The number of payments indicator measures the frequency with which the company has to file and pay different types of taxes and contributions, adjusted for the way in which those payments are made. The time indicator captures the number of hours it takes to prepare, file

and pay 3 major types of taxes: profit taxes, consumption taxes and labor taxes and mandatory contributions. The total tax rate measures the tax cost borne by the standard firm (figure 8.2).[8]

With these indicators, *Doing Business* compares tax systems and tracks tax reforms around the world from the perspective of local businesses, covering both the direct cost of taxes and the administrative burden of complying with them. It does not measure the fiscal health of economies, the macroeconomic conditions under which governments collect revenue or the provision of public services supported by taxation.

The top 10 economies on the ease of paying taxes represent a range of revenue models, each with different implications for the tax burden of a domestic medium-size business (table 8.1). The top 10 include several economies that are small or

FIGURE 8.3

Tax reforms implemented by more than 60% of economies in the past 6 years

Number of *Doing Business* reforms making it easier to pay taxes by *Doing Business* report year

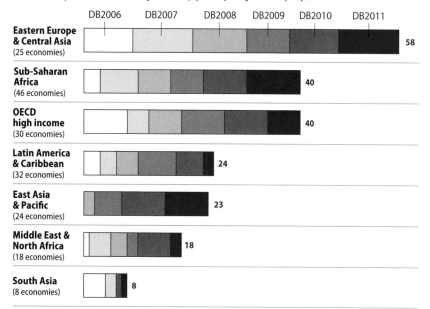

Note: A *Doing Business* reform is counted as 1 reform per reforming economy per year. The data sample for DB2006 (2004) includes 174 economies. The sample for DB2011 (2009) also includes The Bahamas, Bahrain, Brunei Darussalam, Cyprus, Kosovo, Liberia, Luxembourg, Montenegro and Qatar, for a total of 183 economies.
Source: Doing Business database.

resource rich. But these characteristics do not necessarily matter for the administrative burden or total tax rate faced by businesses (box 8.1).

Also among the top 10, Hong Kong SAR (China), Singapore, Ireland and Canada apply a low tax cost, with total tax rates averaging less than 30% of profit. They also stand out for their low administrative burdens. They levy up to 9 different taxes on businesses, yet for a local business to comply with taxes takes only about 1 day a month and 6 payments. Electronic filing and payment and joint forms for multiple taxes are common practice among these 4 economies.

Tunisia, the economy that improved the ease of paying taxes the most in 2009/10, followed their example. It fully implemented electronic payment systems for corporate income tax and value added tax and broadened their use to most firms. The changes reduced the number of payments a year by 14 and compliance time by 84 hours.

Thirty-nine other economies also made it easier for businesses to pay taxes in 2009/10.[9] Governments continued to lower tax rates, broaden the tax base and make compliance easier so as to reduce costs for firms and encourage job creation. As in previous years, the most popular measure was to reduce profit tax rates.

WHAT ARE THE TRENDS?

In the past 6 years more than 60% of the economies covered by *Doing Business* made paying taxes easier or lowered the tax burden for local enterprises (figure 8.3). Globally on average, firms spend 35 days (282 hours) a year complying with 30 tax payments. A comparison with global averages in 2004 shows that payments have been reduced by 4 and compliance time by 5 days (39 hours).[10] Companies in high-income economies have it easiest. On average, they spend 22 days (172 hours) on 15 tax payments a year. Businesses in low-income economies continue to face the highest administrative burden (table 8.2). Globally on average, businesses pay 47.8% of commercial profit in taxes and mandatory contributions, 5.0 percentage points less than in 2004.

TAX COMPLIANCE BECOMING EASIER

Eleven economies in Eastern Europe and Central Asia simplified tax payment in the 6 years since 2004. Average compliance time for businesses fell by about 2 working weeks as a result. The momentum for change started building in Bulgaria and Latvia in 2005 and swept across the region to Azerbaijan, Turkey and Uzbekistan in 2006, Belarus and Ukraine in 2007, the Kyrgyz Republic and FYR Macedonia in 2008 and Albania and Montenegro in 2009. But the administrative burden generally remains high. Five of the region's economies rank among those with the highest number of payments globally (table 8.3).

Some Sub-Saharan African economies also focused on easing tax compliance. In 2010 Sierra Leone introduced administrative reforms at the tax authority and replaced 4 different sales taxes with a value added tax. In the past 5 years 7 other economies—Burkina Faso, Cameroon, Cape Verde, Ghana, Madagascar, South Africa and Sudan—reduced the number of payments by eliminating, merging or reducing the frequency of filings and payments. Mozambique, São Tomé and Principe, Sierra Leone, Sudan and Zambia revamped existing tax codes or enacted new ones in the past 6 years.

TABLE 8.2

Administrative burden lowest in high-income economies

Income group	Payments (number per year)	Time (hours per year)	Total tax rate (% of profit)
Low	38	295	71.0
Lower middle	35	359	40.3
Upper middle	31	272	43.4
High	15	172	38.8
Average	30	282	47.8

Source: Doing Business database.

TABLE 8.3
Who makes paying taxes easy and who does not—and where is the total tax rate highest and lowest?

Payments (number per year)			
Fewest		**Most**	
Sweden	2	Sri Lanka	62
Hong Kong SAR, China	3	Côte d'Ivoire	64
Maldives	3	Nicaragua	64
Qatar	3	Serbia	66
Norway	4	Venezuela, RB	70
Singapore	5	Jamaica	72
Mexico	6	Montenegro	77
Timor-Leste	6	Belarus	82
Kiribati	7	Romania	113
Mauritius	7	Ukraine	135

Time (hours per year)			
Fastest		**Slowest**	
Maldives	0	Ukraine	657
United Arab Emirates	12	Senegal	666
Bahrain	36	Mauritania	696
Qatar	36	Chad	732
Bahamas, The	58	Belarus	798
Luxembourg	59	Venezuela, RB	864
Oman	62	Nigeria	938
Switzerland	63	Vietnam	941
Ireland	76	Bolivia	1,080
Seychelles	76	Brazil	2,600

Total tax rate (% of profit)			
Lowest		**Highest**	
Timor-Leste	0.2	Eritrea	84.5
Vanuatu	8.4	Tajikistan	86.0
Maldives	9.3	Uzbekistan	95.6
Namibia	9.6	Argentina	108.2
Macedonia, FYR	10.6	Burundi	153.4
Qatar	11.3	Central African Republic	203.8
United Arab Emirates	14.1	Comoros	217.9
Saudi Arabia	14.5	Sierra Leone	235.6
Bahrain	15.0	Gambia, The	292.3
Georgia	15.3	Congo, Dem. Rep.	339.7

Note: The indicator on payments is adjusted for the possibility of electronic or joint filing and payment when used by the majority of firms in an economy. See Data notes for more details.
Source: Doing Business database.

Firms in OECD high-income economies have the lowest administrative burden. Businesses in these economies spend on average 25 days a year complying with 14 tax payments. All but 2, the Slovak Republic and Switzerland, have fully implemented electronic filing and payment for firms. Between 2006 and 2009 the Czech Republic, Finland, Greece, the Netherlands, Poland and Spain mandated or enhanced electronic filing or simplified the process of paying taxes, reducing compliance time by 13 days (101 hours) on average.

In the Middle East and North Africa businesses must comply with only 22 payments a year on average, the second lowest among regions. Yet there is great variation, with up to 44 payments in the Republic of Yemen and as few as 3 payments in Qatar. In 2009/10 only 2 tax reforms were recorded, in Jordan and Tunisia.

In Latin America and the Caribbean firms continue to spend substantial time paying taxes—385 hours a year on average. They have to make an average of 33 payments a year (figure 8.4). Thankfully,

many economies in the region have simplified the process of paying taxes since 2004, saving businesses an average of 3 days a year. Still, only 12 of the region's 32 economies offer electronic filing and payment for firms. Colombia, the Dominican Republic, Guatemala, Honduras, Mexico and Peru have introduced online filing and payment systems since 2004, eliminating the need for 25 separate tax payments a year and reducing compliance time by 11 days (83 hours) on average. The boldest measures: since 2004 Colombia has reduced the number of payments by 49 and compliance time by 248 hours, the Dominican Republic has cut payments by 65 and time by 156 hours, and Mexico has reduced the number of payments by 21 and the time to comply with them by 148 hours. And these economies continue work to further reduce the administrative burden for firms.

Economies in East Asia and the Pacific have reduced compliance time since 2004 by about 8 business days, the most after Eastern Europe and Central Asia. Most recently, Lao PDR consolidated the filings for business turnover tax and excise tax as well as personal income tax withholding in a single tax return. Businesses now spend 25 fewer days a year complying with tax laws. China unified accounting methods and expanded the use of electronic tax filing and payment systems in 2007, saving firms 368 hours and 26 payments a year. In 2008 and 2009 China unified criteria for corporate income tax deduction and shifted from a production-oriented value added system to a consumption-oriented one, saving firms another 106 hours a year. Brunei Darussalam, Malaysia, Taiwan (China) and Thailand introduced or enhanced electronic systems in the past 6 years.

In South Asia payments and compliance time changed little overall. In 2009/10 *Doing Business* recorded only 1 tax reform—in India, which abolished fringe benefit tax and enhanced electronic filing.

FIGURE 8.4
Paying taxes easier in East Asia and the Pacific
Regional averages in paying taxes

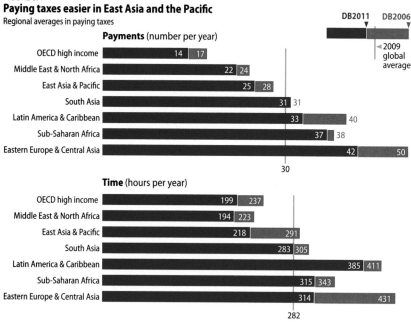

Note: The data sample for DB2006 (2004) includes 174 economies. The sample for DB2011 (2009) also includes The Bahamas, Bahrain, Brunei Darussalam, Cyprus, Kosovo, Liberia, Luxembourg, Montenegro and Qatar, for a total of 183 economies.
Source: Doing Business database.

TOTAL TAX RATES BECOMING LOWER

When considering the burden of taxes on business, it is important to look at all the taxes that companies pay. These may include labor taxes and mandatory contributions paid by employers, sales tax, property tax and other smaller taxes such as property transfer tax, dividend tax, capital gains tax, financial transactions tax, waste collection tax and vehicle and road tax. In 7 economies around the world, taxes and mandatory contributions add up to more than 100% of assumed profit, ranging from 108.2% to 339.7%. *Doing Business* assumes that the standard firm in its tax case study has a fixed gross profit margin of 20%. Where the indicator shows that taxes exceed profit, the company has to earn a gross profit margin in excess of 20% to pay its taxes. Corporate income tax is only one of many taxes with which the company has to comply. The total tax rate

for most economies is between 30% and 50% of profit.

Economies in Eastern Europe and Central Asia have implemented the most reforms affecting the paying taxes indicators since 2004, with 23 of the region's 25 economies implementing 58 such reforms. The most popular feature in the past 6 years was lowering profit tax rates (done by 19 economies). The changes reduced the average total tax rate in the region by 13.1 percentage points (figure 8.5).

In the past year economies in Sub-Saharan Africa implemented almost a quarter of all reforms affecting the paying taxes indicators, a record for the region compared with previous years. In the past 6 years the most popular feature in the region was reducing profit tax rates (28 reforms). The reductions lowered the average total tax rate for the region by 2.7 percentage points. But profit tax, just one of many taxes for businesses in Africa, accounts for only a third of the total tax paid. Firms in the region still face the highest average total tax rate in the world, 68% of profit.

Firms in OECD high-income economies pay 43.0% of profit in taxes on average. Nineteen of these economies lowered profit tax rates in the past 6 years. And more changes are on the horizon. Australia, Finland and the United Kingdom have announced major reforms of their tax systems in the next few years.[11]

The average total tax rate in the Middle East and North Africa, at 32.8% of profit, is the lowest in the world—thanks in part to tax reforms reducing it by 10.8 percentage points since 2004. Algeria, Djibouti, Egypt, Morocco, Syria, Tunisia, West Bank and Gaza and the Republic of Yemen have all lowered profit tax rates, abolished taxes or replaced cascading taxes.

The average total tax rate for Latin America and the Caribbean is the second highest, amounting to 48% of profit. Seven economies, including Mexico, Paraguay and Uruguay, reduced tax rates in the past 6 years, lowering the region's total tax rate by 2.3 percentage points.

The total tax rate in East Asia and

FIGURE 8.5
Eastern Europe and Central Asia has biggest reduction in total tax rate

Total tax rate (% of profit)

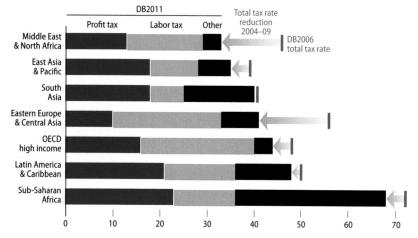

Note: The data sample for DB2006 (2004) includes 174 economies. The sample for DB2011 (2009) also includes The Bahamas, Bahrain, Brunei Darussalam, Cyprus, Kosovo, Liberia, Luxembourg, Montenegro and Qatar, for a total of 183 economies.
Source: Doing Business database.

the Pacific is relatively low. At 35.4% of profit, it is the second lowest after that in the Middle East and North Africa. Still, 13 economies in the region reduced profit tax rates in the past 6 years, including China, Indonesia, Malaysia, the Philippines, Thailand and Vietnam.

Few economies in South Asia have made changes affecting the paying taxes indicators since 2004. Afghanistan, Bangladesh, India and Pakistan reduced profit tax rates, but the reductions had little effect on the region's average total tax rate.

WHAT HAS WORKED?

Worldwide, economies that make paying taxes easy for domestic firms typically offer electronic systems for tax filing and payment, have one tax per tax base and use a filing system based on self-assessment (table 8.4). They also focus on lower tax rates accompanied by wider tax bases.

OFFERING AN ELECTRONIC OPTION

Electronic filing and payment of taxes eliminates excessive paperwork and interaction with tax officers. Offered by 61 economies, this option can reduce the time businesses spend in complying with tax laws, increase tax compliance and reduce the cost of revenue administration. But this is possible only with effective implementation. Simple processes and high-quality security systems are needed.

In Tunisia, thanks to a now fully implemented electronic filing and payment system, businesses spend 37% less time complying with corporate income tax and value added tax. Azerbaijan introduced electronic systems and online payment for value added tax in 2007 and expanded them to property and land taxes in 2009. Belarus enhanced electronic filing and payment systems, reducing the compliance time for value added tax, corporate income tax and labor taxes by 14 days. The reverse happened in Uganda. There, compliance time has increased despite the introduction of an electronic system. Online forms were simply too complex.

TABLE 8.4
Good practices around the world in making it easy to pay taxes

Practice	Economies[a]	Examples
Allowing self-assessment	136	Botswana, Georgia, India, Malaysia, Oman, Peru, United Kingdom
Allowing electronic filing and payment	61	Australia, Dominican Republic, India, Lithuania, Singapore, South Africa, Tunisia
Having one tax per tax base	50	Afghanistan, Hong Kong SAR (China), FYR Macedonia, Morocco, Namibia, Paraguay, Sweden

a. Among 183 economies surveyed.
Source: Doing Business database.

KEEPING IT SIMPLE: ONE TAX BASE, ONE TAX

Multiple taxation—where the same tax base is subject to more than one tax treatment—makes efficient tax management challenging. It increases firms' cost of doing business as well as the government's cost of revenue administration and risks damaging investor confidence.

Fifty economies have one tax per tax base. Having more types of taxes requires more interaction between businesses and tax agencies. In Nigeria corporate income tax, education tax and information technology tax are all levied on a company's taxable income. In New York City taxes are levied at the municipal, state and federal levels. Each is calculated on a different tax base, so businesses must do 3 different calculations.

This is no longer the case in Ontario. The Canadian province harmonized its corporate income tax base with the federal one. And the Canada Revenue Agency now administers Ontario's corporate capital tax and corporate minimum tax. Starting with the 2009 tax year, Ontario businesses have been able to make combined payments and file a single corporate tax return.

Brazil also aims to simplify a system that requires businesses to interact with 3 levels of government. In 2010 it introduced a new system of digital bookkeeping (Sistema Público de Escrituração Digitalor, or SPED) to integrate federal, state and municipal tax agencies. The successful implementation of SPED will ease the administrative burden of complying with taxes in Brazil by reducing the number of tax payments and possibly the time for compliance.

TABLE 8.5
Major cuts in corporate income tax rates in 2009/10

Region	Reduction in corporate income tax rate (%)	Year effective
Sub-Saharan Africa	Burkina Faso from 30 to 27.5	2010
	Republic of Congo from 38 to 36	2010
	Madagascar from 25 to 23	2010
	Niger from 35 to 30	2010
	São Tomé and Principe from 30 to 25	2009
	Seychelles from progressive 0–40 to 25–33	2010
	Zimbabwe from 30 to 25	2010
Eastern Europe & Central Asia	Azerbaijan from 22 to 20	2010
	Lithuania from 20 to 15	2010
	FYR Macedonia from 10 to 0 (for undistributed profits)	2009
	Tajikistan from 25 to 15	2009
East Asia & Pacific	Brunei Darussalam from 23.5 to 22	2010
	Indonesia from 28 to 25	2009
	Taiwan (China) from 25 to 17	2010
	Tonga from progressive 15–30 to 25	2009
Latin America & Caribbean	Panama from 30 to 25	2010

Source: Doing Business database.

TABLE 8.6

Who made paying taxes easier and lowered the tax burden in 2009/10—and what did they do?

	Feature	Economies	Some highlights
Easing compliance	Merged or eliminated taxes other than profit tax	Belarus, Bosnia and Herzegovina, Burkina Faso, Cape Verde, Hong Kong SAR (China), Hungary, India, Jordan, Montenegro, Slovenia, República Bolivariana de Venezuela	Cape Verde eliminated all stamp duties.
	Simplified tax compliance process	Azerbaijan, Belarus, Canada, China, Czech Republic, FYR Macedonia, Montenegro, Netherlands, Sierra Leone, Taiwan (China), Ukraine, Zimbabwe	The Netherlands made value added tax filings and payments quarterly and eased profit tax calculations. Belarus changed from monthly to quarterly payments for several taxes.
	Introduced or enhanced electronic systems	Albania, Azerbaijan, Belarus, Brunei Darussalam, India, Jordan, Tunisia, Ukraine	A big increase in online filing in Azerbaijan reduced the time for filing and the number of payments.
Reducing tax rates	Reduced profit tax rate by 2 percentage points or more	Azerbaijan, Brunei Darussalam, Burkina Faso, Republic of Congo, Indonesia, Lithuania, FYR Macedonia, Madagascar, Niger, Panama, São Tomé and Principe, Seychelles, Taiwan (China), Tajikistan, Thailand, Tonga, Zimbabwe	Burkina Faso reduced the profit tax rate from 30% to 27.5% and merged 3 taxes. Niger lowered the rate from 35% to 30%. Lithuania reversed an increase (from 15% to 20%) made the previous year.
	Reduced labor taxes and mandatory contributions	Albania, Bosnia and Herzegovina, Bulgaria, Canada, Hungary, Moldova, Portugal	Hungary reduced employers' social security contribution rate from 29% of gross salaries to 26%.
Introducing new systems	Introduced new or substantially revised tax law	Azerbaijan, Belarus, Hungary, Jordan, Panama, Portugal, São Tomé and Principe	Jordan's new tax law abolished certain taxes and reduced rates.
	Introduced change in cascading sales tax	Burundi, Lao PDR, Sierra Leone	Burundi introduced a value added tax in place of its transactions tax.

Source: Doing Business database.

TRUSTING THE TAXPAYER

Voluntary compliance and self-assessment have become a popular way to efficiently administer a country's tax system. Taxpayers are expected and trusted to determine their own liability under the law and pay the correct amount. With high rates of voluntary compliance, administrative costs are much lower and so is the burden of compliance actions.[12] Self-assessment systems also reduce the discretionary powers of tax officials and opportunities for corruption.[13] To be effective, however, self-assessment needs to be properly introduced and implemented, with transparent rules, penalties for noncompliance and established audit processes.

Of the 183 economies covered by *Doing Business*, 74% allow firms to calculate their own tax bills and file the returns. These include all economies in Eastern Europe and Central Asia and almost two-thirds in East Asia and the Pacific, the Middle East and North Africa and South Asia. Both taxpayers and revenue authorities can benefit. Malaysia shifted to a self-assessment system for businesses in stages starting in 2001. Taxpayer compliance increased, and so did revenue collection.[14]

WHAT ARE SOME RESULTS?

Franklin D. Roosevelt once said, "Taxes, after all, are the dues that we pay for the privileges of membership in an organized society."[15] There is no doubt about the need for and benefits of taxation. But how economies approach taxation for small and medium-size businesses varies substantially. More than 119 economies made their business tax systems more efficient and effective in the past 6 years—and have seen concrete results.

EASIER PROCESS, MORE REVENUE

Colombia introduced a new electronic system, PILA, that unified in one online payment all contributions to social security, the welfare security system and labor risk insurance. Its use became mandatory for all companies in 2007. By 2008 the number of companies registered to pay contributions through PILA had increased by 55%. The social security contributions collected that year from small and medium-size companies rose by 42%, to 550 billion pesos.

Mauritius implemented a major tax reform in 2006. It reduced the corporate income tax rate from 25% to 15% and re-

moved exemptions and industry-specific allowances, such as its investment allowance and tax holidays for manufacturing. Authorities aimed to increase revenue by combining a low tax rate, a transparent system, a reinforced tax administration and efficient collection—and they did. In the 2007/08 fiscal year corporate income tax revenue grew by 27%, and in 2008/09 it increased by 65%.

FYR Macedonia has implemented major tax reforms for the past several years in a row. In 2007 it introduced a

FIGURE 8.6

Size of informal sector is associated with ease of paying taxes

Informal sector share of GDP

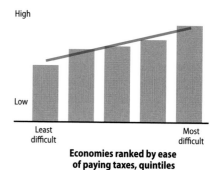

Note: Relationships are significant at the 1% level and remain significant when controlling for income per capita.
Source: Doing Business database; Schneider and Buehn (2009).

new electronic tax service. In 2008 it amended the tax law to cut the profit tax rate from 15% to 10%. In 2009 it implemented a new, clearer Law on Contributions for Mandatory Social Security—and imposed the corporate income tax only on distributed profits. Despite the global downturn, the number of companies registered as taxpayers in FYR Macedonia increased by 16% between 2008 and 2009.

In an effort to stimulate economic growth and create a more business-friendly environment, Korea reduced the corporate income tax rate from 25% to 22% in 2009 and plans to reduce it even further in future years. The revenue collected by the government in 2009 did not fall. Instead, the number of companies registered for corporate income tax increased by 7%—and the corporate income tax revenue by 11%.

WHAT FIRMS VALUE

These results illustrate some of the benefits of more effective tax systems and appropriate tax rates. Recent research has found that in developing economies, where many firms are likely to be small and heavily involved in informal activity, reducing profit tax rates helps reduce informality and raise tax compliance, increasing growth and revenue.[16]

The size of the informal sector, which in many developing economies accounts for as much as half of GDP, can significantly affect the tax revenue collected as a percentage of GDP.[17] But the reverse is also true: the structure of the tax system and the perception of the quality of government services can affect the size of the informal sector in a country. Larger informal sectors as well as greater corruption are found where the majority of firms perceive taxes as not "worth paying" because of low-quality public goods and poor infrastructure. This view is supported by a recent survey of business and law students in Guatemala. Most participants believed that tax evasion was ethical where tax systems are unfair or corrupt and where government commits human rights abuses.[18] *Doing Business* data show that economies where it is more difficult and costly to pay taxes have larger shares of informal sector activity (figure 8.6).

Sensitivity to tax reforms is affected by firm size. Large firms are usually more directly affected by changes. But small firms have a higher tendency to be unregistered if tax rates are high, and tend to underreport income and size if higher incomes and bigger firms are taxed at a higher rate.[19] In Côte d'Ivoire, where firms must pay 44% of profit and make more than 64 payments a year to comply with 14 different taxes, a recent study finds that firms avoid growing in order to pay less tax.[20]

FIGURE 8.7
Total tax rates between 30% and 50% are most common

Number of economies by income group

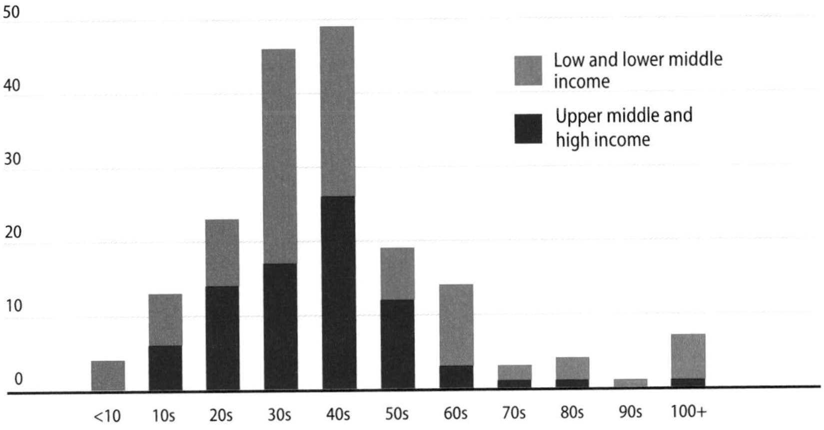

Total tax rate (% of profit)

Source: Doing Business database.

1. Days refer to working days, calculated by assuming 8 working hours a day. Months are calculated by assuming 20 working days a month.

2. Ellis, Manuel and Blackden (2006).

3. World Bank (2010b).

4. Globally, companies ranked tax rates 4th among 16 obstacles to business in World Bank Enterprise Surveys in 2006–09 (http://www.enterprisesurveys.org).

5. Canada, as part of a plan to stimulate growth and restore confidence, reduced the general corporate tax rate to 19% as of January 1, 2009. In Germany a stimulus package adopted in November 2008 introduced declining balance depreciation at 25% for movable assets for 2 years and temporarily expanded special depreciation allowances for small and medium-size enterprises. A second stimulus package, approved in February 2009, provided further tax cuts. In January 2009 Singapore's Ministry of Finance announced a $15 billion "resilience package" to help businesses and workers and reduced the corporate income tax rate from 18% to 17%.

6. International Tax Dialogue (2007).

7. Djankov and others (2010).

8. The company has 60 employees and start-up capital of 102 times income per capita.

9. This year's report records all reforms with an impact on the paying taxes indicators between June 2009 and May 2010. Because the case study underlying the paying taxes indicators refers to the financial year ending December 31, 2009, reforms on the paying taxes indicators implemented between January 2010 and May 2010 are recorded in this year's report, but the impact will be reflected in the data in next year's report.

10. The comparison of global averages refers to the 174 economies included in *Doing Business 2006*. Additional economies were added in subsequent years.

11. Australia intends to reduce the corporate income tax rate from 30% to 29% from July 1, 2013, and then to 28% from July 1, 2014. In Finland an initial proposal includes reducing the corporate income tax rate from 26% to 22% and increasing the standard value added tax rate of 22% by 2 percentage points. In the United Kingdom the emergency budget for 2010–11 calls for reducing the corporation tax rate to 27% for the 2011 financial year and then, through cuts over the next 4 years, to 24%. It also calls for

reducing the small company tax rate to 20% and increasing the standard value added tax rate from 17.5% to 20%.

12. Ricard (2008).

13. Imam and Davina (2007).

14. bin Haji Ridzuan (2006).

15. Address delivered at Worcester, Mass., October 21, 1936. John T. Woolley and Gerhard Peters, *The American Presidency Project*, http://www.presidency.ucsb .edu/.

16. Hibbs and Piculescu (2010).

17. Gordon and Li (2009).

18. McGee and Lingle (2008).

19. OECD (2008).

20. Klapper and Richmond (2010).

Trading across borders

FIGURE 9.1

Traders in Peru benefit from risk-based inspections and electronic systems

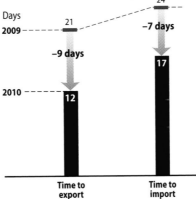

Source: Doing Business database.

Who improved the most in trading across borders?

1. *Peru*
2. *Grenada*
3. *Armenia*
4. *Montenegro*
5. *Nicaragua*
6. *Rwanda*
7. *Cambodia*
8. *Egypt, Arab Rep.*
9. *Spain*
10. *Philippines*

Traders at the Chirundu crossing between Zambia and Zimbabwe have long dealt with congestion and delays at the busy border post. Procedures duplicated on each side of the border and involving up to 15 government agencies often require a wait of 2–3 days to clear goods. This is starting to change, thanks to a one-stop border post that was recently established. Trucking companies will save, because delays "cost each truck $140 per day in fixed costs and driver's time," notes Juma Mwapachu, the secretary general of the East African Community. "The potential cost saving is about $486 million per year, which accrues to our economies and competitiveness."[1]

In a globalized world, making trade between countries easier is increasingly important for business. Bedi Limited, a garment producer in Nakuru, Kenya, spent 18 months pursuing a trial order for school items from Tesco, one of the United Kingdom's largest retail chains. Bedi landed the order and the delivery date was set for early July, in time for the August back-to-school promotions. Bedi's goods arrived in Kenya's port city of Mombasa at the end of June, ready for shipment. But they were delayed at the port due to congestion and didn't arrive in the United Kingdom until August. Bedi missed Tesco's school promotions— and lost out on the chance to become part of its global supply chain.[2]

The ability of firms and economies to compete in global markets has been put to the test in the past 2 years of economic turmoil. In 2009 world trade recorded its largest decline in more than 70 years. No region was left untouched.[3] But

one study shows that during the recent slump in global demand, making trade easier helped to mitigate the drop in an economy's exports by promoting stronger links between suppliers and buyers. By contrast, an extra day's delay led to about an additional 0.5% fall in exports to the United States.[4]

While trade recovered in 2010 and fears of a surge in protectionism have largely subsided, burdensome documentation requirements, time-consuming customs procedures, inefficient port operations and inadequate transport infrastructure still lead to unnecessary costs and delays for traders. Poor performance in just 1 or 2 of these areas can have serious repercussions for an economy's overall trade competitiveness, as shown by the World Bank's Logistics Performance Index.[5] By removing these obstacles, governments can create an environment

TABLE 9.1

Where is trading across borders easy— and where not?

Easiest	RANK	Most difficult	RANK
Singapore	1	Niger	174
Hong Kong SAR, China	2	Burkina Faso	175
		Burundi	176
United Arab Emirates	3	Azerbaijan	177
		Tajikistan	178
Estonia	4	Iraq	179
Finland	5	Congo, Rep.	180
Denmark	6	Kazakhstan	181
Sweden	7	Central African Republic	182
Korea, Rep.	8		
Norway	9	Afghanistan	183
Israel	10		

Note: Rankings are the average of the economy's rankings on the documents, time and cost required to export and import. See Data notes for details.
Source: Doing Business database.

FIGURE 9.2

How much time, how many documents and what cost to export and import across borders by ocean transport?

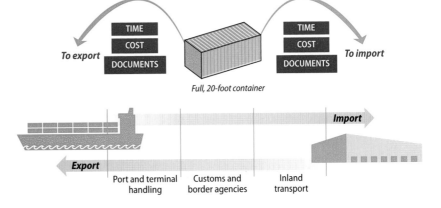

TABLE 9.2
Who made trading across borders easier in 2009/10—and what did they do?

Feature	Economies	Some highlights
Introduced or improved electronic data interchange system	Bahrain, Belarus, Brunei Darussalam, Arab Republic of Egypt, Israel, Kazakhstan, Latvia, Lithuania, Nicaragua, Pakistan, Peru, Philippines, Swaziland, Tunisia, United Arab Emirates, Zambia	Latvia and Lithuania improved their electronic declaration systems to comply with EU requirements on paperless customs that entered into force in 2009.
Improved customs administration	Armenia, Arab Republic of Egypt, Ethiopia, Fiji, Grenada, Mali, Peru, West Bank and Gaza	Traders in Grenada are benefiting from the modernization of the customs administration, in the context of a World Bank Technical Assistance Project.
Improved procedures at ports	Angola, Bahrain, Kenya, Nicaragua, Pakistan, Saudi Arabia	Containers can now move more easily through the Port of Luanda in Angola thanks to the completion of 2 dry ports and new equipment.
Reduced number of trade documents	Burkina Faso, Cambodia, Kazakhstan, Montenegro, Rwanda, Spain	Imports and exports in Cambodia no longer require preshipment inspection.
Introduced or improved risk-based inspections	Armenia, Guyana, Kazakhstan, Peru	Improved risk profiling along with the use of new equipment reduced the time for inspections at Armenia's border posts.
Introduced or improved single window	Indonesia, Israel, Madagascar	An integrated electronic national single window service system became operational in 2010 at several of Indonesia's main seaports.
Implemented border cooperation agreements	Rwanda, Zambia	Better cooperation between the agencies involved in customs clearance at the border between Zambia and Zimbabwe reduced waiting time for traders.

Source: *Doing Business* database.

that encourages entrepreneurs to look beyond their own borders for business opportunities (table 9.1).

Doing Business measures the time and cost (excluding tariffs) associated with exporting and importing by ocean transport, and the number of documents necessary to complete the transaction (figure 9.2). The indicators cover procedural requirements such as documentation requirements and procedures at customs and other regulatory agencies as well as at the port. They also cover trade logistics, including the time and cost of inland transport to the largest business city. These are key dimensions of the ease of trading—the more time consuming and costly it is to export or import, the more difficult it is for traders to be competitive and to reach international markets.

In 2009/10, 33 economies made it easier to trade. Sub-Saharan Africa accounted for the most improvements in trading across borders, followed by the Middle East and North Africa and Eastern Europe and Central Asia. Introducing or enhancing electronic data inter-change systems was the most popular change, followed by improving customs administration and port performance (table 9.2).

Peru improved the ease of trading across borders the most. A new web-based electronic data interchange system is helping to speed up document submission as well as clearance time. Fewer physical inspections of cargo are now needed at customs offices thanks to further implementation of risk-based inspections, though there remains room for improvement. The introduction of payment deferrals for import duties and taxes has also reduced import time, since cargo no longer needs to sit at the port until tariffs and tax payments are settled. Rwanda further improved its trade logistics environment by reducing the number of trade documents required and continuing its efforts toward establishing joint border management procedures with Uganda and other neighbors. The improvements build on earlier efforts in Rwanda to implement electronic submission of customs declarations and increase acceptance points for submission.

WHAT ARE THE TRENDS?

Trading across borders as measured by *Doing Business* has become faster and easier over the years. From the conclusion of a contractual agreement between the exporter and importer to the moment goods are shipped or received (excluding maritime transport) takes 23.1 days on average for exporting and 25.8 for importing. In 2006 it took 26.4 days on average to export and 30.9 to import. Traders in OECD high-income economies have it easiest: to export or import takes about 11 days and fewer than 5 documents on average. Traders in Sub-Saharan Africa, where trade is slowest and most expensive, typically face delays 3 times as long, with the time to export averaging 32 days and the time to import 38 (figure 9.3).

Disparities among regions have changed little over the years. Exporting and importing remain least expensive in East Asia and the Pacific. Inland transport is a challenge for many economies of Eastern Europe and Central Asia because of their distance from ports. And

FIGURE 9.3

Trade becoming faster around the world—with biggest gains in the Middle East and North Africa

Regional averages in trading across borders

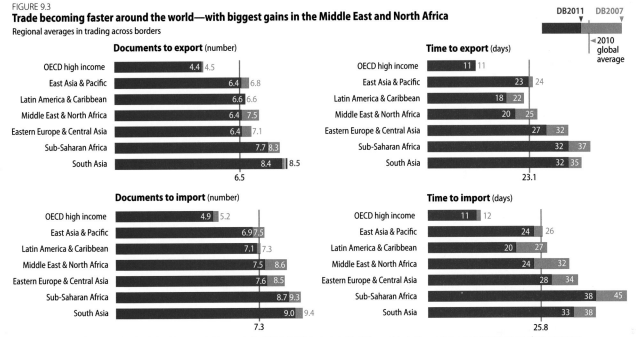

DB2011 DB2007

◄ 2010 global average

Documents to export (number)

OECD high income	4.4 / 4.5
East Asia & Pacific	6.4 / 6.8
Latin America & Caribbean	6.6 / 6.6
Middle East & North Africa	6.4 / 7.5
Eastern Europe & Central Asia	6.4 / 7.1
Sub-Saharan Africa	7.7 / 8.3
South Asia	8.4 / 8.5

6.5

Time to export (days)

OECD high income	11 / 11
East Asia & Pacific	23 / 24
Latin America & Caribbean	18 / 22
Middle East & North Africa	20 / 25
Eastern Europe & Central Asia	27 / 32
Sub-Saharan Africa	32 / 37
South Asia	32 / 35

23.1

Documents to import (number)

OECD high income	4.9 / 5.2
East Asia & Pacific	6.9 / 7.5
Latin America & Caribbean	7.1 / 7.3
Middle East & North Africa	7.5 / 8.6
Eastern Europe & Central Asia	7.6 / 8.5
Sub-Saharan Africa	8.7 / 9.3
South Asia	9.0 / 9.4

7.3

Time to import (days)

OECD high income	11 / 12
East Asia & Pacific	24 / 26
Latin America & Caribbean	20 / 27
Middle East & North Africa	24 / 32
Eastern Europe & Central Asia	28 / 34
Sub-Saharan Africa	38 / 45
South Asia	33 / 38

25.8

Note: The data sample for DB2007 (2006) includes 178 economies. The sample for DB2011 (2010) also includes The Bahamas, Bahrain, Cyprus, Kosovo and Qatar, for a total of 183 economies.
Source: Doing Business database.

economies in South Asia require the largest number of trade-related documents on average. Nevertheless, thanks to efforts at global, regional and national levels, the global trade environment has improved. Trade facilitation has become an important part of governments' strategies to increase national competitiveness and diversify exports, often supported by multilateral organizations—including the World Trade Organization, the World Customs Organization and the World Bank—and bilateral donors.

CUTTING RED TAPE

Trade agreements and customs unions have spurred reforms around the world making it easier to trade across borders. Cargo can move more easily within trade blocs such as the Southern African Customs Union thanks to a common transit document that can be used in all member nations. The Association of Southeast Asian Nations (ASEAN) has been working on an ASEAN-wide single window since 2004. Negotiations on free trade agreements with the United States have often been a driving force for improvements in trade facilitation in Latin America and the Caribbean, as in Colombia, the Dominican Republic

and Peru.[6] Efforts in several Eastern European economies to ease trade were motivated by the need to comply with EU trade regulations or by the conditions for accession to EU membership.

The time to trade has fallen in all regions, for a number of reasons. In Sub-Saharan Africa much of the drop in the time for exporting and importing was achieved by introducing electronic data interchange systems—as in Madagascar, Mali and Tanzania—and by reducing delays at ports and customs through infrastructure improvements—as in Benin and Eritrea. Sometimes simply extending office hours—as in Kenya, Rwanda and Senegal—made processes faster.

OECD high-income economies have advanced the most in the use of electronic customs declarations. Economies now achieve customs clearance times of hours or even minutes, as in France, Korea and New Zealand. In the European Union paperless electronic declaration became mandatory in January 2010.

Elimination of unnecessary documentation was popular in Latin America and the Caribbean. The Dominican Republic, Ecuador and Honduras eliminated notarization requirements. Large investments in infrastructure, including

ports, were common in the Middle East. These were motivated by years of record-high oil prices coupled with integration with global markets, as seen in Dubai, for example.

OVERCOMING GEOGRAPHIC BARRIERS

The geographic characteristics of economies can also influence their approach to trade reforms. For small island states, trade is often critical. Some, such as Singapore, have used their reliance on sea transport to their advantage and become trade hubs for their region. The close proximity of the largest business city to the port and the small volume of cargo can mean speedy inland transport and customs clearance. But many islands are isolated—container vessels call at the port only every 35–40 days in São Tomé and Principe, for example—and lack economies of scale.

By contrast, many landlocked economies face high inland transport costs to reach ports and delays at border posts. Not surprisingly, traders in landlocked economies face a higher average time and cost to export and import than traders elsewhere. But geography is not destiny. Border cooperation agreements can en-

TABLE 9.3

Good practices around the world in making it easy to trade across borders

Practice	Economies[a]	Examples
Using electronic data interchange	116[b]	Chile, Malaysia, Slovenia, United Arab Emirates
Using risk-based inspections	112	Arab Republic of Egypt, Estonia, Kenya, Thailand
Providing a single window	40	Colombia, Israel, Senegal, Singapore

a. Among 149 economies surveyed.
b. Twenty-eight have a full electronic data interchange system, 88 a partial one.
Source: Doing Business database.

able cargo to move freely—without being stopped for customs—until it reaches its destination. A trader in Vienna, in landlocked Austria, needs only 2 days to arrange for and complete the transport of cargo to the German port of Hamburg despite the distance of 900 kilometers. This is similar to the distance that cargo in Ouagadougou, in landlocked Burkina Faso, must travel to reach a port in neighboring Ghana or Togo. Yet transporting a container between Ouagadougou and Tema (in Ghana) or Lomé (in Togo) can take a week or considerably longer. The difference is due in part to inadequate infrastructure. But it also results from additional controls and waiting time at border posts.

To ensure speed while addressing security concerns, some developing economies are introducing fast-track systems for traders with a good track record—"compliant trader" or "gold card trader" programs. The European Union and OECD high-income economies such as the United States have developed a more sophisticated but complex certification system that authorizes certain businesses to move faster through the logistics of importing and exporting.

WHAT HAS WORKED?

The economies with the most efficient trade share common features. They allow traders to exchange information with customs and other control agencies electronically. And they use risk-based assessments to limit physical inspections to only a small percentage of shipments, reducing customs clearance times. Many OECD high-income economies rank high on the ease of trading across borders,

but so do developing economies such as Mauritius, Panama and Thailand.

LINKING UP ELECTRONICALLY

Electronic data interchange systems have become common around the world: 78% of the 149 surveyed economies allow traders to submit at least some of their export and import declarations, manifests and other trade-related documents to customs authorities electronically (table 9.3). Traders can submit all trade documents electronically in half of OECD high-income economies but only in less than 5% of economies in Sub-Saharan Africa and Eastern Europe and Central Asia. The newest systems are web-based, allowing traders to submit their documents from anywhere and at any time. This saves precious time and money (not to mention paper). And fewer interactions with officials mean fewer opportunities for corruption.

Electronic data interchange systems can support regional integration. In Central America the International Goods in Transit (TIM) system harmonizes previously cumbersome procedures in a single electronic document for managing the movement of goods across 9 economies. At some border locations this has reduced clearance times for goods in transit by up to 90%.[7]

But simply having an electronic system in place is not enough. Other factors have to be considered. To function properly, electronic data interchange systems require basic infrastructure such as adequate electricity supply and reliable internet connections—a challenge for many low-income economies. Electronic signature and transaction laws must be in place to ensure legal validity and avoid

disputes. In addition, users will benefit only if they have received adequate training and if systems are user friendly and easy to install. In many economies that have electronic systems, such as Botswana, The Gambia and St. Vincent and the Grenadines, customs authorities still require traders to submit hard copies. This neutralizes potential benefits and may even generate extra work for users.

OPENING A SINGLE WINDOW

Some economies go a step further by linking not only traders and customs but all agencies involved in trade. An electronic single-window system allows users to submit their export or import information in a virtual location that communicates with all the relevant authorities for obtaining documents and approvals. Traders no longer need to visit different physical locations. The most advanced systems, such as the electronic trade portal in Korea, also connect private sector participants such as banks, customs brokers, insurance companies and freight forwarders.

Single-window systems are most prevalent among OECD high-income economies. Given the cost and complexity of setting up such systems, this is not surprising. But Colombia and Senegal have also successfully implemented single-window systems.

FACTORING IN RISK

Requiring imports and exports to undergo several types of inspections—for tax, security, environmental, border control and health and safety reasons—is a normal thing. But how these inspections are carried out is critical. Done with a heavy hand, they can be a serious obstacle to efficient and transparent trade.

Over the years customs administrations around the world have developed systems for establishing risk profiles that allow them to limit physical inspections to only the riskiest consignments. The use of scanners in conjunction with risk-based profiling eliminates the need to open cargo, contributing to the efficiency of inspections. Traders in landlocked Kazakhstan face shorter customs clearance delays at the border with China thanks to the installation and implementation of a TC-SCAN system in recent years. Albania, Cameroon, the Islamic Republic of Iran, FYR Macedonia, Nigeria and the Philippines are other examples of economies that use scanners. But in some cases, such as in Zambia, the use of scanners alone has made delays worse—because customs authorities scan all consignments that pass through the border rather than using risk management to select just the risky ones for scanning.

Risk-based inspections are the norm in OECD high-income economies. They are also becoming increasingly common elsewhere. In Eastern Europe and Central Asia 86% of surveyed economies have adopted risk-based inspections.

WHAT ARE SOME RESULTS?

Implementing new services to ease trade matters only if they provide real benefits to both users and providers. In the best cases they can lead to economy-wide gains. More than 100 economies improved trade procedures in the past 5 years and are reaping the benefits of more efficient systems (figure 9.4).

COMPETITIVE EDGE FOR BUSINESSES

Ahmet Baslikaya, a Turkish exporter of industrial equipment, reports that customs reforms have reduced his clearance costs by 10–15%. "I can send all documents by e-mail to the customs authorities. Apart from the savings in time, we are also saving on labor costs. I used to employ a courier to deliver these documents on my behalf to customs, paying him $400 a month. This is now savings to my company." Rasheed, an exporter in the United Arab Emirates, tells a similar story. "Formerly we were employing 2 people working full time; each one was paid a salary of $500 a month. Now we need only one person, and even that one person needs to work for only about 5–6 hours a day for the customs clearance tasks and spends the rest of the time doing other data entry work."

In an increasingly competitive

FIGURE 9.4

Sub-Saharan Africa continues to lead in trade reforms

Number of *Doing Business* reforms making it easier to trade across borders by *Doing Business* report year

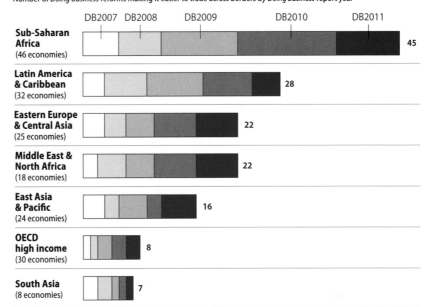

Note: A *Doing Business* reform is counted as 1 reform per reforming economy per year. The data sample for DB2007 (2006) includes 178 economies. The sample for DB2011 (2010) also includes The Bahamas, Bahrain, Cyprus, Kosovo and Qatar, for a total of 183 economies. *Source: Doing Business* database.

global economy, improving the trade facilitation environment can help give businesses a competitive edge. This is often a major impetus for government action. Yet support from the private sector cannot be taken for granted. When Kenya introduced its electronic customs system, Simba, in 2005, the Kenya International Freight and Warehousing Association initiated a court action. Members felt that Simba imposed unfair and costly requirements, such as the need for computerization and training.[8] Traders in the Dominican Republic make similar complaints, claiming that the country's electronic system creates more obstacles than benefits. They report technical glitches and feel that the system was developed without getting input from users or adequately preparing them for the change.

Transitions are challenging. But policy makers can avoid bigger problems down the road by involving stakeholders throughout the process. Implemented correctly, trade facilitation reforms can yield big cost savings. Such reforms in Georgia reduced the customs clearance time for a commercial truck by a day. That saves a day's operating cost, $288 per

truck. In 2006, with about 139,000 truck crossings, this translated into estimated annual savings of $40 million. Two years later the number of truck crossings had grown to more than 600,000 annually—and the annual savings by an additional $133 million.[9]

GREATER INTEGRATION

Easing trade can also open opportunities for domestic firms to be part of global production networks. Firms in developing economies often miss out on global production links because of unfavorable trade facilitation environments that create delays—like those encountered by Bedi.

Traders in Korea need not worry about such delays. Korea Customs Service estimates that predictable cargo processing times and rapid cargo turnover by ports and warehouses provide a benefit to the Korean economy of some $2 billion annually.[10] Indeed, for Korean-based companies such as Samsung and LG, global leaders in the electronics industry, the rapid and predictable turnaround times are an important part of their competitiveness strategies.

TABLE 9.4

Where is exporting easy—and where not?				
Documents (number)				
Fewest		**Most**		
France	2	Burkina Faso	10	
Armenia	3	Cambodia	10	
Canada	3	Kazakhstan	10	
Estonia	3	Angola	11	
Korea, Rep.	3	Cameroon	11	
Micronesia, Fed. Sts.	3	Congo, Rep.	11	
Panama	3	Malawi	11	
Sweden	3	Mauritania	11	
Finland	4	Namibia	11	
Hong Kong SAR, China	4	Afghanistan	12	
Time (days)				
Fastest		**Slowest**		
Denmark	5	Zimbabwe	53	
Estonia	5	Central African Republic	54	
Singapore	5	Niger	59	
Hong Kong SAR, China	6	Kyrgyz Republic	63	
Luxembourg	6	Uzbekistan	71	
Netherlands	6	Afghanistan	74	
United States	6	Chad	75	
Cyprus	7	Iraq	80	
Germany	7	Kazakhstan	81	
Norway	7	Tajikistan	82	
Cost (US$ per container)				
Least		**Most**		
Malaysia	450	Rwanda	3,275	
Singapore	456	Zimbabwe	3,280	
China	500	Tajikistan	3,350	
United Arab Emirates	521	Congo, Dem. Rep.	3,505	
Finland	540	Niger	3,545	
Vietnam	555	Iraq	3,550	
Saudi Arabia	580	Congo, Rep.	3,818	
Latvia	600	Afghanistan	3,865	
Pakistan	611	Central African Republic	5,491	
Egypt, Arab Rep.	613	Chad	5,902	

Where is importing easy—and where not?			
Documents (number)			
Fewest		**Most**	
France	2	Burkina Faso	10
Denmark	3	Afghanistan	11
Korea, Rep.	3	Bhutan	11
Sweden	3	Mauritania	11
Thailand	3	Cameroon	12
Estonia	4	Kazakhstan	12
Hong Kong SAR, China	4	Eritrea	13
Norway	4	Russian Federation	13
Panama	4	Azerbaijan	14
Singapore	4	Central African Republic	17
Time (days)			
Fastest		**Slowest**	
Singapore	4	Kazakhstan	67
Cyprus	5	Burundi	71
Denmark	5	Venezuela, RB	71
Estonia	5	Kyrgyz Republic	72
Hong Kong SAR, China	5	Zimbabwe	73
United States	5	Afghanistan	77
Luxembourg	6	Iraq	83
Netherlands	6	Tajikistan	83
Sweden	6	Uzbekistan	92
United Kingdom	6	Chad	101
Cost (US$ per container)			
Least		**Most**	
Singapore	439	Afghanistan	3,830
Malaysia	450	Burkina Faso	4,030
United Arab Emirates	542	Burundi	4,285
China	545	Tajikistan	4,550
São Tomé and Principe	577	Uzbekistan	4,650
Hong Kong SAR, China	600	Rwanda	4,990
Israel	605	Zimbabwe	5,101
Finland	620	Central African Republic	5,554
Fiji	630	Congo, Rep.	7,709
Vietnam	645	Chad	8,150

Source: Doing Business database.

GAINS FOR GOVERNMENTS

Businesses are not the only ones to benefit. Making it easier to trade across borders can lead to significant benefits for the government by boosting customs revenue. In Angola between 2001 and 2008, customs revenue increased by more than 1,600%, though from a low base. Not all governments experience such big surges in revenue, but steady increases add up. In Georgia improvements in customs clearance procedures, coupled with greater trade, contributed to a 92% increase in value added tax revenue (60–65% of which is collected at the border) between 2005 and 2009. Ghana saw customs revenue grow by 49% in the first 18 months after implementing GCNet, its electronic data interchange system for customs procedures.[11]

Making it easier to trade across borders also assists government operations. Rwanda's consistent reforms easing trade have led to increased productivity of customs officials (figure 9.5). The implementation of single windows in Korea and Singapore also led to big gains in productivity. Singapore, which established the world's first national single window (TradeNet) in 1989 by bringing together more than 35 border agencies, estimates that for every $1 earned in customs revenue it spends only 1 cent—a profit margin of 9,900%.[12] Such gains have allowed it to pass on the benefits to traders. In 1988, under the manual system, traders were charged a processing and transmission fee of S$10. Today the fee is only S$1.80.

While electronic systems can yield big gains, initial investments and operations can be costly. Korea Customs Service estimates that it spends some $38 million annually on its information technology infrastructure, $9 million of

FIGURE 9.5
Improvements in customs administration boost efficiency in Rwanda

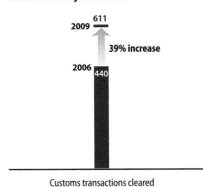

Customs transactions cleared
per customs official per year

Source: Government of Rwanda.

which is for the single-window system. But the estimated benefits, $2–3.3 billion a year according to the agency, far outweigh the costs. For economies with basic computer systems, however, the cost of implementing automated systems can be significant.

Moreover, automated systems can speed up customs procedures only if customs officials and private sector users are adequately trained to use the new technology. Inadequate infrastructure can also be a constraint, such as when customs officials are forced to stop working every time an unreliable electricity supply disrupts internet connections. Nevertheless, many economies continue to learn from Singapore's experience. Ghana, Madagascar, Mauritius, Panama and Saudi Arabia are all using adapted versions of TradeNet.

BEYOND ANECDOTES

The case for trade facilitation reforms goes beyond anecdotal evidence. It is well grounded in the economics literature. A study in Sub-Saharan Africa finds that a 10% reduction in exporting costs increases exports by 4.7%, a greater impact than would come from further reductions in tariffs by richer economies.[13] According to another study, African economies' limited participation in global supply chains for textiles and garments—both time-sensitive products—can be attributed to delays at customs.[14]

A study focusing on Asia-Pacific Economic Cooperation (APEC) economies shows that cutting the days to clear exports by half could enable a small to medium-size enterprise to increase its share of exports in total sales from 1.6% to 4.5%.[15] Another study on APEC economies finds that eliminating layers of trade regulation and improving institutions would cut information and compliance costs for businesses—and lead to an estimated 7.5% increase in intraregional trade and $406 billion in global welfare gains.[16] Transport constraints can play an important part in trade competitiveness, according to a recent study. In the Middle East and North Africa, reducing transport constraints to the world average could increase exports by about 10% and imports by more than 11%.[17]

But trade facilitation alone is not enough. Other factors in the business environment, some of which are considered elsewhere in this report, play a complementary part in boosting trade. Recent studies point to the importance of such factors as the depth of credit information, enforcement of contracts and flexibility of labor markets.[18]

1. Statement during the official launch of the Chirundu one-stop border post, December 5, 2009.

2. Bedi (2009).

3. WTO (2010).

4. Dennis (2010).

5. World Bank, Logistics Performance Index, 2007 and 2010 (http://www.worldbank.org/lpi).

6. The United States–Colombia Trade Promotion Agreement was signed on November 22, 2006, but is awaiting approval by the U.S. Congress before it can enter into force.

7. Sarmiento, Lucenti and Garcia (2010).

8. BIZCLIR (2007).

9. Beruashvili and McGill (2010).

10. Korea Customs Service (2010).

11. De Wulf and Sokol (2004).

12. Singapore Customs Service (2007).

13. Hoekman and Nicita (2009).

14. Yoshino (2008).

15. Li and Wilson (2009).

16. Helble, Shepherd and Wilson (2009).

17. Bhattacharya and Wolde (2010).

18. Cuñat and Melitz (2007), Depken and Sonora (2005), Levchenko (2007) and Ranjan and Lee (2007).

Enforcing contracts

FIGURE 10.1

Higher ceiling for claims made enforcing contracts faster and cheaper in Malawi

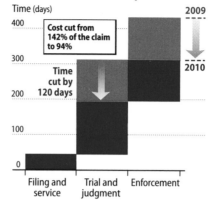

Source: Doing Business database.

Businesses worldwide continue to face challenges as a result of the global financial crisis—and are more concerned than ever about recovering losses fast. In the past 2 years more disputes involving property, supply contracts and banking transactions ended up in court, increasing caseloads and backlogs. Ireland's commercial court had a record number of cases listed in 2009.[1] In the first 6 months of the year it had 192 cases entered, compared with 76 in the same period of 2007.[2] In Denmark caseloads in enforcement courts increased by 38% in 2009 compared with 2007.[3] In the United States, New York State courts finished the year with the highest ever annual tally of cases. In the past 5 years foreclosure cases in the state doubled while contract disputes increased by 23%.[4]

In China in 2009 the number of contract disputes was up by 8.6% from the year before.[5] In Montenegro the commercial court of Podgorica had a nearly 300% jump in cases in 2009.[6] In Serbia the 17 commercial courts saw incoming cases grow from 135,497 in 2008 to 165,013 in 2009, an increase of 22%—more than 3 times the 7% increase in 2007 and 2008.[7] The Belgrade commercial court experienced an even larger increase: about 40% more cases were brought in 2009 than in the year before.

Reflecting the effects of the global crisis, most cases were filed by large creditors, such as utility companies and mobile phone providers trying to collect from defaulting debtors. Efficient processes for dispute resolution are needed now more than ever (table 10.1).

For some economies growing caseloads have offered an opportunity to come up with new solutions to improve the working of their courts. Dubai responded to pressures on its legal system by creating specialized courts. While the volume of cases has continued to grow, the courts in Dubai can now handle a greater number—resolving 58% more cases in 2009 than in the previous year.[8] Improving court functions remains essential to sustaining a healthy, stable economy, especially during a credit crunch. A recent study found that efficient contract enforcement is associated with greater access to credit for firms.[9]

Thirteen economies made it faster, cheaper or less cumbersome to enforce a contract through the courts in 2009/10 (table 10.2). Malawi improved the ease of enforcing contracts the most by raising the ceiling for commercial claims that small magistrates courts can hear (figure 10.1).

Doing Business measures the time, cost and procedural complexity of resolving a commercial lawsuit between 2 domestic businesses. The dispute involves the breach of a sales contract worth twice the income per capita of the economy. The case study assumes that the court hears an expert on the quality of the goods in dispute. This distinguishes the case from simple debt enforcement (figure 10.2).

TABLE 10.1

Where is enforcing contracts easy—and where not?

Easiest	RANK	Most difficult	RANK
Luxembourg	1	Central African Republic	174
Hong Kong SAR, China	2		
		Honduras	175
Iceland	3	Syrian Arab Republic	176
Norway	4		
Korea, Rep.	5	Benin	177
Germany	6	Suriname	178
France	7	Bangladesh	179
United States	8	São Tomé and Principe	180
Austria	9		
New Zealand	10	Angola	181
		India	182
		Timor-Leste	183

Note: Rankings are the average of the economy's rankings on the procedures, time and cost to resolve a commercial dispute through the courts. See Data notes for details.

Source: Doing Business database.

FIGURE 10.2

What are the time, cost and number of procedures to resolve a commercial dispute through the courts?

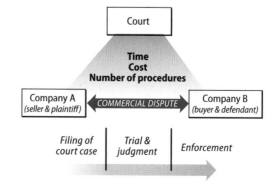

TABLE 10.2
Who made enforcing contracts easier in 2009/10—and what did they do?

Feature	Economies	Some highlights
Increased procedural efficiency at main trial court	Burkina Faso, Canada, Hong Kong SAR (China), Malawi, Mauritius, New Zealand, Timor-Leste, Uganda	In Hong Kong SAR (China) civil justice reforms improved case management, imposed limits on certain applications and appeals, limited the time for witness examination and oral submissions and extended discovery procedures.
Introduced or expanded computerized case management system	Canada, Hong Kong SAR (China), United Kingdom, Zambia	Zambia is moving to electronic forms, real-time court reporting, electronic storage and computer searches of registry files. Records of court proceedings are immediately available to litigants and court officials—as well as to the public, through computer terminals in the courts.
Introduced or expanded specialized commercial court	Burkina Faso, Guinea-Bissau	In Guinea-Bissau the new commercial court was set up, and judges as well as clerks and other support personnel received training.
Made enforcement of judgment more efficient	Georgia	In Georgia private enforcement officers were introduced alongside state enforcement agents, increasing enforcement capacity. And debtors can now pay creditors the outstanding debt before the closing of an auction to avoid the sale of their assets.
Reviewed rules on modes of service and notification	Islamic Republic of Iran	The Islamic Republic of Iran is introducing electronic filing, allowing parties to file petitions electronically with certain courts. Several courts have also implemented text message notification. An electronic case management system has been implemented in branches of Tehran's court of first instance.

Source: Doing Business database.

WHAT ARE THE TRENDS?

Economies in all regions have implemented reforms easing contract enforcement in the past 7 years (figure 10.3). A judiciary can be improved in different ways. Higher-income economies tend to look for ways to enhance efficiency by introducing new technology. Lower-income economies often work on reducing backlogs by introducing periodic reviews to clear inactive cases from the docket and by making procedures faster.

MORE AUTOMATION IN OECD HIGH-INCOME ECONOMIES

OECD high-income economies lead in the ease of enforcing contracts, with court processes that are the cheapest and among the fastest for commercial litigants. For a plaintiff to go from filing a claim to collecting the proceeds from the sale of movable assets costs 19% of the claim value and takes about 518 days on average.

What has driven the advances made? Investing in automation. Half of OECD high-income economies have set up electronic processes for filing claims in commercial disputes, far more than in any other region (table 10.3). Tech-

nological innovations include systems to electronically store court documents on microfilm (as in Germany) and the use of electronic communication through data mailboxes to serve process (as in the Czech Republic). In Norway a computer system that tracks deadlines and requires judges to justify postponements, together with new procedural rules since 2008, helped reduce the time for trial by a month. The United Kingdom recently introduced an electronic system in its commercial court that allows filings 24 hours a day, so litigants can now initiate lawsuits outside normal court hours.

MORE SPEED IN EASTERN EUROPE AND CENTRAL ASIA

Courts in Eastern Europe and Central Asia are the fastest globally, resolving commercial disputes in 402 days on average. Thanks to consistent efforts to streamline courts, they have also accelerated the process the most since 2003—by nearly 7 weeks on average. Many in the region focused on the enforcement of judgments after the trial, reducing the time it takes by an average of 15 days since 2003.

A trend that started in Estonia in 2001 and Latvia in 2002 is to move en-

forcement of judgments to the private sector. In 2003, inspired by the French model, Lithuania introduced private enforcement officers. In 2006 Bulgaria and FYR Macedonia followed suit, replacing state enforcement officers with self-employed private bailiffs.[10] Georgia combined the state and private models, introducing private bailiffs in 2008 alongside the state bailiffs to increase enforcement capacity. Since 2009 the Georgian Ministry of Justice has issued 38 licenses to private enforcement agents. Kazakhstan has a draft law aimed at introducing private enforcement agents by 2011. Armenia studied the introduction of private bailiffs but decided to focus for now on improving the performance of state enforcement agencies.

INCREASED EFFICIENCY IN SUB-SAHARAN AFRICA

Court reforms in Sub-Saharan Africa have had the second greatest impact in speeding up the enforcement of contracts. New case management systems, commercial courts and measures to reduce backlogs have cut the time it takes to resolve a commercial dispute by an average of nearly 4 weeks since 2005. But resolving a commercial dispute still costs businesses 50% of the claim value on average. The main reason: high lawyers' fees relative to the value of the claim.

One solution being explored by some African countries is to introduce small claims courts or small claims procedures. These offer simplified processes that take less time. Parties can often represent themselves, saving fees that they would normally spend on lawyers. In addition, filing fees are lower, and judges issue decisions more quickly.[11] Particularly for female entrepreneurs, who typically own small businesses, small claims courts can be a preferable forum for resolving simple disputes. In Zimbabwe the small claims court takes cases up to $250, and no lawyers are allowed. In neighboring Zambia a new small claims court for cases up to about $5,000 started operating in 2009. One limitation is that a company cannot file a claim in the court but can appear only to respond to a claim filed against it by an individual. Kampala, Uganda, is piloting a small claims procedure with magistrates dedicated to hearing simple cases.

LESS COMPLEXITY IN EAST ASIA AND THE PACIFIC

In East Asia and the Pacific changes to civil procedure laws have been aimed at reducing procedural complexity. In 2009/10 Hong Kong SAR (China) introduced wide-ranging civil justice reforms, including procedural deadlines, case management, limits on appeals, flexible settlement arrangements and an emphasis on alternative dispute resolution. The previous year Malaysia introduced stricter enforcement of procedural deadlines to process documents and created a separate "fast track" for disposing of interlocutory matters. Among the Pacific islands, Papua New Guinea introduced a specialized commercial division in its national court in 2007, now fully operational. Tonga set up court-referred mediation in 2008. The Solomon Islands is scheduled to launch it in 2010.

TABLE 10.3

Good practices around the world in making it easy to enforce contracts

Practice	Economies[a]	Examples
Using active case management	100[b]	Armenia, Ghana, Japan, Jordan, Malaysia, Puerto Rico, Sri Lanka
Maintaining specialized commercial court, division or judge	85	El Salvador, Germany, Malaysia, Maldives, Mauritius, Russian Federation, Tunisia
Allowing electronic filing of complaints	19	Australia, Czech Republic, Estonia, Singapore, Turkey, United Arab Emirates, United States

a. Among 183 economies surveyed, unless otherwise specified.
b. Among 164 economies surveyed.
Source: Doing Business database.

FEW COURT REFORMS IN SOUTH ASIA

In some parts of the world slow courts still risk delaying commercial justice. South Asia has the longest court delays. The process of deciding a standard commercial dispute and enforcing the judgment takes on average more than 1,000 days, or nearly 3 years—almost twice as much time as the average for other regions, 585 days (figure 10.4). Contributing to the delays are the inadequate number of judges; the lack of strict deadlines, which encourages constant adjournments; and the large caseloads and backlogs.

South Asian economies have been slow to make changes. Doing Business recorded no major court reforms in the region in the past 2 years. To avoid lengthy court trials, the private sector has introduced systems of alternative dispute resolution as a way to bypass the courts in such countries as Bangladesh, India and Pakistan.

BUT A PICKUP IN PACE IN 2 REGIONS

Efforts to reduce delays in the judicial system have also been slow to get off the ground in the Middle East and North Africa and in Latin America and the Caribbean. But the pace has recently picked up. Doing Business recorded 5 major reforms to improve court efficiency in the Middle East and North Africa in the

FIGURE 10.3

Pace of reform in enforcing contracts picks up in Sub-Saharan Africa

Number of Doing Business reforms making it easier to enforce contracts by Doing Business report year

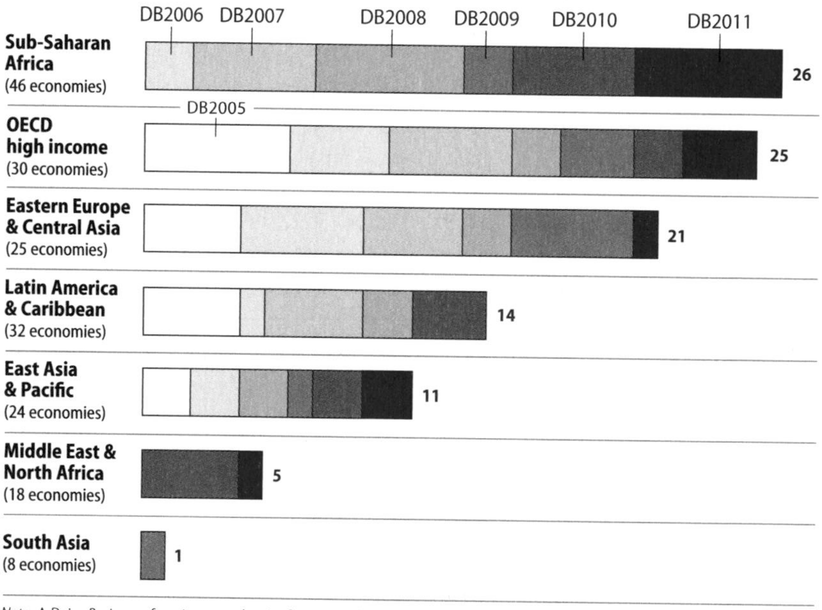

Note: A Doing Business reform is counted as 1 reform per reforming economy per year. The data sample for DB2005 (2004) includes 155 economies. Twenty-eight more were added in subsequent years.
Source: Doing Business database.

FIGURE 10 .4
Fastest courts in Eastern Europe and Central Asia

Regional averages in enforcing contracts

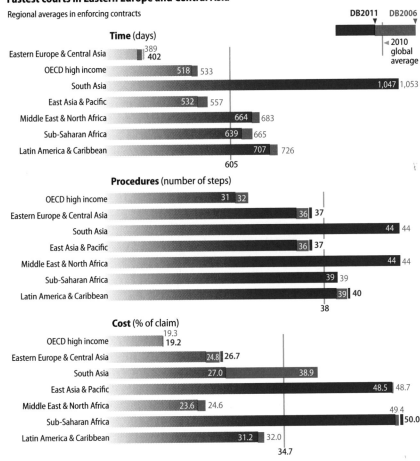

DB2011   DB2006

Time (days)

- Eastern Europe & Central Asia: 389 / 402
- OECD high income: 518 / 533
- South Asia: 1,047 / 1,053
- East Asia & Pacific: 532 / 557
- Middle East & North Africa: 664 / 683
- Sub-Saharan Africa: 639 / 665
- Latin America & Caribbean: 707 / 726

◄ 2010 global average

605

Procedures (number of steps)

- OECD high income: 31 / 32
- Eastern Europe & Central Asia: 36 / 37
- South Asia: 44 / 44
- East Asia & Pacific: 36 / 37
- Middle East & North Africa: 44 / 44
- Sub-Saharan Africa: 39 / 39
- Latin America & Caribbean: 39 / 40

38

Cost (% of claim)

- OECD high income: 19.3 / 19.2
- Eastern Europe & Central Asia: 24.8 / 26.7
- South Asia: 27.0 / 38.9
- East Asia & Pacific: 48.5 / 48.7
- Middle East & North Africa: 23.6 / 24.6
- Sub-Saharan Africa: 49 4 / 50.0
- Latin America & Caribbean: 31.2 / 32.0

34.7

Note: The data sample for DB2006 (2005) includes 174 economies. The sample for DB2011 (2010) also includes The Bahamas, Bahrain, Brunei Darussalam, Cyprus, Kosovo, Liberia, Luxembourg, Montenegro and Qatar, for a total of 183 economies.

Source: Doing Business database.

past 2 years. Some solutions involved introducing computer-aided case management systems. Jordan and West Bank and Gaza introduced software featuring online access to court records and automated notification and case tracking. Algeria and Saudi Arabia are also developing automated case management systems. Saudi Arabia's will allow electronic filing and automatic assignment of court dates as well as keep a log of all proceedings.

In Latin America and the Caribbean improvements have speeded up contract enforcement by an average of 3 weeks since 2004. In the past several years such economies as Brazil, Colombia and Peru have aimed to increase procedural efficiency and reduce backlogs. Brazil has been pioneering change at the federal level. Since 2006 it has limited recourse to interlocutory appeals, eliminated the need for a separate enforcement procedure and introduced electronic filing of certain documents in court. Brazil's superior court has scanned 231,000 paper proceedings since 2007, saving 108 million sheets of paper. This spares 1,836 hectares of forest—covering the equivalent of more than 300 soccer fields—annually.[12]

WHAT HAS WORKED?

In the past 7 years *Doing Business* recorded 103 reforms to improve court efficiency. Few have been successful, and many have been slow to show impact. Court reform takes time to show results. As the courts and users become accustomed to the new system, efficiency can continue to improve for years after the change. In the past year, thanks to previous years' reforms to improve efficiency, Botswana, Mali, Rwanda and West Bank and Gaza reduced the time to file and try a case by 40 days on average (table 10.4).

SPECIALIZING FOR SPEED

Introducing specialized courts has been a popular improvement. A specialized commercial procedure can be established by setting up a dedicated stand-alone court, a specialized commercial section within existing courts or specialized judges within a general civil court. Economies with stand-alone commercial courts include Sierra Leone, Sri Lanka and Tanzania. Those with commercial divisions within high courts include Ireland, Kenya, Nigeria, Uganda and the United Kingdom. In some economies the specialized commercial courts decide only cases relating to bankruptcy, securities, maritime transport or intellectual property while general commercial cases remain with the ordinary courts. This is the case in such economies as Algeria, Indonesia, the Slovak Republic, Thailand and Uruguay. Specialized courts, besides offering the benefits of specialization, also generally resolve commercial disputes faster.

Several economies have recently introduced reforms increasing court specialization. Jordan set up commercial divisions in its courts of first instance and its conciliation courts in 2008, assigning judges to hear solely commercial cases. In Mauritius a specialized commercial division in the supreme court began hearing cases in 2009. Burkina Faso and Guinea-Bissau established dedicated commercial courts the same year. Syria plans to follow suit. If creating specialized courts yields satisfied users, it can embolden governments to try broader judicial reforms.

INTRODUCING TECHNOLOGY

Using technology to track court processes can make managing cases easier while increasing transparency and limiting opportunities for corruption in the judiciary. Automated court processes

BOX 10.1
Civil conflict and the courts

War and civil strife in a country disrupt the judicial system by destroying court buildings and records and driving qualified professionals out of the country. Uncertainty about the legitimacy of the courts often discourages their use. Fragile states commonly face broad strikes in the judiciary. Chad and Zimbabwe have contended with judges' strikes for higher salaries in recent years. Burundi had to overcome a lawyers' strike in 2006. In West Bank and Gaza increased security threats against judges triggered a strike by all courts in 2005.

During a conflict, informal economic activity increases. Once the conflict ends, a key issue is how to efficiently resolve disputes over property.[1] Rebuilding the judiciary can take years, and legal professionals may be in short supply. Chad has only about 150 practicing lawyers, and in 2009 it had only 6 new law graduates. Liberia has only about 300 practicing lawyers for a population of 3.4 million, and some have little legal training. But judges are being trained, courts equipped with new resources and legal academies given the support they need.

Despite the challenges, postconflict economies are revitalizing their judiciaries. Burundi and Rwanda have enacted new civil procedure codes and reorganized their judiciaries since 2004. Before the new commercial courts were established in Kigali, Rwanda had to change its law to allow the hiring of non-Rwandese expatriate judges. In May 2008, 2 Mauritian judges were sworn in to help local judges run the new courts during the first 3 years of operation.[2] Sierra Leone is creating a new division of its high court for commercial cases, expected to start operating by the end of 2010, and is also working toward launching a fast-track commercial court. Liberia is creating a new commercial court. Timor-Leste is improving the internal organization of the district court of Dili, including by training and recruiting new judges.

1. Samuels (2006).
2. Hertveldt (2008).

can also prevent the loss, destruction or concealment of court records.[13] And allowing litigants to file complaints electronically in commercial cases, as the United Kingdom recently did, makes initiating a lawsuit faster. In Armenia the introduction of electronic case management has increased transparency. Public kiosks with touch screens located in court buildings make case information available to the public. But simply introducing information technology does not solve underlying procedural inefficiency. A thorough overhaul of court processes is also necessary.

Electronic systems also improve efficiency within the courts, making the work of judges and staff easier. In Egypt employees in the Alexandria and El Mansûra courts of first instance used to transcribe judges' handwritten decisions on typewriters. But thanks to court modernization efforts, now they can transcribe decisions directly into an electronic system, to be archived and promptly produced for docketing and

distribution.[14] In 2008 Moldova computerized its courts and introduced websites and audio recording equipment. Court administrators reported that the changes made the courts' work faster, easier and more efficient.[15] Bulgaria's supreme courts computerized their court records system in 2006, enabling litigants to access court documents and track a case to its completion.[16] All judgments of the supreme courts have been accessible online since October 2008.

MANAGING CASES

Judicial case management has proved to be effective in reducing procedural delays. It also helps in monitoring performance. Croatia is adopting an automated case management system that it expects will not only improve efficiency but also produce better statistical data for monitoring the performance of judges.[17]

Botswana introduced case management in its high court rules in 2008. The average duration of trials has since fallen from 912 days to 550. In 2006 Fiji ap-

pointed and trained a master to improve case management in the high court. In the country's magistrates' courts case management reportedly reduced the backlog of cases from 5 months to 2.5.[18]

Case management includes the possibility for a judge to conduct preparatory hearings to help the parties narrow the issues in dispute, to encourage them to settle and to fix procedural timelines and monitor compliance. In Norway preparatory meetings held in civil cases at the Midhordland district court led to settlement in more than 80% of cases.[19]

In the Slovak Republic the Bratislava district court keeps cases moving by allowing adjournments only when there is a compelling reason.[20] In Israel in 2009 the chief justice of the supreme court issued an official instruction requiring the courts to refuse adjournments and prevent delay tactics in all but the most serious situations. In Ireland the Dublin commercial court has the power to strike out cases or order fines for failure to follow the court's directions and timelines.[21]

MEASURING PERFORMANCE

Measuring the performance of courts and individual judges can increase efficiency. Assessments of a court's performance can help its personnel set concrete targets and aid in evaluating the court's progress toward its goals, in setting budgets and in motivating staff to improve performance.[22] What gets measured can range from user satisfaction to costs, timeliness and clearance rates.[23] Economies such as Australia, Singapore and the United States have been using tools to measure performance in the judicial sector since the late 1990s.[24] Others started more recently.

In 2005 the Netherlands introduced an innovative system that ties court performance to budget allocation. The new system measures the output of the courts—the number of cases resolved in each case category—and the Ministry of Justice then allocates a budget to each court on that basis. Any operating surplus can be added to a court's future budget, giving the court an incentive to

TABLE 10.4
Who makes enforcing contracts easy—and who does not?

Procedures (number of steps)			
Fewest		**Most**	
Ireland	20	Guinea	50
Singapore	21	Kuwait	50
Hong Kong SAR, China	24	Belize	51
Rwanda	24	Iraq	51
Austria	25	Oman	51
Belgium	26	Timor-Leste	51
Luxembourg	26	Kosovo	53
Netherlands	26	Sudan	53
Czech Republic	27	Syrian Arab Republic	55
Iceland	27	Brunei Darussalam	58

Time (days)			
Fastest		**Slowest**	
Singapore	150	Timor-Leste	1,285
Uzbekistan	195	Slovenia	1,290
New Zealand	216	Sri Lanka	1,318
Belarus	225	Trinidad and Tobago	1,340
Bhutan	225	Colombia	1,346
Korea, Rep.	230	India	1,420
Rwanda	230	Bangladesh	1,442
Azerbaijan	237	Guatemala	1,459
Kyrgyz Republic	260	Afghanistan	1,642
Namibia	270	Suriname	1,715

Cost (% of claim)			
Least		**Most**	
Bhutan	0.1	Comoros	89.4
Iceland	8.2	Malawi	94.1
Luxembourg	9.7	Cambodia	102.7
Norway	9.9	Papua New Guinea	110.3
Korea, Rep.	10.3	Zimbabwe	113.1
China	11.1	Indonesia	122.7
Poland	12.0	Mozambique	142.5
Thailand	12.3	Sierra Leone	149.5
Slovenia	12.7	Congo, Dem. Rep.	151.8
Portugal	13.0	Timor-Leste	163.2

Source: Doing Business database.

improve its efficiency. Besides output, the Dutch system also evaluates judicial quality, which includes the quality of judicial decisions, the timeliness of proceedings, the degree to which court officials treat the parties in a case with due respect and the expertise, independence and impartiality of judges.[25]

Finland introduced quality benchmarks in a number of courts in 2006. These are used to measure the operational performance of courts, the quality

of decisions, the treatment of the parties, the promptness of the proceedings, the competence of the judge and the organization and management of adjudication.[26] Malaysia introduced a performance index for judges in 2009. The index, fixed by the judges themselves, is aimed at allowing them to assess and monitor their performance. The result: case disposal rates in Malaysian courts are already improving.

WHAT ARE SOME RESULTS?

Well-functioning courts help businesses expand their networks and markets. Without effective contract enforcement, people might well do business only with family, friends and others with whom they have established relationships.

Successful court reforms increase efficiency and save time. That's the case in Rwanda. The commercial courts inaugurated in Kigali in May 2008 have completed more than 81.5% of the cases received. Because half the 6,806 cases that the Kigali commercial courts received and resolved in 2008–09 had been transferred from other courts, that means a big reduction in the case backlog.[27] The improved infrastructure of the new commercial courts also reduced delays in commercial dispute resolution. The registry, having mastered the new case registration system, now enters cases into the system swiftly. And time for service by bailiffs has decreased. Since 2008 the average time to resolve a commercial dispute has declined by nearly 3 months, from 310 days to 230.

In 2002 Pakistan implemented the Access to Justice Program to reduce delays in a number of pilot courts. The improvements cost $350 million and focused on providing more training, such as in case management techniques. Research analyzing court data for 2001–03 shows that after the court reform, 25% more cases were decided in the affected districts.[28] In 1993 India introduced debt recovery tribunals, an expedited enforcement mechanism that bypasses normal court procedures. Research drawing on data for 2000–03 finds that introducing the tribunals reduced nonpayment of debt by 3–11% and made loans 1.4–2 percentage points cheaper.[29]

Extending the use of information and communication technology can reduce costs. In Austria a "data highway" for the courts that allows documents to be sent electronically has produced huge savings. In 2009 there were about 3.4 million electronic exchanges of documents related to summary proceedings

FIGURE 10.5

Information technology in Austrian courts saved more than €11 million over 3 years

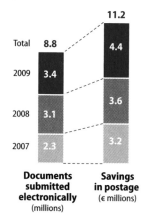

Source: Austrian Judicial System, http://www.justiz.gv.at.

(figure 10.5). The savings in postage alone amounted to €4.4 million. In Turkey the use of text messaging for legal notifications—such as to communicate the dates of court hearings—has allowed savings in postage of up to 7 million Turkish liras (about €3.3 million) a year. By early 2010 nearly 2,000 lawyers and 80,000 citizens in Turkey were using the system, and the numbers were growing by 500 a day.[30]

1. Dearbhail McDonald, "Disputes before the Commercial Court Soar to Record Level," *Irish Independent,* July 6, 2009, http://www.independent.ie/.

2. Dearbhail McDonald, "Business and Debt Lawsuits Double in Wake of Downturn," *Irish Independent,* July 24, 2009, http://www.independent.ie/.

3. Courts of Denmark, "Statistics," http://www.domstol.dk/.

4. Lippman (2010) and William Glaberson "The Recession Begins Flooding into the Courts," *New York Times,* December 28, 2009.

5. Zhu Zhe and Yang Wanli, "Court Cases Reach Record High in 2009," *China Daily,* March 12, 2010, http://www.chinadaily.com.cn.

6. Commercial Court of Podgorica (2009).

7. Commercial Courts of Serbia, http://www.portal.sud.rs.

8. Awad Mustafa, "Specialised Courts Tackle 51% Increase in Cases," *The National* (Dubai), April 18, 2010, http://www.thenational.ae/.

9. Bae and Goyal (2009, p. 823) show that "banks respond to poor enforceability of contracts by reducing loan amounts, shortening loan maturities, and increasing loan spreads."

10. See EBRD (2006).

11. World Bank (2010b, p. 34), citing Zucker and Herr (2003).

12. Electronic Proceedings Project (2010).

13. See Pepys (2003).

14. U.S. Agency for International Development, "Egypt—Before & After: Modernization Raises Court's Efficiency," http://www.usaid.gov/stories/.

15. Millennium Partners, "The Moldova Governance Threshold Country Program (MCC)/USAID," http://www.millenniumpartners.org. See also USAID (2010).

16. See Pepys (2003) and Supreme Administrative Court of the Republic of Bulgaria, http://www.sac.government.bg/.

17. Botero and others (2003).

18. AusAID (2005, p. 51).

19. CEPEJ (2006).

20. CEPEJ (2006).

21. CEPEJ (2006).

22. See National Center for State Courts (2005a).

23. National Center for State Courts (2005a, 2005b).

24. For the United States, see the official website of the National Center for State Courts (http://www.ncsconline.org/) and North Carolina Court System, "Court Performance Management System," http://www.nccourts.org/.

25. Albers (2009).

26. See Finland Judiciary (2006).

27. Interview by the *Business Times* (Kigali) with the vice president of the commercial high court, Benoit Gatete, January 12, 2010, http://allafrica.com/.

28. Chemin (2009).

29. Visaria (2009).

30. European Commission (2010).

Closing a business

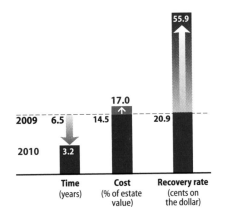

FIGURE 11.1

Insolvency act starts to pay off in the Czech Republic

Time (years): 2009 6.5 → 2010 3.2
Cost (% of estate value): 2009 14.5 ↑ 17.0 → 2010
Recovery rate (cents on the dollar): 2009 20.9 ↑ 55.9 → 2010

Who improved the most in closing a business?

1. *Czech Republic*
2. *Serbia*
3. *Latvia*
4. *United Kingdom*
5. *Belgium*
6. *Japan*
7. *Spain*
8. *Korea, Rep.*
9. *Lithuania*
10. *Hungary*

Source: Doing Business database.

When Jan checked into Starý zámek, a business hotel in downtown Prague, he found everything just as expected: a polite greeting from the reception staff, a comfortable room, neatly arranged towels. Imagine his surprise when a waiter serving him breakfast in the café the next morning mentioned that the hotel could close any day—because the company running it had been badly hit by the crisis. Jan, an attorney, checked the online insolvency register. He was relieved to find documents showing that the company was being reorganized. So the hotel was likely to continue operating well beyond his planned 3-week stay.

Saving viable businesses becomes especially important in times of recession.

Historically, crises have been used as an opportunity to improve insolvency laws. As anticipated in *Doing Business 2010*, several legislative changes in 2009/10 were inspired by the recent global financial and economic crisis. Germany extended until 2013 its suspension of the obligation to file for insolvency for overindebted companies whose business would be likely to continue. The suspension, made in 2008 and initially scheduled to run only until the end of 2010, is aimed at keeping courts from being overwhelmed by the many filings resulting from the crisis.

Other changes addressed increases in insolvency cases. Latvia introduced a new out-of-court procedure in 2009. Romania established special preinsolvency procedures in 2010 for distressed companies trying to avoid bankruptcy. In another response to the crisis, Spain passed a new law in 2009 introducing

out-of-court debt restructuring. In Hong Kong SAR (China), following an increase in bankruptcy petitions from 10,918 in 2007 to 15,784 in 2009,[1] a new "corporate rescue" reorganization procedure was under consideration in June 2010.

Keeping viable businesses operating is one of the important goals of bankruptcy systems.[2] A firm suffering from bad management choices or a temporary economic downturn may still be capable of being turned around. In most cases keeping the business alive is the most efficient outcome. Creditors get a chance to recover a larger part of their credit, more employees keep their jobs, and the network of suppliers and customers is preserved. But not all businesses that become insolvent are viable. A good bankruptcy system weeds out the bad from the good.

Many recent reforms of bankruptcy laws have been aimed at promoting reor-

TABLE 11.1

Where is closing a business easy— and where not?

Easiest	RECOVERY RATE	Most difficult	RECOVERY RATE
Japan	92.7	Liberia	8.4
Singapore	91.3	Sierra Leone	8.4
Canada	91.2	Ukraine	7.9
Norway	90.9	Haiti	6.7
Denmark	89.4	Venezuela, RB	5.9
Finland	89.4	Philippines	4.5
United Kingdom	88.6	Micronesia, Fed. Sts.	3.2
Belgium	87.6	Congo, Dem. Rep.	1.1
Ireland	87.4	Zimbabwe	0.2
Taiwan, China	82.2	Central African Republic	0.0

Note: Rankings are based on the recovery rate: how many cents on the dollar creditors recover from an insolvent firm. See Data notes for details.

Source: Doing Business database.

FIGURE 11.2

What are the time, cost and outcome of the insolvency proceedings against a local company?

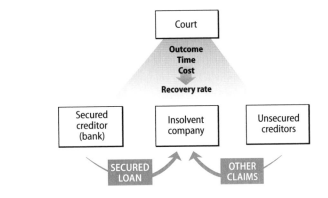

ganization as the most intuitively effective way for viable businesses to survive. The new bankruptcy law that went into effect in Brazil in 2005 is one example. Estonia passed a special reorganization act in 2008. In 2009 Japan made it easier to transfer necessary business permits to the new companies created as a result of reorganization. In June 2010 new legislation focusing on the reorganization of small and medium-size enterprises was being discussed in India.

The Czech Republic adopted a new insolvency act in 2006 to help more viable businesses survive. Under the previous law, adopted in 1991, insolvency always resulted in liquidation. Debt could be restructured, but only through informal means, outside the official bankruptcy procedures. By June 2010 more than 50 filings for reorganization had been recorded and 31 reorganizations approved under the new law.[3] The full benefits of the new law will take time to materialize. Insolvency proceedings in the Czech Republic can still take more than 3 years, and the number of approved reorganizations remains low, with 6 in 2008, 16 in 2009 and 9 in the first 6 months of 2010.[4]

Doing Business studies the time, cost and outcome of insolvency proceedings involving domestic entities (figure 11.2).[5] Speed, low costs and continuation of viable businesses characterize the top-performing economies. *Doing Business* does not measure insolvency proceedings of individuals and financial institutions.[6]

WHAT ARE THE TRENDS?

Bankruptcy regulation continues to vary across regions, and so does the pace of bankruptcy reform (figure 11.3). And while some economies have made continual efforts to improve their insolvency laws, implementing the new legal provisions and supporting them with adequate infrastructure remain crucial.

A declaration of bankruptcy originally carried great stigma. This is clear from the word's origins in the Italian

FIGURE 11.3

Rapid pace of bankruptcy reforms in OECD high-income economies and Eastern Europe and Central Asia

Number of *Doing Business* reforms making it easier to close a business by *Doing Business* report year

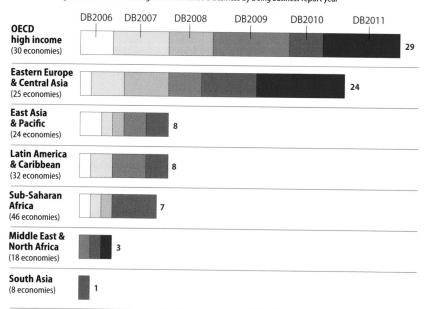

Note: A *Doing Business* reform is counted as 1 reform per reforming economy per year. The data sample for DB2006 (2005) includes 174 economies. The sample for DB2011 (2010) also includes The Bahamas, Bahrain, Brunei Darussalam, Cyprus, Kosovo, Liberia, Luxembourg, Montenegro and Qatar, for a total of 183 economies.
Source: Doing Business database.

banca rupta, referring to the practice of breaking a moneylender's bench, sometimes over his head. Today the stigma of bankruptcy continues to be among the reasons that debtors in many economies in the Caribbean, Central America, the Middle East and North Africa and Sub-Saharan Africa do not easily resort to insolvency procedures. Older laws take a much more punitive approach than newer ones. Modern bankruptcy laws focus on the survival of viable businesses and the creation of solid reorganization procedures.

EVER-GREATER EFFICIENCY IN OECD HIGH-INCOME ECONOMIES

Bankruptcy processes tend to be more efficient in OECD high-income economies (figure 11.4). This is reflected in their average recovery rate of 69.1 cents on the dollar, the highest rate globally. These economies also have the fastest proceedings, taking an average of 1.7 years (down from 2.0 in 2004). And they have the cheapest proceedings after South Asia's, costing an average of 9.1%

of the value of the estate.

In 22 of the 30 OECD high-income economies, businesses have a chance to survive as a going concern following insolvency proceedings. In the past 20 years many OECD high-income economies introduced or strengthened insolvency regimes along the principles of the U.S. chapter 11 process. Sweden reformed insolvency regulations in 1996, Belgium in 1997, Germany in 1999, France and Italy in 2006 and Finland in 2007, among others.[7] A parallel trend was to improve the infrastructure of bankruptcy systems. In 2006 the Czech Republic increased transparency by introducing an online register for documents produced in the course of proceedings. In 2009 the United Kingdom allowed court documents to be signed and filed electronically as part of the courts' greater use of information technology. In June 2010 Poland was in the early stages of implementing a comprehensive training program for insolvency judges. The country plans to position its training institutions as international leaders.

FIGURE 11.4
Big increase in recovery rate in Eastern Europe and Central Asia
Regional averages in closing a business

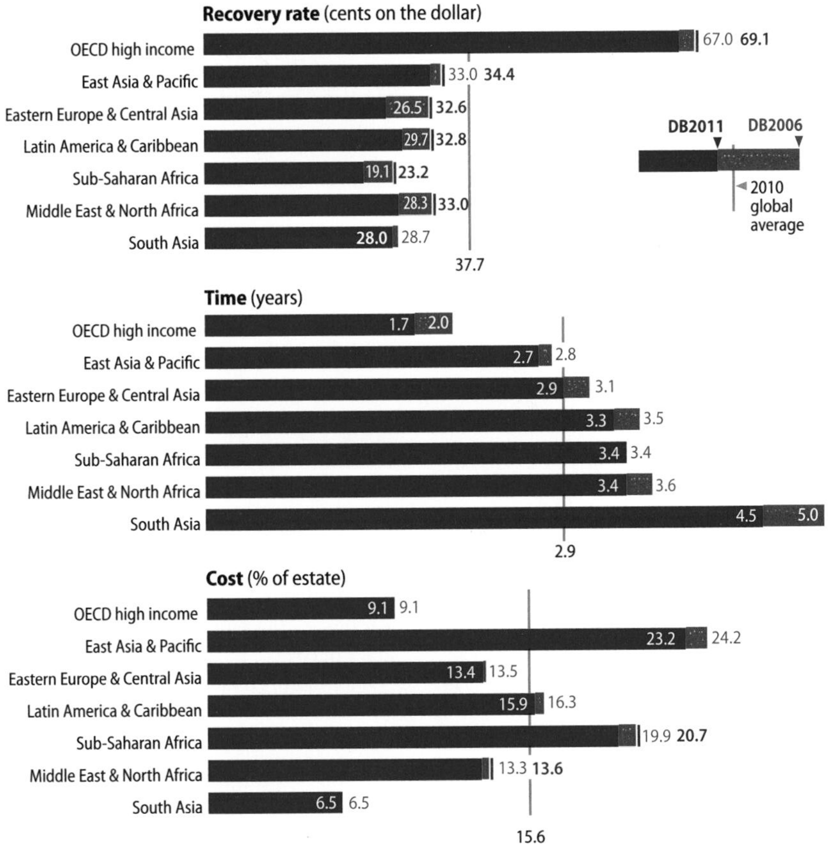

Recovery rate (cents on the dollar)

Region	DB2011	DB2006
OECD high income	67.0	**69.1**
East Asia & Pacific	33.0	**34.4**
Eastern Europe & Central Asia	26.5	**32.6**
Latin America & Caribbean	29.7	**32.8**
Sub-Saharan Africa	19.1	**23.2**
Middle East & North Africa	28.3	**33.0**
South Asia	28.0	28.7

◄ 2010 global average 37.7

Time (years)

Region	DB2011	DB2006
OECD high income	1.7	2.0
East Asia & Pacific	2.7	2.8
Eastern Europe & Central Asia	2.9	3.1
Latin America & Caribbean	3.3	3.5
Sub-Saharan Africa	3.4	3.4
Middle East & North Africa	3.4	3.6
South Asia	4.5	5.0

2.9

Cost (% of estate)

Region	DB2011	DB2006
OECD high income	9.1	9.1
East Asia & Pacific	23.2	24.2
Eastern Europe & Central Asia	13.4	13.5
Latin America & Caribbean	15.9	16.3
Sub-Saharan Africa	19.9	**20.7**
Middle East & North Africa	13.3	**13.6**
South Asia	6.5	6.5

15.6

Note: The data sample for DB2006 (2005) includes 174 economies. The sample for DB2011 (2010) also includes The Bahamas, Bahrain, Brunei Darussalam, Cyprus, Kosovo, Liberia, Luxembourg, Montenegro and Qatar, for a total of 183 economies.
Source: Doing Business database.

A MIXED STORY IN EAST ASIA AND THE PACIFIC

Bankruptcy systems in East Asia and the Pacific show a mixed story. The average recovery rate in Hong Kong SAR (China), Singapore and Taiwan (China) is 84.9 cents on the dollar, while the region-wide average is 34.4. The average cost of insolvency proceedings in the region is the highest in the world, at 23.2% of the value of the debtor's estate. On the other hand, proceedings take 2.7 years on average, making the region the second fastest after the OECD high-income economies.

Many of the region's economies are small island nations where bankruptcy proceedings are naturally rare because creditors and debtors tend to resolve insolvency situations through informal means. Among the formal mechanisms to address defaults, foreclosure is com-mon. Reorganization rarely happens. Recent changes include a new company law and a receivership law that went into effect in Samoa in 2008. In June 2010 new insolvency legislation, modeled on the New Zealand system, was pending in Tonga.

BANKRUPTCY REFORMS RARE IN THE MIDDLE EAST AND NORTH AFRICA

The average recovery rate in the Middle East and North Africa is low, at 33.0 cents on the dollar. And changes to improve in-solvency regulations are rare. In the past year Saudi Arabia established additional committees for amicable settlement of insolvencies. Egypt consulted interna-tional experts and insolvency judges on a new bill, to be aligned with its recently created commercial courts. Jordan is contemplating new regulations on insol-vency administrators. In May 2009, 10 economies signed a joint declaration on intended reforms of their insolvency re-gimes. The legislative changes in Egypt, Jordan and the other economies were still being discussed in June 2010.

Insolvency proceedings in the Mid-dle East and North Africa are the lon-gest after South Asia's. The number of cases that go through court remains low. Creditors and debtors rarely resort to collective procedures.

NEW LAWS AND INCENTIVES IN LATIN AMERICA

Several economies in Latin America and the Caribbean have recently introduced or are contemplating changes to the reg-ulation of insolvency administrators. In 2005 Chile linked the calculation of ad-ministrators' fees to the amounts realized from the sale of distressed companies' assets. This was done to encourage quick and efficient sales. Similarly, in 2009 Colombia introduced monetary incen-tives for speedy resolution of bankruptcy processes by insolvency representatives, along with additional rules on their qual-ifications and training. In June 2010 Peru was considering a reform of its regula-tion of insolvency administrators.

A regional trend in the past 3 years was to focus on improving reorganiza-tion procedures. Colombia and Mexico passed reorganization laws in 2007. Uru-guay did the same in 2008.

BROAD PROGRESS IN EASTERN EUROPE AND CENTRAL ASIA

In Eastern Europe and Central Asia most of the economies have postsocialist legal systems. Bankruptcy was virtually nonex-istent there 20 years ago. This is no longer the case regionwide, with Albania, Azer-baijan and Tajikistan among the few ex-ceptions. Improvements have been made in a range of areas, from regulation of in-solvency administrators (Belarus, Estonia, Lithuania and Russia) and out-of-court settlements (Latvia, Romania and Serbia) to the prevention of fraud and abuse in insolvency proceedings (Romania, Russia and Serbia; table 11.2).

TABLE 11.2
Who made closing a business easier in 2009/10—and what did they do?

Feature	Economies	Some highlights
Established or promoted reorganization procedures or prepackaged reorganizations	Belgium, Czech Republic, Hungary, Japan, Republic of Korea, Latvia, Romania, Russian Federation, Saudi Arabia, Serbia, Spain	Korea granted superpriority to postfiling financings in reorganizations.
Eliminated formalities or introduced or tightened time limits	Estonia, Georgia, Latvia, Saudi Arabia, Serbia, Spain, United Kingdom	Serbia passed a new bankruptcy law aimed at, among other aspects, reducing the length of insolvency procedures.
Regulated the profession of insolvency administrators	Belarus, Estonia, Lithuania, Russian Federation, United Kingdom	The United Kingdom improved the calculation of insolvency administrators' fees.
Took steps to prevent abuse	Romania, Russian Federation, Serbia	Russia enhanced the voidable transactions regime.
Modified obligation for management to file for insolvency	Czech Republic, Russian Federation	The Czech Republic suspended management's obligation to file for insolvency in certain circumstances.
Promoted specialized courts	Romania	Special insolvency departments were created within Romanian courts.

Source: Doing Business database.

Despite improvements, the average recovery rate in Eastern Europe and Central Asia remains low, at 32.6 cents on the dollar, mainly because of the weak institutional framework. The implementation of insolvency laws and professional standards for administrators is lagging behind the rapid pace of reform in bankruptcy regimes.

NEW INSOLVENCY REGULATIONS EXPECTED IN SOUTH ASIA

In South Asia outdated laws based on the British "winding-up" model are still binding in several economies. Insolvency proceedings in the region are the longest in the world, taking 4.5 years on average. But the cost of proceedings is the lowest globally, averaging 6.5% of the value of the debtor's estate.

In June 2010 bankruptcy reforms were being discussed in at least 3 economies. Afghanistan was working with international insolvency experts on ways to improve its insolvency framework. India and Pakistan were considering passing laws on restructuring.

LITTLE PRACTICE IN AFRICA

Sub-Saharan Africa has the largest share of economies with little or no insolvency practice. Twelve of the region's 46 economies—more than a quarter—have had fewer than 5 insolvency cases annually in recent years. In these economies the law still contemplates imprisonment (*contrainte par corps*) as a method of debt

enforcement, judges have little or no experience in handling bankruptcy cases, and costs are prohibitive. Indeed, only East Asia and the Pacific has more expensive insolvency proceedings on average, and only South Asia and the Middle East and North Africa have longer ones. To close a business in Sub-Saharan Africa costs 20.7% of the value of the debtor's estate and takes 3.4 years on average.

Only a small number of economies in the region have improved their insolvency systems in recent years. Mauritius and Rwanda implemented new insolvency acts in 2009. In June 2010 Malawi was working on a new insolvency act, and South Africa was contemplating a reform of its regulation of insolvency administrators. Meanwhile, the 16 member states of the Organization for the Harmonization of Business Law in Africa were discussing an amendment of the uniform act on insolvency.

WHAT HAS WORKED?

Many features can enhance a bankruptcy system. Key are the mechanisms for creditor coordination, qualified insolvency administrators and a framework that enables parties to negotiate out of court. An efficient judicial process is also critical.

EMPOWERING CREDITORS

Creditors' committees ensure control for the creditors over bankruptcy proceedings. They supervise the operation of a business by a debtor-in-possession and sometimes participate in the preparation of a reorganization plan. In Finland creditors' committees play a significant role in reorganization proceedings.

More than half the 183 economies covered by *Doing Business* recognize creditors' committees (table 11.3). Almost all insolvency laws in Eastern Europe and Central Asia, OECD high-income

TABLE 11.3
Good practices around the world in making it easy to close a business

Practice	Economies[a]	Examples
Allowing creditors' committees a say in relevant decisions	100	Colombia, Finland, Singapore
Requiring professional or academic qualifications for insolvency administrators by law	62[b]	Botswana, Hong Kong SAR (China), Mexico
Providing a legal framework for out-of-court workouts	45	Cyprus, Italy, Puerto Rico

a. Among 149 economies surveyed, unless otherwise specified.
b. Among 147 economies surveyed.
Source: Doing Business database.

economies and South Asia acknowledge a creditors' committee as a participant in bankruptcy proceedings. In the Middle East and North Africa, by contrast, creditors' committees are not popular. In Sub-Saharan Africa 69% of the surveyed economies allow creditors' committees a say in insolvency proceedings, while 65% do in East Asia and the Pacific.

INSISTING ON QUALIFICATIONS

Professional insolvency administrators assist and sometimes replace the management of an insolvent company. Their tasks normally include registering all the creditors' claims, assessing and administering the company's assets (on their own or with the debtor's management or creditors' committee), recovering assets disposed of shortly before the insolvency and liquidating a bankrupt estate. National laws vary in their approaches to determining whether insolvency administrators are qualified for these tasks.

Only 42% of the economies surveyed by *Doing Business* have established specific professional or academic requirements to ensure that the person replacing management has the knowledge and skills to do so. Most of the surveyed economies in Eastern Europe and Central Asia and the OECD high-income group have done so. But approaches differ. Germany's insolvency act only has a general requirement that an administrator be qualified for the case and experienced in business. By contrast, in Canada trustees in bankruptcy are licensed by the Office of the Superintendent of Bankruptcy. The Canadian Association of Insolvency and Restructuring Professionals administers the official qualification process for individuals seeking to become licensed trustees and establishes the rules of professional conduct and standards of professional practice for the members.

The insolvency laws of most of the surveyed economies in East Asia and the Pacific, Latin America and the Caribbean and Sub-Saharan Africa contain no requirements for insolvency administrators. In South Asia none of the economies surveyed by *Doing Business* legally requires professional qualifications for administrators. In the Middle East and North Africa only 3 economies do.

Mandatory qualification requirements are based on the notion that where qualified insolvency professionals are involved, viable businesses should have higher chances of survival and nonviable ones should generate higher proceeds in liquidation. Where the law has no requirements, the insolvency administrator is generally a trusted representative of the creditors or a person deemed by a court to be up to the job.

PROMOTING OUT-OF-COURT WORKOUTS

The global financial crisis caused a surge in insolvency filings, especially in Eastern Europe and Central Asia and OECD high-income economies. In Hungary the number of bankruptcy filings increased by 29% in 2009 compared with 2008.[8] In England and Wales the number of company liquidations rose by 22.8% in 2009 compared with the previous year.[9]

One way to ease the burden on courts is to limit their involvement to cases where parties cannot agree on their own. Yet only about 45 economies in a sample of 149 have a framework for out-of-court workouts that allows creditors and debtors to bring to a court a prenegotiated reorganization plan. The restructuring framework that the Bank of England began to develop after the recession of the mid-1970s in the United Kingdom, known as the "London approach," ensured the survival of many companies in later crises. And it inspired similar sets of rules in other economies, including Indonesia, Korea, Malaysia, Thailand and Turkey.[10]

Out-of-court workouts are most common in OECD high-income economies. In Sub-Saharan Africa only 22% of the surveyed economies have rules on out-of-court settlement for bankruptcy. Where there are no explicit rules, creditors and debtors can usually negotiate the restructuring of debt by using the generally applicable laws on contracts

TABLE 11.4
Who makes closing a business easy—and who does not?

Time *(years)*			
Fastest		**Slowest**	
Ireland	0.4	Ecuador	5.3
Japan	0.6	Micronesia, Fed. Sts.	5.3
Canada	0.8	Indonesia	5.5
Singapore	0.8	Haiti	5.7
Belgium	0.9	Philippines	5.7
Finland	0.9	Belarus	5.8
Norway	0.9	Angola	6.2
Australia	1.0	Maldives	6.7
Belize	1.0	India	7.0
Iceland	1.0	Mauritania	8.0
Cost *(% of estate)*			
Least		**Most**	
Colombia	1.0	Micronesia, Fed. Sts.	38.0
Kuwait	1.0	Philippines	38.0
Norway	1.0	Samoa	38.0
Singapore	1.0	Solomon Islands	38.0
Bahamas, The	3.5	Vanuatu	38.0
Belgium	3.5	Venezuela, RB	38.0
Brunei Darussalam	3.5	Sierra Leone	42.0
Canada	3.5	Ukraine	42.0
Finland	3.5	Liberia	42.5
Georgia	3.5	Central African Republic	76.0

Source: Doing Business database.

FIGURE 11.5
Big jump in reorganization filings after a new law in the Republic of Korea

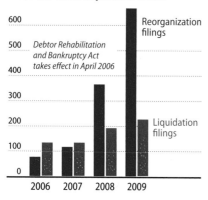

Source: Supreme Court of Korea.

and obligations. The disadvantage of such agreements is that they are not opposable to any of the creditors who did not participate in the settlement negotiations or become party to the ultimate agreement.

KEEPING ABUSE IN CHECK

Debtors filing for reorganization often do so because once a court accepts the case, it usually puts the enforcement of claims of individual creditors on hold. This allows management and shareholders to gain time, often for legitimate reasons but sometimes to tunnel valuable assets out of the company. Moreover, debtors may threaten to file for reorganization and use this threat as leverage in restructuring negotiations with creditors.

Creditors too can use the threat to file for bankruptcy, to force their terms on debtors. In many economies banks and companies prefer to avoid doing business with a bankrupt firm, so a debtor will go to great lengths to try to avoid bankruptcy. Where the law establishes criminal liability of managers and shareholders for the company's simple failure to repay regular commercial debt, this often leads to abuse by creditors. This happens in some Sub-Saharan African economies and in the Middle East and North Africa. A more reasonable option is for the law to establish managers' personal liability for failure to file for insolvency when mandated by law or criminal liability only for engaging in fraudulent transactions.

Thus to avoid abuse of well-intended provisions, the law should always include a system of checks and balances—such as liability for frivolous filings or robust practices for bringing assets tunneled out of a debtor's business back into the estate.

WHAT ARE SOME RESULTS?

A well-balanced bankruptcy system functions as a filter, separating companies that are financially distressed but economically viable from inefficient companies that should be liquidated.[11] By giving efficient companies a chance at a fresh start, bankruptcy law helps maintain a higher overall level of entrepreneurship in an economy.[12] And by letting inefficient companies go, it fosters an efficient reallocation of resources.

Well-functioning insolvency regimes can facilitate access to finance, especially for small and medium-size enterprises, and thereby improve growth in the economy overall.[13] A study of the 2005 bankruptcy reform in Brazil finds that it led to an average reduction of 22% in the cost of debt for Brazilian companies, a 39% increase in overall credit and a 79% increase in long-term credit in the economy.[14] Improvements in protection for creditors led them to expect that more assets would be available to them in insolvency. Since the risks for creditors were reduced, the costs for debtors were reduced as well.[15]

The efficiency of bankruptcy systems can be tested only if they are used. Cambodia passed an insolvency law in 2007, but by the end of 2009 not a single case had been filed under the new law. While Mexico introduced a framework for out-of-court workouts in 2007, this option has not been widely used. Korea had a different experience after it adopted the 2006 Debtor Rehabilitation and Bankruptcy Act introducing debtor-in-possession reorganization and allowing management to remain onboard to administer the company's turnaround. The number of reorganization filings jumped from 76 in 2006 to 670 in 2009 (figure 11.5).

A reform of bankruptcy laws can lead to important time and cost savings. In 1999 Colombia limited the duration of a reorganization procedure by setting a maximum of 8 months for negotiations. If no agreement is reached within 8 months, liquidation becomes mandatory. According to a study of Colombian firms that filed for insolvency between 1995/96 and 2003/04, the duration and cost of the reorganization process fell. Moreover, the selection of viable firms into reorganization improved.[16] In 2009 Spain raised the ceiling for its expedited bankruptcy procedure from a debt value of €1 million to €10 million. As a result, about 70% of bankruptcy proceedings in Spain are now eligible for the expedited procedure. This procedure is less costly than the regular one because it requires appointing only 1 insolvency administrator (rather than 3). The changes are expected to reduce the backlog in insolvency courts, which may also result in shorter proceedings.

A study of the 2000 bankruptcy reform in Mexico also shows clear gains. Looking at a sample of 78 bankruptcy cases in 1991–2005, the study finds that the average time to go through bankruptcy fell from 7.8 years to 2.3 years, thus increasing the amounts recovered by creditors.[17] In 2008 Lithuania eliminated a statutory prefiling waiting period of 3 months. Creditors could give debtors 1 month's notice of their intention to file for bankruptcy, and insolvency proceedings could commence 2 months earlier than before.

1. Official Receiver's Office of the government of Hong Kong SAR (China), http://www.oro.gov.hk.

2. See Djankov, Hart, McLiesh and Shleifer (2008).

3. Ministry of Justice of the Czech Republic, http://portal.justice.cz.

4. Ministry of Justice of the Czech Republic, http://portal.justice.cz.

5. *Outcome* refers to whether the hotel business in the *Doing Business* case study emerges from the proceedings as a going

concern or whether the company's assets are sold piecemeal (see Data notes).

6. See Djankov (2009a).

7. See Dewaelheyns and Van Hulle (2009a).

8. Hungarian Association of Insolvency Practitioners, http://www.foe.hu.

9. Insolvency Service of the United Kingdom, http://www.insolvency.gov.uk.

10. See Lieberman and others (2005) and Mako (2005).

11. See Dewaelheyns and Van Hulle (2009b).

12. See Armour and Cumming (2008).

13. See Uttamchandani and Menezes (2010).

14. See Funchal (2008).

15. See Funchal (2008).

16. See Giné and Love (2006).

17. See Gamboa-Cavazos and Schneider (2007).

Annex: pilot indicators on getting electricity

FIGURE 12.1

Getting Electricity **measures the connection process at the level of distribution utilities**

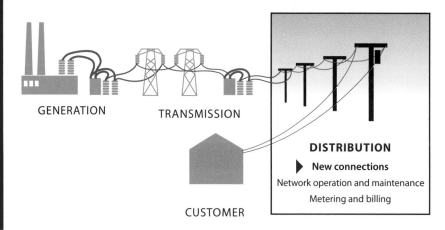

A young entrepreneur who manufactures home furnishings in Moscow is working hard to expand her business by setting up a new warehouse. She negotiated financing with the bank, spent weeks getting building and operating permits and invested in new machinery as well as a new building. She has employees lined up and is ready to get started. But the young entrepreneur will have to wait. She needs to obtain a new electricity connection for the warehouse, and in Moscow that requires many interactions with the utility, takes more than 10 months on average and costs more than 40 times the income per capita.[1]

Compare the experience of a similar entrepreneur in Germany, constructing a warehouse in Berlin-Westhafen. His warehouse is hooked up to electricity in less than 3 weeks. The process involves just 3 interactions with the utility and costs only half the country's income per capita.

World Bank Enterprise Surveys in 108 economies show that firms consider electricity to be among the biggest constraints to their business.[2] Poor electricity supply has adverse effects on firms' productivity and the investments they make in their productive capacity.[3] To counter weak electricity supply, many firms in developing economies have to rely on self-supply through a generator.[4] The cost of self-supply is often prohibitively high, especially for small firms,[5] underlining the importance of utilities'

providing reliable and affordable electricity to businesses.

Whether electricity is reliably available or not, the first step for a customer is always to gain access by obtaining a connection. It is this first and key step that *Doing Business* aims to measure through a new set of indicators. Introduced in *Doing Business 2010* with data for an initial 140 economies, these indicators measure the procedures, time and cost for obtaining a new electricity connection. The *Getting Electricity* data set covers only a small part of electricity service (figure 12.1). Yet it provides information on a number of issues for which data previously did not exist for such a large number of economies.

FIGURE 12.2

Procedures to obtain an electricity connection in Azerbaijan add up to an 8-month process

1. Application and technical conditions
2. External inspection by utility
3. Technical design
4. Design approval from utility
5. Excavation permit
6. External connection works
7. External inspection by Ministry of Emergency Situations
8. External and internal inspection by Energy Inspectorate
9. Supply contract

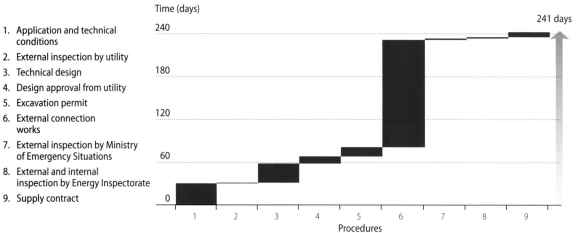

Source: Getting Electricity database.

In 2009/10 *Doing Business* disseminated a report with more detailed findings among regulators and academics to solicit feedback on the *Getting Electricity* methodology and increased the sample of economies surveyed to 176.[6] As a result of the additional research and feedback, minor changes were made to the methodology to clarify the underlying case study (for details on the methodology, see Data notes).

WHERE ARE CONNECTION PROCESSES LONG AND CUMBERSOME—AND WHY?

In Baku, Azerbaijan, to get connected to electricity by the local distribution utility requires 9 procedures, including undergoing multiple inspections by the utility and 2 outside agencies and getting a permit from the Ministry of Transport (figure 12.2). The cumbersome process takes 241 days and costs $31,848, or 658% of income per capita.

Among the 176 economies surveyed, Azerbaijan ranks among the 10 with the most procedures. Economies such as Germany, Japan, Mauritius and the Federated States of Micronesia make it much easier for businesses to connect to electricity (table 12.1).

The economies where the connection process involves relatively few procedures are also those where customers get connected faster. Where businesses have to go through 3–5 procedures to get connected, the process takes 99 days on average. But in economies with 6–11 procedures, it takes 138 days on average. And in the 10 economies with the most, it takes 233.

Why are particular procedures needed, and how can utilities minimize their effect in delaying connections?

MISSED OPPORTUNITIES FOR STREAMLINING

Connection delays increase significantly where utilities and other public agencies miss opportunities to streamline approvals. Take Cyprus. Before the utility can issue an estimate to a new customer, it must contact several government au-

thorities, including the telecommunications authority, sewerage authority, public works department, municipality, archaeological department and fire brigade. This clearance process alone takes 3–6 months. Meanwhile, the work to install the connection must wait.

Where delays occur because other public agencies are excessively slow and bureaucratic, utilities may be tempted to shift the administrative hassle to their customers.[7] Among the procedures most commonly transferred to customers is applying to the municipality or the department of roads or transport for an excavation permit or right of way so that the utility can lay the cables or extend wires for the connection. Customers seeking a connection undertake such procedures in 39 economies. Wait times range from 1 day in Algeria to 60 in Madagascar, Mongolia and República Bolivariana de Venezuela. In Egypt customers have to contact 2 agencies to obtain an excavation permit: the district office and the Greater Cairo Utility Data Center.

But relegating the administrative

burden to customers is not the only option. Successful utilities engage actively with other service providers to ensure that working relationships are clear and function smoothly. Take recent efforts in Hong Kong SAR (China). In March 2010 the utility established a working group with the police force and highway and transport departments to work out performance pledges that would allow quicker turnaround of approvals for excavation permits.

DIFFERENT WAYS TO DEAL WITH SAFETY CONCERNS

According to a survey by the Vietnam Standards and Consumer Protection Association, 83% of electrical wiring in Ho Chi Minh City fails to meet quality standards.[8] In the United States during a typical year, home electrical problems account for 67,800 fires, 485 deaths and $868 million in property losses. In urban areas faulty wiring accounts for 33% of residential electrical fires.[9]

The safety of internal wiring installations is a concern not only for those

TABLE 12.1

Who makes getting electricity easy—and who does not?

Procedures (number)			
Fewest		**Most**	
Germany	3	Armenia	8
Japan	3	Kyrgyz Republic	8
Mauritius	3	Mongolia	8
Micronesia, Fed. Sts.	3	Nigeria	8
Qatar	3	Sierra Leone	8
St. Vincent and the Grenadines	3	Azerbaijan	9
Sweden	3	Russian Federation	9
Switzerland	3	Tajikistan	9
Timor-Leste	3	Uzbekistan	9
Iceland	4	Ukraine	11

Time (days)			
Fastest		**Slowest**	
Germany	17	Vanuatu	257
St. Kitts and Nevis	18	Nigeria	260
Iceland	22	Pakistan	266
Austria	23	Czech Republic	279
Samoa	23	Russian Federation	302
Taiwan, China	23	Ukraine	309
St. Lucia	25	Kyrgyz Republic	337
Rwanda	30	Madagascar	419
Chile	31	Guinea-Bissau	455
Puerto Rico	32	Liberia	586

Source: Getting Electricity database.

FIGURE 12.3
Who is responsible for enforcing safety standards?
Economies by type of safety certification for internal wiring (%)

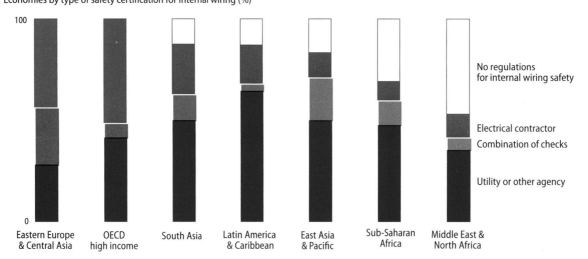

Source: Getting Electricity database.

using a building but also for utilities. One customer's faulty internal wiring can lead to power outages affecting other customers connected to the same distribution line. Because the quality of the internal installation matters to utilities and the public alike, in most economies customers seeking a connection for their business need to go through some procedure to ensure that quality.

The approach taken to address safety issues varies. Some economies regulate the electrical profession by establishing clear liability arrangements for electrical contractors. Others regulate the connection process by requiring customers to obtain additional inspections and certifications from the utility or outside agencies before a new connection is granted (figure 12.3).

Getting Electricity data suggest that economies that regulate the electrical profession rather than the connection process itself not only lessen the burden on customers but also have shorter average connection delays. In economies such as Denmark, Germany and Japan the quality of the internal wiring is the responsibility of the electrical contractor who did the installation. The utility simply requests certification by the electrical contractor that the internal wiring was done in accordance with the prevailing standards, usually established by the rel-

evant professional bodies. The customer is not involved.

But where professional standards are poorly established or qualified electrical professionals are in short supply, utilities or designated agencies may be better placed to carry out inspections that ensure the safety of customers, even if this leads to connection delays. In 15 of the 31 economies surveyed in Latin America and the Caribbean, customers are required to contact an outside agency—often a regulatory agency, municipality or fire department—to inspect the internal wiring.

Economies seeking to shift from regulating the connection process to regulating the electrical profession have to be careful not to transfer responsibility to private professionals too early. Take the experience in South Africa.[10] In 1992, in an attempt to free utilities from the burden of inspecting internal wiring, the government made private electricians liable for the quality of their wiring installations. But the shortage of qualified electrical professionals, and the ambiguity of the regulations in assigning responsibilities, led to an increase in customer complaints about substandard wiring. After 8 years of heated debate the government introduced new internal wiring regulations in May 2009, clarifying standards for electrical installations and the is-

suance of compliance certificates and introducing nonmandatory inspections by a new independent authority. The government is also working to reduce the shortage of skilled electricians in the country.

While different approaches to dealing with the safety of internal wiring installations can make sense in different environments, some cases emerging from the *Getting Electricity* data clearly suggest room for immediate improvement. Because electrical safety is a public concern, governments that require no checks of electrical installations may fail to provide an important public good. Twenty-nine economies, many of them in the Middle East and North Africa and Sub-Saharan Africa, fall into this category. At the other extreme are governments that require multiple checks, imposing an excessive burden on customers seeking to get connected. Twenty-two economies, many of them in Eastern Europe and Central Asia, are in this category.

MATERIAL SHORTAGES

Connecting a new customer to an electricity network requires materials and equipment. If the new connection is through an overhead line, wires must be extended; if it is through an underground connection, cables must be laid. Often the utility will also have to install

FIGURE 12.4
Lack of materials causes delays for utilities in 56% of low-income economies

Share of economies where lack of materials delays new electricity connections (%)

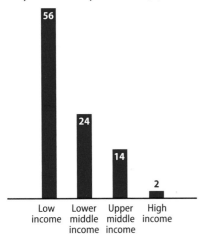

Source: Getting Electricity database.

meters, new electricity poles and heavy equipment such as distribution transformers. Requirements for materials not only translate into costs; they also can lead to longer wait times.

Utilities, especially those in low- and lower-middle-income economies, often have to delay new connections because they lack the materials needed (figure 12.4). In 39 economies survey respondents reported additional wait times—up to 180 days in Vanuatu—because in more than 50% of cases where new connections were requested, the utility did not have such critical materials as meters or distribution transformers in stock and had to order them specially. This suggests that the utility faces either financial or inventory and procurement management constraints.

In 16 economies the utility completing the external connection works asked customers to provide such materials as poles, meter boxes or transformers because it did not have them in stock. Requiring individual customers to purchase materials is not a cost-effective way to maintain a distribution network. But customers are often happy to comply. In Malawi customers purchasing the materials themselves reduced the time required for obtaining a connection from 2–3 years to 8 months on average.

Just buying the materials sometimes is not enough. Where utilities shift this responsibility to customers, they have to ensure that the customers buy the right materials. This can mean additional procedures. Customers in such economies as Côte d'Ivoire, Guyana, Kosovo, Madagascar, Nepal and Sierra Leone have to prove to the utility that the materials they purchased comply with the standards. Sometimes they must even present the materials for testing at the utility.

WHAT DOES IT COST TO GET CONNECTED?

The same electricity need can require different connection works, depending on how constrained installed capacity is. In some economies the *Getting Electricity* customer requesting a not trivial but still relatively modest 140-kilovolt-ampere (kVA) connection would simply receive an overhead line or underground cable connection.[11] But in many others the capacity of the existing network is constrained, and 140-kVA electricity therefore requires a more complicated connection effectively leading to an expansion of the distribution network. Such connections require significant capital investments (such as the installation of distribution transformers), often covered by the new customer.

Accommodating the demand of the *Getting Electricity* customer is naturally more likely to require additional capital investment in low-income economies,

where the installed electrical capacity tends to be more constrained—driving up absolute connection costs for new customers. The 10 economies with the lowest costs are all high income except the Marshall Islands and Panama. The 10 with the highest costs are all low income except Djibouti (table 12.2). Yet connection costs are not just a function of the general infrastructure in an economy. They vary significantly among economies within income groups, suggesting room to reduce the cost regardless of existing infrastructure (figure 12.5).

TRANSPARENCY AND ACCOUNTABILITY MATTER

As utilities allocate the costs for new connections between existing and prospective customers, they have to balance considerations of economic efficiency and fairness. In practice, it is often difficult to distinguish between capital works needed to connect specific customers and those needed to accommodate projected growth or to improve the safety or reliability of the distribution network. This leaves room to make new customers pay for investments in the network that will benefit other customers as well. Connection costs should therefore be as transparent as possible, to allow customers to contest them when they feel they are paying more than they should.

But connection costs in many of the economies surveyed are not fully transparent. Utilities far too often present customers with individual budgets rather

TABLE 12.2
Who makes getting electricity least costly—and who most costly?

Cost (% of income per capita)			
Least		**Most**	
Japan	0.0	Madagascar	8,268.0
Hong Kong SAR, China	1.9	Djibouti	10,008.1
Trinidad and Tobago	2.5	Malawi	11,703.7
Qatar	5.1	Guinea	13,275.4
Marshall Islands	6.5	Central African Republic	13,298.3
Iceland	6.6	Chad	14,719.8
Norway	7.3	Burkina Faso	14,901.3
Australia	9.5	Benin	15,452.0
Panama	9.9	Congo, Dem. Rep.	27,089.4
Israel	12.6	Burundi	36,696.7

Source: Getting Electricity database.

FIGURE 12.5

Connection costs vary by type of connection and among economies within income groups

US$ thousands

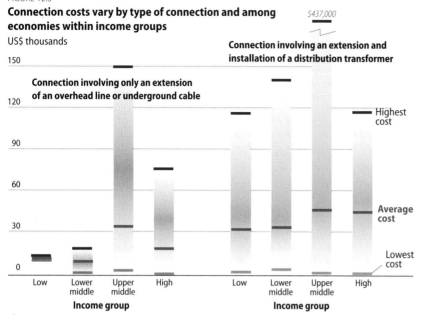

Source: Getting Electricity database.

than follow clearly regulated capital contribution policies aimed at spreading the fixed costs of expanding the network over several customers. To illustrate, *Getting Electricity* divides costs into 2 main categories: a fixed connection fee based on a clear formula (often linked to the peak electricity demand of the customer to be connected), which is usually publicly available; and the variable costs for the connection, accounting for the labor,

material and inspections required.[12]

The fixed connection fee represents a far bigger share of the total cost in high-income economies than in low- and middle-income economies (figure 12.6). And where the share of those fixed costs is higher, connection costs also tend to be lower. This suggests a potential for lowering connection costs by improving the transparency of the costs and strengthening the accountability of utilities.

BURDENSOME SECURITY DEPOSITS

Security deposits are one cost item worth highlighting. Utilities in 82 of the 176 economies surveyed charge customers security deposits as a guarantee against nonpayment of future electricity bills.[13] Security deposits are particularly common in Latin America and the Caribbean and in Sub-Saharan Africa. While they average $9,988, they can run as high as $55,609, as in Dominica.[14]

Because most utilities hold the deposit until the end of the contract and repay it without interest, this requirement can impose a substantial financial burden on small and medium-size businesses, especially those facing credit constraints. In Ethiopia a medium-size company is effectively granting the utility an interest-free credit equivalent to

121% of income per capita—and being prevented from putting the money to a more productive use.

Not surprisingly, where court systems are inefficient and contracts can be enforced only with significant delays, utilities are more likely to request a security deposit (figure 12.7).

Where utilities feel that they have to rely on security deposits, they should at least consider lessening the financial burden for customers. In 20 economies utilities do so by allowing customers to settle the security deposit with a bank guarantee or bond rather than deposit the entire amount with the utility. The service cost for such bank guarantees usually amounts to less than the interest that customers lose on the deposit. More important, bank guarantees both allow customers to keep control of their financial assets and improve their cash flow.

Where credit reports are widely available, utilities can be more selective, asking only customers with a weak credit history to put up a security deposit. This is done in Australia and Austria. Where credit reports are hard to come by, ownership can also be used as a screening device. In Argentina and El Salvador only customers that do not own the property being connected must put up a deposit.

FIGURE 12.6

Variable fees a big share of the cost in low- and middle-income economies

Share of total connection cost (%)

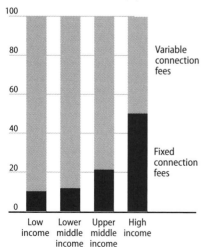

Source: Getting Electricity database.

FIGURE 12.7

Utilities more likely to require security deposits where courts are inefficient

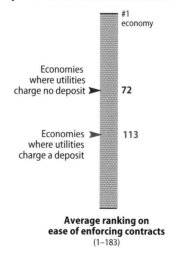

Average ranking on ease of enforcing contracts
(1–183)

Note: Relationships are significant at the 1% level and remain significant when controlling for income per capita.

Source: Getting Electricity database; Doing Business database.

WHO MADE GETTING ELECTRICITY EASIER IN 2009/10?

Reforms making it easier to get an electricity connection are complex—often involving such stakeholders as regulatory agencies and other public service providers—and take time to implement. Connection processes were reformed in 8 economies in 2009/10.

Mexico had the most radical reform in getting electricity. The government liquidated the state-owned electrical utility company that served Mexico City because severe structural problems had made the company financially nonviable. The distribution concession for the city was transferred to Mexico's largest state power company. In less than a year the new concessionaire was able to substantially shorten connection delays. Before, customers in Mexico City had to be prepared to wait 10 months to get a new electricity connection, the longest wait in Latin America and the Caribbean. Now the average wait is 4 months.

Several other utilities also cut connection times by streamlining internal procedures. Changing procurement practices for materials and making application procedures faster cut wait times at the utility in Tanzania by 9 months. In Suriname the utility introduced an improved customer service policy in the second quarter of 2009 that reduced the wait for inspections and external connection works. Other efforts under way are expected to further streamline internal procedures. In Bosnia and Herzegovina a new law shifted responsibility for external connection works from the client to the utility. This cut 2 procedures for the customer. In Uganda the utility began outsourcing external connection works to registered construction firms, cutting connection times by 60 days.

Serving customers faster by improving working relationships with other public agencies was the aim of the initiative by the utility in Hong Kong SAR (China).[15] The performance pledges developed by the working group it formed are expected to reduce the time for the utility to obtain an excavation permit from 2 months to 23 days.

Changes to the system for checking internal wiring can also cut connection delays. Moldova eliminated duplication in inspections. Before, both the utility and the State Energy Inspectorate inspected internal wiring installations, effectively doing the same job twice. Now only the State Energy Inspectorate inspects the installations.

Trinidad and Tobago clarified connection costs through a new capital contribution policy that took effect in August 2009. Before, connection costs were calculated case by case, making it difficult for customers to assess whether they were charged too much or not. Now the utility bears the connection costs, then distributes them across all customers through clearly regulated consumption tariffs. This reduced the connection cost for the *Getting Electricity* customer in Port of Spain by 52% of income per capita. More important, the new policy increased the transparency of connection costs for customers.

Important improvements substantially increased the electricity supply in 2 postconflict economies, Afghanistan and Sierra Leone. Customers that would have had no choice before but to buy their own generator can now obtain a connection to the local electricity network. In Afghanistan a new transmission line is bringing electricity from neighboring Uzbekistan to Kabul. In Sierra Leone a long-awaited hydroelectric power project started generating electricity, bringing more power to Freetown. An entrepreneur running an internet café in western Freetown reports that 1 month's electricity supply now costs him what he used to spend for 4 days of power from a generator. But, he says, there is room for improvement.[16] Connection costs went up, and wait times remain long as utilities in both countries work through a backlog of connection applications.

WHAT'S NEXT?

This annex presents findings on the kinds of constraints entrepreneurs in 176 economies face in getting access to electricity and illustrates patterns in connection processes. By measuring the procedures, time and cost for obtaining a new electricity connection, *Getting Electricity* allows an objective comparison from the perspective of businesses (table 12.3). And it provides insights into the efficiency of distribution utilities and the environment in which they operate. Feedback from governments and utilities on the *Getting Electricity* indicators and the findings presented in this report is welcome and will be used to further refine the methodology.

Electricity connections are provided by distribution utilities that retain monopolistic positions even in otherwise liberalized electricity markets. Businesses and other customers are therefore captive to the utility. By providing data for benchmarking, *Getting Electricity* can benefit these distribution utilities and their customers. With more economies included next year and more years of data, *Getting Electricity* can help identify good practices that can inform future efforts to improve interactions between utility service providers and businesses.

TABLE 12.3
Getting electricity data

Economy	Procedures (number)	Time (days)	Cost (% of income per capita)	Economy	Procedures (number)	Time (days)	Cost (% of income per capita)
Afghanistan	4	191	5,768.2	France	5	123	39.6
Albania	5	162	614.9	Gabon	6	160	316.8
Algeria	6	119	1,430.4	Gambia, The	4	178	6,526.3
Angola	8	48	1,278.5	Georgia	5	97	759.4
Antigua and Barbuda	4	42	132.2	Germany	3	17	51.9
Argentina	6	74	25.2	Ghana	4	78	2,423.5
Armenia	8	242	787.0	Greece	6	77	57.5
Australia	5	81	9.5	Grenada	5	49	370.2
Austria	5	23	113.0	Guatemala	4	39	655.5
Azerbaijan	9	241	658.0	Guinea	5	69	13,275.4
Bahamas, The	7	101	101.5	Guinea-Bissau	7	455	2,133.5
Bahrain	5	90	67.0	Guyana	7	109	568.5
Bangladesh	7	109	2,762.0	Haiti	4	66	3,345.3
Belarus	7	254	1,383.0	Honduras	8	33	1,109.9
Belgium	6	88	96.7	Hong Kong SAR, China	4	93	1.9
Belize	5	66	369.4	Hungary	5	252	126.5
Benin	4	172	15,452.0	Iceland	4	22	6.6
Bhutan	5	225	1,493.9	India	7	67	400.6
Bolivia	8	42	1,297.3	Indonesia	7	108	1,350.0
Bosnia and Herzegovina	8	125	535.6	Iran, Islamic Rep.	7	140	1,108.4
Botswana	5	121	495.3	Ireland	5	205	86.6
Brazil	6	59	150.5	Israel	6	132	12.6
Brunei Darussalam	5	86	46.7	Italy	5	192	332.9
Bulgaria	6	137	381.5	Jamaica	6	86	222.5
Burkina Faso	4	158	14,901.3	Japan	3	105	0.0
Burundi	4	188	36,696.7	Jordan	5	43	323.8
Cambodia	4	183	3,581.5	Kazakhstan	6	88	111.3
Cameroon	4	67	1,846.0	Kenya	4	163	1,449.6
Canada	8	168	152.3	Kiribati	6	142	4,297.0
Cape Verde	5	58	1,217.5	Kosovo	7	60	910.1
Central African Republic	6	210	13,298.3	Kuwait	7	36	63.4
Chad	5	66.5	14,719.8	Kyrgyz Republic	8	337	2,111.1
Chile	6	31	82.8	Lao PDR	5	134	2,734.3
China	5	132	755.2	Latvia	6	198	405.2
Colombia	5	165	1,182.7	Lebanon	5	75	23.9
Congo, Dem. Rep.	6	58	27,089.4	Lesotho	5	140	2,664.0
Congo, Rep.	5	55	7,647.2	Liberia	4	586	5,294.1
Costa Rica	5	62	316.7	Lithuania	4	98	46.0
Côte d'Ivoire	5	44	4,137.0	Luxembourg	5	120	66.1
Croatia	5	70	327.5	Macedonia, FYR	5	151	34.5
Cyprus	5	247	88.9	Madagascar	6	419	8,268.0
Czech Republic	6	279	187.2	Malawi	5	244	11,703.7
Denmark	4	38	128.2	Malaysia	6	51	55.8
Djibouti	4	180	10,008.1	Maldives	6	101	761.6
Dominica	5	73	1,187.7	Mali	4	120	3,877.9
Dominican Republic	7	87	405.3	Marshall Islands	5	172	6.5
Ecuador	6	89	899.4	Mauritania	5	80	7,591.9
Egypt, Arab Rep.	7	54	499.9	Mauritius	3	59	212.7
El Salvador	7	78	522.2	Mexico	7	114	436.0
Eritrea	5	59	4,156.7	Micronesia, Fed. Sts.	3	75	519.9
Estonia	4	111	229.1	Moldova	7	140	796.0
Ethiopia	4	75	3,734.8	Mongolia	8	156	1,261.7
Fiji	6	57	1,209.2	Montenegro	5	71	458.0
Finland	5	53	33.9	Morocco	5	71	2,725.5

TABLE 12.3
Getting electricity data

Economy	Procedures (number)	Time (days)	Cost (% of income per capita)
Mozambique	7	87	2,523.9
Namibia	7	55	576.6
Nepal	5	74	2,370.7
Netherlands	5	143	29.5
New Zealand	5	47	66.8
Nicaragua	6	70	1,768.4
Niger	4	120	4,419.9
Nigeria	8	260	1,180.3
Norway	4	66	7.3
Oman	6	62	66.3
Pakistan	6	266	1,829.2
Palau	5	125	132.7
Panama	5	35	9.9
Papua New Guinea	4	66	2,230.3
Paraguay	4	53	287.5
Peru	5	100	500.0
Philippines	5	63	479.2
Poland	4	143	303.4
Portugal	5	64	57.3
Puerto Rico	5	32	428.6
Qatar	3	90	5.1
Romania	7	244	544.7
Russian Federation	9	302	4,671.7
Rwanda	4	30	5,513.6
Samoa	5	23	881.9
Saudi Arabia	4	71	21.3
Senegal	7	125	6,018.5
Serbia	4	131	574.7
Seychelles	6	147	565.6
Sierra Leone	8	137	2,914.1
Singapore	4	36	33.9
Slovak Republic	5	177	197.5
Slovenia	5	38	122.9
Solomon Islands	4	39	2,244.6

Economy	Procedures (number)	Time (days)	Cost (% of income per capita)
South Africa	4	214	1,780.4
Spain	4	101	229.8
Sri Lanka	4	132	1,381.6
St. Kitts and Nevis	5	18	377.1
St. Lucia	4	25	212.6
St. Vincent and the Grenadines	3	52	280.7
Suriname	5	58	795.3
Swaziland	6	137	1,472.2
Sweden	3	52	21.8
Switzerland	3	39	70.7
Syrian Arab Republic	5	71	1,045.9
Taiwan, China	4	23	56.8
Tajikistan	9	224	1,240.9
Tanzania	4	109	265.3
Thailand	4	35	86.3
Timor-Leste	3	39	7,389.0
Togo	4	89	6,020.7
Tonga	5	50	115.1
Trinidad and Tobago	5	61	2.5
Tunisia	4	65	1,062.8
Turkey	5	70	714.3
Uganda	5	91	5,793.4
Ukraine	11	309	275.6
United Arab Emirates	4	55	18.6
United Kingdom	5	111	43.3
United States	4	68	16.9
Uzbekistan	9	117	2,070.8
Vanuatu	5	257	1,200.1
Venezuela, RB	6	125	1,461.3
Vietnam	5	142	1,536.0
West Bank and Gaza	5	63	1,560.6
Yemen, Rep.	4	35	4,973.4
Zambia	5	117	1,250.5
Zimbabwe	6	125	6,511.9

Source: Getting Electricity database.

1. World Bank (2009c), comparing the ease of doing business across 10 cities in Russia, shows that dealing with construction permits is more complex in Moscow than in the other cities in part because of differences in the number of procedures required to obtain an electricity hookup.

2. According to the survey data, which cover the years 2006–09, 15.2% of managers consider electricity the most serious constraint, while 15.68% consider access to finance the most serious (http://www.enterprisesurveys.org).

3. See, for example, Calderon and Servén (2003), Dollar, Hallward-Driemeier and Mengistae (2005), Reinikka and Svensson (1999) and Eifert (2007). Using firm-level data, Iimi (2008) finds that in Eastern Europe and Central Asia eliminating electricity outages could increase GDP by 0.5–6%.

4. Foster and Steinbuks (2009).

5. Lee, Anas and Oh (1996).

6. The report is available for further comments on the *Doing Business* website (http://www.doingbusiness.org). A final draft of the methodology paper is under preparation.

7. Geginat and Ramalho (2010) find that connecting a new customer to electricity takes more than twice as long on average in low-income economies as in high-income ones. They find that the differences can be explained in part by the overall level of bureaucracy in an economy, especially where utilities are majority state owned.

8. Th. H. (translated by Cong Dung), "83% of Electrical Wiring Fails to Meet Quality Standards," *Saigon-GP Daily*, May 19, 2010, http://www.saigon-gpdaily.com.vn.

9. U.S. Fire Administration (2008).

10. Srinivasan and Turlakova (2010).

11. By comparison, the demand of a residential connection is about 20 kVA.

12. Detailed information on cost components for each economy can be found on the *Doing Business* website (http://www.doingbusiness.org).

13. The number of economies where utilities charge security deposits does not include those where security deposits are rolled over into consumption bills for the first 3 months (Malaysia and the United States).

14. Although *Getting Electricity* records only the present value of the interest lost on the security deposit, even those amounts can be high—in Haiti, as high as $11,421. On average, the present value of the interest lost on the security deposit accounts for 13% of the entire connection cost for the customer.

15. GovHK, "Process Review: Application for Excavation Permit," http://www.gov.hk/.

16. Fid Thompson, "Sierra Leone's Hydro-Power Dam Lighting Up Freetown," *VOA News*, February 10, 2010, http://www1.voanews.com/.

Annex: employing workers

Before the global economic crisis Slovenia was among the fastest-growing economies in Europe, with an unemployment rate hovering near 4% at its 2008 low. But the country, with an export-focused economy, was hit hard by the crisis. By early 2010 the unemployment rate had risen to 6.3%. The government responded with 2 new laws. Under the Partial Reimbursement of Payment Compensation Act, a temporary measure expiring in 2011, the government reimburses employers for education expenses and wages paid to employees put on temporary leave because of work shortages. This helps employers stay in business while keeping workers on the payroll. And workers use their time off to receive training that can help them and their employers in the future. Another provisional measure enables employers facing work shortages to reduce their employees' workweek from 40 hours to 32. The employer pays only for the 32 hours worked, and the government makes up the difference. This way workers still receive their full wages, while struggling employers face lower costs.

Maintaining and creating productive jobs and businesses is a priority for economies recovering from the crisis. As the International Labour Organization's (ILO) Decent Work Agenda acknowledges, work plays a central part in people's lives,[1] providing economic and social opportunities. When the World Bank study *Voices of the Poor* asked 60,000 poor people around the world how they thought they might escape poverty, the majority of men and women pinned their hopes above all on income from their own business or wages earned in employment.[2] Smart employment regulation, which enhances job security and improves productivity through employer-worker cooperation, means that both workers and firms benefit.[3]

Good labor regulation promotes new businesses and can help shift workers to the formal sector, where they will benefit the most from worker protection and where higher productivity boosts economic growth.[4] By contrast, labor market restrictions can be an obstacle to the development of businesses, which is consistently apparent in surveys of entrepreneurs in more than 80 countries.[5] Moreover, strict labor rules and policies that increase the cost of formality are considered one of the main contributors to the persistence and growth of the informal sector in low-income economies, where it accounts for an estimated 30–70% of the workforce.[6] Workers often become caught in the "informality trap": those who do not leave the informal sector soon enough may find themselves remaining there for a long time.[7] As a result, in developing economies excessively rigid employment rules can end up providing a relatively high standard of protection to a few workers in the formal sector—but minimal protection or none at all for the majority of workers, employed in the informal sector.[8] Workers in the informal sector are twice as likely to become unemployed as those in the formal sector.[9]

Creating productive jobs in the formal sector is key. So is shielding workers from abusive or arbitrary treatment. Where labor rules do not exist, or where the rules are too flexible and fail to offer sufficient protection, workers are at risk of abusive work conditions—such as working long hours without rest periods. When employers are hit by difficult times and economic redundancy becomes inevitable, lack of sufficient severance pay or unemployment benefits can also leave workers in precarious conditions. In Latin American countries, for example, workers dismissed from a job often turn to the informal sector because the lack of unemployment benefits prevents a proper search for another formal sector job.[10]

Evidence suggests that unemployment benefits can have a strong effect in reducing poverty.[11] Lack of access to insurance among poor rural households pushes them to take up low-risk activities with lower returns. This reduces their income potential—by 25% in rural Tanzania and by 50% in a sample of rural villages in India, according to a recent study.[12] Mauritius took such considerations into account when it implemented a new labor law in 2008 aimed at balancing flexibility and worker protection. As part of the unemployment protection

FIGURE 13.1

Most economies balance flexibility and protection in the length of the workweek

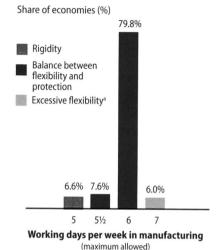

Share of economies (%)

a. Accords with ILO Convention 14.
Source: Doing Business database.

scheme, the law introduced a recycling fee—a lump sum payment from a national savings fund account to which employers contribute over time—rather than severance pay in the case of justified economic redundancies. Economies achieve this balance in different ways, depending in part on their organizational and financial means. Some establish a centralized system of government payments. Others mandate direct payments from employers.

CHANGES IN METHODOLOGY

Doing Business, in its indicators on employing workers, measures flexibility in the regulation of hiring, working hours and redundancy in a manner consistent with the ILO conventions. Changes in the methodology for these indicators have been made in the past 3 years so as to ensure consistency with relevant ILO conventions and to avoid scoring that rewards economies for flexibility that comes at the cost of a basic level of social protection (including unemployment protection). In *Doing Business 2010*, for example, the indicators started taking into account the existence of unemployment protection schemes in cases of redundancy dismissal where workers receive less than 8 weeks of severance pay.

Further changes have been made to take into account the need for a balance between worker protection and flexibility in employment regulation that favors job creation. Over the past year a consultative group—including labor lawyers, employer and employee representatives and experts from the ILO, the OECD, civil society and the private sector—has been meeting to review the methodology as well as to suggest future areas of research. Because this consultation is not yet complete, this year's report does not rank economies on the employing workers indicators or include the indicators in the aggregate ranking on the ease of doing business.

The consultative process has informed several changes in the methodology for the employing workers indicators, some of which have been implemented in this year's report. New thresholds have been introduced to recognize minimum levels of protection in line with relevant ILO conventions. This provides a framework for balancing worker protection against employment restrictions in the areas measured by the indicators.

Four main aspects are affected by the changes in methodology: the minimum wage, paid annual leave, the maximum number of working days per week and the tenure of the worker in the case study.

For the minimum wage, an economy would receive a score indicating excessive flexibility if it has no minimum wage at all, if the law provides a regulatory mechanism for the minimum wage that is not enforced in practice, if there is only a customary minimum wage or if the minimum wage applies only to the public sector. For paid annual leave there is now a minimum threshold of 15 working days below which scoring would indicate excessive flexibility. For paid annual leave above 26 working days, scoring would indicate excessive rigidity. For paid annual leave between 22 and 26 working days, an intermediate score would be assigned indicating semirigidity. For the number of working days per week there is now a maximum of 6 above which scoring would reflect excessive flexibility.

The change in the worker's tenure affects the measurements of annual leave, notice period and severance pay. Before, all these related to a worker with 20 years of tenure. Now they relate to the average for a worker with 1 year of tenure, a worker with 5 years and a worker with 10 years (see Data notes for a full description).

For working days per week, for example, the new methodology is in accord with ILO Convention 14, which states that every worker "shall enjoy in every period of seven days a period of rest comprising at least twenty-four consecutive hours." Under the new methodology economies requiring less than 1 day (24 hours) of rest time a week receive a lower score, indicating excessive flexibility. Economies achieve the highest score by striking a balance between flexibility and worker protection (figure 13.1). For a discussion of the results of some of the other changes in methodology, see the section in this chapter on emerging patterns.

WHO REFORMED LABOR REGULATIONS IN 2009/10?

Governments have continued to respond to the global economic crisis with short-term, emergency legislation aimed at mitigating its adverse effects. Some have focused on combating unemployment by attempting to help businesses adjust and recover, others on increasing assistance for those already unemployed. Spain now exempts a portion of severance payments from taxation. Romania exempts employers that hire previously unemployed workers from paying the workers' social insurance contributions for 6 months. Poland and Serbia have adopted legislative measures allowing employers to respond to a decline in work volume by reducing their workers' hours or placing workers on temporary leave with reduced pay. Eleven economies made changes to their labor regulations in 2009/10 that affect the employing workers indicators.

Australia passed the Fair Work Act

in 2009 and National Employment Standards in 2010. These led to significant changes, including the introduction of a severance pay requirement when before there had been none. Now workers in manufacturing are entitled to up to 12 weeks of severance pay, depending on the length of their tenure. In addition, an employer must look into the feasibility of reassigning an employee to another position before considering redundancy. Annual leave requirements changed from 20 working days (4 weeks for a worker with a 5-day workweek) to 4 weeks for a nonshift worker and 5 for a shift worker.

Bhutan set a minimum for paid annual leave, having previously required none. Under the 2009 Leave Regulation most workers are entitled to a minimum of 18 days of leave a year. The regulation was one in a series Bhutan adopted in 2009 to further implement aspects of its 2007 Labor and Employment Act.

Estonia adopted a new Employment Contracts Act in 2009. Under the new law there are no priority rules for rehiring. Collective dismissals meeting threshold numbers trigger requirements for notification of and consultation with employee representatives and government authorities. Notice periods were reduced to a range of 15–90 calendar days, depending on an employee's seniority, and severance payments to 1 month's wages. But now an unemployment insurance fund disburses an additional 1–3 months' wages, a solution that balances flexibility and worker protection.

Kuwait increased its notice period for dismissal from 15 calendar days to 3 months. It expanded minimum requirements for annual leave from 14 or 21 calendar days, depending on a worker's tenure, to 26 working days for all.

Malaysia changed its restrictions on redundancy dismissals. Before, an employer had to notify the Department of Labor in writing of all redundancy dismissals. A 2009 circular now limits that requirement to the redundancy dismissal of 5 or more employees.

Poland, which previously had no restriction on the maximum duration of fixed-term contracts, introduced a limit of 24 months. The Slovak Republic reduced its limit from 36 months to 24.

Spain passed a royal decree-law to urgently implement several changes. One measure reduced the notice period for redundancy dismissal for workers with all lengths of tenure from 30 calendar days to 15.

Syria passed a new labor law in 2010 to replace its 1959 law. Among other changes, the new law increases notice periods to 2 months, introduces new restrictions on weekly holiday work and slightly increases annual leave—now 14–30 working days a year, depending on a worker's tenure.

Zimbabwe lowered its severance pay requirements. When the country converted its wages into U.S. dollars in response to hyperinflation, it also converted severance pay amounts. As a result, common law practices shifted. Retrenchment boards now grant 2–4 months' wages as severance rather than 4–6 months' wages.

WHAT PATTERNS ARE EMERGING?

Since its inception *Doing Business* has been collecting increasingly detailed information on labor regulation as a basis for the employing workers indicators.[13] The employing workers data set has expanded over the years. The following additional data are presented in this year's report or on the *Doing Business* website: the generally applicable minimum wage as well as any minimum wage applying to a 19-year-old worker, or an apprentice, in the manufacturing sector; the maximum duration for a single fixed-term contract; and provisions relating to the work schedule, such as the length of a standard workday, the limit on overtime both in normal and in exceptional circumstances, the minimum number of rest hours between working days required by law and premiums for overtime work, night work and weekly holiday work.

Doing Business also gathered new information on regulations according to length of job tenure (9 months, 1 year, 5 years and 10 years). Some aspects measured by the employing workers indicators—such as paid annual leave, notice period and severance payment—can vary with different tenures. And while the indicators previously considered a worker with 20 years of tenure, this length of tenure may not be typical for small and medium-size businesses in many economies.

The data *Doing Business* has gathered on employment and labor laws and regulations point to global and regional patterns in how the 183 economies it covers regulate the conditions on which

FIGURE 13.2

Almost half of economies balance flexibility and protection in annual leave

Share of economies (%)

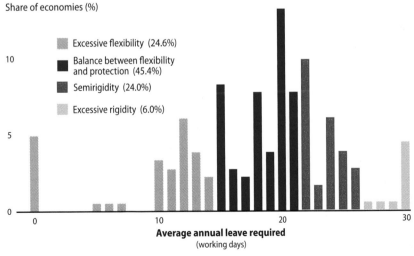

Note: The designation *excessive flexibility* accords with ILO Convention 132. Annual leave is the average for 1, 5 and 10 years of tenure.
Source: *Doing Business* database.

FIGURE 13.3

The most common premium for work done on the weekly holiday is 100%

Share of economies (%)

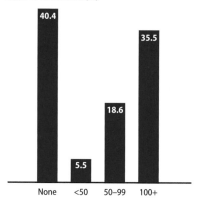

Premium for work on weekly holiday
(% of normal hourly wage)

Source: Doing Business database.

firms employ workers. These data can also be used to assess how regulation balances worker protection and employment flexibility.

FIXED OR PROPORTIONAL REDUNDANCY COSTS

In cases of redundancy dismissal, how do severance pay and notice period requirements vary for workers with different tenures? Eleven economies require no severance payment or notice period, which together make up the redundancy cost (expressed in weeks of wages). Among the rest, economies take 2 broad approaches: they set the same requirements for workers with different tenures, or they set requirements proportional to a worker's tenure.

Thirty-one economies take a fixed-cost approach. In Montenegro, for example, the redundancy cost is 28.1 weeks of wages whether the worker has 1, 5, 10 or 20 years of service. Six economies follow a proportional approach. One is the Islamic Republic of Iran, where workers are granted severance pay equal to 1 month's salary for each year worked.

The majority, 117 economies, fall between these 2 approaches. In these economies the redundancy cost is proportionally higher at the beginning of the worker's service. In most, this is because of a fixed notice period and a severance payment proportional to the

worker's tenure. Cape Verde, where the severance payment is 1 month's wages for each year of work, is an example. In other economies the notice period is fixed but the severance payment is proportionally higher at the beginning of the worker's tenure. In Thailand, for example, a worker with 5 years of tenure is given 180 days of severance pay while a worker with 20 years is given 300.

In 18 economies governments adopt yet another approach, which results in redundancy costs being proportionally higher toward the end of service. This is the case in Paraguay, where workers with 5 years of tenure are granted 75 calendar days of severance pay while those with 20 years receive 600.

BALANCING PROTECTION AND FLEXIBILITY IN ANNUAL LEAVE

Previously, the employing workers indicators scored economies on the basis of excessive rigidity in the number of days of annual leave. Now the data also highlight excessive flexibility—a change that reflects input from the consultative process. To illustrate, economies are divided into 4 groups based on average mandatory paid annual leave (figure 13.2). The first group consists of 43 economies that on the basis of ILO Convention 132 can be considered to have excessive flexibility, with average paid annual leave of less than 15 working days. The second group, 85 economies, shows a balance between flexibility and worker protection, with average paid annual leave of between 15 and 21 working days. The third group is formed of 44 economies that can be

considered to have semirigid regulations, with average paid annual leave of between 22 and 26 working days. The 11 economies in the last group have the most rigid regulations, requiring more than 26 working days of paid annual leave for workers.

VARYING PREMIUMS FOR WEEKLY HOLIDAY WORK

Economies also vary in the premium they require for work performed on the weekly holiday, with 74 economies requiring no premium. The most common holiday work premium is 100% of the hourly pay, while the highest observed premium is 150% of the hourly pay (figure 13.3).

High-income economies have lower premiums on average than low- and middle-income economies. But there is a significant difference within this group, with non-OECD high-income economies having a lower average premium than OECD high-income economies. Among regions, Latin America and the Caribbean has the highest average premium, and South Asia the lowest (figure 13.4).

LOOKING FORWARD

The employing workers indicators are changing to reflect a balance between worker protection and flexibility in employment regulation that favors job creation. The changes are being driven by the useful engagement with experts and stakeholders through the ongoing consultative process. Initial analysis of the impact of the changes to the indicators il-

FIGURE 13.4

Where are premiums for working on the weekly holiday highest?

Average premium for work on weekly holiday (% of normal hourly wage)

Source: Doing Business database.

lustrates how economies tend to regulate the employment of workers and which regulations are excessively rigid, excessively flexible or balanced between them. Further analysis of the data collected will provide a deeper understanding of labor regulation and the patterns that emerge globally.

Following is some of the information collected for the employing workers data set across 183 economies. The complete data set is available on the *Doing Business* website.

1. ILO, "Decent Work FAQ: Making Decent Work a Global Goal," accessed June 23, 2010, http://www.ilo.org/.

2. Narayan and others (2000).

3. Pierre and Scarpetta (2007).

4. La Porta and Shleifer (2008).

5. World Business Environment Surveys and Investment Climate Surveys, conducted in more than 80 countries by the World Bank in 1999–2000.

6. Bosch and Esteban-Pretel (2009).

7. Masatlioglu and Rigolini (2008).

8. Pierre and Scarpetta (2007).

9. Duryea and others (2006).

10. Pierre and Scarpetta (2007).

11. Vodopivec (2009).

12. Pierre and Scarpetta (2007) citing Rosenzweig and Binswanger (1993).

13. Detailed data are available for 183 economies on the *Doing Business* website (http://www.doingbusiness.org).

	Difficulty of hiring index				Rigidity of hours index							Difficulty of redundancy index								Redundancy cost	
	Fixed-term contracts prohibited for permanent tasks?	Maximum length of fixed-term contracts (months) [a]	Minimum wage for a 19-year-old worker or an apprentice (US$ per month) [b]	Ratio of minimum wage to value added per worker	50-hour workweek allowed? [c]	Maximum working days per week	Premium for night work (% of hourly pay) [d]	Premium for work on weekly rest day (% of hourly pay) [d]	Major restrictions on night work? [d]	Major restrictions on weekly holiday work? [d]	Paid annual leave (working days) [e]	Dismissal due to redundancy allowed by law?	Third-party notification if 1 worker is dismissed?	Third-party approval if 1 worker is dismissed?	Third-party notification if 9 workers are dismissed?	Third-party approval if 9 workers are dismissed?	Retraining or reassignment? [f]	Priority rules for redundancies?	Priority rules for reemployment?	Notice period for redundancy dismissal (weeks of salary) [e]	Severance pay for redundancy dismissal (weeks of salary) [e]
Afghanistan	No	NO LIMIT	0.0	0.00	Yes	5.6	25	50	No	No	20.0	Yes	No	No	Yes	No	No	No	No	4.3	17.3
Albania	Yes	NO LIMIT	201.3	0.41	Yes	6.0	50	25	Yes	No	20.0	Yes	No	No	No	No	No	No	No	4.3	10.7
Algeria	Yes	NO LIMIT	228.1	0.42	No	6.0	0	0	No	No	22.0	Yes	No	No	No	No	No	No	No	11.6	13.0
Angola	Yes	12	122.0	0.22	Yes	6.0	0	100	No	No	22.0	Yes	Yes	No	Yes	No	No	No	No	4.3	13.0
Antigua and Barbuda	No	NO LIMIT	576.5	0.36	Yes	6.0	25	0	No	No	12.0	Yes	No	No	No	No	No	No	No	3.4	10.7
Argentina	Yes	60	447.6	0.45	Yes	6.0	13	50	No	No	18.0	Yes	No	No	No	No	No	No	No	7.2	23.1
Armenia	Yes	60	88.3	0.23	Yes	6.0	150	100	No	No	20.0	Yes	No	No	No	No	Yes	No	No	8.7	4.3
Australia	No	NO LIMIT	1,291.1	0.24	Yes	7.0	0	0	No	Yes	20.0	Yes	No	No	Yes	No	No	No	No	4.0	8.7
Austria	No	NO LIMIT	716.3	0.12	Yes	5.5	17	100	No	No	25.0	Yes	No	No	Yes	No	Yes	No	No	2.0	0.0
Azerbaijan	No	60	98.6	0.17	Yes	6.0	40	150	Yes	No	17.0	Yes	No	No	Yes	No	No	No	No	8.7	13.0
Bahamas, The	No	NO LIMIT	693.3	0.24	Yes	5.5	0	0	No	No	11.7	Yes	No	No	No	No	No	No	No	2.0	10.7
Bahrain	No	NO LIMIT	0.0	0.00	Yes	6.0	50	0	No	No	18.3	Yes	No	No	No	No	No	No	No	4.3	0.0
Bangladesh	Yes	NO LIMIT	23.2	0.30	Yes	6.0	0	0	No	No	17.0	Yes	Yes	No	Yes	No	No	Yes	Yes	4.3	26.7
Belarus	No	NO LIMIT	102.7	0.16	Yes	6.0	20	100	No	No	18.0	Yes	No	No	Yes	No	Yes	Yes	No	8.7	13.0
Belgium	No	NO LIMIT	1,746.7	0.30	Yes	6.0	4	100	No	No	20.0	Yes	No	No	Yes	No	No	No	No	6.0	0.0
Belize	No	NO LIMIT	291.7	0.50	Yes	6.0	0	50	No	No	10.0	Yes	No	No	No	No	No	No	No	3.3	5.0
Benin	No	48	67.7	0.58	Yes	6.0	0	0	No	No	24.0	Yes	Yes	Yes	Yes	Yes	No	Yes	Yes	4.3	7.3
Bhutan	No	NO LIMIT	33.0	0.13	Yes	6.0	0	0	No	No	15.0	Yes	No	No	Yes	No	No	No	No	8.3	0.0
Bolivia [g]	Yes	24	88.8	0.38	Yes	6.0	30	100	No	No	21.7	No	n.a.	n.a.	n.a.	n.a.	n.a.	n.a.	n.a.	n.a.	n.a.
Bosnia and Herzegovina	No	24	529.6	0.95	Yes	6.0	30	20	No	No	18.0	Yes	Yes	No	Yes	No	Yes	Yes	Yes	2.0	7.2
Botswana	No	NO LIMIT	110.5	0.13	Yes	6.0	0	100	No	No	15.0	Yes	No	No	No	No	No	No	No	4.9	16.8
Brazil	Yes	24	279.3	0.28	Yes	6.0	20	100	No	No	26.0	Yes	No	No	No	No	No	No	No	4.3	8.9
Brunei Darussalam	No	NO LIMIT	0.0	0.00	Yes	6.0	0	50	No	No	13.3	Yes	No	No	No	No	No	No	No	3.0	0.0
Bulgaria	No	36	166.2	0.24	Yes	6.0	10	0	Yes	No	20.0	Yes	No	No	Yes	No	No	No	No	4.3	3.2
Burkina Faso	No	NO LIMIT	65.1	0.79	Yes	6.0	0	0	No	No	22.0	Yes	No	No	Yes	No	No	Yes	Yes	4.3	6.1
Burundi	No	NO LIMIT	3.0	0.14	Yes	6.0	0	0	No	Yes	21.0	Yes	No	No	Yes	No	Yes	No	Yes	8.7	7.2
Cambodia	No	24	41.0	0.47	Yes	6.0	30	100	No	No	19.3	Yes	No	No	Yes	No	No	No	Yes	7.9	10.7
Cameroon	No	48	63.3	0.36	Yes	6.0	50	0	No	No	26.0	Yes	Yes	Yes	Yes	Yes	No	Yes	Yes	6.5	8.1

	Difficulty of hiring index				Rigidity of hours index							Difficulty of redundancy index								Redundancy cost	
	Fixed-term contracts prohibited for permanent tasks?	Maximum length of fixed-term contracts (months) [a]	Minimum wage for a 19-year-old worker or an apprentice (US$ per month) [b]	Ratio of minimum wage to value added per worker	50-hour workweek allowed? [c]	Maximum working days per week	Premium for night work (% of hourly pay) [d]	Premium for work on weekly rest day (% of hourly pay) [d]	Major restrictions on night work? [d]	Major restrictions on weekly holiday work? [d]	Paid annual leave (working days) [e]	Dismissal due to redundancy allowed by law?	Third-party notification if 1 worker is dismissed?	Third-party approval if 1 worker is dismissed?	Third-party notification if 9 workers are dismissed?	Third-party approval if 9 workers are dismissed?	Retraining or reassignment? [f]	Priority rules for redundancies?	Priority rules for reemployment?	Notice period for redundancy dismissal (weeks of salary) [e]	Severance pay for redundancy dismissal (weeks of salary) [e]
Canada	No	NO LIMIT	1,703.7	0.34	Yes	6.0	0	0	No	No	10.0	Yes	No	No	No	No	No	No	No	7.0	5.0
Cape Verde	Yes	60	0.0	0.00	Yes	6.0	25	100	No	No	22.0	Yes	Yes	Yes	Yes	Yes	Yes	Yes	No	6.4	23.1
Central African Republic	Yes	48	39.8	0.59	Yes	5.0	0	50	Yes	Yes	25.3	Yes	Yes	Yes	Yes	Yes	No	Yes	Yes	4.3	17.3
Chad	No	48	71.9	0.71	Yes	6.0	0	100	No	No	24.7	Yes	No	No	Yes	No	No	Yes	Yes	7.2	5.8
Chile	No	24	0.0	0.00	Yes	6.0	0	0	No	No	15.0	Yes	No	No	No	No	No	No	No	4.3	12.0
China	No	NO LIMIT	159.9	0.38	Yes	6.0	0	100	No	No	6.7	Yes	Yes	No	Yes	No	Yes	Yes	Yes	4.3	23.1
Colombia	No	NO LIMIT	244.2	0.39	Yes	6.0	35	75	No	No	15.0	Yes	No	No	No	No	No	No	No	0.0	19.0
Comoros	No	36	64.8	0.52	Yes	6.0	0	0	No	Yes	22.0	Yes	Yes	No	Yes	No	Yes	Yes	Yes	0.0	0.0
Congo, Dem. Rep.	Yes	48	65.0	2.46	Yes	5.0	25	0	No	No	13.0	Yes	Yes	No	Yes	Yes	No	Yes	Yes	13.0	23.1
Congo, Rep.	Yes	24	119.7	0.44	Yes	6.0	0	50	Yes	Yes	29.0	Yes	Yes	Yes	Yes	Yes	No	Yes	Yes	10.3	6.5
Costa Rica	Yes	12	334.5	0.43	Yes	6.0	0	100	No	No	12.0	Yes	No	No	No	No	No	No	No	4.3	14.4
Côte d'Ivoire	No	24	0.0	0.00	No	6.0	38	35	No	No	27.4	Yes	Yes	No	Yes	No	Yes	Yes	Yes	5.8	7.3
Croatia	Yes	36	534.3	0.31	Yes	6.0	10	0	No	Yes	20.0	Yes	Yes	No	Yes	No	Yes	No	Yes	7.9	7.2
Cyprus	No	30	0.0	0.00	Yes	6.0	0	0	No	No	20.0	Yes	No	No	No	No	No	No	No	5.7	0.0
Czech Republic	No	24	427.8	0.21	Yes	6.0	10	10	No	No	20.0	Yes	No	No	Yes	No	No	No	No	8.7	13.0
Denmark	No	NO LIMIT	0.0	0.00	Yes	6.0	0	0	No	No	25.0	Yes	No	No	Yes	No	No	No	No	0.0	0.0
Djibouti	Yes	24	0.0	0.00	Yes	6.0	0	0	Yes	No	30.0	Yes	Yes	No	Yes	No	No	Yes	Yes	4.3	0.0
Dominica	No	NO LIMIT	257.2	0.40	Yes	6.0	0	100	Yes	Yes	15.0	Yes	No	No	Yes	No	No	No	No	4.3	9.3
Dominican Republic	Yes	NO LIMIT	226.0	0.37	Yes	6.0	0	100	No	No	14.0	Yes	Yes	No	No	No	No	No	No	4.0	22.2
Ecuador	No	24	229.7	0.43	Yes	5.0	25	100	No	No	12.3	Yes	Yes	Yes	Yes	Yes	No	No	No	4.3	31.8
Egypt, Arab Rep.	No	NO LIMIT	31.4	0.11	Yes	6.0	0	0	No	No	24.0	Yes	Yes	Yes	Yes	Yes	No	Yes	No	10.1	26.7
El Salvador	Yes	NO LIMIT	80.1	0.17	Yes	6.0	25	100	No	Yes	11.0	Yes	Yes	No	Yes	No	No	No	Yes	0.0	22.9
Equatorial Guinea	Yes	24	291.4	0.16	Yes	6.0	25	50	No	No	22.0	Yes	No	No	Yes	Yes	No	Yes	Yes	4.3	34.3
Eritrea	Yes	NO LIMIT	0.0	0.00	Yes	6.0	0	0	No	No	19.0	Yes	No	No	No	No	No	No	No	3.1	12.3
Estonia	Yes	120	393.0	0.23	Yes	5.0	25	0	Yes	No	24.0	Yes	No	No	No	No	Yes	No	No	8.6	4.3
Ethiopia	Yes	NO LIMIT	0.0	0.00	Yes	6.0	0	0	No	No	18.3	Yes	Yes	No	Yes	No	Yes	Yes	No	10.1	10.5
Fiji	No	NO LIMIT	290.8	0.56	Yes	6.0	6	100	No	No	10.0	Yes	Yes	No	Yes	No	No	No	No	4.3	5.3

	Difficulty of hiring index				Rigidity of hours index							Difficulty of redundancy index								Redundancy cost	
	Fixed-term contracts prohibited for permanent tasks?	Maximum length of fixed-term contracts (months) [a]	Minimum wage for a 19-year-old worker or an apprentice (US$ per month) [b]	Ratio of minimum wage to value added per worker	50-hour workweek allowed? [c]	Maximum working days per week	Premium for night work (% of hourly pay) [d]	Premium for work on weekly rest day (% of hourly pay) [d]	Major restrictions on night work? [d]	Major restrictions on weekly holiday work? [d]	Paid annual leave (working days) [e]	Dismissal due to redundancy allowed by law?	Third-party notification if 1 worker is dismissed?	Third-party approval if 1 worker is dismissed?	Third-party notification if 9 workers are dismissed?	Third-party approval if 9 workers are dismissed?	Retraining or reassignment? [f]	Priority rules for redundancies?	Priority rules for reemployment?	Notice period for redundancy dismissal (weeks of salary) [e]	Severance pay for redundancy dismissal (weeks of salary) [e]
Finland	Yes	60	2,063.9	0.36	Yes	6.0	8	100	No	No	30.0	Yes	No	No	Yes	No	Yes	No	Yes	10.1	0.0
France	Yes	18	788.2	0.14	No	6.0	0	0	No	No	30.0	Yes	Yes	No	Yes	No	Yes	Yes	Yes	7.2	4.6
Gabon	No	48	48.2	0.05	Yes	6.0	50	100	No	No	24.0	Yes	Yes	No	Yes	No	No	Yes	Yes	10.4	4.3
Gambia, The	No	NO LIMIT	0.0	0.00	Yes	5.0	0	0	No	No	21.0	Yes	No	No	No	No	Yes	No	No	26.0	0.0
Georgia	No	NO LIMIT	25.1	0.08	Yes	7.0	0	0	No	No	24.0	Yes	No	No	No	No	No	No	No	0.0	0.0
Germany	No	24	1,139.6	0.21	Yes	6.0	0	0	No	No	24.0	Yes	Yes	No	Yes	No	Yes	Yes	No	0.0	0.0
Ghana	No	NO LIMIT	25.8	0.26	Yes	6.0	13	0	No	No	15.0	Yes	Yes	No	Yes	No	Yes	Yes	Yes	3.6	46.2
Greece	Yes	NO LIMIT	1,015.8	0.29	Yes	5.0	25	75	No	No	15.0	Yes	Yes	No	Yes	No	Yes	No	No	0.0	24.0
Grenada	Yes	NO LIMIT	225.3	0.31	Yes	6.0	0	0	No	No	13.3	Yes	No	No	No	No	No	No	No	7.2	5.3
Guatemala	Yes	NO LIMIT	169.8	0.41	Yes	6.0	50	100	Yes	Yes	15.0	Yes	Yes	Yes	Yes	Yes	No	No	No	0.0	27.0
Guinea	No	24	0.0	0.00	Yes	6.0	20	45	No	No	30.0	Yes	No	No	Yes	No	No	Yes	Yes	2.1	5.8
Guinea-Bissau	Yes	12	0.0	0.00	Yes	6.0	25	50	No	No	21.0	Yes	Yes	No	Yes	No	Yes	Yes	Yes	26.0	26.0
Guyana	No	NO LIMIT	145.0	0.45	Yes	7.0	0	100	No	No	12.0	Yes	No	No	Yes	No	No	No	No	4.3	12.3
Haiti	No	NO LIMIT	43.2	0.41	Yes	6.0	50	50	No	No	13.0	Yes	No	No	Yes	No	No	No	No	10.1	0.0
Honduras	Yes	24	259.2	0.99	Yes	6.0	25	100	Yes	Yes	16.7	Yes	Yes	No	Yes	No	No	Yes	No	7.2	23.1
Hong Kong SAR, China	No	NO LIMIT	0.0	0.00	Yes	6.0	0	0	No	No	11.3	Yes	No	No	No	No	No	No	No	4.3	1.5
Hungary	No	60	390.0	0.25	Yes	5.0	40	100	No	No	21.3	Yes	No	No	Yes	No	No	No	No	6.2	7.2
Iceland	No	24	1,707.7	0.32	Yes	6.0	80	80	No	No	24.0	Yes	No	No	Yes	No	No	No	No	10.1	0.0
India	No	NO LIMIT	24.1	0.16	Yes	6.0	0	0	No	No	15.0	Yes	Yes	No	Yes	Yes	No	Yes	Yes	4.3	11.4
Indonesia	Yes	36	105.9	0.38	Yes	6.0	0	0	No	No	12.0	Yes	Yes	Yes	Yes	Yes	Yes	No	Yes	0.0	34.7
Iran, Islamic Rep.	No	NO LIMIT	309.1	0.58	Yes	6.0	23	40	No	No	24.0	Yes	Yes	Yes	Yes	Yes	No	No	No	0.0	23.1
Iraq	Yes	NO LIMIT	115.5	0.35	Yes	5.0	100	50	No	No	22.0	Yes	No	No	Yes	No	No	No	No	0.0	0.0
Ireland	No	NO LIMIT	1,793.9	0.33	Yes	6.0	0	0	No	No	20.0	Yes	No	No	Yes	No	No	No	No	4.0	2.8
Israel	No	NO LIMIT	985.7	0.29	Yes	5.5	0	50	No	Yes	18.0	Yes	No	No	No	No	No	No	No	4.3	23.1
Italy	Yes	NO LIMIT	1,582.7	0.36	Yes	6.0	30	50	Yes	Yes	20.3	Yes	Yes	No	Yes	No	No	Yes	No	8.7	0.0
Jamaica	No	NO LIMIT	207.3	0.31	Yes	7.0	0	0	No	No	11.3	Yes	No	No	No	No	No	No	No	4.0	10.0
Japan	No	NO LIMIT	1,361.4	0.28	Yes	6.0	25	35	No	No	15.3	Yes	Yes	No	Yes	No	Yes	No	No	4.3	0.0
Jordan	No	NO LIMIT	201.0	0.40	Yes	6.0	0	150	No	No	18.7	Yes	Yes	Yes	Yes	Yes	No	No	Yes	4.3	0.0
Kazakhstan	No	NO LIMIT	111.6	0.14	Yes	6.0	50	100	No	No	18.0	Yes	Yes	No	Yes	No	Yes	No	No	4.3	4.3

	Difficulty of hiring index				Rigidity of hours index							Difficulty of redundancy index								Redundancy cost	
	Fixed-term contracts prohibited for permanent tasks?	Maximum length of fixed-term contracts (months) [a]	Minimum wage for a 19-year-old worker or an apprentice (US$ per month) [b]	Ratio of minimum wage to value added per worker	50-hour workweek allowed? [c]	Maximum working days per week	Premium for night work (% of hourly pay) [d]	Premium for work on weekly rest day (% of hourly pay) [d]	Major restrictions on night work? [d]	Major restrictions on weekly holiday work? [d]	Paid annual leave (working days) [e]	Dismissal due to redundancy allowed by law?	Third-party notification if 1 worker is dismissed?	Third-party approval if 1 worker is dismissed?	Third-party notification if 9 workers are dismissed?	Third-party approval if 9 workers are dismissed?	Retraining or reassignment? [f]	Priority rules for redundancies?	Priority rules for reemployment?	Notice period for redundancy dismissal (weeks of salary) [e]	Severance pay for redundancy dismissal (weeks of salary) [e]
Kenya	No	NO LIMIT	67.4	0.57	Yes	6.0	0	50	No	No	21.0	Yes	No	No	Yes	No	No	Yes	No	4.3	11.4
Kiribati	No	NO LIMIT	0.0	0.00	Yes	7.0	0	0	No	No	0.0	Yes	No	No	Yes	No	No	No	Yes	4.3	0.0
Korea, Rep.	No	24	579.9	0.25	Yes	6.0	50	50	No	No	17.0	Yes	No	No	Yes	No	Yes	No	Yes	4.3	23.1
Kosovo	No	NO LIMIT	0.0	0.00	Yes	6.0	20	0	Yes	No	16.0	Yes	Yes	No	Yes	Yes	No	Yes	Yes	13.0	7.2
Kuwait	No	NO LIMIT	0.0	0.00	Yes	6.0	0	50	No	No	26.0	Yes	No	No	No	No	No	No	No	13.0	15.1
Kyrgyz Republic	Yes	60	12.2	0.11	Yes	6.0	50	100	No	No	20.0	Yes	No	No	Yes	No	No	Yes	No	4.3	13.0
Lao PDR	No	NO LIMIT	63.9	0.51	Yes	6.0	15	150	No	No	15.0	Yes	No	No	Yes	No	No	No	Yes	6.4	40.7
Latvia	Yes	36	354.4	0.24	Yes	5.5	50	0	Yes	No	20.0	Yes	No	No	Yes	No	Yes	Yes	Yes	1.0	8.7
Lebanon	No	24	317.3	0.32	Yes	6.0	0	50	No	No	15.0	Yes	No	No	Yes	No	No	No	No	8.7	0.0
Lesotho	No	NO LIMIT	93.8	0.62	Yes	6.0	0	0	No	No	12.0	Yes	No	No	No	No	No	Yes	No	4.3	10.7
Liberia	No	NO LIMIT	52.0	2.11	Yes	6.0	0	100	Yes	Yes	16.0	Yes	No	No	No	No	No	No	No	4.3	21.3
Lithuania	Yes	60	329.7	0.24	No	5.5	50	50	No	No	20.0	Yes	No	No	Yes	No	Yes	Yes	Yes	8.7	15.9
Luxembourg	Yes	24	2,407.2	0.26	No	5.5	15	70	No	Yes	25.0	Yes	No	No	Yes	No	No	No	No	17.3	4.3
Macedonia, FYR	No	60	169.0	0.32	Yes	6.0	35	50	Yes	No	20.0	Yes	No	No	Yes	No	No	No	Yes	4.3	8.7
Madagascar	Yes	24	34.0	0.47	Yes	6.0	30	40	No	No	24.0	Yes	Yes	No	Yes	No	No	Yes	Yes	3.4	8.9
Malawi	Yes	NO LIMIT	22.6	0.49	Yes	6.0	0	100	No	No	15.0	Yes	Yes	No	Yes	No	No	No	No	4.3	14.0
Malaysia	No	NO LIMIT	0.0	0.00	Yes	6.0	0	0	No	No	13.3	Yes	No	No	No	No	No	Yes	Yes	6.7	17.2
Maldives	No	24	0.0	0.00	Yes	6.0	0	50	No	No	30.0	Yes	No	No	No	No	No	No	No	5.8	0.0
Mali	Yes	72	14.8	0.14	Yes	6.0	0	0	No	No	22.0	Yes	Yes	No	Yes	No	No	Yes	Yes	4.3	9.3
Marshall Islands	No	NO LIMIT	0.0	0.00	Yes	7.0	0	0	No	No	0.0	Yes	No	No	No	No	No	No	No	0.0	0.0
Mauritania	No	24	83.1	0.60	Yes	6.0	0	50	Yes	No	18.0	Yes	Yes	No	Yes	No	No	Yes	Yes	4.3	6.1
Mauritius	No	NO LIMIT	156.5	0.18	Yes	6.0	0	100	No	No	22.0	Yes	Yes	No	Yes	No	No	No	No	4.3	6.3
Mexico	Yes	NO LIMIT	123.6	0.11	Yes	6.0	0	25	Yes	No	12.0	Yes	Yes	No	Yes	Yes	No	Yes	No	0.0	22.0
Micronesia, Fed. Sts.	No	NO LIMIT	212.7	0.68	Yes	7.0	0	0	No	No	0.0	Yes	No	No	No	No	No	No	No	0.0	0.0
Moldova	Yes	NO LIMIT	96.6	0.52	Yes	6.0	50	100	Yes	Yes	20.0	Yes	No	No	Yes	No	Yes	No	No	8.7	13.9
Mongolia	No	NO LIMIT	82.4	0.42	Yes	5.0	0	0	No	No	17.7	Yes	No	No	No	No	No	No	No	4.3	4.3
Montenegro	No	NO LIMIT	76.4	0.09	Yes	6.0	40	0	No	No	19.0	Yes	No	No	No	No	Yes	Yes	Yes	2.1	26.0
Morocco	Yes	12	254.1	0.72	Yes	6.0	0	0	No	Yes	19.5	Yes	No	No	Yes	Yes	Yes	Yes	Yes	7.2	13.5

	Difficulty of hiring index				Rigidity of hours index							Difficulty of redundancy index								Redundancy cost	
	Fixed-term contracts prohibited for permanent tasks?	Maximum length of fixed-term contracts (months) [a]	Minimum wage for a 19-year-old worker or an apprentice (US$ per month) [b]	Ratio of minimum wage to value added per worker	50-hour workweek allowed? [c]	Maximum working days per week	Premium for night work (% of hourly pay) [d]	Premium for work on weekly rest day (% of hourly pay) [d]	Major restrictions on night work? [d]	Major restrictions on weekly holiday work? [d]	Paid annual leave (working days) [e]	Dismissal due to redundancy allowed by law?	Third-party notification if 1 worker is dismissed?	Third-party approval if 1 worker is dismissed?	Third-party notification if 9 workers are dismissed?	Third-party approval if 9 workers are dismissed?	Retraining or reassignment? [f]	Priority rules for redundancies?	Priority rules for reemployment?	Notice period for redundancy dismissal (weeks of salary) [e]	Severance pay for redundancy dismissal (weeks of salary) [e]
Mozambique	Yes	72	87.9	1.26	Yes	6.0	0	100	No	Yes	21.3	Yes	No	No	Yes	No	No	No	No	4.3	36.8
Namibia	No	NO LIMIT	0.0	0.00	Yes	6.0	6	100	No	No	20.0	Yes	No	No	Yes	No	No	No	No	4.3	5.3
Nepal	Yes	NO LIMIT	60.8	0.97	Yes	6.0	0	50	No	No	0.0	Yes	Yes	No	Yes	Yes	Yes	Yes	Yes	4.3	22.9
Netherlands	No	36	1,062.7	0.17	Yes	5.5	0	0	Yes	Yes	20.0	Yes	No	Yes	No	Yes	Yes	Yes	No	8.7	0.0
New Zealand	No	NO LIMIT	1,552.3	0.45	Yes	7.0	0	0	No	No	20.0	Yes	No	No	No	No	Yes	No	No	0.0	0.0
Nicaragua	No	NO LIMIT	121.5	0.86	Yes	6.0	0	100	No	No	30.0	Yes	No	No	No	No	No	No	No	0.0	14.9
Niger	Yes	24	59.1	1.01	No	6.0	38	0	Yes	Yes	22.0	Yes	Yes	No	Yes	No	Yes	Yes	Yes	4.3	5.8
Nigeria	No	NO LIMIT	0.0	0.00	Yes	6.0	0	0	No	No	20.0	Yes	No	No	No	No	No	No	No	4.0	12.2
Norway	Yes	48	3,647.4	0.34	Yes	6.0	0	0	Yes	Yes	21.0	Yes	Yes	No	Yes	No	Yes	Yes	Yes	8.7	0.0
Oman	No	NO LIMIT	363.6	0.15	Yes	6.0	50	100	No	No	18.3	Yes	No	No	No	No	No	No	No	4.3	22.9
Pakistan	Yes	9	44.8	0.31	Yes	6.0	0	100	No	Yes	14.0	Yes	No	No	Yes	Yes	No	Yes	Yes	4.3	22.9
Palau	No	NO LIMIT	450.6	0.38	Yes	7.0	0	0	No	No	0.0	Yes	No	No	No	No	No	No	No	0.0	0.0
Panama	Yes	12	370.3	0.42	Yes	6.0	0	50	Yes	Yes	22.0	Yes	No	Yes	Yes	Yes	No	Yes	No	0.0	19.0
Papua New Guinea	No	NO LIMIT	119.8	0.70	Yes	6.0	0	0	No	No	11.0	Yes	No	No	No	No	No	No	No	3.3	9.2
Paraguay	Yes	NO LIMIT	168.6	0.54	Yes	6.0	30	100	No	No	20.0	Yes	Yes	No	Yes	No	No	Yes	Yes	7.5	18.6
Peru	Yes	60	185.8	0.34	Yes	6.0	35	100	No	No	13.0	Yes	No	No	Yes	Yes	No	No	No	0.0	11.4
Philippines	Yes	NO LIMIT	173.2	0.72	Yes	6.0	10	30	No	No	5.0	Yes	Yes	No	Yes	No	Yes	No	No	4.3	23.1
Poland	No	24	379.4	0.27	Yes	6.0	20	100	No	No	26.0	Yes	No	No	Yes	No	No	No	No	10.1	0.0
Portugal	Yes	72	677.9	0.26	Yes	6.0	25	100	No	No	22.0	Yes	No	No	Yes	No	Yes	Yes	No	7.9	26.0
Puerto Rico	No	NO LIMIT	1,256.7	0.64	Yes	7.0	0	100	No	No	15.0	Yes	No	No	No	No	No	No	No	0.0	26.0
Qatar	No	NO LIMIT	0.0	0.00	Yes	6.0	0	0	No	No	22.0	Yes	Yes	No	Yes	No	No	No	No	7.2	16.0
Romania	Yes	24	214.5	0.22	Yes	5.0	25	100	No	No	21.0	Yes	No	No	Yes	No	Yes	Yes	Yes	4.0	4.3
Russian Federation	Yes	60	150.8	0.14	Yes	6.0	20	100	No	No	22.0	Yes	Yes	No	Yes	No	Yes	Yes	No	8.7	8.7
Rwanda	No	NO LIMIT	17.6	0.25	Yes	6.0	0	0	No	No	19.3	Yes	No	No	No	No	No	No	No	4.3	8.7
Samoa	No	NO LIMIT	128.7	0.30	Yes	6.0	0	100	No	No	10.0	Yes	No	No	No	No	No	No	No	5.8	0.0
São Tomé and Principe	Yes	36	0.0	0.00	No	6.0	25	0	No	Yes	26.0	Yes	Yes	Yes	Yes	Yes	No	No	No	4.3	26.0
Saudi Arabia	No	NO LIMIT	0.0	0.00	Yes	6.0	0	0	No	No	20.7	Yes	No	No	No	No	No	No	No	4.3	15.2
Senegal	Yes	48	77.3	0.48	Yes	6.0	38	0	No	Yes	24.3	Yes	Yes	No	Yes	No	No	Yes	Yes	3.2	10.5

	Difficulty of hiring index				Rigidity of hours index							Difficulty of redundancy index								Redundancy cost	
	Fixed-term contracts prohibited for permanent tasks?	Maximum length of fixed-term contracts (months) [a]	Minimum wage for a 19-year-old worker or an apprentice (US$ per month) [b]	Ratio of minimum wage to value added per worker	50-hour workweek allowed? [c]	Maximum working days per week	Premium for night work (% of hourly pay) [d]	Premium for work on weekly rest day (% of hourly pay) [d]	Major restrictions on night work? [d]	Major restrictions on weekly holiday work? [d]	Paid annual leave (working days) [e]	Dismissal due to redundancy allowed by law?	Third-party notification if 1 worker is dismissed?	Third-party approval if 1 worker is dismissed?	Third-party notification if 9 workers are dismissed?	Third-party approval if 9 workers are dismissed?	Retraining or reassignment? [f]	Priority rules for redundancies?	Priority rules for reemployment?	Notice period for redundancy dismissal (weeks of salary) [e]	Severance pay for redundancy dismissal (weeks of salary) [e]
Serbia	Yes	12	186.8	0.25	Yes	6.0	26	26	No	No	20.0	Yes	No	No	No	No	Yes	Yes	No	0.0	7.7
Seychelles	Yes	NO LIMIT	287.0	0.26	Yes	6.0	0	100	No	No	21.0	Yes	Yes	Yes	Yes	Yes	No	No	No	4.3	9.1
Sierra Leone	Yes	NO LIMIT	12.7	0.25	Yes	5.0	15	0	No	No	21.7	Yes	Yes	No	Yes	No	Yes	Yes	Yes	8.7	34.8
Singapore	No	NO LIMIT	0.0	0.00	Yes	6.0	0	100	No	No	10.7	Yes	No	No	No	No	No	No	No	3.0	0.0
Slovak Republic	No	24	441.2	0.24	Yes	6.0	20	0	No	No	25.0	Yes	No	No	Yes	No	Yes	No	No	11.6	11.6
Slovenia	Yes	24	1,036.7	0.37	Yes	6.0	30	50	No	No	21.0	Yes	Yes	No	Yes	No	Yes	Yes	No	5.7	5.7
Solomon Islands	No	NO LIMIT	96.3	0.73	Yes	6.0	0	0	No	No	15.0	Yes	No	No	No	No	No	No	No	4.3	10.7
South Africa	Yes	NO LIMIT	516.4	0.70	Yes	6.0	0	100	Yes	No	15.0	Yes	No	No	Yes	No	No	No	No	4.0	5.3
Spain	Yes	12	1,059.4	0.27	Yes	5.5	25	0	No	Yes	22.0	Yes	Yes	No	Yes	No	Yes	Yes	No	2.1	15.2
Sri Lanka	No	NO LIMIT	35.6	0.15	Yes	5.5	0	50	No	Yes	14.0	Yes	Yes	Yes	Yes	Yes	No	No	No	4.3	54.2
St. Kitts and Nevis	No	NO LIMIT	505.1	0.38	Yes	7.0	0	0	No	No	14.0	Yes	No	No	No	No	No	No	No	8.7	0.0
St. Lucia	No	NO LIMIT	0.0	0.00	Yes	6.0	0	150	No	No	21.0	Yes	No	No	No	No	Yes	No	Yes	3.7	9.7
St. Vincent and the Grenadines	No	NO LIMIT	176.0	0.27	Yes	6.0	0	0	No	No	19.3	Yes	No	No	No	No	No	No	No	4.0	10.0
Sudan	No	48	90.6	0.50	Yes	6.0	0	0	No	No	23.3	Yes	Yes	No	Yes	No	No	No	No	4.3	21.7
Suriname	No	NO LIMIT	0.0	0.00	Yes	6.0	0	100	No	No	16.0	Yes	No	No	Yes	No	No	No	No	0.0	8.8
Swaziland	No	NO LIMIT	85.5	0.25	Yes	5.5	0	0	No	No	11.0	Yes	No	No	No	No	Yes	Yes	No	5.9	8.7
Sweden	No	NO LIMIT	0.0	0.00	Yes	5.5	0	0	No	No	25.0	Yes	Yes	No	Yes	No	Yes	Yes	Yes	14.4	0.0
Switzerland	No	120	0.0	0.00	Yes	6.0	0	0	No	No	20.0	Yes	No	No	Yes	No	No	No	No	10.1	0.0
Syrian Arab Republic	No	60	133.7	0.41	Yes	6.0	0	100	No	Yes	19.3	Yes	Yes	Yes	Yes	Yes	No	Yes	No	8.7	0.0
Taiwan, China	Yes	12	525.2	0.26	Yes	6.0	0	100	No	No	12.0	Yes	No	No	Yes	No	Yes	No	Yes	4.3	18.8
Tajikistan	Yes	NO LIMIT	14.3	0.14	No	6.0	0	100	Yes	No	23.3	Yes	Yes	No	Yes	No	Yes	No	No	8.7	6.9
Tanzania	Yes	0	60.0	0.75	Yes	6.0	0	0	No	No	20.0	Yes	Yes	No	Yes	No	No	No	No	4.0	5.3
Thailand	Yes	NO LIMIT	78.9	0.18	Yes	6.0	0	0	No	No	6.0	Yes	No	No	No	No	No	No	No	4.3	31.7
Timor-Leste	Yes	NO LIMIT	0.0	0.00	Yes	6.0	0	100	No	No	12.0	Yes	No	No	Yes	Yes	No	No	No	4.3	0.0
Togo	Yes	48	0.0	0.92	Yes	6.0	38	60	Yes	No	30.0	Yes	Yes	Yes	Yes	No	No	Yes	Yes	4.3	7.3
Tonga	No	NO LIMIT	0.0	0.00	Yes	6.0	0	0	No	Yes	0.0	Yes	No	No	No	No	No	No	No	0.0	0.0
Trinidad and Tobago	No	NO LIMIT	0.0	0.00	Yes	6.0	0	100	No	No	10.0	Yes	No	No	Yes	No	No	Yes	No	6.4	14.1

	Difficulty of hiring index				Rigidity of hours index							Difficulty of redundancy index								Redundancy cost	
	Fixed-term contracts prohibited for permanent tasks?	Maximum length of fixed-term contracts (months) [a]	Minimum wage for a 19-year-old worker or an apprentice (US$ per month) [b]	Ratio of minimum wage to value added per worker	50-hour workweek allowed? [c]	Maximum working days per week	Premium for night work (% of hourly pay) [d]	Premium for work on weekly rest day (% of hourly pay) [d]	Major restrictions on night work? [d]	Major restrictions on weekly holiday work? [d]	Paid annual leave (working days) [e]	Dismissal due to redundancy allowed by law?	Third-party notification if 1 worker is dismissed?	Third-party approval if 1 worker is dismissed?	Third-party notification if 9 workers are dismissed?	Third-party approval if 9 workers are dismissed?	Retraining or reassignment? [f]	Priority rules for redundancies?	Priority rules for reemployment?	Notice period for redundancy dismissal (weeks of salary) [e]	Severance pay for redundancy dismissal (weeks of salary) [e]
Tunisia	No	48	120.5	0.27	Yes	6.0	0	0	No	No	13.0	Yes	No	No	Yes	No	No	No	No	4.3	7.8
Turkey	Yes	NO LIMIT	505.4	0.47	Yes	6.0	0	100	No	No	18.0	Yes	No	No	Yes	No	No	No	No	6.7	23.1
Uganda	No	NO LIMIT	3.1	0.04	Yes	6.0	0	0	No	No	21.0	Yes	No	No	No	No	Yes	No	No	8.7	0.0
Ukraine	Yes	NO LIMIT	125.1	0.38	No	5.5	20	100	No	No	18.0	Yes	Yes	No	Yes	No	Yes	No	Yes	8.7	4.3
United Arab Emirates	No	NO LIMIT	0.0	0.00	Yes	6.0	0	50	No	No	26.0	Yes	No	No	No	No	No	No	No	4.3	18.1
United Kingdom	No	NO LIMIT	1,805.0	0.35	Yes	6.0	0	0	No	No	28.0	Yes	No	No	No	No	No	No	No	5.3	2.6
United States	No	NO LIMIT	1,252.9	0.21	Yes	6.0	0	0	No	No	0.0	Yes	No	No	No	No	No	No	No	0.0	0.0
Uruguay	Yes	NO LIMIT	235.2	0.19	Yes	6.0	0	100	No	No	21.0	Yes	No	No	No	No	Yes	No	No	0.0	20.8
Uzbekistan	Yes	60	23.9	0.17	Yes	6.0	50	100	No	No	15.0	Yes	No	No	No	No	Yes	No	No	0.0	0.0
Vanuatu	No	NO LIMIT	247.0	0.65	Yes	6.0	75	50	No	No	15.0	Yes	No	No	Yes	No	No	Yes	No	8.7	13.0
Venezuela, RB [g]	Yes	24	326.4	0.25	Yes	6.0	30	50	No	No	15.0	No	n.a.	n.a.	n.a.	n.a.	n.a.	n.a.	n.a.	9.3	23.1
Vietnam	No	72	40.7	0.33	Yes	6.0	30	100	No	No	13.0	Yes	No	No	No	No	Yes	Yes	Yes	0.0	23.1
West Bank and Gaza	No	24	0.0	0.00	Yes	6.0	0	150	No	Yes	18.0	Yes	Yes	No	Yes	No	Yes	No	No	4.3	23.1
Yemen, Rep.	No	NO LIMIT	99.1	0.60	Yes	6.0	15	100	No	No	30.0	Yes	Yes	No	Yes	No	Yes	No	Yes	4.3	23.1
Zambia	No	NO LIMIT	63.7	0.40	Yes	5.5	4	100	No	No	24.0	Yes	Yes	No	Yes	No	No	No	No	4.3	46.2
Zimbabwe	No	NO LIMIT	90.0	1.80	Yes	6.0	0	0	No	No	22.0	Yes	Yes	Yes	Yes	Yes	Yes	No	No	13.0	69.3

a. Including renewals.
b. Economies for which 0.0 is shown have no minimum wage.
c. For 2 months a year in case of increase in production.
d. In case of continuous operations.
e. Average for workers with 1, 5 and 10 years of tenure.
f. Whether compulsory before redundancy.
g. Some questions are not applicable ("n.a.") for economies where dismissal due to redundancy is disallowed.

Source: Doing Business database.

References

Aghion, Philippe, Robin Burgess, Stephen Redding and Fabrizio Zilibotti. 2008. "The Unequal Effects of Liberalization: Evidence from Dismantling the License Raj in India." *American Economic Review* 98 (4): 1397–412.

Albers, Pim. 2009. "Justice Sector Performance Measurement: Experiences from the Netherlands." Available at http://serbiamdtf.org/.

Alesina, Alberto, Silvia Ardagna, Giuseppe Nicoletti and Fabio Schiantarelli. 2005. "Regulation and Investment." *Journal of the European Economic Association* 3 (4): 791–825.

Alvarez de la Campa, Alejandro, Everett T. Wohlers, Yair Baranes and Sevi Simavi. 2010. *Secured Transactions Systems and Collateral Registries.* Washington, DC: International Finance Corporation.

Amin, Mohammad. 2010. "Gender and Firm-Size: Evidence from Africa." *Economics Bulletin* 30 (1): 663–68.

Amin, Mohammad, and Rita Ramalho. Forthcoming. "Micro Reforms and Labor Productivity." Enterprise Notes Series, Enterprise Analysis Unit, World Bank Group. http://www.enterprisesurveys.org/.

Antunes, Antonio, and Tiago Cavalcanti. 2007. "Start Up Costs, Limited Enforcement, and the Hidden Economy." *European Economic Review* 51 (1): 203–24.

Anzoategui, Diego, María Soledad Martinez Pería and Roberto Rocha. 2010. "Bank Competition in the Middle East and Northern Africa Region." Policy Research Working Paper 5363, World Bank, Washington, DC.

Ardagna, Silvia, and Annamaria Lusardi. 2008. "Explaining International Differences in Entrepreneurship: The Role of Individual Characteristics and Regulatory Constraints." NBER Working Paper 14012, National Bureau of Economic Research, Cambridge, MA.

___. 2009. "Where Does Regulation Hurt? Evidence from New Businesses across Countries." NBER Working Paper 14747, National Bureau of Economic Research, Cambridge, MA.

___. 2010. "Heterogeneity in the Effect of Regulation on Entrepreneurship and Entry Size." *Journal of the European Economic Association* 8 (2–3): 594–605.

Armour, John, and Douglas Cumming. 2008. "Bankruptcy Law and Entrepreneurship." *American Law and Economics Review* 10 (2): 303–50.

AusAID. 2005. *Annual Report 2004–2005.* Commonwealth of Australia. http://www.ausaid.gov.au/.

Ayyagari, Meghana, Thorsten Beck and Asli Demirgüç-Kunt. 2007. "Small and Medium Enterprises across the Globe." *Small Business Economics* 29: 415–34.

Bae, Kee-Hong, and Vidhan K. Goyal. 2009. "Creditor Rights, Enforcement, and Bank Loans." *Journal of Finance* 64 (2): 823–60.

Baker, Edward, Matthew Morey, Aron Gottesman and Benjamin Godridge. 2007. "Corporate Governance Ratings in Emerging Markets: Implications for Market Valuation, Internal Firm-Performance, Dividend Payouts and Policy." CRIF Seminar series, paper 5, Frank J. Petrilli Center for Research in International Finance, Fordham University. http://fordham.bepress.com/.

Barseghyan, Levon. 2008. "Entry Costs and Cross-Country Differences in Productivity and Output." *Journal of Economic Growth* 13 (2): 145–67.

Barseghyan, Levon, and Riccardo DiCecio. 2009. "Entry Costs, Industry Structure and Cross-Country Income and TFP Differences." Working Paper 2009-005C, Federal Reserve Bank of St. Louis.

Barth, James, Chen Lin, Ping Lin and Frank M. Song. 2009. "Corruption in Bank Lending to Firms: Cross-Country Micro Evidence on the Beneficial Role of Competition and Information Sharing." *Journal of Financial Economics* 91: 361–88.

Bauer, Rob, Nadja Gunster and Roger Otten. 2004. "Empirical Evidence on Corporate Governance in Europe." *Journal of Asset Management* 5 (2): 91–104.

Bayerisches Staatsministerium des Innern. 2002. *Erfahrungsbericht BayBO 1998.* Munich.

Bedi, Jaswinder. 2009. "Impact of Existing Transit/Transport Regimes on Exports: Experiences from the Cotton Sector." Paper presented at the Northern Corridor Transport and Transit Facilitation Conference, Mombasa, Kenya, September 30.

Beruashvili, Nato, and Olin McGill. 2010. "Breaking Up the Logjam: Automated Customs Risk Management System Implementation in Georgia." IFC SmartLessons, World Bank Group, Washington, DC.

Bhatia, Deepak, Subhash C. Bhatnagar and Jiro Tominaga. 2009. "How Do Manual and E-Government Services Compare? Experiences from India." In World Bank, *Information and Communications for Development 2009: Extending Reach and Increasing Impact.* Washington, DC: World Bank.

Bhattacharya, Rina, and Hirut Wolde. 2010. "Constraints on Trade in the MENA Region." IMF Working Paper WP/10/31, International Monetary Fund, Washington, DC.

bin Haji Ridzuan, Datuk Mohad Salan. 2006. "Tax Reform and the Self-Assessment in Malaysia." Paper presented at the Asian Development Bank Tax Administration Course 2006, Siem Reap, Cambodia, March 21–23.

BIZCLIR (Business Climate Legal & Institutional Reform). 2007. "Customs Automation and Process Reform: Lessons from Kenya." Best Practices for the Business Environment 12. http://bizclir.com/.

Bosch, Mariano, and Julen Esteban-Pretel. 2009. "Cyclical Informality and Unemployment." CIRJE Discussion Paper F-613, Center for International Research on the Japanese Economy, Faculty of Economics, University of Tokyo.

Botero, Juan Carlos, Simeon Djankov, Rafael La Porta, Florencio López-de-Silanes and Andrei Shleifer. 2004. "The Regulation of Labor." *Quarterly Journal of Economics* 119 (4): 1339–82.

Botero, Juan Carlos, Rafael La Porta, Florencio López-de-Silanes, Andrei Shleifer and Alexander Volokh. 2003. "Judicial Reform." *World Bank Research Observer* 18 (1): 67–88.

BOVESPA (São Paulo Stock Exchange). 2010. *Annual Report 2009.* http://www.bmfbovespa.com.br/.

Brown, Martin, Tullio Jappelli and Marco Pagano. 2009. "Information Sharing and Credit: Firm-Level Evidence from Transition Countries." *Journal of Financial Intermediation* 18: 151–72.

Bruhn, Miriam. 2008. "License to Sell: The Effect of Business Registration Reform on Entrepreneurial Activity in Mexico." Policy Research Working Paper 4538, World Bank, Washington, DC.

Calderon, César, and Luis Servén. 2003. "The Output Cost of Latin America's Infrastructure Gap." In *The Limits of Stabilization: Infrastructure, Public Deficits, and Growth in Latin America*, ed. William R. Easterly and Luis Servén. Washington, DC: World Bank.

Cardenas, Mauricio, and Sandra Rozo. 2009. "Firm Informality in Colombia: Problems and Solutions." *Desarrollo y Sociedad*, no. 63: 211–43.

CEPEJ (European Commission for the Efficiency of Justice). 2006. *Compendium of "Best Practices" on Time Management of Judicial Proceedings*. Strasbourg: Council of Europe.

CGAP (Consultative Group to Assist the Poor) and World Bank. 2010. *Financial Access 2010: The State of Financial Inclusion through the Crisis*. Washington, DC: World Bank.

Chang, Roberto, Linda Kaltani and Norman Loayza. 2009. "Openness Can Be Good for Growth: The Role of Policy Complementarities." *Journal of Development Economics* 90: 33–49.

Chemin, Matthieu. 2009. "The Impact of the Judiciary on Entrepreneurship: Evaluation of Pakistan's 'Access to Justice Programme.'" *Journal of Public Economics* 93: 114–25.

Cheung, Yan-Leung, P. Raghavendra Rau and Aris Stouraitis. 2006. "Tunneling, Propping, and Expropriation: Evidence from Connected-Party Transactions in Hong Kong." *Journal of Financial Economics* 82 (2): 343–86.

Chhabra, Rama. 2003. "Women in Informal Sector." *Indian Journal of Training and Development* 33 (1–2): 127–34.

Ciccone, Antonio, and Elias Papaioannou. 2007. "Red Tape and Delayed Entry." *Journal of the European Economic Association* 5 (2–3): 444–58.

Commercial Court of Podgorica. 2009. *Annual Report of the Commercial Court 2009* (Godisnji izvjestaj za 2009). Podgorica, Montenegro.

Crain, Mark. 2005. "The Impact of Regulatory Costs on Small Firms." Office of Advocacy, U.S. Small Business Administration, Washington, DC.

Cuñat, Alejandro, and Marc Melitz. 2007. "Volatility, Labor Market Flexibility and the Pattern of Comparative Advantage." NBER Working Paper 13062, National Bureau of Economic Research, Cambridge, MA.

Dabla-Norris, Era, and Gabriela Inchauste. 2008. "Informality and Regulations: What Drives the Growth of Firms?" *IMF Staff Papers* 5 (1): 50–82.

Dahya, Jay, Orlin Dimitrov and John McConnell. 2008. "Dominant Shareholders, Corporate Boards, and Corporate Value: A Cross-Country Analysis." *Journal of Financial Economics* 87 (1): 73–100.

Deininger, Klaus, and Juan Sebastian Chamorro. 2002. "Investment and Equity Effects of Land Regularization: The Case of Nicaragua." World Bank, Washington, DC.

Dennis, Allen. 2010. "Global Economic Crisis and Trade: The Role of Trade Facilitation." *Applied Economics Letters*. Published electronically May 19 (iFirst).

Depken, Craig, and Robert Sonora. 2005. "Asymmetric Effects of Economic Freedom on International Trade Flows." *International Journal of Business and Economics* 4 (2): 141–55.

de Soto, Hernando. 2000. *The Mystery of Capital: Why Capitalism Triumphs in the West and Fails Everywhere Else*. New York: Basic Books.

Dewaelheyns, Nico, and Cynthia Van Hulle. 2009a. "Bankruptcy Reform: Evidence from a Survey among Judges and Receivers." *Applied Economics Letters*. Published electronically September 24 (iFirst).

———. 2009b. "Filtering Speed in a Continental European Reorganization Procedure." *International Review of Law and Economics* 29 (4): 375–87.

De Wulf, Luc, and Jose B. Sokol. 2004. *Customs Modernization Initiatives: Case Studies*. Washington, DC: World Bank.

Djankov, Simeon. 2009a. "Bankruptcy Regimes during Financial Distress." World Bank, Washington, DC.

———. 2009b. "The Regulation of Entry: A Survey." *World Bank Research Observer* 24 (2): 183–203.

Djankov, Simeon, Caroline Freund and Cong S. Pham. 2010. "Trading on Time." *Review of Economics and Statistics* 92 (1): 166–73.

Djankov, Simeon, Caralee McLiesh and Rita Ramalho. 2006. "Regulation and Growth." *Economics Letters* 92 (3): 395–401.

Djankov, Simeon, Caralee McLiesh and Andrei Shleifer. 2007. "Private Credit in 129 Countries." *Journal of Financial Economics* 84 (2): 299–329.

Djankov, Simeon, Oliver Hart, Caralee McLiesh and Andrei Shleifer. 2008. "Debt Enforcement around the World." *Journal of Political Economy* 116 (6): 1105–49.

Djankov, Simeon, Rafael La Porta, Florencio López-de-Silanes and Andrei Shleifer. 2002. "The Regulation of Entry." *Quarterly Journal of Economics* 117 (1): 1–37.

———. 2003. "Courts." *Quarterly Journal of Economics* 118 (2): 453–517.

———. 2008. "The Law and Economics of Self-Dealing." *Journal of Financial Economics* 88 (3): 430–65.

Djankov, Simeon, Darshini Manraj, Caralee McLiesh and Rita Ramalho. 2005. "Doing Business Indicators: Why Aggregate, and How to Do It." World Bank, Washington, DC.

Djankov, Simeon, Tim Ganser, Caralee McLeish, Rita Ramalho and Andrei Shleifer. 2010. "The Effect of Corporate Taxes on Investment and Entrepreneurship." *American Economic Journal: Macroeconomics* 2 (3): 31–64.

Dollar, David, Mary Hallward-Driemeier and Taye Mengistae. 2005. "Investment Climate and International Integration." Policy Research Working Paper 3323, World Bank, Washington, DC.

Durnev, Art, and E. Han Kim. 2005. "To Steal or Not to Steal: Firm Attributes, Legal Environment, and Valuation." *Journal of Finance* 60: 1461–93.

Duryea, Suzanne, Gustavo Marquéz, Carmen Pagés and Stefano Scarpetta. 2006. "For Better or for Worse? Job and Earnings Mobility in Nine Middle- and Low-Income Countries." *Brookings Trade Forum 2006*, pp. 187–203.

EBRD (European Bank for Reconstruction and Development). 2006. "The Enforcement of Judgments in Civil and Commercial Cases in the New EU Member States." In *Law in Transition Online 2006*. London: EBRD. http://www.ebrd.com/.

Eifert, Benjamin. 2007. "Infrastructure and Market Structure in Least-Developed Countries." Department of Economics, University of California, Berkeley.

Electronic Proceedings Project. 2010. "Brazilian Justice in the Virtual Era." Handout at World Bank conference. Superior Court of Justice, Brasília.

Ellis, Amanda, Claire Manuel and C. Mark Blackden. 2006. *Gender and Economic Growth in Uganda: Unleashing the Power of Women*. Washington, DC: World Bank.

Espinosa-Wang, Alejandro. Forthcoming. "Private Help for a Public Problem." World Bank, Washington, DC. http://www.reformersclub.org/.

European Commission. 2010. "European Good Practices: European eGovernment Awards—Winners 2009." Brussels. Available at http://www.uyap.gov.tr/english/makale/awards-articles2009.pdf.

Field, Erica. 2007. "Entitled to Work: Urban Property Rights and Labor Supply in Peru." *Quarterly Journal of Economics* 122 (4): 1561–602.

Field, Erica, and Maximo Torero. 2006. "Do Property Titles Increase Credit Access among the Urban Poor? Evidence from a Nationwide Titling Program." Department of Economics, Harvard University, Cambridge, MA; Group for Development Analysis, Lima; and International Food Policy Research Institute, Washington, DC.

Finland Judiciary. 2006. "How to Assess Quality in the Courts?" http://www.oikeus.fi/.

Fisman, Raymond, and Virginia Sarria-Allende. 2004. "Regulation of Entry and the Distortion of Industrial Organization." NBER Working Paper 10929, National Bureau of Economic Research, Cambridge, MA.

Fleisig, Heywood, and Nuria de la Peña. 2003. "Legal and Regulatory Requirements for Effective Rural Financial Markets." Center for the Economic Analysis of Law, Washington, DC.

Fleisig, Heywood, Mehnaz Safavian and Nuria de la Peña. 2006. *Reforming Collateral Laws to Expand Access to Finance.* Washington, DC: World Bank.

Fonseca, Raquel, Paloma Lopez-Garcia and Christopher Pissarides. 2001. "Entrepreneurship, Start-Up Costs and Employment." *European Economic Review* 45 (4–6): 692–705.

Foster, Vivien, and Jevgenijs Steinbuks. 2009. "Paying the Price for Unreliable Power Supplies." Policy Research Working Paper 4913, World Bank, Washington, DC.

Freund, Caroline, and Bineswaree Bolaky. 2008. "Trade, Regulations and Income." *Journal of Development Economics* 87: 309–21.

Funchal, Bruno. 2008. "The Effects of the 2005 Bankruptcy Reform in Brazil." *Economics Letters* 101: 84–86.

Galiani, Sebastian, and Ernesto Schargrodsky. 2006. "Property Rights for the Poor: Effects of Land Titling." Business School Working Paper, Universidad Torcuato Di Tella, Buenos Aires.

Gamboa-Cavazos, Mario, and Frank Schneider. 2007. "Bankruptcy as a Legal Process." Draft, Department of Economics, Harvard University, Cambridge, MA.

Geginat, Carolin, and Rita Ramalho. 2010. "Connecting Businesses to the Electrical Grid in 140 Economies." Paper presented at the International Conference on Infrastructure Economics and Development, Toulouse, January 14–15.

Giné, Xavier, and Inessa Love. 2006. "Do Reorganization Costs Matter for Efficiency? Evidence from a Bankruptcy Reform in Colombia." Policy Research Working Paper 3970, World Bank, Washington, DC.

Gordon, Roger, and Wei Li. 2009. "Tax Structures in Developing Countries: Many Puzzles and a Possible Explanation." *Journal of Public Economics* 93: 855–66.

Grandmont, Renato, Gavin Grant and Flavia Silva. 2004. "Beyond the Numbers—Corporate Governance: Implications for Investors." Deutsche Bank, Frankfurt.

Helble, Matthias Carl, Ben Shepherd and John S. Wilson. 2009. "Transparency and Regional Integration in the Asia Pacific." *World Economy* 32 (3): 479–508.

Helpman, Elhanan, Marc Melitz and Yona Rubinstein. 2008. "Estimating Trade Flows: Trading Partners and Trading Volumes." *Quarterly Journal of Economics* 123 (2): 441–87.

Hertveldt, Sabine. 2008. "Pragmatism Leads the Way in Setting Up Specialized Commercial Courts." *Doing Business* case study: Rwanda. World Bank Group, Washington, DC.

Hibbs, Douglas A., and Violeta Piculescu. 2010. "Tax Toleration and Tax Compliance: How Government Affects the Propensity of Firms to Enter the Unofficial Economy." *American Journal of Political Science* 54 (1): 18–33.

Ho, Yuen-Ping, and Poh-Kam Wong. 2006. "Financing, Regulatory Costs and Entrepreneurial Propensity." *Small Business Economics* 28: 187–204.

Hoekman, Bernard, and Alessandro Nicita. 2009. "Trade Policy, Trade Cost, and Developing Country Trade." Policy Research Working Paper 4797, World Bank, Washington, DC.

Houston, Joel, Chen Lin, Ping Lin and Yue Ma. 2010. "Creditor Rights, Information Sharing, and Bank Risk Taking." *Journal of Financial Economics* 96 (3): 485–512.

IFC (International Finance Corporation). 2006. *Case Studies in Good Corporate Governance Practices.* Companies Circle of the Latin American Corporate Governance Roundtable. Washington, DC: World Bank Group.

____. 2008a. "Georgia: After Three Years of Licensing Reform." Analytical Note, World Bank Group, Washington, DC.

____. 2008b. *Novo Mercado and Its Followers: Case Studies in Corporate Governance Reform.* Washington, DC: World Bank Group.

Iimi, Atsushi. 2008. "Effects of Improving Infrastructure Quality on Business Costs: Evidence from Firm-Level Data." Policy Research Working Paper 4581, World Bank, Washington, DC.

ILO (International Labour Organization). 2009. *World of Work* 66. Geneva: ILO.

ILO and SERCOTEC (Servicio de Cooperación Técnica). 2010. *La situación de la micro y pequeña empresa en Chile.* Santiago.

Imam, Patrick A., and Jacob F. Davina. 2007. "Effect of Corruption on Tax Revenues in the Middle East." IMF Working Paper WP/07/270, International Monetary Fund, Washington, DC.

Indonesia Stock Exchange. 2009. *Annual Report 2008.* http://www.idx.co.id/.

International Tax Dialogue. 2007. "Taxation of Small and Medium-Size Enterprises." Background paper for the International Tax Dialogue Conference on Taxation of SMEs, Buenos Aires, October 17–19.

Johns, Melissa, and Jean Michel Lobet. 2007. "Protecting Investors from Self-Dealing." In World Bank, *Celebrating Reform 2007.* Washington, DC: World Bank Group and U.S. Agency for International Development.

Kaplan, David, Eduardo Piedra and Enrique Seira. 2007. "Entry Regulation and Business Start-Ups: Evidence from Mexico." Policy Research Working Paper 4322, World Bank, Washington, DC.

Kauffman Foundation. n.d. "Young People Want to Be Their Own Boss to Realize Their Ideas." http://www.kauffman,org/.

Kendall, Jake, Nataliya Mylenko and Alejandro Ponce. 2010. "Measuring Financial Access around the World." Policy Research Working Paper 5253, World Bank, Washington, DC.

Kenny, Charles. 2007. "Construction, Corruption, and Developing Countries." Policy Research Working Paper 4271, World Bank, Washington, DC.

Klapper, Leora, and Inessa Love. 2004. "Corporate Governance, Investor Protection, and Performance in Emerging Markets." *Journal of Corporate Finance* 10 (5): 703–28.

____. 2010. "The Impact of the Financial Crisis on New Firm Registration." Policy Research Working Paper 5444, World Bank, Washington, DC.

Klapper, Leora, and Simon Parker. 2010. "Gender and Business Environment for New Firm Creation." *World Bank Research Observer*. Published electronically February 25. doi:10.1093/wbro/lkp032.

Klapper, Leora, and Christine Richmond. 2010. "The Political Economy of Firm Size." Paper presented at the World Bank–Kauffman Foundation Conference on Entrepreneurship and Growth.

Klapper, Leora, Luc Laeven and Raghuram Rajan. 2006. "Entry Regulation as a Barrier to Entrepreneurship." *Journal of Financial Economics* 82 (3): 591–629.

Klapper, Leora, Anat Lewin and Juan Manuel Quesada Delgado. 2009. "The Impact of the Business Environment on the Business Creation Process." Policy Research Working Paper 4937, World Bank, Washington, DC.

Korea Customs Service. 2010. "The KCS' Challenging Drive for Trade Facilitation." http://www.customs.go.kr.

Kozolchyk, Boris. 2009. "Modernization of Commercial Law: International Uniformity and Economic Development." *Brooklyn Journal of International Law* 34 (3): 709–47.

Kozolchyk, Boris, and Dale Furnish. 2006. "The OAS Model Law on Secured Transactions: A Comparative Analysis." Arizona Legal Studies Discussion Paper 06-39, University of Arizona Rogers College of Law, Tucson.

KPMG. 2009. "Competitive Alternatives: KPMG's Guide to International Business Location." http://www.competitivealternatives.com.

La Porta, Rafael, and Andrei Shleifer. 2008. "The Unofficial Economy and Economic Development." Tuck School of Business Working Paper 2009-57. Available at http://ssrn.com/abstract=1304760.

Lee, Kyu Sik, Alex Anas and Gi-Taik Oh. 1996. "Cost of Infrastructure Deficiencies in Manufacturing in Indonesia, Nigeria and Thailand." Policy Research Working Paper 1604, World Bank, Washington, DC.

Levchenko, Andrei. 2007. "Institutional Quality and International Trade." *Review of Economic Studies* 74 (3): 791–819.

Li, Yue, and John Wilson. 2009. "Trade Facilitation and Expanding the Benefits of Trade: Evidence from the Firm-Level Data." ARTNet Working Paper Series, no. 71, Asia Pacific Research and Training Network on Trade, Bangkok.

Lieberman, Ira, Mario Gobbo, William P. Mako and Ruth L. Neyens. 2005. "Recent International Experiences in the Use of Voluntary Workouts under Distressed Conditions." In *Corporate Restructuring: Lessons from Experience*, ed. Michael Pomerleano and William Shaw. Washington, DC: World Bank.

Lippman, Jonathan. 2010. *The State of the Judiciary 2010*. New York State Unified Court System. http://www.courts.state.ny.us/.

Lobet, Jean Michel. 2009. "Seizing the Opportunity for Effective Legal Reform in Albania." Celebrating Reform 2009 case study. World Bank Group, Washington, DC. http://www.doingbusiness.org.

Love, Inessa. 2010. "Corporate Governance and Performance around the World: What We Know and What We Don't." *World Bank Research Observer*. Published electronically February 4. doi:10.1093/wbro/lkp030.

Mako, William P. 2005. "Emerging-Market and Crisis Applications for Out-of-Court Workouts: Lessons from East Asia, 1998–2001." In *Corporate Restructuring: Lessons from Experience*, ed. Michael Pomerleano and William Shaw. Washington, DC: World Bank.

Masatlioglu, Yusufcan, and Jamele Rigolini. 2008. "Informality Traps." *B.E. Journal of Economic Analysis & Policy* 8 (1).

McGee, Robert, and Christopher Lingle. 2008. "The Ethics of Tax Evasion: A Survey of Guatemalan Opinion." *Taxation and Public Finance in Transition and Developing Economies* 3: 481–95.

McGinty, Andrew, and V. C. Leow. 2009. "China's Insolvency Law Two Years On: Are Government-Driven Restructurings the New Trend?" *Butterworths Journal of International Banking and Financial Law* 24 (11): 689–92.

Motta, Marialisa, Ana Maria Oviedo and Massimiliano Santini. 2010. "An Open Door for Firms: The Impact of Business Entry Reforms." Viewpoint Note 323, World Bank Group, Washington, DC.

Moullier, Thomas. 2009. "Reforming Building Permits: Why Is It Important and What Can IFC Really Do?" International Finance Corporation, Washington, DC.

Narayan, Deepa, Robert Chambers, Meer Kaul Shah and Patti Petesh. 2000. *Voices of the Poor: Crying Out for Change*. Washington, DC: World Bank.

National Center for State Courts. 2005a. "CourTools: Giving Courts the Tools to Measure Success." Williamsburg, VA. http://www.ncsconline.org/.

———. 2005b. "CourTools: Trial Court Performance Measures." Williamsburg, VA. http://www.ncsconline.org/.

Nunn, Nathan. 2007. "Relationship-Specificity, Incomplete Contracts, and the Pattern of Trade." *Quarterly Journal of Economics* 122 (2): 569–600.

OECD (Organisation for Economic Co-operation and Development). 2004a. *OECD Principles of Corporate Governance*. Paris: OECD.

———. 2004b. "Promoting SMEs for Development." Background report prepared for Second OECD Conference of Ministers Responsible for Small and Medium-Sized Enterprises, Istanbul, June 3–5.

———. 2008. *Employment Outlook: 2008*. Paris: OECD.

———. 2009. *Guide on Fighting Abusive Related-Party Transactions in Asia*. Paris: OECD.

———. 2010. "Construction Industry." *OECD Journal of Competition Law and Policy* 10 (1).

Pal, Mariam. 1997. "Women Entrepreneurs and the Need for Financial Sector Reform." *Economic Reform Today* 2: 26–30.

Pande, Rohini, and Christopher Udry. 2005. "Institutions and Development: A View from Below." Economic Growth Center Working Paper 928, Yale University, New Haven, CT.

Pepys, Mary Noel. 2003. "Corruption and the Justice Sector." U.S. Agency for International Development and Management Systems International, Washington, DC. http://www.usaid.gov/.

Perotti, Enrico, and Paolo Volpin. 2004. "Lobbying on Entry." CEPR Discussion Paper 4519, Centre for Economic Policy Research, London.

Pierre, Gaëlle, and Stefano Scarpetta. 2007. "How Labor Market Policies Can Combine Workers' Protection with Job Creation: A Partial Review of Some Key Issues and Policy Options." Social Protection Discussion Paper 716, World Bank, Washington, DC.

PricewaterhouseCoopers. 2005. "The Economic Impact of Accelerating Permit Processes on Local Development and Government Revenues." Report prepared for the American Institute of Architects, Washington, DC.

Qian, Jun, and Philip E. Strahan. 2007. "How Laws and Institutions Shape Financial Contracts: The Case of Bank Loans." *Journal of Finance* 62 (6): 2803–34.

Ranjan, Priya, and Jae Young Lee. 2007. "Contract Enforcement and International Trade." *Economics and Politics* 19 (2): 191–218.

Reinikka, Ritva, and Jakob Svensson. 1999. "Confronting Competition: Investment Response and Constraints in Uganda." Policy Research Working Paper 2242, World Bank, Washington, DC.

Ricard, Lyse. 2008. "Strategies for the Control of Tax Compliance." Paper presented at the 42nd CIAT (Inter-American Center of Tax Administrations) General Assembly, Antigua, Guatemala, April 21–24.

Rocha, Roberto, Subika Farazi, Rania Khouri and Douglas Pearce. 2010. "The Status of Bank Lending to SMEs in the Middle East and North Africa Region: The Results of a Joint Survey of the Union of Arab Banks and the World Bank." World Bank, Washington, DC; and Union of Arab Banks, Beirut.

Samuels, Kristi. 2006. "Rule of Law Reform in Post-Conflict Countries: Operational Initiatives and Lessons Learnt." Social Development Paper 37, World Bank, Washington, DC.

Sarmiento, Alvaro, Krista Lucenti and Aurelio Garcia. 2010. "Automating the Control of Goods in International Transit in Goods: Implementing the TIM in Central America." IFC SmartLessons, World Bank Group, Washington, DC.

Schindler, Kati. 2010. "Credit for What? Informal Credit as a Coping Strategy of Market Women in Northern Ghana." *Journal of Development Studies* 46 (2): 234–53.

Schneider, Friedrich. 2005. "The Informal Sector in 145 Countries." Department of Economics, University Linz.

Schneider, Eriedrich, and Andres Buehn. 2009. "Shadow Economics and Corruption All Over the World: Estimates for 120 countries." *Economics*. Published electronically October 27. doi: 10.5018/economics-ejournal.ja.2007-9.

Simavi, Sevi, Clare Manuel and Mark Blackden. 2010. *Gender Dimensions of Investment Climate Reform: A Guide for Policy Makers and Practitioners.* Washington, DC: World Bank.

Simovic, Vladimir, Vojkan Vaskovic and Dusan Poznanovic. 2009. "A Model of Credit Bureau in Serbia: Instrument for Preserving Stability of the Banking Sector in Conditions of the Global Economic Crisis." *Journal of Applied Quantitative Methods* 4 (4): 429–39.

Simpson, John, and Joachim Menze. 2000. "Ten Years of Secured Transactions Reforms." European Bank for Reconstruction and Development, London.

Singapore Customs Service. 2007. *Annual Report 2006/07.* Singapore.

South Africa, Department of Trade and Industry. 2004. "Review of Ten Years of Small Business Support in South Africa, 1994–2004." Enterprise Development Unit, Department of Trade and Industry, Pretoria.

Srinivasan, Jayashree, and Marina Turlakova. 2010. "Trade-Offs in Reforming Internal Wiring Regulations in South Africa." Draft, World Bank, Washington, DC.

Stein, Peer. 2010. "Towards Universal Access: Addressing the Global Challenge of Financial Inclusion—Challenges and the Way Forward." Paper presented at Korea–World Bank High-Level Conference on Post-Crisis Growth and Development, Busan, Korea, June 3–4.

Turner, Michael, and Robin Varghese. 2007. *Economic Impacts of Payment Reporting Participation in Latin America.* Chapel Hill, NC: PERC Press.

Turner, Michael, Robin Varghese and Patrick Walker. 2007. *On the Impact of Credit Payment Reporting on the Financial Sector and Overall Economic Performance in Japan.* Chapel Hill, NC: PERC Press.

Turner, Michael, Robin Varghese, Patrick Walker and Katrina Dusek. 2009. *Credit Reporting Customer Payment Data: Impact on Customer Payment Behavior and Furnisher Costs and Benefits.* Chapel Hill, NC: PERC Press.

USAID (U.S. Agency for International Development). 2010. "Report on the Use of Audio Recording Equipment, Integrated Case Management System and Web-Pages by Moldova Courts." Moldova Rapid Governance Support Program, Chisinau, Moldova.

U.S. Fire Administration. 2008. "Electrical Fire Safety: A Factsheet on Home Electrical Fire Prevention." http://www.usfa.dhs.gov/.

Uttamchandani, Mahesh, and Antonia Menezes. 2010. "The Freedom to Fail: Why Small Business Insolvency Regimes Are Critical for Emerging Markets." *International Corporate Rescue* 7 (4): 262–68.

Van Stel, Andre, David Storey and Roy Thurik. 2007. "The Effect of Business Regulations on Nascent and Young Business Entrepreneurship." *Small Business Economics* 28 (2–3): 171–86.

Visaria, Sujata. 2009. "Legal Reform and Loan Repayment: The Microeconomic Impact of Debt Recovery Tribunals in India." *American Economic Journal: Applied Economics* 1 (3): 59–81.

Vodopivec, Milan. 2009. "Introducing Unemployment Insurance to Developing Countries." Social Protection Discussion Paper 907, World Bank, Washington, DC.

World Bank. 2003. *Doing Business in 2004: Understanding Regulation.* Washington, DC: World Bank Group.

___. 2008. *Finance for All: Policies and Pitfalls in Expanding Access.* World Bank Policy Research Report. Washington, DC: World Bank.

___. 2009a. *Doing Business in India 2009.* Washington, DC: World Bank Group. http://www.doingbusiness.org.

___. 2009b. *Doing Business in Indonesia 2010.* Washington, DC: World Bank Group. http://www.doingbusiness.org.

___. 2009c. *Doing Business in Russia 2009.* Washington, DC: World Bank Group. http://www.doingbusiness.org.

___. 2009d. *Doing Business 2010: Reforming through Difficult Times.* Washington, DC: World Bank Group.

___. 2009e. "Guidance Note for World Bank Group Staff on the Use of the Doing Business Employing Workers Indicator for Policy Advice." http://www.doingbusiness.org.

___. 2009f. *How Many Stops in a One-Stop Shop?* Washington, DC: World Bank Group.

___. 2009g. *Information and Communications for Development 2009: Extending Reach and Increasing Impact.* Washington, DC: World Bank.

___. 2009h. "Running a Business in Georgia." Country Notes Series, Enterprise Analysis Unit, World Bank Group. http://www.enterprisesurveys.org/.

___. 2010a. *Doing Business in Nigeria 2010.* Washington, DC: World Bank Group.

___. 2010b. *Women, Business and the Law 2010: Measuring Legal Gender Parity for Entrepreneurs and Workers in 128 Economies.* Washington, DC: World Bank Group.

___. 2010c. *World Development Indicators 2010.* Washington, DC: World Bank.

World Bank Independent Evaluation Group. 2008. *Doing Business: An Independent Evaluation—Taking the Measure of the World Bank–IFC Doing Business Indicators.* Washington, DC: World Bank.

WTO (World Trade Organization). 2010. *World Trade Report 2010.* Geneva: WTO.

Yoshino, Yutaka. 2008. "Domestic Constraints, Firm Characteristics, and Geographical Diversification of Firm-Level Manufacturing Exports in Africa." Policy Research Working Paper 4575, World Bank, Washington, DC.

Data notes

The indicators presented and analyzed in *Doing Business* measure business regulation and the protection of property rights—and their effect on businesses, especially small and medium-size domestic firms. First, the indicators document the degree of regulation, such as the number of procedures to start a business or to register and transfer commercial property. Second, they gauge regulatory outcomes, such as the time and cost to enforce a contract, go through bankruptcy or trade across borders. Third, they measure the extent of legal protections of property, for example, the protections of investors against looting by company directors or the range of assets that can be used as collateral according to secured transactions laws. Fourth, a set of indicators documents the tax

TABLE 14.1

How many experts does *Doing Business* consult?

Indicator set	Contributors
Starting a business	1,406
Dealing with construction permits	605
Registering property	1,128
Getting credit	1,127
Protecting investors	874
Paying taxes	891
Trading across borders	1,279
Enforcing contracts	984
Closing a business	852
Getting electricity	602
Employing workers	862

burden on businesses. Finally, a set of indicators measures different aspects of employment regulation.

The data for all sets of indicators in *Doing Business 2011* are for June 2010.[1]

METHODOLOGY

The *Doing Business* data are collected in a standardized way. To start, the *Doing Business* team, with academic advisers, designs a survey. The survey uses a simple business case to ensure comparability across economies and over time—with assumptions about the legal form of the business, its size, its location and the nature of its operations. Surveys are administered through more than 8,200 local experts, including lawyers, business consultants, accountants, freight forwarders, government officials and other professionals routinely administering or advising on legal and regulatory requirements (table 14.1). These experts have several rounds of interaction with the *Doing Business* team, involving conference calls, written correspondence and visits by the team. For *Doing Business 2011* team members visited 33 economies to verify data and recruit respondents. The data from surveys are subjected to numerous tests for robustness, which lead to revisions or expansions of the information collected.

The *Doing Business* methodology offers several advantages. It is transparent, using factual information about what laws and regulations say and allowing multiple interactions with local respondents to clarify potential misinterpretations of questions. Having representative samples of respondents is not an issue, as the texts of the relevant laws and regulations are collected and answers checked for accuracy. The methodology is inexpensive and easily replicable, so data can be collected in a large sample of economies. Because standard assumptions are used in the data collection, comparisons and benchmarks are valid across economies. Finally, the data not only highlight the extent of specific regulatory obstacles to business but also identify their source and point to what might be reformed.

LIMITS TO WHAT IS MEASURED

The *Doing Business* methodology has 5 limitations that should be considered when interpreting the data. First, the collected data refer to businesses in the economy's largest business city and may not be representative of regulation in other parts of the economy. To address this limitation, subnational *Doing Business* indicators were created for 6 economies in 2009/10: Colombia, Indonesia, Kenya, Nigeria, Pakistan and Russia.[2] A city profile on Zanzibar, Tanzania, was also published in 2009/10. A subnational study is under way in the Philippines. In addition, a city profile is under way for Juba, Southern Sudan, and a regional report has been started in Southeastern Europe, covering 7 economies—Albania, Bosnia and Herzegovina, Kosovo, FYR Macedonia, Moldova, Montenegro and Serbia—and 16 cities. Increasingly, such studies are being periodically updated to measure progress over time or to expand geographic coverage to additional cities. This year that is the case for the subnational studies in Colombia, Nigeria, Pakistan and the Philippines and for the regional study in Southeast Europe. The subnational studies point to significant differences in the speed of reform and the ease of doing business across cities in the same economy.

Second, the data often focus on a specific business form—generally a limited liability company (or its legal equivalent) of a specified size—and may not be representative of the regulation on other businesses, for example, sole proprietorships. Third, transactions described in a standardized case scenario refer to a specific set of issues and may not represent the full set of issues a business encounters. Fourth, the measures of time involve an element of judgment by the expert respondents. When sources indicate different estimates, the time indicators reported in *Doing Business* represent the median values of several responses given under the assumptions of the standardized case.

Finally, the methodology assumes that a business has full information on what is required and does not waste time when completing procedures. In practice, completing a procedure may take longer if the business lacks information or is unable to follow up promptly. Alternatively, the business may choose to disregard some burdensome procedures. For both reasons the time delays reported in *Doing Business 2011* would differ from the recollection of entrepreneurs reported in the World Bank Enterprise Surveys or other perception surveys.

CHANGES IN WHAT IS MEASURED

The methodology for the employing workers indicators was updated this year, with guidance from a consultative group of relevant experts and stakeholders.[3] The employing workers indicators are not included in this year's aggregate ranking on the ease of doing business.

Changes agreed as of the date of publication are the following: the calculation of the minimum wage ratio was changed to ensure that no economy can receive the highest score if it has no minimum wage at all, if the law provides a regulatory mechanism for the minimum wage that is not enforced in practice, if there is only a customary minimum wage or if the minimum wage applies only to the public sector. A minimum threshold was set for paid annual leave and a ceiling for working days allowed per week to ensure that no economy benefits in the scoring from excessive flexibility in these areas. Finally, the calculation of the redundancy cost and of the annual leave period for the rigidity of hours index was changed to refer to the average value for a worker with 1 year of tenure, a worker with 5 years and a worker with 10 years rather than the value for a worker with 20 years of tenure.

Economy characteristics

GROSS NATIONAL INCOME (GNI) PER CAPITA

Doing Business 2011 reports 2009 income per capita as published in the World Bank's *World Development Indicators 2010*. Income is calculated using the Atlas method (current US$). For cost indicators expressed as a percentage of income per capita, 2009 GNI in U.S. dollars is used as the denominator. GNI data were not available from the World Bank for Afghanistan, The Bahamas, Bahrain, Belize, Cyprus, Eritrea, Guyana, Haiti, Hong Kong SAR (China), Madagascar, New Zealand, Oman, Puerto Rico, Qatar, Saudi Arabia, Suriname, Switzerland, Taiwan (China), Timor-Leste, the United Arab Emirates, West Bank and Gaza and Zimbabwe. In these cases GDP or GNP per capita data and growth rates from the International Monetary Fund's World Economic Outlook database

DATA CHALLENGES AND REVISIONS

Most laws and regulations underlying the *Doing Business* data are available on the *Doing Business* website at http://www.doingbusiness.org. All the sample surveys and the details underlying the indicators are also published on the website. Questions on the methodology and challenges to data can be submitted through the website's "Ask a Question" function at http://www.doingbusiness.org.

Doing Business publishes 8,967 indicators each year. To create these indicators, the team measures more than 52,000 data points, each of which is made available on the *Doing Business* website. Historical data for each indicator and economy are available on the website, beginning with the first year the indicator or economy was included in the report. To provide a comparable time series for research, the *Doing Business* website provides historical data sets adjusted for changes in methodology and

and the Economist Intelligence Unit were used.

REGION AND INCOME GROUP

Doing Business uses the World Bank regional and income group classifications, available at http://www.worldbank.org/data/countryclass. The World Bank does not assign regional classifications to high-income economies. For the purpose of the *Doing Business* report, high-income OECD economies are assigned the "regional" classification *OECD high income*. Figures and tables presenting regional averages include economies from all income groups (low, lower middle, upper middle and high income).

POPULATION

Doing Business 2011 reports midyear 2009 population statistics as published in *World Development Indicators 2010*.

any revisions in data due to corrections. The website also makes available all original data sets used for background papers. The correction rate between *Doing Business 2010* and *Doing Business 2011* is 5.7%.

FIVE-YEAR MEASURE OF CUMULATIVE CHANGE: DB CHANGE SCORE

Doing Business 2011 is introducing a new measure to illustrate how the regulatory environment for business has changed in absolute terms in each economy over the 5 years since *Doing Business 2006* was published. This measure is called the DB change score. In the 9 areas of business regulation included in the aggregate ranking on the ease of doing business in *Doing Business 2011*, the new measure assigns a neutral score if there were no changes in the underlying data, a positive score for changes leading to improvements in the indicators and a negative score for changes having an adverse impact on the indicators.

This measure complements the aggregate ease of doing business ranking, which benchmarks each economy's current performance on the indicators against that of all other economies in the *Doing Business* sample. By showing absolute change over time, the measure illustrates for each economy how much its regulatory environment for business as measured through the *Doing Business* indicators has changed compared with 5 years ago. Economies that achieved the biggest cumulative change in the past 5 years are assigned the highest DB change score.

The DB change score is constructed in 4 steps.

1. As a first step, the absolute difference in scores is calculated for each of the component indicators of the 9 *Doing Business* topics, 28 in all. For example, for starting a business there are 4 indicators: procedures, time, cost (as a percentage of GNI per capita) and paid-in minimum capital requirement (as a percentage of GNI per capita). Annual absolute changes are calculated economy by economy for each of these indicators. For example, if starting a business in an economy took 200 days as measured in *Doing Business 2006* and only 50 as measured in *Doing Business 2007*, a

change of 150 would be recorded for the economy. If instead the time had increased to 350 days, a change of −150 would be recorded.

2. To allow aggregation across all indicators, the results for each indicator are made comparable by normalizing the change values on a scale of 0–1, where a higher value indicates that an economy made a larger absolute improvement on a particular indicator than other economies. As a second step, the values are rescaled once more so that any lowering of an indicator is reflected by a negative score and any improvement by a positive score. A score of 0 indicates that no change occurred.[4]

3. To illustrate the change across all 9 areas of business regulation, a simple average of all scores obtained for the different indicators is taken to calculate a total annual measure of change for each economy. By using a simple average, the new measure follows the approach used in the ease of doing business ranking.

4. Finally, the annual measures of change for each economy are added to illustrate the cumulative change in its business regulatory environment over the past 5 years.

EASE OF DOING BUSINESS RANKING

The ease of doing business index ranks economies from 1 to 183. For each economy the index is calculated as the ranking on the simple average of its percentile rankings on each of the 9 topics included in the index in *Doing Business 2011*: starting a business, dealing with construction permits, registering property, getting credit, protecting investors, paying taxes, trading across borders, enforcing contracts and closing a business. The ranking on each topic is the simple average of the percentile rankings on its component indicators (table 14.2).

If an economy has no laws or regulations covering a specific area—for example, bankruptcy—it receives a "no practice" mark. Similarly, an economy receives a "no practice" or "not possible" mark if regulation exists but is never used in practice or if a competing regulation prohibits such practice. Either way, a "no practice" mark puts the economy at the bottom of the ranking on the relevant indicator.

Here is one example of how the ranking is constructed. In Iceland it takes 5 procedures, 5 days and 2.3% of annual income per capita in fees to open a business. The minimum capital required amounts to 11.97% of income per capita. On these 4 indicators Iceland ranks in

TABLE 14.2

Which indicators make up the ranking?

Starting a business	*Paying taxes*
Procedures, time, cost and paid-in minimum capital to open a new business	Number of tax payments, time to prepare and file tax returns and to pay taxes, total taxes as a share of profit before all taxes borne
Dealing with construction permits	*Trading across borders*
Procedures, time and cost to obtain construction permits, inspections and utility connections	Documents, time and cost to export and import
Registering property	*Enforcing contracts*
Procedures, time and cost to transfer commercial real estate	Procedures, time and cost to resolve a commercial dispute
Getting credit	*Closing a business*
Strength of legal rights index, depth of credit information index	Recovery rate in bankruptcy
Protecting investors	
Strength of investor protection index: extent of disclosure index, extent of director liability index and ease of shareholder suits index	

the 13th, 4th, 15th and 63th percentiles. So on average Iceland ranks in the 24th percentile on the ease of starting a business. It ranks in the 50th percentile on protecting investors, 40th percentile on trading across borders, 10th percentile on enforcing contracts, 9th percentile on closing a business and so on. Higher rankings indicate simpler regulation and stronger protection of property rights. The simple average of Iceland's percentile rankings on all topics is 25%. When all economies are ordered by their average percentile rank, Iceland is in 15th place.

More complex aggregation methods—such as principal components and unobserved components—yield a nearly identical ranking.[5] The choice of aggregation method has little influence on the rankings because the 9 sets of indicators provide sufficiently broad coverage across topics. So *Doing Business* uses the simplest method.

The ease of doing business index is limited in scope. It does not account for an economy's proximity to large markets, the quality of its infrastructure services (other than services related to trading across borders), the strength of its financial system, the security of property from theft and looting, its macroeconomic conditions or the strength of underlying institutions. There remains a large unfinished agenda for research into what regulation constitutes binding constraints, what package of reforms is most effective and how these issues are shaped by the context in an economy. The *Doing Business* indicators provide a new empirical data set that may improve understanding of these issues.

Doing Business 2011 also uses a simple method to calculate which economies improve the most on the ease of doing business. First, it selects the economies that reformed in 3 or more of the 9 topics included in this year's ease of doing business ranking. Twenty-five economies met this criterion: Belarus, Brunei Darussalam, Burkina Faso, Cape Verde, the Democratic Republic of Congo, Georgia, Grenada, Guyana, Hungary, Indonesia, the Islamic Republic of Iran, Kazakh-

stan, Lithuania, Mali, Montenegro, Peru, Rwanda, Saudi Arabia, Sierra Leone, Slovenia, Sweden, Tajikistan, Ukraine, Vietnam and Zambia. Second, *Doing Business* ranks these economies on the increase in their ranking on the ease of doing business from the previous year using comparable rankings.

IN THE EASE OF DOING BUSINESS RANKING

This year's aggregate ranking on the ease of doing business is based on 9 indicator sets: starting a business, dealing with construction permits, registering property, getting credit, protecting investors, paying taxes, trading across borders, enforcing contracts and closing a business.

STARTING A BUSINESS

Doing Business records all procedures that are officially required for an entrepreneur to start up and formally operate an industrial or commercial business. These include obtaining all necessary licenses and permits and completing any required notifications, verifications or inscriptions for the company and employees with relevant authorities. The ranking on the ease of starting a business is the simple average of the percentile rankings on its component indicators (figure 14.1).

After a study of laws, regulations and publicly available information on business entry, a detailed list of procedures is developed, along with the time and cost of complying with each procedure under normal circumstances and the paid-in minimum capital requirements. Subsequently, local incorporation lawyers and government officials complete and verify the data.

Information is also collected on the sequence in which procedures are to be completed and whether procedures may be carried out simultaneously. It is assumed that any required information is readily available and that all agencies involved in the start-up process function without corruption. If answers by local

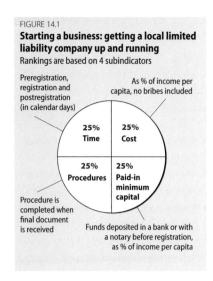

FIGURE 14.1
Starting a business: getting a local limited liability company up and running
Rankings are based on 4 subindicators

Preregistration, registration and postregistration (in calendar days)

As % of income per capita, no bribes included

25% Time   25% Cost

25% Procedures   25% Paid-in minimum capital

Procedure is completed when final document is received

Funds deposited in a bank or with a notary before registration, as % of income per capita

experts differ, inquiries continue until the data are reconciled.

To make the data comparable across economies, several assumptions about the business and the procedures are used.

ASSUMPTIONS ABOUT THE BUSINESS

The business:

- Is a limited liability company. If there is more than one type of limited liability company in the economy, the limited liability form most popular among domestic firms is chosen. Information on the most popular form is obtained from incorporation lawyers or the statistical office.
- Operates in the economy's largest business city.
- Is 100% domestically owned and has 5 owners, none of whom is a legal entity.
- Has start-up capital of 10 times income per capita at the end of 2009, paid in cash.
- Performs general industrial or commercial activities, such as the production or sale to the public of products or services. The business does not perform foreign trade activities and does not handle products subject to a special tax regime, for example, liquor or tobacco. It is not using heavily polluting production processes.

- Leases the commercial plant and offices and is not a proprietor of real estate.
- Does not qualify for investment incentives or any special benefits.
- Has at least 10 and up to 50 employees 1 month after the commencement of operations, all of them nationals.
- Has a turnover of at least 100 times income per capita.
- Has a company deed 10 pages long.

PROCEDURES

A procedure is defined as any interaction of the company founders with external parties (for example, government agencies, lawyers, auditors or notaries). Interactions between company founders or company officers and employees are not counted as procedures. Procedures that must be completed in the same building but in different offices are counted as separate procedures. If founders have to visit the same office several times for different sequential procedures, each is counted separately. The founders are assumed to complete all procedures themselves, without middlemen, facilitators, accountants or lawyers, unless the use of such a third party is mandated by law. If the services of professionals are required, procedures conducted by such

professionals on behalf of the company are counted separately. Each electronic procedure is counted separately. If 2 procedures can be completed through the same website but require separate filings, they are counted as 2 procedures.

Both pre- and postincorporation procedures that are officially required for an entrepreneur to formally operate a business are recorded (table 14.3).

Procedures required for official correspondence or transactions with public agencies are also included. For example, if a company seal or stamp is required on official documents, such as tax declarations, obtaining the seal or stamp is counted. Similarly, if a company must open a bank account before registering for sales tax or value added tax, this transaction is included as a procedure. Shortcuts are counted only if they fulfill 4 criteria: they are legal, they are available to the general public, they are used by the majority of companies, and avoiding them causes substantial delays.

Only procedures required of all businesses are covered. Industry-specific procedures are excluded. For example, procedures to comply with environmental regulations are included only when they apply to all businesses conducting general commercial or industrial activities. Procedures that the company un-

dergoes to connect to electricity, water, gas and waste disposal services are not included.

TIME

Time is recorded in calendar days. The measure captures the median duration that incorporation lawyers indicate is necessary to complete a procedure with minimum follow-up with government agencies and no extra payments. It is assumed that the minimum time required for each procedure is 1 day. Although procedures may take place simultaneously, they cannot start on the same day (that is, simultaneous procedures start on consecutive days). A procedure is considered completed once the company has received the final document, such as the company registration certificate or tax number. If a procedure can be accelerated for an additional cost, the fastest procedure is chosen. It is assumed that the entrepreneur does not waste time and commits to completing each remaining procedure without delay. The time that the entrepreneur spends on gathering information is ignored. It is assumed that the entrepreneur is aware of all entry regulations and their sequence from the beginning but has had no prior contact with any of the officials.

COST

Cost is recorded as a percentage of the economy's income per capita. It includes all official fees and fees for legal or professional services if such services are required by law. Fees for purchasing and legalizing company books are included if these transactions are required by law. The company law, the commercial code and specific regulations and fee schedules are used as sources for calculating costs. In the absence of fee schedules, a government officer's estimate is taken as an official source. In the absence of a government officer's estimate, estimates of incorporation lawyers are used. If several incorporation lawyers provide different estimates, the median reported value is applied. In all cases the cost excludes bribes.

TABLE 14.3

What do the starting a business indicators measure?

Procedures to legally start and operate a company (number)

- Preregistration (for example, name verification or reservation, notarization)
- Registration in the economy's largest business city
- Postregistration (for example, social security registration, company seal)

Time required to complete each procedure (calendar days)

- Does not include time spent gathering information
- Each procedure starts on a separate day
- Procedure completed once final document is received
- No prior contact with officials

Cost required to complete each procedure (% of income per capita)

- Official costs only, no bribes
- No professional fees unless services required by law

Paid-in minimum capital (% of income per capita)

- Deposited in a bank or with a notary before registration begins

Source: Doing Business database.

PAID-IN MINIMUM CAPITAL

The paid-in minimum capital requirement reflects the amount that the entrepreneur needs to deposit in a bank or with a notary before registration and up to 3 months following incorporation and is recorded as a percentage of the economy's income per capita. The amount is typically specified in the commercial code or the company law. Many economies have a minimum capital requirement but allow businesses to pay only a part of it before registration, with the rest to be paid after the first year of operation. In Italy in June 2009 the minimum capital requirement for limited liability companies was €10,000, of which at least €2,500 was payable before registration. The paid-in minimum capital recorded for Italy is therefore €2,500, or 10.1% of income per capita. In Mexico the minimum capital requirement was 50,000 pesos, of which one-fifth needed to be paid before registration. The paid-in minimum capital recorded for Mexico is therefore 10,000 pesos, or 9.2% of income per capita.

The data details on starting a business can be found for each economy at http://www.doingbusiness.org by selecting the economy in the drop-down list. This methodology was developed in Djankov and others (2002) and is adopted here with minor changes.

DEALING WITH CONSTRUCTION PERMITS

Doing Business records all procedures required for a business in the construction industry to build a standardized warehouse. These procedures include submitting all relevant project-specific documents (for example, building plans and site maps) to the authorities; obtaining all necessary clearances, licenses, permits and certificates; completing all required notifications; and receiving all necessary inspections. *Doing Business* also records procedures for obtaining connections for electricity, water, sew-

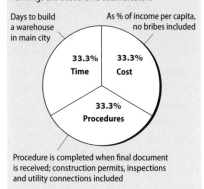

FIGURE 14.2

Dealing with construction permits: building a warehouse

Rankings are based on 3 subindicators

Procedure is completed when final document is received; construction permits, inspections and utility connections included

erage and a fixed land line. Procedures necessary to register the property so that it can be used as collateral or transferred to another entity are also counted. The survey divides the process of building a warehouse into distinct procedures and calculates the time and cost of completing each procedure in practice under normal circumstances. The ranking on the ease of dealing with construction permits is the simple average of the percentile rankings on its component indicators (figure 14.2).

Information is collected from experts in construction licensing, including architects, construction lawyers, construction firms, utility service providers and public officials who deal with building regulations, including approvals and inspections. To make the data comparable across economies, several assumptions about the business, the warehouse project and the utility connections are used.

ASSUMPTIONS ABOUT THE CONSTRUCTION COMPANY

The business (BuildCo):
- Is a limited liability company.
- Operates in the economy's largest business city.
- Is 100% domestically and privately owned.
- Has 5 owners, none of whom is a legal entity.
- Is fully licensed and insured to carry out construction projects, such as building warehouses.
- Has 60 builders and other employees, all of them nationals with the technical expertise and professional experience necessary to obtain construction permits and approvals.
- Has at least 1 employee who is a licensed architect and registered with the local association of architects.
- Has paid all taxes and taken out all necessary insurance applicable to its general business activity (for example, accidental insurance for construction workers and third-person liability).
- Owns the land on which the warehouse is built.

ASSUMPTIONS ABOUT THE WAREHOUSE

The warehouse:
- Will be used for general storage activities, such as storage of books or stationery. The warehouse will not be used for any goods requiring special conditions, such as food, chemicals or pharmaceuticals.
- Has 2 stories, both above ground, with a total surface of approximately 1,300.6 square meters (14,000 square feet). Each floor is 3 meters (9 feet, 10 inches) high.
- Has road access and is located in the periurban area of the economy's largest business city (that is, on the fringes of the city but still within its official limits).
- Is not located in a special economic or industrial zone. The zoning requirements for warehouses are met by building in an area where similar warehouses can be found.
- Is located on a land plot of 929 square meters (10,000 square feet) that is 100% owned by BuildCo and is accurately registered in the cadastre and land registry.
- Is a new construction (there was no previous construction on the land).
- Has complete architectural and technical plans prepared by a licensed architect.

- Will include all technical equipment required to make the warehouse fully operational.
- Will take 30 weeks to construct (excluding all delays due to administrative and regulatory requirements).

ASSUMPTIONS ABOUT THE UTILITY CONNECTIONS

The electricity connection:
- Is 10 meters (32 feet, 10 inches) from the main electricity network.
- Is a medium-tension, 3-phase, 4-wire Y, 140-kilovolt-ampere (kVA) connection. Three-phase service is available in the construction area.
- Will be delivered by an overhead service, unless overhead service is not available in the periurban area.
- Consists of a simple hookup unless installation of a private substation (transformer) or extension of network is required.
- Requires the installation of only one electricity meter.

BuildCo is assumed to have a licensed electrician on its team to complete the internal wiring for the warehouse.

The water and sewerage connection:
- Is 10 meters (32 feet, 10 inches) from the existing water source and sewer tap.
- Does not require water for fire protection reasons; a fire extinguishing system (dry system) will be used instead. If a wet fire protection system is required by law, it is assumed that the water demand specified below also covers the water needed for fire protection.
- Has an average water use of 662 liters (175 gallons) a day and an average wastewater flow of 568 liters (150 gallons) a day.
- Has a peak water use of 1,325 liters (350 gallons) a day and a peak wastewater flow of 1,136 liters (300 gallons) a day.
- Will have a constant level of water demand and wastewater flow throughout the year.

The telephone connection:

- Is 10 meters (32 feet, 10 inches) from the main telephone network.
- Is a fixed land line.

PROCEDURES

A procedure is any interaction of the company's employees or managers with external parties, including government agencies, notaries, the land registry, the cadastre, utility companies, public and private inspectors and technical experts apart from in-house architects and engineers. Interactions between company employees, such as development of the warehouse plans and inspections conducted by employees, are not counted as procedures. Procedures that the company undergoes to connect to electricity, water, sewerage and telephone services are included. All procedures that are legally or in practice required for building a warehouse are counted, even if they may be avoided in exceptional cases (table 14.4).

TIME

Time is recorded in calendar days. The measure captures the median duration that local experts indicate is necessary to complete a procedure in practice. It is assumed that the minimum time required for each procedure is 1 day. Although procedures may take place simultaneously, they cannot start on the same day

(that is, simultaneous procedures start on consecutive days). If a procedure can be accelerated legally for an additional cost, the fastest procedure is chosen. It is assumed that BuildCo does not waste time and commits to completing each remaining procedure without delay. The time that BuildCo spends on gathering information is ignored. It is assumed that BuildCo is aware of all building requirements and their sequence from the beginning.

COST

Cost is recorded as a percentage of the economy's income per capita. Only official costs are recorded. All the fees associated with completing the procedures to legally build a warehouse are recorded, including those associated with obtaining land use approvals and preconstruction design clearances; receiving inspections before, during and after construction; getting utility connections; and registering the warehouse property. Nonrecurring taxes required for the completion of the warehouse project also are recorded. The building code, information from local experts and specific regulations and fee schedules are used as sources for costs. If several local partners provide different estimates, the median reported value is used.

TABLE 14.4

What do the dealing with construction permits indicators measure?

Procedures to legally build a warehouse (number)
Submitting all relevant documents and obtaining all necessary clearances, licenses, permits and certificates
Completing all required notifications and receiving all necessary inspections
Obtaining utility connections for electricity, water, sewerage and a land telephone line
Registering the warehouse after its completion (if required for use as collateral or for transfer of warehouse)

Time required to complete each procedure (calendar days)
Does not include time spent gathering information
Each procedure starts on a separate day
Procedure completed once final document is received
No prior contact with officials

Cost required to complete each procedure (% of income per capita)
Official costs only, no bribes

Source: Doing Business database.

The data details on dealing with construction permits can be found for each economy at http://www.doingbusiness.org by selecting the economy in the drop-down list.

REGISTERING PROPERTY

Doing Business records the full sequence of procedures necessary for a business (buyer) to purchase a property from another business (seller) and to transfer the property title to the buyer's name so that the buyer can use the property for expanding its business, use the property as collateral in taking new loans or, if necessary, sell the property to another business. The process starts with obtaining the necessary documents, such as a copy of the seller's title if necessary, and conducting due diligence if required. The transaction is considered complete when it is opposable to third parties and when the buyer can use the property, use it as collateral for a bank loan or resell it. The ranking on the ease of registering property is the simple average of the percentile rankings on its component indicators (figure 14.3).

Every procedure required by law or necessary in practice is included, whether it is the responsibility of the seller or the buyer or must be completed by a third party on their behalf. Local property lawyers, notaries and property registries provide information on pro-cedures as well as the time and cost to complete each of them.

To make the data comparable across economies, several assumptions about the parties to the transaction, the property and the procedures are used.

ASSUMPTIONS ABOUT THE PARTIES

The parties (buyer and seller):
- Are limited liability companies.
- Are located in the periurban area of the economy's largest business city.
- Are 100% domestically and privately owned.
- Have 50 employees each, all of whom are nationals.
- Perform general commercial activities.

ASSUMPTIONS ABOUT THE PROPERTY

The property:
- Has a value of 50 times income per capita. The sale price equals the value.
- Is fully owned by the seller.
- Has no mortgages attached and has been under the same ownership for the past 10 years.
- Is registered in the land registry or cadastre, or both, and is free of title disputes.
- Is located in a periurban commercial zone, and no rezoning is required.
- Consists of land and a building. The land area is 557.4 square meters (6,000 square feet). A 2-story warehouse of 929 square meters

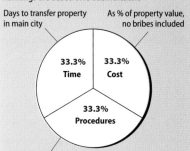

FIGURE 14.3

Registering property: transfer of property between 2 local companies

Rankings are based on 3 subindicators

Days to transfer property in main city

As % of property value, no bribes included

33.3% Time

33.3% Cost

33.3% Procedures

Steps to check encumbrances, obtain clearance certificates, prepare deed and transfer title so that the property can be occupied, sold or used as collateral

(10,000 square feet) is located on the land. The warehouse is 10 years old, is in good condition and complies with all safety standards, building codes and other legal requirements. The property of land and building will be transferred in its entirety.
- Will not be subject to renovations or additional building following the purchase.
- Has no trees, natural water sources, natural reserves or historical monuments of any kind.
- Will not be used for special purposes, and no special permits, such as for residential use, industrial plants, waste storage or certain types of agricultural activities, are required.
- Has no occupants (legal or illegal), and no other party holds a legal interest in it.

PROCEDURES

A procedure is defined as any interaction of the buyer or the seller, their agents (if an agent is legally or in practice required) or the property with external parties, including government agencies, inspectors, notaries and lawyers. Interactions between company officers and employees are not considered. All procedures that are legally or in practice required for registering property are recorded, even if they may be avoided in exceptional cases (table 14.5). It is assumed that the buyer follows the fastest legal option available and used

TABLE 14.5

What do the registering property indicators measure?

Procedures to legally transfer title on immovable property *(number)*
Preregistration (for example, checking for liens, notarizing sales agreement, paying property transfer taxes)
Registration in the economy's largest business city
Postregistration (for example, transactions with the local authority, tax authority or cadastre)

Time required to complete each procedure *(calendar days)*
Does not include time spent gathering information
Each procedure starts on a separate day
Procedure completed once final document is received
No prior contact with officials

Cost required to complete each procedure *(% of property value)*
Official costs only, no bribes
No value added or capital gains taxes included

Source: Doing Business database.

by the majority of property owners. Although the buyer may use lawyers or other professionals where necessary in the registration process, it is assumed that it does not employ an outside facilitator in the registration process unless legally or in practice required to do so.

TIME

Time is recorded in calendar days. The measure captures the median duration that property lawyers, notaries or registry officials indicate is necessary to complete a procedure. It is assumed that the minimum time required for each procedure is 1 day. Although procedures may take place simultaneously, they cannot start on the same day. It is assumed that the buyer does not waste time and commits to completing each remaining procedure without delay. If a procedure can be accelerated for an additional cost, the fastest legal procedure available and used by the majority of property owners is chosen. If procedures can be undertaken simultaneously, it is assumed that they are. It is assumed that the parties involved are aware of all regulations and their sequence from the beginning. Time spent on gathering information is not considered.

COST

Cost is recorded as a percentage of the property value, assumed to be equivalent to 50 times income per capita. Only official costs required by law are recorded, including fees, transfer taxes, stamp duties and any other payment to the property registry, notaries, public agencies or lawyers. Other taxes, such as capital gains tax or value added tax, are excluded from the cost measure. Both costs borne by the buyer and those borne by the seller are included. If cost estimates differ among sources, the median reported value is used.

The data details on registering property can be found for each economy at http://www.doingbusiness.org by selecting the economy in the drop-down list.

FIGURE 14.4

Getting credit: collateral rules and credit information

Rankings are based on 2 subindicators

Regulations on nonpossessory security interests in movable property

62.5%
Strength of legal rights index
(0–10)

37.5%
Depth of credit information index
(0–6)

Scope, quality and accessibility of credit information through public and private credit registries

Note: Private bureau coverage and public registry coverage are measured but do not count for the rankings.

GETTING CREDIT

Doing Business measures the legal rights of borrowers and lenders with respect to secured transactions through one set of indicators and the sharing of credit information through another. The first set of indicators describes how well collateral and bankruptcy laws facilitate lending. The second set measures the coverage, scope and accessibility of credit information available through public credit registries and private credit bureaus. The ranking on the ease of getting credit is the simple average of the percentile rankings on its component indicators (figure 14.4).

The data on the legal rights of borrowers and lenders are gathered through a survey of financial lawyers and verified through analysis of laws and regulations as well as public sources of information on collateral and bankruptcy laws. The data on credit information sharing are built in 2 stages. First, banking supervision authorities and public information sources are surveyed to confirm the presence of a public credit registry or private credit bureau. Second, when applicable, a detailed survey on the public credit registry's or private credit bureau's structure, laws and associated rules is administered to the entity itself. Survey responses are verified through several rounds of follow-up communication with respondents as well as by contact-

ing third parties and consulting public sources. The survey data are confirmed through teleconference calls or on-site visits in all economies.

STRENGTH OF LEGAL RIGHTS INDEX

The strength of legal rights index measures the degree to which collateral and bankruptcy laws protect the rights of borrowers and lenders and thus facilitate lending (table 14.6). Two case scenarios, case A and case B, are used to determine the scope of the secured transactions system, involving a secured borrower, the company ABC, and a secured lender, BizBank. In certain economies the legal framework on secured transactions means that only case A or case B can apply (not both). Both cases examine the same set of legal restrictions on the use of movable collateral.

Several assumptions about the secured borrower and lender are used:

- ABC is a domestic, limited liability company.
- ABC has its headquarters and only base of operations in the economy's largest business city.
- To fund its business expansion plans, ABC obtains a loan from BizBank for an amount up to 10 times income per capita in local currency.

TABLE 14.6

What do the getting credit indicators measure?

Strength of legal rights index (0–10)

- Protection of rights of borrowers and lenders through collateral laws
- Protection of secured creditors' rights through bankruptcy laws

Depth of credit information index (0–6)

- Scope and accessibility of credit information distributed by public credit registries and private credit bureaus

Public credit registry coverage (% of adults)

- Number of individuals and firms listed in public credit registry as percentage of adult population

Private credit bureau coverage (% of adults)

- Number of individuals and firms listed in largest private credit bureau as percentage of adult population

Source: Doing Business database.

- Both ABC and BizBank are 100% domestically owned.

The case scenarios also involve assumptions. In case A, as collateral for the loan, ABC grants BizBank a nonpossessory security interest in one category of movable assets, for example, its accounts receivable or its inventory. ABC wants to keep both possession and ownership of the collateral. In economies in which the law does not allow nonpossessory security interests in movable property, ABC and BizBank use a fiduciary transfer-of-title arrangement (or a similar substitute for nonpossessory security interests).

In case B, ABC grants BizBank a business charge, enterprise charge, floating charge or any charge that gives BizBank a security interest over ABC's combined movable assets (or as much of ABC's movable assets as possible). ABC keeps ownership and possession of the assets.

The strength of legal rights index includes 8 aspects related to legal rights in collateral law and 2 aspects in bankruptcy law. A score of 1 is assigned for each of the following features of the laws:

- Any business may use movable assets as collateral while keeping possession of the assets, and any financial institution may accept such assets as collateral.
- The law allows a business to grant a nonpossessory security right in a single category of movable assets (such as accounts receivable or inventory), without requiring a specific description of the collateral.
- The law allows a business to grant a nonpossessory security right in substantially all its movable assets, without requiring a specific description of the collateral.
- A security right may extend to future or after-acquired assets and may extend automatically to the products, proceeds or replacements of the original assets.

- A general description of debts and obligations is permitted in the collateral agreements and in registration documents: all types of debts and obligations can be secured between the parties, and the collateral agreement can include a maximum amount for which the assets are encumbered.
- A collateral registry or registration institution is in operation, unified geographically and by asset type, with an electronic database indexed by debtors' names.
- Secured creditors are paid first (for example, before general tax claims and employee claims) when a debtor defaults outside an insolvency procedure.
- Secured creditors are paid first (for example, before general tax claims and employee claims) when a business is liquidated.
- Secured creditors are not subject to an automatic stay or moratorium on enforcement procedures when a debtor enters a court-supervised reorganization procedure.
- The law allows parties to agree in a collateral agreement that the lender may enforce its security right out of court.

The index ranges from 0 to 10, with higher scores indicating that collateral and bankruptcy laws are better designed to expand access to credit.

DEPTH OF CREDIT INFORMATION INDEX

The depth of credit information index measures rules and practices affecting the coverage, scope and accessibility of credit information available through either a public credit registry or a private credit bureau. A score of 1 is assigned for each of the following 6 features of the public credit registry or private credit bureau (or both):

- Both positive credit information (for example, outstanding loan amounts and pattern of on-time repayments) and negative information (for example, late payments, number and

amount of defaults and bankruptcies) are distributed.
- Data on both firms and individuals are distributed.
- Data from retailers and utility companies as well as financial institutions are distributed.
- More than 2 years of historical data are distributed. Credit registries and bureaus that erase data on defaults as soon as they are repaid obtain a score of 0 for this indicator.
- Data on loan amounts below 1% of income per capita are distributed. Note that a credit registry or bureau must have a minimum coverage of 1% of the adult population to score a 1 on this indicator.
- By law, borrowers have the right to access their data in the largest credit registry or bureau in the economy.

The index ranges from 0 to 6, with higher values indicating the availability of more credit information, from either a public credit registry or a private credit bureau, to facilitate lending decisions. If the credit registry or bureau is not operational or has a coverage of less than 0.1% of the adult population, the score on the depth of credit information index is 0.

In Lithuania, for example, both a public credit registry and a private credit bureau operate. Both distribute positive and negative information (a score of 1). Both distribute data on firms and individuals (a score of 1). Although the public credit registry does not distribute data from retailers or utilities, the private credit bureau does do so (a score of 1). Although the private credit bureau does not distribute more than 2 years of historical data, the public credit registry does do so (a score of 1). Although the public credit registry has a threshold of 50,000 litai, the private credit bureau distributes data on loans of any value (a score of 1). Borrowers have the right to access their data in both the public credit registry and the private credit bureau (a score of 1). Summing across the indicators gives Lithuania a total score of 6.

FIGURE 14.5

Protecting investors: minority shareholder rights in related-party transactions

Rankings are based on 3 subindicators

PUBLIC CREDIT REGISTRY COVERAGE

The public credit registry coverage indicator reports the number of individuals and firms listed in a public credit registry with information on their borrowing history from the past 5 years. The number is expressed as a percentage of the adult population (the population age 15 and above in 2009 according to the World Bank's *World Development Indicators*). A public credit registry is defined as a database managed by the public sector, usually by the central bank or the superintendent of banks, that collects information on the creditworthiness of borrowers (individuals or firms) in the financial system and facilitates the exchange of credit information among banks and financial institutions. If no public registry operates, the coverage value is 0.

PRIVATE CREDIT BUREAU COVERAGE

The private credit bureau coverage indicator reports the number of individuals and firms listed by a private credit bureau with information on their borrowing history from the past 5 years. The number is expressed as a percentage of the adult population (the population age 15 and above in 2009 according to the World Bank's *World Development Indicators*). A private credit bureau is defined as a private firm or nonprofit organization that maintains a database on the creditworthiness of borrowers (individuals or firms) in the financial system and facili-

tates the exchange of credit information among banks and financial institutions. Credit investigative bureaus and credit reporting firms that do not directly facilitate information exchange among banks and other financial institutions are not considered. If no private bureau operates, the coverage value is 0.

The data details on getting credit can be found for each economy at http://www.doingbusiness.org by selecting the economy in the drop-down list. This methodology was developed in Djankov, McLiesh and Shleifer (2007) and is adopted here with minor changes.

PROTECTING INVESTORS

Doing Business measures the strength of minority shareholder protections against directors' misuse of corporate assets for personal gain. The indicators distinguish 3 dimensions of investor protections: transparency of related-party transactions (extent of disclosure index), liability for self-dealing (extent of director liability index) and shareholders' ability to sue officers and directors for misconduct (ease of shareholder suits index). The data come from a survey of corporate and securities lawyers and are based on securities regulations, company laws and court rules of evidence. The ranking on the strength of investor protection index is the simple average of the percentile rankings on its component indicators (figure 14.5).

To make the data comparable across economies, several assumptions about the business and the transaction are used.

ASSUMPTIONS ABOUT THE BUSINESS

The business (Buyer):
- Is a publicly traded corporation listed on the economy's most important stock exchange. If the number of publicly traded companies listed on that exchange is less than 10, or if there is no stock exchange in the economy, it is assumed that Buyer is a large private company with multiple shareholders.

- Has a board of directors and a chief executive officer (CEO) who may legally act on behalf of Buyer where permitted, even if this is not specifically required by law.
- Is a food manufacturer.
- Has its own distribution network.

ASSUMPTIONS ABOUT THE TRANSACTION

- Mr. James is Buyer's controlling shareholder and a member of Buyer's board of directors. He owns 60% of Buyer and elected 2 directors to Buyer's 5-member board.
- Mr. James also owns 90% of Seller, a company that operates a chain of retail hardware stores. Seller recently closed a large number of its stores.
- Mr. James proposes that Buyer purchase Seller's unused fleet of trucks to expand Buyer's distribution of its food products, a proposal to which Buyer agrees. The price is equal to 10% of Buyer's assets and is higher than the market value.
- The proposed transaction is part of the company's ordinary course of business and is not outside the authority of the company.
- Buyer enters into the transaction. All required approvals are obtained, and all required disclosures made (that is, the transaction is not fraudulent).
- The transaction causes damages to Buyer. Shareholders sue Mr. James and the other parties that approved the transaction.

EXTENT OF DISCLOSURE INDEX

The extent of disclosure index has 5 components (table 14.7):
- What corporate body can provide legally sufficient approval for the transaction. A score of 0 is assigned if it is the CEO or the managing director alone; 1 if the board of directors or shareholders must vote and Mr. James is permitted to vote; 2 if the board of directors must vote and Mr. James is not permitted to vote; 3 if

shareholders must vote and Mr. James is not permitted to vote.

- Whether immediate disclosure of the transaction to the public, the regulator or the shareholders is required.[6] A score of 0 is assigned if no disclosure is required; 1 if disclosure on the terms of the transaction is required but not on Mr. James's conflict of interest; 2 if disclosure on both the terms and Mr. James's conflict of interest is required.
- Whether disclosure in the annual report is required. A score of 0 is assigned if no disclosure on the transaction is required; 1 if disclosure on the terms of the transaction is required but not on Mr. James's conflict of interest; 2 if disclosure on both the terms and Mr. James's conflict of interest is required.
- Whether disclosure by Mr. James to the board of directors is required. A score of 0 is assigned if no disclosure is required; 1 if a general disclosure of the existence of a conflict of interest is required without any specifics; 2 if full disclosure of all material facts relating to Mr. James's interest in the Buyer-Seller transaction is required.
- Whether it is required that an external body, for example, an external auditor, review the

transaction before it takes place. A score of 0 is assigned if no; 1 if yes.

The index ranges from 0 to 10, with higher values indicating greater disclosure. In Poland, for example, the board of directors must approve the transaction and Mr. James is not allowed to vote (a score of 2). Buyer is required to disclose immediately all information affecting the stock price, including the conflict of interest (a score of 2). In its annual report Buyer must also disclose the terms of the transaction and Mr. James's ownership in Buyer and Seller (a score of 2). Before the transaction Mr. James must disclose his conflict of interest to the other directors, but he is not required to provide specific information about it (a score of 1). Poland does not require an external body to review the transaction (a score of 0). Adding these numbers gives Poland a score of 7 on the extent of disclosure index.

EXTENT OF DIRECTOR LIABILITY INDEX

The extent of director liability index has 7 components:[7]

- Whether a shareholder plaintiff is able to hold Mr. James liable for damage the Buyer-Seller transaction causes to the company. A score of 0 is assigned if Mr. James cannot be held

liable or can be held liable only for fraud or bad faith; 1 if Mr. James can be held liable only if he influenced the approval of the transaction or was negligent; 2 if Mr. James can be held liable when the transaction is unfair or prejudicial to the other shareholders.

- Whether a shareholder plaintiff is able to hold the approving body (the CEO or board of directors) liable for the damage the transaction causes to the company. A score of 0 is assigned if the approving body cannot be held liable or can be held liable only for fraud or bad faith; 1 if the approving body can be held liable for negligence; 2 if the approving body can be held liable when the transaction is unfair or prejudicial to the other shareholders.
- Whether a court can void the transaction upon a successful claim by a shareholder plaintiff. A score of 0 is assigned if rescission is unavailable or is available only in case of fraud or bad faith; 1 if rescission is available when the transaction is oppressive or prejudicial to the other shareholders; 2 if rescission is available when the transaction is unfair or entails a conflict of interest.
- Whether Mr. James pays damages for the harm caused to the company upon a successful claim by the shareholder plaintiff. A score of 0 is assigned if no; 1 if yes.
- Whether Mr. James repays profits made from the transaction upon a successful claim by the shareholder plaintiff. A score of 0 is assigned if no; 1 if yes.
- Whether both fines and imprisonment can be applied against Mr. James. A score of 0 is assigned if no; 1 if yes.
- Whether shareholder plaintiffs are able to sue directly or derivatively for the damage the transaction causes to the company. A score of 0 is assigned if suits are unavailable or are available only for shareholders holding more than 10% of the company's share

TABLE 14.7
What do the protecting investors indicators measure?

Extent of disclosure index (0–10)

- Who can approve related-party transactions
- Requirements for external and internal disclosure in case of related-party transactions

Extent of director liability index (0–10)

- Ability of shareholders to hold the interested party and the approving body liable in case of a prejudicial related-party transaction
- Available legal remedies (damages, repayment of profits, fines, imprisonment and rescission of the transaction)
- Ability of shareholders to sue directly or derivatively

Ease of shareholder suits index (0–10)

- Documents and information available during trial
- Access to internal corporate documents (directly and/or through a government inspector)

Strength of investor protection index (0–10)

- Simple average of the extent of disclosure, extent of director liability and ease of shareholder suits indices

Source: Doing Business database.

capital; 1 if direct or derivative suits are available for shareholders holding 10% or less of share capital.

The index ranges from 0 to 10, with higher values indicating greater liability of directors. Assuming that the prejudicial transaction was duly approved and disclosed, in order to hold Mr. James liable in Panama, for example, a plaintiff must prove that Mr. James influenced the approving body or acted negligently (a score of 1). To hold the other directors liable, a plaintiff must prove that they acted negligently (a score of 1). The prejudicial transaction cannot be voided (a score of 0). If Mr. James is found liable, he must pay damages (a score of 1) but he is not required to disgorge his profits (a score of 0). Mr. James cannot be fined and imprisoned (a score of 0). Direct or derivative suits are available for shareholders holding 10% or less of share capital (a score of 1). Adding these numbers gives Panama a score of 4 on the extent of director liability index.

EASE OF SHAREHOLDER SUITS INDEX

The ease of shareholder suits index has 6 components:

- What range of documents is available to the shareholder plaintiff from the defendant and witnesses during trial. A score of 1 is assigned for each of the following types of documents available: information that the defendant has indicated he intends to rely on for his defense; information that directly proves specific facts in the plaintiff's claim; any information relevant to the subject matter of the claim; and any information that may lead to the discovery of relevant information.
- Whether the plaintiff can directly examine the defendant and witnesses during trial. A score of 0 is assigned if no; 1 if yes, with prior approval of the questions by the judge; 2 if yes, without prior approval.
- Whether the plaintiff can obtain categories of relevant documents from the defendant without identifying

each document specifically. A score of 0 is assigned if no; 1 if yes.
- Whether shareholders owning 10% or less of the company's share capital can request that a government inspector investigate the Buyer-Seller transaction without filing suit in court. A score of 0 is assigned if no; 1 if yes.
- Whether shareholders owning 10% or less of the company's share capital have the right to inspect the transaction documents before filing suit. A score of 0 is assigned if no; 1 if yes.
- Whether the standard of proof for civil suits is lower than that for a criminal case. A score of 0 is assigned if no; 1 if yes.

The index ranges from 0 to 10, with higher values indicating greater powers of shareholders to challenge the transaction. In Greece, for example, the plaintiff can access documents that the defendant intends to rely on for his defense and that directly prove facts in the plaintiff's claim (a score of 2). The plaintiff can examine the defendant and witnesses during trial, though only with prior approval of the questions by the court (a score of 1). The plaintiff must specifically identify the documents being sought (for example, the Buyer-Seller purchase agreement of July 15, 2006) and cannot just request categories (for example, all documents related to the transaction) (a score of 0). A shareholder holding 5% of Buyer's shares can request that a government inspector review suspected mismanagement by Mr. James and the CEO without filing suit in court (a score of 1). Any shareholder can inspect the transaction documents before deciding whether to sue (a score of 1). The standard of proof for civil suits is the same as that for a criminal case (a score of 0). Adding these numbers gives Greece a score of 5 on the ease of shareholder suits index.

STRENGTH OF INVESTOR PROTECTION INDEX

The strength of investor protection index is the average of the extent of disclosure index, the extent of director liability index and the ease of shareholder suits index. The index ranges from 0 to 10, with higher values indicating more investor protection.

The data details on protecting investors can be found for each economy at http://www.doingbusiness.org by selecting the economy in the drop-down list. This methodology was developed in Djankov, La Porta, López-de-Silanes and Shleifer (2008).

PAYING TAXES

Doing Business records the taxes and mandatory contributions that a medium-size company must pay in a given year as well as measures of the administrative burden of paying taxes and contributions. The project was developed and implemented in cooperation with PricewaterhouseCoopers. Taxes and contributions measured include the profit or corporate income tax, social contributions and labor taxes paid by the employer, property taxes, property transfer taxes, dividend tax, capital gains tax, financial transactions tax, waste collection taxes, vehicle and road taxes and any other small taxes or fees. The ranking on the ease of paying taxes is the simple average of the percentile rankings on its compo-

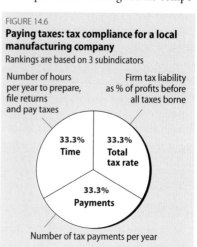

FIGURE 14.6

Paying taxes: tax compliance for a local manufacturing company

Rankings are based on 3 subindicators

nent indicators (figure 14.6).

Doing Business measures all taxes and contributions that are government mandated (at any level—federal, state or local) and that apply to the standardized business and have an impact in its financial statements. In doing so, *Doing Business* goes beyond the traditional definition of a tax. As defined for the purposes of government national accounts, taxes include only compulsory, unrequited payments to general government. *Doing Business* departs from this definition because it measures imposed charges that affect business accounts, not government accounts. The main differences relate to labor contributions. The *Doing Business* measure includes government-mandated contributions paid by the employer to a requited private pension fund or workers' insurance fund. The indicator includes, for example, Australia's compulsory superannuation guarantee and workers' compensation insurance. For the purpose of calculating the total tax rate (defined below), only taxes borne are included. For example, value added taxes are generally excluded (provided they are not irrecoverable) because they do not affect the accounting profits of the business—that is, they are not reflected in the income statement. They are, however, included for the purpose of the compliance measures (time and payments), as they add to the burden of complying with the tax system.

Doing Business uses a case scenario to measure the taxes and contributions paid by a standardized business and the complexity of an economy's tax compliance system. This case scenario uses a set of financial statements and assumptions about transactions made over the year. In each economy tax experts from a number of different firms (in many economies these include PricewaterhouseCoopers) compute the taxes and mandatory contributions due in their jurisdiction based on the standardized case study facts. Information is also compiled on the frequency of filing and payments

as well as time taken to comply with tax laws in an economy. To make the data comparable across economies, several assumptions about the business and the taxes and contributions are used.

ASSUMPTIONS ABOUT THE BUSINESS

The business:

- Is a limited liability, taxable company. If there is more than one type of limited liability company in the economy, the limited liability form most popular among domestic firms is chosen. The most popular form is reported by incorporation lawyers or the statistical office.
- Started operations on January 1, 2008. At that time the company purchased all the assets shown in its balance sheet and hired all its workers.
- Operates in the economy's largest business city.
- Is 100% domestically owned and has 5 owners, all of whom are natural persons.
- At the end of 2008, has a start-up capital of 102 times income per capita.
- Performs general industrial or commercial activities. Specifically, it produces ceramic flowerpots and sells them at retail. It does not participate in foreign trade (no import or export) and does not handle products subject to a special tax regime, for example, liquor or tobacco.
- At the beginning of 2009, owns 2 plots of land, 1 building, machinery, office equipment, computers and 1 truck and leases 1 truck.
- Does not qualify for investment incentives or any benefits apart from those related to the age or size of the company.
- Has 60 employees—4 managers, 8 assistants and 48 workers. All are nationals, and 1 manager is also an owner. The company pays for additional medical insurance for employees (not mandated by any law) as an additional benefit. In addition, in some economies reimbursable business travel and client entertainment

expenses are considered fringe benefits. When applicable, it is assumed that the company pays the fringe benefit tax on this expense or that the benefit becomes taxable income for the employee. The case study assumes no additional salary additions for meals, transportation, education or others. Therefore, even when such benefits are frequent, they are not added to or removed from the taxable gross salaries to arrive at the labor tax or contribution calculation.

- Has a turnover of 1,050 times income per capita.
- Makes a loss in the first year of operation.
- Has a gross margin (pretax) of 20% (that is, sales are 120% of the cost of goods sold).
- Distributes 50% of its net profits as dividends to the owners at the end of the second year.
- Sells one of its plots of land at a profit at the beginning of the second year.
- Has annual fuel costs for its trucks equal to twice income per capita.
- Is subject to a series of detailed assumptions on expenses and transactions to further standardize the case. All financial statement variables are proportional to 2005 income per capita. For example, the owner who is also a manager spends 10% of income per capita on traveling for the company (20% of this owner's expenses are purely private, 20% are for entertaining customers and 60% for business travel).

ASSUMPTIONS ABOUT THE TAXES AND CONTRIBUTIONS

- All the taxes and contributions recorded are those paid in the second year of operation (calendar year 2009). A tax or contribution is considered distinct if it has a different name or is collected by a different agency. Taxes and contributions with the same name and agency, but charged at different rates depending on the business, are counted as the same tax or contribution.

- The number of times the company pays taxes and contributions in a year is the number of different taxes or contributions multiplied by the frequency of payment (or withholding) for each tax. The frequency of payment includes advance payments (or withholding) as well as regular payments (or withholding).

TAX PAYMENTS

The tax payments indicator reflects the total number of taxes and contributions paid, the method of payment, the frequency of payment, the frequency of filing and the number of agencies involved for this standardized case study company during the second year of operation (table 14.8). It includes consumption taxes paid by the company, such as sales tax or value added tax. These taxes are traditionally collected from the consumer on behalf of the tax agencies. Although they do not affect the income statements of the company, they add to the administrative burden of complying with the tax system and so are included in the tax payments measure.

The number of payments takes into account electronic filing. Where full electronic filing and payment is allowed and it is used by the majority of medium-size businesses, the tax is counted as paid

once a year even if filings and payments are more frequent. For payments made through third parties, such as tax on interest paid by a financial institution or fuel tax paid by a fuel distributor, only one payment is included even if payments are more frequent.

Where 2 or more taxes or contributions are filed for and paid jointly using the same form, each of these joint payments is counted once. For example, if mandatory health insurance contributions and mandatory pension contributions are filed for and paid together, only one of these contributions would be included in the number of payments.

TIME

Time is recorded in hours per year. The indicator measures the time taken to prepare, file and pay 3 major types of taxes and contributions: the corporate income tax, value added or sales tax and labor taxes, including payroll taxes and social contributions. Preparation time includes the time to collect all information necessary to compute the tax payable and to calculate the amount payable. If separate accounting books must be kept for tax purposes—or separate calculations made—the time associated with these processes is included. This extra time is included only if the regular accounting

work is not enough to fulfill the tax accounting requirements. Filing time includes the time to complete all necessary tax return forms and file the relevant returns at the tax authority. Payment time considers the hours needed to make the payment online or at the tax authorities. Where taxes and contributions are paid in person, the time includes delays while waiting.

TOTAL TAX RATE

The total tax rate measures the amount of taxes and mandatory contributions borne by the business in the second year of operation, expressed as a share of commercial profit. *Doing Business 2011* reports the total tax rate for calendar year 2009. The total amount of taxes borne is the sum of all the different taxes and contributions payable after accounting for allowable deductions and exemptions. The taxes withheld (such as personal income tax) or collected by the company and remitted to the tax authorities (such as value added tax, sales tax or goods and service tax) but not borne by the company are excluded. The taxes included can be divided into 5 categories: profit or corporate income tax, social contributions and labor taxes paid by the employer (in respect of which all mandatory contributions are included, even if paid to a private entity such as a requited pension fund), property taxes, turnover taxes and other taxes (such as municipal fees and vehicle and fuel taxes).

The total tax rate is designed to provide a comprehensive measure of the cost of all the taxes a business bears. It differs from the statutory tax rate, which merely provides the factor to be applied to the tax base. In computing the total tax rate, the actual tax payable is divided by commercial profit. Data for Sweden illustrate (table 14.9).

Commercial profit is essentially net profit before all taxes borne. It differs from the conventional profit before tax, reported in financial statements. In computing profit before tax, many of the taxes borne by a firm are deductible. In computing commercial profit, these

TABLE 14.8

What do the paying taxes indicators measure?

Tax payments for a manufacturing company in 2009 (number per year adjusted for electronic or joint filing and payment)

- Total number of taxes and contributions paid, including consumption taxes (value added tax, sales tax or goods and service tax)
- Method and frequency of filing and payment

Time required to comply with 3 major taxes (hours per year)

- Collecting information and computing the tax payable
- Completing tax return forms, filing with proper agencies
- Arranging payment or withholding
- Preparing separate tax accounting books, if required

Total tax rate (% of profit)

- Profit or corporate income tax
- Social contributions and labor taxes paid by the employer
- Property and property transfer taxes
- Dividend, capital gains and financial transactions taxes
- Waste collection, vehicle, road and other taxes

Source: Doing Business database.

TABLE 14.9

Computing the total tax rate for Sweden

Type of tax (tax base)	Statutory rate (r)	Statutory tax base (b)	Actual tax payable (a) $a = r \times b$	Commercial profit[1] (c)	Total tax rate (t) $t = a/c$
		SKr	SKr	SKr	
Corporate income tax (taxable income)	28%	10,330,966	2,892,670	17,619,223	16.4%
Real estate tax (land and buildings)	0.38%	26,103,545	97,888	17,619,223	0.6%
Payroll tax (taxable wages)	32.42%	19,880,222	6,445,168	17,619,223	36.6%
Fuel tax (fuel price)	SKr 4.16 per liter	45,565 liters	189,550	17,619,223	1.1%
TOTAL			**9,625,276**		**54.6%**

1. Profit before all taxes borne.
Note: SKr is Swedish kronor. Commercial profit is assumed to be 59.4 times income per capita.
Source: Doing Business database.

taxes are not deductible. Commercial profit therefore presents a clear picture of the actual profit of a business before any of the taxes it bears in the course of the fiscal year.

Commercial profit is computed as sales minus cost of goods sold, minus gross salaries, minus administrative expenses, minus other expenses, minus provisions, plus capital gains (from the property sale) minus interest expense, plus interest income and minus commercial depreciation. To compute the commercial depreciation, a straight-line depreciation method is applied, with the following rates: 0% for the land, 5% for the building, 10% for the machinery, 33% for the computers, 20% for the office equipment, 20% for the truck and 10% for business development expenses. Commercial profit amounts to 59.4 times income per capita.

The methodology for calculating the total tax rate is broadly consistent with the Total Tax Contribution framework developed by PricewaterhouseCoopers and the calculation within this framework for taxes borne. But while the work undertaken by PricewaterhouseCoopers is usually based on data received from the largest companies in the economy, *Doing Business* focuses on a case study for standardized medium-size company.

The methodology for the paying taxes indicators has further benefited from discussion with members of the International Tax Dialogue, which led to a refinement of the questions on the time to pay taxes indicator in the survey instrument and the collection of pilot data on the labor tax wedge for further research.

The data details on paying taxes can be found for each economy at http://www. doingbusiness.org by selecting the economy in the drop-down list. This methodology was developed in Djankov and others (2010).

TRADING ACROSS BORDERS

Doing Business compiles procedural requirements for exporting and importing a standardized cargo of goods by ocean transport. Every official procedure for exporting and importing the goods is recorded—from the contractual agreement between the 2 parties to the delivery of goods—along with the time and cost necessary for completion. All documents needed by the trader to export or import the goods across the border are also recorded. For exporting goods, procedures range from packing the goods at the warehouse to their departure from the port of exit. For importing goods, procedures range from the vessel's arrival at the port of entry to the cargo's delivery at the warehouse. The time and cost for ocean transport are not included. Payment is made by letter of credit, and the time, cost and documents required for the issuance or advising of a letter of credit are taken into account. The ranking on the ease of trading across borders is the simple average of the percentile rankings on its component indicators (figure 14.7).

Local freight forwarders, shipping lines, customs brokers, port officials and banks provide information on required documents and cost as well as the time to complete each procedure. To make the data comparable across economies, several assumptions about the business and the traded goods are used.

ASSUMPTIONS ABOUT THE BUSINESS

The business:

- Has at least 60 employees.
- Is located in the economy's largest business city.
- Is a private, limited liability company. It does not operate in an export processing zone or an industrial estate with special export or import privileges.
- Is domestically owned with no foreign ownership.
- Exports more than 10% of its sales.

FIGURE 14.7

Trading across borders: exporting and importing by ocean transport

Rankings are based on 3 subindicators

All documents required by customs and other agencies

Document preparation, customs clearance and technical control, port and terminal handling, inland transport and handling

33.3% Documents to export and import

33.3% Time to export and import

33.3% Cost to export and import

US$ per 20-foot container, no bribes or tariffs included

ASSUMPTIONS ABOUT THE TRADED GOODS

The traded product travels in a dry-cargo, 20-foot, full container load. It weighs 10 tons and is valued at $20,000. The product:

- Is not hazardous nor does it include military items.
- Does not require refrigeration or any other special environment.
- Does not require any special phytosanitary or environmental safety standards other than accepted international standards.
- Is one of the economy's leading export or import products.

DOCUMENTS

All documents required per shipment to export and import the goods are recorded (table 14.10). It is assumed that the contract has already been agreed upon and signed by both parties. Documents required for clearance by government ministries, customs authorities, port and container terminal authorities, health and technical control agencies and banks are taken into account. Since payment is by letter of credit, all documents required by banks for the issuance or se-

TABLE 14.10

What do the trading across borders indicators measure?

Documents required to export and import (number)

- Bank documents
- Customs clearance documents
- Port and terminal handling documents
- Transport documents

Time required to export and import (days)

- Obtaining all the documents
- Inland transport and handling
- Customs clearance and inspections
- Port and terminal handling
- Does not include ocean transport time

Cost required to export and import (US$ per container)

- All documentation
- Inland transport and handling
- Customs clearance and inspections
- Port and terminal handling
- Official costs only, no bribes

Source: Doing Business database.

curing of a letter of credit are also taken into account. Documents that are renewed annually and that do not require renewal per shipment (for example, an annual tax clearance certificate) are not included.

TIME

The time for exporting and importing is recorded in calendar days. The time calculation for a procedure starts from the moment it is initiated and runs until it is completed. If a procedure can be accelerated for an additional cost and is available to all trading companies, the fastest legal procedure is chosen. Fast-track procedures applying to firms located in an export processing zone are not taken into account because they are not available to all trading companies. Ocean transport time is not included. It is assumed that neither the exporter nor the importer wastes time and that each commits to completing each remaining procedure without delay. Procedures that can be completed in parallel are measured as simultaneous. The waiting time between procedures—for example, during unloading of the cargo—is included in the measure.

COST

Cost measures the fees levied on a 20-foot container in U.S. dollars. All the fees associated with completing the procedures to export or import the goods are included. These include costs for documents, administrative fees for customs clearance and technical control, customs broker fees, terminal handling charges and inland transport. The cost does not include customs tariffs and duties or costs related to ocean transport. Only official costs are recorded.

The data details on trading across borders can be found for each economy at http://www.doingbusiness.org by selecting the economy in the drop-down list. This methodology was developed in Djankov, Freund and Pham (2010) and is adopted here with minor changes.

ENFORCING CONTRACTS

Indicators on enforcing contracts measure the efficiency of the judicial system in resolving a commercial dispute. The data are built by following the step-by-step evolution of a commercial sale dispute before local courts. The data are collected through study of the codes of civil procedure and other court regulations as well as surveys completed by local litigation lawyers and by judges. The ranking on the ease of enforcing contracts is the simple average of the percentile rankings on its component indicators (figure 14.8).

The name of the relevant court in each economy—the court in the largest business city with jurisdiction over commercial cases worth 200% of income per capita—is published at http://www.doingbusiness.org/ExploreTopics/EnforcingContracts/.

ASSUMPTIONS ABOUT THE CASE

- The value of the claim equals 200% of the economy's income per capita.
- The dispute concerns a lawful transaction between 2 businesses (Seller and Buyer), located in the economy's largest business city. Seller sells goods worth 200% of the economy's income per capita to Buyer. After Seller delivers the goods to Buyer, Buyer refuses to pay for the goods on the grounds that the delivered goods were not of adequate quality.

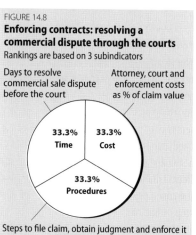

FIGURE 14.8

Enforcing contracts: resolving a commercial dispute through the courts

Rankings are based on 3 subindicators

Days to resolve commercial sale dispute before the court

Attorney, court and enforcement costs as % of claim value

33.3% Time

33.3% Cost

33.3% Procedures

Steps to file claim, obtain judgment and enforce it

- Seller (the plaintiff) sues Buyer (the defendant) to recover the amount under the sales agreement (that is, 200% of the economy's income per capita). Buyer opposes Seller's claim, saying that the quality of the goods is not adequate. The claim is disputed on the merits.
- A court in the economy's largest business city with jurisdiction over commercial cases worth 200% of income per capita decides the dispute.
- Seller attaches Buyer's movable assets (for example, office equipment and vehicles) before obtaining a judgment because Seller fears that Buyer may become insolvent.
- An expert opinion is given on the quality of the delivered goods. If it is standard practice in the economy for each party to call its own expert witness, the parties each call one expert witness. If it is standard practice for the judge to appoint an independent expert, the judge does so. In this case the judge does not allow opposing expert testimony.
- The judgment is 100% in favor of Seller: the judge decides that the goods are of adequate quality and that Buyer must pay the agreed price.
- Buyer does not appeal the judgment. The judgment becomes final.
- Seller takes all required steps for prompt enforcement of the judgment. The money is successfully collected through a public sale of Buyer's movable assets (for example, office equipment and vehicles).

PROCEDURES

The list of procedural steps compiled for each economy traces the chronology of a commercial dispute before the relevant court. A procedure is defined as any interaction, required by law or commonly used in practice, between the parties or between them and the judge or court officer. This includes steps to file and serve the case, steps for trial and judgment and steps necessary to enforce the judgment (table 14.11).

The survey allows respondents to record procedures that exist in civil law but not common law jurisdictions and vice versa. For example, in civil law countries the judge can appoint an independent expert, while in common law countries each party submits a list of expert witnesses to the court. To indicate overall efficiency, 1 procedure is subtracted from the total number for economies that have specialized commercial courts, and 1 procedure for economies that allow electronic filing of court cases. Some procedural steps that take place simultaneously with or are included in other procedural steps are not counted in the total number of procedures.

TIME

Time is recorded in calendar days, counted from the moment the plaintiff decides to file the lawsuit in court until payment. This includes both the days when actions take place and the waiting periods between. The average duration of different stages of dispute resolution is recorded: the completion of service of process (time to file and serve the case), the issuance of judgment (time for the trial and obtaining the judgment) and the moment of payment (time for enforcement of judgment).

COST

Cost is recorded as a percentage of the claim, assumed to be equivalent to 200% of income per capita. No bribes are recorded. Three types of costs are recorded: court costs, enforcement costs and average attorney fees.

Court costs include all court costs and expert fees that Seller (plaintiff) must advance to the court, regardless of the final cost to Seller. Expert fees, if required by law or commonly used in practice, are included in court costs. Enforcement costs are all costs that Seller (plaintiff) must advance to enforce the judgment through a public sale of Buyer's movable assets, regardless of the final cost to Seller. Average attorney fees are the fees that Seller (plaintiff) must advance to a local attorney to represent Seller in the standardized case.

TABLE 14.11

What do the enforcing contracts indicators measure?

Procedures to enforce a contract (number)

- Any interaction between the parties in a commercial dispute, or between them and the judge or court officer
- Steps to file the case
- Steps for trial and judgment
- Steps to enforce the judgment

Time required to complete procedures (calendar days)

- Time to file and serve the case
- Time for trial and obtaining judgment
- Time to enforce the judgment

Cost required to complete procedures (% of claim)

- No bribes
- Average attorney fees
- Court costs, including expert fees
- Enforcement costs

Source: Doing Business database.

The data details on enforcing contracts can be found for each economy at http://www.doingbusiness.org by selecting the economy in the drop-down list. This methodology was developed in Djankov and others (2003) and is adopted here with minor changes.

CLOSING A BUSINESS

Doing Business studies the time, cost and outcome of insolvency proceedings involving domestic entities. The data are derived from survey responses by local insolvency practitioners and verified through a study of laws and regulations as well as public information on bankruptcy systems. The ranking on the ease of closing a business is based on the recovery rate (figure 14.9).

To make the data comparable across economies, several assumptions about the business and the case are used.

ASSUMPTIONS ABOUT THE BUSINESS

The business:
- Is a limited liability company.
- Operates in the economy's largest business city.

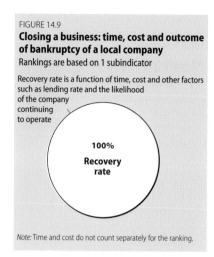

FIGURE 14.9

Closing a business: time, cost and outcome of bankruptcy of a local company

Rankings are based on 1 subindicator

Recovery rate is a function of time, cost and other factors such as lending rate and the likelihood of the company continuing to operate

100% Recovery rate

Note: Time and cost do not count separately for the ranking.

- Is 100% domestically owned, with the founder, who is also the chairman of the supervisory board, owning 51% (no other shareholder holds more than 5% of shares).
- Has downtown real estate, where it runs a hotel, as its major asset. The hotel is valued at 100 times income per capita or $200,000, whichever is larger.
- Has a professional general manager.
- Has 201 employees and 50 suppliers, each of which is owed money for the last delivery.
- Has a 10-year loan agreement with a domestic bank secured by a universal business charge (for example, a floating charge) in economies where such collateral is recognized or by the hotel property. If the laws of the economy do not specifically provide for a universal business charge but contracts commonly use some other provision to that effect, this provision is specified in the loan agreement.
- Has observed the payment schedule and all other conditions of the loan up to now.
- Has a mortgage, with the value of the mortgage principal being exactly equal to the market value of the hotel.

ASSUMPTIONS ABOUT THE CASE

The business is experiencing liquidity problems. The company's loss in 2009 reduced its net worth to a negative figure. It is January 1, 2010. There is no cash to pay

the bank interest or principal in full, due the next day, January 2. The business will therefore default on its loan. Management believes that losses will be incurred in 2010 and 2011 as well.

The amount outstanding under the loan agreement is exactly equal to the market value of the hotel business and represents 74% of the company's total debt. The other 26% of its debt is held by unsecured creditors (suppliers, employees, tax authorities).

The company has too many creditors to negotiate an informal out-of-court workout. The following options are available: a judicial procedure aimed at the rehabilitation or reorganization of the company to permit its continued operation; a judicial procedure aimed at the liquidation or winding-up of the company; or a debt enforcement or foreclosure procedure against the company, enforced either in court (or through another government authority) or out of court (for example, by appointing a receiver).

ASSUMPTIONS ABOUT THE PARTIES

The bank wants to recover as much as possible of its loan, as quickly and cheaply as possible. The unsecured creditors will do everything permitted under the applicable laws to avoid a piecemeal sale of the assets. The majority shareholder wants to keep the company operating and under its control. Management wants to keep the company operating and preserve their jobs. All the parties are local entities or citizens; no foreign parties are involved.

TIME

Time for creditors to recover their credit is recorded in calendar years (table 14.12). The period of time measured by *Doing Business* is from the company's default until the payment of some or all of the money owed to the bank. Potential delay tactics by the parties, such as the filing of dilatory appeals or requests for extension, are taken into consideration.

TABLE 14.12

What do the closing a business indicators measure?

Time required to recover debt (years)
- Measured in calendar years
- Appeals and requests for extension are included

Cost required to recover debt (% of debtor's estate)
- Measured as percentage of estate value
- Court fees
- Fees of insolvency administrators
- Lawyers' fees
- Assessors' and auctioneers' fees

Recovery rate for creditors (cents on the dollar)
- Measures the cents on the dollar recovered by creditors
- Present value of debt recovered
- Official costs of the insolvency proceedings are deducted
- Depreciation of furniture is taken into account
- Outcome for the business (survival or not) affects the maximum value that can be recovered

Source: Doing Business database.

COST

The cost of the proceedings is recorded as a percentage of the value of the debtor's estate. The cost is calculated on the basis of survey responses and includes court fees and government levies; fees of insolvency administrators, auctioneers, assessors and lawyers; and all other fees and costs. Respondents provide cost estimates from among the following options: less than 2%, 2–5%, 5–8%, 8–11%, 11–18%, 18–25%, 25–33%, 33–50%, 50–75% and more than 75% of the value of the estate.

OUTCOME

Recovery by creditors depends on whether the hotel business emerges from the proceedings as a going concern or the company's assets are sold piecemeal. If the business keeps operating, no value is lost and the bank can satisfy its claim in full, or recover 100 cents on the dollar. If the assets are sold piecemeal, the maximum amount that can be recovered will not exceed 70% of the bank's claim, which translates into 70 cents on the dollar.

RECOVERY RATE

The recovery rate is recorded as cents on the dollar recouped by creditors through reorganization, liquidation or debt enforcement (foreclosure) proceedings. The calculation takes into account the outcome: whether the business emerges from the proceedings as a going concern or the assets are sold piecemeal. Then the costs of the proceedings are deducted (1 cent for each percentage point of the value of the debtor's estate). Finally, the value lost as a result of the time the money remains tied up in insolvency proceedings is taken into account, including the loss of value due to depreciation of the hotel furniture. Consistent with international accounting practice, the annual depreciation rate for furniture is taken to be 20%. The furniture is assumed to account for a quarter of the total value of assets. The recovery rate is the present value of the remaining proceeds, based on end-2009 lending rates from the International Monetary Fund's *International Financial Statistics*, supplemented with data from central banks and the Economist Intelligence Unit.

NO PRACTICE

If an economy has had fewer than 5 cases a year over the past 5 years involving a judicial reorganization, judicial liquidation or debt enforcement procedure (foreclosure), the economy receives a "no practice" ranking. This means that creditors are unlikely to recover their money through a formal legal process (in or out of court). The recovery rate for "no practice" economies is zero.

This methodology was developed in Djankov, Hart, McLiesh and Shleifer (2008) and is adopted here with minor changes.

NOT IN THE EASE OF DOING BUSINESS RANKING

Two indicator sets are not included in this year's aggregate ranking on the ease of doing business: the getting electricity indicators, a pilot data set, and the employing workers indicators, for which the methodology is being refined.

GETTING ELECTRICITY

Doing Business records all procedures required for a business to obtain a permanent electricity connection and supply for a standardized warehouse. These procedures include applications and contracts with electricity utilities, all necessary clearances from other agencies and the external and final connection works (table 14.13).

Data are collected from the electricity distribution utility, then completed and verified by electricity regulatory agencies and independent professionals such as electrical engineers, electrical contractors and construction companies. The electricity distribution utility surveyed is the one serving the area (or areas) in which warehouses are located. If there is a choice of distribution utilities, the one serving the largest number of customers is selected.

To make the data comparable across economies, several assumptions about

the warehouse and the electricity connection are used.

ASSUMPTIONS ABOUT THE WAREHOUSE

The warehouse:

- Is owned by a local entrepreneur.
- Is located in the economy's largest business city.
- Is located within the city's official limits and in an area in which other warehouses are located (a nonresidential area).
- Is not located in a special economic or investment zone; that is, the electricity connection is not eligible for subsidization or faster service under a special investment promotion regime. If several options for location are available, the warehouse is located where electricity is most easily available.
- Has road access. The connection works involve the crossing of a road or roads (for excavation, overhead lines and the like), but they are all carried out on public land; that is, there is no crossing into other private property.
- Is located in an area with no physical constraints. For example, the property is not near a railway.
- Is used for storage of refrigerated goods.
- Is a new construction (that is, there was no previous construction on the

TABLE 14.13

What do the getting electricity indicators measure?

Procedures to obtain an electricity connection (number)

- Submitting all relevant documents and obtaining all necessary clearances and permits
- Completing all required notifications and receiving all necessary inspections
- Obtaining external installation works and possibly purchasing any needed material
- Concluding any necessary supply contract and obtaining final supply

Time required to complete each procedure (calendar days)

- Is at least 1 calendar day
- Each procedure starts on a separate day
- Does not include time spent gathering information
- Reflects the time spent in practice, with little follow-up and no prior contact with officials

Cost required to complete each procedure (% of income per capita)

- Official costs only, no bribes
- Excludes value added tax

Source: Doing Business database.

land where it is located). It is being connected to electricity for the first time.

- Has 2 stories, both above ground, with a total surface of approximately 1,300.6 square meters (14,000 square feet). The plot of land on which it is built is 929 square meters (10,000 square feet).

ASSUMPTIONS ABOUT THE ELECTRICITY CONNECTION

The electricity connection:
- Is a permanent one.
- Is a 3-phase, 4-wire Y, 140-kVA (subscribed capacity) connection.
- Is a low-voltage connection 150 meters long (unless a distribution transformer is installed on the customer's property, in which case the length of the low-voltage connection is 0).[8] The connection is overhead or underground, whichever is more common in the economy and in the area in which the warehouse is located. The length in the customer's private domain is negligible.
- Involves the installation of only one electricity meter. The monthly electricity consumption will be 0.07 gigawatt-hour (GWh).

The internal electrical wiring has already been completed.

PROCEDURES

A procedure is defined as any interaction of the company's employees or its main electrician or electrical engineer (that is, the one who may have done the internal wiring) with external parties such as the electricity distribution utility, electricity supply utilities, government agencies, electrical contractors and electrical firms. Interactions between company employees and steps related to the internal electrical wiring, such as the design and execution of the internal electrical installation plans, are not counted as procedures. Procedures that must be completed with the same utility but with different departments are counted as separate procedures.

The company's employees are as-

sumed to complete all procedures themselves unless the use of a third party is mandated (for example, if only an electrician registered with the utility is allowed to submit an application). If the company can, but is not required to, request the services of professionals (such as a private firm rather than the utility for the external works), these procedures are recorded if they are commonly done. For all procedures, only the most likely cases (for example, more than 50% of the time the utility has the material) and those followed in practice for connecting a warehouse to electricity are counted.

TIME

Time is recorded in calendar days. The measure captures the median duration that the electricity utility and experts indicate is necessary in practice, rather than required by law, to complete a procedure with minimum follow-up and no extra payments. It is also assumed that the minimum time required for each procedure is 1 day. Although procedures may take place simultaneously, they cannot start on the same day (that is, simultaneous procedures start on consecutive days). It is assumed that the company does not waste time and commits to completing each remaining procedure without delay. The time that the company spends on gathering information is ignored. It is assumed that the company is aware of all electricity connection requirements and their sequence from the beginning.

COST

Cost is recorded as a percentage of the economy's income per capita. Costs are recorded exclusive of value added tax. All the fees and costs associated with completing the procedures to connect a warehouse to electricity are recorded, including those related to obtaining clearances from government agencies, applying for the connection, receiving inspections of both the site and the internal wiring, purchasing material, getting the actual connection works and paying a security deposit. Information from local experts

and specific regulations and fee schedules are used as sources for costs. If several local partners provide different estimates, the median reported value is used. In all cases the cost excludes bribes.

SECURITY DEPOSIT

Utilities require security deposits as a guarantee against the possible failure of customers to pay their consumption bills. For this reason the security deposit for a new customer is most often calculated as a function of the customer's estimated consumption.

Doing Business does not record the full amount of the security deposit. Instead, it records the present value of the losses in interest earnings experienced by the customer because the utility holds the security deposit over a prolonged period, in most cases until the end of the contract (assumed to be after 5 years). In cases in which the security deposit is used to cover the first monthly consumption bills, it is not recorded. To calculate the present value of the lost interest earnings, the end-2009 lending rates from the International Monetary Fund's *International Financial Statistics* are used. In cases in which the security deposit is returned with interest, the difference between the lending rate and the interest paid by the utility is used to calculate the present value.

In some economies the security deposit can be put up in the form of a bond: the company can obtain from a bank or an insurance company a guarantee issued on the assets it holds with that financial institution. In contrast to the scenario in which the customer pays the deposit in cash to the utility, in this scenario the company does not lose ownership control over the full amount and can continue using it. In return the company will pay the bank a commission for obtaining the bond. The commission charged may vary depending on the credit standing of the company. The best possible credit standing and thus the lowest possible commission are assumed. Where a bond can be put up, the value recorded for the deposit is the annual commission times the 5 years assumed to be the length of the contract. If both options exist, the cheaper alternative is recorded.

In Belize in June 2010 a customer requesting a 140-kVA electricity connection would have had to put up a security deposit of 22,662 Belize dollars in cash or check, and the deposit would be returned only at the end of the contract. The customer could instead have invested this money at the prevailing lending rate of 14.05%. Over the 5 years of the contract this would imply a present value of lost interest earnings of BZ$10,918. In contrast, if the customer had been allowed to settle the deposit with a bank guarantee at an annual rate of 1.75%, the amount lost over the 5 years would have been just BZ$1,983.

The data details on getting electricity can be found for each economy at http://www.doingbusiness.org.

EMPLOYING WORKERS

Doing Business measures the regulation of employment, specifically as it affects the hiring and redundancy of workers and the rigidity of working hours. In 2007 improvements were made to align the methodology for the employing workers indicators with the International Labour Organization (ILO) conventions. Only 4 of the 188 ILO conventions cover areas measured by *Doing Business*: employee termination, weekend work, holiday with pay and night work. The *Doing Business* methodology is fully consistent with these 4 conventions. It is possible for an economy to receive the best score on the ease of employing workers and comply with all relevant ILO conventions (specifically, the 4 covering areas measured by *Doing Business*)—and no economy can achieve a better score by failing to comply with these conventions.

The ILO conventions covering areas related to the employing workers indicators do not include the ILO core labor standards—8 conventions covering the right to collective bargaining, the elimination of forced labor, the abolition of

child labor and equitable treatment in employment practices.

In 2009 additional changes were made to the methodology for the employing workers indicators.

First, the standardized case study was changed to refer to a small to medium-size company with 60 employees rather than 201. Second, restrictions on night and weekly holiday work are taken into account if they apply to manufacturing activities in which continuous operation is economically necessary. Third, legally mandated wage premiums for work performed on the designated weekly holiday or for night work are scored on the basis of a 4-tiered scale. Fourth, economies that mandate 8 or fewer weeks of severance pay and do not offer unemployment protection do not receive the highest score. Finally, the calculation of the minimum wage ratio was modified to ensure that an economy would not benefit in the scoring from lowering the minimum wage to below $1.25 a day, adjusted for purchasing power parity. This level is consistent with recent adjustments to the absolute poverty line.

This year further modifications were made to the methodology based on consultations with a consultative group of relevant stakeholders. For more information on the consultation process, see the *Doing Business* website (http://www.doingbusiness.org). Changes agreed as of the date of publication are the following: For the scoring of the minimum wage, no economy can receive the highest score if it has no minimum wage at all, if the law provides a regulatory mechanism for the minimum wage that is not enforced in practice, if there is only a customary minimum wage or if the minimum wage applies only to the public sector. A threshold was set for excessive flexibility in the paid annual leave period and the maximum number of working days per week. In addition, for the scoring of the annual leave period for the rigidity of hours index and the notice period and severance pay for the redundancy cost, the average value for a worker with 1 year

of tenure, a worker with 5 years and a worker with 10 years is used rather than the value for a worker with 20 years of tenure.

The data on employing workers are based on a detailed survey of employment regulations that is completed by local lawyers and public officials. Employment laws and regulations as well as secondary sources are reviewed to ensure accuracy. To make the data comparable across economies, several assumptions about the worker and the business are used.

ASSUMPTIONS ABOUT THE WORKER

The worker:

- Is a 42-year-old, nonexecutive, full-time, male employee.
- Earns a salary plus benefits equal to the economy's average wage during the entire period of his employment.
- Has a pay period that is the most common for workers in the economy.
- Is a lawful citizen who belongs to the same race and religion as the majority of the economy's population.
- Resides in the economy's largest business city.
- Is not a member of a labor union, unless membership is mandatory.

ASSUMPTIONS ABOUT THE BUSINESS

The business:

- Is a limited liability company.
- Operates in the economy's largest business city.
- Is 100% domestically owned.
- Operates in the manufacturing sector.
- Has 60 employees.
- Is subject to collective bargaining agreements in economies where such agreements cover more than half the manufacturing sector and apply even to firms not party to them.
- Abides by every law and regulation but does not grant workers more benefits than mandated by law, regulation or (if applicable) collective bargaining agreement.

TABLE 14.14

What do the employing workers indicators measure?

Difficulty of hiring index (0–100)

- Applicability and maximum duration of fixed-term contracts
- Minimum wage for trainee or first-time employee

Rigidity of hours index (0–100)

- Restrictions on night work and weekend work
- Allowed maximum length of the workweek in days and hours, including overtime
- Paid annual vacation days

Difficulty of redundancy index (0–100)

- Notification and approval requirements for termination of a redundant worker or group of redundant workers
- Obligation to reassign or retrain and priority rules for redundancy and reemployment

Rigidity of employment index (0–100)

- Simple average of the difficulty of hiring, rigidity of hours and difficulty of redundancy indices

Redundancy cost (weeks of salary)

- Notice requirements, severance payments and penalties due when terminating a redundant worker, expressed in weeks of salary

Source: Doing Business database.

RIGIDITY OF EMPLOYMENT INDEX

The rigidity of employment index is the average of 3 subindices: a difficulty of hiring index, a rigidity of hours index and a difficulty of redundancy index (table 14.14). All the subindices have several components. And all take values between 0 and 100, with higher values indicating more rigid regulation.

The difficulty of hiring index measures (i) whether fixed-term contracts are prohibited for permanent tasks; (ii) the maximum cumulative duration of fixed-term contracts; and (iii) the ratio of the minimum wage for a trainee or first-time employee to the average value added per worker.[9] An economy is assigned a score of 1 if fixed-term contracts are prohibited for permanent tasks and a score of 0 if they can be used for any task. A score of 1 is assigned if the maximum cumulative duration of fixed-term contracts is less than 3 years; 0.5 if it is 3 years or more but less than 5 years; and 0 if fixed-term contracts can last 5 years or more. Finally, a score of 1 is assigned if the ratio of the minimum wage to the average value added per worker is 0.75 or more; 0.67 for a ratio of 0.50 or more but less than 0.75; 0.33 for a ratio of 0.25 or more but less than 0.50; and 0 for a

ratio of less than 0.25. A score of 0 is also assigned if the minimum wage is set by a collective bargaining agreement that applies to less than half the manufacturing sector or does not apply to firms not party to it, or if the minimum wage is set by law but does not apply to workers who are in their apprentice period. A ratio of 0.251 (and therefore a score of 0.33) is automatically assigned in 4 cases: if there is no minimum wage, if the law provides a regulatory mechanism for the minimum wage that is not enforced in practice, if there is no minimum wage set by law but there is a wage amount that is customarily used as a minimum or if there is no minimum wage set by law in the private sector but there is one in the public sector.

In Benin, for example, fixed-term contracts are not prohibited for permanent tasks (a score of 0), and they can be used for a maximum of 4 years (a score of 0.5). The ratio of the mandated minimum wage to the value added per worker is 0.58 (a score of 0.67). Averaging the 3 values and scaling the index to 100 gives Benin a score of 39.

The rigidity of hours index has 5 components: (i) whether there are restrictions on night work; (ii) whether

there are restrictions on weekly holiday work; (iii) whether the workweek can consist of 5.5 days or is more than 6 days; (iv) whether the workweek can extend to 50 hours or more (including overtime) for 2 months a year to respond to a seasonal increase in production; and (v) whether the average paid annual leave for a worker with 1 year of tenure, a worker with 5 years and a worker with 10 years is more than 26 working days or fewer than 15 working days. For questions (i) and (ii), if restrictions other than premiums apply, a score of 1 is given. If the only restriction is a premium for night work or weekly holiday work, a score of 0, 0.33, 0.66 or 1 is given, depending on the quartile in which the economy's premium falls. If there are no restrictions, the economy receives a score of 0. For question (iii) a score of 1 is assigned if the legally permitted workweek is less than 5.5 days or more than 6 days; otherwise a score of 0 is assigned. For question (iv), if the answer is "no", a score of 1 is assigned; otherwise a score of 0 is assigned. For question (v) a score of 0 is assigned if the average paid annual leave is between 15 and 21 working days, a score of 0.5 if it is between 22 and 26 working days and a score of 1 if it is less than 15 or more than 26 working days.

For example, Honduras imposes restrictions on night work (a score of 1) but not on weekly holiday work (a score of 0), allows 6-day workweeks (a score of 0), permits 50-hour workweeks for 2 months (a score of 0) and requires average paid annual leave of 16.7 working days (a score of 0). Averaging the scores and scaling the result to 100 gives a final index of 20 for Honduras.

The difficulty of redundancy index has 8 components: (i) whether redundancy is disallowed as a basis for terminating workers; (ii) whether the employer needs to notify a third party (such as a government agency) to terminate 1 redundant worker; (iii) whether the employer needs to notify a third party to terminate a group of 9 redundant workers; (iv) whether the employer needs approval from a third party to terminate

1 redundant worker; (v) whether the employer needs approval from a third party to terminate a group of 9 redundant workers; (vi) whether the law requires the employer to reassign or retrain a worker before making the worker redundant; (vii) whether priority rules apply for redundancies; and (viii) whether priority rules apply for reemployment. For question (i) an answer of "yes" for workers of any income level gives a score of 10 and means that the rest of the questions do not apply. An answer of "yes" to question (iv) gives a score of 2. For every other question, if the answer is "yes," a score of 1 is assigned; otherwise a score of 0 is given. Questions (i) and (iv), as the most restrictive regulations, have greater weight in the construction of the index.

In Tunisia, for example, redundancy is allowed as grounds for termination (a score of 0). An employer has to both notify a third party (a score of 1) and obtain its approval (a score of 2) to terminate a single redundant worker, and has to both notify a third party (a score of 1) and obtain its approval (a score of 1) to terminate a group of 9 redundant workers. The law mandates retraining or alternative placement before termination (a score of 1). There are priority rules for termination (a score of 1) and reemployment (a score of 1). Adding the scores and scaling to 100 gives a final index of 80.

REDUNDANCY COST

The redundancy cost indicator measures the cost of advance notice requirements, severance payments and penalties due when terminating a redundant worker, expressed in weeks of salary. The average value of notice requirements and severance payments applicable to a worker with 1 year of tenure, a worker with 5 years and a worker with 10 years is used to assign the score. If the redundancy cost adds up to 8 or fewer weeks of salary and the workers can benefit from unemployment protection, a score of 0 is assigned, but the actual number of weeks is published. If the redundancy cost adds up to 8 or fewer weeks of salary and the workers cannot benefit from any type of

unemployment protection, a score of 8.1 weeks is assigned, although the actual number of weeks is published. If the cost adds up to more than 8 weeks of salary, the score is the number of weeks. One month is recorded as 4 and 1/3 weeks.

In Mauritania, for example, an employer is required to give an average of 1 month's notice before a redundancy termination, and the average severance pay for a worker with 1 year of service, a worker with 5 years and a worker with 10 years equals 1.42 months of wages. No penalty is levied. Altogether, the employer pays the equivalent of 10.5 weeks of salary to dismiss a worker.

The data details on employing workers can be found for each economy at http:// www.doingbusiness.org by selecting the economy in the drop-down list. This methodology was developed in Botero and others (2004) and is adopted here with changes.

---

1. The data for paying taxes refer to January–December 2009.
2. These are available at http://www.doingbusiness.org/Subnational/.
3. The *Doing Business* website (http://www.doingbusiness.org) provides a comparable time series of historical data for research, with a data set back-calculated to adjust for changes in methodology and data revisions due to corrections.

   For the terms of reference and composition of the consultative group, see World Bank, "Doing Business Employing Workers Indicator Consultative Group," http://www.doingbusiness.org.
4. Changes in *Doing Business* indicators follow very different increments. For example, the possible scores an economy can obtain on the protecting investors indicators can range from 0 to 10, while the procedures, time and cost for, say, starting a business can potentially range from 1 to infinity.

   Because normalizing the scores introduces an element of relativeness, a normalization approach has been chosen that minimizes this element: scores are normalized on a scale of 0–1 by subtracting from each value the smallest change and dividing the result by the differ-

ence between the highest and lowest observations. An alternative approach is to subtract from each value the mean value within each indicator's distribution and divide the result by the standard deviation within that same distribution. The resulting statistic is what is widely referred to as the Z-score. The main point of divergence between the normalization approach chosen for the new measure and the Z-score method is the reference point to which an economy's improvement is benchmarked. In the first approach an economy's measure of improvement on a particular indicator is benchmarked to the best and worst performance on that indicator. In the second approach the reference point for benchmarking an economy's performance is the average for the other 182 economies in the sample. This means that an economy's reform efforts again are ultimately scored relative to all other economies. Because the new measure is aimed at moving away from the relativeness of the ease of doing business ranking to focus on absolute improvements within economies, the first approach was chosen.

Given the alternatives available, a sensitivity analysis was carried out to see how much the results would differ if a Z-score were adopted instead. Using data from *Doing Business 2009* and *Doing Business 2010,* the correlation coefficient of results between the main approach used and the Z-score approach was computed. The results show a strong degree of correlation between the 2 approaches (correlation coefficient of 0.81).

5. See Djankov and others (2005).
6. This question is usually regulated by stock exchange or securities laws. Points are awarded only to economies with more than 10 listed firms in their most important stock exchange.
7. When evaluating the regime of liability for company directors for a prejudicial related-party transaction, *Doing Business* assumes that the transaction was duly disclosed and approved. *Doing Business* does not measure director liability in the event of fraud.
8. The distance of the assumed electricity connection was increased from 10 meters to what respondents considered to be a more realistic 150 meters. This change translated in some cases into a higher cost or longer time (or both) for the connection.
9. The average value added per worker is the ratio of an economy's GNI per capita to the working-age population as a percentage of the total population.

Summaries of *Doing Business* reforms in 2009/10

Doing Business reforms affecting all sets of indicators included in this year's ranking on the ease of doing business, implemented between June 2009 and May 2010.

✔ *Doing Business* reform making it easier to do business

✗ *Doing Business* reform making it more difficult to do business

ALBANIA

✔ Paying taxes

Albania made it easier and less costly for companies to pay taxes by amending several laws, reducing social security contributions and introducing electronic filing and payment.

ANGOLA

✔ Trading across borders

Angola reduced the time for trading across borders by making investments in port infrastructure and administration.

ANTIGUA AND BARBUDA

✗ Registering property

In Antigua and Barbuda, to transfer property now requires clearance by the chief surveyor to avoid mischievous declarations.

ARMENIA

✔ Trading across borders

Armenia made trading easier by introducing self-declaration desks at customs houses and warehouses, investing in new equipment to improve border operations and introducing a risk management system.

AUSTRIA

✔ Registering property

Austria made it easier to transfer property by requiring online submission of all applications to register property transfers.

AZERBAIJAN

✔ Getting credit

Azerbaijan improved access to credit by establishing an online platform allowing financial institutions to provide information to, and retrieve it from, the public credit registry.

✔ Paying taxes

A revision of Azerbaijan's tax code lowered several tax rates, including the profit tax rate, and simplified the process of paying corporate income tax and value added tax.

BAHRAIN

✗ Registering property

Bahrain made registering property more burdensome by increasing the fees at the Survey and Land Registration Bureau.

✔ Trading across borders

Bahrain made it easier to trade by building a modern new port, improving the electronic data interchange system and introducing risk-based inspections.

BANGLADESH

✔ Starting a business

Bangladesh made business start-up easier by eliminating the requirement to buy adhesive stamps and further enhancing the online registration system.

✔ Registering property

Bangladesh reduced the property transfer tax to 6.7% of the property value.

BELARUS

✔ Getting credit

Belarus enhanced access to credit by facilitating the use of the pledge as a security arrangement and providing for out-of-court enforcement of the pledge on default.

✔ Paying taxes

Reductions in the turnover tax, social security contributions and the base for property taxes along with continued efforts to encourage electronic filing made it easier and less costly for companies in Belarus to pay taxes.

✔ Trading across borders

Belarus reduced the time to trade by introducing electronic declaration of exports and imports.

✔ Closing a business

Belarus amended regulations governing the activities of insolvency administrators and strengthened the protection of creditor rights in bankruptcy.

BELGIUM

✗ Registering property

Belgium's capital city, Brussels, made it more difficult to transfer property by requiring a clean-soil certificate.

✔ Closing a business

Belgium introduced a new law that will promote and facilitate the survival of viable businesses experiencing financial difficulties.

BENIN

✔ Dealing with construction permits

Benin created a new municipal commission to streamline construction permitting and set up an ad hoc commission to deal with the backlog in permit application

BOSNIA AND HERZEGOVINA

✔ Registering property

Bosnia and Herzegovina reduced delays in property registration at the land registry in Sarajevo.

✔ Paying taxes

Bosnia and Herzegovina simplified its labor tax processes, reduced employer contribution rates for social security and abolished its payroll tax.

BRAZIL

✔ Starting a business

Brazil eased business start-up by further enhancing the electronic synchronization between federal and state tax authorities.

BRUNEI DARUSSALAM

✔ Starting a business

Brunei Darussalam made starting a business easier by improving efficiency at the company registrar and implementing an electronic system for name searches.

✔ Paying taxes

Brunei Darussalam reduced the corporate income tax rate from 23.5% to 22% while also introducing a lower tax rate for small businesses, ranging from 5.5% to 11%.

✔ Trading across borders

The introduction of an electronic customs system in Brunei Darussalam made trading easier.

BULGARIA

✔ Starting a business

Bulgaria eased business start-up by reducing the minimum capital requirement from 5,000 leva ($3,250) to 2 leva ($1.30).

✔ Paying taxes

Bulgaria reduced employer contribution rates for social security.

BURKINA FASO

✔ Dealing with construction permits

Burkina Faso made dealing with construction permits easier by cutting the cost of the soil survey in half and the time to process a building permit application by a third.

✔ Paying taxes

Burkina Faso reduced the statutory tax rate and the number of taxes for business and introduced simpler, uniform compliance procedures.

✔ Trading across borders

Burkina Faso reduced documentation requirements for importers and exporters, making it easier to trade.

✔ Enforcing contracts

Burkina Faso made enforcing contracts easier by setting up a specialized commercial court and abolishing the fee to register judicial decisions.

BURUNDI

✔ Paying taxes

Burundi made paying taxes simpler by replacing the transactions tax with a value added tax.

CAMBODIA

✔ Trading across borders

Cambodia eliminated preshipment inspections, reducing the time and number of documents required for importing and exporting.

CAMEROON

✔ Starting a business

Cameroon made starting a business easier by establishing a new one-stop shop and abolishing the requirement for verifying business premises and its corresponding fees.

CANADA

✔ Paying taxes

Canada harmonized the Ontario and federal tax returns and reduced the corporate and employee tax rates.

✔ Enforcing contracts

Canada increased the efficiency of the courts by expanding electronic document submission and streamlining procedures.

CAPE VERDE

✔ Starting a business

Cape Verde made start-up easier by eliminating the need for a municipal inspection before a business begins operations and computerizing the system for delivering the municipal license.

✔ Registering property

Cape Verde eased property registration by switching from fees based on a percentage of the property value to lower fixed rates.

✔ Paying taxes

Cape Verde abolished the stamp duties on sales and checks.

CHAD

✗ Paying taxes

Chad increased taxes on business through changes to its social security contribution rates.

CHILE

✔ Starting a business

Chile made business start-up easier by introducing an online system for registration and for filing the request for publication.

✔ Protecting investors

An amendment to Chile's securities law strengthened investor protections by requiring greater corporate disclosure and regulating the approval of transactions between interested parties.

CHINA

✔ Paying taxes

China's new corporate income tax law unified the tax regimes for domestic and foreign enterprises and clarified the calculation of taxable income for corporate income tax purposes.

COLOMBIA

✔ Dealing with construction permits

Colombia eased construction permitting by improving the electronic verification of prebuilding certificates.

CONGO, DEM. REP.

✔ Starting a business

The Democratic Republic of Congo eased business start-up by eliminating procedures, including the company seal.

✔ Dealing with construction permits

Dealing with construction permits became easier in the Democratic Republic of Congo thanks to a reduction in the cost of a building permit from 1% of the estimated construction cost to 0.6% and a time limit for issuing building permits.

✔ Registering property

The Democratic Republic of Congo reduced by half the property transfer tax to 3% of the property value.

CONGO, REP.

✔ Paying taxes

The Republic of Congo reduced its corporate income tax rate from 38% to 36% in 2010.

CÔTE D'IVOIRE

✔ **Dealing with construction permits**

Côte d'Ivoire eased construction permitting by eliminating the need to obtain a preliminary approval.

CROATIA

✔ **Starting a business**

Croatia eased business start-up by allowing limited liability companies to file their registration application with the court registries electronically through the notary public.

✔ **Dealing with construction permits**

Croatia replaced the location permit and project design confirmation with a single certificate, simplifying and speeding up the construction permitting process.

CZECH REPUBLIC

✔ **Paying taxes**

The Czech Republic simplified its labor tax processes and reduced employer contribution rates for social security.

✔ **Closing a business**

The Czech Republic made it easier to deal with insolvency by introducing further legal amendments to restrict setoffs in insolvency cases and suspending for some insolvent debtors the obligation to file for bankruptcy.

DENMARK

✔ **Starting a business**

Denmark eased business start-up by reducing the minimum capital requirement for limited liability companies from 125,000 Danish kroner ($22,850) to 80,000 Danish kroner ($14,620).

✔ **Registering property**

Computerization of Denmark's land registry cut the number of procedures required to register property by half.

DOMINICAN REPUBLIC

✗ **Starting a business**

The Dominican Republic made it more difficult to start a business by setting a minimum capital requirement of 100,000 Dominican pesos ($2,855) for its new type of company, *sociedad de responsabilidad limitada* (limited liability company).

ECUADOR

✔ **Starting a business**

Ecuador made starting a business easier by introducing an online registration system for social security.

EGYPT, ARAB REP.

✔ **Starting a business**

Egypt reduced the cost to start a business.

✔ **Trading across borders**

Egypt made trading easier by introducing an electronic system for submitting export and import documents.

ESTONIA

✗ **Dealing with construction permits**

Estonia made dealing with construction permits more complex by increasing the time for obtaining design criteria from the municipality.

✔ **Getting credit**

Estonia improved access to credit by amending the Code of Enforcement Procedure and allowing out-of-court enforcement of collateral by secured creditors.

✗ **Paying taxes**

Estonia increased the unemployment insurance contribution rate and raised the standard value added tax rate from 18% to 20%.

✔ **Closing a business**

Amendments to Estonia's recent insolvency law increased the chances that viable businesses will survive insolvency by improving procedures and changing the qualification requirements for insolvency administrators.

ETHIOPIA

✔ **Trading across borders**

Ethiopia made trading easier by addressing internal bureaucratic inefficiencies.

FIJI

✔ **Trading across borders**

Fiji made trading easier by opening customer care service centers and improving customs operations.

GEORGIA

✔ **Getting credit**

Georgia improved access to credit by implementing a central collateral registry with an electronic database accessible online.

✔ **Protecting investors**

Georgia strengthened investor protections by allowing greater access to corporate information during the trial.

✔ **Enforcing contracts**

Georgia made the enforcement of contracts easier by streamlining the procedures for public auctions, intrducing private enforcement officers and modernizing its dispute resolution system.

✔ **Closing a business**

Georgia improved insolvency proceedings by streamlining the regulation of auction sales.

GERMANY

✔ **Starting a business**

Germany eased business start-up by increasing the efficiency of communications between the notary and the commercial registry and eliminating the need to publish an announcement in a newspaper.

GHANA

✔ **Getting credit**

Ghana enhanced access to credit by establishing a centralized collateral registry and by granting an operating license to a private credit bureau that began operations in April 2010.

GREECE

✗ **Registering property**

Greece made transferring property more costly by increasing the transfer tax from 1% of the property value to 10%.

GRENADA

✔ **Starting a business**

Grenada eased business start-up by transferring responsibility for the commercial registry from the courts to the civil administration.

✔ Registering property

The appointment of a registrar focusing only on property cut the time needed to transfer property in Grenada by almost half.

✔ Trading across borders

Grenada's customs administration made trading faster by simplifying procedures, reducing inspections, improving staff training and enhancing communication with users.

GUINEA

✗ Dealing with construction permits

Guinea increased the cost of obtaining a building permit.

GUINEA-BISSAU

✔ Enforcing contracts

Guinea-Bissau established a specialized commercial court, speeding up the enforcement of contracts.

GUYANA

✔ Starting a business

Guyana eased business start-up by digitizing company records, which speeded up the process of company name search and reservation.

✔ Getting credit

Guyana enhanced access to credit by establishing a regulatory framework that allows the licensing of private credit bureaus and gives borrowers the right to inspect their data.

✔ Trading across borders

Guyana improved its risk profiling system for customs inspection, reducing physical inspections of shipments and the time to trade.

HAITI

✔ Starting a business

Haiti eased business start-up by eliminating the review by the president's or the prime minister's office of the incorporation act submitted for publication.

HONG KONG SAR, CHINA

✔ Paying taxes

Hong Kong SAR (China) abolished the fuel tax on diesel.

✔ Enforcing contracts

Reforms implemented in the civil justice system of Hong Kong SAR (China) will help increase the efficiency and cost-effectiveness of commercial dispute resolution.

HUNGARY

✔ Dealing with construction permits

Hungary implemented a time limit for the issuance of building permits.

✔ Registering property

Hungary reduced the property registration fee by 6% of the property value.

✔ Paying taxes

Hungary simplified taxes and tax bases.

✔ Closing a business

Amendments to Hungary's bankruptcy law encourage insolvent companies to consider reaching agreements with creditors out of court so as to avoid bankruptcy.

ICELAND

✗ Dealing with construction permits

Iceland made dealing with construction permits more costly by increasing the fees to obtain the design approval and receive inspections.

✗ Paying taxes

Iceland increased the corporate income tax rate from 15% to 18% and raised social security and pension contribution rates.

INDIA

✔ Starting a business

India eased business start-up by establishing an online VAT registration system and replacing the physical stamp previously required with an online version.

✔ Paying taxes

India reduced the administrative burden of paying taxes by abolishing the fringe benefit tax and improving electronic payment.

INDONESIA

✔ Starting a business

Indonesia eased business start-up by reducing the cost for company name clearance and reservation and the time required to reserve the name and approve the deed of incorporation.

✔ Paying taxes

Indonesia reduced its corporate income tax rate.

✔ Trading across borders

Indonesia reduced the time to export by launching a single-window service.

IRAN, ISLAMIC REP.

✔ Starting a business

The Islamic Republic of Iran eased business start-up by installing a web portal allowing entrepreneurs to search for and reserve a unique company name.

✔ Getting credit

The establishment of a new private credit bureau improved access to credit information.

✔ Enforcing contracts

The Islamic Republic of Iran made enforcing contracts easier and faster by introducing electronic filing of some documents, text message notification and an electronic case management system.

ISRAEL

✔ Trading across borders

Israel is expanding its electronic data interchange system and developing a single-window framework, allowing easier assembly of documents required by different authorities and reducing the time to trade.

ITALY

✔ Starting a business

Italy made starting a business easier by enhancing an online registration system.

JAMAICA

✔ Registering property

Jamaica eased the transfer of property by lowering transfer taxes and fees, offering expedited registration procedures and making information from the company registrar available online.

JAPAN

✔ Closing a business

Japan made it easier to deal with insolvency by establishing a new entity, the Enterprise Turnaround Initiative Corporation, to support the revitalization of companies suffering from excessive debt but professionally managed.

JORDAN

✔ Getting credit

Jordan improved its credit information system by setting up a regulatory framework for establishing a private credit bureau as well as lowering the threshold for loans to be reported to the public credit registry.

✔ Paying taxes

Jordan abolished certain taxes and made it possible to file income and sales tax returns electronically.

KAZAKHSTAN

✔ Starting a business

Kazakhstan eased business start-up by reducing the minimum capital requirement to 100 tenge ($0.70) and eliminating the need to have the memorandum of association and company charter notarized.

✔ Dealing with construction permits

Kazakhstan made dealing with construction permits easier by implementing a one-stop shop related to technical conditions for utilities.

✔ Protecting investors

Kazakhstan strengthened investor protections by requiring greater corporate disclosure in company annual reports.

✔ Trading across borders

Kazakhstan speeded up trade through efforts to modernize customs, including implementation of a risk management system and improvements in customs automation.

KENYA

✔ Starting a business

Kenya eased business start-up by reducing the time it takes to get the memorandum and articles of association stamped, merging the tax and value added tax registration procedures and digitizing records at the registrar.

✗ Paying taxes

Kenya increased the administrative burden of paying taxes by requiring quarterly filing of payroll taxes.

✔ Trading across borders

Kenya speeded up trade by implementing an electronic cargo tracking system and linking this system to the Kenya Revenue Authority's electronic data interchange system for customs clearance.

KOREA, REP.

✔ Closing a business

Korea made it easier to deal with insolvency by introducing postfiling financing, granting superpriority to the repayment of loans given to companies undergoing reorganization.

KOSOVO

✗ Starting a business

Kosovo made business start-up more difficult by replacing the tax number previously required with a "fiscal number," which takes longer to issue and requires the tax administration to first inspect the business premises.

KYRGYZ REPUBLIC

✔ Starting a business

The Kyrgyz Republic eased business start-up by eliminating the requirement to have the signatures of company founders notarized.

✗ Closing a business

The Kyrgyz Republic streamlined insolvency proceedings and updated requirements for administrators, but new formalities added to prevent abuse of proceedings made closing a business more difficult.

LAO PDR

✔ Paying taxes

Lao PDR replaced the business turnover tax with a new value added tax.

LATVIA

✔ Trading across borders

Latvia reduced the time to export and import by introducing electronic submission of customs declarations.

✔ Closing a business

Latvia introduced a mechanism for out-of-court settlement of insolvencies to alleviate pressure on courts and tightened some procedural deadlines.

LEBANON

✗ Starting a business

Lebanon increased the cost of starting a business.

✔ Getting credit

Lebanon improved its credit information system by allowing banks online access to the public credit registry's reports.

LITHUANIA

✔ Starting a business

Lithuania tightened the time limit for completing the registration of a company.

✔ Getting credit

Lithuania's private credit bureau now collects and distributes positive information on borrowers.

✔ Paying taxes

Lithuania reduced corporate tax rates.

✔ Trading across borders

Lithuania reduced the time to import by introducing, in compliance with EU law, an electronic system for submitting customs declarations.

✔ Closing a business

Lithuania introduced regulations relating to insolvency administrators that set out clear rules of liability for violations of law.

LUXEMBOURG

✔ **Starting a business**

Luxembourg eased business start-up by speeding up the delivery of the business license.

MACEDONIA, FYR

✔ **Starting a business**

FYR Macedonia made it easier to start a business by further improving its one-stop shop.

✔ **Paying taxes**

FYR Macedonia lowered tax costs for businesses by requiring that corporate income tax be paid only on distributed profits.

MADAGASCAR

✔ **Paying taxes**

Madagascar continued to reduce corporate tax rates.

✔ **Trading across borders**

Madagascar improved communication and coordination between customs and the terminal port operators through its single-window system (GASYNET), reducing both the time and the cost to export and import.

MALAWI

✔ **Registering property**

Malawi eased property transfers by cutting the wait for consents and registration of legal instruments by half.

✔ **Enforcing contracts**

Malawi simplified the enforcement of contracts by raising the ceiling for commercial claims that can be brought to the magistrate's courts.

MALAYSIA

✔ **Starting a business**

Malaysia eased business start-up by introducing more online services.

✔ **Registering property**

Malaysia's introduction of online stamping reduced the time and cost to transfer property.

MALDIVES

✔ **Registering property**

Maldives now allows registered companies to own land as long as all company shares are owned by Maldivians.

MALI

✔ **Dealing with construction permits**

Mali eased construction permitting by implementing a simplified environmental impact assessment for noncomplex commercial buildings.

✔ **Registering property**

Mali eased property transfers by reducing the property transfer tax for firms from 15% of the property value to 7%.

✔ **Trading across borders**

Mali eliminated redundant inspections of imported goods, reducing the time for trading across borders.

MARSHALL ISLANDS

✔ **Getting credit**

The Marshall Islands improved access to credit through a new law on secured transactions that establishes a central collateral registry, broadens the range of assets that can be used as collateral, allows a general description of debts and obligations and assets granted as collateral and establishes clear priority rules outside bankruptcy for secured creditors.

MAURITIUS

✘ **Paying taxes**

Mauritius introduced a new corporate social responsibility tax.

✔ **Enforcing contracts**

Mauritius speeded up the resolution of commercial disputes by recruiting more judges and adding more courtrooms.

MEXICO

✔ **Starting a business**

Mexico launched an online one-stop shop for initiating business registration.

✔ **Dealing with construction permits**

Mexico improved construction permitting by merging and streamlining procedures related to zoning and utilities.

✘ **Paying taxes**

Mexico increased taxes on companies by raising several tax rates, including the corporate income tax and the rate on cash deposits. At the same time, the administrative burden continued to decrease with more options for online payment and increased use of accounting software.

MOLDOVA

✔ **Paying taxes**

Moldova reduced employer contribution rates for social security.

MONTENEGRO

✔ **Starting a business**

Montenegro eliminated several procedures for business start-up by introducing a single registration form for submission to the tax administration.

✔ **Paying taxes**

An amendment to Montenegro's corporate income tax law removed the obligation for advance payments and abolished the construction land charge.

✔ **Trading across borders**

Montenegro's customs administration simplified trade by eliminating the requirement to present a terminal handling receipt for exporting and importing.

MOROCCO

✔ **Protecting investors**

Morocco strengthened investor protections by requiring greater disclosure in companies' annual reports.

MOZAMBIQUE

✔ **Starting a business**

Mozambique eased business start-up by introducing a simplified licensing process.

NETHERLANDS

✔ **Paying taxes**

The Netherlands reduced the frequency of filing and paying value added taxes from monthly to quarterly and allowed small entities to use their annual accounts as the basis for computing their corporate income tax.

NEW ZEALAND

✔ Enforcing contracts

New Zealand enacted new district court rules that make the process for enforcing contracts user friendly.

NICARAGUA

✗ Paying taxes

Nicaragua increased taxes on firms by raising social security contribution rates and introducing a 10% withholding tax on the gross interest accrued from deposits. It also improved electronic payment of taxes through bank transfer.

✔ Trading across borders

Nicaragua expedited trade by migrating to a new electronic data interchange system for customs, setting up a physical one-stop shop for exports and investing in new equipment at the port of Corinto.

NIGER

✔ Paying taxes

Niger reduced its corporate income tax rate.

PAKISTAN

✗ Registering property

Pakistan made registering property more expensive by doubling the capital value tax to 4%.

✔ Trading across borders

Pakistan reduced the time to export by improving electronic communication between the Karachi Port authorities and the private terminals, which have also boosted efficiency by introducing new equipment.

PANAMA

✔ Starting a business

Panama eased business start-up by increasing efficiency at the registrar.

✗ Registering property

Panama made it more expensive to transfer property by requiring that an amount equal to 3% of the property value be paid upon registration.

✔ Paying taxes

Panama reduced the corporate income tax rate, modified various taxes and created a new tax court of appeals.

PAPUA NEW GUINEA

✔ Getting credit

Operation of a new private credit bureau improved the credit information system in Papua New Guinea.

PARAGUAY

✔ Dealing with construction permits

Paraguay made dealing with construction permits easier by creating a new administrative structure and a better tracking system in the municipality of Asunción.

PERU

✔ Starting a business

Peru eased business start-up by simplifying the requirements for operating licenses and creating an online one-stop shop for business registration.

✔ Dealing with construction permits

Peru streamlined construction permitting by implementing administrative reforms.

✔ Registering property

Peru introduced fast-track procedures at the land registry, cutting by half the time needed to register property.

✔ Trading across borders

Peru made trading easier by implementing a new web-based electronic data interchange system, risk-based inspections and payment deferrals.

PHILIPPINES

✔ Starting a business

The Philippines eased business start-up by setting up a one-stop shop at the municipal level.

✗ Dealing with construction permits

The Philippines made construction permitting more cumbersome through updated electricity connection costs.

✔ Trading across borders

The Philippines reduced the time and cost to trade by improving its electronic customs systems, adding such functions as electronic payments and online submission of declarations.

POLAND

✔ Registering property

Poland eased property registration by computerizing its land registry.

PORTUGAL

✔ Registering property

Portugal established a one-stop shop for property registration.

✔ Paying taxes

Portugal introduced a new social security code and lowered corporate tax rates.

PUERTO RICO

✗ Paying taxes

Puerto Rico made paying taxes more costly for business by introducing a special surtax of 5% on the tax liability in addition to the normal corporate income tax.

QATAR

✗ Starting a business

Qatar made starting a business more difficult by adding a procedure to register for taxes and obtain a company seal.

ROMANIA

✔ Dealing with construction permits

Romania amended regulations related to construction permitting to reduce fees and expedite the process.

✗ Paying taxes

Romania introduced tax changes, including a new minimum tax on profit, that made paying taxes more costly for companies.

✔ Closing a business

Substantial amendments to Romania's bankruptcy laws—introducing, among other things, a procedure for out-of-court workouts—made dealing with insolvency easier.

RUSSIAN FEDERATION

✔ **Dealing with construction permits**

Russia eased construction permitting by implementing a single window for all procedures related to land use.

✔ **Closing a business**

Russia introduced a series of legislative measures in 2009 to improve creditor rights and the insolvency system.

RWANDA

✔ **Dealing with construction permits**

Rwanda made dealing with construction permits easier by passing new building regulations at the end of April 2010 and implementing new time limits for the issuance of various permits.

✔ **Getting credit**

Rwanda enhanced access to credit by allowing borrowers the right to inspect their own credit report and mandating that loans of all sizes be reported to the central bank's public credit registry.

✔ **Trading across borders**

Rwanda reduced the number of trade documents required and enhanced its joint border management procedures with Uganda and other neighbors, leading to an improvement in the trade logistics environment.

SAMOA

✔ **Registering property**

Samoa shifted from a deed system to a title system and fully computerized its land registry, which reduced the time required to register property by 4 months.

SÃO TOMÉ AND PRINCIPE

✗ **Starting a business**

São Tomé and Principe made starting a business more difficult by introducing a minimum capital requirement for limited liability companies.

✔ **Paying taxes**

São Tomé and Principe reduced the corporate income tax rate to a standard 25%.

SAUDI ARABIA

✔ **Dealing with construction permits**

Saudi Arabia made dealing with construction permits easier for the second year in a row by introducing a new, streamlined process.

✔ **Getting credit**

An amendment to Saudi Arabia's commercial lien law enhanced access to credit by making secured lending more flexible and allowing out-of-court enforcement in case of default.

✔ **Trading across borders**

Saudi Arabia reduced the time to import by launching a new container terminal at the Jeddah Islamic Port.

✔ **Closing a business**

Saudi Arabia speeded up the insolvency process by providing earlier access to amicable settlements and putting time limits on the settlements to encourage creditors to participate.

SERBIA

✔ **Closing a business**

Serbia passed a new bankruptcy law that introduced out-of-court workouts and a unified reorganization procedure.

SEYCHELLES

✔ **Paying taxes**

The Seychelles removed the tax-free threshold limit and lowered corporate income tax rates.

SIERRA LEONE

✔ **Dealing with construction permits**

Sierra Leone made dealing with construction permits easier by streamlining the issuance of location clearances and building permits.

✔ **Registering property**

Sierra Leone lifted a moratorium on sales of privately owned properties.

✔ **Paying taxes**

Sierra Leone replaced sales and service taxes with a goods and service tax.

SLOVENIA

✔ **Starting a business**

Slovenia made starting a business easier through improvements to its one-stop shop that allowed more online services.

✔ **Registering property**

Greater computerization in Slovenia's land registry reduced delays in property registration by 75%.

✔ **Paying taxes**

Slovenia abolished its payroll tax and reduced its corporate income tax rate.

SOLOMON ISLANDS

✔ **Getting credit**

The Solomon Islands strengthened access to credit by passing a new secured transactions law that broadens the range of assets that can be used as collateral, allows a general description of debts and obligations secured by collateral, permits out-of-court enforcement and creates a collateral registry.

SPAIN

✔ **Trading across borders**

Spain streamlined the documentation for imports by including tax-related information on its single administrative document.

✔ **Closing a business**

Spain amended its regulations governing insolvency proceedings with the aim of reducing the cost and time. The new regulations also introduced out-of-court workouts.

SWAZILAND

✔ **Protecting investors**

Swaziland strengthened investor protections by requiring greater corporate disclosure, higher standards of accountability for company directors and greater access to corporate information for minority investors.

✔ **Trading across borders**

Swaziland reduced the time to import by implementing an electronic data interchange system for customs at its border posts.

SWEDEN

✔ Starting a business

Sweden cut the minimum capital requirement for limited liability companies by half, making it easier to start a business.

✔ Registering property

Sweden made registering property easier by eliminating the requirement to obtain a preemption waiver from the municipality.

✔ Protecting investors

Sweden strengthened investor protections by requiring greater corporate disclosure and regulating the approval of transactions between interested parties.

SYRIAN ARAB REPUBLIC

✔ Starting a business

Syria eased business start-up by reducing the minimum capital requirement for limited liability companies by two-thirds. It also decentralized approval of the company memorandum.

✔ Getting credit

Syria enhanced access to credit by eliminating the minimum threshold for loans included in the database, which expanded the coverage of individuals and firms to 2.2% of the adult population.

TAIWAN, CHINA

✔ Starting a business

Taiwan (China) eased business start-up by reducing the time required to check company names, register retirement plans and apply for health, pension and labor insurance.

✔ Paying taxes

Taiwan (China) reduced the corporate income tax rate and simplified tax return forms, rules for assessing corporate income tax and the calculation of interim tax payments.

TAJIKISTAN

✔ Starting a business

Tajikistan made starting a business easier by creating a one-stop shop that consolidates registration with the state and the tax authority.

✔ Protecting investors

Tajikistan strengthened investor protections by requiring greater corporate disclosure in the annual report and greater access to corporate information for minority investors.

✔ Paying taxes

Tajikistan lowered its corporate income tax rate.

THAILAND

✗ Registering property

Thailand made registering property more costly by repealing a 2-year temporary tax reduction for property transfers.

✔ Paying taxes

Thailand temporarily lowered taxes on business by reducing its specific business tax for 12 months.

TIMOR-LESTE

✔ Enforcing contracts

Timor-Leste increased court efficiency by training and appointing new judges and passing a new civil procedure code.

TONGA

✔ Paying taxes

Tonga simplified the payment of taxes by replacing a 2-tier system with a 25% corporate income tax rate for both domestic and foreign companies and introducing tax incentives with a broad-based capital allowance system to replace tax holidays and other tax concessions.

TUNISIA

✔ Paying taxes

Tunisia introduced the use of electronic systems for payment of corporate income tax and value added tax.

✔ Trading across borders

Tunisia upgraded its electronic data interchange system for imports and exports, speeding up the assembly of import documents.

UGANDA

✗ Starting a business

Uganda made it more difficult to start a business by increasing the trade licensing fees.

✔ Getting credit

Uganda enhanced access to credit by establishing a new private credit bureau.

✔ Enforcing contracts

Uganda continues to improve the efficiency of its court system, greatly reducing the time to file and serve a claim.

UKRAINE

✔ Starting a business

Ukraine eased business start-up by substantially reducing the minimum capital requirement.

✔ Dealing with construction permits

Ukraine made dealing with construction permits easier by implementing national and local regulations that streamlined procedures.

✔ Paying taxes

Ukraine eased tax compliance by introducing and continually enhancing an electronic filing system for value added tax.

UNITED ARAB EMIRATES

✔ Getting credit

The United Arab Emirates enhanced access to credit by setting up a legal framework for the operation of the private credit bureau and requiring that financial institutions share credit information.

✔ Trading across borders

The United Arab Emirates streamlined document preparation and reduced the time to trade with the launch of Dubai Customs' comprehensive new customs system, Mirsal 2.

UNITED KINGDOM

✔ **Enforcing contracts**

The United Kingdom improved the process for enforcing contracts by modernizing civil procedures in the commercial court.

✔ **Closing a business**

Amendments to the United Kingdom's insolvency rules streamline bankruptcy procedures, favor the sale of the firm as a whole and improve the calculation of administrators' fees.

UNITED STATES

✗ **Paying taxes**

In the United States the introduction of a new tax on payroll increased taxes on companies operating within the New York City metropolitan commuter transportation district.

URUGUAY

✔ **Registering property**

In Uruguay the Municipality of Montevideo made registering property easier by eliminating the need to obtain a mandatory waiver for preemption rights.

UZBEKISTAN

✗ **Dealing with construction permits**

Uzbekistan increased all fees for procedures relating to construction permits.

VENEZUELA, RB

✗ **Starting a business**

República Bolivariana de Venezuela made starting a business more difficult by introducing a new procedure for registering a company.

✔ **Paying taxes**

República Bolivariana de Venezuela abolished the tax on financial transactions.

VIETNAM

✔ **Starting a business**

Vietnam eased company start-up by creating a one-stop shop that combines the processes for obtaining a business license and tax license and by eliminating the need for a seal for company licensing.

✔ **Dealing with construction permits**

Vietnam made dealing with construction permits easier by reducing the cost to register newly completed buildings by 50% and transferring the authority to register buildings from local authorities to the Department of National Resources and Environment.

✔ **Getting credit**

Vietnam improved its credit information system by allowing borrowers to examine their own credit report and correct errors.

WEST BANK AND GAZA

✗ **Starting a business**

West Bank and Gaza made starting a business more difficult by increasing the lawyers' fees that must be paid for incorporation.

✔ **Trading across borders**

More efficient processes at Palestinian customs made trading easier in the West Bank.

ZAMBIA

✔ **Starting a business**

Zambia eased business start-up by eliminating the minimum capital requirement.

✔ **Trading across borders**

Zambia eased trade by implementing a one-stop border post with Zimbabwe, launching web-based submission of customs declarations and introducing scanning machines at border posts.

✔ **Enforcing contracts**

Zambia improved contract enforcement by introducing an electronic case management system in the courts that provides electronic referencing of cases, a database of laws, real-time court reporting and public access to court records.

ZIMBABWE

✔ **Starting a business**

Zimbabwe eased business start-up by reducing registration fees and speeding up the name search process and company and tax registration.

✔ **Paying taxes**

Zimbabwe reduced the corporate income tax rate from 30% to 25%, lowered the capital gains tax from 20% to 5% and simplified the payment of corporate income tax by allowing quarterly payment through commercial banks.

Country
tables

AFGHANISTAN

		South Asia		GNI per capita (US$)	486
Ease of doing business (rank)	167	Low income		Population (m)	29.8
Starting a business (rank)	25	**Getting credit** (rank)	128	**Trading across borders** (rank)	183
Procedures (number)	4	Strength of legal rights index (0-10)	6	Documents to export (number)	12
Time (days)	7	Depth of credit information index (0-6)	0	Time to export (days)	74
Cost (% of income per capita)	26.7	Public registry coverage (% of adults)	0.0	Cost to export (US$ per container)	3,865
Minimum capital (% of income per capita)	0.0	Private bureau coverage (% of adults)	0.0	Documents to import (number)	11
				Time to import (days)	77
Dealing with construction permits (rank)	149	**Protecting investors** (rank)	183	Cost to import (US$ per container)	3,830
Procedures (number)	13	Extent of disclosure index (0-10)	1		
Time (days)	340	Extent of director liability index (0-10)	1	**Enforcing contracts** (rank)	162
Cost (% of income per capita)	11,355.3	Ease of shareholder suits index (0-10)	1	Procedures (number)	47
		Strength of investor protection index (0-10)	1.0	Time (days)	1,642
Registering property (rank)	170			Cost (% of claim)	25.0
Procedures (number)	9	**Paying taxes** (rank)	53		
Time (days)	250	Payments (number per year)	8	**Closing a business** (rank)	183
Cost (% of property value)	5.0	Time (hours per year)	275	Time (years)	NO PRACTICE
		Total tax rate (% of profit)	36.4	Cost (% of estate)	NO PRACTICE
				Recovery rate (cents on the dollar)	0.0

ALBANIA

		Eastern Europe & Central Asia		GNI per capita (US$)	3,950
Ease of doing business (rank)	82	Upper middle income		Population (m)	3.2
Starting a business (rank)	45	**Getting credit** (rank)	15	**Trading across borders** (rank)	75
Procedures (number)	5	Strength of legal rights index (0-10)	9	Documents to export (number)	7
Time (days)	5	Depth of credit information index (0-6)	4	Time to export (days)	19
Cost (% of income per capita)	16.8	Public registry coverage (% of adults)	8.3	Cost to export (US$ per container)	725
Minimum capital (% of income per capita)	0.0	Private bureau coverage (% of adults)	0.0	Documents to import (number)	9
				Time to import (days)	18
Dealing with construction permits (rank)	170	**Protecting investors** (rank)	15	Cost to import (US$ per container)	710
Procedures (number)	24	Extent of disclosure index (0-10)	8		
Time (days)	331	Extent of director liability index (0-10)	9	**Enforcing contracts** (rank)	89
Cost (% of income per capita)	381.3	Ease of shareholder suits index (0-10)	5	Procedures (number)	39
		Strength of investor protection index (0-10)	7.3	Time (days)	390
Registering property (rank)	72			Cost (% of claim)	38.7
Procedures (number)	6	✔ **Paying taxes** (rank)	149		
Time (days)	42	Payments (number per year)	44	**Closing a business** (rank)	183
Cost (% of property value)	3.4	Time (hours per year)	360	Time (years)	NO PRACTICE
		Total tax rate (% of profit)	40.6	Cost (% of estate)	NO PRACTICE
				Recovery rate (cents on the dollar)	0.0

ALGERIA

		Middle East & North Africa		GNI per capita (US$)	4,420
Ease of doing business (rank)	136	Upper middle income		Population (m)	34.9
Starting a business (rank)	150	**Getting credit** (rank)	138	**Trading across borders** (rank)	124
Procedures (number)	14	Strength of legal rights index (0-10)	3	Documents to export (number)	8
Time (days)	24	Depth of credit information index (0-6)	2	Time to export (days)	17
Cost (% of income per capita)	12.9	Public registry coverage (% of adults)	0.2	Cost to export (US$ per container)	1,248
Minimum capital (% of income per capita)	34.4	Private bureau coverage (% of adults)	0.0	Documents to import (number)	9
				Time to import (days)	23
Dealing with construction permits (rank)	113	**Protecting investors** (rank)	74	Cost to import (US$ per container)	1,428
Procedures (number)	22	Extent of disclosure index (0-10)	6		
Time (days)	240	Extent of director liability index (0-10)	6	**Enforcing contracts** (rank)	127
Cost (% of income per capita)	44.0	Ease of shareholder suits index (0-10)	4	Procedures (number)	46
		Strength of investor protection index (0-10)	5.3	Time (days)	630
Registering property (rank)	165			Cost (% of claim)	21.9
Procedures (number)	11	**Paying taxes** (rank)	168		
Time (days)	47	Payments (number per year)	34	**Closing a business** (rank)	51
Cost (% of property value)	7.1	Time (hours per year)	451	Time (years)	2.5
		Total tax rate (% of profit)	72.0	Cost (% of estate)	7
				Recovery rate (cents on the dollar)	41.7

✔ Reforms making it easier to do business   ✘ Reforms making it more difficult to do business

ANGOLA

		Sub-Saharan Africa		GNI per capita (US$)	3,490
Ease of doing business (rank)	163	Lower middle income		Population (m)	18.5
Starting a business (rank)	164	**Getting credit** (rank)	116	✔ **Trading across borders** (rank)	166
Procedures (number)	8	Strength of legal rights index (0-10)	4	Documents to export (number)	11
Time (days)	68	Depth of credit information index (0-6)	3	Time to export (days)	52
Cost (% of income per capita)	163.0	Public registry coverage (% of adults)	2.4	Cost to export (US$ per container)	1,850
Minimum capital (% of income per capita)	28.7	Private bureau coverage (% of adults)	0.0	Documents to import (number)	8
				Time to import (days)	49
Dealing with construction permits (rank)	128	**Protecting investors** (rank)	59	Cost to import (US$ per container)	2,840
Procedures (number)	12	Extent of disclosure index (0-10)	5		
Time (days)	328	Extent of director liability index (0-10)	6	**Enforcing contracts** (rank)	181
Cost (% of income per capita)	694.3	Ease of shareholder suits index (0-10)	6	Procedures (number)	46
		Strength of investor protection index (0-10)	5.7	Time (days)	1,011
Registering property (rank)	174			Cost (% of claim)	44.4
Procedures (number)	7	**Paying taxes** (rank)	142		
Time (days)	184	Payments (number per year)	31	**Closing a business** (rank)	147
Cost (% of property value)	11.5	Time (hours per year)	282	Time (years)	6.2
		Total tax rate (% of profit)	53.2	Cost (% of estate)	22
				Recovery rate (cents on the dollar)	8.4

ANTIGUA AND BARBUDA

		Latin America & Caribbean		GNI per capita (US$)	12,130
Ease of doing business (rank)	64	Upper middle income		Population (m)	0.1
Starting a business (rank)	72	**Getting credit** (rank)	116	**Trading across borders** (rank)	63
Procedures (number)	8	Strength of legal rights index (0-10)	7	Documents to export (number)	5
Time (days)	21	Depth of credit information index (0-6)	0	Time to export (days)	15
Cost (% of income per capita)	11.0	Public registry coverage (% of adults)	0.0	Cost to export (US$ per container)	1,133
Minimum capital (% of income per capita)	0.0	Private bureau coverage (% of adults)	0.0	Documents to import (number)	5
				Time to import (days)	15
Dealing with construction permits (rank)	25	**Protecting investors** (rank)	28	Cost to import (US$ per container)	1,633
Procedures (number)	13	Extent of disclosure index (0-10)	4		
Time (days)	156	Extent of director liability index (0-10)	8	**Enforcing contracts** (rank)	73
Cost (% of income per capita)	24.2	Ease of shareholder suits index (0-10)	7	Procedures (number)	45
		Strength of investor protection index (0-10)	6.3	Time (days)	351
✘ **Registering property** (rank)	123			Cost (% of claim)	22.7
Procedures (number)	7	**Paying taxes** (rank)	132		
Time (days)	26	Payments (number per year)	56	**Closing a business** (rank)	66
Cost (% of property value)	10.9	Time (hours per year)	207	Time (years)	3.0
		Total tax rate (% of profit)	41.5	Cost (% of estate)	7
				Recovery rate (cents on the dollar)	36.7

ARGENTINA

		Latin America & Caribbean		GNI per capita (US$)	7,600
Ease of doing business (rank)	115	Upper middle income		Population (m)	40.3
Starting a business (rank)	142	**Getting credit** (rank)	65	**Trading across borders** (rank)	115
Procedures (number)	14	Strength of legal rights index (0-10)	4	Documents to export (number)	9
Time (days)	26	Depth of credit information index (0-6)	6	Time to export (days)	13
Cost (% of income per capita)	14.2	Public registry coverage (% of adults)	30.8	Cost to export (US$ per container)	1,480
Minimum capital (% of income per capita)	2.7	Private bureau coverage (% of adults)	100.0	Documents to import (number)	7
				Time to import (days)	16
Dealing with construction permits (rank)	168	**Protecting investors** (rank)	109	Cost to import (US$ per container)	1,810
Procedures (number)	28	Extent of disclosure index (0-10)	6		
Time (days)	338	Extent of director liability index (0-10)	2	**Enforcing contracts** (rank)	45
Cost (% of income per capita)	133.9	Ease of shareholder suits index (0-10)	6	Procedures (number)	36
		Strength of investor protection index (0-10)	4.7	Time (days)	590
Registering property (rank)	118			Cost (% of claim)	16.5
Procedures (number)	6	**Paying taxes** (rank)	143		
Time (days)	52	Payments (number per year)	9	**Closing a business** (rank)	77
Cost (% of property value)	7.0	Time (hours per year)	453	Time (years)	2.8
		Total tax rate (% of profit)	108.2	Cost (% of estate)	12
				Recovery rate (cents on the dollar)	32.8

ARMENIA

		Eastern Europe & Central Asia		GNI per capita (US$)		3,100
Ease of doing business (rank)	48	Lower middle income		Population (m)		3.1
Starting a business (rank)	22	**Getting credit** (rank)	46	✔ **Trading across borders** (rank)		82
Procedures (number)	6	Strength of legal rights index (0-10)	6	Documents to export (number)		3
Time (days)	15	Depth of credit information index (0-6)	5	Time to export (days)		13
Cost (% of income per capita)	3.1	Public registry coverage (% of adults)	16.9	Cost to export (US$ per container)		1,665
Minimum capital (% of income per capita)	0.0	Private bureau coverage (% of adults)	38.3	Documents to import (number)		6
				Time to import (days)		18
Dealing with construction permits (rank)	78	**Protecting investors** (rank)	93	Cost to import (US$ per container)		2,045
Procedures (number)	20	Extent of disclosure index (0-10)	5			
Time (days)	137	Extent of director liability index (0-10)	2	**Enforcing contracts** (rank)		63
Cost (% of income per capita)	122.7	Ease of shareholder suits index (0-10)	8	Procedures (number)		49
		Strength of investor protection index (0-10)	5.0	Time (days)		285
Registering property (rank)	5			Cost (% of claim)		19.0
Procedures (number)	3	**Paying taxes** (rank)	159			
Time (days)	7	Payments (number per year)	50	**Closing a business** (rank)		54
Cost (% of property value)	0.3	Time (hours per year)	581	Time (years)		1.9
		Total tax rate (% of profit)	40.7	Cost (% of estate)		4
				Recovery rate (cents on the dollar)		40.6

AUSTRALIA

		OECD high income		GNI per capita (US$)		43,770
Ease of doing business (rank)	10	High income		Population (m)		21.9
Starting a business (rank)	2	**Getting credit** (rank)	6	**Trading across borders** (rank)		29
Procedures (number)	2	Strength of legal rights index (0-10)	9	Documents to export (number)		6
Time (days)	2	Depth of credit information index (0-6)	5	Time to export (days)		9
Cost (% of income per capita)	0.7	Public registry coverage (% of adults)	0.0	Cost to export (US$ per container)		1,060
Minimum capital (% of income per capita)	0.0	Private bureau coverage (% of adults)	100.0	Documents to import (number)		5
				Time to import (days)		8
Dealing with construction permits (rank)	63	**Protecting investors** (rank)	59	Cost to import (US$ per container)		1,119
Procedures (number)	16	Extent of disclosure index (0-10)	8			
Time (days)	221	Extent of director liability index (0-10)	2	**Enforcing contracts** (rank)		16
Cost (% of income per capita)	11.7	Ease of shareholder suits index (0-10)	7	Procedures (number)		28
		Strength of investor protection index (0-10)	5.7	Time (days)		395
Registering property (rank)	35			Cost (% of claim)		20.7
Procedures (number)	5	**Paying taxes** (rank)	48			
Time (days)	5	Payments (number per year)	11	**Closing a business** (rank)		12
Cost (% of property value)	5.0	Time (hours per year)	109	Time (years)		1.0
		Total tax rate (% of profit)	47.9	Cost (% of estate)		8
				Recovery rate (cents on the dollar)		81.8

AUSTRIA

		OECD high income		GNI per capita (US$)		46,850
Ease of doing business (rank)	32	High income		Population (m)		8.4
Starting a business (rank)	125	**Getting credit** (rank)	15	**Trading across borders** (rank)		25
Procedures (number)	8	Strength of legal rights index (0-10)	7	Documents to export (number)		4
Time (days)	28	Depth of credit information index (0-6)	6	Time to export (days)		7
Cost (% of income per capita)	5.2	Public registry coverage (% of adults)	1.4	Cost to export (US$ per container)		1,180
Minimum capital (% of income per capita)	53.1	Private bureau coverage (% of adults)	40.6	Documents to import (number)		5
				Time to import (days)		8
Dealing with construction permits (rank)	57	**Protecting investors** (rank)	132	Cost to import (US$ per container)		1,195
Procedures (number)	14	Extent of disclosure index (0-10)	3			
Time (days)	194	Extent of director liability index (0-10)	5	**Enforcing contracts** (rank)		9
Cost (% of income per capita)	72.9	Ease of shareholder suits index (0-10)	4	Procedures (number)		25
		Strength of investor protection index (0-10)	4.0	Time (days)		397
✔ **Registering property** (rank)	33			Cost (% of claim)		18.0
Procedures (number)	3	**Paying taxes** (rank)	104			
Time (days)	21	Payments (number per year)	22	**Closing a business** (rank)		20
Cost (% of property value)	4.5	Time (hours per year)	170	Time (years)		1.1
		Total tax rate (% of profit)	55.5	Cost (% of estate)		18
				Recovery rate (cents on the dollar)		73.1

✔ Reforms making it easier to do business ✘ Reforms making it more difficult to do business

AZERBAIJAN

		Eastern Europe & Central Asia		GNI per capita (US$)	4,840
Ease of doing business (rank)	54	Upper middle income		Population (m)	8.8
Starting a business (rank)	15	✔ **Getting credit** (rank)	46	**Trading across borders** (rank)	177
Procedures (number)	6	Strength of legal rights index (0-10)	6	Documents to export (number)	9
Time (days)	8	Depth of credit information index (0-6)	5	Time to export (days)	43
Cost (% of income per capita)	3.1	Public registry coverage (% of adults)	7.0	Cost to export (US$ per container)	2,980
Minimum capital (% of income per capita)	0.0	Private bureau coverage (% of adults)	0.0	Documents to import (number)	14
				Time to import (days)	46
Dealing with construction permits (rank)	160	**Protecting investors** (rank)	20	Cost to import (US$ per container)	3,480
Procedures (number)	31	Extent of disclosure index (0-10)	7		
Time (days)	207	Extent of director liability index (0-10)	5	**Enforcing contracts** (rank)	27
Cost (% of income per capita)	388.9	Ease of shareholder suits index (0-10)	8	Procedures (number)	39
		Strength of investor protection index (0-10)	6.7	Time (days)	237
Registering property (rank)	10			Cost (% of claim)	18.5
Procedures (number)	4	✔ **Paying taxes** (rank)	103		
Time (days)	11	Payments (number per year)	18	**Closing a business** (rank)	88
Cost (% of property value)	0.2	Time (hours per year)	306	Time (years)	2.7
		Total tax rate (% of profit)	40.9	Cost (% of estate)	8
				Recovery rate (cents on the dollar)	28.8

BAHAMAS, THE

		Latin America & Caribbean		GNI per capita (US$)	21,529
Ease of doing business (rank)	77	High income		Population (m)	0.3
Starting a business (rank)	66	**Getting credit** (rank)	72	**Trading across borders** (rank)	45
Procedures (number)	7	Strength of legal rights index (0-10)	9	Documents to export (number)	5
Time (days)	31	Depth of credit information index (0-6)	0	Time to export (days)	19
Cost (% of income per capita)	9.1	Public registry coverage (% of adults)	0.0	Cost to export (US$ per container)	930
Minimum capital (% of income per capita)	0.0	Private bureau coverage (% of adults)	0.0	Documents to import (number)	5
				Time to import (days)	13
Dealing with construction permits (rank)	107	**Protecting investors** (rank)	109	Cost to import (US$ per container)	1,380
Procedures (number)	18	Extent of disclosure index (0-10)	2		
Time (days)	197	Extent of director liability index (0-10)	5	**Enforcing contracts** (rank)	120
Cost (% of income per capita)	222.0	Ease of shareholder suits index (0-10)	7	Procedures (number)	49
		Strength of investor protection index (0-10)	4.7	Time (days)	427
Registering property (rank)	154			Cost (% of claim)	28.9
Procedures (number)	7	**Paying taxes** (rank)	50		
Time (days)	48	Payments (number per year)	18	**Closing a business** (rank)	34
Cost (% of property value)	12.5	Time (hours per year)	58	Time (years)	5.0
		Total tax rate (% of profit)	46.1	Cost (% of estate)	4
				Recovery rate (cents on the dollar)	54.7

BAHRAIN

		Middle East & North Africa		GNI per capita (US$)	19,455
Ease of doing business (rank)	28	High income		Population (m)	0.8
Starting a business (rank)	78	**Getting credit** (rank)	89	✔ **Trading across borders** (rank)	33
Procedures (number)	7	Strength of legal rights index (0-10)	4	Documents to export (number)	5
Time (days)	9	Depth of credit information index (0-6)	4	Time to export (days)	11
Cost (% of income per capita)	0.8	Public registry coverage (% of adults)	0.0	Cost to export (US$ per container)	955
Minimum capital (% of income per capita)	273.4	Private bureau coverage (% of adults)	35.9	Documents to import (number)	6
				Time to import (days)	15
Dealing with construction permits (rank)	17	**Protecting investors** (rank)	59	Cost to import (US$ per container)	995
Procedures (number)	13	Extent of disclosure index (0-10)	8		
Time (days)	43	Extent of director liability index (0-10)	4	**Enforcing contracts** (rank)	117
Cost (% of income per capita)	78.3	Ease of shareholder suits index (0-10)	5	Procedures (number)	48
		Strength of investor protection index (0-10)	5.7	Time (days)	635
✘ **Registering property** (rank)	29			Cost (% of claim)	14.7
Procedures (number)	2	**Paying taxes** (rank)	14		
Time (days)	31	Payments (number per year)	25	**Closing a business** (rank)	26
Cost (% of property value)	2.7	Time (hours per year)	36	Time (years)	2.5
		Total tax rate (% of profit)	15.0	Cost (% of estate)	10
				Recovery rate (cents on the dollar)	64.2

BANGLADESH

		South Asia		GNI per capita (US$)	590
Ease of doing business (rank)	107	Low income		Population (m)	162.2
✔ **Starting a business** (rank)	79	**Getting credit** (rank)	72	**Trading across borders** (rank)	112
Procedures (number)	7	Strength of legal rights index (0-10)	7	Documents to export (number)	6
Time (days)	19	Depth of credit information index (0-6)	2	Time to export (days)	25
Cost (% of income per capita)	33.3	Public registry coverage (% of adults)	0.6	Cost to export (US$ per container)	985
Minimum capital (% of income per capita)	0.0	Private bureau coverage (% of adults)	0.0	Documents to import (number)	8
				Time to import (days)	31
Dealing with construction permits (rank)	116	**Protecting investors** (rank)	20	Cost to import (US$ per container)	1,390
Procedures (number)	14	Extent of disclosure index (0-10)	6		
Time (days)	231	Extent of director liability index (0-10)	7	**Enforcing contracts** (rank)	179
Cost (% of income per capita)	558.1	Ease of shareholder suits index (0-10)	7	Procedures (number)	41
		Strength of investor protection index (0-10)	6.7	Time (days)	1,442
✔ **Registering property** (rank)	172			Cost (% of claim)	63.3
Procedures (number)	8	**Paying taxes** (rank)	93		
Time (days)	245	Payments (number per year)	21	**Closing a business** (rank)	101
Cost (% of property value)	6.6	Time (hours per year)	302	Time (years)	4.0
		Total tax rate (% of profit)	35.0	Cost (% of estate)	8
				Recovery rate (cents on the dollar)	25.8

BELARUS

		Eastern Europe & Central Asia		GNI per capita (US$)	5,540
Ease of doing business (rank)	68	Upper middle income		Population (m)	9.7
Starting a business (rank)	7	✔ **Getting credit** (rank)	89	✔ **Trading across borders** (rank)	128
Procedures (number)	5	Strength of legal rights index (0-10)	3	Documents to export (number)	8
Time (days)	5	Depth of credit information index (0-6)	5	Time to export (days)	15
Cost (% of income per capita)	1.6	Public registry coverage (% of adults)	33.5	Cost to export (US$ per container)	1,772
Minimum capital (% of income per capita)	0.0	Private bureau coverage (% of adults)	0.0	Documents to import (number)	8
				Time to import (days)	20
Dealing with construction permits (rank)	44	**Protecting investors** (rank)	109	Cost to import (US$ per container)	1,770
Procedures (number)	16	Extent of disclosure index (0-10)	5		
Time (days)	151	Extent of director liability index (0-10)	1	**Enforcing contracts** (rank)	12
Cost (% of income per capita)	50.9	Ease of shareholder suits index (0-10)	8	Procedures (number)	28
		Strength of investor protection index (0-10)	4.7	Time (days)	225
Registering property (rank)	6			Cost (% of claim)	23.4
Procedures (number)	3	✔ **Paying taxes** (rank)	183		
Time (days)	15	Payments (number per year)	82	✔ **Closing a business** (rank)	93
Cost (% of property value)	0.0	Time (hours per year)	798	Time (years)	5.8
		Total tax rate (% of profit)	80.4	Cost (% of estate)	22
				Recovery rate (cents on the dollar)	28.0

BELGIUM

		OECD high income		GNI per capita (US$)	45,310
Ease of doing business (rank)	25	High income		Population (m)	10.8
Starting a business (rank)	31	**Getting credit** (rank)	46	**Trading across borders** (rank)	44
Procedures (number)	3	Strength of legal rights index (0-10)	7	Documents to export (number)	4
Time (days)	4	Depth of credit information index (0-6)	4	Time to export (days)	8
Cost (% of income per capita)	5.4	Public registry coverage (% of adults)	57.2	Cost to export (US$ per container)	1,619
Minimum capital (% of income per capita)	19.6	Private bureau coverage (% of adults)	0.0	Documents to import (number)	5
				Time to import (days)	9
Dealing with construction permits (rank)	41	**Protecting investors** (rank)	16	Cost to import (US$ per container)	1,600
Procedures (number)	14	Extent of disclosure index (0-10)	8		
Time (days)	169	Extent of director liability index (0-10)	6	**Enforcing contracts** (rank)	21
Cost (% of income per capita)	64.1	Ease of shareholder suits index (0-10)	7	Procedures (number)	26
		Strength of investor protection index (0-10)	7.0	Time (days)	505
✗ **Registering property** (rank)	177			Cost (% of claim)	16.6
Procedures (number)	8	**Paying taxes** (rank)	70		
Time (days)	79	Payments (number per year)	11	✔ **Closing a business** (rank)	8
Cost (% of property value)	12.7	Time (hours per year)	156	Time (years)	0.9
		Total tax rate (% of profit)	57.0	Cost (% of estate)	4
				Recovery rate (cents on the dollar)	87.6

✔ Reforms making it easier to do business   ✘ Reforms making it more difficult to do business

BELIZE

		Latin America & Caribbean		GNI per capita (US$)	4,045
Ease of doing business (rank)	99	Lower middle income		Population (m)	0.3
Starting a business (rank)	148	**Getting credit** (rank)	89	**Trading across borders** (rank)	119
Procedures (number)	9	Strength of legal rights index (0-10)	8	Documents to export (number)	7
Time (days)	44	Depth of credit information index (0-6)	0	Time to export (days)	21
Cost (% of income per capita)	47.9	Public registry coverage (% of adults)	0.0	Cost to export (US$ per container)	1,710
Minimum capital (% of income per capita)	0.0	Private bureau coverage (% of adults)	0.0	Documents to import (number)	6
				Time to import (days)	21
Dealing with construction permits (rank)	4	**Protecting investors** (rank)	120	Cost to import (US$ per container)	1,870
Procedures (number)	11	Extent of disclosure index (0-10)	3		
Time (days)	66	Extent of director liability index (0-10)	4	**Enforcing contracts** (rank)	168
Cost (% of income per capita)	16.7	Ease of shareholder suits index (0-10)	6	Procedures (number)	51
		Strength of investor protection index (0-10)	4.3	Time (days)	892
Registering property (rank)	134			Cost (% of claim)	27.5
Procedures (number)	8	**Paying taxes** (rank)	69		
Time (days)	60	Payments (number per year)	40	**Closing a business** (rank)	28
Cost (% of property value)	4.8	Time (hours per year)	147	Time (years)	1.0
		Total tax rate (% of profit)	33.2	Cost (% of estate)	23
				Recovery rate (cents on the dollar)	63.6

BENIN

		Sub-Saharan Africa		GNI per capita (US$)	750
Ease of doing business (rank)	170	Low income		Population (m)	8.9
Starting a business (rank)	157	**Getting credit** (rank)	152	**Trading across borders** (rank)	127
Procedures (number)	7	Strength of legal rights index (0-10)	3	Documents to export (number)	7
Time (days)	31	Depth of credit information index (0-6)	1	Time to export (days)	30
Cost (% of income per capita)	152.6	Public registry coverage (% of adults)	10.4	Cost to export (US$ per container)	1,251
Minimum capital (% of income per capita)	285.3	Private bureau coverage (% of adults)	0.0	Documents to import (number)	7
				Time to import (days)	32
✔ **Dealing with construction permits** (rank)	125	**Protecting investors** (rank)	154	Cost to import (US$ per container)	1,400
Procedures (number)	15	Extent of disclosure index (0-10)	6		
Time (days)	320	Extent of director liability index (0-10)	1	**Enforcing contracts** (rank)	177
Cost (% of income per capita)	249.6	Ease of shareholder suits index (0-10)	3	Procedures (number)	42
		Strength of investor protection index (0-10)	3.3	Time (days)	825
Registering property (rank)	129			Cost (% of claim)	64.7
Procedures (number)	4	**Paying taxes** (rank)	167		
Time (days)	120	Payments (number per year)	55	**Closing a business** (rank)	118
Cost (% of property value)	11.8	Time (hours per year)	270	Time (years)	4.0
		Total tax rate (% of profit)	66.0	Cost (% of estate)	22
				Recovery rate (cents on the dollar)	20.2

BHUTAN

		South Asia		GNI per capita (US$)	2,020
Ease of doing business (rank)	142	Lower middle income		Population (m)	0.7
Starting a business (rank)	84	**Getting credit** (rank)	176	**Trading across borders** (rank)	161
Procedures (number)	8	Strength of legal rights index (0-10)	2	Documents to export (number)	8
Time (days)	46	Depth of credit information index (0-6)	0	Time to export (days)	38
Cost (% of income per capita)	7.2	Public registry coverage (% of adults)	0.0	Cost to export (US$ per container)	1,352
Minimum capital (% of income per capita)	0.0	Private bureau coverage (% of adults)	0.0	Documents to import (number)	11
				Time to import (days)	38
Dealing with construction permits (rank)	123	**Protecting investors** (rank)	132	Cost to import (US$ per container)	2,665
Procedures (number)	25	Extent of disclosure index (0-10)	5		
Time (days)	183	Extent of director liability index (0-10)	3	**Enforcing contracts** (rank)	33
Cost (% of income per capita)	132.8	Ease of shareholder suits index (0-10)	4	Procedures (number)	47
		Strength of investor protection index (0-10)	4.0	Time (days)	225
Registering property (rank)	48			Cost (% of claim)	0.1
Procedures (number)	5	**Paying taxes** (rank)	94		
Time (days)	64	Payments (number per year)	18	**Closing a business** (rank)	183
Cost (% of property value)	0.0	Time (hours per year)	274	Time (years)	NO PRACTICE
		Total tax rate (% of profit)	40.6	Cost (% of estate)	NO PRACTICE
				Recovery rate (cents on the dollar)	0.0

BOLIVIA

		Latin America & Caribbean		GNI per capita (US$)	1,630
Ease of doing business (rank)	149	Lower middle income		Population (m)	9.9
Starting a business (rank)	166	**Getting credit** (rank)	116	**Trading across borders** (rank)	125
Procedures (number)	15	Strength of legal rights index (0-10)	1	Documents to export (number)	8
Time (days)	50	Depth of credit information index (0-6)	6	Time to export (days)	19
Cost (% of income per capita)	100.8	Public registry coverage (% of adults)	11.3	Cost to export (US$ per container)	1,425
Minimum capital (% of income per capita)	2.5	Private bureau coverage (% of adults)	31.4	Documents to import (number)	7
				Time to import (days)	23
Dealing with construction permits (rank)	98	**Protecting investors** (rank)	132	Cost to import (US$ per container)	1,747
Procedures (number)	17	Extent of disclosure index (0-10)	1		
Time (days)	249	Extent of director liability index (0-10)	5	**Enforcing contracts** (rank)	136
Cost (% of income per capita)	109.1	Ease of shareholder suits index (0-10)	6	Procedures (number)	40
		Strength of investor protection index (0-10)	4.0	Time (days)	591
Registering property (rank)	139			Cost (% of claim)	33.2
Procedures (number)	7	**Paying taxes** (rank)	177		
Time (days)	92	Payments (number per year)	42	**Closing a business** (rank)	58
Cost (% of property value)	4.8	Time (hours per year)	1,080	Time (years)	1.8
		Total tax rate (% of profit)	80.0	Cost (% of estate)	15
				Recovery rate (cents on the dollar)	39.3

BOSNIA AND HERZEGOVINA

		Eastern Europe & Central Asia		GNI per capita (US$)	4,700
Ease of doing business (rank)	110	Upper middle income		Population (m)	3.8
Starting a business (rank)	160	**Getting credit** (rank)	65	**Trading across borders** (rank)	71
Procedures (number)	12	Strength of legal rights index (0-10)	5	Documents to export (number)	5
Time (days)	55	Depth of credit information index (0-6)	5	Time to export (days)	16
Cost (% of income per capita)	17.7	Public registry coverage (% of adults)	30.2	Cost to export (US$ per container)	1,240
Minimum capital (% of income per capita)	30.5	Private bureau coverage (% of adults)	47.2	Documents to import (number)	7
				Time to import (days)	16
Dealing with construction permits (rank)	139	**Protecting investors** (rank)	93	Cost to import (US$ per container)	1,200
Procedures (number)	16	Extent of disclosure index (0-10)	3		
Time (days)	255	Extent of director liability index (0-10)	6	**Enforcing contracts** (rank)	124
Cost (% of income per capita)	578.1	Ease of shareholder suits index (0-10)	6	Procedures (number)	37
		Strength of investor protection index (0-10)	5.0	Time (days)	595
✔ **Registering property** (rank)	103			Cost (% of claim)	40.4
Procedures (number)	7	✔ **Paying taxes** (rank)	127		
Time (days)	33	Payments (number per year)	51	**Closing a business** (rank)	73
Cost (% of property value)	5.3	Time (hours per year)	422	Time (years)	3.3
		Total tax rate (% of profit)	23.0	Cost (% of estate)	9
				Recovery rate (cents on the dollar)	34.7

BOTSWANA

		Sub-Saharan Africa		GNI per capita (US$)	6,260
Ease of doing business (rank)	52	Upper middle income		Population (m)	1.9
Starting a business (rank)	90	**Getting credit** (rank)	46	**Trading across borders** (rank)	151
Procedures (number)	10	Strength of legal rights index (0-10)	7	Documents to export (number)	6
Time (days)	61	Depth of credit information index (0-6)	4	Time to export (days)	28
Cost (% of income per capita)	2.2	Public registry coverage (% of adults)	0.0	Cost to export (US$ per container)	3,010
Minimum capital (% of income per capita)	0.0	Private bureau coverage (% of adults)	57.6	Documents to import (number)	9
				Time to import (days)	41
Dealing with construction permits (rank)	127	**Protecting investors** (rank)	44	Cost to import (US$ per container)	3,390
Procedures (number)	24	Extent of disclosure index (0-10)	7		
Time (days)	167	Extent of director liability index (0-10)	8	**Enforcing contracts** (rank)	70
Cost (% of income per capita)	264.5	Ease of shareholder suits index (0-10)	3	Procedures (number)	29
		Strength of investor protection index (0-10)	6.0	Time (days)	625
Registering property (rank)	44			Cost (% of claim)	28.1
Procedures (number)	5	**Paying taxes** (rank)	21		
Time (days)	16	Payments (number per year)	19	**Closing a business** (rank)	27
Cost (% of property value)	5.0	Time (hours per year)	152	Time (years)	1.7
		Total tax rate (% of profit)	19.5	Cost (% of estate)	15
				Recovery rate (cents on the dollar)	63.7

✔ Reforms making it easier to do business   ✘ Reforms making it more difficult to do business

BRAZIL

		Latin America & Caribbean		GNI per capita (US$)	8,070
Ease of doing business (rank)	127	Upper middle income		Population (m)	193.7
✔ **Starting a business** (rank)	128	**Getting credit** (rank)	89	**Trading across borders** (rank)	114
Procedures (number)	15	Strength of legal rights index (0-10)	3	Documents to export (number)	8
Time (days)	120	Depth of credit information index (0-6)	5	Time to export (days)	13
Cost (% of income per capita)	7.3	Public registry coverage (% of adults)	26.9	Cost to export (US$ per container)	1,790
Minimum capital (% of income per capita)	0.0	Private bureau coverage (% of adults)	53.5	Documents to import (number)	7
				Time to import (days)	17
Dealing with construction permits (rank)	112	**Protecting investors** (rank)	74	Cost to import (US$ per container)	1,730
Procedures (number)	18	Extent of disclosure index (0-10)	6		
Time (days)	411	Extent of director liability index (0-10)	7	**Enforcing contracts** (rank)	98
Cost (% of income per capita)	46.6	Ease of shareholder suits index (0-10)	3	Procedures (number)	45
		Strength of investor protection index (0-10)	5.3	Time (days)	616
Registering property (rank)	122			Cost (% of claim)	16.5
Procedures (number)	14	**Paying taxes** (rank)	152		
Time (days)	42	Payments (number per year)	10	**Closing a business** (rank)	132
Cost (% of property value)	2.7	Time (hours per year)	2,600	Time (years)	4.0
		Total tax rate (% of profit)	69.0	Cost (% of estate)	12
				Recovery rate (cents on the dollar)	17.1

BRUNEI DARUSSALAM

		East Asia & Pacific		GNI per capita (US$)	26,325
Ease of doing business (rank)	112	High income		Population (m)	0.4
✔ **Starting a business** (rank)	133	**Getting credit** (rank)	116	✔ **Trading across borders** (rank)	52
Procedures (number)	15	Strength of legal rights index (0-10)	7	Documents to export (number)	6
Time (days)	105	Depth of credit information index (0-6)	0	Time to export (days)	25
Cost (% of income per capita)	13.5	Public registry coverage (% of adults)	0.0	Cost to export (US$ per container)	630
Minimum capital (% of income per capita)	0.0	Private bureau coverage (% of adults)	0.0	Documents to import (number)	6
				Time to import (days)	20
Dealing with construction permits (rank)	74	**Protecting investors** (rank)	120	Cost to import (US$ per container)	708
Procedures (number)	32	Extent of disclosure index (0-10)	3		
Time (days)	163	Extent of director liability index (0-10)	2	**Enforcing contracts** (rank)	159
Cost (% of income per capita)	6.7	Ease of shareholder suits index (0-10)	8	Procedures (number)	58
		Strength of investor protection index (0-10)	4.3	Time (days)	540
Registering property (rank)	183			Cost (% of claim)	36.6
Procedures (number)	NO PRACTICE	✔ **Paying taxes** (rank)	22		
Time (days)	NO PRACTICE	Payments (number per year)	15	**Closing a business** (rank)	42
Cost (% of property value)	NO PRACTICE	Time (hours per year)	144	Time (years)	2.5
		Total tax rate (% of profit)	29.8	Cost (% of estate)	4
				Recovery rate (cents on the dollar)	47.2

BULGARIA

		Eastern Europe & Central Asia		GNI per capita (US$)	5,770
Ease of doing business (rank)	51	Upper middle income		Population (m)	7.6
✔ **Starting a business** (rank)	43	**Getting credit** (rank)	6	**Trading across borders** (rank)	108
Procedures (number)	4	Strength of legal rights index (0-10)	8	Documents to export (number)	5
Time (days)	18	Depth of credit information index (0-6)	6	Time to export (days)	23
Cost (% of income per capita)	1.6	Public registry coverage (% of adults)	37.0	Cost to export (US$ per container)	1,551
Minimum capital (% of income per capita)	0.0	Private bureau coverage (% of adults)	13.1	Documents to import (number)	7
				Time to import (days)	21
Dealing with construction permits (rank)	119	**Protecting investors** (rank)	44	Cost to import (US$ per container)	1,666
Procedures (number)	24	Extent of disclosure index (0-10)	10		
Time (days)	139	Extent of director liability index (0-10)	1	**Enforcing contracts** (rank)	87
Cost (% of income per capita)	442.3	Ease of shareholder suits index (0-10)	7	Procedures (number)	39
		Strength of investor protection index (0-10)	6.0	Time (days)	564
Registering property (rank)	62			Cost (% of claim)	23.8
Procedures (number)	8	✔ **Paying taxes** (rank)	85		
Time (days)	15	Payments (number per year)	17	**Closing a business** (rank)	83
Cost (% of property value)	3.0	Time (hours per year)	616	Time (years)	3.3
		Total tax rate (% of profit)	29.0	Cost (% of estate)	9
				Recovery rate (cents on the dollar)	31.0

BURKINA FASO

Ease of doing business (rank)	151	Sub-Saharan Africa			GNI per capita (US$)	510
		Low income			Population (m)	15.8

Starting a business (rank)	119
Procedures (number)	4
Time (days)	14
Cost (% of income per capita)	49.8
Minimum capital (% of income per capita)	416.2

Getting credit (rank)	152
Strength of legal rights index (0-10)	3
Depth of credit information index (0-6)	1
Public registry coverage (% of adults)	0.2
Private bureau coverage (% of adults)	0.0

✔ **Trading across borders** (rank)	175
Documents to export (number)	10
Time to export (days)	41
Cost to export (US$ per container)	2,412
Documents to import (number)	10
Time to import (days)	49
Cost to import (US$ per container)	4,030

✔ **Dealing with construction permits** (rank)	77
Procedures (number)	15
Time (days)	122
Cost (% of income per capita)	576.1

Protecting investors (rank)	147
Extent of disclosure index (0-10)	6
Extent of director liability index (0-10)	1
Ease of shareholder suits index (0-10)	4
Strength of investor protection index (0-10)	3.7

✔ **Enforcing contracts** (rank)	108
Procedures (number)	37
Time (days)	446
Cost (% of claim)	81.7

Registering property (rank)	118
Procedures (number)	4
Time (days)	59
Cost (% of property value)	13.1

✔ **Paying taxes** (rank)	148
Payments (number per year)	46
Time (hours per year)	270
Total tax rate (% of profit)	44.9

Closing a business (rank)	100
Time (years)	4.0
Cost (% of estate)	9
Recovery rate (cents on the dollar)	26.8

BURUNDI

Ease of doing business (rank)	181	Sub-Saharan Africa			GNI per capita (US$)	150
		Low income			Population (m)	8.3

Starting a business (rank)	135
Procedures (number)	11
Time (days)	32
Cost (% of income per capita)	129.3
Minimum capital (% of income per capita)	0.0

Getting credit (rank)	168
Strength of legal rights index (0-10)	2
Depth of credit information index (0-6)	1
Public registry coverage (% of adults)	0.2
Private bureau coverage (% of adults)	0.0

Trading across borders (rank)	176
Documents to export (number)	9
Time to export (days)	47
Cost to export (US$ per container)	2,747
Documents to import (number)	10
Time to import (days)	71
Cost to import (US$ per container)	4,285

Dealing with construction permits (rank)	175
Procedures (number)	25
Time (days)	212
Cost (% of income per capita)	7,047.6

Protecting investors (rank)	154
Extent of disclosure index (0-10)	4
Extent of director liability index (0-10)	1
Ease of shareholder suits index (0-10)	5
Strength of investor protection index (0-10)	3.3

Enforcing contracts (rank)	171
Procedures (number)	44
Time (days)	832
Cost (% of claim)	38.6

Registering property (rank)	115
Procedures (number)	5
Time (days)	94
Cost (% of property value)	5.8

✔ **Paying taxes** (rank)	141
Payments (number per year)	32
Time (hours per year)	211
Total tax rate (% of profit)	153.4

Closing a business (rank)	183
Time (years)	NO PRACTICE
Cost (% of estate)	NO PRACTICE
Recovery rate (cents on the dollar)	0.0

CAMBODIA

Ease of doing business (rank)	147	East Asia & Pacific			GNI per capita (US$)	650
		Low income			Population (m)	14.8

Starting a business (rank)	170
Procedures (number)	9
Time (days)	85
Cost (% of income per capita)	128.3
Minimum capital (% of income per capita)	37.0

Getting credit (rank)	89
Strength of legal rights index (0-10)	8
Depth of credit information index (0-6)	0
Public registry coverage (% of adults)	0.0
Private bureau coverage (% of adults)	0.0

✔ **Trading across borders** (rank)	118
Documents to export (number)	10
Time to export (days)	22
Cost to export (US$ per container)	732
Documents to import (number)	10
Time to import (days)	26
Cost to import (US$ per container)	872

Dealing with construction permits (rank)	146
Procedures (number)	23
Time (days)	709
Cost (% of income per capita)	54.2

Protecting investors (rank)	74
Extent of disclosure index (0-10)	5
Extent of director liability index (0-10)	9
Ease of shareholder suits index (0-10)	2
Strength of investor protection index (0-10)	5.3

Enforcing contracts (rank)	142
Procedures (number)	44
Time (days)	401
Cost (% of claim)	102.7

Registering property (rank)	117
Procedures (number)	7
Time (days)	56
Cost (% of property value)	4.3

Paying taxes (rank)	57
Payments (number per year)	39
Time (hours per year)	173
Total tax rate (% of profit)	22.5

Closing a business (rank)	183
Time (years)	NO PRACTICE
Cost (% of estate)	NO PRACTICE
Recovery rate (cents on the dollar)	0.0

CAMEROON

		Sub-Saharan Africa		GNI per capita (US$)	1,170
Ease of doing business (rank)	168	Lower middle income		Population (m)	19.5
✔ **Starting a business** (rank)	131	**Getting credit** (rank)	138	**Trading across borders** (rank)	155
Procedures (number)	6	Strength of legal rights index (0-10)	3	Documents to export (number)	11
Time (days)	19	Depth of credit information index (0-6)	2	Time to export (days)	23
Cost (% of income per capita)	51.2	Public registry coverage (% of adults)	2.9	Cost to export (US$ per container)	1,379
Minimum capital (% of income per capita)	191.8	Private bureau coverage (% of adults)	0.0	Documents to import (number)	12
				Time to import (days)	26
Dealing with construction permits (rank)	118	**Protecting investors** (rank)	120	Cost to import (US$ per container)	1,978
Procedures (number)	14	Extent of disclosure index (0-10)	6		
Time (days)	213	Extent of director liability index (0-10)	1	**Enforcing contracts** (rank)	173
Cost (% of income per capita)	1,235.8	Ease of shareholder suits index (0-10)	6	Procedures (number)	43
		Strength of investor protection index (0-10)	4.3	Time (days)	800
Registering property (rank)	149			Cost (% of claim)	46.6
Procedures (number)	5	**Paying taxes** (rank)	169		
Time (days)	93	Payments (number per year)	44	**Closing a business** (rank)	141
Cost (% of property value)	19.3	Time (hours per year)	654	Time (years)	3.2
		Total tax rate (% of profit)	49.1	Cost (% of estate)	34
				Recovery rate (cents on the dollar)	13.6

CANADA

		OECD high income		GNI per capita (US$)	42,170
Ease of doing business (rank)	7	High income		Population (m)	33.7
Starting a business (rank)	3	**Getting credit** (rank)	32	**Trading across borders** (rank)	41
Procedures (number)	1	Strength of legal rights index (0-10)	6	Documents to export (number)	3
Time (days)	5	Depth of credit information index (0-6)	6	Time to export (days)	7
Cost (% of income per capita)	0.4	Public registry coverage (% of adults)	0.0	Cost to export (US$ per container)	1,610
Minimum capital (% of income per capita)	0.0	Private bureau coverage (% of adults)	100.0	Documents to import (number)	4
				Time to import (days)	11
Dealing with construction permits (rank)	29	**Protecting investors** (rank)	5	Cost to import (US$ per container)	1,660
Procedures (number)	14	Extent of disclosure index (0-10)	8		
Time (days)	75	Extent of director liability index (0-10)	9	✔ **Enforcing contracts** (rank)	58
Cost (% of income per capita)	101.0	Ease of shareholder suits index (0-10)	8	Procedures (number)	36
		Strength of investor protection index (0-10)	8.3	Time (days)	570
Registering property (rank)	37			Cost (% of claim)	22.3
Procedures (number)	6	✔ **Paying taxes** (rank)	10		
Time (days)	17	Payments (number per year)	8	**Closing a business** (rank)	3
Cost (% of property value)	1.8	Time (hours per year)	131	Time (years)	0.8
		Total tax rate (% of profit)	29.2	Cost (% of estate)	4
				Recovery rate (cents on the dollar)	91.2

CAPE VERDE

		Sub-Saharan Africa		GNI per capita (US$)	3,010
Ease of doing business (rank)	132	Lower middle income		Population (m)	0.5
✔ **Starting a business** (rank)	120	**Getting credit** (rank)	152	**Trading across borders** (rank)	55
Procedures (number)	8	Strength of legal rights index (0-10)	2	Documents to export (number)	5
Time (days)	11	Depth of credit information index (0-6)	2	Time to export (days)	19
Cost (% of income per capita)	18.5	Public registry coverage (% of adults)	22.1	Cost to export (US$ per container)	1,200
Minimum capital (% of income per capita)	42.4	Private bureau coverage (% of adults)	0.0	Documents to import (number)	5
				Time to import (days)	18
Dealing with construction permits (rank)	89	**Protecting investors** (rank)	132	Cost to import (US$ per container)	1,000
Procedures (number)	18	Extent of disclosure index (0-10)	1		
Time (days)	120	Extent of director liability index (0-10)	5	**Enforcing contracts** (rank)	38
Cost (% of income per capita)	570.7	Ease of shareholder suits index (0-10)	6	Procedures (number)	37
		Strength of investor protection index (0-10)	4.0	Time (days)	425
✔ **Registering property** (rank)	104			Cost (% of claim)	21.8
Procedures (number)	6	✔ **Paying taxes** (rank)	100		
Time (days)	73	Payments (number per year)	43	**Closing a business** (rank)	183
Cost (% of property value)	3.9	Time (hours per year)	186	Time (years)	NO PRACTICE
		Total tax rate (% of profit)	37.1	Cost (% of estate)	NO PRACTICE
				Recovery rate (cents on the dollar)	0.0

CENTRAL AFRICAN REPUBLIC

		Sub-Saharan Africa		GNI per capita (US$)	450
Ease of doing business (rank)	182	Low income		Population (m)	4.4
Starting a business (rank)	161	**Getting credit** (rank)	138	**Trading across borders** (rank)	182
Procedures (number)	8	Strength of legal rights index (0-10)	3	Documents to export (number)	9
Time (days)	22	Depth of credit information index (0-6)	2	Time to export (days)	54
Cost (% of income per capita)	228.4	Public registry coverage (% of adults)	2.0	Cost to export (US$ per container)	5,491
Minimum capital (% of income per capita)	468.6	Private bureau coverage (% of adults)	0.0	Documents to import (number)	17
				Time to import (days)	62
Dealing with construction permits (rank)	148	**Protecting investors** (rank)	132	Cost to import (US$ per container)	5,554
Procedures (number)	21	Extent of disclosure index (0-10)	6		
Time (days)	239	Extent of director liability index (0-10)	1	**Enforcing contracts** (rank)	173
Cost (% of income per capita)	259.5	Ease of shareholder suits index (0-10)	5	Procedures (number)	43
		Strength of investor protection index (0-10)	4.0	Time (days)	660
Registering property (rank)	141			Cost (% of claim)	82.0
Procedures (number)	5	**Paying taxes** (rank)	182		
Time (days)	75	Payments (number per year)	54	**Closing a business** (rank)	183
Cost (% of property value)	18.5	Time (hours per year)	504	Time (years)	4.8
		Total tax rate (% of profit)	203.8	Cost (% of estate)	76
				Recovery rate (cents on the dollar)	0.0

CHAD

		Sub-Saharan Africa		GNI per capita (US$)	620
Ease of doing business (rank)	183	Low income		Population (m)	11.2
Starting a business (rank)	182	**Getting credit** (rank)	152	**Trading across borders** (rank)	171
Procedures (number)	13	Strength of legal rights index (0-10)	3	Documents to export (number)	6
Time (days)	75	Depth of credit information index (0-6)	1	Time to export (days)	75
Cost (% of income per capita)	226.9	Public registry coverage (% of adults)	0.8	Cost to export (US$ per container)	5,902
Minimum capital (% of income per capita)	386.7	Private bureau coverage (% of adults)	0.0	Documents to import (number)	10
				Time to import (days)	101
Dealing with construction permits (rank)	101	**Protecting investors** (rank)	154	Cost to import (US$ per container)	8,150
Procedures (number)	14	Extent of disclosure index (0-10)	6		
Time (days)	164	Extent of director liability index (0-10)	1	**Enforcing contracts** (rank)	164
Cost (% of income per capita)	6,684.4	Ease of shareholder suits index (0-10)	3	Procedures (number)	41
		Strength of investor protection index (0-10)	3.3	Time (days)	743
Registering property (rank)	137			Cost (% of claim)	45.7
Procedures (number)	6	✗ **Paying taxes** (rank)	179		
Time (days)	44	Payments (number per year)	54	**Closing a business** (rank)	183
Cost (% of property value)	18.2	Time (hours per year)	732	Time (years)	NO PRACTICE
		Total tax rate (% of profit)	65.4	Cost (% of estate)	NO PRACTICE
				Recovery rate (cents on the dollar)	0.0

CHILE

		Latin America & Caribbean		GNI per capita (US$)	9,460
Ease of doing business (rank)	43	Upper middle income		Population (m)	17.0
✔ **Starting a business** (rank)	62	**Getting credit** (rank)	72	**Trading across borders** (rank)	68
Procedures (number)	8	Strength of legal rights index (0-10)	4	Documents to export (number)	6
Time (days)	22	Depth of credit information index (0-6)	5	Time to export (days)	21
Cost (% of income per capita)	6.8	Public registry coverage (% of adults)	30.9	Cost to export (US$ per container)	745
Minimum capital (% of income per capita)	0.0	Private bureau coverage (% of adults)	22.9	Documents to import (number)	7
				Time to import (days)	21
Dealing with construction permits (rank)	68	✔ **Protecting investors** (rank)	28	Cost to import (US$ per container)	795
Procedures (number)	18	Extent of disclosure index (0-10)	8		
Time (days)	155	Extent of director liability index (0-10)	6	**Enforcing contracts** (rank)	68
Cost (% of income per capita)	93.8	Ease of shareholder suits index (0-10)	5	Procedures (number)	36
		Strength of investor protection index (0-10)	6.3	Time (days)	480
Registering property (rank)	45			Cost (% of claim)	28.6
Procedures (number)	6	**Paying taxes** (rank)	46		
Time (days)	31	Payments (number per year)	9	**Closing a business** (rank)	91
Cost (% of property value)	1.3	Time (hours per year)	316	Time (years)	4.5
		Total tax rate (% of profit)	25.0	Cost (% of estate)	15
				Recovery rate (cents on the dollar)	28.2

CHINA

Ease of doing business (rank)	79	East Asia & Pacific		GNI per capita (US$)		3,620
Starting a business (rank)	151	Lower middle income		Population (m)		1,331.5
Procedures (number)	14	**Getting credit** (rank)	65	**Trading across borders** (rank)		50
Time (days)	38	Strength of legal rights index (0-10)	6	Documents to export (number)		7
Cost (% of income per capita)	4.5	Depth of credit information index (0-6)	4	Time to export (days)		21
Minimum capital (% of income per capita)	118.3	Public registry coverage (% of adults)	63.9	Cost to export (US$ per container)		500
		Private bureau coverage (% of adults)	0.0	Documents to import (number)		5
				Time to import (days)		24
Dealing with construction permits (rank)	181	**Protecting investors** (rank)	93	Cost to import (US$ per container)		545
Procedures (number)	37	Extent of disclosure index (0-10)	10			
Time (days)	336	Extent of director liability index (0-10)	1	**Enforcing contracts** (rank)		15
Cost (% of income per capita)	523.4	Ease of shareholder suits index (0-10)	4	Procedures (number)		34
		Strength of investor protection index (0-10)	5.0	Time (days)		406
Registering property (rank)	38			Cost (% of claim)		11.1
Procedures (number)	4	✔ **Paying taxes** (rank)	114			
Time (days)	29	Payments (number per year)	7	**Closing a business** (rank)		68
Cost (% of property value)	3.6	Time (hours per year)	398	Time (years)		1.7
		Total tax rate (% of profit)	63.5	Cost (% of estate)		22
				Recovery rate (cents on the dollar)		36.4

COLOMBIA

Ease of doing business (rank)	39	Latin America & Caribbean		GNI per capita (US$)		4,950
Starting a business (rank)	73	Upper middle income		Population (m)		45.7
Procedures (number)	9	**Getting credit** (rank)	65	**Trading across borders** (rank)		99
Time (days)	14	Strength of legal rights index (0-10)	5	Documents to export (number)		6
Cost (% of income per capita)	14.7	Depth of credit information index (0-6)	5	Time to export (days)		14
Minimum capital (% of income per capita)	0.0	Public registry coverage (% of adults)	0.0	Cost to export (US$ per container)		1,770
		Private bureau coverage (% of adults)	63.1	Documents to import (number)		8
				Time to import (days)		13
✔ **Dealing with construction permits** (rank)	32	**Protecting investors** (rank)	5	Cost to import (US$ per container)		1,700
Procedures (number)	10	Extent of disclosure index (0-10)	8			
Time (days)	50	Extent of director liability index (0-10)	8	**Enforcing contracts** (rank)		150
Cost (% of income per capita)	405.9	Ease of shareholder suits index (0-10)	9	Procedures (number)		34
		Strength of investor protection index (0-10)	8.3	Time (days)		1,346
Registering property (rank)	55			Cost (% of claim)		47.9
Procedures (number)	7	**Paying taxes** (rank)	118			
Time (days)	20	Payments (number per year)	20	**Closing a business** (rank)		29
Cost (% of property value)	2.0	Time (hours per year)	208	Time (years)		3.0
		Total tax rate (% of profit)	78.7	Cost (% of estate)		1
				Recovery rate (cents on the dollar)		62.4

COMOROS

Ease of doing business (rank)	159	Sub-Saharan Africa		GNI per capita (US$)		870
Starting a business (rank)	168	Low income		Population (m)		0.7
Procedures (number)	11	**Getting credit** (rank)	168	**Trading across borders** (rank)		135
Time (days)	24	Strength of legal rights index (0-10)	3	Documents to export (number)		10
Cost (% of income per capita)	176.5	Depth of credit information index (0-6)	0	Time to export (days)		30
Minimum capital (% of income per capita)	245.5	Public registry coverage (% of adults)	0.0	Cost to export (US$ per container)		1,073
		Private bureau coverage (% of adults)	0.0	Documents to import (number)		10
				Time to import (days)		21
Dealing with construction permits (rank)	68	**Protecting investors** (rank)	132	Cost to import (US$ per container)		1,057
Procedures (number)	18	Extent of disclosure index (0-10)	6			
Time (days)	164	Extent of director liability index (0-10)	1	**Enforcing contracts** (rank)		152
Cost (% of income per capita)	68.1	Ease of shareholder suits index (0-10)	5	Procedures (number)		43
		Strength of investor protection index (0-10)	4.0	Time (days)		506
Registering property (rank)	99			Cost (% of claim)		89.4
Procedures (number)	5	**Paying taxes** (rank)	96			
Time (days)	24	Payments (number per year)	20	**Closing a business** (rank)		183
Cost (% of property value)	20.8	Time (hours per year)	100	Time (years)		NO PRACTICE
		Total tax rate (% of profit)	217.9	Cost (% of estate)		NO PRACTICE
				Recovery rate (cents on the dollar)		0.0

CONGO, DEM. REP.

		Sub-Saharan Africa		GNI per capita (US$)	160
Ease of doing business (rank)	175	Low income		Population (m)	66.0
✔ **Starting a business** (rank)	146	**Getting credit** (rank)	168	**Trading across borders** (rank)	172
Procedures (number)	10	Strength of legal rights index (0-10)	3	Documents to export (number)	8
Time (days)	84	Depth of credit information index (0-6)	0	Time to export (days)	44
Cost (% of income per capita)	735.1	Public registry coverage (% of adults)	0.0	Cost to export (US$ per container)	3,505
Minimum capital (% of income per capita)	0.0	Private bureau coverage (% of adults)	0.0	Documents to import (number)	9
				Time to import (days)	63
✔ **Dealing with construction permits** (rank)	81	**Protecting investors** (rank)	154	Cost to import (US$ per container)	3,735
Procedures (number)	14	Extent of disclosure index (0-10)	3		
Time (days)	128	Extent of director liability index (0-10)	3	**Enforcing contracts** (rank)	172
Cost (% of income per capita)	2,692.2	Ease of shareholder suits index (0-10)	4	Procedures (number)	43
		Strength of investor protection index (0-10)	3.3	Time (days)	625
✔ **Registering property** (rank)	118			Cost (% of claim)	151.8
Procedures (number)	6	**Paying taxes** (rank)	163		
Time (days)	54	Payments (number per year)	32	**Closing a business** (rank)	155
Cost (% of property value)	7.0	Time (hours per year)	336	Time (years)	5.2
		Total tax rate (% of profit)	339.7	Cost (% of estate)	29
				Recovery rate (cents on the dollar)	1.1

CONGO, REP.

		Sub-Saharan Africa		GNI per capita (US$)	1,830
Ease of doing business (rank)	177	Lower middle income		Population (m)	3.7
Starting a business (rank)	176	**Getting credit** (rank)	138	**Trading across borders** (rank)	180
Procedures (number)	10	Strength of legal rights index (0-10)	3	Documents to export (number)	11
Time (days)	160	Depth of credit information index (0-6)	2	Time to export (days)	50
Cost (% of income per capita)	111.4	Public registry coverage (% of adults)	2.9	Cost to export (US$ per container)	3,818
Minimum capital (% of income per capita)	129.8	Private bureau coverage (% of adults)	0.0	Documents to import (number)	10
				Time to import (days)	62
Dealing with construction permits (rank)	83	**Protecting investors** (rank)	154	Cost to import (US$ per container)	7,709
Procedures (number)	17	Extent of disclosure index (0-10)	6		
Time (days)	169	Extent of director liability index (0-10)	1	**Enforcing contracts** (rank)	158
Cost (% of income per capita)	241.1	Ease of shareholder suits index (0-10)	3	Procedures (number)	44
		Strength of investor protection index (0-10)	3.3	Time (days)	560
Registering property (rank)	133			Cost (% of claim)	53.2
Procedures (number)	6	✔ **Paying taxes** (rank)	180		
Time (days)	55	Payments (number per year)	61	**Closing a business** (rank)	128
Cost (% of property value)	10.7	Time (hours per year)	606	Time (years)	3.3
		Total tax rate (% of profit)	65.5	Cost (% of estate)	25
				Recovery rate (cents on the dollar)	17.8

COSTA RICA

		Latin America & Caribbean		GNI per capita (US$)	6,260
Ease of doing business (rank)	125	Upper middle income		Population (m)	4.6
Starting a business (rank)	116	**Getting credit** (rank)	65	**Trading across borders** (rank)	69
Procedures (number)	12	Strength of legal rights index (0-10)	5	Documents to export (number)	6
Time (days)	60	Depth of credit information index (0-6)	5	Time to export (days)	13
Cost (% of income per capita)	10.5	Public registry coverage (% of adults)	23.3	Cost to export (US$ per container)	1,190
Minimum capital (% of income per capita)	0.0	Private bureau coverage (% of adults)	64.8	Documents to import (number)	7
				Time to import (days)	15
Dealing with construction permits (rank)	131	**Protecting investors** (rank)	167	Cost to import (US$ per container)	1,190
Procedures (number)	23	Extent of disclosure index (0-10)	2		
Time (days)	191	Extent of director liability index (0-10)	5	**Enforcing contracts** (rank)	130
Cost (% of income per capita)	172.2	Ease of shareholder suits index (0-10)	2	Procedures (number)	40
		Strength of investor protection index (0-10)	3.0	Time (days)	852
Registering property (rank)	52			Cost (% of claim)	24.3
Procedures (number)	6	**Paying taxes** (rank)	155		
Time (days)	21	Payments (number per year)	42	**Closing a business** (rank)	114
Cost (% of property value)	3.4	Time (hours per year)	272	Time (years)	3.5
		Total tax rate (% of profit)	55.0	Cost (% of estate)	15
				Recovery rate (cents on the dollar)	21.2

✔ Reforms making it easier to do business   ✘ Reforms making it more difficult to do business

CÔTE D'IVOIRE

		Sub-Saharan Africa		GNI per capita (US$)	1,060
Ease of doing business (rank)	169	Lower middle income		Population (m)	21.1
Starting a business (rank)	172	**Getting credit** (rank)	152	**Trading across borders** (rank)	160
Procedures (number)	10	Strength of legal rights index (0-10)	3	Documents to export (number)	10
Time (days)	40	Depth of credit information index (0-6)	1	Time to export (days)	25
Cost (% of income per capita)	133.0	Public registry coverage (% of adults)	0.2	Cost to export (US$ per container)	1,969
Minimum capital (% of income per capita)	202.9	Private bureau coverage (% of adults)	0.0	Documents to import (number)	9
				Time to import (days)	36
✔ **Dealing with construction permits** (rank)	165	**Protecting investors** (rank)	154	Cost to import (US$ per container)	2,577
Procedures (number)	21	Extent of disclosure index (0-10)	6		
Time (days)	592	Extent of director liability index (0-10)	1	**Enforcing contracts** (rank)	126
Cost (% of income per capita)	227.6	Ease of shareholder suits index (0-10)	3	Procedures (number)	33
		Strength of investor protection index (0-10)	3.3	Time (days)	770
Registering property (rank)	151			Cost (% of claim)	41.7
Procedures (number)	6	**Paying taxes** (rank)	153		
Time (days)	62	Payments (number per year)	64	**Closing a business** (rank)	76
Cost (% of property value)	13.9	Time (hours per year)	270	Time (years)	2.2
		Total tax rate (% of profit)	44.4	Cost (% of estate)	18
				Recovery rate (cents on the dollar)	32.8

CROATIA

		Eastern Europe & Central Asia		GNI per capita (US$)	13,810
Ease of doing business (rank)	84	High income		Population (m)	4.4
✔ **Starting a business** (rank)	56	**Getting credit** (rank)	65	**Trading across borders** (rank)	98
Procedures (number)	6	Strength of legal rights index (0-10)	6	Documents to export (number)	7
Time (days)	7	Depth of credit information index (0-6)	4	Time to export (days)	20
Cost (% of income per capita)	8.6	Public registry coverage (% of adults)	0.0	Cost to export (US$ per container)	1,281
Minimum capital (% of income per capita)	13.7	Private bureau coverage (% of adults)	81.2	Documents to import (number)	8
				Time to import (days)	16
✔ **Dealing with construction permits** (rank)	132	**Protecting investors** (rank)	132	Cost to import (US$ per container)	1,141
Procedures (number)	13	Extent of disclosure index (0-10)	1		
Time (days)	315	Extent of director liability index (0-10)	5	**Enforcing contracts** (rank)	47
Cost (% of income per capita)	850.9	Ease of shareholder suits index (0-10)	6	Procedures (number)	38
		Strength of investor protection index (0-10)	4.0	Time (days)	561
Registering property (rank)	110			Cost (% of claim)	13.8
Procedures (number)	5	**Paying taxes** (rank)	42		
Time (days)	104	Payments (number per year)	17	**Closing a business** (rank)	89
Cost (% of property value)	5.0	Time (hours per year)	196	Time (years)	3.1
		Total tax rate (% of profit)	32.5	Cost (% of estate)	15
				Recovery rate (cents on the dollar)	28.7

CYPRUS

		Eastern Europe & Central Asia		GNI per capita (US$)	29,620
Ease of doing business (rank)	37	High income		Population (m)	0.9
Starting a business (rank)	26	**Getting credit** (rank)	72	**Trading across borders** (rank)	19
Procedures (number)	6	Strength of legal rights index (0-10)	9	Documents to export (number)	5
Time (days)	8	Depth of credit information index (0-6)	0	Time to export (days)	7
Cost (% of income per capita)	12.6	Public registry coverage (% of adults)	0.0	Cost to export (US$ per container)	820
Minimum capital (% of income per capita)	0.0	Private bureau coverage (% of adults)	0.0	Documents to import (number)	6
				Time to import (days)	5
Dealing with construction permits (rank)	75	**Protecting investors** (rank)	93	Cost to import (US$ per container)	1,030
Procedures (number)	13	Extent of disclosure index (0-10)	4		
Time (days)	677	Extent of director liability index (0-10)	4	**Enforcing contracts** (rank)	104
Cost (% of income per capita)	45.0	Ease of shareholder suits index (0-10)	7	Procedures (number)	43
		Strength of investor protection index (0-10)	5.0	Time (days)	735
Registering property (rank)	66			Cost (% of claim)	16.4
Procedures (number)	3	**Paying taxes** (rank)	32		
Time (days)	34	Payments (number per year)	27	**Closing a business** (rank)	22
Cost (% of property value)	10.0	Time (hours per year)	149	Time (years)	1.5
		Total tax rate (% of profit)	23.2	Cost (% of estate)	15
				Recovery rate (cents on the dollar)	70.4

CZECH REPUBLIC

Ease of doing business (rank)	63	OECD high income		GNI per capita (US$)	17,310	
		High income		Population (m)	10.5	
Starting a business (rank)	130	**Getting credit** (rank)	46	**Trading across borders** (rank)	62	
Procedures (number)	9	Strength of legal rights index (0-10)	6	Documents to export (number)	4	
Time (days)	20	Depth of credit information index (0-6)	5	Time to export (days)	17	
Cost (% of income per capita)	9.3	Public registry coverage (% of adults)	4.9	Cost to export (US$ per container)	1,060	
Minimum capital (% of income per capita)	30.9	Private bureau coverage (% of adults)	73.2	Documents to import (number)	7	
				Time to import (days)	20	
Dealing with construction permits (rank)	76	**Protecting investors** (rank)	93	Cost to import (US$ per container)	1,165	
Procedures (number)	36	Extent of disclosure index (0-10)	2			
Time (days)	150	Extent of director liability index (0-10)	5	**Enforcing contracts** (rank)	78	
Cost (% of income per capita)	16.4	Ease of shareholder suits index (0-10)	8	Procedures (number)	27	
		Strength of investor protection index (0-10)	5.0	Time (days)	611	
Registering property (rank)	47			Cost (% of claim)	33.0	
Procedures (number)	4	✔ **Paying taxes** (rank)	128			
Time (days)	43	Payments (number per year)	12	✔ **Closing a business** (rank)	32	
Cost (% of property value)	3.0	Time (hours per year)	557	Time (years)	3.2	
		Total tax rate (% of profit)	48.8	Cost (% of estate)	17	
				Recovery rate (cents on the dollar)	55.9	

DENMARK

Ease of doing business (rank)	6	OECD high income		GNI per capita (US$)	58,930	
		High income		Population (m)	5.5	
✔ **Starting a business** (rank)	27	**Getting credit** (rank)	15	**Trading across borders** (rank)	5	
Procedures (number)	4	Strength of legal rights index (0-10)	9	Documents to export (number)	4	
Time (days)	6	Depth of credit information index (0-6)	4	Time to export (days)	5	
Cost (% of income per capita)	0.0	Public registry coverage (% of adults)	0.0	Cost to export (US$ per container)	744	
Minimum capital (% of income per capita)	26.0	Private bureau coverage (% of adults)	5.4	Documents to import (number)	3	
				Time to import (days)	5	
Dealing with construction permits (rank)	10	**Protecting investors** (rank)	28	Cost to import (US$ per container)	744	
Procedures (number)	6	Extent of disclosure index (0-10)	7			
Time (days)	69	Extent of director liability index (0-10)	5	**Enforcing contracts** (rank)	30	
Cost (% of income per capita)	61.7	Ease of shareholder suits index (0-10)	7	Procedures (number)	35	
		Strength of investor protection index (0-10)	6.3	Time (days)	410	
✔ **Registering property** (rank)	30			Cost (% of claim)	23.3	
Procedures (number)	3	**Paying taxes** (rank)	13			
Time (days)	42	Payments (number per year)	9	**Closing a business** (rank)	5	
Cost (% of property value)	0.6	Time (hours per year)	135	Time (years)	1.1	
		Total tax rate (% of profit)	29.2	Cost (% of estate)	4	
				Recovery rate (cents on the dollar)	89.4	

DJIBOUTI

Ease of doing business (rank)	158	Middle East & North Africa		GNI per capita (US$)	1,280	
		Lower middle income		Population (m)	0.9	
Starting a business (rank)	175	**Getting credit** (rank)	176	**Trading across borders** (rank)	38	
Procedures (number)	11	Strength of legal rights index (0-10)	1	Documents to export (number)	5	
Time (days)	37	Depth of credit information index (0-6)	1	Time to export (days)	19	
Cost (% of income per capita)	169.9	Public registry coverage (% of adults)	0.2	Cost to export (US$ per container)	836	
Minimum capital (% of income per capita)	434.1	Private bureau coverage (% of adults)	0.0	Documents to import (number)	5	
				Time to import (days)	18	
Dealing with construction permits (rank)	125	**Protecting investors** (rank)	179	Cost to import (US$ per container)	911	
Procedures (number)	16	Extent of disclosure index (0-10)	5			
Time (days)	179	Extent of director liability index (0-10)	2	**Enforcing contracts** (rank)	160	
Cost (% of income per capita)	1,862.8	Ease of shareholder suits index (0-10)	0	Procedures (number)	40	
		Strength of investor protection index (0-10)	2.3	Time (days)	1,225	
Registering property (rank)	140			Cost (% of claim)	34.0	
Procedures (number)	7	**Paying taxes** (rank)	60			
Time (days)	40	Payments (number per year)	35	**Closing a business** (rank)	137	
Cost (% of property value)	13.0	Time (hours per year)	90	Time (years)	5.0	
		Total tax rate (% of profit)	38.7	Cost (% of estate)	18	
				Recovery rate (cents on the dollar)	15.6	

✔ Reforms making it easier to do business   ✘ Reforms making it more difficult to do business

DOMINICA

		Latin America & Caribbean		GNI per capita (US$)	4,900
Ease of doing business (rank)	88	Upper middle income		Population (m)	0.1
Starting a business (rank)	38	**Getting credit** (rank)	72	**Trading across borders** (rank)	90
Procedures (number)	5	Strength of legal rights index (0-10)	9	Documents to export (number)	7
Time (days)	14	Depth of credit information index (0-6)	0	Time to export (days)	13
Cost (% of income per capita)	22.0	Public registry coverage (% of adults)	0.0	Cost to export (US$ per container)	1,297
Minimum capital (% of income per capita)	0.0	Private bureau coverage (% of adults)	0.0	Documents to import (number)	8
				Time to import (days)	15
Dealing with construction permits (rank)	28	**Protecting investors** (rank)	28	Cost to import (US$ per container)	1,310
Procedures (number)	13	Extent of disclosure index (0-10)	4		
Time (days)	182	Extent of director liability index (0-10)	8	**Enforcing contracts** (rank)	167
Cost (% of income per capita)	11.0	Ease of shareholder suits index (0-10)	7	Procedures (number)	47
		Strength of investor protection index (0-10)	6.3	Time (days)	681
Registering property (rank)	112			Cost (% of claim)	36.0
Procedures (number)	5	**Paying taxes** (rank)	67		
Time (days)	42	Payments (number per year)	38	**Closing a business** (rank)	183
Cost (% of property value)	13.7	Time (hours per year)	120	Time (years)	NO PRACTICE
		Total tax rate (% of profit)	37.0	Cost (% of estate)	NO PRACTICE
				Recovery rate (cents on the dollar)	0.0

DOMINICAN REPUBLIC

		Latin America & Caribbean		GNI per capita (US$)	4,530
Ease of doing business (rank)	91	Upper middle income		Population (m)	10.1
✘ **Starting a business** (rank)	137	**Getting credit** (rank)	72	**Trading across borders** (rank)	40
Procedures (number)	8	Strength of legal rights index (0-10)	3	Documents to export (number)	6
Time (days)	19	Depth of credit information index (0-6)	6	Time to export (days)	9
Cost (% of income per capita)	19.2	Public registry coverage (% of adults)	28.5	Cost to export (US$ per container)	916
Minimum capital (% of income per capita)	62.6	Private bureau coverage (% of adults)	47.3	Documents to import (number)	7
				Time to import (days)	10
Dealing with construction permits (rank)	89	**Protecting investors** (rank)	59	Cost to import (US$ per container)	1,150
Procedures (number)	17	Extent of disclosure index (0-10)	5		
Time (days)	214	Extent of director liability index (0-10)	4	**Enforcing contracts** (rank)	84
Cost (% of income per capita)	126.7	Ease of shareholder suits index (0-10)	8	Procedures (number)	34
		Strength of investor protection index (0-10)	5.7	Time (days)	460
Registering property (rank)	114			Cost (% of claim)	40.9
Procedures (number)	7	**Paying taxes** (rank)	76		
Time (days)	60	Payments (number per year)	9	**Closing a business** (rank)	145
Cost (% of property value)	3.7	Time (hours per year)	324	Time (years)	3.5
		Total tax rate (% of profit)	40.7	Cost (% of estate)	38
				Recovery rate (cents on the dollar)	9.1

ECUADOR

		Latin America & Caribbean		GNI per capita (US$)	3,940
Ease of doing business (rank)	130	Lower middle income		Population (m)	13.6
✔ **Starting a business** (rank)	158	**Getting credit** (rank)	89	**Trading across borders** (rank)	126
Procedures (number)	13	Strength of legal rights index (0-10)	3	Documents to export (number)	9
Time (days)	56	Depth of credit information index (0-6)	5	Time to export (days)	20
Cost (% of income per capita)	32.6	Public registry coverage (% of adults)	36.5	Cost to export (US$ per container)	1,345
Minimum capital (% of income per capita)	4.9	Private bureau coverage (% of adults)	45.0	Documents to import (number)	7
				Time to import (days)	29
Dealing with construction permits (rank)	88	**Protecting investors** (rank)	132	Cost to import (US$ per container)	1,332
Procedures (number)	19	Extent of disclosure index (0-10)	1		
Time (days)	155	Extent of director liability index (0-10)	5	**Enforcing contracts** (rank)	100
Cost (% of income per capita)	213.2	Ease of shareholder suits index (0-10)	6	Procedures (number)	39
		Strength of investor protection index (0-10)	4.0	Time (days)	588
Registering property (rank)	69			Cost (% of claim)	27.2
Procedures (number)	9	**Paying taxes** (rank)	81		
Time (days)	16	Payments (number per year)	8	**Closing a business** (rank)	133
Cost (% of property value)	2.2	Time (hours per year)	654	Time (years)	5.3
		Total tax rate (% of profit)	35.3	Cost (% of estate)	18
				Recovery rate (cents on the dollar)	17.0

EGYPT, ARAB REP.

		Middle East & North Africa		GNI per capita (US$)	2,070
Ease of doing business (rank)	94	Lower middle income		Population (m)	83.0
✔ **Starting a business** (rank)	18	**Getting credit** (rank)	72	✔ **Trading across borders** (rank)	21
Procedures (number)	6	Strength of legal rights index (0-10)	3	Documents to export (number)	6
Time (days)	7	Depth of credit information index (0-6)	6	Time to export (days)	12
Cost (% of income per capita)	6.3	Public registry coverage (% of adults)	2.9	Cost to export (US$ per container)	613
Minimum capital (% of income per capita)	0.0	Private bureau coverage (% of adults)	10.3	Documents to import (number)	6
				Time to import (days)	12
Dealing with construction permits (rank)	154	**Protecting investors** (rank)	74	Cost to import (US$ per container)	698
Procedures (number)	25	Extent of disclosure index (0-10)	8		
Time (days)	218	Extent of director liability index (0-10)	3	**Enforcing contracts** (rank)	143
Cost (% of income per capita)	293.7	Ease of shareholder suits index (0-10)	5	Procedures (number)	41
		Strength of investor protection index (0-10)	5.3	Time (days)	1,010
Registering property (rank)	93			Cost (% of claim)	26.2
Procedures (number)	7	**Paying taxes** (rank)	136		
Time (days)	72	Payments (number per year)	29	**Closing a business** (rank)	131
Cost (% of property value)	0.8	Time (hours per year)	433	Time (years)	4.2
		Total tax rate (% of profit)	42.6	Cost (% of estate)	22
				Recovery rate (cents on the dollar)	17.4

EL SALVADOR

		Latin America & Caribbean		GNI per capita (US$)	3,370
Ease of doing business (rank)	86	Lower middle income		Population (m)	6.2
Starting a business (rank)	129	**Getting credit** (rank)	46	**Trading across borders** (rank)	65
Procedures (number)	8	Strength of legal rights index (0-10)	5	Documents to export (number)	8
Time (days)	17	Depth of credit information index (0-6)	6	Time to export (days)	14
Cost (% of income per capita)	45.0	Public registry coverage (% of adults)	21.8	Cost to export (US$ per container)	845
Minimum capital (% of income per capita)	3.0	Private bureau coverage (% of adults)	95.0	Documents to import (number)	8
				Time to import (days)	10
Dealing with construction permits (rank)	124	**Protecting investors** (rank)	120	Cost to import (US$ per container)	845
Procedures (number)	34	Extent of disclosure index (0-10)	5		
Time (days)	155	Extent of director liability index (0-10)	2	**Enforcing contracts** (rank)	51
Cost (% of income per capita)	171.7	Ease of shareholder suits index (0-10)	6	Procedures (number)	30
		Strength of investor protection index (0-10)	4.3	Time (days)	786
Registering property (rank)	49			Cost (% of claim)	19.2
Procedures (number)	5	**Paying taxes** (rank)	137		
Time (days)	31	Payments (number per year)	53	**Closing a business** (rank)	87
Cost (% of property value)	3.8	Time (hours per year)	320	Time (years)	4.0
		Total tax rate (% of profit)	35.0	Cost (% of estate)	9
				Recovery rate (cents on the dollar)	29.2

EQUATORIAL GUINEA

		Sub-Saharan Africa		GNI per capita (US$)	12,420
Ease of doing business (rank)	164	High income		Population (m)	0.7
Starting a business (rank)	179	**Getting credit** (rank)	138	**Trading across borders** (rank)	137
Procedures (number)	20	Strength of legal rights index (0-10)	3	Documents to export (number)	7
Time (days)	136	Depth of credit information index (0-6)	2	Time to export (days)	29
Cost (% of income per capita)	104.3	Public registry coverage (% of adults)	2.5	Cost to export (US$ per container)	1,411
Minimum capital (% of income per capita)	21.3	Private bureau coverage (% of adults)	0.0	Documents to import (number)	7
				Time to import (days)	48
Dealing with construction permits (rank)	109	**Protecting investors** (rank)	147	Cost to import (US$ per container)	1,411
Procedures (number)	18	Extent of disclosure index (0-10)	6		
Time (days)	201	Extent of director liability index (0-10)	1	**Enforcing contracts** (rank)	72
Cost (% of income per capita)	220.7	Ease of shareholder suits index (0-10)	4	Procedures (number)	40
		Strength of investor protection index (0-10)	3.7	Time (days)	553
Registering property (rank)	79			Cost (% of claim)	18.5
Procedures (number)	6	**Paying taxes** (rank)	170		
Time (days)	23	Payments (number per year)	46	**Closing a business** (rank)	183
Cost (% of property value)	6.3	Time (hours per year)	492	Time (years)	NO PRACTICE
		Total tax rate (% of profit)	59.5	Cost (% of estate)	NO PRACTICE
				Recovery rate (cents on the dollar)	0.0

ERITREA

		Sub-Saharan Africa		GNI per capita (US$)	363
Ease of doing business (rank)	180	Low income		Population (m)	5.1
Starting a business (rank)	180	**Getting credit** (rank)	176	**Trading across borders** (rank)	165
Procedures (number)	13	Strength of legal rights index (0-10)	2	Documents to export (number)	9
Time (days)	84	Depth of credit information index (0-6)	0	Time to export (days)	50
Cost (% of income per capita)	69.2	Public registry coverage (% of adults)	0.0	Cost to export (US$ per container)	1,431
Minimum capital (% of income per capita)	268.4	Private bureau coverage (% of adults)	0.0	Documents to import (number)	13
				Time to import (days)	59
Dealing with construction permits (rank)	183	**Protecting investors** (rank)	109	Cost to import (US$ per container)	1,581
Procedures (number)	NO PRACTICE	Extent of disclosure index (0-10)	4		
Time (days)	NO PRACTICE	Extent of director liability index (0-10)	5	**Enforcing contracts** (rank)	48
Cost (% of income per capita)	NO PRACTICE	Ease of shareholder suits index (0-10)	5	Procedures (number)	39
		Strength of investor protection index (0-10)	4.7	Time (days)	405
Registering property (rank)	178			Cost (% of claim)	22.6
Procedures (number)	11	**Paying taxes** (rank)	113		
Time (days)	78	Payments (number per year)	18	**Closing a business** (rank)	183
Cost (% of property value)	9.1	Time (hours per year)	216	Time (years)	NO PRACTICE
		Total tax rate (% of profit)	84.5	Cost (% of estate)	NO PRACTICE
				Recovery rate (cents on the dollar)	0.0

ESTONIA

		Eastern Europe & Central Asia		GNI per capita (US$)	14,060
Ease of doing business (rank)	17	High income		Population (m)	1.3
Starting a business (rank)	37	✔ **Getting credit** (rank)	32	**Trading across borders** (rank)	4
Procedures (number)	5	Strength of legal rights index (0-10)	7	Documents to export (number)	3
Time (days)	7	Depth of credit information index (0-6)	5	Time to export (days)	5
Cost (% of income per capita)	1.9	Public registry coverage (% of adults)	0.0	Cost to export (US$ per container)	725
Minimum capital (% of income per capita)	25.7	Private bureau coverage (% of adults)	22.4	Documents to import (number)	4
				Time to import (days)	5
✗ **Dealing with construction permits** (rank)	24	**Protecting investors** (rank)	59	Cost to import (US$ per container)	725
Procedures (number)	14	Extent of disclosure index (0-10)	8		
Time (days)	134	Extent of director liability index (0-10)	3	**Enforcing contracts** (rank)	50
Cost (% of income per capita)	29.9	Ease of shareholder suits index (0-10)	6	Procedures (number)	36
		Strength of investor protection index (0-10)	5.7	Time (days)	425
Registering property (rank)	13			Cost (% of claim)	26.3
Procedures (number)	3	✗ **Paying taxes** (rank)	30		
Time (days)	18	Payments (number per year)	7	✔ **Closing a business** (rank)	70
Cost (% of property value)	0.5	Time (hours per year)	81	Time (years)	3.0
		Total tax rate (% of profit)	49.6	Cost (% of estate)	9
				Recovery rate (cents on the dollar)	35.5

ETHIOPIA

		Sub-Saharan Africa		GNI per capita (US$)	330
Ease of doing business (rank)	104	Low income		Population (m)	82.8
Starting a business (rank)	89	**Getting credit** (rank)	128	✔ **Trading across borders** (rank)	157
Procedures (number)	5	Strength of legal rights index (0-10)	4	Documents to export (number)	8
Time (days)	9	Depth of credit information index (0-6)	2	Time to export (days)	44
Cost (% of income per capita)	14.1	Public registry coverage (% of adults)	0.1	Cost to export (US$ per container)	1,890
Minimum capital (% of income per capita)	367.7	Private bureau coverage (% of adults)	0.0	Documents to import (number)	8
				Time to import (days)	45
Dealing with construction permits (rank)	53	**Protecting investors** (rank)	120	Cost to import (US$ per container)	2,993
Procedures (number)	12	Extent of disclosure index (0-10)	4		
Time (days)	128	Extent of director liability index (0-10)	4	**Enforcing contracts** (rank)	57
Cost (% of income per capita)	419.6	Ease of shareholder suits index (0-10)	5	Procedures (number)	37
		Strength of investor protection index (0-10)	4.3	Time (days)	620
Registering property (rank)	109			Cost (% of claim)	15.2
Procedures (number)	10	**Paying taxes** (rank)	47		
Time (days)	41	Payments (number per year)	19	**Closing a business** (rank)	82
Cost (% of property value)	2.1	Time (hours per year)	198	Time (years)	3.0
		Total tax rate (% of profit)	31.1	Cost (% of estate)	15
				Recovery rate (cents on the dollar)	31.3

FIJI

East Asia & Pacific		GNI per capita (US$)	3,950
		Population (m)	0.8

Ease of doing business (rank)	62

Starting a business (rank)	104
Procedures (number)	8
Time (days)	46
Cost (% of income per capita)	23.8
Minimum capital (% of income per capita)	0.0

Getting credit (rank)	46
Strength of legal rights index (0-10)	7
Depth of credit information index (0-6)	4
Public registry coverage (% of adults)	0.0
Private bureau coverage (% of adults)	47.7

✔ **Trading across borders** (rank)	103
Documents to export (number)	10
Time to export (days)	22
Cost to export (US$ per container)	654
Documents to import (number)	10
Time to import (days)	23
Cost to import (US$ per container)	630

Dealing with construction permits (rank)	58
Procedures (number)	19
Time (days)	135
Cost (% of income per capita)	47.4

Protecting investors (rank)	44
Extent of disclosure index (0-10)	3
Extent of director liability index (0-10)	8
Ease of shareholder suits index (0-10)	7
Strength of investor protection index (0-10)	6.0

Enforcing contracts (rank)	63
Procedures (number)	34
Time (days)	397
Cost (% of claim)	38.9

Registering property (rank)	50
Procedures (number)	3
Time (days)	68
Cost (% of property value)	2.0

Paying taxes (rank)	77
Payments (number per year)	33
Time (hours per year)	163
Total tax rate (% of profit)	39.3

Closing a business (rank)	117
Time (years)	1.8
Cost (% of estate)	38
Recovery rate (cents on the dollar)	20.5

FINLAND

OECD high income		GNI per capita (US$)	45,680
High income		Population (m)	5.3

Ease of doing business (rank)	13

Starting a business (rank)	32
Procedures (number)	3
Time (days)	14
Cost (% of income per capita)	1.1
Minimum capital (% of income per capita)	7.9

Getting credit (rank)	32
Strength of legal rights index (0-10)	7
Depth of credit information index (0-6)	5
Public registry coverage (% of adults)	0.0
Private bureau coverage (% of adults)	14.9

Trading across borders (rank)	6
Documents to export (number)	4
Time to export (days)	8
Cost to export (US$ per container)	540
Documents to import (number)	5
Time to import (days)	8
Cost to import (US$ per container)	620

Dealing with construction permits (rank)	55
Procedures (number)	18
Time (days)	66
Cost (% of income per capita)	134.2

Protecting investors (rank)	59
Extent of disclosure index (0-10)	6
Extent of director liability index (0-10)	4
Ease of shareholder suits index (0-10)	7
Strength of investor protection index (0-10)	5.7

Enforcing contracts (rank)	11
Procedures (number)	32
Time (days)	375
Cost (% of claim)	13.3

Registering property (rank)	26
Procedures (number)	3
Time (days)	14
Cost (% of property value)	4.0

Paying taxes (rank)	65
Payments (number per year)	8
Time (hours per year)	243
Total tax rate (% of profit)	44.6

Closing a business (rank)	6
Time (years)	0.9
Cost (% of estate)	4
Recovery rate (cents on the dollar)	89.4

FRANCE

OECD high income		GNI per capita (US$)	43,990
High income		Population (m)	62.6

Ease of doing business (rank)	26

Starting a business (rank)	21
Procedures (number)	5
Time (days)	7
Cost (% of income per capita)	0.9
Minimum capital (% of income per capita)	0.0

Getting credit (rank)	46
Strength of legal rights index (0-10)	7
Depth of credit information index (0-6)	4
Public registry coverage (% of adults)	33.3
Private bureau coverage (% of adults)	0.0

Trading across borders (rank)	26
Documents to export (number)	2
Time to export (days)	9
Cost to export (US$ per container)	1,078
Documents to import (number)	2
Time to import (days)	11
Cost to import (US$ per container)	1,248

Dealing with construction permits (rank)	19
Procedures (number)	13
Time (days)	137
Cost (% of income per capita)	23.6

Protecting investors (rank)	74
Extent of disclosure index (0-10)	10
Extent of director liability index (0-10)	1
Ease of shareholder suits index (0-10)	5
Strength of investor protection index (0-10)	5.3

Enforcing contracts (rank)	7
Procedures (number)	29
Time (days)	331
Cost (% of claim)	17.4

Registering property (rank)	142
Procedures (number)	8
Time (days)	59
Cost (% of property value)	6.1

Paying taxes (rank)	55
Payments (number per year)	7
Time (hours per year)	132
Total tax rate (% of profit)	65.8

Closing a business (rank)	44
Time (years)	1.9
Cost (% of estate)	9
Recovery rate (cents on the dollar)	45.2

GABON

		Sub-Saharan Africa		GNI per capita (US$)	7,370
Ease of doing business (rank)	156	Upper middle income		Population (m)	1.5
Starting a business (rank)	153	**Getting credit** (rank)	138	**Trading across borders** (rank)	134
Procedures (number)	9	Strength of legal rights index (0-10)	3	Documents to export (number)	7
Time (days)	58	Depth of credit information index (0-6)	2	Time to export (days)	20
Cost (% of income per capita)	21.9	Public registry coverage (% of adults)	22.5	Cost to export (US$ per container)	1,945
Minimum capital (% of income per capita)	32.7	Private bureau coverage (% of adults)	0.0	Documents to import (number)	8
				Time to import (days)	22
Dealing with construction permits (rank)	67	**Protecting investors** (rank)	154	Cost to import (US$ per container)	1,955
Procedures (number)	16	Extent of disclosure index (0-10)	6		
Time (days)	210	Extent of director liability index (0-10)	1	**Enforcing contracts** (rank)	148
Cost (% of income per capita)	42.9	Ease of shareholder suits index (0-10)	3	Procedures (number)	38
		Strength of investor protection index (0-10)	3.3	Time (days)	1,070
Registering property (rank)	132			Cost (% of claim)	34.3
Procedures (number)	7	**Paying taxes** (rank)	140		
Time (days)	39	Payments (number per year)	26	**Closing a business** (rank)	139
Cost (% of property value)	10.5	Time (hours per year)	488	Time (years)	5.0
		Total tax rate (% of profit)	43.5	Cost (% of estate)	15
				Recovery rate (cents on the dollar)	15.2

GAMBIA, THE

		Sub-Saharan Africa		GNI per capita (US$)	440
Ease of doing business (rank)	146	Low income		Population (m)	1.7
Starting a business (rank)	115	**Getting credit** (rank)	138	**Trading across borders** (rank)	87
Procedures (number)	8	Strength of legal rights index (0-10)	5	Documents to export (number)	6
Time (days)	27	Depth of credit information index (0-6)	0	Time to export (days)	23
Cost (% of income per capita)	199.6	Public registry coverage (% of adults)	0.0	Cost to export (US$ per container)	831
Minimum capital (% of income per capita)	0.0	Private bureau coverage (% of adults)	0.0	Documents to import (number)	8
				Time to import (days)	23
Dealing with construction permits (rank)	80	**Protecting investors** (rank)	173	Cost to import (US$ per container)	975
Procedures (number)	17	Extent of disclosure index (0-10)	2		
Time (days)	146	Extent of director liability index (0-10)	1	**Enforcing contracts** (rank)	67
Cost (% of income per capita)	314.9	Ease of shareholder suits index (0-10)	5	Procedures (number)	32
		Strength of investor protection index (0-10)	2.7	Time (days)	434
Registering property (rank)	121			Cost (% of claim)	37.9
Procedures (number)	5	**Paying taxes** (rank)	176		
Time (days)	66	Payments (number per year)	50	**Closing a business** (rank)	121
Cost (% of property value)	7.6	Time (hours per year)	376	Time (years)	3.0
		Total tax rate (% of profit)	292.3	Cost (% of estate)	15
				Recovery rate (cents on the dollar)	19.8

GEORGIA

		Eastern Europe & Central Asia		GNI per capita (US$)	2,530
Ease of doing business (rank)	12	Lower middle income		Population (m)	4.3
Starting a business (rank)	8	✔ **Getting credit** (rank)	15	**Trading across borders** (rank)	35
Procedures (number)	3	Strength of legal rights index (0-10)	7	Documents to export (number)	4
Time (days)	3	Depth of credit information index (0-6)	6	Time to export (days)	10
Cost (% of income per capita)	5.0	Public registry coverage (% of adults)	0.0	Cost to export (US$ per container)	1,329
Minimum capital (% of income per capita)	0.0	Private bureau coverage (% of adults)	16.4	Documents to import (number)	4
				Time to import (days)	13
Dealing with construction permits (rank)	7	✔ **Protecting investors** (rank)	20	Cost to import (US$ per container)	1,316
Procedures (number)	10	Extent of disclosure index (0-10)	8		
Time (days)	98	Extent of director liability index (0-10)	6	✔ **Enforcing contracts** (rank)	41
Cost (% of income per capita)	23.2	Ease of shareholder suits index (0-10)	6	Procedures (number)	36
		Strength of investor protection index (0-10)	6.7	Time (days)	285
Registering property (rank)	2			Cost (% of claim)	29.9
Procedures (number)	1	**Paying taxes** (rank)	61		
Time (days)	2	Payments (number per year)	18	✔ **Closing a business** (rank)	105
Cost (% of property value)	0.1	Time (hours per year)	387	Time (years)	3.3
		Total tax rate (% of profit)	15.3	Cost (% of estate)	4
				Recovery rate (cents on the dollar)	25.1

GERMANY

Ease of doing business (rank)	22

✔ **Starting a business** (rank)	88
Procedures (number)	9
Time (days)	15
Cost (% of income per capita)	4.8
Minimum capital (% of income per capita)	0.0

Dealing with construction permits (rank)	18
Procedures (number)	12
Time (days)	100
Cost (% of income per capita)	61.8

Registering property (rank)	67
Procedures (number)	5
Time (days)	40
Cost (% of property value)	5.1

OECD high income	
High income	

Getting credit (rank)	15
Strength of legal rights index (0-10)	7
Depth of credit information index (0-6)	6
Public registry coverage (% of adults)	1.0
Private bureau coverage (% of adults)	98.4

Protecting investors (rank)	93
Extent of disclosure index (0-10)	5
Extent of director liability index (0-10)	5
Ease of shareholder suits index (0-10)	5
Strength of investor protection index (0-10)	5.0

Paying taxes (rank)	88
Payments (number per year)	16
Time (hours per year)	215
Total tax rate (% of profit)	48.2

GNI per capita (US$)	42,560
Population (m)	81.9

Trading across borders (rank)	14
Documents to export (number)	4
Time to export (days)	7
Cost to export (US$ per container)	872
Documents to import (number)	5
Time to import (days)	7
Cost to import (US$ per container)	937

Enforcing contracts (rank)	6
Procedures (number)	30
Time (days)	394
Cost (% of claim)	14.4

Closing a business (rank)	35
Time (years)	1.2
Cost (% of estate)	8
Recovery rate (cents on the dollar)	53.1

GHANA

Ease of doing business (rank)	67

Starting a business (rank)	99
Procedures (number)	7
Time (days)	12
Cost (% of income per capita)	20.3
Minimum capital (% of income per capita)	11.0

Dealing with construction permits (rank)	151
Procedures (number)	18
Time (days)	220
Cost (% of income per capita)	1,017.7

Registering property (rank)	36
Procedures (number)	5
Time (days)	34
Cost (% of property value)	1.0

Sub-Saharan Africa	
Low income	

✔ **Getting credit** (rank)	46
Strength of legal rights index (0-10)	8
Depth of credit information index (0-6)	3
Public registry coverage (% of adults)	0.0
Private bureau coverage (% of adults)	10.3

Protecting investors (rank)	44
Extent of disclosure index (0-10)	7
Extent of director liability index (0-10)	5
Ease of shareholder suits index (0-10)	6
Strength of investor protection index (0-10)	6.0

Paying taxes (rank)	78
Payments (number per year)	33
Time (hours per year)	224
Total tax rate (% of profit)	32.7

GNI per capita (US$)	700
Population (m)	23.8

Trading across borders (rank)	89
Documents to export (number)	6
Time to export (days)	19
Cost to export (US$ per container)	1,013
Documents to import (number)	7
Time to import (days)	29
Cost to import (US$ per container)	1,203

Enforcing contracts (rank)	45
Procedures (number)	36
Time (days)	487
Cost (% of claim)	23.0

Closing a business (rank)	109
Time (years)	1.9
Cost (% of estate)	22
Recovery rate (cents on the dollar)	23.7

GREECE

Ease of doing business (rank)	109

Starting a business (rank)	149
Procedures (number)	15
Time (days)	19
Cost (% of income per capita)	20.7
Minimum capital (% of income per capita)	22.3

Dealing with construction permits (rank)	51
Procedures (number)	15
Time (days)	169
Cost (% of income per capita)	52.9

✗ **Registering property** (rank)	153
Procedures (number)	11
Time (days)	22
Cost (% of property value)	12.7

OECD high income	
High income	

Getting credit (rank)	89
Strength of legal rights index (0-10)	3
Depth of credit information index (0-6)	5
Public registry coverage (% of adults)	0.0
Private bureau coverage (% of adults)	61.5

Protecting investors (rank)	154
Extent of disclosure index (0-10)	1
Extent of director liability index (0-10)	4
Ease of shareholder suits index (0-10)	5
Strength of investor protection index (0-10)	3.3

Paying taxes (rank)	74
Payments (number per year)	10
Time (hours per year)	224
Total tax rate (% of profit)	47.2

GNI per capita (US$)	28,630
Population (m)	11.3

Trading across borders (rank)	84
Documents to export (number)	5
Time to export (days)	20
Cost to export (US$ per container)	1,153
Documents to import (number)	6
Time to import (days)	25
Cost to import (US$ per container)	1,265

Enforcing contracts (rank)	88
Procedures (number)	39
Time (days)	819
Cost (% of claim)	14.4

Closing a business (rank)	49
Time (years)	2.0
Cost (% of estate)	9
Recovery rate (cents on the dollar)	43.2

✔ Reforms making it easier to do business   ✘ Reforms making it more difficult to do business

GRENADA

		Latin America & Caribbean		GNI per capita (US$)	5,580
Ease of doing business (rank)	92	Upper middle income		Population (m)	0.1
✔ **Starting a business** (rank)	49	**Getting credit** (rank)	89	✔ **Trading across borders** (rank)	57
Procedures (number)	6	Strength of legal rights index (0-10)	8	Documents to export (number)	6
Time (days)	15	Depth of credit information index (0-6)	0	Time to export (days)	10
Cost (% of income per capita)	25.2	Public registry coverage (% of adults)	0.0	Cost to export (US$ per container)	876
Minimum capital (% of income per capita)	0.0	Private bureau coverage (% of adults)	0.0	Documents to import (number)	5
				Time to import (days)	15
Dealing with construction permits (rank)	15	**Protecting investors** (rank)	28	Cost to import (US$ per container)	2,129
Procedures (number)	10	Extent of disclosure index (0-10)	4		
Time (days)	149	Extent of director liability index (0-10)	8	**Enforcing contracts** (rank)	161
Cost (% of income per capita)	25.9	Ease of shareholder suits index (0-10)	7	Procedures (number)	47
		Strength of investor protection index (0-10)	6.3	Time (days)	688
✔ **Registering property** (rank)	145			Cost (% of claim)	32.6
Procedures (number)	8	**Paying taxes** (rank)	79		
Time (days)	47	Payments (number per year)	30	**Closing a business** (rank)	183
Cost (% of property value)	7.4	Time (hours per year)	140	Time (years)	NO PRACTICE
		Total tax rate (% of profit)	45.3	Cost (% of estate)	NO PRACTICE
				Recovery rate (cents on the dollar)	0.0

GUATEMALA

		Latin America & Caribbean		GNI per capita (US$)	2,630
Ease of doing business (rank)	101	Lower middle income		Population (m)	14.0
Starting a business (rank)	162	**Getting credit** (rank)	6	**Trading across borders** (rank)	122
Procedures (number)	12	Strength of legal rights index (0-10)	8	Documents to export (number)	10
Time (days)	37	Depth of credit information index (0-6)	6	Time to export (days)	17
Cost (% of income per capita)	49.1	Public registry coverage (% of adults)	16.4	Cost to export (US$ per container)	1,182
Minimum capital (% of income per capita)	24.2	Private bureau coverage (% of adults)	8.8	Documents to import (number)	10
				Time to import (days)	17
Dealing with construction permits (rank)	144	**Protecting investors** (rank)	132	Cost to import (US$ per container)	1,302
Procedures (number)	22	Extent of disclosure index (0-10)	3		
Time (days)	178	Extent of director liability index (0-10)	3	**Enforcing contracts** (rank)	101
Cost (% of income per capita)	599.4	Ease of shareholder suits index (0-10)	6	Procedures (number)	31
		Strength of investor protection index (0-10)	4.0	Time (days)	1,459
Registering property (rank)	23			Cost (% of claim)	26.5
Procedures (number)	4	**Paying taxes** (rank)	116		
Time (days)	23	Payments (number per year)	24	**Closing a business** (rank)	94
Cost (% of property value)	1.0	Time (hours per year)	344	Time (years)	3.0
		Total tax rate (% of profit)	40.9	Cost (% of estate)	15
				Recovery rate (cents on the dollar)	27.5

GUINEA

		Sub-Saharan Africa		GNI per capita (US$)	370
Ease of doing business (rank)	179	Low income		Population (m)	10.1
Starting a business (rank)	181	**Getting credit** (rank)	168	**Trading across borders** (rank)	129
Procedures (number)	13	Strength of legal rights index (0-10)	3	Documents to export (number)	7
Time (days)	41	Depth of credit information index (0-6)	0	Time to export (days)	35
Cost (% of income per capita)	146.6	Public registry coverage (% of adults)	0.0	Cost to export (US$ per container)	855
Minimum capital (% of income per capita)	519.1	Private bureau coverage (% of adults)	0.0	Documents to import (number)	9
				Time to import (days)	32
✘ **Dealing with construction permits** (rank)	171	**Protecting investors** (rank)	173	Cost to import (US$ per container)	1,391
Procedures (number)	32	Extent of disclosure index (0-10)	6		
Time (days)	255	Extent of director liability index (0-10)	1	**Enforcing contracts** (rank)	130
Cost (% of income per capita)	419.0	Ease of shareholder suits index (0-10)	1	Procedures (number)	50
		Strength of investor protection index (0-10)	2.7	Time (days)	276
Registering property (rank)	166			Cost (% of claim)	45.0
Procedures (number)	6	**Paying taxes** (rank)	173		
Time (days)	104	Payments (number per year)	56	**Closing a business** (rank)	123
Cost (% of property value)	14.0	Time (hours per year)	416	Time (years)	3.8
		Total tax rate (% of profit)	54.6	Cost (% of estate)	8
				Recovery rate (cents on the dollar)	19.4

GUINEA-BISSAU

		Sub-Saharan Africa		GNI per capita (US$)	510
Ease of doing business (rank)	176	Low income		Population (m)	1.6
Starting a business (rank)	183	**Getting credit** (rank)	152	**Trading across borders** (rank)	117
Procedures (number)	17	Strength of legal rights index (0-10)	3	Documents to export (number)	6
Time (days)	216	Depth of credit information index (0-6)	1	Time to export (days)	23
Cost (% of income per capita)	183.3	Public registry coverage (% of adults)	0.3	Cost to export (US$ per container)	1,545
Minimum capital (% of income per capita)	415.1	Private bureau coverage (% of adults)	0.0	Documents to import (number)	6
				Time to import (days)	22
Dealing with construction permits (rank)	103	**Protecting investors** (rank)	132	Cost to import (US$ per container)	2,349
Procedures (number)	15	Extent of disclosure index (0-10)	6		
Time (days)	167	Extent of director liability index (0-10)	1	✔ **Enforcing contracts** (rank)	139
Cost (% of income per capita)	1,075.0	Ease of shareholder suits index (0-10)	5	Procedures (number)	40
		Strength of investor protection index (0-10)	4.0	Time (days)	1,140
Registering property (rank)	175			Cost (% of claim)	25.0
Procedures (number)	9	**Paying taxes** (rank)	133		
Time (days)	211	Payments (number per year)	46	**Closing a business** (rank)	183
Cost (% of property value)	6.1	Time (hours per year)	208	Time (years)	NO PRACTICE
		Total tax rate (% of profit)	45.9	Cost (% of estate)	NO PRACTICE
				Recovery rate (cents on the dollar)	0.0

GUYANA

		Latin America & Caribbean		GNI per capita (US$)	2,629
Ease of doing business (rank)	100	Lower middle income		Population (m)	0.8
✔ **Starting a business** (rank)	90	✔ **Getting credit** (rank)	152	✔ **Trading across borders** (rank)	78
Procedures (number)	8	Strength of legal rights index (0-10)	4	Documents to export (number)	7
Time (days)	30	Depth of credit information index (0-6)	0	Time to export (days)	19
Cost (% of income per capita)	18.7	Public registry coverage (% of adults)	0.0	Cost to export (US$ per container)	730
Minimum capital (% of income per capita)	0.0	Private bureau coverage (% of adults)	0.0	Documents to import (number)	8
				Time to import (days)	22
Dealing with construction permits (rank)	33	**Protecting investors** (rank)	74	Cost to import (US$ per container)	745
Procedures (number)	11	Extent of disclosure index (0-10)	5		
Time (days)	133	Extent of director liability index (0-10)	5	**Enforcing contracts** (rank)	74
Cost (% of income per capita)	130.5	Ease of shareholder suits index (0-10)	6	Procedures (number)	36
		Strength of investor protection index (0-10)	5.3	Time (days)	581
Registering property (rank)	75			Cost (% of claim)	25.2
Procedures (number)	6	**Paying taxes** (rank)	119		
Time (days)	34	Payments (number per year)	34	**Closing a business** (rank)	130
Cost (% of property value)	4.5	Time (hours per year)	288	Time (years)	3.0
		Total tax rate (% of profit)	38.9	Cost (% of estate)	29
				Recovery rate (cents on the dollar)	17.6

HAITI

		Latin America & Caribbean		GNI per capita (US$)	733
Ease of doing business (rank)	162	Low income		Population (m)	10.0
✔ **Starting a business** (rank)	178	**Getting credit** (rank)	138	**Trading across borders** (rank)	145
Procedures (number)	13	Strength of legal rights index (0-10)	3	Documents to export (number)	8
Time (days)	105	Depth of credit information index (0-6)	2	Time to export (days)	35
Cost (% of income per capita)	212.0	Public registry coverage (% of adults)	0.7	Cost to export (US$ per container)	1,005
Minimum capital (% of income per capita)	20.7	Private bureau coverage (% of adults)	0.0	Documents to import (number)	10
				Time to import (days)	33
Dealing with construction permits (rank)	122	**Protecting investors** (rank)	167	Cost to import (US$ per container)	1,545
Procedures (number)	11	Extent of disclosure index (0-10)	2		
Time (days)	1,179	Extent of director liability index (0-10)	3	**Enforcing contracts** (rank)	91
Cost (% of income per capita)	525.3	Ease of shareholder suits index (0-10)	4	Procedures (number)	35
		Strength of investor protection index (0-10)	3.0	Time (days)	508
Registering property (rank)	128			Cost (% of claim)	42.6
Procedures (number)	5	**Paying taxes** (rank)	97		
Time (days)	405	Payments (number per year)	42	**Closing a business** (rank)	151
Cost (% of property value)	6.3	Time (hours per year)	160	Time (years)	5.7
		Total tax rate (% of profit)	40.1	Cost (% of estate)	30
				Recovery rate (cents on the dollar)	6.7

✔ Reforms making it easier to do business   ✘ Reforms making it more difficult to do business

HONDURAS

		Latin America & Caribbean		GNI per capita (US$)		1,820
Ease of doing business (rank)	131	Lower middle income		Population (m)		7.5
Starting a business (rank)	145	**Getting credit** (rank)	32	**Trading across borders** (rank)		110
Procedures (number)	13	Strength of legal rights index (0-10)	6	Documents to export (number)		6
Time (days)	14	Depth of credit information index (0-6)	6	Time to export (days)		19
Cost (% of income per capita)	47.2	Public registry coverage (% of adults)	22.7	Cost to export (US$ per container)		1,193
Minimum capital (% of income per capita)	17.5	Private bureau coverage (% of adults)	100.0	Documents to import (number)		10
				Time to import (days)		23
Dealing with construction permits (rank)	73	**Protecting investors** (rank)	167	Cost to import (US$ per container)		1,205
Procedures (number)	17	Extent of disclosure index (0-10)	0			
Time (days)	106	Extent of director liability index (0-10)	5	**Enforcing contracts** (rank)		175
Cost (% of income per capita)	469.3	Ease of shareholder suits index (0-10)	4	Procedures (number)		45
		Strength of investor protection index (0-10)	3.0	Time (days)		900
Registering property (rank)	89			Cost (% of claim)		35.2
Procedures (number)	7	**Paying taxes** (rank)	147			
Time (days)	23	Payments (number per year)	47	**Closing a business** (rank)		120
Cost (% of property value)	5.5	Time (hours per year)	224	Time (years)		3.8
		Total tax rate (% of profit)	48.3	Cost (% of estate)		15
				Recovery rate (cents on the dollar)		19.9

HONG KONG SAR, CHINA

		East Asia & Pacific		GNI per capita (US$)		29,826
Ease of doing business (rank)	2	High income		Population (m)		7.0
Starting a business (rank)	6	**Getting credit** (rank)	2	**Trading across borders** (rank)		2
Procedures (number)	3	Strength of legal rights index (0-10)	10	Documents to export (number)		4
Time (days)	6	Depth of credit information index (0-6)	5	Time to export (days)		6
Cost (% of income per capita)	2.0	Public registry coverage (% of adults)	0.0	Cost to export (US$ per container)		625
Minimum capital (% of income per capita)	0.0	Private bureau coverage (% of adults)	72.0	Documents to import (number)		4
				Time to import (days)		5
Dealing with construction permits (rank)	1	**Protecting investors** (rank)	3	Cost to import (US$ per container)		600
Procedures (number)	7	Extent of disclosure index (0-10)	10			
Time (days)	67	Extent of director liability index (0-10)	8	✔ **Enforcing contracts** (rank)		2
Cost (% of income per capita)	19.4	Ease of shareholder suits index (0-10)	9	Procedures (number)		24
		Strength of investor protection index (0-10)	9.0	Time (days)		280
Registering property (rank)	56			Cost (% of claim)		19.5
Procedures (number)	5	✔ **Paying taxes** (rank)	3			
Time (days)	36	Payments (number per year)	3	**Closing a business** (rank)		15
Cost (% of property value)	4.2	Time (hours per year)	80	Time (years)		1.1
		Total tax rate (% of profit)	24.1	Cost (% of estate)		9
				Recovery rate (cents on the dollar)		81.2

HUNGARY

		OECD high income		GNI per capita (US$)		12,980
Ease of doing business (rank)	46	High income		Population (m)		10.0
Starting a business (rank)	35	**Getting credit** (rank)	32	**Trading across borders** (rank)		73
Procedures (number)	4	Strength of legal rights index (0-10)	7	Documents to export (number)		5
Time (days)	4	Depth of credit information index (0-6)	5	Time to export (days)		18
Cost (% of income per capita)	8.2	Public registry coverage (% of adults)	0.0	Cost to export (US$ per container)		1,225
Minimum capital (% of income per capita)	10.2	Private bureau coverage (% of adults)	11.4	Documents to import (number)		7
				Time to import (days)		17
✔ **Dealing with construction permits** (rank)	86	**Protecting investors** (rank)	120	Cost to import (US$ per container)		1,215
Procedures (number)	31	Extent of disclosure index (0-10)	2			
Time (days)	189	Extent of director liability index (0-10)	4	**Enforcing contracts** (rank)		22
Cost (% of income per capita)	9.8	Ease of shareholder suits index (0-10)	7	Procedures (number)		35
		Strength of investor protection index (0-10)	4.3	Time (days)		395
✔ **Registering property** (rank)	41			Cost (% of claim)		15.0
Procedures (number)	4	✔ **Paying taxes** (rank)	109			
Time (days)	17	Payments (number per year)	14	✔ **Closing a business** (rank)		62
Cost (% of property value)	5.0	Time (hours per year)	277	Time (years)		2.0
		Total tax rate (% of profit)	53.3	Cost (% of estate)		15
				Recovery rate (cents on the dollar)		37.9

ICELAND

		OECD high income		GNI per capita (US$)		43,220
Ease of doing business (rank)	15	High income		Population (m)		0.3

Starting a business (rank)	29	**Getting credit** (rank)	32
Procedures (number)	5	Strength of legal rights index (0-10)	7
Time (days)	5	Depth of credit information index (0-6)	5
Cost (% of income per capita)	2.3	Public registry coverage (% of adults)	0.0
Minimum capital (% of income per capita)	12.0	Private bureau coverage (% of adults)	100.0

Trading across borders (rank) 79
Documents to export (number) 5
Time to export (days) 19
Cost to export (US$ per container) 1,532
Documents to import (number) 5
Time to import (days) 14
Cost to import (US$ per container) 1,674

✗ **Dealing with construction permits** (rank) 31
Procedures (number) 18
Time (days) 75
Cost (% of income per capita) 19.6

Protecting investors (rank) 74
Extent of disclosure index (0-10) 5
Extent of director liability index (0-10) 5
Ease of shareholder suits index (0-10) 6
Strength of investor protection index (0-10) 5.3

Enforcing contracts (rank) 3
Procedures (number) 27
Time (days) 417
Cost (% of claim) 8.2

Registering property (rank) 11
Procedures (number) 3
Time (days) 4
Cost (% of property value) 2.4

✗ **Paying taxes** (rank) 35
Payments (number per year) 31
Time (hours per year) 140
Total tax rate (% of profit) 26.8

Closing a business (rank) 17
Time (years) 1.0
Cost (% of estate) 4
Recovery rate (cents on the dollar) 78.5

INDIA

South Asia · Lower middle income · GNI per capita (US$) 1,170 · Population (m) 1,155.3

Ease of doing business (rank) 134

✔ **Starting a business** (rank) 165
Procedures (number) 12
Time (days) 29
Cost (% of income per capita) 56.5
Minimum capital (% of income per capita) 188.8

Getting credit (rank) 32
Strength of legal rights index (0-10) 8
Depth of credit information index (0-6) 4
Public registry coverage (% of adults) 0.0
Private bureau coverage (% of adults) 10.0

Trading across borders (rank) 100
Documents to export (number) 8
Time to export (days) 17
Cost to export (US$ per container) 1,055
Documents to import (number) 9
Time to import (days) 20
Cost to import (US$ per container) 1,025

Dealing with construction permits (rank) 177
Procedures (number) 37
Time (days) 195
Cost (% of income per capita) 2,143.7

Protecting investors (rank) 44
Extent of disclosure index (0-10) 7
Extent of director liability index (0-10) 4
Ease of shareholder suits index (0-10) 7
Strength of investor protection index (0-10) 6.0

Enforcing contracts (rank) 182
Procedures (number) 46
Time (days) 1,420
Cost (% of claim) 39.6

Registering property (rank) 94
Procedures (number) 5
Time (days) 44
Cost (% of property value) 7.4

✔ **Paying taxes** (rank) 164
Payments (number per year) 56
Time (hours per year) 258
Total tax rate (% of profit) 63.3

Closing a business (rank) 134
Time (years) 7.0
Cost (% of estate) 9
Recovery rate (cents on the dollar) 16.3

INDONESIA

East Asia & Pacific · Lower middle income · GNI per capita (US$) 2,230 · Population (m) 230.0

Ease of doing business (rank) 121

✔ **Starting a business** (rank) 155
Procedures (number) 9
Time (days) 47
Cost (% of income per capita) 22.3
Minimum capital (% of income per capita) 53.1

Getting credit (rank) 116
Strength of legal rights index (0-10) 3
Depth of credit information index (0-6) 4
Public registry coverage (% of adults) 25.2
Private bureau coverage (% of adults) 0.0

✔ **Trading across borders** (rank) 47
Documents to export (number) 5
Time to export (days) 20
Cost to export (US$ per container) 704
Documents to import (number) 6
Time to import (days) 27
Cost to import (US$ per container) 660

Dealing with construction permits (rank) 60
Procedures (number) 14
Time (days) 160
Cost (% of income per capita) 173.3

Protecting investors (rank) 44
Extent of disclosure index (0-10) 10
Extent of director liability index (0-10) 5
Ease of shareholder suits index (0-10) 3
Strength of investor protection index (0-10) 6.0

Enforcing contracts (rank) 154
Procedures (number) 40
Time (days) 570
Cost (% of claim) 122.7

Registering property (rank) 98
Procedures (number) 6
Time (days) 22
Cost (% of property value) 10.9

✔ **Paying taxes** (rank) 130
Payments (number per year) 51
Time (hours per year) 266
Total tax rate (% of profit) 37.3

Closing a business (rank) 142
Time (years) 5.5
Cost (% of estate) 18
Recovery rate (cents on the dollar) 13.2

✔ Reforms making it easier to do business   ✘ Reforms making it more difficult to do business

IRAN, ISLAMIC REP.

		Middle East & North Africa		GNI per capita (US$)	4,530
Ease of doing business (rank)	129	Upper middle income		Population (m)	72.9
✔ **Starting a business** (rank)	42	✔ **Getting credit** (rank)	89	**Trading across borders** (rank)	131
Procedures (number)	6	Strength of legal rights index (0-10)	4	Documents to export (number)	7
Time (days)	8	Depth of credit information index (0-6)	4	Time to export (days)	25
Cost (% of income per capita)	4.0	Public registry coverage (% of adults)	22.7	Cost to export (US$ per container)	1,090
Minimum capital (% of income per capita)	0.8	Private bureau coverage (% of adults)	4.5	Documents to import (number)	8
				Time to import (days)	32
Dealing with construction permits (rank)	143	**Protecting investors** (rank)	167	Cost to import (US$ per container)	1,735
Procedures (number)	17	Extent of disclosure index (0-10)	5		
Time (days)	322	Extent of director liability index (0-10)	4	✔ **Enforcing contracts** (rank)	49
Cost (% of income per capita)	382.3	Ease of shareholder suits index (0-10)	0	Procedures (number)	39
		Strength of investor protection index (0-10)	3.0	Time (days)	505
Registering property (rank)	156			Cost (% of claim)	17.0
Procedures (number)	9	**Paying taxes** (rank)	115		
Time (days)	36	Payments (number per year)	20	**Closing a business** (rank)	111
Cost (% of property value)	10.5	Time (hours per year)	344	Time (years)	4.5
		Total tax rate (% of profit)	44.1	Cost (% of estate)	9
				Recovery rate (cents on the dollar)	23.1

IRAQ

		Middle East & North Africa		GNI per capita (US$)	2,210
Ease of doing business (rank)	166	Lower middle income		Population (m)	31.5
Starting a business (rank)	174	**Getting credit** (rank)	168	**Trading across borders** (rank)	179
Procedures (number)	11	Strength of legal rights index (0-10)	3	Documents to export (number)	10
Time (days)	77	Depth of credit information index (0-6)	0	Time to export (days)	80
Cost (% of income per capita)	107.8	Public registry coverage (% of adults)	0.0	Cost to export (US$ per container)	3,550
Minimum capital (% of income per capita)	43.6	Private bureau coverage (% of adults)	0.0	Documents to import (number)	10
				Time to import (days)	83
Dealing with construction permits (rank)	102	**Protecting investors** (rank)	120	Cost to import (US$ per container)	3,650
Procedures (number)	14	Extent of disclosure index (0-10)	4		
Time (days)	215	Extent of director liability index (0-10)	5	**Enforcing contracts** (rank)	141
Cost (% of income per capita)	506.8	Ease of shareholder suits index (0-10)	4	Procedures (number)	51
		Strength of investor protection index (0-10)	4.3	Time (days)	520
Registering property (rank)	96			Cost (% of claim)	28.1
Procedures (number)	5	**Paying taxes** (rank)	54		
Time (days)	51	Payments (number per year)	13	**Closing a business** (rank)	183
Cost (% of property value)	6.4	Time (hours per year)	312	Time (years)	NO PRACTICE
		Total tax rate (% of profit)	28.4	Cost (% of estate)	NO PRACTICE
				Recovery rate (cents on the dollar)	0.0

IRELAND

		OECD high income		GNI per capita (US$)	44,310
Ease of doing business (rank)	9	High income		Population (m)	4.5
Starting a business (rank)	11	**Getting credit** (rank)	15	**Trading across borders** (rank)	23
Procedures (number)	4	Strength of legal rights index (0-10)	8	Documents to export (number)	4
Time (days)	13	Depth of credit information index (0-6)	5	Time to export (days)	7
Cost (% of income per capita)	0.4	Public registry coverage (% of adults)	0.0	Cost to export (US$ per container)	1,109
Minimum capital (% of income per capita)	0.0	Private bureau coverage (% of adults)	100.0	Documents to import (number)	4
				Time to import (days)	12
Dealing with construction permits (rank)	38	**Protecting investors** (rank)	5	Cost to import (US$ per container)	1,121
Procedures (number)	11	Extent of disclosure index (0-10)	10		
Time (days)	192	Extent of director liability index (0-10)	6	**Enforcing contracts** (rank)	37
Cost (% of income per capita)	57.8	Ease of shareholder suits index (0-10)	9	Procedures (number)	20
		Strength of investor protection index (0-10)	8.3	Time (days)	515
Registering property (rank)	78			Cost (% of claim)	26.9
Procedures (number)	5	**Paying taxes** (rank)	7		
Time (days)	38	Payments (number per year)	9	**Closing a business** (rank)	9
Cost (% of property value)	6.3	Time (hours per year)	76	Time (years)	0.4
		Total tax rate (% of profit)	26.5	Cost (% of estate)	9
				Recovery rate (cents on the dollar)	87.4

ISRAEL

Ease of doing business (rank)	29	OECD high income		GNI per capita (US$)		25,740
		High income		Population (m)		7.4
Starting a business (rank)	36	**Getting credit** (rank)	6	✔ **Trading across borders** (rank)		10
Procedures (number)	5	Strength of legal rights index (0-10)	9	Documents to export (number)		5
Time (days)	34	Depth of credit information index (0-6)	5	Time to export (days)		11
Cost (% of income per capita)	4.3	Public registry coverage (% of adults)	0.0	Cost to export (US$ per container)		670
Minimum capital (% of income per capita)	0.0	Private bureau coverage (% of adults)	88.2	Documents to import (number)		4
				Time to import (days)		10
Dealing with construction permits (rank)	121	**Protecting investors** (rank)	5	Cost to import (US$ per container)		605
Procedures (number)	20	Extent of disclosure index (0-10)	7			
Time (days)	235	Extent of director liability index (0-10)	9	**Enforcing contracts** (rank)		96
Cost (% of income per capita)	104.0	Ease of shareholder suits index (0-10)	9	Procedures (number)		35
		Strength of investor protection index (0-10)	8.3	Time (days)		890
Registering property (rank)	147			Cost (% of claim)		25.3
Procedures (number)	7	**Paying taxes** (rank)	82			
Time (days)	144	Payments (number per year)	33	**Closing a business** (rank)		40
Cost (% of property value)	5.0	Time (hours per year)	235	Time (years)		4.0
		Total tax rate (% of profit)	31.7	Cost (% of estate)		23
				Recovery rate (cents on the dollar)		49.1

ITALY

Ease of doing business (rank)	80	OECD high income		GNI per capita (US$)		35,080
		High income		Population (m)		60.2
✔ **Starting a business** (rank)	68	**Getting credit** (rank)	89	**Trading across borders** (rank)		59
Procedures (number)	6	Strength of legal rights index (0-10)	3	Documents to export (number)		4
Time (days)	6	Depth of credit information index (0-6)	5	Time to export (days)		20
Cost (% of income per capita)	18.5	Public registry coverage (% of adults)	16.6	Cost to export (US$ per container)		1,245
Minimum capital (% of income per capita)	10.1	Private bureau coverage (% of adults)	80.5	Documents to import (number)		4
				Time to import (days)		18
Dealing with construction permits (rank)	92	**Protecting investors** (rank)	59	Cost to import (US$ per container)		1,245
Procedures (number)	14	Extent of disclosure index (0-10)	7			
Time (days)	257	Extent of director liability index (0-10)	4	**Enforcing contracts** (rank)		157
Cost (% of income per capita)	142.3	Ease of shareholder suits index (0-10)	6	Procedures (number)		41
		Strength of investor protection index (0-10)	5.7	Time (days)		1,210
Registering property (rank)	95			Cost (% of claim)		29.9
Procedures (number)	8	**Paying taxes** (rank)	128			
Time (days)	27	Payments (number per year)	15	**Closing a business** (rank)		30
Cost (% of property value)	4.5	Time (hours per year)	285	Time (years)		1.8
		Total tax rate (% of profit)	68.6	Cost (% of estate)		22
				Recovery rate (cents on the dollar)		58.0

JAMAICA

Ease of doing business (rank)	81	Latin America & Caribbean		GNI per capita (US$)		5,020
		Upper middle income		Population (m)		2.7
Starting a business (rank)	18	**Getting credit** (rank)	89	**Trading across borders** (rank)		104
Procedures (number)	6	Strength of legal rights index (0-10)	8	Documents to export (number)		6
Time (days)	8	Depth of credit information index (0-6)	0	Time to export (days)		21
Cost (% of income per capita)	5.2	Public registry coverage (% of adults)	0.0	Cost to export (US$ per container)		1,750
Minimum capital (% of income per capita)	0.0	Private bureau coverage (% of adults)	0.0	Documents to import (number)		6
				Time to import (days)		22
Dealing with construction permits (rank)	47	**Protecting investors** (rank)	74	Cost to import (US$ per container)		1,420
Procedures (number)	10	Extent of disclosure index (0-10)	4			
Time (days)	156	Extent of director liability index (0-10)	8	**Enforcing contracts** (rank)		128
Cost (% of income per capita)	258.3	Ease of shareholder suits index (0-10)	4	Procedures (number)		35
		Strength of investor protection index (0-10)	5.3	Time (days)		655
✔ **Registering property** (rank)	106			Cost (% of claim)		45.6
Procedures (number)	6	**Paying taxes** (rank)	174			
Time (days)	37	Payments (number per year)	72	**Closing a business** (rank)		24
Cost (% of property value)	7.5	Time (hours per year)	414	Time (years)		1.1
		Total tax rate (% of profit)	50.1	Cost (% of estate)		18
				Recovery rate (cents on the dollar)		65.1

✔ Reforms making it easier to do business   ✘ Reforms making it more difficult to do business

JAPAN

		OECD high income		GNI per capita (US$)	37,870
Ease of doing business (rank)	18	High income		Population (m)	127.6
Starting a business (rank)	98	**Getting credit** (rank)	15	**Trading across borders** (rank)	24
Procedures (number)	8	Strength of legal rights index (0-10)	7	Documents to export (number)	4
Time (days)	23	Depth of credit information index (0-6)	6	Time to export (days)	10
Cost (% of income per capita)	7.5	Public registry coverage (% of adults)	0.0	Cost to export (US$ per container)	1,010
Minimum capital (% of income per capita)	0.0	Private bureau coverage (% of adults)	76.1	Documents to import (number)	5
				Time to import (days)	11
Dealing with construction permits (rank)	44	**Protecting investors** (rank)	16	Cost to import (US$ per container)	1,060
Procedures (number)	15	Extent of disclosure index (0-10)	7		
Time (days)	187	Extent of director liability index (0-10)	6	**Enforcing contracts** (rank)	19
Cost (% of income per capita)	20.8	Ease of shareholder suits index (0-10)	8	Procedures (number)	30
		Strength of investor protection index (0-10)	7.0	Time (days)	360
Registering property (rank)	59			Cost (% of claim)	22.7
Procedures (number)	6	**Paying taxes** (rank)	112		
Time (days)	14	Payments (number per year)	14	✔ **Closing a business** (rank)	1
Cost (% of property value)	5.5	Time (hours per year)	355	Time (years)	0.6
		Total tax rate (% of profit)	48.6	Cost (% of estate)	4
				Recovery rate (cents on the dollar)	92.7

JORDAN

		Middle East & North Africa		GNI per capita (US$)	3,740
Ease of doing business (rank)	111	Lower middle income		Population (m)	6.0
Starting a business (rank)	127	✔ **Getting credit** (rank)	128	**Trading across borders** (rank)	77
Procedures (number)	8	Strength of legal rights index (0-10)	4	Documents to export (number)	7
Time (days)	13	Depth of credit information index (0-6)	2	Time to export (days)	14
Cost (% of income per capita)	44.6	Public registry coverage (% of adults)	1.5	Cost to export (US$ per container)	825
Minimum capital (% of income per capita)	17.9	Private bureau coverage (% of adults)	0.0	Documents to import (number)	7
				Time to import (days)	18
Dealing with construction permits (rank)	92	**Protecting investors** (rank)	120	Cost to import (US$ per container)	1,335
Procedures (number)	19	Extent of disclosure index (0-10)	5		
Time (days)	87	Extent of director liability index (0-10)	4	**Enforcing contracts** (rank)	129
Cost (% of income per capita)	634.1	Ease of shareholder suits index (0-10)	4	Procedures (number)	38
		Strength of investor protection index (0-10)	4.3	Time (days)	689
Registering property (rank)	106			Cost (% of claim)	31.2
Procedures (number)	7	✔ **Paying taxes** (rank)	29		
Time (days)	21	Payments (number per year)	26	**Closing a business** (rank)	98
Cost (% of property value)	7.5	Time (hours per year)	101	Time (years)	4.3
		Total tax rate (% of profit)	31.2	Cost (% of estate)	9
				Recovery rate (cents on the dollar)	26.9

KAZAKHSTAN

		Eastern Europe & Central Asia		GNI per capita (US$)	6,740
Ease of doing business (rank)	59	Upper middle income		Population (m)	15.9
✔ **Starting a business** (rank)	47	**Getting credit** (rank)	72	✔ **Trading across borders** (rank)	181
Procedures (number)	6	Strength of legal rights index (0-10)	4	Documents to export (number)	10
Time (days)	19	Depth of credit information index (0-6)	5	Time to export (days)	81
Cost (% of income per capita)	1.0	Public registry coverage (% of adults)	0.0	Cost to export (US$ per container)	3,005
Minimum capital (% of income per capita)	0.0	Private bureau coverage (% of adults)	29.9	Documents to import (number)	12
				Time to import (days)	67
✔ **Dealing with construction permits** (rank)	147	✔ **Protecting investors** (rank)	44	Cost to import (US$ per container)	3,055
Procedures (number)	34	Extent of disclosure index (0-10)	8		
Time (days)	219	Extent of director liability index (0-10)	1	**Enforcing contracts** (rank)	36
Cost (% of income per capita)	119.8	Ease of shareholder suits index (0-10)	9	Procedures (number)	38
		Strength of investor protection index (0-10)	6.0	Time (days)	390
Registering property (rank)	28			Cost (% of claim)	22.0
Procedures (number)	4	**Paying taxes** (rank)	39		
Time (days)	40	Payments (number per year)	9	**Closing a business** (rank)	48
Cost (% of property value)	0.1	Time (hours per year)	271	Time (years)	1.5
		Total tax rate (% of profit)	29.6	Cost (% of estate)	15
				Recovery rate (cents on the dollar)	43.3

KENYA

		Sub-Saharan Africa		GNI per capita (US$)	770
Ease of doing business (rank)	98	Low income		Population (m)	39.8
✔ **Starting a business** (rank)	125	**Getting credit** (rank)	6	✔ **Trading across borders** (rank)	144
Procedures (number)	11	Strength of legal rights index (0-10)	10	Documents to export (number)	8
Time (days)	33	Depth of credit information index (0-6)	4	Time to export (days)	26
Cost (% of income per capita)	38.3	Public registry coverage (% of adults)	0.0	Cost to export (US$ per container)	2,055
Minimum capital (% of income per capita)	0.0	Private bureau coverage (% of adults)	3.3	Documents to import (number)	7
				Time to import (days)	24
Dealing with construction permits (rank)	35	**Protecting investors** (rank)	93	Cost to import (US$ per container)	2,190
Procedures (number)	11	Extent of disclosure index (0-10)	3		
Time (days)	120	Extent of director liability index (0-10)	2	**Enforcing contracts** (rank)	125
Cost (% of income per capita)	167.8	Ease of shareholder suits index (0-10)	10	Procedures (number)	40
		Strength of investor protection index (0-10)	5.0	Time (days)	465
Registering property (rank)	129			Cost (% of claim)	47.2
Procedures (number)	8	✗ **Paying taxes** (rank)	162		
Time (days)	64	Payments (number per year)	41	**Closing a business** (rank)	85
Cost (% of property value)	4.2	Time (hours per year)	393	Time (years)	4.5
		Total tax rate (% of profit)	49.7	Cost (% of estate)	22
				Recovery rate (cents on the dollar)	29.8

KIRIBATI

		East Asia & Pacific		GNI per capita (US$)	1,890
Ease of doing business (rank)	93	Lower middle income		Population (m)	0.1
Starting a business (rank)	123	**Getting credit** (rank)	138	**Trading across borders** (rank)	83
Procedures (number)	6	Strength of legal rights index (0-10)	5	Documents to export (number)	6
Time (days)	21	Depth of credit information index (0-6)	0	Time to export (days)	21
Cost (% of income per capita)	40.2	Public registry coverage (% of adults)	0.0	Cost to export (US$ per container)	1,070
Minimum capital (% of income per capita)	21.7	Private bureau coverage (% of adults)	0.0	Documents to import (number)	7
				Time to import (days)	21
Dealing with construction permits (rank)	72	**Protecting investors** (rank)	44	Cost to import (US$ per container)	1,070
Procedures (number)	14	Extent of disclosure index (0-10)	6		
Time (days)	160	Extent of director liability index (0-10)	5	**Enforcing contracts** (rank)	80
Cost (% of income per capita)	446.5	Ease of shareholder suits index (0-10)	7	Procedures (number)	32
		Strength of investor protection index (0-10)	6.0	Time (days)	660
Registering property (rank)	68			Cost (% of claim)	25.8
Procedures (number)	5	**Paying taxes** (rank)	10		
Time (days)	513	Payments (number per year)	7	**Closing a business** (rank)	183
Cost (% of property value)	0.0	Time (hours per year)	120	Time (years)	NO PRACTICE
		Total tax rate (% of profit)	31.8	Cost (% of estate)	NO PRACTICE
				Recovery rate (cents on the dollar)	0.0

KOREA, REP.

		OECD high income		GNI per capita (US$)	19,830
Ease of doing business (rank)	16	High income		Population (m)	48.7
Starting a business (rank)	60	**Getting credit** (rank)	15	**Trading across borders** (rank)	8
Procedures (number)	8	Strength of legal rights index (0-10)	7	Documents to export (number)	3
Time (days)	14	Depth of credit information index (0-6)	6	Time to export (days)	8
Cost (% of income per capita)	14.7	Public registry coverage (% of adults)	0.0	Cost to export (US$ per container)	790
Minimum capital (% of income per capita)	0.0	Private bureau coverage (% of adults)	93.3	Documents to import (number)	3
				Time to import (days)	7
Dealing with construction permits (rank)	22	**Protecting investors** (rank)	74	Cost to import (US$ per container)	790
Procedures (number)	13	Extent of disclosure index (0-10)	7		
Time (days)	34	Extent of director liability index (0-10)	2	**Enforcing contracts** (rank)	5
Cost (% of income per capita)	131.2	Ease of shareholder suits index (0-10)	7	Procedures (number)	35
		Strength of investor protection index (0-10)	5.3	Time (days)	230
Registering property (rank)	74			Cost (% of claim)	10.3
Procedures (number)	7	**Paying taxes** (rank)	49		
Time (days)	11	Payments (number per year)	14	✔ **Closing a business** (rank)	13
Cost (% of property value)	5.1	Time (hours per year)	250	Time (years)	1.5
		Total tax rate (% of profit)	29.8	Cost (% of estate)	4
				Recovery rate (cents on the dollar)	81.7

✔ Reforms making it easier to do business ✘ Reforms making it more difficult to do business

KOSOVO

			Eastern Europe & Central Asia		GNI per capita (US$)	3,240
Ease of doing business (rank)	119		Lower middle income		Population (m)	1.8
✘ **Starting a business** (rank)	163		**Getting credit** (rank)	32	**Trading across borders** (rank)	130
Procedures (number)	10		Strength of legal rights index (0-10)	8	Documents to export (number)	8
Time (days)	58		Depth of credit information index (0-6)	4	Time to export (days)	17
Cost (% of income per capita)	28.7		Public registry coverage (% of adults)	16.9	Cost to export (US$ per container)	2,230
Minimum capital (% of income per capita)	112.4		Private bureau coverage (% of adults)	0.0	Documents to import (number)	8
					Time to import (days)	16
Dealing with construction permits (rank)	173		**Protecting investors** (rank)	173	Cost to import (US$ per container)	2,280
Procedures (number)	21		Extent of disclosure index (0-10)	3		
Time (days)	320		Extent of director liability index (0-10)	2	**Enforcing contracts** (rank)	155
Cost (% of income per capita)	856.5		Ease of shareholder suits index (0-10)	3	Procedures (number)	53
			Strength of investor protection index (0-10)	2.7	Time (days)	420
Registering property (rank)	65				Cost (% of claim)	61.2
Procedures (number)	8		**Paying taxes** (rank)	41		
Time (days)	33		Payments (number per year)	33	**Closing a business** (rank)	31
Cost (% of property value)	0.6		Time (hours per year)	163	Time (years)	2
			Total tax rate (% of profit)	16.5	Cost (% of estate)	15
					Recovery rate (cents on the dollar)	57.4

KUWAIT

			Middle East & North Africa		GNI per capita (US$)	31,482
Ease of doing business (rank)	74		High income		Population (m)	2.8
Starting a business (rank)	141		**Getting credit** (rank)	89	**Trading across borders** (rank)	113
Procedures (number)	13		Strength of legal rights index (0-10)	4	Documents to export (number)	8
Time (days)	35		Depth of credit information index (0-6)	4	Time to export (days)	17
Cost (% of income per capita)	1.3		Public registry coverage (% of adults)	0.0	Cost to export (US$ per container)	1,060
Minimum capital (% of income per capita)	82.7		Private bureau coverage (% of adults)	29.6	Documents to import (number)	10
					Time to import (days)	19
Dealing with construction permits (rank)	91		**Protecting investors** (rank)	28	Cost to import (US$ per container)	1,217
Procedures (number)	25		Extent of disclosure index (0-10)	7		
Time (days)	104		Extent of director liability index (0-10)	7	**Enforcing contracts** (rank)	114
Cost (% of income per capita)	173.4		Ease of shareholder suits index (0-10)	5	Procedures (number)	50
			Strength of investor protection index (0-10)	6.3	Time (days)	566
Registering property (rank)	90				Cost (% of claim)	18.8
Procedures (number)	8		**Paying taxes** (rank)	9		
Time (days)	55		Payments (number per year)	15	**Closing a business** (rank)	61
Cost (% of property value)	0.5		Time (hours per year)	118	Time (years)	4.2
			Total tax rate (% of profit)	15.5	Cost (% of estate)	1
					Recovery rate (cents on the dollar)	37.9

KYRGYZ REPUBLIC

			Eastern Europe & Central Asia		GNI per capita (US$)	870
Ease of doing business (rank)	44		Low income		Population (m)	5.3
✔ **Starting a business** (rank)	14		**Getting credit** (rank)	15	**Trading across borders** (rank)	156
Procedures (number)	2		Strength of legal rights index (0-10)	10	Documents to export (number)	7
Time (days)	10		Depth of credit information index (0-6)	3	Time to export (days)	63
Cost (% of income per capita)	3.7		Public registry coverage (% of adults)	0.0	Cost to export (US$ per container)	3,010
Minimum capital (% of income per capita)	0.0		Private bureau coverage (% of adults)	11.9	Documents to import (number)	7
					Time to import (days)	72
Dealing with construction permits (rank)	43		**Protecting investors** (rank)	12	Cost to import (US$ per container)	3,280
Procedures (number)	13		Extent of disclosure index (0-10)	8		
Time (days)	143		Extent of director liability index (0-10)	7	**Enforcing contracts** (rank)	54
Cost (% of income per capita)	153.9		Ease of shareholder suits index (0-10)	8	Procedures (number)	39
			Strength of investor protection index (0-10)	7.7	Time (days)	260
Registering property (rank)	17				Cost (% of claim)	29.0
Procedures (number)	4		**Paying taxes** (rank)	150		
Time (days)	5		Payments (number per year)	48	✘ **Closing a business** (rank)	138
Cost (% of property value)	2.3		Time (hours per year)	202	Time (years)	4.0
			Total tax rate (% of profit)	57.2	Cost (% of estate)	15
					Recovery rate (cents on the dollar)	15.3

LAO PDR

Ease of doing business (rank)	171	East Asia & Pacific		GNI per capita (US$)		880
		Low income		Population (m)		6.3
Starting a business (rank)	93	**Getting credit** (rank)	152	**Trading across borders** (rank)		170
Procedures (number)	7	Strength of legal rights index (0-10)	4	Documents to export (number)		9
Time (days)	100	Depth of credit information index (0-6)	0	Time to export (days)		48
Cost (% of income per capita)	11.3	Public registry coverage (% of adults)	0.0	Cost to export (US$ per container)		1,860
Minimum capital (% of income per capita)	0.0	Private bureau coverage (% of adults)	0.0	Documents to import (number)		10
				Time to import (days)		50
Dealing with construction permits (rank)	115	**Protecting investors** (rank)	182	Cost to import (US$ per container)		2,040
Procedures (number)	24	Extent of disclosure index (0-10)	2			
Time (days)	172	Extent of director liability index (0-10)	1	**Enforcing contracts** (rank)		110
Cost (% of income per capita)	131.3	Ease of shareholder suits index (0-10)	2	Procedures (number)		42
		Strength of investor protection index (0-10)	1.7	Time (days)		443
Registering property (rank)	163			Cost (% of claim)		31.6
Procedures (number)	9	✔ **Paying taxes** (rank)	116			
Time (days)	135	Payments (number per year)	34	**Closing a business** (rank)		183
Cost (% of property value)	4.1	Time (hours per year)	362	Time (years)	NO PRACTICE	
		Total tax rate (% of profit)	33.7	Cost (% of estate)	NO PRACTICE	
				Recovery rate (cents on the dollar)		0.0

LATVIA

Ease of doing business (rank)	24	Eastern Europe & Central Asia		GNI per capita (US$)	12,390
		High income		Population (m)	2.3
Starting a business (rank)	53	**Getting credit** (rank)	6	✔ **Trading across borders** (rank)	16
Procedures (number)	5	Strength of legal rights index (0-10)	9	Documents to export (number)	5
Time (days)	16	Depth of credit information index (0-6)	5	Time to export (days)	10
Cost (% of income per capita)	1.5	Public registry coverage (% of adults)	57.2	Cost to export (US$ per container)	600
Minimum capital (% of income per capita)	15.9	Private bureau coverage (% of adults)	0.0	Documents to import (number)	6
				Time to import (days)	11
Dealing with construction permits (rank)	79	**Protecting investors** (rank)	59	Cost to import (US$ per container)	801
Procedures (number)	24	Extent of disclosure index (0-10)	5		
Time (days)	186	Extent of director liability index (0-10)	4	**Enforcing contracts** (rank)	14
Cost (% of income per capita)	19.3	Ease of shareholder suits index (0-10)	8	Procedures (number)	27
		Strength of investor protection index (0-10)	5.7	Time (days)	309
Registering property (rank)	57			Cost (% of claim)	23.1
Procedures (number)	6	**Paying taxes** (rank)	59		
Time (days)	42	Payments (number per year)	7	✔ **Closing a business** (rank)	80
Cost (% of property value)	2.0	Time (hours per year)	293	Time (years)	3.0
		Total tax rate (% of profit)	38.5	Cost (% of estate)	13
				Recovery rate (cents on the dollar)	31.9

LEBANON

Ease of doing business (rank)	113	Middle East & North Africa		GNI per capita (US$)	7,970
		Upper middle income		Population (m)	4.2
✗ **Starting a business** (rank)	103	✔ **Getting credit** (rank)	89	**Trading across borders** (rank)	95
Procedures (number)	5	Strength of legal rights index (0-10)	3	Documents to export (number)	5
Time (days)	9	Depth of credit information index (0-6)	5	Time to export (days)	26
Cost (% of income per capita)	75.0	Public registry coverage (% of adults)	8.7	Cost to export (US$ per container)	1,000
Minimum capital (% of income per capita)	39.8	Private bureau coverage (% of adults)	0.0	Documents to import (number)	7
				Time to import (days)	35
Dealing with construction permits (rank)	142	**Protecting investors** (rank)	93	Cost to import (US$ per container)	1,200
Procedures (number)	21	Extent of disclosure index (0-10)	9		
Time (days)	218	Extent of director liability index (0-10)	1	**Enforcing contracts** (rank)	122
Cost (% of income per capita)	284.7	Ease of shareholder suits index (0-10)	5	Procedures (number)	37
		Strength of investor protection index (0-10)	5.0	Time (days)	721
Registering property (rank)	111			Cost (% of claim)	30.8
Procedures (number)	8	**Paying taxes** (rank)	36		
Time (days)	25	Payments (number per year)	19	**Closing a business** (rank)	122
Cost (% of property value)	5.8	Time (hours per year)	180	Time (years)	4.0
		Total tax rate (% of profit)	30.2	Cost (% of estate)	22
				Recovery rate (cents on the dollar)	19.8

✔ Reforms making it easier to do business   ✗ Reforms making it more difficult to do business

LESOTHO

		Sub-Saharan Africa		GNI per capita (US$)	1,020
Ease of doing business (rank)	138	Lower middle income		Population (m)	2.1
Starting a business (rank)	140	**Getting credit** (rank)	128	**Trading across borders** (rank)	140
Procedures (number)	7	Strength of legal rights index (0-10)	6	Documents to export (number)	6
Time (days)	40	Depth of credit information index (0-6)	0	Time to export (days)	31
Cost (% of income per capita)	26.0	Public registry coverage (% of adults)	0.0	Cost to export (US$ per container)	1,680
Minimum capital (% of income per capita)	12.0	Private bureau coverage (% of adults)	0.0	Documents to import (number)	8
				Time to import (days)	35
Dealing with construction permits (rank)	163	**Protecting investors** (rank)	147	Cost to import (US$ per container)	1,610
Procedures (number)	15	Extent of disclosure index (0-10)	2		
Time (days)	601	Extent of director liability index (0-10)	1	**Enforcing contracts** (rank)	116
Cost (% of income per capita)	1,290.7	Ease of shareholder suits index (0-10)	8	Procedures (number)	41
		Strength of investor protection index (0-10)	3.7	Time (days)	785
Registering property (rank)	146			Cost (% of claim)	19.5
Procedures (number)	6	**Paying taxes** (rank)	64		
Time (days)	101	Payments (number per year)	21	**Closing a business** (rank)	69
Cost (% of property value)	8.0	Time (hours per year)	324	Time (years)	2.6
		Total tax rate (% of profit)	19.6	Cost (% of estate)	8
				Recovery rate (cents on the dollar)	36.4

LIBERIA

		Sub-Saharan Africa		GNI per capita (US$)	160
Ease of doing business (rank)	155	Low income		Population (m)	4.0
Starting a business (rank)	64	**Getting credit** (rank)	138	**Trading across borders** (rank)	116
Procedures (number)	5	Strength of legal rights index (0-10)	4	Documents to export (number)	10
Time (days)	20	Depth of credit information index (0-6)	1	Time to export (days)	17
Cost (% of income per capita)	54.6	Public registry coverage (% of adults)	0.2	Cost to export (US$ per container)	1,232
Minimum capital (% of income per capita)	0.0	Private bureau coverage (% of adults)	0.0	Documents to import (number)	9
				Time to import (days)	15
Dealing with construction permits (rank)	135	**Protecting investors** (rank)	147	Cost to import (US$ per container)	1,212
Procedures (number)	24	Extent of disclosure index (0-10)	4		
Time (days)	77	Extent of director liability index (0-10)	1	**Enforcing contracts** (rank)	166
Cost (% of income per capita)	29,574.4	Ease of shareholder suits index (0-10)	6	Procedures (number)	41
		Strength of investor protection index (0-10)	3.7	Time (days)	1,280
Registering property (rank)	176			Cost (% of claim)	35.0
Procedures (number)	10	**Paying taxes** (rank)	84		
Time (days)	50	Payments (number per year)	32	**Closing a business** (rank)	148
Cost (% of property value)	13.2	Time (hours per year)	158	Time (years)	3.0
		Total tax rate (% of profit)	43.7	Cost (% of estate)	43
				Recovery rate (cents on the dollar)	8.4

LITHUANIA

		Eastern Europe & Central Asia		GNI per capita (US$)	11,410
Ease of doing business (rank)	23	Upper middle income		Population (m)	3.3
✔ **Starting a business** (rank)	87	✔ **Getting credit** (rank)	46	✔ **Trading across borders** (rank)	31
Procedures (number)	6	Strength of legal rights index (0-10)	5	Documents to export (number)	6
Time (days)	22	Depth of credit information index (0-6)	6	Time to export (days)	10
Cost (% of income per capita)	2.8	Public registry coverage (% of adults)	20.0	Cost to export (US$ per container)	870
Minimum capital (% of income per capita)	36.1	Private bureau coverage (% of adults)	67.8	Documents to import (number)	6
				Time to import (days)	10
Dealing with construction permits (rank)	59	**Protecting investors** (rank)	93	Cost to import (US$ per container)	980
Procedures (number)	17	Extent of disclosure index (0-10)	5		
Time (days)	162	Extent of director liability index (0-10)	4	**Enforcing contracts** (rank)	17
Cost (% of income per capita)	68.8	Ease of shareholder suits index (0-10)	6	Procedures (number)	30
		Strength of investor protection index (0-10)	5.0	Time (days)	275
Registering property (rank)	7			Cost (% of claim)	23.6
Procedures (number)	3	✔ **Paying taxes** (rank)	44		
Time (days)	3	Payments (number per year)	11	✔ **Closing a business** (rank)	39
Cost (% of property value)	1.9	Time (hours per year)	175	Time (years)	1.5
		Total tax rate (% of profit)	38.7	Cost (% of estate)	7
				Recovery rate (cents on the dollar)	49.6

LUXEMBOURG

Ease of doing business (rank)	45	OECD high income		GNI per capita (US$)		74,430
		High income		Population (m)		0.5
✔ **Starting a business** (rank)	77	**Getting credit** (rank)	116	**Trading across borders** (rank)		32
Procedures (number)	6	Strength of legal rights index (0-10)	7	Documents to export (number)		5
Time (days)	19	Depth of credit information index (0-6)	0	Time to export (days)		6
Cost (% of income per capita)	2.1	Public registry coverage (% of adults)	0.0	Cost to export (US$ per container)		1,420
Minimum capital (% of income per capita)	23.8	Private bureau coverage (% of adults)	0.0	Documents to import (number)		4
				Time to import (days)		6
Dealing with construction permits (rank)	42	**Protecting investors** (rank)	120	Cost to import (US$ per container)		1,420
Procedures (number)	13	Extent of disclosure index (0-10)	6			
Time (days)	217	Extent of director liability index (0-10)	4	**Enforcing contracts** (rank)		1
Cost (% of income per capita)	23.8	Ease of shareholder suits index (0-10)	3	Procedures (number)		26
		Strength of investor protection index (0-10)	4.3	Time (days)		321
Registering property (rank)	129			Cost (% of claim)		9.7
Procedures (number)	8	**Paying taxes** (rank)	15			
Time (days)	29	Payments (number per year)	22	**Closing a business** (rank)		45
Cost (% of property value)	10.2	Time (hours per year)	59	Time (years)		2.0
		Total tax rate (% of profit)	21.1	Cost (% of estate)		15
				Recovery rate (cents on the dollar)		43.7

MACEDONIA, FYR

Ease of doing business (rank)	38	Eastern Europe & Central Asia		GNI per capita (US$)	4,400
		Upper middle income		Population (m)	2.0
✔ **Starting a business** (rank)	5	**Getting credit** (rank)	46	**Trading across borders** (rank)	66
Procedures (number)	3	Strength of legal rights index (0-10)	7	Documents to export (number)	6
Time (days)	3	Depth of credit information index (0-6)	4	Time to export (days)	12
Cost (% of income per capita)	2.5	Public registry coverage (% of adults)	39.4	Cost to export (US$ per container)	1,376
Minimum capital (% of income per capita)	0.0	Private bureau coverage (% of adults)	0.0	Documents to import (number)	6
				Time to import (days)	11
Dealing with construction permits (rank)	136	**Protecting investors** (rank)	20	Cost to import (US$ per container)	1,380
Procedures (number)	21	Extent of disclosure index (0-10)	9		
Time (days)	146	Extent of director liability index (0-10)	7	**Enforcing contracts** (rank)	65
Cost (% of income per capita)	1,601.4	Ease of shareholder suits index (0-10)	4	Procedures (number)	37
		Strength of investor protection index (0-10)	6.7	Time (days)	370
Registering property (rank)	69			Cost (% of claim)	33.1
Procedures (number)	5	✔ **Paying taxes** (rank)	33		
Time (days)	58	Payments (number per year)	40	**Closing a business** (rank)	116
Cost (% of property value)	3.2	Time (hours per year)	119	Time (years)	2.9
		Total tax rate (% of profit)	10.6	Cost (% of estate)	28
				Recovery rate (cents on the dollar)	20.7

MADAGASCAR

Ease of doing business (rank)	140	Sub-Saharan Africa		GNI per capita (US$)	412
		Low income		Population (m)	19.6
Starting a business (rank)	70	**Getting credit** (rank)	176	✔ **Trading across borders** (rank)	106
Procedures (number)	2	Strength of legal rights index (0-10)	2	Documents to export (number)	4
Time (days)	7	Depth of credit information index (0-6)	0	Time to export (days)	21
Cost (% of income per capita)	12.9	Public registry coverage (% of adults)	0.0	Cost to export (US$ per container)	1,197
Minimum capital (% of income per capita)	248.1	Private bureau coverage (% of adults)	0.0	Documents to import (number)	9
				Time to import (days)	24
Dealing with construction permits (rank)	110	**Protecting investors** (rank)	59	Cost to import (US$ per container)	1,555
Procedures (number)	16	Extent of disclosure index (0-10)	5		
Time (days)	178	Extent of director liability index (0-10)	6	**Enforcing contracts** (rank)	153
Cost (% of income per capita)	654.9	Ease of shareholder suits index (0-10)	6	Procedures (number)	38
		Strength of investor protection index (0-10)	5.7	Time (days)	871
Registering property (rank)	162			Cost (% of claim)	42.4
Procedures (number)	7	✔ **Paying taxes** (rank)	72		
Time (days)	74	Payments (number per year)	23	**Closing a business** (rank)	183
Cost (% of property value)	9.8	Time (hours per year)	201	Time (years)	NO PRACTICE
		Total tax rate (% of profit)	37.7	Cost (% of estate)	NO PRACTICE
				Recovery rate (cents on the dollar)	0.0

MALAWI

Ease of doing business (rank)	133	

Sub-Saharan Africa	
Low income	

GNI per capita (US$)	280
Population (m)	15.3

Starting a business (rank)	132
Procedures (number)	10
Time (days)	39
Cost (% of income per capita)	108.4
Minimum capital (% of income per capita)	0.0

Getting credit (rank)	116
Strength of legal rights index (0-10)	7
Depth of credit information index (0-6)	0
Public registry coverage (% of adults)	0.0
Private bureau coverage (% of adults)	0.0

Trading across borders (rank)	173
Documents to export (number)	11
Time to export (days)	41
Cost to export (US$ per container)	1,713
Documents to import (number)	10
Time to import (days)	51
Cost to import (US$ per container)	2,570

Dealing with construction permits (rank)	174
Procedures (number)	21
Time (days)	268
Cost (% of income per capita)	1,316.7

Protecting investors (rank)	74
Extent of disclosure index (0-10)	4
Extent of director liability index (0-10)	7
Ease of shareholder suits index (0-10)	5
Strength of investor protection index (0-10)	5.3

✔ **Enforcing contracts** (rank)	121
Procedures (number)	42
Time (days)	312
Cost (% of claim)	94.1

✔ **Registering property** (rank)	81
Procedures (number)	6
Time (days)	49
Cost (% of property value)	3.2

Paying taxes (rank)	25
Payments (number per year)	19
Time (hours per year)	157
Total tax rate (% of profit)	25.1

Closing a business (rank)	126
Time (years)	2.6
Cost (% of estate)	25
Recovery rate (cents on the dollar)	17.9

MALAYSIA

Ease of doing business (rank)	21

East Asia & Pacific	
Upper middle income	

GNI per capita (US$)	7,230
Population (m)	27.5

✔ **Starting a business** (rank)	113
Procedures (number)	9
Time (days)	17
Cost (% of income per capita)	17.5
Minimum capital (% of income per capita)	0.0

Getting credit (rank)	1
Strength of legal rights index (0-10)	10
Depth of credit information index (0-6)	6
Public registry coverage (% of adults)	62.0
Private bureau coverage (% of adults)	100.0

Trading across borders (rank)	37
Documents to export (number)	7
Time to export (days)	18
Cost to export (US$ per container)	450
Documents to import (number)	7
Time to import (days)	14
Cost to import (US$ per container)	450

Dealing with construction permits (rank)	108
Procedures (number)	25
Time (days)	261
Cost (% of income per capita)	7.9

Protecting investors (rank)	4
Extent of disclosure index (0-10)	10
Extent of director liability index (0-10)	9
Ease of shareholder suits index (0-10)	7
Strength of investor protection index (0-10)	8.7

Enforcing contracts (rank)	59
Procedures (number)	30
Time (days)	585
Cost (% of claim)	27.5

✔ **Registering property** (rank)	60
Procedures (number)	5
Time (days)	56
Cost (% of property value)	2.5

Paying taxes (rank)	23
Payments (number per year)	12
Time (hours per year)	145
Total tax rate (% of profit)	33.7

Closing a business (rank)	55
Time (years)	2.3
Cost (% of estate)	15
Recovery rate (cents on the dollar)	39.8

MALDIVES

Ease of doing business (rank)	85

South Asia	
Lower middle income	

GNI per capita (US$)	3,870
Population (m)	0.3

Starting a business (rank)	50
Procedures (number)	5
Time (days)	9
Cost (% of income per capita)	9.4
Minimum capital (% of income per capita)	3.7

Getting credit (rank)	152
Strength of legal rights index (0-10)	4
Depth of credit information index (0-6)	0
Public registry coverage (% of adults)	0.0
Private bureau coverage (% of adults)	0.0

Trading across borders (rank)	138
Documents to export (number)	8
Time to export (days)	21
Cost to export (US$ per container)	1,550
Documents to import (number)	9
Time to import (days)	22
Cost to import (US$ per container)	1,526

Dealing with construction permits (rank)	9
Procedures (number)	9
Time (days)	118
Cost (% of income per capita)	20.3

Protecting investors (rank)	74
Extent of disclosure index (0-10)	0
Extent of director liability index (0-10)	8
Ease of shareholder suits index (0-10)	8
Strength of investor protection index (0-10)	5.3

Enforcing contracts (rank)	92
Procedures (number)	41
Time (days)	665
Cost (% of claim)	16.5

✔ **Registering property** (rank)	147
Procedures (number)	6
Time (days)	57
Cost (% of property value)	16.9

Paying taxes (rank)	1
Payments (number per year)	3
Time (hours per year)	0
Total tax rate (% of profit)	9.3

Closing a business (rank)	125
Time (years)	6.7
Cost (% of estate)	4
Recovery rate (cents on the dollar)	18.2

MALI

		Sub-Saharan Africa		GNI per capita (US$)	680
Ease of doing business (rank)	153	Low income		Population (m)	13.0
Starting a business (rank)	117	**Getting credit** (rank)	152	✔ **Trading across borders** (rank)	154
Procedures (number)	6	Strength of legal rights index (0-10)	3	Documents to export (number)	7
Time (days)	8	Depth of credit information index (0-6)	1	Time to export (days)	26
Cost (% of income per capita)	79.7	Public registry coverage (% of adults)	0.1	Cost to export (US$ per container)	2,202
Minimum capital (% of income per capita)	306.8	Private bureau coverage (% of adults)	0.0	Documents to import (number)	10
				Time to import (days)	31
✔ **Dealing with construction permits** (rank)	87	**Protecting investors** (rank)	147	Cost to import (US$ per container)	3,067
Procedures (number)	15	Extent of disclosure index (0-10)	6		
Time (days)	168	Extent of director liability index (0-10)	1	**Enforcing contracts** (rank)	133
Cost (% of income per capita)	505.0	Ease of shareholder suits index (0-10)	4	Procedures (number)	36
		Strength of investor protection index (0-10)	3.7	Time (days)	620
✔ **Registering property** (rank)	88			Cost (% of claim)	52.0
Procedures (number)	5	**Paying taxes** (rank)	159		
Time (days)	29	Payments (number per year)	59	**Closing a business** (rank)	106
Cost (% of property value)	11.9	Time (hours per year)	270	Time (years)	3.6
		Total tax rate (% of profit)	52.2	Cost (% of estate)	18
				Recovery rate (cents on the dollar)	24.6

MARSHALL ISLANDS

		East Asia & Pacific		GNI per capita (US$)	3,060
Ease of doing business (rank)	108	Lower middle income		Population (m)	0.1
Starting a business (rank)	39	✔ **Getting credit** (rank)	89	**Trading across borders** (rank)	70
Procedures (number)	5	Strength of legal rights index (0-10)	8	Documents to export (number)	5
Time (days)	17	Depth of credit information index (0-6)	0	Time to export (days)	21
Cost (% of income per capita)	17.3	Public registry coverage (% of adults)	0.0	Cost to export (US$ per container)	945
Minimum capital (% of income per capita)	0.0	Private bureau coverage (% of adults)	0.0	Documents to import (number)	5
				Time to import (days)	33
Dealing with construction permits (rank)	6	**Protecting investors** (rank)	154	Cost to import (US$ per container)	945
Procedures (number)	10	Extent of disclosure index (0-10)	2		
Time (days)	55	Extent of director liability index (0-10)	0	**Enforcing contracts** (rank)	62
Cost (% of income per capita)	36.0	Ease of shareholder suits index (0-10)	8	Procedures (number)	36
		Strength of investor protection index (0-10)	3.3	Time (days)	476
Registering property (rank)	183			Cost (% of claim)	27.4
Procedures (number)	NO PRACTICE	**Paying taxes** (rank)	90		
Time (days)	NO PRACTICE	Payments (number per year)	21	**Closing a business** (rank)	127
Cost (% of property value)	NO PRACTICE	Time (hours per year)	128	Time (years)	2.0
		Total tax rate (% of profit)	64.9	Cost (% of estate)	38
				Recovery rate (cents on the dollar)	17.9

MAURITANIA

		Sub-Saharan Africa		GNI per capita (US$)	960
Ease of doing business (rank)	165	Low income		Population (m)	3.3
Starting a business (rank)	152	**Getting credit** (rank)	152	**Trading across borders** (rank)	163
Procedures (number)	9	Strength of legal rights index (0-10)	3	Documents to export (number)	11
Time (days)	19	Depth of credit information index (0-6)	1	Time to export (days)	39
Cost (% of income per capita)	33.6	Public registry coverage (% of adults)	0.1	Cost to export (US$ per container)	1,520
Minimum capital (% of income per capita)	412.1	Private bureau coverage (% of adults)	0.0	Documents to import (number)	11
				Time to import (days)	42
Dealing with construction permits (rank)	153	**Protecting investors** (rank)	147	Cost to import (US$ per container)	1,523
Procedures (number)	25	Extent of disclosure index (0-10)	5		
Time (days)	201	Extent of director liability index (0-10)	3	**Enforcing contracts** (rank)	83
Cost (% of income per capita)	463.2	Ease of shareholder suits index (0-10)	3	Procedures (number)	46
		Strength of investor protection index (0-10)	3.7	Time (days)	370
Registering property (rank)	73			Cost (% of claim)	23.2
Procedures (number)	4	**Paying taxes** (rank)	172		
Time (days)	49	Payments (number per year)	38	**Closing a business** (rank)	144
Cost (% of property value)	5.2	Time (hours per year)	696	Time (years)	8.0
		Total tax rate (% of profit)	68.4	Cost (% of estate)	9
				Recovery rate (cents on the dollar)	10.3

✔ Reforms making it easier to do business   ✘ Reforms making it more difficult to do business

MAURITIUS

		Sub-Saharan Africa		GNI per capita (US$)	7,240
Ease of doing business (rank)	20	Upper middle income		Population (m)	1.3
Starting a business (rank)	12	**Getting credit** (rank)	89	**Trading across borders** (rank)	22
Procedures (number)	5	Strength of legal rights index (0-10)	5	Documents to export (number)	5
Time (days)	6	Depth of credit information index (0-6)	3	Time to export (days)	13
Cost (% of income per capita)	3.8	Public registry coverage (% of adults)	49.8	Cost to export (US$ per container)	737
Minimum capital (% of income per capita)	0.0	Private bureau coverage (% of adults)	0.0	Documents to import (number)	6
				Time to import (days)	13
Dealing with construction permits (rank)	39	**Protecting investors** (rank)	12	Cost to import (US$ per container)	689
Procedures (number)	18	Extent of disclosure index (0-10)	6		
Time (days)	107	Extent of director liability index (0-10)	8	✔ **Enforcing contracts** (rank)	61
Cost (% of income per capita)	32.3	Ease of shareholder suits index (0-10)	9	Procedures (number)	36
		Strength of investor protection index (0-10)	7.7	Time (days)	645
				Cost (% of claim)	17.4
Registering property (rank)	69				
Procedures (number)	4	✘ **Paying taxes** (rank)	12	**Closing a business** (rank)	71
Time (days)	26	Payments (number per year)	7	Time (years)	1.7
Cost (% of property value)	10.6	Time (hours per year)	161	Cost (% of estate)	15
		Total tax rate (% of profit)	24.1	Recovery rate (cents on the dollar)	35.1

MEXICO

		Latin America & Caribbean		GNI per capita (US$)	8,960
Ease of doing business (rank)	35	Upper middle income		Population (m)	107.4
✔ **Starting a business** (rank)	67	**Getting credit** (rank)	46	**Trading across borders** (rank)	58
Procedures (number)	6	Strength of legal rights index (0-10)	5	Documents to export (number)	5
Time (days)	9	Depth of credit information index (0-6)	6	Time to export (days)	12
Cost (% of income per capita)	12.3	Public registry coverage (% of adults)	0.0	Cost to export (US$ per container)	1,420
Minimum capital (% of income per capita)	9.2	Private bureau coverage (% of adults)	71.6	Documents to import (number)	4
				Time to import (days)	12
✔ **Dealing with construction permits** (rank)	22	**Protecting investors** (rank)	44	Cost to import (US$ per container)	1,880
Procedures (number)	11	Extent of disclosure index (0-10)	8		
Time (days)	105	Extent of director liability index (0-10)	5	**Enforcing contracts** (rank)	81
Cost (% of income per capita)	117.0	Ease of shareholder suits index (0-10)	5	Procedures (number)	38
		Strength of investor protection index (0-10)	6.0	Time (days)	415
				Cost (% of claim)	32.0
Registering property (rank)	105				
Procedures (number)	5	✘ **Paying taxes** (rank)	107	**Closing a business** (rank)	23
Time (days)	74	Payments (number per year)	6	Time (years)	1.8
Cost (% of property value)	5.2	Time (hours per year)	404	Cost (% of estate)	18
		Total tax rate (% of profit)	50.5	Recovery rate (cents on the dollar)	66.7

MICRONESIA, FED. STS.

		East Asia & Pacific		GNI per capita (US$)	2,220
Ease of doing business (rank)	141	Lower middle income		Population (m)	0.1
Starting a business (rank)	92	**Getting credit** (rank)	116	**Trading across borders** (rank)	97
Procedures (number)	7	Strength of legal rights index (0-10)	7	Documents to export (number)	3
Time (days)	16	Depth of credit information index (0-6)	0	Time to export (days)	30
Cost (% of income per capita)	150.5	Public registry coverage (% of adults)	0.0	Cost to export (US$ per container)	1,295
Minimum capital (% of income per capita)	0.0	Private bureau coverage (% of adults)	0.0	Documents to import (number)	6
				Time to import (days)	30
Dealing with construction permits (rank)	11	**Protecting investors** (rank)	173	Cost to import (US$ per container)	1,295
Procedures (number)	14	Extent of disclosure index (0-10)	0		
Time (days)	73	Extent of director liability index (0-10)	0	**Enforcing contracts** (rank)	147
Cost (% of income per capita)	19.2	Ease of shareholder suits index (0-10)	8	Procedures (number)	34
		Strength of investor protection index (0-10)	2.7	Time (days)	965
				Cost (% of claim)	66.0
Registering property (rank)	183				
Procedures (number)	NO PRACTICE	**Paying taxes** (rank)	83	**Closing a business** (rank)	154
Time (days)	NO PRACTICE	Payments (number per year)	21	Time (years)	5.3
Cost (% of property value)	NO PRACTICE	Time (hours per year)	128	Cost (% of estate)	38
		Total tax rate (% of profit)	58.7	Recovery rate (cents on the dollar)	3.2

MOLDOVA

		Eastern Europe & Central Asia		GNI per capita (US$)		1,590
Ease of doing business (rank)	90	Lower middle income		Population (m)		3.6
Starting a business (rank)	94	**Getting credit** (rank)	89	**Trading across borders** (rank)		141
Procedures (number)	8	Strength of legal rights index (0-10)	8	Documents to export (number)		6
Time (days)	10	Depth of credit information index (0-6)	0	Time to export (days)		32
Cost (% of income per capita)	10.9	Public registry coverage (% of adults)	0.0	Cost to export (US$ per container)		1,765
Minimum capital (% of income per capita)	11.9	Private bureau coverage (% of adults)	0.0	Documents to import (number)		7
				Time to import (days)		35
Dealing with construction permits (rank)	159	**Protecting investors** (rank)	109	Cost to import (US$ per container)		1,960
Procedures (number)	30	Extent of disclosure index (0-10)	7			
Time (days)	292	Extent of director liability index (0-10)	1	**Enforcing contracts** (rank)		20
Cost (% of income per capita)	120.9	Ease of shareholder suits index (0-10)	6	Procedures (number)		31
		Strength of investor protection index (0-10)	4.7	Time (days)		365
Registering property (rank)	18			Cost (% of claim)		20.9
Procedures (number)	5	✔ **Paying taxes** (rank)	106			
Time (days)	5	Payments (number per year)	48	**Closing a business** (rank)		92
Cost (% of property value)	0.9	Time (hours per year)	228	Time (years)		2.8
		Total tax rate (% of profit)	30.9	Cost (% of estate)		9
				Recovery rate (cents on the dollar)		28.2

MONGOLIA

		East Asia & Pacific		GNI per capita (US$)		1,630
Ease of doing business (rank)	73	Lower middle income		Population (m)		2.7
Starting a business (rank)	86	**Getting credit** (rank)	72	**Trading across borders** (rank)		158
Procedures (number)	7	Strength of legal rights index (0-10)	6	Documents to export (number)		8
Time (days)	13	Depth of credit information index (0-6)	3	Time to export (days)		46
Cost (% of income per capita)	3.2	Public registry coverage (% of adults)	19.2	Cost to export (US$ per container)		2,131
Minimum capital (% of income per capita)	46.8	Private bureau coverage (% of adults)	0.0	Documents to import (number)		8
				Time to import (days)		47
Dealing with construction permits (rank)	104	**Protecting investors** (rank)	28	Cost to import (US$ per container)		2,274
Procedures (number)	21	Extent of disclosure index (0-10)	5			
Time (days)	215	Extent of director liability index (0-10)	8	**Enforcing contracts** (rank)		35
Cost (% of income per capita)	65.1	Ease of shareholder suits index (0-10)	6	Procedures (number)		32
		Strength of investor protection index (0-10)	6.3	Time (days)		314
Registering property (rank)	27			Cost (% of claim)		30.6
Procedures (number)	5	**Paying taxes** (rank)	66			
Time (days)	11	Payments (number per year)	43	**Closing a business** (rank)		119
Cost (% of property value)	2.2	Time (hours per year)	192	Time (years)		4.0
		Total tax rate (% of profit)	23.0	Cost (% of estate)		8
				Recovery rate (cents on the dollar)		20.0

MONTENEGRO

		Eastern Europe & Central Asia		GNI per capita (US$)		6,550
Ease of doing business (rank)	66	Upper middle income		Population (m)		0.6
✔ **Starting a business** (rank)	51	**Getting credit** (rank)	32	✔ **Trading across borders** (rank)		34
Procedures (number)	7	Strength of legal rights index (0-10)	10	Documents to export (number)		6
Time (days)	10	Depth of credit information index (0-6)	2	Time to export (days)		14
Cost (% of income per capita)	1.9	Public registry coverage (% of adults)	26.7	Cost to export (US$ per container)		775
Minimum capital (% of income per capita)	0.0	Private bureau coverage (% of adults)	0.0	Documents to import (number)		6
				Time to import (days)		14
Dealing with construction permits (rank)	161	**Protecting investors** (rank)	28	Cost to import (US$ per container)		890
Procedures (number)	19	Extent of disclosure index (0-10)	5			
Time (days)	230	Extent of director liability index (0-10)	8	**Enforcing contracts** (rank)		135
Cost (% of income per capita)	1,215.0	Ease of shareholder suits index (0-10)	6	Procedures (number)		49
		Strength of investor protection index (0-10)	6.3	Time (days)		545
Registering property (rank)	116			Cost (% of claim)		25.7
Procedures (number)	7	✔ **Paying taxes** (rank)	139			
Time (days)	71	Payments (number per year)	77	**Closing a business** (rank)		47
Cost (% of property value)	3.3	Time (hours per year)	372	Time (years)		2.0
		Total tax rate (% of profit)	26.6	Cost (% of estate)		8
				Recovery rate (cents on the dollar)		43.4

MOROCCO

		Middle East & North Africa		GNI per capita (US$)	2,790
Ease of doing business (rank)	114	Lower middle income		Population (m)	32.0
Starting a business (rank)	82	**Getting credit** (rank)	89	**Trading across borders** (rank)	80
Procedures (number)	6	Strength of legal rights index (0-10)	3	Documents to export (number)	7
Time (days)	12	Depth of credit information index (0-6)	5	Time to export (days)	14
Cost (% of income per capita)	15.8	Public registry coverage (% of adults)	0.0	Cost to export (US$ per container)	700
Minimum capital (% of income per capita)	11.2	Private bureau coverage (% of adults)	9.9	Documents to import (number)	10
				Time to import (days)	17
Dealing with construction permits (rank)	98	✔ **Protecting investors** (rank)	154	Cost to import (US$ per container)	1,000
Procedures (number)	19	Extent of disclosure index (0-10)	7		
Time (days)	163	Extent of director liability index (0-10)	2	**Enforcing contracts** (rank)	106
Cost (% of income per capita)	251.5	Ease of shareholder suits index (0-10)	1	Procedures (number)	40
		Strength of investor protection index (0-10)	3.3	Time (days)	615
Registering property (rank)	124			Cost (% of claim)	25.2
Procedures (number)	8	**Paying taxes** (rank)	124		
Time (days)	47	Payments (number per year)	28	**Closing a business** (rank)	59
Cost (% of property value)	4.9	Time (hours per year)	358	Time (years)	1.8
		Total tax rate (% of profit)	41.7	Cost (% of estate)	18
				Recovery rate (cents on the dollar)	38.4

MOZAMBIQUE

		Sub-Saharan Africa		GNI per capita (US$)	440
Ease of doing business (rank)	126	Low income		Population (m)	22.9
✔ **Starting a business** (rank)	65	**Getting credit** (rank)	128	**Trading across borders** (rank)	133
Procedures (number)	9	Strength of legal rights index (0-10)	2	Documents to export (number)	7
Time (days)	13	Depth of credit information index (0-6)	4	Time to export (days)	23
Cost (% of income per capita)	13.9	Public registry coverage (% of adults)	2.2	Cost to export (US$ per container)	1,100
Minimum capital (% of income per capita)	0.0	Private bureau coverage (% of adults)	0.0	Documents to import (number)	10
				Time to import (days)	30
Dealing with construction permits (rank)	155	**Protecting investors** (rank)	44	Cost to import (US$ per container)	1,475
Procedures (number)	17	Extent of disclosure index (0-10)	5		
Time (days)	381	Extent of director liability index (0-10)	4	**Enforcing contracts** (rank)	132
Cost (% of income per capita)	530.3	Ease of shareholder suits index (0-10)	9	Procedures (number)	30
		Strength of investor protection index (0-10)	6.0	Time (days)	730
Registering property (rank)	144			Cost (% of claim)	142.5
Procedures (number)	8	**Paying taxes** (rank)	101		
Time (days)	42	Payments (number per year)	37	**Closing a business** (rank)	129
Cost (% of property value)	9.9	Time (hours per year)	230	Time (years)	5.0
		Total tax rate (% of profit)	34.3	Cost (% of estate)	9
				Recovery rate (cents on the dollar)	17.7

NAMIBIA

		Sub-Saharan Africa		GNI per capita (US$)	4,310
Ease of doing business (rank)	69	Upper middle income		Population (m)	2.2
Starting a business (rank)	124	**Getting credit** (rank)	15	**Trading across borders** (rank)	153
Procedures (number)	10	Strength of legal rights index (0-10)	8	Documents to export (number)	11
Time (days)	66	Depth of credit information index (0-6)	5	Time to export (days)	29
Cost (% of income per capita)	18.5	Public registry coverage (% of adults)	0.0	Cost to export (US$ per container)	1,686
Minimum capital (% of income per capita)	0.0	Private bureau coverage (% of adults)	58.5	Documents to import (number)	9
				Time to import (days)	24
Dealing with construction permits (rank)	36	**Protecting investors** (rank)	74	Cost to import (US$ per container)	1,813
Procedures (number)	12	Extent of disclosure index (0-10)	5		
Time (days)	139	Extent of director liability index (0-10)	5	**Enforcing contracts** (rank)	41
Cost (% of income per capita)	113.0	Ease of shareholder suits index (0-10)	6	Procedures (number)	33
		Strength of investor protection index (0-10)	5.3	Time (days)	270
Registering property (rank)	136			Cost (% of claim)	35.8
Procedures (number)	9	**Paying taxes** (rank)	99		
Time (days)	23	Payments (number per year)	37	**Closing a business** (rank)	53
Cost (% of property value)	9.6	Time (hours per year)	375	Time (years)	1.5
		Total tax rate (% of profit)	9.6	Cost (% of estate)	15
				Recovery rate (cents on the dollar)	41.5

NEPAL

		South Asia		GNI per capita (US$)	440
Ease of doing business (rank)	116	Low income		Population (m)	29.3
Starting a business (rank)	96	**Getting credit** (rank)	89	**Trading across borders** (rank)	164
Procedures (number)	7	Strength of legal rights index (0-10)	6	Documents to export (number)	9
Time (days)	31	Depth of credit information index (0-6)	2	Time to export (days)	41
Cost (% of income per capita)	46.6	Public registry coverage (% of adults)	0.0	Cost to export (US$ per container)	1,960
Minimum capital (% of income per capita)	0.0	Private bureau coverage (% of adults)	0.3	Documents to import (number)	10
				Time to import (days)	35
Dealing with construction permits (rank)	130	**Protecting investors** (rank)	74	Cost to import (US$ per container)	2,095
Procedures (number)	15	Extent of disclosure index (0-10)	6		
Time (days)	424	Extent of director liability index (0-10)	1	**Enforcing contracts** (rank)	123
Cost (% of income per capita)	192.1	Ease of shareholder suits index (0-10)	9	Procedures (number)	39
		Strength of investor protection index (0-10)	5.3	Time (days)	735
Registering property (rank)	25			Cost (% of claim)	26.8
Procedures (number)	3	**Paying taxes** (rank)	123		
Time (days)	5	Payments (number per year)	34	**Closing a business** (rank)	107
Cost (% of property value)	4.8	Time (hours per year)	338	Time (years)	5.0
		Total tax rate (% of profit)	38.2	Cost (% of estate)	9
				Recovery rate (cents on the dollar)	24.5

NETHERLANDS

		OECD high income		GNI per capita (US$)	49,350
Ease of doing business (rank)	30	High income		Population (m)	16.5
Starting a business (rank)	71	**Getting credit** (rank)	46	**Trading across borders** (rank)	13
Procedures (number)	6	Strength of legal rights index (0-10)	6	Documents to export (number)	4
Time (days)	8	Depth of credit information index (0-6)	5	Time to export (days)	6
Cost (% of income per capita)	5.7	Public registry coverage (% of adults)	0.0	Cost to export (US$ per container)	895
Minimum capital (% of income per capita)	52.4	Private bureau coverage (% of adults)	100.0	Documents to import (number)	5
				Time to import (days)	6
Dealing with construction permits (rank)	105	**Protecting investors** (rank)	109	Cost to import (US$ per container)	942
Procedures (number)	18	Extent of disclosure index (0-10)	4		
Time (days)	230	Extent of director liability index (0-10)	4	**Enforcing contracts** (rank)	29
Cost (% of income per capita)	113.8	Ease of shareholder suits index (0-10)	6	Procedures (number)	26
		Strength of investor protection index (0-10)	4.7	Time (days)	514
Registering property (rank)	46			Cost (% of claim)	24.4
Procedures (number)	5	✔ **Paying taxes** (rank)	27		
Time (days)	7	Payments (number per year)	9	**Closing a business** (rank)	11
Cost (% of property value)	6.1	Time (hours per year)	134	Time (years)	1.1
		Total tax rate (% of profit)	40.5	Cost (% of estate)	4
				Recovery rate (cents on the dollar)	81.9

NEW ZEALAND

		OECD high income		GNI per capita (US$)	27,259
Ease of doing business (rank)	3	High income		Population (m)	4.3
Starting a business (rank)	1	**Getting credit** (rank)	2	**Trading across borders** (rank)	28
Procedures (number)	1	Strength of legal rights index (0-10)	10	Documents to export (number)	7
Time (days)	1	Depth of credit information index (0-6)	5	Time to export (days)	10
Cost (% of income per capita)	0.4	Public registry coverage (% of adults)	0.0	Cost to export (US$ per container)	855
Minimum capital (% of income per capita)	0.0	Private bureau coverage (% of adults)	100.0	Documents to import (number)	5
				Time to import (days)	9
Dealing with construction permits (rank)	5	**Protecting investors** (rank)	1	Cost to import (US$ per container)	825
Procedures (number)	7	Extent of disclosure index (0-10)	10		
Time (days)	65	Extent of director liability index (0-10)	9	✔ **Enforcing contracts** (rank)	9
Cost (% of income per capita)	35.1	Ease of shareholder suits index (0-10)	10	Procedures (number)	30
		Strength of investor protection index (0-10)	9.7	Time (days)	216
Registering property (rank)	3			Cost (% of claim)	22.4
Procedures (number)	2	**Paying taxes** (rank)	26		
Time (days)	2	Payments (number per year)	8	**Closing a business** (rank)	16
Cost (% of property value)	0.1	Time (hours per year)	192	Time (years)	1.3
		Total tax rate (% of profit)	34.3	Cost (% of estate)	4
				Recovery rate (cents on the dollar)	79.1

✔ Reforms making it easier to do business   ✗ Reforms making it more difficult to do business

NICARAGUA

		Latin America & Caribbean		GNI per capita (US$)	1,010
Ease of doing business (rank)	117	Lower middle income		Population (m)	5.7

Starting a business (rank)	97	**Getting credit** (rank)	89	✔ **Trading across borders** (rank)	85
Procedures (number)	6	Strength of legal rights index (0-10)	3	Documents to export (number)	5
Time (days)	39	Depth of credit information index (0-6)	5	Time to export (days)	26
Cost (% of income per capita)	117.9	Public registry coverage (% of adults)	14.0	Cost to export (US$ per container)	1,140
Minimum capital (% of income per capita)	0.0	Private bureau coverage (% of adults)	21.4	Documents to import (number)	5
				Time to import (days)	26
Dealing with construction permits (rank)	138	**Protecting investors** (rank)	93	Cost to import (US$ per container)	1,220
Procedures (number)	17	Extent of disclosure index (0-10)	4		
Time (days)	219	Extent of director liability index (0-10)	5	**Enforcing contracts** (rank)	66
Cost (% of income per capita)	767.1	Ease of shareholder suits index (0-10)	6	Procedures (number)	35
		Strength of investor protection index (0-10)	5.0	Time (days)	540
Registering property (rank)	142			Cost (% of claim)	26.8
Procedures (number)	8	✗ **Paying taxes** (rank)	158		
Time (days)	124	Payments (number per year)	64	**Closing a business** (rank)	75
Cost (% of property value)	3.9	Time (hours per year)	222	Time (years)	2.2
		Total tax rate (% of profit)	63.2	Cost (% of estate)	15
				Recovery rate (cents on the dollar)	33.7

NIGER

		Sub-Saharan Africa		GNI per capita (US$)	340
Ease of doing business (rank)	173	Low income		Population (m)	15.3

Starting a business (rank)	159	**Getting credit** (rank)	152	**Trading across borders** (rank)	174
Procedures (number)	9	Strength of legal rights index (0-10)	3	Documents to export (number)	8
Time (days)	17	Depth of credit information index (0-6)	1	Time to export (days)	59
Cost (% of income per capita)	118.6	Public registry coverage (% of adults)	0.1	Cost to export (US$ per container)	3,545
Minimum capital (% of income per capita)	613.0	Private bureau coverage (% of adults)	0.0	Documents to import (number)	10
				Time to import (days)	64
Dealing with construction permits (rank)	162	**Protecting investors** (rank)	154	Cost to import (US$ per container)	3,545
Procedures (number)	17	Extent of disclosure index (0-10)	6		
Time (days)	265	Extent of director liability index (0-10)	1	**Enforcing contracts** (rank)	138
Cost (% of income per capita)	2,352.3	Ease of shareholder suits index (0-10)	3	Procedures (number)	39
		Strength of investor protection index (0-10)	3.3	Time (days)	545
Registering property (rank)	84			Cost (% of claim)	59.6
Procedures (number)	4	✔ **Paying taxes** (rank)	144		
Time (days)	35	Payments (number per year)	41	**Closing a business** (rank)	136
Cost (% of property value)	11.0	Time (hours per year)	270	Time (years)	5.0
		Total tax rate (% of profit)	46.5	Cost (% of estate)	18
				Recovery rate (cents on the dollar)	16.0

NIGERIA

		Sub-Saharan Africa		GNI per capita (US$)	1,140
Ease of doing business (rank)	137	Lower middle income		Population (m)	154.7

Starting a business (rank)	110	**Getting credit** (rank)	89	**Trading across borders** (rank)	146
Procedures (number)	8	Strength of legal rights index (0-10)	8	Documents to export (number)	10
Time (days)	31	Depth of credit information index (0-6)	0	Time to export (days)	24
Cost (% of income per capita)	78.9	Public registry coverage (% of adults)	0.0	Cost to export (US$ per container)	1,263
Minimum capital (% of income per capita)	0.0	Private bureau coverage (% of adults)	0.0	Documents to import (number)	9
				Time to import (days)	39
Dealing with construction permits (rank)	167	**Protecting investors** (rank)	59	Cost to import (US$ per container)	1,440
Procedures (number)	18	Extent of disclosure index (0-10)	5		
Time (days)	350	Extent of director liability index (0-10)	7	**Enforcing contracts** (rank)	97
Cost (% of income per capita)	597.5	Ease of shareholder suits index (0-10)	5	Procedures (number)	40
		Strength of investor protection index (0-10)	5.7	Time (days)	457
Registering property (rank)	179			Cost (% of claim)	32.0
Procedures (number)	13	**Paying taxes** (rank)	134		
Time (days)	82	Payments (number per year)	35	**Closing a business** (rank)	99
Cost (% of property value)	20.9	Time (hours per year)	938	Time (years)	2.0
		Total tax rate (% of profit)	32.2	Cost (% of estate)	22
				Recovery rate (cents on the dollar)	26.8

NORWAY

Ease of doing business (rank)	8

OECD high income	
High income	

GNI per capita (US$)	86,440
Population (m)	4.8

Starting a business (rank)	33
Procedures (number)	5
Time (days)	7
Cost (% of income per capita)	1.8
Minimum capital (% of income per capita)	20.0

Getting credit (rank)	46
Strength of legal rights index (0-10)	7
Depth of credit information index (0-6)	4
Public registry coverage (% of adults)	0.0
Private bureau coverage (% of adults)	100.0

Trading across borders (rank)	9
Documents to export (number)	4
Time to export (days)	7
Cost to export (US$ per container)	830
Documents to import (number)	4
Time to import (days)	7
Cost to import (US$ per container)	729

Dealing with construction permits (rank)	65
Procedures (number)	14
Time (days)	252
Cost (% of income per capita)	43.8

Protecting investors (rank)	20
Extent of disclosure index (0-10)	7
Extent of director liability index (0-10)	6
Ease of shareholder suits index (0-10)	7
Strength of investor protection index (0-10)	6.7

Enforcing contracts (rank)	4
Procedures (number)	33
Time (days)	280
Cost (% of claim)	9.9

Registering property (rank)	8
Procedures (number)	1
Time (days)	3
Cost (% of property value)	2.5

Paying taxes (rank)	18
Payments (number per year)	4
Time (hours per year)	87
Total tax rate (% of profit)	41.6

Closing a business (rank)	4
Time (years)	0.9
Cost (% of estate)	1
Recovery rate (cents on the dollar)	90.9

OMAN

Ease of doing business (rank)	57

Middle East & North Africa	
High income	

GNI per capita (US$)	18,013
Population (m)	2.8

Starting a business (rank)	76
Procedures (number)	5
Time (days)	12
Cost (% of income per capita)	3.3
Minimum capital (% of income per capita)	288.4

Getting credit (rank)	128
Strength of legal rights index (0-10)	4
Depth of credit information index (0-6)	2
Public registry coverage (% of adults)	19.6
Private bureau coverage (% of adults)	0.0

Trading across borders (rank)	88
Documents to export (number)	9
Time to export (days)	14
Cost to export (US$ per container)	766
Documents to import (number)	9
Time to import (days)	17
Cost to import (US$ per container)	890

Dealing with construction permits (rank)	70
Procedures (number)	15
Time (days)	186
Cost (% of income per capita)	106.2

Protecting investors (rank)	93
Extent of disclosure index (0-10)	8
Extent of director liability index (0-10)	5
Ease of shareholder suits index (0-10)	2
Strength of investor protection index (0-10)	5.0

Enforcing contracts (rank)	104
Procedures (number)	51
Time (days)	598
Cost (% of claim)	13.5

Registering property (rank)	21
Procedures (number)	2
Time (days)	16
Cost (% of property value)	3.0

Paying taxes (rank)	8
Payments (number per year)	14
Time (hours per year)	62
Total tax rate (% of profit)	21.6

Closing a business (rank)	72
Time (years)	4.0
Cost (% of estate)	4
Recovery rate (cents on the dollar)	34.9

PAKISTAN

Ease of doing business (rank)	83

South Asia	
Lower middle income	

GNI per capita (US$)	1,020
Population (m)	169.7

Starting a business (rank)	85
Procedures (number)	10
Time (days)	21
Cost (% of income per capita)	10.7
Minimum capital (% of income per capita)	0.0

Getting credit (rank)	65
Strength of legal rights index (0-10)	6
Depth of credit information index (0-6)	4
Public registry coverage (% of adults)	5.8
Private bureau coverage (% of adults)	1.4

✔ **Trading across borders** (rank)	81
Documents to export (number)	9
Time to export (days)	21
Cost to export (US$ per container)	611
Documents to import (number)	8
Time to import (days)	18
Cost to import (US$ per container)	680

Dealing with construction permits (rank)	98
Procedures (number)	12
Time (days)	223
Cost (% of income per capita)	575.7

Protecting investors (rank)	28
Extent of disclosure index (0-10)	6
Extent of director liability index (0-10)	6
Ease of shareholder suits index (0-10)	7
Strength of investor protection index (0-10)	6.3

Enforcing contracts (rank)	155
Procedures (number)	47
Time (days)	976
Cost (% of claim)	23.8

✗ **Registering property** (rank)	126
Procedures (number)	6
Time (days)	50
Cost (% of property value)	9.2

Paying taxes (rank)	145
Payments (number per year)	47
Time (hours per year)	560
Total tax rate (% of profit)	31.6

Closing a business (rank)	67
Time (years)	2.8
Cost (% of estate)	4
Recovery rate (cents on the dollar)	36.5

✔ Reforms making it easier to do business   ✗ Reforms making it more difficult to do business

PALAU

Ease of doing business (rank)	120	East Asia & Pacific		GNI per capita (US$)		8,940	
		Upper middle income		Population (m)		0.02	
Starting a business (rank)	105	**Getting credit** (rank)	183	**Trading across borders** (rank)		121	
Procedures (number)	8	Strength of legal rights index (0-10)	0	Documents to export (number)		6	
Time (days)	28	Depth of credit information index (0-6)	0	Time to export (days)		29	
Cost (% of income per capita)	4.2	Public registry coverage (% of adults)	0.0	Cost to export (US$ per container)		1,070	
Minimum capital (% of income per capita)	11.2	Private bureau coverage (% of adults)	0.0	Documents to import (number)		10	
				Time to import (days)		33	
Dealing with construction permits (rank)	54	**Protecting investors** (rank)	173	Cost to import (US$ per container)		1,022	
Procedures (number)	25	Extent of disclosure index (0-10)	0				
Time (days)	118	Extent of director liability index (0-10)	0	**Enforcing contracts** (rank)		145	
Cost (% of income per capita)	5.1	Ease of shareholder suits index (0-10)	8	Procedures (number)		38	
		Strength of investor protection index (0-10)	2.7	Time (days)		885	
Registering property (rank)	20			Cost (% of claim)		35.3	
Procedures (number)	5	**Paying taxes** (rank)	89				
Time (days)	14	Payments (number per year)	19	**Closing a business** (rank)		60	
Cost (% of property value)	0.3	Time (hours per year)	128	Time (years)		1.0	
		Total tax rate (% of profit)	73.0	Cost (% of estate)		23	
				Recovery rate (cents on the dollar)		37.9	

PANAMA

Ease of doing business (rank)	72	Latin America & Caribbean		GNI per capita (US$)	6,740
		Upper middle income		Population (m)	3.5
✔ **Starting a business** (rank)	23	**Getting credit** (rank)	32	**Trading across borders** (rank)	11
Procedures (number)	6	Strength of legal rights index (0-10)	6	Documents to export (number)	3
Time (days)	9	Depth of credit information index (0-6)	6	Time to export (days)	9
Cost (% of income per capita)	10.3	Public registry coverage (% of adults)	0.0	Cost to export (US$ per container)	765
Minimum capital (% of income per capita)	0.0	Private bureau coverage (% of adults)	31.9	Documents to import (number)	4
				Time to import (days)	9
Dealing with construction permits (rank)	66	**Protecting investors** (rank)	109	Cost to import (US$ per container)	915
Procedures (number)	20	Extent of disclosure index (0-10)	1		
Time (days)	116	Extent of director liability index (0-10)	4	**Enforcing contracts** (rank)	119
Cost (% of income per capita)	99.1	Ease of shareholder suits index (0-10)	9	Procedures (number)	31
		Strength of investor protection index (0-10)	4.7	Time (days)	686
✗ **Registering property** (rank)	113			Cost (% of claim)	50.0
Procedures (number)	8	✔ **Paying taxes** (rank)	175		
Time (days)	32	Payments (number per year)	62	**Closing a business** (rank)	78
Cost (% of property value)	5.4	Time (hours per year)	482	Time (years)	2.5
		Total tax rate (% of profit)	50.1	Cost (% of estate)	18
				Recovery rate (cents on the dollar)	32.4

PAPUA NEW GUINEA

Ease of doing business (rank)	103	East Asia & Pacific		GNI per capita (US$)	1,180
		Lower middle income		Population (m)	6.7
Starting a business (rank)	81	✔ **Getting credit** (rank)	89	**Trading across borders** (rank)	96
Procedures (number)	6	Strength of legal rights index (0-10)	5	Documents to export (number)	7
Time (days)	51	Depth of credit information index (0-6)	3	Time to export (days)	26
Cost (% of income per capita)	17.7	Public registry coverage (% of adults)	0.0	Cost to export (US$ per container)	664
Minimum capital (% of income per capita)	0.0	Private bureau coverage (% of adults)	0.6	Documents to import (number)	9
				Time to import (days)	29
Dealing with construction permits (rank)	120	**Protecting investors** (rank)	44	Cost to import (US$ per container)	722
Procedures (number)	24	Extent of disclosure index (0-10)	5		
Time (days)	217	Extent of director liability index (0-10)	5	**Enforcing contracts** (rank)	163
Cost (% of income per capita)	77.5	Ease of shareholder suits index (0-10)	8	Procedures (number)	42
		Strength of investor protection index (0-10)	6.0	Time (days)	591
Registering property (rank)	85			Cost (% of claim)	110.3
Procedures (number)	4	**Paying taxes** (rank)	101		
Time (days)	72	Payments (number per year)	33	**Closing a business** (rank)	108
Cost (% of property value)	5.1	Time (hours per year)	194	Time (years)	3.0
		Total tax rate (% of profit)	42.3	Cost (% of estate)	23
				Recovery rate (cents on the dollar)	23.9

PARAGUAY

		Latin America & Caribbean		GNI per capita (US$)	2,280
Ease of doing business (rank)	106	Lower middle income		Population (m)	6.3
Starting a business (rank)	102	**Getting credit** (rank)	72	**Trading across borders** (rank)	152
Procedures (number)	7	Strength of legal rights index (0-10)	3	Documents to export (number)	8
Time (days)	35	Depth of credit information index (0-6)	6	Time to export (days)	33
Cost (% of income per capita)	55.1	Public registry coverage (% of adults)	13.9	Cost to export (US$ per container)	1,440
Minimum capital (% of income per capita)	0.0	Private bureau coverage (% of adults)	0.0	Documents to import (number)	10
				Time to import (days)	33
✔ **Dealing with construction permits** (rank)	71	**Protecting investors** (rank)	59	Cost to import (US$ per container)	1,750
Procedures (number)	13	Extent of disclosure index (0-10)	6		
Time (days)	179	Extent of director liability index (0-10)	5	**Enforcing contracts** (rank)	107
Cost (% of income per capita)	298.9	Ease of shareholder suits index (0-10)	6	Procedures (number)	38
		Strength of investor protection index (0-10)	5.7	Time (days)	591
				Cost (% of claim)	30.0
Registering property (rank)	60				
Procedures (number)	6	**Paying taxes** (rank)	110	**Closing a business** (rank)	135
Time (days)	46	Payments (number per year)	35	Time (years)	3.9
Cost (% of property value)	1.9	Time (hours per year)	311	Cost (% of estate)	9
		Total tax rate (% of profit)	35.0	Recovery rate (cents on the dollar)	16.1

PERU

		Latin America & Caribbean		GNI per capita (US$)	4,160
Ease of doing business (rank)	36	Upper middle income		Population (m)	29.2
✔ **Starting a business** (rank)	54	**Getting credit** (rank)	15	✔ **Trading across borders** (rank)	53
Procedures (number)	6	Strength of legal rights index (0-10)	7	Documents to export (number)	6
Time (days)	27	Depth of credit information index (0-6)	6	Time to export (days)	12
Cost (% of income per capita)	13.6	Public registry coverage (% of adults)	25.5	Cost to export (US$ per container)	860
Minimum capital (% of income per capita)	0.0	Private bureau coverage (% of adults)	33.3	Documents to import (number)	8
				Time to import (days)	17
✔ **Dealing with construction permits** (rank)	97	**Protecting investors** (rank)	20	Cost to import (US$ per container)	880
Procedures (number)	19	Extent of disclosure index (0-10)	8		
Time (days)	188	Extent of director liability index (0-10)	5	**Enforcing contracts** (rank)	110
Cost (% of income per capita)	128.1	Ease of shareholder suits index (0-10)	7	Procedures (number)	41
		Strength of investor protection index (0-10)	6.7	Time (days)	428
				Cost (% of claim)	35.7
✔ **Registering property** (rank)	24				
Procedures (number)	4	**Paying taxes** (rank)	86	**Closing a business** (rank)	96
Time (days)	7	Payments (number per year)	9	Time (years)	3.1
Cost (% of property value)	3.3	Time (hours per year)	380	Cost (% of estate)	7
		Total tax rate (% of profit)	40.2	Recovery rate (cents on the dollar)	27.2

PHILIPPINES

		East Asia & Pacific		GNI per capita (US$)	1,790
Ease of doing business (rank)	148	Lower middle income		Population (m)	92.0
✔ **Starting a business** (rank)	156	**Getting credit** (rank)	128	✔ **Trading across borders** (rank)	61
Procedures (number)	15	Strength of legal rights index (0-10)	3	Documents to export (number)	8
Time (days)	38	Depth of credit information index (0-6)	3	Time to export (days)	15
Cost (% of income per capita)	29.7	Public registry coverage (% of adults)	0.0	Cost to export (US$ per container)	675
Minimum capital (% of income per capita)	6.0	Private bureau coverage (% of adults)	7.4	Documents to import (number)	8
				Time to import (days)	14
✗ **Dealing with construction permits** (rank)	156	**Protecting investors** (rank)	132	Cost to import (US$ per container)	730
Procedures (number)	26	Extent of disclosure index (0-10)	2		
Time (days)	169	Extent of director liability index (0-10)	2	**Enforcing contracts** (rank)	118
Cost (% of income per capita)	778.5	Ease of shareholder suits index (0-10)	8	Procedures (number)	37
		Strength of investor protection index (0-10)	4.0	Time (days)	842
				Cost (% of claim)	26.0
Registering property (rank)	102				
Procedures (number)	8	**Paying taxes** (rank)	124	**Closing a business** (rank)	153
Time (days)	33	Payments (number per year)	47	Time (years)	5.7
Cost (% of property value)	4.3	Time (hours per year)	195	Cost (% of estate)	38
		Total tax rate (% of profit)	45.8	Recovery rate (cents on the dollar)	4.5

POLAND

Ease of doing business (rank)	70	OECD high income		GNI per capita (US$)	12,260
		High income		Population (m)	38.1
Starting a business (rank)	113	**Getting credit** (rank)	15	**Trading across borders** (rank)	49
Procedures (number)	6	Strength of legal rights index (0-10)	9	Documents to export (number)	5
Time (days)	32	Depth of credit information index (0-6)	4	Time to export (days)	17
Cost (% of income per capita)	17.5	Public registry coverage (% of adults)	0.0	Cost to export (US$ per container)	884
Minimum capital (% of income per capita)	14.7	Private bureau coverage (% of adults)	91.7	Documents to import (number)	5
				Time to import (days)	25
Dealing with construction permits (rank)	164	**Protecting investors** (rank)	44	Cost to import (US$ per container)	884
Procedures (number)	32	Extent of disclosure index (0-10)	7		
Time (days)	311	Extent of director liability index (0-10)	2	**Enforcing contracts** (rank)	77
Cost (% of income per capita)	121.8	Ease of shareholder suits index (0-10)	9	Procedures (number)	38
		Strength of investor protection index (0-10)	6.0	Time (days)	830
✔ **Registering property** (rank)	86			Cost (% of claim)	12.0
Procedures (number)	6	**Paying taxes** (rank)	121		
Time (days)	152	Payments (number per year)	29	**Closing a business** (rank)	81
Cost (% of property value)	0.4	Time (hours per year)	325	Time (years)	3.0
		Total tax rate (% of profit)	42.3	Cost (% of estate)	20
				Recovery rate (cents on the dollar)	31.3

PORTUGAL

Ease of doing business (rank)	31	OECD high income		GNI per capita (US$)	20,940
		High income		Population (m)	10.6
Starting a business (rank)	59	**Getting credit** (rank)	89	**Trading across borders** (rank)	27
Procedures (number)	6	Strength of legal rights index (0-10)	3	Documents to export (number)	4
Time (days)	6	Depth of credit information index (0-6)	5	Time to export (days)	16
Cost (% of income per capita)	6.5	Public registry coverage (% of adults)	67.1	Cost to export (US$ per container)	685
Minimum capital (% of income per capita)	34.1	Private bureau coverage (% of adults)	16.3	Documents to import (number)	5
				Time to import (days)	15
Dealing with construction permits (rank)	111	**Protecting investors** (rank)	44	Cost to import (US$ per container)	999
Procedures (number)	19	Extent of disclosure index (0-10)	6		
Time (days)	272	Extent of director liability index (0-10)	5	**Enforcing contracts** (rank)	24
Cost (% of income per capita)	53.9	Ease of shareholder suits index (0-10)	7	Procedures (number)	31
		Strength of investor protection index (0-10)	6.0	Time (days)	547
✔ **Registering property** (rank)	31			Cost (% of claim)	13.0
Procedures (number)	1	✔ **Paying taxes** (rank)	73		
Time (days)	1	Payments (number per year)	8	**Closing a business** (rank)	21
Cost (% of property value)	7.4	Time (hours per year)	298	Time (years)	2.0
		Total tax rate (% of profit)	43.3	Cost (% of estate)	9
				Recovery rate (cents on the dollar)	72.6

PUERTO RICO

Ease of doing business (rank)	47	Latin America & Caribbean		GNI per capita (US$)	15,819
		High income		Population (m)	4.0
Starting a business (rank)	16	**Getting credit** (rank)	32	**Trading across borders** (rank)	107
Procedures (number)	7	Strength of legal rights index (0-10)	7	Documents to export (number)	7
Time (days)	7	Depth of credit information index (0-6)	5	Time to export (days)	15
Cost (% of income per capita)	0.7	Public registry coverage (% of adults)	0.0	Cost to export (US$ per container)	1,250
Minimum capital (% of income per capita)	0.0	Private bureau coverage (% of adults)	71.5	Documents to import (number)	10
				Time to import (days)	16
Dealing with construction permits (rank)	150	**Protecting investors** (rank)	16	Cost to import (US$ per container)	1,250
Procedures (number)	22	Extent of disclosure index (0-10)	7		
Time (days)	209	Extent of director liability index (0-10)	6	**Enforcing contracts** (rank)	99
Cost (% of income per capita)	500.4	Ease of shareholder suits index (0-10)	8	Procedures (number)	39
		Strength of investor protection index (0-10)	7.0	Time (days)	620
Registering property (rank)	127			Cost (% of claim)	25.6
Procedures (number)	8	✗ **Paying taxes** (rank)	108		
Time (days)	194	Payments (number per year)	16	**Closing a business** (rank)	25
Cost (% of property value)	0.9	Time (hours per year)	218	Time (years)	3.8
		Total tax rate (% of profit)	67.7	Cost (% of estate)	8
				Recovery rate (cents on the dollar)	64.7

QATAR

		Middle East & North Africa		GNI per capita (US$)	68,872
Ease of doing business (rank)	50	High income		Population (m)	1.4
✗ **Starting a business** (rank)	111	**Getting credit** (rank)	138	**Trading across borders** (rank)	46
Procedures (number)	8	Strength of legal rights index (0-10)	3	Documents to export (number)	5
Time (days)	12	Depth of credit information index (0-6)	2	Time to export (days)	21
Cost (% of income per capita)	9.7	Public registry coverage (% of adults)	0.1	Cost to export (US$ per container)	735
Minimum capital (% of income per capita)	79.8	Private bureau coverage (% of adults)	0.0	Documents to import (number)	7
				Time to import (days)	20
Dealing with construction permits (rank)	30	**Protecting investors** (rank)	93	Cost to import (US$ per container)	657
Procedures (number)	19	Extent of disclosure index (0-10)	5		
Time (days)	76	Extent of director liability index (0-10)	6	**Enforcing contracts** (rank)	95
Cost (% of income per capita)	0.8	Ease of shareholder suits index (0-10)	4	Procedures (number)	43
		Strength of investor protection index (0-10)	5.0	Time (days)	570
				Cost (% of claim)	21.6
Registering property (rank)	58				
Procedures (number)	10	**Paying taxes** (rank)	2	**Closing a business** (rank)	36
Time (days)	16	Payments (number per year)	3	Time (years)	2.8
Cost (% of property value)	0.3	Time (hours per year)	36	Cost (% of estate)	22
		Total tax rate (% of profit)	11.3	Recovery rate (cents on the dollar)	53.0

ROMANIA

		Eastern Europe & Central Asia		GNI per capita (US$)	8,330
Ease of doing business (rank)	56	Upper middle income		Population (m)	21.5
Starting a business (rank)	44	**Getting credit** (rank)	15	**Trading across borders** (rank)	47
Procedures (number)	6	Strength of legal rights index (0-10)	8	Documents to export (number)	5
Time (days)	10	Depth of credit information index (0-6)	5	Time to export (days)	12
Cost (% of income per capita)	2.6	Public registry coverage (% of adults)	13.0	Cost to export (US$ per container)	1,275
Minimum capital (% of income per capita)	0.9	Private bureau coverage (% of adults)	33.3	Documents to import (number)	6
				Time to import (days)	13
✔ **Dealing with construction permits** (rank)	84	**Protecting investors** (rank)	44	Cost to import (US$ per container)	1,175
Procedures (number)	17	Extent of disclosure index (0-10)	9		
Time (days)	228	Extent of director liability index (0-10)	5	**Enforcing contracts** (rank)	54
Cost (% of income per capita)	73.9	Ease of shareholder suits index (0-10)	4	Procedures (number)	31
		Strength of investor protection index (0-10)	6.0	Time (days)	512
				Cost (% of claim)	28.9
Registering property (rank)	92				
Procedures (number)	8	✗ **Paying taxes** (rank)	151	✔ **Closing a business** (rank)	102
Time (days)	48	Payments (number per year)	113	Time (years)	3.3
Cost (% of property value)	1.3	Time (hours per year)	222	Cost (% of estate)	11
		Total tax rate (% of profit)	44.9	Recovery rate (cents on the dollar)	25.7

RUSSIAN FEDERATION

		Eastern Europe & Central Asia		GNI per capita (US$)	9,370
Ease of doing business (rank)	123	Upper middle income		Population (m)	141.9
Starting a business (rank)	108	**Getting credit** (rank)	89	**Trading across borders** (rank)	162
Procedures (number)	9	Strength of legal rights index (0-10)	3	Documents to export (number)	8
Time (days)	30	Depth of credit information index (0-6)	5	Time to export (days)	36
Cost (% of income per capita)	3.6	Public registry coverage (% of adults)	0.0	Cost to export (US$ per container)	1,850
Minimum capital (% of income per capita)	1.9	Private bureau coverage (% of adults)	14.4	Documents to import (number)	13
				Time to import (days)	36
✔ **Dealing with construction permits** (rank)	182	**Protecting investors** (rank)	93	Cost to import (US$ per container)	1,850
Procedures (number)	53	Extent of disclosure index (0-10)	6		
Time (days)	540	Extent of director liability index (0-10)	2	**Enforcing contracts** (rank)	18
Cost (% of income per capita)	4,141.0	Ease of shareholder suits index (0-10)	7	Procedures (number)	37
		Strength of investor protection index (0-10)	5.0	Time (days)	281
				Cost (% of claim)	13.4
Registering property (rank)	51				
Procedures (number)	6	**Paying taxes** (rank)	105	✔ **Closing a business** (rank)	103
Time (days)	43	Payments (number per year)	11	Time (years)	3.8
Cost (% of property value)	0.1	Time (hours per year)	320	Cost (% of estate)	9
		Total tax rate (% of profit)	46.5	Recovery rate (cents on the dollar)	25.3

✔ Reforms making it easier to do business   ✗ Reforms making it more difficult to do business

RWANDA

		Sub-Saharan Africa		GNI per capita (US$)		460
Ease of doing business (rank)	58	Low income		Population (m)		10.0
Starting a business (rank)	9	✔ **Getting credit** (rank)	32	✔ **Trading across borders** (rank)		159
Procedures (number)	2	Strength of legal rights index (0-10)	8	Documents to export (number)		8
Time (days)	3	Depth of credit information index (0-6)	4	Time to export (days)		35
Cost (% of income per capita)	8.8	Public registry coverage (% of adults)	0.7	Cost to export (US$ per container)		3,275
Minimum capital (% of income per capita)	0.0	Private bureau coverage (% of adults)	0.0	Documents to import (number)		8
				Time to import (days)		34
✔ **Dealing with construction permits** (rank)	82	**Protecting investors** (rank)	28	Cost to import (US$ per container)		4,990
Procedures (number)	14	Extent of disclosure index (0-10)	7			
Time (days)	195	Extent of director liability index (0-10)	9	**Enforcing contracts** (rank)		39
Cost (% of income per capita)	353.6	Ease of shareholder suits index (0-10)	3	Procedures (number)		24
		Strength of investor protection index (0-10)	6.3	Time (days)		230
Registering property (rank)	41			Cost (% of claim)		78.7
Procedures (number)	4	**Paying taxes** (rank)	43			
Time (days)	55	Payments (number per year)	26	**Closing a business** (rank)		183
Cost (% of property value)	0.4	Time (hours per year)	148	Time (years)		NO PRACTICE
		Total tax rate (% of profit)	31.3	Cost (% of estate)		NO PRACTICE
				Recovery rate (cents on the dollar)		0.0

SAMOA

		East Asia & Pacific		GNI per capita (US$)		2,840
Ease of doing business (rank)	61	Lower middle income		Population (m)		0.2
Starting a business (rank)	20	**Getting credit** (rank)	128	**Trading across borders** (rank)		94
Procedures (number)	5	Strength of legal rights index (0-10)	6	Documents to export (number)		7
Time (days)	9	Depth of credit information index (0-6)	0	Time to export (days)		27
Cost (% of income per capita)	9.8	Public registry coverage (% of adults)	0.0	Cost to export (US$ per container)		820
Minimum capital (% of income per capita)	0.0	Private bureau coverage (% of adults)	0.0	Documents to import (number)		7
				Time to import (days)		31
Dealing with construction permits (rank)	47	**Protecting investors** (rank)	28	Cost to import (US$ per container)		848
Procedures (number)	18	Extent of disclosure index (0-10)	5			
Time (days)	88	Extent of director liability index (0-10)	6	**Enforcing contracts** (rank)		82
Cost (% of income per capita)	78.7	Ease of shareholder suits index (0-10)	8	Procedures (number)		44
		Strength of investor protection index (0-10)	6.3	Time (days)		455
✔ **Registering property** (rank)	34			Cost (% of claim)		19.7
Procedures (number)	5	**Paying taxes** (rank)	68			
Time (days)	27	Payments (number per year)	37	**Closing a business** (rank)		140
Cost (% of property value)	1.6	Time (hours per year)	224	Time (years)		2.5
		Total tax rate (% of profit)	18.9	Cost (% of estate)		38
				Recovery rate (cents on the dollar)		14.6

SÃO TOMÉ AND PRINCIPE

		Sub-Saharan Africa		GNI per capita (US$)		1,140
Ease of doing business (rank)	178	Lower middle income		Population (m)		0.2
✗ **Starting a business** (rank)	177	**Getting credit** (rank)	176	**Trading across borders** (rank)		92
Procedures (number)	10	Strength of legal rights index (0-10)	2	Documents to export (number)		8
Time (days)	144	Depth of credit information index (0-6)	0	Time to export (days)		27
Cost (% of income per capita)	77.3	Public registry coverage (% of adults)	0.0	Cost to export (US$ per container)		690
Minimum capital (% of income per capita)	385.7	Private bureau coverage (% of adults)	0.0	Documents to import (number)		8
				Time to import (days)		29
Dealing with construction permits (rank)	113	**Protecting investors** (rank)	154	Cost to import (US$ per container)		577
Procedures (number)	13	Extent of disclosure index (0-10)	3			
Time (days)	255	Extent of director liability index (0-10)	1	**Enforcing contracts** (rank)		179
Cost (% of income per capita)	565.1	Ease of shareholder suits index (0-10)	6	Procedures (number)		43
		Strength of investor protection index (0-10)	3.3	Time (days)		1,185
Registering property (rank)	161			Cost (% of claim)		50.5
Procedures (number)	7	✔ **Paying taxes** (rank)	135			
Time (days)	62	Payments (number per year)	42	**Closing a business** (rank)		183
Cost (% of property value)	10.9	Time (hours per year)	424	Time (years)		NO PRACTICE
		Total tax rate (% of profit)	33.3	Cost (% of estate)		NO PRACTICE
				Recovery rate (cents on the dollar)		0.0

SAUDI ARABIA

		Middle East & North Africa		GNI per capita (US$)	14,486
Ease of doing business (rank)	11	High income		Population (m)	25.4

Starting a business (rank)	13	✔ **Getting credit** (rank)	46	✔ **Trading across borders** (rank)	18
Procedures (number)	4	Strength of legal rights index (0-10)	5	Documents to export (number)	5
Time (days)	5	Depth of credit information index (0-6)	6	Time to export (days)	13
Cost (% of income per capita)	7.0	Public registry coverage (% of adults)	0.0	Cost to export (US$ per container)	580
Minimum capital (% of income per capita)	0.0	Private bureau coverage (% of adults)	18.0	Documents to import (number)	5
				Time to import (days)	17
✔ **Dealing with construction permits** (rank)	14	**Protecting investors** (rank)	16	Cost to import (US$ per container)	686
Procedures (number)	12	Extent of disclosure index (0-10)	9		
Time (days)	89	Extent of director liability index (0-10)	8	**Enforcing contracts** (rank)	140
Cost (% of income per capita)	43.8	Ease of shareholder suits index (0-10)	4	Procedures (number)	43
		Strength of investor protection index (0-10)	7.0	Time (days)	635
				Cost (% of claim)	27.5
Registering property (rank)	1				
Procedures (number)	2	**Paying taxes** (rank)	6	✔ **Closing a business** (rank)	65
Time (days)	2	Payments (number per year)	14	Time (years)	1.5
Cost (% of property value)	0.0	Time (hours per year)	79	Cost (% of estate)	22
		Total tax rate (% of profit)	14.5	Recovery rate (cents on the dollar)	36.8

SENEGAL

		Sub-Saharan Africa		GNI per capita (US$)	1,040
Ease of doing business (rank)	152	Lower middle income		Population (m)	12.5

Starting a business (rank)	101	**Getting credit** (rank)	152	**Trading across borders** (rank)	67
Procedures (number)	4	Strength of legal rights index (0-10)	3	Documents to export (number)	6
Time (days)	8	Depth of credit information index (0-6)	1	Time to export (days)	11
Cost (% of income per capita)	63.1	Public registry coverage (% of adults)	0.4	Cost to export (US$ per container)	1,098
Minimum capital (% of income per capita)	205.1	Private bureau coverage (% of adults)	0.0	Documents to import (number)	5
				Time to import (days)	14
Dealing with construction permits (rank)	117	**Protecting investors** (rank)	167	Cost to import (US$ per container)	1,940
Procedures (number)	16	Extent of disclosure index (0-10)	6		
Time (days)	210	Extent of director liability index (0-10)	1	**Enforcing contracts** (rank)	148
Cost (% of income per capita)	459.0	Ease of shareholder suits index (0-10)	2	Procedures (number)	44
		Strength of investor protection index (0-10)	3.0	Time (days)	780
				Cost (% of claim)	26.5
Registering property (rank)	167				
Procedures (number)	6	**Paying taxes** (rank)	170	**Closing a business** (rank)	79
Time (days)	122	Payments (number per year)	59	Time (years)	3.0
Cost (% of property value)	20.6	Time (hours per year)	666	Cost (% of estate)	7
		Total tax rate (% of profit)	46.0	Recovery rate (cents on the dollar)	32.0

SERBIA

		Eastern Europe & Central Asia		GNI per capita (US$)	5,990
Ease of doing business (rank)	89	Upper middle income		Population (m)	7.3

Starting a business (rank)	83	**Getting credit** (rank)	15	**Trading across borders** (rank)	74
Procedures (number)	7	Strength of legal rights index (0-10)	8	Documents to export (number)	6
Time (days)	13	Depth of credit information index (0-6)	5	Time to export (days)	12
Cost (% of income per capita)	7.9	Public registry coverage (% of adults)	0.0	Cost to export (US$ per container)	1,398
Minimum capital (% of income per capita)	6.0	Private bureau coverage (% of adults)	100.0	Documents to import (number)	6
				Time to import (days)	14
Dealing with construction permits (rank)	176	**Protecting investors** (rank)	74	Cost to import (US$ per container)	1,559
Procedures (number)	20	Extent of disclosure index (0-10)	7		
Time (days)	279	Extent of director liability index (0-10)	6	**Enforcing contracts** (rank)	94
Cost (% of income per capita)	1,821.4	Ease of shareholder suits index (0-10)	3	Procedures (number)	36
		Strength of investor protection index (0-10)	5.3	Time (days)	635
				Cost (% of claim)	28.9
Registering property (rank)	100				
Procedures (number)	6	**Paying taxes** (rank)	138	✔ **Closing a business** (rank)	86
Time (days)	91	Payments (number per year)	66	Time (years)	2.7
Cost (% of property value)	2.7	Time (hours per year)	279	Cost (% of estate)	23
		Total tax rate (% of profit)	34.0	Recovery rate (cents on the dollar)	29.5

✔ Reforms making it easier to do business   ✘ Reforms making it more difficult to do business

SEYCHELLES

		Sub-Saharan Africa		GNI per capita (US$)	8,480
Ease of doing business (rank)	95	Upper middle income		Population (m)	0.1
Starting a business (rank)	109	**Getting credit** (rank)	152	**Trading across borders** (rank)	36
Procedures (number)	10	Strength of legal rights index (0-10)	4	Documents to export (number)	5
Time (days)	39	Depth of credit information index (0-6)	0	Time to export (days)	17
Cost (% of income per capita)	17.5	Public registry coverage (% of adults)	0.0	Cost to export (US$ per container)	876
Minimum capital (% of income per capita)	0.0	Private bureau coverage (% of adults)	0.0	Documents to import (number)	5
				Time to import (days)	18
Dealing with construction permits (rank)	61	**Protecting investors** (rank)	59	Cost to import (US$ per container)	876
Procedures (number)	20	Extent of disclosure index (0-10)	4		
Time (days)	144	Extent of director liability index (0-10)	8	**Enforcing contracts** (rank)	69
Cost (% of income per capita)	38.0	Ease of shareholder suits index (0-10)	5	Procedures (number)	37
		Strength of investor protection index (0-10)	5.7	Time (days)	720
Registering property (rank)	62			Cost (% of claim)	15.4
Procedures (number)	4	✔ **Paying taxes** (rank)	38		
Time (days)	33	Payments (number per year)	16	**Closing a business** (rank)	183
Cost (% of property value)	7.0	Time (hours per year)	76	Time (years)	NO PRACTICE
		Total tax rate (% of profit)	44.1	Cost (% of estate)	NO PRACTICE
				Recovery rate (cents on the dollar)	0.0

SIERRA LEONE

		Sub-Saharan Africa		GNI per capita (US$)	340
Ease of doing business (rank)	143	Low income		Population (m)	5.7
Starting a business (rank)	61	**Getting credit** (rank)	128	**Trading across borders** (rank)	136
Procedures (number)	6	Strength of legal rights index (0-10)	6	Documents to export (number)	7
Time (days)	12	Depth of credit information index (0-6)	0	Time to export (days)	26
Cost (% of income per capita)	110.7	Public registry coverage (% of adults)	0.0	Cost to export (US$ per container)	1,573
Minimum capital (% of income per capita)	0.0	Private bureau coverage (% of adults)	0.0	Documents to import (number)	7
				Time to import (days)	31
✔ **Dealing with construction permits** (rank)	166	**Protecting investors** (rank)	28	Cost to import (US$ per container)	1,639
Procedures (number)	25	Extent of disclosure index (0-10)	6		
Time (days)	252	Extent of director liability index (0-10)	7	**Enforcing contracts** (rank)	144
Cost (% of income per capita)	343.3	Ease of shareholder suits index (0-10)	6	Procedures (number)	40
		Strength of investor protection index (0-10)	6.3	Time (days)	515
✔ **Registering property** (rank)	169			Cost (% of claim)	149.5
Procedures (number)	7	✔ **Paying taxes** (rank)	159		
Time (days)	86	Payments (number per year)	29	**Closing a business** (rank)	149
Cost (% of property value)	12.2	Time (hours per year)	357	Time (years)	2.6
		Total tax rate (% of profit)	235.6	Cost (% of estate)	42
				Recovery rate (cents on the dollar)	8.4

SINGAPORE

		East Asia & Pacific		GNI per capita (US$)	37,220
Ease of doing business (rank)	1	High income		Population (m)	5.0
Starting a business (rank)	4	**Getting credit** (rank)	6	**Trading across borders** (rank)	1
Procedures (number)	3	Strength of legal rights index (0-10)	10	Documents to export (number)	4
Time (days)	3	Depth of credit information index (0-6)	4	Time to export (days)	5
Cost (% of income per capita)	0.7	Public registry coverage (% of adults)	0.0	Cost to export (US$ per container)	456
Minimum capital (% of income per capita)	0.0	Private bureau coverage (% of adults)	60.8	Documents to import (number)	4
				Time to import (days)	4
Dealing with construction permits (rank)	2	**Protecting investors** (rank)	2	Cost to import (US$ per container)	439
Procedures (number)	11	Extent of disclosure index (0-10)	10		
Time (days)	25	Extent of director liability index (0-10)	9	**Enforcing contracts** (rank)	13
Cost (% of income per capita)	19.7	Ease of shareholder suits index (0-10)	9	Procedures (number)	21
		Strength of investor protection index (0-10)	9.3	Time (days)	150
Registering property (rank)	15			Cost (% of claim)	25.8
Procedures (number)	3	**Paying taxes** (rank)	4		
Time (days)	5	Payments (number per year)	5	**Closing a business** (rank)	2
Cost (% of property value)	2.8	Time (hours per year)	84	Time (years)	0.8
		Total tax rate (% of profit)	25.4	Cost (% of estate)	1
				Recovery rate (cents on the dollar)	91.3

SLOVAK REPUBLIC

		OECD high income		GNI per capita (US$)	16,130
Ease of doing business (rank)	41	High income		Population (m)	5.4
Starting a business (rank)	68	**Getting credit** (rank)	15	**Trading across borders** (rank)	102
Procedures (number)	6	Strength of legal rights index (0-10)	9	Documents to export (number)	6
Time (days)	16	Depth of credit information index (0-6)	4	Time to export (days)	17
Cost (% of income per capita)	1.9	Public registry coverage (% of adults)	2.2	Cost to export (US$ per container)	1,530
Minimum capital (% of income per capita)	22.2	Private bureau coverage (% of adults)	44.5	Documents to import (number)	8
				Time to import (days)	19
Dealing with construction permits (rank)	56	**Protecting investors** (rank)	109	Cost to import (US$ per container)	1,505
Procedures (number)	13	Extent of disclosure index (0-10)	3		
Time (days)	287	Extent of director liability index (0-10)	4	**Enforcing contracts** (rank)	71
Cost (% of income per capita)	12.7	Ease of shareholder suits index (0-10)	7	Procedures (number)	31
		Strength of investor protection index (0-10)	4.7	Time (days)	565
Registering property (rank)	9			Cost (% of claim)	30.0
Procedures (number)	3	**Paying taxes** (rank)	122		
Time (days)	17	Payments (number per year)	31	**Closing a business** (rank)	33
Cost (% of property value)	0.0	Time (hours per year)	257	Time (years)	4.0
		Total tax rate (% of profit)	48.7	Cost (% of estate)	18
				Recovery rate (cents on the dollar)	55.3

SLOVENIA

		OECD high income		GNI per capita (US$)	23,520
Ease of doing business (rank)	42	High income		Population (m)	2.0
✔ **Starting a business** (rank)	28	**Getting credit** (rank)	116	**Trading across borders** (rank)	56
Procedures (number)	2	Strength of legal rights index (0-10)	5	Documents to export (number)	6
Time (days)	6	Depth of credit information index (0-6)	2	Time to export (days)	19
Cost (% of income per capita)	0.0	Public registry coverage (% of adults)	2.7	Cost to export (US$ per container)	710
Minimum capital (% of income per capita)	45.0	Private bureau coverage (% of adults)	0.0	Documents to import (number)	8
				Time to import (days)	17
Dealing with construction permits (rank)	63	**Protecting investors** (rank)	20	Cost to import (US$ per container)	765
Procedures (number)	14	Extent of disclosure index (0-10)	3		
Time (days)	199	Extent of director liability index (0-10)	9	**Enforcing contracts** (rank)	60
Cost (% of income per capita)	85.1	Ease of shareholder suits index (0-10)	8	Procedures (number)	32
		Strength of investor protection index (0-10)	6.7	Time (days)	1,290
✔ **Registering property** (rank)	97			Cost (% of claim)	12.7
Procedures (number)	6	✔ **Paying taxes** (rank)	80		
Time (days)	113	Payments (number per year)	22	**Closing a business** (rank)	38
Cost (% of property value)	2.1	Time (hours per year)	260	Time (years)	2.0
		Total tax rate (% of profit)	35.4	Cost (% of estate)	4
				Recovery rate (cents on the dollar)	50.9

SOLOMON ISLANDS

		East Asia & Pacific		GNI per capita (US$)	910
Ease of doing business (rank)	96	Low income		Population (m)	0.5
Starting a business (rank)	112	✔ **Getting credit** (rank)	89	**Trading across borders** (rank)	86
Procedures (number)	7	Strength of legal rights index (0-10)	8	Documents to export (number)	7
Time (days)	57	Depth of credit information index (0-6)	0	Time to export (days)	24
Cost (% of income per capita)	68.1	Public registry coverage (% of adults)	0.0	Cost to export (US$ per container)	1,023
Minimum capital (% of income per capita)	0.0	Private bureau coverage (% of adults)	0.0	Documents to import (number)	4
				Time to import (days)	21
Dealing with construction permits (rank)	46	**Protecting investors** (rank)	59	Cost to import (US$ per container)	1,237
Procedures (number)	12	Extent of disclosure index (0-10)	3		
Time (days)	62	Extent of director liability index (0-10)	7	**Enforcing contracts** (rank)	108
Cost (% of income per capita)	665.4	Ease of shareholder suits index (0-10)	7	Procedures (number)	37
		Strength of investor protection index (0-10)	5.7	Time (days)	455
Registering property (rank)	173			Cost (% of claim)	78.9
Procedures (number)	10	**Paying taxes** (rank)	51		
Time (days)	297	Payments (number per year)	33	**Closing a business** (rank)	110
Cost (% of property value)	4.9	Time (hours per year)	80	Time (years)	1.0
		Total tax rate (% of profit)	36.4	Cost (% of estate)	38
				Recovery rate (cents on the dollar)	23.4

✔ Reforms making it easier to do business   ✘ Reforms making it more difficult to do business

SOUTH AFRICA

		Sub-Saharan Africa		GNI per capita (US$)		5,770
Ease of doing business (rank)	34	Upper middle income		Population (m)		49.3
Starting a business (rank)	75	**Getting credit** (rank)	2	**Trading across borders** (rank)		149
Procedures (number)	6	Strength of legal rights index (0-10)	9	Documents to export (number)		8
Time (days)	22	Depth of credit information index (0-6)	6	Time to export (days)		30
Cost (% of income per capita)	6.0	Public registry coverage (% of adults)	0.0	Cost to export (US$ per container)		1,531
Minimum capital (% of income per capita)	0.0	Private bureau coverage (% of adults)	54.9	Documents to import (number)		9
				Time to import (days)		35
Dealing with construction permits (rank)	52	**Protecting investors** (rank)	10	Cost to import (US$ per container)		1,807
Procedures (number)	17	Extent of disclosure index (0-10)	8			
Time (days)	174	Extent of director liability index (0-10)	8	**Enforcing contracts** (rank)		85
Cost (% of income per capita)	23.1	Ease of shareholder suits index (0-10)	8	Procedures (number)		30
		Strength of investor protection index (0-10)	8.0	Time (days)		600
Registering property (rank)	91			Cost (% of claim)		33.2
Procedures (number)	6	**Paying taxes** (rank)	24			
Time (days)	24	Payments (number per year)	9	**Closing a business** (rank)		74
Cost (% of property value)	8.8	Time (hours per year)	200	Time (years)		2.0
		Total tax rate (% of profit)	30.5	Cost (% of estate)		18
				Recovery rate (cents on the dollar)		34.4

SPAIN

		OECD high income		GNI per capita (US$)		31,870
Ease of doing business (rank)	49	High income		Population (m)		46.0
Starting a business (rank)	147	**Getting credit** (rank)	46	✔ **Trading across borders** (rank)		54
Procedures (number)	10	Strength of legal rights index (0-10)	6	Documents to export (number)		6
Time (days)	47	Depth of credit information index (0-6)	5	Time to export (days)		9
Cost (% of income per capita)	15.1	Public registry coverage (% of adults)	54.6	Cost to export (US$ per container)		1,221
Minimum capital (% of income per capita)	13.5	Private bureau coverage (% of adults)	10.7	Documents to import (number)		7
				Time to import (days)		10
Dealing with construction permits (rank)	49	**Protecting investors** (rank)	93	Cost to import (US$ per container)		1,221
Procedures (number)	11	Extent of disclosure index (0-10)	5			
Time (days)	233	Extent of director liability index (0-10)	6	**Enforcing contracts** (rank)		52
Cost (% of income per capita)	47.4	Ease of shareholder suits index (0-10)	4	Procedures (number)		39
		Strength of investor protection index (0-10)	5.0	Time (days)		515
Registering property (rank)	54			Cost (% of claim)		17.2
Procedures (number)	4	**Paying taxes** (rank)	71			
Time (days)	18	Payments (number per year)	8	✔ **Closing a business** (rank)		19
Cost (% of property value)	7.1	Time (hours per year)	197	Time (years)		1.0
		Total tax rate (% of profit)	56.5	Cost (% of estate)		11
				Recovery rate (cents on the dollar)		76.3

SRI LANKA

		South Asia		GNI per capita (US$)		1,990
Ease of doing business (rank)	102	Lower middle income		Population (m)		20.3
Starting a business (rank)	34	**Getting credit** (rank)	72	**Trading across borders** (rank)		72
Procedures (number)	4	Strength of legal rights index (0-10)	4	Documents to export (number)		8
Time (days)	35	Depth of credit information index (0-6)	5	Time to export (days)		21
Cost (% of income per capita)	5.4	Public registry coverage (% of adults)	0.0	Cost to export (US$ per container)		715
Minimum capital (% of income per capita)	0.0	Private bureau coverage (% of adults)	18.6	Documents to import (number)		6
				Time to import (days)		19
Dealing with construction permits (rank)	169	**Protecting investors** (rank)	74	Cost to import (US$ per container)		745
Procedures (number)	22	Extent of disclosure index (0-10)	4			
Time (days)	214	Extent of director liability index (0-10)	5	**Enforcing contracts** (rank)		137
Cost (% of income per capita)	1,335.2	Ease of shareholder suits index (0-10)	7	Procedures (number)		40
		Strength of investor protection index (0-10)	5.3	Time (days)		1,318
Registering property (rank)	155			Cost (% of claim)		22.8
Procedures (number)	8	**Paying taxes** (rank)	166			
Time (days)	83	Payments (number per year)	62	**Closing a business** (rank)		43
Cost (% of property value)	5.1	Time (hours per year)	256	Time (years)		1.7
		Total tax rate (% of profit)	64.7	Cost (% of estate)		5
				Recovery rate (cents on the dollar)		47.0

ST. KITTS AND NEVIS

		Latin America & Caribbean		GNI per capita (US$)	10,150
Ease of doing business (rank)	87	Upper middle income		Population (m)	0.05
Starting a business (rank)	55	**Getting credit** (rank)	116	**Trading across borders** (rank)	39
Procedures (number)	7	Strength of legal rights index (0-10)	7	Documents to export (number)	4
Time (days)	19	Depth of credit information index (0-6)	0	Time to export (days)	12
Cost (% of income per capita)	11.3	Public registry coverage (% of adults)	0.0	Cost to export (US$ per container)	850
Minimum capital (% of income per capita)	0.0	Private bureau coverage (% of adults)	0.0	Documents to import (number)	5
				Time to import (days)	13
Dealing with construction permits (rank)	8	**Protecting investors** (rank)	28	Cost to import (US$ per container)	2,138
Procedures (number)	14	Extent of disclosure index (0-10)	4		
Time (days)	67	Extent of director liability index (0-10)	8	**Enforcing contracts** (rank)	115
Cost (% of income per capita)	4.8	Ease of shareholder suits index (0-10)	7	Procedures (number)	47
		Strength of investor protection index (0-10)	6.3	Time (days)	578
Registering property (rank)	160			Cost (% of claim)	20.5
Procedures (number)	6	**Paying taxes** (rank)	98		
Time (days)	81	Payments (number per year)	24	**Closing a business** (rank)	183
Cost (% of property value)	13.3	Time (hours per year)	155	Time (years)	NO PRACTICE
		Total tax rate (% of profit)	52.7	Cost (% of estate)	NO PRACTICE
				Recovery rate (cents on the dollar)	0.0

ST. LUCIA

		Latin America & Caribbean		GNI per capita (US$)	5,190
Ease of doing business (rank)	53	Upper middle income		Population (m)	0.2
Starting a business (rank)	41	**Getting credit** (rank)	89	**Trading across borders** (rank)	105
Procedures (number)	5	Strength of legal rights index (0-10)	8	Documents to export (number)	5
Time (days)	14	Depth of credit information index (0-6)	0	Time to export (days)	14
Cost (% of income per capita)	23.8	Public registry coverage (% of adults)	0.0	Cost to export (US$ per container)	1,700
Minimum capital (% of income per capita)	0.0	Private bureau coverage (% of adults)	0.0	Documents to import (number)	8
				Time to import (days)	18
Dealing with construction permits (rank)	13	**Protecting investors** (rank)	28	Cost to import (US$ per container)	2,745
Procedures (number)	9	Extent of disclosure index (0-10)	4		
Time (days)	139	Extent of director liability index (0-10)	8	**Enforcing contracts** (rank)	165
Cost (% of income per capita)	32.2	Ease of shareholder suits index (0-10)	7	Procedures (number)	47
		Strength of investor protection index (0-10)	6.3	Time (days)	635
Registering property (rank)	77			Cost (% of claim)	37.3
Procedures (number)	6	**Paying taxes** (rank)	45		
Time (days)	16	Payments (number per year)	32	**Closing a business** (rank)	52
Cost (% of property value)	7.4	Time (hours per year)	92	Time (years)	2.0
		Total tax rate (% of profit)	34.0	Cost (% of estate)	9
				Recovery rate (cents on the dollar)	41.5

ST. VINCENT AND THE GRENADINES

		Latin America & Caribbean		GNI per capita (US$)	5,130
Ease of doing business (rank)	75	Upper middle income		Population (m)	0.1
Starting a business (rank)	52	**Getting credit** (rank)	116	**Trading across borders** (rank)	41
Procedures (number)	7	Strength of legal rights index (0-10)	7	Documents to export (number)	5
Time (days)	10	Depth of credit information index (0-6)	0	Time to export (days)	12
Cost (% of income per capita)	21.2	Public registry coverage (% of adults)	0.0	Cost to export (US$ per container)	1,075
Minimum capital (% of income per capita)	0.0	Private bureau coverage (% of adults)	0.0	Documents to import (number)	4
				Time to import (days)	12
Dealing with construction permits (rank)	3	**Protecting investors** (rank)	28	Cost to import (US$ per container)	1,605
Procedures (number)	11	Extent of disclosure index (0-10)	4		
Time (days)	74	Extent of director liability index (0-10)	8	**Enforcing contracts** (rank)	103
Cost (% of income per capita)	7.0	Ease of shareholder suits index (0-10)	7	Procedures (number)	45
		Strength of investor protection index (0-10)	6.3	Time (days)	394
Registering property (rank)	138			Cost (% of claim)	30.3
Procedures (number)	7	**Paying taxes** (rank)	55		
Time (days)	38	Payments (number per year)	32	**Closing a business** (rank)	183
Cost (% of property value)	11.9	Time (hours per year)	111	Time (years)	NO PRACTICE
		Total tax rate (% of profit)	38.7	Cost (% of estate)	NO PRACTICE
				Recovery rate (cents on the dollar)	0.0

✔ Reforms making it easier to do business   ✘ Reforms making it more difficult to do business

SUDAN

Ease of doing business (rank)	154	Sub-Saharan Africa		GNI per capita (US$)			1,230
		Lower middle income		Population (m)			42.3
Starting a business (rank)	121	**Getting credit** (rank)	138	**Trading across borders** (rank)			143
Procedures (number)	10	Strength of legal rights index (0-10)	5	Documents to export (number)			6
Time (days)	36	Depth of credit information index (0-6)	0	Time to export (days)			32
Cost (% of income per capita)	33.6	Public registry coverage (% of adults)	0.0	Cost to export (US$ per container)			2,050
Minimum capital (% of income per capita)	0.0	Private bureau coverage (% of adults)	0.0	Documents to import (number)			6
				Time to import (days)			46
Dealing with construction permits (rank)	139	**Protecting investors** (rank)	154	Cost to import (US$ per container)			2,900
Procedures (number)	19	Extent of disclosure index (0-10)	0				
Time (days)	271	Extent of director liability index (0-10)	6	**Enforcing contracts** (rank)			146
Cost (% of income per capita)	192.2	Ease of shareholder suits index (0-10)	4	Procedures (number)			53
		Strength of investor protection index (0-10)	3.3	Time (days)			810
Registering property (rank)	40			Cost (% of claim)			19.8
Procedures (number)	6	**Paying taxes** (rank)	94				
Time (days)	9	Payments (number per year)	42	**Closing a business** (rank)			183
Cost (% of property value)	3.0	Time (hours per year)	180	Time (years)			NO PRACTICE
		Total tax rate (% of profit)	36.1	Cost (% of estate)			NO PRACTICE
				Recovery rate (cents on the dollar)			0.0

SURINAME

Ease of doing business (rank)	161	Latin America & Caribbean		GNI per capita (US$)			5,676
		Upper middle income		Population (m)			0.5
Starting a business (rank)	171	**Getting credit** (rank)	138	**Trading across borders** (rank)			101
Procedures (number)	13	Strength of legal rights index (0-10)	5	Documents to export (number)			8
Time (days)	694	Depth of credit information index (0-6)	0	Time to export (days)			25
Cost (% of income per capita)	119.9	Public registry coverage (% of adults)	0.0	Cost to export (US$ per container)			995
Minimum capital (% of income per capita)	0.6	Private bureau coverage (% of adults)	0.0	Documents to import (number)			7
				Time to import (days)			25
Dealing with construction permits (rank)	94	**Protecting investors** (rank)	181	Cost to import (US$ per container)			945
Procedures (number)	14	Extent of disclosure index (0-10)	1				
Time (days)	431	Extent of director liability index (0-10)	0	**Enforcing contracts** (rank)			178
Cost (% of income per capita)	88.9	Ease of shareholder suits index (0-10)	5	Procedures (number)			44
		Strength of investor protection index (0-10)	2.0	Time (days)			1,715
Registering property (rank)	168			Cost (% of claim)			37.1
Procedures (number)	6	**Paying taxes** (rank)	34				
Time (days)	197	Payments (number per year)	17	**Closing a business** (rank)			146
Cost (% of property value)	13.8	Time (hours per year)	199	Time (years)			5.0
		Total tax rate (% of profit)	27.9	Cost (% of estate)			30
				Recovery rate (cents on the dollar)			8.7

SWAZILAND

Ease of doing business (rank)	118	Sub-Saharan Africa		GNI per capita (US$)			2,350
		Lower middle income		Population (m)			1.2
Starting a business (rank)	153	**Getting credit** (rank)	46	✔ **Trading across borders** (rank)			147
Procedures (number)	12	Strength of legal rights index (0-10)	6	Documents to export (number)			9
Time (days)	56	Depth of credit information index (0-6)	5	Time to export (days)			18
Cost (% of income per capita)	33.0	Public registry coverage (% of adults)	0.0	Cost to export (US$ per container)			1,754
Minimum capital (% of income per capita)	0.5	Private bureau coverage (% of adults)	35.7	Documents to import (number)			10
				Time to import (days)			27
Dealing with construction permits (rank)	40	✔ **Protecting investors** (rank)	120	Cost to import (US$ per container)			1,849
Procedures (number)	14	Extent of disclosure index (0-10)	2				
Time (days)	116	Extent of director liability index (0-10)	5	**Enforcing contracts** (rank)			170
Cost (% of income per capita)	143.0	Ease of shareholder suits index (0-10)	6	Procedures (number)			40
		Strength of investor protection index (0-10)	4.3	Time (days)			972
Registering property (rank)	156			Cost (% of claim)			56.1
Procedures (number)	9	**Paying taxes** (rank)	52				
Time (days)	44	Payments (number per year)	33	**Closing a business** (rank)			63
Cost (% of property value)	7.1	Time (hours per year)	104	Time (years)			2.0
		Total tax rate (% of profit)	36.8	Cost (% of estate)			15
				Recovery rate (cents on the dollar)			37.6

SWEDEN

		OECD high income		GNI per capita (US$)		48,930
Ease of doing business (rank)	14	High income		Population (m)		9.3
✔ **Starting a business** (rank)	39	**Getting credit** (rank)	72	**Trading across borders** (rank)		7
Procedures (number)	3	Strength of legal rights index (0-10)	5	Documents to export (number)		3
Time (days)	15	Depth of credit information index (0-6)	4	Time to export (days)		8
Cost (% of income per capita)	0.6	Public registry coverage (% of adults)	0.0	Cost to export (US$ per container)		697
Minimum capital (% of income per capita)	14.7	Private bureau coverage (% of adults)	100.0	Documents to import (number)		3
				Time to import (days)		6
Dealing with construction permits (rank)	20	✔ **Protecting investors** (rank)	28	Cost to import (US$ per container)		735
Procedures (number)	8	Extent of disclosure index (0-10)	8			
Time (days)	116	Extent of director liability index (0-10)	4	**Enforcing contracts** (rank)		52
Cost (% of income per capita)	106.5	Ease of shareholder suits index (0-10)	7	Procedures (number)		30
		Strength of investor protection index (0-10)	6.3	Time (days)		508
✔ **Registering property** (rank)	15			Cost (% of claim)		31.2
Procedures (number)	1	**Paying taxes** (rank)	39			
Time (days)	7	Payments (number per year)	2	**Closing a business** (rank)		18
Cost (% of property value)	3.0	Time (hours per year)	122	Time (years)		2.0
		Total tax rate (% of profit)	54.6	Cost (% of estate)		9
				Recovery rate (cents on the dollar)		77.3

SWITZERLAND

		OECD high income		GNI per capita (US$)		67,560
Ease of doing business (rank)	27	High income		Population (m)		7.7
Starting a business (rank)	80	**Getting credit** (rank)	15	**Trading across borders** (rank)		43
Procedures (number)	6	Strength of legal rights index (0-10)	8	Documents to export (number)		4
Time (days)	20	Depth of credit information index (0-6)	5	Time to export (days)		8
Cost (% of income per capita)	2.1	Public registry coverage (% of adults)	0.0	Cost to export (US$ per container)		1,537
Minimum capital (% of income per capita)	27.2	Private bureau coverage (% of adults)	22.3	Documents to import (number)		5
				Time to import (days)		9
Dealing with construction permits (rank)	37	**Protecting investors** (rank)	167	Cost to import (US$ per container)		1,540
Procedures (number)	14	Extent of disclosure index (0-10)	0			
Time (days)	154	Extent of director liability index (0-10)	5	**Enforcing contracts** (rank)		28
Cost (% of income per capita)	51.3	Ease of shareholder suits index (0-10)	4	Procedures (number)		31
		Strength of investor protection index (0-10)	3.0	Time (days)		417
Registering property (rank)	14			Cost (% of claim)		24.0
Procedures (number)	4	**Paying taxes** (rank)	16			
Time (days)	16	Payments (number per year)	19	**Closing a business** (rank)		41
Cost (% of property value)	0.4	Time (hours per year)	63	Time (years)		3.0
		Total tax rate (% of profit)	30.1	Cost (% of estate)		4
				Recovery rate (cents on the dollar)		47.5

SYRIAN ARAB REPUBLIC

		Middle East & North Africa		GNI per capita (US$)		2,410
Ease of doing business (rank)	144	Lower middle income		Population (m)		21.1
✔ **Starting a business** (rank)	134	✔ **Getting credit** (rank)	168	**Trading across borders** (rank)		120
Procedures (number)	7	Strength of legal rights index (0-10)	1	Documents to export (number)		8
Time (days)	13	Depth of credit information index (0-6)	2	Time to export (days)		15
Cost (% of income per capita)	38.1	Public registry coverage (% of adults)	2.2	Cost to export (US$ per container)		1,190
Minimum capital (% of income per capita)	355.1	Private bureau coverage (% of adults)	0.0	Documents to import (number)		9
				Time to import (days)		21
Dealing with construction permits (rank)	134	**Protecting investors** (rank)	109	Cost to import (US$ per container)		1,625
Procedures (number)	26	Extent of disclosure index (0-10)	7			
Time (days)	128	Extent of director liability index (0-10)	5	**Enforcing contracts** (rank)		176
Cost (% of income per capita)	568.4	Ease of shareholder suits index (0-10)	2	Procedures (number)		55
		Strength of investor protection index (0-10)	4.7	Time (days)		872
Registering property (rank)	80			Cost (% of claim)		29.3
Procedures (number)	4	**Paying taxes** (rank)	110			
Time (days)	19	Payments (number per year)	20	**Closing a business** (rank)		95
Cost (% of property value)	27.9	Time (hours per year)	336	Time (years)		4.1
		Total tax rate (% of profit)	42.9	Cost (% of estate)		9
				Recovery rate (cents on the dollar)		27.4

✔ Reforms making it easier to do business   ✘ Reforms making it more difficult to do business

TAIWAN, CHINA

		East Asia & Pacific		GNI per capita (US$)	16,392
Ease of doing business (rank)	33	High income		Population (m)	23.1
✔ **Starting a business** (rank)	24	**Getting credit** (rank)	72	**Trading across borders** (rank)	17
Procedures (number)	6	Strength of legal rights index (0-10)	4	Documents to export (number)	5
Time (days)	15	Depth of credit information index (0-6)	5	Time to export (days)	12
Cost (% of income per capita)	4.1	Public registry coverage (% of adults)	0.0	Cost to export (US$ per container)	645
Minimum capital (% of income per capita)	0.0	Private bureau coverage (% of adults)	90.4	Documents to import (number)	6
				Time to import (days)	12
Dealing with construction permits (rank)	95	**Protecting investors** (rank)	74	Cost to import (US$ per container)	700
Procedures (number)	28	Extent of disclosure index (0-10)	7		
Time (days)	142	Extent of director liability index (0-10)	4	**Enforcing contracts** (rank)	90
Cost (% of income per capita)	100.9	Ease of shareholder suits index (0-10)	5	Procedures (number)	47
		Strength of investor protection index (0-10)	5.3	Time (days)	510
Registering property (rank)	32			Cost (% of claim)	17.7
Procedures (number)	3	✔ **Paying taxes** (rank)	87		
Time (days)	5	Payments (number per year)	17	**Closing a business** (rank)	10
Cost (% of property value)	6.2	Time (hours per year)	269	Time (years)	1.9
		Total tax rate (% of profit)	41.9	Cost (% of estate)	4
				Recovery rate (cents on the dollar)	82.2

TAJIKISTAN

		Eastern Europe & Central Asia		GNI per capita (US$)	700
Ease of doing business (rank)	139	Low income		Population (m)	7.0
✔ **Starting a business** (rank)	136	**Getting credit** (rank)	168	**Trading across borders** (rank)	178
Procedures (number)	8	Strength of legal rights index (0-10)	3	Documents to export (number)	10
Time (days)	27	Depth of credit information index (0-6)	0	Time to export (days)	82
Cost (% of income per capita)	36.9	Public registry coverage (% of adults)	0.0	Cost to export (US$ per container)	3,350
Minimum capital (% of income per capita)	8.5	Private bureau coverage (% of adults)	0.0	Documents to import (number)	9
				Time to import (days)	83
Dealing with construction permits (rank)	178	✔ **Protecting investors** (rank)	59	Cost to import (US$ per container)	4,550
Procedures (number)	30	Extent of disclosure index (0-10)	8		
Time (days)	228	Extent of director liability index (0-10)	3	**Enforcing contracts** (rank)	40
Cost (% of income per capita)	996.1	Ease of shareholder suits index (0-10)	6	Procedures (number)	34
		Strength of investor protection index (0-10)	5.7	Time (days)	430
Registering property (rank)	87			Cost (% of claim)	25.5
Procedures (number)	6	✔ **Paying taxes** (rank)	165		
Time (days)	37	Payments (number per year)	54	**Closing a business** (rank)	64
Cost (% of property value)	5.5	Time (hours per year)	224	Time (years)	1.7
		Total tax rate (% of profit)	86.0	Cost (% of estate)	9
				Recovery rate (cents on the dollar)	37.4

TANZANIA

		Sub-Saharan Africa		GNI per capita (US$)	500
Ease of doing business (rank)	128	Low income		Population (m)	43.7
Starting a business (rank)	122	**Getting credit** (rank)	89	**Trading across borders** (rank)	109
Procedures (number)	12	Strength of legal rights index (0-10)	8	Documents to export (number)	5
Time (days)	29	Depth of credit information index (0-6)	0	Time to export (days)	24
Cost (% of income per capita)	30.9	Public registry coverage (% of adults)	0.0	Cost to export (US$ per container)	1,262
Minimum capital (% of income per capita)	0.0	Private bureau coverage (% of adults)	0.0	Documents to import (number)	7
				Time to import (days)	31
Dealing with construction permits (rank)	179	**Protecting investors** (rank)	93	Cost to import (US$ per container)	1,475
Procedures (number)	22	Extent of disclosure index (0-10)	3		
Time (days)	328	Extent of director liability index (0-10)	4	**Enforcing contracts** (rank)	32
Cost (% of income per capita)	2,756.3	Ease of shareholder suits index (0-10)	8	Procedures (number)	38
		Strength of investor protection index (0-10)	5.0	Time (days)	462
Registering property (rank)	151			Cost (% of claim)	14.3
Procedures (number)	9	**Paying taxes** (rank)	120		
Time (days)	73	Payments (number per year)	48	**Closing a business** (rank)	113
Cost (% of property value)	4.4	Time (hours per year)	172	Time (years)	3.0
		Total tax rate (% of profit)	45.2	Cost (% of estate)	22
				Recovery rate (cents on the dollar)	21.9

THAILAND

		East Asia & Pacific		GNI per capita (US$)		3,760
Ease of doing business (rank)	19	Lower middle income		Population (m)		67.8

Starting a business (rank)	95	**Getting credit** (rank)	72	**Trading across borders** (rank)	12
Procedures (number)	7	Strength of legal rights index (0-10)	4	Documents to export (number)	4
Time (days)	32	Depth of credit information index (0-6)	5	Time to export (days)	14
Cost (% of income per capita)	5.6	Public registry coverage (% of adults)	0.0	Cost to export (US$ per container)	625
Minimum capital (% of income per capita)	0.0	Private bureau coverage (% of adults)	35.7	Documents to import (number)	3
				Time to import (days)	13
Dealing with construction permits (rank)	12	**Protecting investors** (rank)	12	Cost to import (US$ per container)	795
Procedures (number)	11	Extent of disclosure index (0-10)	10		
Time (days)	156	Extent of director liability index (0-10)	7	**Enforcing contracts** (rank)	25
Cost (% of income per capita)	9.5	Ease of shareholder suits index (0-10)	6	Procedures (number)	36
		Strength of investor protection index (0-10)	7.7	Time (days)	479
✗ **Registering property** (rank)	19			Cost (% of claim)	12.3
Procedures (number)	2	✔ **Paying taxes** (rank)	91		
Time (days)	2	Payments (number per year)	23	**Closing a business** (rank)	46
Cost (% of property value)	4.3	Time (hours per year)	264	Time (years)	2.7
		Total tax rate (% of profit)	37.4	Cost (% of estate)	36
				Recovery rate (cents on the dollar)	43.5

TIMOR-LESTE

		East Asia & Pacific		GNI per capita (US$)		543
Ease of doing business (rank)	174	Lower middle income		Population (m)		1.1

Starting a business (rank)	167	**Getting credit** (rank)	182	**Trading across borders** (rank)	91
Procedures (number)	10	Strength of legal rights index (0-10)	1	Documents to export (number)	6
Time (days)	83	Depth of credit information index (0-6)	0	Time to export (days)	25
Cost (% of income per capita)	18.4	Public registry coverage (% of adults)	0.0	Cost to export (US$ per container)	1,010
Minimum capital (% of income per capita)	921.3	Private bureau coverage (% of adults)	0.0	Documents to import (number)	7
				Time to import (days)	26
Dealing with construction permits (rank)	128	**Protecting investors** (rank)	132	Cost to import (US$ per container)	1,015
Procedures (number)	22	Extent of disclosure index (0-10)	3		
Time (days)	208	Extent of director liability index (0-10)	4	✔ **Enforcing contracts** (rank)	183
Cost (% of income per capita)	138.2	Ease of shareholder suits index (0-10)	5	Procedures (number)	51
		Strength of investor protection index (0-10)	4.0	Time (days)	1,285
Registering property (rank)	183			Cost (% of claim)	163.2
Procedures (number)	NO PRACTICE	**Paying taxes** (rank)	20		
Time (days)	NO PRACTICE	Payments (number per year)	6	**Closing a business** (rank)	183
Cost (% of property value)	NO PRACTICE	Time (hours per year)	276	Time (years)	NO PRACTICE
		Total tax rate (% of profit)	0.2	Cost (% of estate)	NO PRACTICE
				Recovery rate (cents on the dollar)	0.0

TOGO

		Sub-Saharan Africa		GNI per capita (US$)		440
Ease of doing business (rank)	160	Low income		Population (m)		6.6

Starting a business (rank)	169	**Getting credit** (rank)	152	**Trading across borders** (rank)	93
Procedures (number)	7	Strength of legal rights index (0-10)	3	Documents to export (number)	6
Time (days)	75	Depth of credit information index (0-6)	1	Time to export (days)	24
Cost (% of income per capita)	178.1	Public registry coverage (% of adults)	0.2	Cost to export (US$ per container)	940
Minimum capital (% of income per capita)	486.9	Private bureau coverage (% of adults)	0.0	Documents to import (number)	8
				Time to import (days)	28
Dealing with construction permits (rank)	152	**Protecting investors** (rank)	147	Cost to import (US$ per container)	963
Procedures (number)	15	Extent of disclosure index (0-10)	6		
Time (days)	277	Extent of director liability index (0-10)	1	**Enforcing contracts** (rank)	151
Cost (% of income per capita)	1,241.9	Ease of shareholder suits index (0-10)	4	Procedures (number)	41
		Strength of investor protection index (0-10)	3.7	Time (days)	588
Registering property (rank)	158			Cost (% of claim)	47.5
Procedures (number)	5	**Paying taxes** (rank)	157		
Time (days)	295	Payments (number per year)	53	**Closing a business** (rank)	84
Cost (% of property value)	13.0	Time (hours per year)	270	Time (years)	3.0
		Total tax rate (% of profit)	50.8	Cost (% of estate)	15
				Recovery rate (cents on the dollar)	30.6

✔ Reforms making it easier to do business ✘ Reforms making it more difficult to do business

TONGA

		East Asia & Pacific		GNI per capita (US$)	3,260
Ease of doing business (rank)	71	Lower middle income		Population (m)	0.1
Starting a business (rank)	30	**Getting credit** (rank)	116	**Trading across borders** (rank)	60
Procedures (number)	4	Strength of legal rights index (0-10)	7	Documents to export (number)	7
Time (days)	25	Depth of credit information index (0-6)	0	Time to export (days)	19
Cost (% of income per capita)	7.0	Public registry coverage (% of adults)	0.0	Cost to export (US$ per container)	650
Minimum capital (% of income per capita)	0.0	Private bureau coverage (% of adults)	0.0	Documents to import (number)	6
				Time to import (days)	24
Dealing with construction permits (rank)	34	**Protecting investors** (rank)	109	Cost to import (US$ per container)	725
Procedures (number)	11	Extent of disclosure index (0-10)	3		
Time (days)	76	Extent of director liability index (0-10)	3	**Enforcing contracts** (rank)	56
Cost (% of income per capita)	269.6	Ease of shareholder suits index (0-10)	8	Procedures (number)	37
		Strength of investor protection index (0-10)	4.7	Time (days)	350
				Cost (% of claim)	30.5
Registering property (rank)	125				
Procedures (number)	4	✔ **Paying taxes** (rank)	31		
Time (days)	108	Payments (number per year)	20	**Closing a business** (rank)	104
Cost (% of property value)	10.2	Time (hours per year)	164	Time (years)	2.7
		Total tax rate (% of profit)	25.5	Cost (% of estate)	22
				Recovery rate (cents on the dollar)	25.3

TRINIDAD AND TOBAGO

		Latin America & Caribbean		GNI per capita (US$)	16,560
Ease of doing business (rank)	97	High income		Population (m)	1.3
Starting a business (rank)	74	**Getting credit** (rank)	32	**Trading across borders** (rank)	51
Procedures (number)	9	Strength of legal rights index (0-10)	8	Documents to export (number)	5
Time (days)	43	Depth of credit information index (0-6)	4	Time to export (days)	14
Cost (% of income per capita)	0.8	Public registry coverage (% of adults)	0.0	Cost to export (US$ per container)	808
Minimum capital (% of income per capita)	0.0	Private bureau coverage (% of adults)	45.2	Documents to import (number)	6
				Time to import (days)	19
Dealing with construction permits (rank)	85	**Protecting investors** (rank)	20	Cost to import (US$ per container)	1,250
Procedures (number)	20	Extent of disclosure index (0-10)	4		
Time (days)	261	Extent of director liability index (0-10)	9	**Enforcing contracts** (rank)	169
Cost (% of income per capita)	5.1	Ease of shareholder suits index (0-10)	7	Procedures (number)	42
		Strength of investor protection index (0-10)	6.7	Time (days)	1,340
				Cost (% of claim)	33.5
Registering property (rank)	171				
Procedures (number)	8	**Paying taxes** (rank)	91		
Time (days)	162	Payments (number per year)	40	**Closing a business** (rank)	183
Cost (% of property value)	7.0	Time (hours per year)	210	Time (years)	NO PRACTICE
		Total tax rate (% of profit)	33.1	Cost (% of estate)	NO PRACTICE
				Recovery rate (cents on the dollar)	0.0

TUNISIA

		Middle East & North Africa		GNI per capita (US$)	3,720
Ease of doing business (rank)	55	Lower middle income		Population (m)	10.4
Starting a business (rank)	48	**Getting credit** (rank)	89	✔ **Trading across borders** (rank)	30
Procedures (number)	10	Strength of legal rights index (0-10)	3	Documents to export (number)	4
Time (days)	11	Depth of credit information index (0-6)	5	Time to export (days)	13
Cost (% of income per capita)	5.0	Public registry coverage (% of adults)	22.9	Cost to export (US$ per container)	773
Minimum capital (% of income per capita)	0.0	Private bureau coverage (% of adults)	0.0	Documents to import (number)	7
				Time to import (days)	17
Dealing with construction permits (rank)	106	**Protecting investors** (rank)	74	Cost to import (US$ per container)	858
Procedures (number)	20	Extent of disclosure index (0-10)	5		
Time (days)	97	Extent of director liability index (0-10)	5	**Enforcing contracts** (rank)	78
Cost (% of income per capita)	858.7	Ease of shareholder suits index (0-10)	6	Procedures (number)	39
		Strength of investor protection index (0-10)	5.3	Time (days)	565
				Cost (% of claim)	21.8
Registering property (rank)	64				
Procedures (number)	4	✔ **Paying taxes** (rank)	58		
Time (days)	39	Payments (number per year)	8	**Closing a business** (rank)	37
Cost (% of property value)	6.1	Time (hours per year)	144	Time (years)	1.3
		Total tax rate (% of profit)	62.8	Cost (% of estate)	7
				Recovery rate (cents on the dollar)	51.7

TURKEY

		Eastern Europe & Central Asia		GNI per capita (US$)	8,730
Ease of doing business (rank)	65	Upper middle income		Population (m)	74.8
Starting a business (rank)	63	**Getting credit** (rank)	72	**Trading across borders** (rank)	76
Procedures (number)	6	Strength of legal rights index (0-10)	4	Documents to export (number)	7
Time (days)	6	Depth of credit information index (0-6)	5	Time to export (days)	14
Cost (% of income per capita)	17.2	Public registry coverage (% of adults)	18.3	Cost to export (US$ per container)	990
Minimum capital (% of income per capita)	9.9	Private bureau coverage (% of adults)	42.2	Documents to import (number)	8
				Time to import (days)	15
Dealing with construction permits (rank)	137	**Protecting investors** (rank)	59	Cost to import (US$ per container)	1,063
Procedures (number)	25	Extent of disclosure index (0-10)	9		
Time (days)	188	Extent of director liability index (0-10)	4	**Enforcing contracts** (rank)	26
Cost (% of income per capita)	231.4	Ease of shareholder suits index (0-10)	4	Procedures (number)	35
		Strength of investor protection index (0-10)	5.7	Time (days)	420
Registering property (rank)	38			Cost (% of claim)	18.8
Procedures (number)	6	**Paying taxes** (rank)	75		
Time (days)	6	Payments (number per year)	15	**Closing a business** (rank)	115
Cost (% of property value)	3.0	Time (hours per year)	223	Time (years)	3.3
		Total tax rate (% of profit)	44.5	Cost (% of estate)	15
				Recovery rate (cents on the dollar)	21.1

UGANDA

		Sub-Saharan Africa		GNI per capita (US$)	460
Ease of doing business (rank)	122	Low income		Population (m)	32.7
✗ **Starting a business** (rank)	137	✔ **Getting credit** (rank)	46	**Trading across borders** (rank)	148
Procedures (number)	18	Strength of legal rights index (0-10)	7	Documents to export (number)	6
Time (days)	25	Depth of credit information index (0-6)	4	Time to export (days)	37
Cost (% of income per capita)	94.4	Public registry coverage (% of adults)	0.0	Cost to export (US$ per container)	2,780
Minimum capital (% of income per capita)	0.0	Private bureau coverage (% of adults)	1.1	Documents to import (number)	8
				Time to import (days)	34
Dealing with construction permits (rank)	133	**Protecting investors** (rank)	132	Cost to import (US$ per container)	2,940
Procedures (number)	18	Extent of disclosure index (0-10)	2		
Time (days)	171	Extent of director liability index (0-10)	5	✔ **Enforcing contracts** (rank)	113
Cost (% of income per capita)	1,287.8	Ease of shareholder suits index (0-10)	5	Procedures (number)	38
		Strength of investor protection index (0-10)	4.0	Time (days)	490
Registering property (rank)	150			Cost (% of claim)	44.9
Procedures (number)	13	**Paying taxes** (rank)	62		
Time (days)	77	Payments (number per year)	32	**Closing a business** (rank)	56
Cost (% of property value)	3.2	Time (hours per year)	161	Time (years)	2.2
		Total tax rate (% of profit)	35.7	Cost (% of estate)	30
				Recovery rate (cents on the dollar)	39.7

UKRAINE

		Eastern Europe & Central Asia		GNI per capita (US$)	2,800
Ease of doing business (rank)	145	Lower middle income		Population (m)	46.0
✔ **Starting a business** (rank)	118	**Getting credit** (rank)	32	**Trading across borders** (rank)	139
Procedures (number)	10	Strength of legal rights index (0-10)	9	Documents to export (number)	6
Time (days)	27	Depth of credit information index (0-6)	3	Time to export (days)	31
Cost (% of income per capita)	6.1	Public registry coverage (% of adults)	0.0	Cost to export (US$ per container)	1,560
Minimum capital (% of income per capita)	2.2	Private bureau coverage (% of adults)	10.1	Documents to import (number)	8
				Time to import (days)	36
✔ **Dealing with construction permits** (rank)	179	**Protecting investors** (rank)	109	Cost to import (US$ per container)	1,580
Procedures (number)	22	Extent of disclosure index (0-10)	5		
Time (days)	374	Extent of director liability index (0-10)	2	**Enforcing contracts** (rank)	43
Cost (% of income per capita)	1,737.6	Ease of shareholder suits index (0-10)	7	Procedures (number)	30
		Strength of investor protection index (0-10)	4.7	Time (days)	345
Registering property (rank)	164			Cost (% of claim)	41.5
Procedures (number)	10	✔ **Paying taxes** (rank)	181		
Time (days)	117	Payments (number per year)	135	**Closing a business** (rank)	150
Cost (% of property value)	4.1	Time (hours per year)	657	Time (years)	2.9
		Total tax rate (% of profit)	55.5	Cost (% of estate)	42
				Recovery rate (cents on the dollar)	7.9

✔ Reforms making it easier to do business   ✗ Reforms making it more difficult to do business

UNITED ARAB EMIRATES

		Middle East & North Africa		GNI per capita (US$)	46,857
Ease of doing business (rank)	40	High income		Population (m)	4.6
Starting a business (rank)	46	✔ **Getting credit** (rank)	72	✔ **Trading across borders** (rank)	3
Procedures (number)	8	Strength of legal rights index (0-10)	4	Documents to export (number)	4
Time (days)	15	Depth of credit information index (0-6)	5	Time to export (days)	7
Cost (% of income per capita)	6.4	Public registry coverage (% of adults)	8.4	Cost to export (US$ per container)	521
Minimum capital (% of income per capita)	0.0	Private bureau coverage (% of adults)	17.7	Documents to import (number)	5
				Time to import (days)	7
Dealing with construction permits (rank)	26	**Protecting investors** (rank)	120	Cost to import (US$ per container)	542
Procedures (number)	17	Extent of disclosure index (0-10)	4		
Time (days)	64	Extent of director liability index (0-10)	7	**Enforcing contracts** (rank)	134
Cost (% of income per capita)	35.8	Ease of shareholder suits index (0-10)	2	Procedures (number)	49
		Strength of investor protection index (0-10)	4.3	Time (days)	537
Registering property (rank)	4			Cost (% of claim)	26.2
Procedures (number)	1	**Paying taxes** (rank)	5		
Time (days)	2	Payments (number per year)	14	**Closing a business** (rank)	143
Cost (% of property value)	2.0	Time (hours per year)	12	Time (years)	5.1
		Total tax rate (% of profit)	14.1	Cost (% of estate)	30
				Recovery rate (cents on the dollar)	11.2

UNITED KINGDOM

		OECD high income		GNI per capita (US$)	41,520
Ease of doing business (rank)	4	High income		Population (m)	61.8
Starting a business (rank)	17	**Getting credit** (rank)	2	**Trading across borders** (rank)	15
Procedures (number)	6	Strength of legal rights index (0-10)	9	Documents to export (number)	4
Time (days)	13	Depth of credit information index (0-6)	6	Time to export (days)	7
Cost (% of income per capita)	0.7	Public registry coverage (% of adults)	0.0	Cost to export (US$ per container)	950
Minimum capital (% of income per capita)	0.0	Private bureau coverage (% of adults)	100.0	Documents to import (number)	4
				Time to import (days)	6
Dealing with construction permits (rank)	16	**Protecting investors** (rank)	10	Cost to import (US$ per container)	1,045
Procedures (number)	11	Extent of disclosure index (0-10)	10		
Time (days)	95	Extent of director liability index (0-10)	7	✔ **Enforcing contracts** (rank)	23
Cost (% of income per capita)	70.9	Ease of shareholder suits index (0-10)	7	Procedures (number)	28
		Strength of investor protection index (0-10)	8.0	Time (days)	399
Registering property (rank)	22			Cost (% of claim)	23.4
Procedures (number)	2	**Paying taxes** (rank)	16		
Time (days)	8	Payments (number per year)	8	✔ **Closing a business** (rank)	7
Cost (% of property value)	4.1	Time (hours per year)	110	Time (years)	1.0
		Total tax rate (% of profit)	37.3	Cost (% of estate)	6
				Recovery rate (cents on the dollar)	88.6

UNITED STATES

		OECD high income		GNI per capita (US$)	47,240
Ease of doing business (rank)	5	High income		Population (m)	307.0
Starting a business (rank)	9	**Getting credit** (rank)	6	**Trading across borders** (rank)	20
Procedures (number)	6	Strength of legal rights index (0-10)	8	Documents to export (number)	4
Time (days)	6	Depth of credit information index (0-6)	6	Time to export (days)	6
Cost (% of income per capita)	1.4	Public registry coverage (% of adults)	0.0	Cost to export (US$ per container)	1,050
Minimum capital (% of income per capita)	0.0	Private bureau coverage (% of adults)	100.0	Documents to import (number)	5
				Time to import (days)	5
Dealing with construction permits (rank)	27	**Protecting investors** (rank)	5	Cost to import (US$ per container)	1,315
Procedures (number)	19	Extent of disclosure index (0-10)	7		
Time (days)	40	Extent of director liability index (0-10)	9	**Enforcing contracts** (rank)	8
Cost (% of income per capita)	12.8	Ease of shareholder suits index (0-10)	9	Procedures (number)	32
		Strength of investor protection index (0-10)	8.3	Time (days)	300
Registering property (rank)	12			Cost (% of claim)	14.4
Procedures (number)	4	✗ **Paying taxes** (rank)	62		
Time (days)	12	Payments (number per year)	11	**Closing a business** (rank)	14
Cost (% of property value)	0.5	Time (hours per year)	187	Time (years)	1.5
		Total tax rate (% of profit)	46.8	Cost (% of estate)	7
				Recovery rate (cents on the dollar)	81.5

URUGUAY

		Latin America & Caribbean		GNI per capita (US$)	9,400
Ease of doing business (rank)	124	Upper middle income		Population (m)	3.3
Starting a business (rank)	139	**Getting credit** (rank)	46	**Trading across borders** (rank)	132
Procedures (number)	11	Strength of legal rights index (0-10)	5	Documents to export (number)	10
Time (days)	65	Depth of credit information index (0-6)	6	Time to export (days)	19
Cost (% of income per capita)	42.1	Public registry coverage (% of adults)	19.4	Cost to export (US$ per container)	1,100
Minimum capital (% of income per capita)	0.0	Private bureau coverage (% of adults)	100.0	Documents to import (number)	10
				Time to import (days)	22
Dealing with construction permits (rank)	141	**Protecting investors** (rank)	93	Cost to import (US$ per container)	1,330
Procedures (number)	30	Extent of disclosure index (0-10)	3		
Time (days)	234	Extent of director liability index (0-10)	4	**Enforcing contracts** (rank)	102
Cost (% of income per capita)	84.5	Ease of shareholder suits index (0-10)	8	Procedures (number)	41
		Strength of investor protection index (0-10)	5.0	Time (days)	720
✔ **Registering property** (rank)	159			Cost (% of claim)	19.0
Procedures (number)	8	**Paying taxes** (rank)	155		
Time (days)	66	Payments (number per year)	53	**Closing a business** (rank)	57
Cost (% of property value)	7.1	Time (hours per year)	336	Time (years)	2.1
		Total tax rate (% of profit)	42.0	Cost (% of estate)	7
				Recovery rate (cents on the dollar)	39.7

UZBEKISTAN

		Eastern Europe & Central Asia		GNI per capita (US$)	1,100
Ease of doing business (rank)	150	Lower middle income		Population (m)	27.8
Starting a business (rank)	106	**Getting credit** (rank)	138	**Trading across borders** (rank)	169
Procedures (number)	7	Strength of legal rights index (0-10)	2	Documents to export (number)	7
Time (days)	15	Depth of credit information index (0-6)	3	Time to export (days)	71
Cost (% of income per capita)	11.9	Public registry coverage (% of adults)	4.5	Cost to export (US$ per container)	3,150
Minimum capital (% of income per capita)	32.5	Private bureau coverage (% of adults)	3.3	Documents to import (number)	9
				Time to import (days)	92
✗ **Dealing with construction permits** (rank)	145	**Protecting investors** (rank)	132	Cost to import (US$ per container)	4,650
Procedures (number)	28	Extent of disclosure index (0-10)	4		
Time (days)	274	Extent of director liability index (0-10)	1	**Enforcing contracts** (rank)	44
Cost (% of income per capita)	67.7	Ease of shareholder suits index (0-10)	7	Procedures (number)	42
		Strength of investor protection index (0-10)	4.0	Time (days)	195
Registering property (rank)	135			Cost (% of claim)	22.2
Procedures (number)	12	**Paying taxes** (rank)	154		
Time (days)	78	Payments (number per year)	44	**Closing a business** (rank)	112
Cost (% of property value)	1.2	Time (hours per year)	205	Time (years)	4.0
		Total tax rate (% of profit)	95.6	Cost (% of estate)	10
				Recovery rate (cents on the dollar)	22.2

VANUATU

		East Asia & Pacific		GNI per capita (US$)	2,620
Ease of doing business (rank)	60	Lower middle income		Population (m)	0.2
Starting a business (rank)	107	**Getting credit** (rank)	72	**Trading across borders** (rank)	142
Procedures (number)	8	Strength of legal rights index (0-10)	9	Documents to export (number)	7
Time (days)	39	Depth of credit information index (0-6)	0	Time to export (days)	26
Cost (% of income per capita)	37.9	Public registry coverage (% of adults)	0.0	Cost to export (US$ per container)	1,565
Minimum capital (% of income per capita)	0.0	Private bureau coverage (% of adults)	0.0	Documents to import (number)	9
				Time to import (days)	30
Dealing with construction permits (rank)	21	**Protecting investors** (rank)	74	Cost to import (US$ per container)	1,465
Procedures (number)	7	Extent of disclosure index (0-10)	5		
Time (days)	51	Extent of director liability index (0-10)	6	**Enforcing contracts** (rank)	76
Cost (% of income per capita)	246.7	Ease of shareholder suits index (0-10)	5	Procedures (number)	30
		Strength of investor protection index (0-10)	5.3	Time (days)	430
Registering property (rank)	108			Cost (% of claim)	74.7
Procedures (number)	2	**Paying taxes** (rank)	19		
Time (days)	188	Payments (number per year)	31	**Closing a business** (rank)	50
Cost (% of property value)	7.0	Time (hours per year)	120	Time (years)	2.6
		Total tax rate (% of profit)	8.4	Cost (% of estate)	38
				Recovery rate (cents on the dollar)	42.7

✔ Reforms making it easier to do business   ✘ Reforms making it more difficult to do business

VENEZUELA, RB

		Latin America & Caribbean		GNI per capita (US$)		10,200
Ease of doing business (rank)	172	Upper middle income		Population (m)		28.4
✘ **Starting a business** (rank)	144	**Getting credit** (rank)	176	**Trading across borders** (rank)		167
Procedures (number)	17	Strength of legal rights index (0-10)	2	Documents to export (number)		8
Time (days)	141	Depth of credit information index (0-6)	0	Time to export (days)		49
Cost (% of income per capita)	30.2	Public registry coverage (% of adults)	0.0	Cost to export (US$ per container)		2,590
Minimum capital (% of income per capita)	0.0	Private bureau coverage (% of adults)	0.0	Documents to import (number)		9
				Time to import (days)		71
Dealing with construction permits (rank)	96	**Protecting investors** (rank)	179	Cost to import (US$ per container)		2,868
Procedures (number)	11	Extent of disclosure index (0-10)	3			
Time (days)	395	Extent of director liability index (0-10)	2	**Enforcing contracts** (rank)		74
Cost (% of income per capita)	227.7	Ease of shareholder suits index (0-10)	2	Procedures (number)		29
		Strength of investor protection index (0-10)	2.3	Time (days)		510
				Cost (% of claim)		43.7
Registering property (rank)	101					
Procedures (number)	8	✔ **Paying taxes** (rank)	178			
Time (days)	47	Payments (number per year)	70	**Closing a business** (rank)		152
Cost (% of property value)	2.2	Time (hours per year)	864	Time (years)		4.0
		Total tax rate (% of profit)	52.6	Cost (% of estate)		38
				Recovery rate (cents on the dollar)		5.9

VIETNAM

		East Asia & Pacific		GNI per capita (US$)		1,010
Ease of doing business (rank)	78	Lower middle income		Population (m)		87.3
✔ **Starting a business** (rank)	100	✔ **Getting credit** (rank)	15	**Trading across borders** (rank)		63
Procedures (number)	9	Strength of legal rights index (0-10)	8	Documents to export (number)		6
Time (days)	44	Depth of credit information index (0-6)	5	Time to export (days)		22
Cost (% of income per capita)	12.1	Public registry coverage (% of adults)	26.4	Cost to export (US$ per container)		555
Minimum capital (% of income per capita)	0.0	Private bureau coverage (% of adults)	0.0	Documents to import (number)		8
				Time to import (days)		21
✔ **Dealing with construction permits** (rank)	62	**Protecting investors** (rank)	173	Cost to import (US$ per container)		645
Procedures (number)	13	Extent of disclosure index (0-10)	6			
Time (days)	194	Extent of director liability index (0-10)	0	**Enforcing contracts** (rank)		31
Cost (% of income per capita)	128.4	Ease of shareholder suits index (0-10)	2	Procedures (number)		34
		Strength of investor protection index (0-10)	2.7	Time (days)		295
				Cost (% of claim)		28.5
Registering property (rank)	43					
Procedures (number)	4	**Paying taxes** (rank)	124			
Time (days)	57	Payments (number per year)	32	**Closing a business** (rank)		124
Cost (% of property value)	0.6	Time (hours per year)	941	Time (years)		5.0
		Total tax rate (% of profit)	33.1	Cost (% of estate)		15
				Recovery rate (cents on the dollar)		18.6

WEST BANK AND GAZA

		Middle East & North Africa		GNI per capita (US$)		1,554
Ease of doing business (rank)	135	Lower middle income		Population (m)		4.0
✘ **Starting a business** (rank)	173	**Getting credit** (rank)	168	✔ **Trading across borders** (rank)		111
Procedures (number)	11	Strength of legal rights index (0-10)	0	Documents to export (number)		6
Time (days)	49	Depth of credit information index (0-6)	3	Time to export (days)		23
Cost (% of income per capita)	93.7	Public registry coverage (% of adults)	5.6	Cost to export (US$ per container)		1,310
Minimum capital (% of income per capita)	211.3	Private bureau coverage (% of adults)	0.0	Documents to import (number)		6
				Time to import (days)		40
Dealing with construction permits (rank)	157	**Protecting investors** (rank)	44	Cost to import (US$ per container)		1,225
Procedures (number)	21	Extent of disclosure index (0-10)	6			
Time (days)	199	Extent of director liability index (0-10)	5	**Enforcing contracts** (rank)		93
Cost (% of income per capita)	1,113.0	Ease of shareholder suits index (0-10)	7	Procedures (number)		44
		Strength of investor protection index (0-10)	6.0	Time (days)		540
				Cost (% of claim)		21.2
Registering property (rank)	76					
Procedures (number)	7	**Paying taxes** (rank)	28			
Time (days)	47	Payments (number per year)	27	**Closing a business** (rank)		183
Cost (% of property value)	0.7	Time (hours per year)	154	Time (years)		NO PRACTICE
		Total tax rate (% of profit)	16.8	Cost (% of estate)		NO PRACTICE
				Recovery rate (cents on the dollar)		0.0

YEMEN, REP.

		Middle East & North Africa			GNI per capita (US$)	1,060
Ease of doing business (rank)	105	Lower middle income			Population (m)	23.6
Starting a business (rank)	57	**Getting credit** (rank)	152		**Trading across borders** (rank)	123
Procedures (number)	6	Strength of legal rights index (0-10)	2		Documents to export (number)	6
Time (days)	12	Depth of credit information index (0-6)	2		Time to export (days)	27
Cost (% of income per capita)	82.1	Public registry coverage (% of adults)	0.3		Cost to export (US$ per container)	1,129
Minimum capital (% of income per capita)	0.0	Private bureau coverage (% of adults)	0.0		Documents to import (number)	9
					Time to import (days)	25
Dealing with construction permits (rank)	50	**Protecting investors** (rank)	132		Cost to import (US$ per container)	1,475
Procedures (number)	15	Extent of disclosure index (0-10)	6			
Time (days)	107	Extent of director liability index (0-10)	4		**Enforcing contracts** (rank)	34
Cost (% of income per capita)	136.6	Ease of shareholder suits index (0-10)	2		Procedures (number)	36
		Strength of investor protection index (0-10)	4.0		Time (days)	520
					Cost (% of claim)	16.5
Registering property (rank)	53					
Procedures (number)	6	**Paying taxes** (rank)	146		**Closing a business** (rank)	90
Time (days)	19	Payments (number per year)	44		Time (years)	3.0
Cost (% of property value)	3.8	Time (hours per year)	248		Cost (% of estate)	8
		Total tax rate (% of profit)	47.8		Recovery rate (cents on the dollar)	28.6

ZAMBIA

		Sub-Saharan Africa			GNI per capita (US$)	970
Ease of doing business (rank)	76	Low income			Population (m)	12.9
✔ **Starting a business** (rank)	57	**Getting credit** (rank)	6		✔ **Trading across borders** (rank)	150
Procedures (number)	6	Strength of legal rights index (0-10)	9		Documents to export (number)	6
Time (days)	18	Depth of credit information index (0-6)	5		Time to export (days)	44
Cost (% of income per capita)	27.9	Public registry coverage (% of adults)	0.0		Cost to export (US$ per container)	2,664
Minimum capital (% of income per capita)	0.0	Private bureau coverage (% of adults)	3.0		Documents to import (number)	8
					Time to import (days)	56
Dealing with construction permits (rank)	158	**Protecting investors** (rank)	74		Cost to import (US$ per container)	3,315
Procedures (number)	17	Extent of disclosure index (0-10)	3			
Time (days)	254	Extent of director liability index (0-10)	6		✔ **Enforcing contracts** (rank)	86
Cost (% of income per capita)	2,454.2	Ease of shareholder suits index (0-10)	7		Procedures (number)	35
		Strength of investor protection index (0-10)	5.3		Time (days)	471
					Cost (% of claim)	38.7
Registering property (rank)	83					
Procedures (number)	5	**Paying taxes** (rank)	37		**Closing a business** (rank)	97
Time (days)	40	Payments (number per year)	37		Time (years)	2.7
Cost (% of property value)	6.6	Time (hours per year)	132		Cost (% of estate)	9
		Total tax rate (% of profit)	16.1		Recovery rate (cents on the dollar)	27.2

ZIMBABWE

		Sub-Saharan Africa			GNI per capita (US$)	375
Ease of doing business (rank)	157	Low income			Population (m)	12.5
✔ **Starting a business** (rank)	143	**Getting credit** (rank)	128		**Trading across borders** (rank)	168
Procedures (number)	9	Strength of legal rights index (0-10)	6		Documents to export (number)	7
Time (days)	90	Depth of credit information index (0-6)	0		Time to export (days)	53
Cost (% of income per capita)	182.8	Public registry coverage (% of adults)	0.0		Cost to export (US$ per container)	3,280
Minimum capital (% of income per capita)	0.0	Private bureau coverage (% of adults)	0.0		Documents to import (number)	9
					Time to import (days)	73
Dealing with construction permits (rank)	172	**Protecting investors** (rank)	120		Cost to import (US$ per container)	5,101
Procedures (number)	17	Extent of disclosure index (0-10)	8			
Time (days)	1,012	Extent of director liability index (0-10)	1		**Enforcing contracts** (rank)	110
Cost (% of income per capita)	8,020.6	Ease of shareholder suits index (0-10)	4		Procedures (number)	38
		Strength of investor protection index (0-10)	4.3		Time (days)	410
					Cost (% of claim)	113.1
Registering property (rank)	82					
Procedures (number)	5	✔ **Paying taxes** (rank)	131		**Closing a business** (rank)	156
Time (days)	31	Payments (number per year)	49		Time (years)	3.3
Cost (% of property value)	8.5	Time (hours per year)	242		Cost (% of estate)	22
		Total tax rate (% of profit)	40.3		Recovery rate (cents on the dollar)	0.2

Acknowledgments

Contact details for local partners are available on the Doing Business website at http://www.doingbusiness.org

Doing Business 2011 was prepared by a team led by Sylvia Solf, Penelope Brook (through May 2010) and Neil Gregory (from June 2010) under the general direction of Janamitra Devan. The team comprised Svetlana Bagaudinova, Jose Becerra Marta, Karim O. Belayachi, Frederic Bustelo, César Chaparro Yedro, Maya Choueiri, Santiago Croci Downes, Karen Sarah Cuttaree, Marie Delion, Allen Dennis, Jacqueline den Otter, Raian Divanbeigi, Alejandro Espinosa-Wang, Antonio Garcia Cueto, Carolin Geginat, Cemile Hacibeyoglu, Betina Hennig, Sabine Hertveldt, Mikiko Imai Ollison, Ludmila Januan, Nan Jiang, Palarp Jumpasut, Dahlia Khalifa, Eugenia Levine, Jean Michel Lobet, Valerie Marechal, Andres Martinez, Frederic Meunier, Alexandra Mincu, Robert Murillo, Joanna Nasr, Titilayo Oke, Oleksandr Olshanskyy, Dana Omran, Caroline Otonglo, Yara Salem, Pilar Salgado-Otónel, Jayashree Srinivasan, Susanne Szymanski, Tea Trumbic, Marina Turlakova and Lior Ziv. Koichi Ito, Lizhi Liu, Junko Miyazaki, Janet Morris, Di Wang and Bryan Welsh assisted in the months prior to publication.

The online service of the *Doing Business* database is managed by Ramin Aliyev, Preeti Endlaw, Felipe Iturralde Escudero, Graeme Littler, Kunal H. Patel, Vinod Thottikkatu and Hashim Zia. The *Doing Business 2011* report media and marketing strategy is managed by Nadine Ghannam. The events and road-show strategy is managed by Jamile Ramadan. All knowledge management and outreach activities are under the direction and guidance of Suzanne Smith.

The *Doing Business* team is grateful for valuable comments provided by colleagues across the World Bank Group and for the guidance of World Bank Group Executive Directors.

Oliver Hart and Andrei Shleifer provided academic advice on the project. The paying taxes project was conducted in collaboration with PricewaterhouseCoopers, led by Robert Morris. The development of the getting electricity indicators was financed by the Norwegian Trust Fund.

Alison Strong copyedited the manuscript. Gerry Quinn designed the report and the graphs. Alexandra Quinn and Karen Jackson provided desktopping services.

The report was made possible by the generous contributions of more than 8,200 lawyers, accountants, judges, business-people and public officials in 183 economies.[1] Global and regional contributors are firms that have completed multiple surveys in their various offices around the world.

Quotations in this report are from *Doing Business* local partners unless otherwise indicated. The names of those wishing to be acknowledged individually are listed below. Contact details are posted on the *Doing Business* website at http://www.doingbusiness.org.

1. The team regrets the loss of Courtney Fowler, who passed away in 2010. A partner at PricewaterhouseCoopers, Ms. Fowler had contributed to the paying taxes indicators since their introduction in *Doing Business 2006* and oversaw surveys for several Central Asian economies.

GLOBAL CONTRIBUTORS

Allen & Overy LLP

Baker & McKenzie

Cleary Gottlieb Steen & Hamilton LLP

Ius Laboris, Alliance of Labor, Employment, Benefits and Pensions Law Firms

KPMG

Law Society of England and Wales

Lex Mundi, Association of Independent Law Firms

Noronha Advogados

Panalpina

PricewaterhouseCoopers

PricewaterhouseCoopers Legal Services

Russell Bedford International

SDV International Logistics

Toboc Inc.

REGIONAL CONTRIBUTORS

Adora Group (Freightnet)

APL

A.P. Moller-Maersk Group

BNT

Consortium of European Building Control

Federación Interamericana de la Industria de la Construcción

García & Bodán

Globalink Transportation & Logistics Worldwide LLP

Grata Law Firm

IKRP Rokas & Partners

Manica Africa Pty. Ltd.

Talal Abu-Ghazaleh Legal (TAG-Legal)

Transunion International

AFGHANISTAN

Khan Afzal
Da Afghanistan Bank

Naseem Akbar
AISA

Katherine Blanchette
Deloitte Consulting LLP

Jay Doeden
Deloitte Consulting LLP

Oliver Dziggel
Deloitte Consulting LLP

Abdul Wassay Haqiqi
Haqiqi Legal Services

Saduddin Haziq
Afghan United Bank

Rashid Ibrahim
A.F. Ferguson & Co.

Gaurav Lekh Raj Kukreja
Afghan Container Transport Company

Richard Laliberte
Deloitte Consulting LLP

Tali Mohammed
Afghanistan Investment Support Agency

Wahidulla Qais
NRC

Mudassir Rizwan
PricewaterhouseCoopers

Richard Scarth
Property Consulting Afghanistan

Mirza Taqi Ud-Din Ahmad
PricewaterhouseCoopers

ALBANIA

Erjola Aliaj
IKRP Rokas & Partners

Artur Asllani
Tonucci & Partners Albania Sh.p.k

Sabina Baboci
Kalo & Associates

BALFIN sh.p.k, Balkan Finance Investment Group

Indrit Banka
Bank of Albania

Ledia Beçi
Hoxha, Memi & Hoxha

Alban Bello
IKRP Rokas & Partners

Jona Bica
Kalo & Associates

Emiliano Bicaku
Bozo & Associates Law Firm

Juna Bozdo
Bank of Albania

Artan Bozo
Bozo & Associates Law Firm

Peter Burnie
PricewaterhouseCoopers

Alban Caushi
Kalo & Associates

Dorian Collaku
Bank of Albania

Ilir Daci
OPTIMA Legal and Financial

Sajmir Dautaj
Tonucci & Partners Albania Sh.p.k

Distribution System Operator Albanian Power Cooperation

Dael Dervishi
OPTIMA Legal and Financial

Eniana Dupi
AECO consulting

Sokol Elmazaj
Boga & Associates

Sokol Elmazaj
Boga & Associates

Lorena Gega
PricewaterhouseCoopers

Aurela Gjokutaj
Al-Tax Studio

Eduart Gjokutaj
Al-Tax Studio

Valbona Gjonçari
Boga & Associates

Anjeza Harizaj
Bank of Albania

Emel Haxhillari
Kalo & Associates

Shpati Hoxha
Hoxha, Memi & Hoxha

Oltjan Hoxholli
Kalo & Associates

Ilir Johollari
Hoxha, Memi & Hoxha

Renata Leka
Boga & Associates

ManeTCI (Mane Trading Construction & Investment)

Aigest Milo
Kalo & Associates

Lorenc Nele
Bozo & Associates Law Firm

Kostanca Papa
Bozo & Associates Law Firm

Loreta Peci
PricewaterhouseCoopers

Florian Piperi
OPTIMA Legal and Financial

Kristaq Profkola
Boga & Associates

Andi Qinam
OPTIMA Legal and Financial

Laura Qorlaze
PricewaterhouseCoopers

Artila Rama
Boga & Associates

Ermira Rapushi
Bozo & Associates Law Firm

Enkelejd Seitllari
Kalo & Associates

Ardjana Shehi
Kalo & Associates

Besa Tauzi
Boga & Associates

Ketrin Topciu
Bozo & Associates Law Firm

Fioralba Trebicka
Hoxha, Memi & Hoxha

Gerhard Velaj
Boga & Associates

Silva Velaj
Boga & Associates

Zamira Xhaferri
IKRP Rokas & Partners

Stefan Xhillari
Kalo & Associates

Selena Ymeri
Hoxha, Memi & Hoxha

Enida Zeneli
Bozo & Associates Law Firm

ALGERIA

Branka Achari-Djokic
Banque d'Algérie

Mohammed Salim Azzouz
Deramchi & Azzouz - Russell Bedford International

Khodja Bachir
SNC Khodja & Co.

Nabil Belloula
Cabinet Belloula

Tayeb Belloula
Cabinet Belloula

Samir Benslimane
Cabinet Benslimane

Adnane Bouchaib
Bouchaib Law Firm

Abdelkader Boussourdi
Société Distribution de l'Electricité et du Gaz d'Alger (SDA)

Abdallah Deramchi
Russell Bedford International

Mohamed Riad Deramchi
Deramchi & Azzouz - Russell Bedford International

Asmaa El Ouazzani
Landwell & Associés - PricewaterhouseCoopers Legal Services

Brahim Embouazza
MCDConsulting

Mohamed El-Amine Haddad
Cabinet Avocat Amine Haddad

Sakina Haddad
Crédit Populaire d'Algerie

Goussanem Khaled
Law Firm Goussanem & Aloui

Karine Lasne
Landwell & Associés - PricewaterhouseCoopers Legal Services

Adnane Merad
Etude de Me Kaddour Merad

Mohamed Mokrane
Ministère des Finances, Direction Generale du Domaine National

Dib Said
Banque d'Algérie

Aloui Salima
Law Firm Goussanem & Aloui

Benabid Mohammed Tahar
Cabinet Mohammed Tahar Benabid

Hassan Yassine
Thompson & Knight LLP

Nabiha Zerigui
Cabinet d'Avocats Samir Hamouda correspondent of PricewaterhouseCoopers

ANGOLA

José Rodrigues Alentejo
Câmara de Comércio e Indústria de Angola

Suely Odete Moreira Arcanjo
AVM Advogados

Fernando Barros
PricewaterhouseCoopers

Pedro Calixto
PricewaterhouseCoopers

Anacleta Cipriano
Faria de Bastos, Sebastião e Lopes - Advogados Associados

Miguel de Avillez Pereira
Abreu Advogados

Joao de Freitas e Costa
Abreu Advogados

Myline Dias
PricewaterhouseCoopers

Alexandre Patrício Fernandes
PricewaterhouseCoopers

Brian Glazier
EDI Architecture Inc.

Victor Leonel
Ordem dos Arquitectos

Paulette Lopes
Faria de Bastos, Sebastião e Lopes - Advogados Associados

Teresinha Lopes
Faria de Bastos, Sebastião e Lopes - Advogados Associados

Josephine Matambo
KPMG

Janota Nzogi
EDEL-EP

Walter Paixão
PricewaterhouseCoopers

Jorge Leão Peres
Banco Nacional de Angola

Elisa Rangel Nunes
ERN Advogados

Víctor Anjos Santos
AVM Advogados

N'Gunu Tiny
CFRA Advogados Associados

ANTIGUA AND BARBUDA

Hastin Barnes
Antigua Public Utilities Authority

Vernon Bird
Land Registry

Neil Coates
PRICEWATERHOUSECOOPERS

Nicolette Doherty
NICOLETTE M. DOHERTY ATTORNEY AT LAW AND NOTARY PUBLIC

Brian D'Ornellas
OBM INTERNATIONAL

Vernon Edwards Jr.
FREIGHT FORWARDING & DECONSOLIDATING

Ann Henry
HENRY & BURNETTE

Jefferson Hunte
PRICEWATERHOUSECOOPERS

Alfred McKelly James
JAMES & ASSOCIATES

Hugh C. Marshall
MARSHALL & CO.

Victor Meade
ANTIGUA PUBLIC UTILITIES AUTHORITY

Septimus A. Rhudd
RHUDD & ASSOCIATES

Stacy A. Richards-Anjo
RICHARDS & CO.

Alice N. Roberts
ROBERTS & CO.

Lestroy Samuel
ANTIGUA AND BARBUDA INVESTMENT AUTHORITY

Sharon Simmons
LAND REGISTRY

Patricia Simon-Forde
CHAMBERS PATRICIA SIMON-FORDE

Arthur Thomas
THOMAS, JOHN & CO.

Charles Walwyn
PRICEWATERHOUSECOOPERS

ARGENTINA

María Victoria Abudara
M. & M. BOMCHIL

Fernando Aguinaga
ZANG, BERGEL & VIÑES ABOGADOS

María Agustina Vítolo
VITOLO ABOGADOS

Dolores Aispuru
PRICEWATERHOUSECOOPERS

Carlos Alfaro
ALFARO ABOGADOS

Lisandro A. Allende
BRONS & SALAS ABOGADOS

María Florencia Angélico
CANOSA ABOGADOS

Ignacio E. Aramburu
RATTAGAN, MACCHIAVELLO AROCENA & PEÑA ROBIROSA ABOGADOS

Tomás M. Araya
M. & M. BOMCHIL

Vanesa Balda
VITALE, MANOFF & FEILBOGEN

Ricardo Balestra
M. & M. BOMCHIL

Gonzalo Carlos Ballester
J.P. O'FARRELL ABOGADOS

Federico Martín Basile
M. & M. BOMCHIL

Gabriela Bindi
ZANG, BERGEL & VIÑES ABOGADOS

Sebastián Bittner
JEBSEN & CO.

Pilar Etcheverry Boneo
MARVAL, O'FARRELL & MAIRAL, member of LEX MUNDI

Julieta Bontempi
ESTUDIO BECCAR VARELA

Matias Borderes
FORTUNATI & ASOCIADOS

Ignacio Fernández Borzese
LUNA REQUENA & FERNÁNDEZ BORZESE TAX LAW FIRM

Mariano Bourdieu
SEVERGNINI ROBIOLA GRINBERG & LARRECHEA

Ivan Burin
ZANG, BERGEL & VIÑES ABOGADOS

Adriana Estefanía Camaño
CANOSA ABOGADOS

Javier Canosa
CANOSA ABOGADOS

Federico Carenzo
LEONHARDT, DIETL, GRAF & VON DER FECHT

Mariano E. Carricart
FORNIELES LAW FIRM

Gustavo Casir
QUATTRINI, LAPRIDA & ASOCIADOS

Agustín Castro Bravo
ESTUDIO BECCAR VARELA

Pablo L. Cavallaro
ESTUDIO CAVALLARO ABOGADOS

Nicolas Cesario
QUATTRINI, LAPRIDA & ASOCIADOS

Jimena Congo
PRICEWATERHOUSECOOPERS

Roberto H. Crouzel
ESTUDIO BECCAR VARELA

Valeria D'Alessandro
MARVAL, O'FARRELL & MAIRAL, member of LEX MUNDI

Ángeles del Prado
ZANG, BERGEL & VIÑES ABOGADOS

Oscar Alberto del Río
CENTRAL BANK OF ARGENTINA

Leonardo Damián Diaz
PRICEWATERHOUSECOOPERS

Marcelo Dinocco
PRICEWATERHOUSECOOPERS

Andrés Edelstein
PRICEWATERHOUSECOOPERS

Mercedes Escriña
QUATTRINI, LAPRIDA & ASOCIADOS

Juan M. Espeso
JEBSEN & CO.

Diego Etchepare
PRICEWATERHOUSECOOPERS

Alejandro D. Fiuza
MARVAL, O'FARRELL & MAIRAL, member of LEX MUNDI

Ignacio Funes de Rioja
FUNES DE RIOJA & ASOCIADOS, MEMBER OF IUS LABORIS

Gianluca Galeotti
M. & M. BOMCHIL

Manuel Garford Nuñez
ALFARO ABOGADOS

Javier M. Gattó Bicain
CANDIOTI GATTO BICAIN & OCANTOS

Giselle Rita Geuna
ALFARO ABOGADOS

Mariano Gonzalez
GONZALEZ & FERRARO MILA

Pablo González del Solar
PRICEWATERHOUSECOOPERS

Matías Grinberg
SEVERGNINI ROBIOLA GRINBERG & LARRECHEA

Eduardo Guglielmini
EDUARDO GUGLIELMINI

Sandra S. Guillan
DE DIOS & GOYENA ABOGADOS CONSULTORES

Daniel Intile
DANIEL INTILE & ASSOC., MEMBER OF RUSSELL BEDFORD INTERNATIONAL

Martín Jebsen
JEBSEN & CO.

Santiago Laclau
MARVAL, O'FARRELL & MAIRAL, member of LEX MUNDI

Francisco Lagger
SEVERGNINI ROBIOLA GRINBERG & LARRECHEA

Bastiana Locurscio
RATTAGAN, MACCHIAVELLO AROCENA & PEÑA ROBIROSA ABOGADOS

Dolores Madueño
JEBSEN & CO.

Rodrigo Marchan
GYPM

Patricio Martin
M. & M. BOMCHIL

Pablo Mastromarino
ESTUDIO BECCAR VARELA

Pedro Mazer
ALFARO ABOGADOS

Sean McCormick
SEVERGNINI ROBIOLA GRINBERG & LARRECHEA

Julian Melis
CANDIOTI GATTO BICAIN & OCANTOS

José Oscar Mira
CENTRAL BANK OF ARGENTINA

Jorge Miranda
CLIPPERS S.A.

Francisco Molinari
PRICEWATERHOUSECOOPERS

Enrique Monsegur
CLIPPERS S.A.

Mariana Morelli
ALFARO ABOGADOS

Natalia Virginia Muller
DE DIOS & GOYENA ABOGADOS CONSULTORES

Miguel P. Murray
MURRAY, D´ANDRÉ & SIRITO DE ZAVALÍA

Pablo Murray
FIORITO MURRAY & DIAZ CORDERO

Damián Mauricio Najenson
ESTUDIO SPOTA

Alfredo Miguel O'Farrell
MARVAL, O'FARRELL & MAIRAL, member of LEX MUNDI

Hernan Papa
ALFARO ABOGADOS

Gustavo Papeschi
ESTUDIO BECCAR VARELA

Mariano Payaslian
GYPM

Javier Martín Petrantonio
M. & M. BOMCHIL

Alejandro Poletto
FORTUNATI & ASOCIADOS

José Miguel Puccinelli
ESTUDIO BECCAR VARELA

Julio Alberto Pueyrredón
PRICEWATERHOUSECOOPERS

Federico José Reibestein
REIBESTEIN ASOCIADOS

Sebastián Rodrigo
ALFARO ABOGADOS

Ignacio Rodriguez
PRICEWATERHOUSECOOPERS

Rocio Rojas Iglesias
FORTUNATI & ASOCIADOS

Juan Rosolen
VITOLO ABOGADOS

Mariana Sanchez
QUATTRINI, LAPRIDA & ASOCIADOS

Jorge Sanchez Diaz
ECOBAMBOO S.A.

Esteban Aguirre Saravia
LUNA REQUENA & FERNÁNDEZ BORZESE TAX LAW FIRM

Florencia Saviotti
CANOSA ABOGADOS

Rocío Soriano
M. & M. BOMCHIL

Adolfo Tombolini
DANIEL INTILE & ASSOC., MEMBER OF RUSSELL BEDFORD INTERNATIONAL

Martín Torres Girotti
M. & M. BOMCHIL

Marcelo Torterola
QUATTRINI, LAPRIDA & ASOCIADOS

Pablo Trevisán
ESTUDIO TREVISÁN

María Paola Trigiani
ALFARO ABOGADOS

Agustin Waisman
FORTUNATI & ASOCIADOS

Silvana Wasersztrom
ZANG, BERGEL & VIÑES ABOGADOS

Carolina Zang
ZANG, BERGEL & VIÑES ABOGADOS

Saúl Zang
ZANG, BERGEL & VIÑES ABOGADOS

Joaquín Emilio Zappa
J.P. O'FARRELL ABOGADOS

Carlos Zima
PRICEWATERHOUSECOOPERS

Sofia Zuloaga
RATTAGAN, MACCHIAVELLO AROCENA & PEÑA ROBIROSA ABOGADOS

ARMENIA

Armen L. Alaverdyan
STATE REVENUE COMMITTEE OF THE GOVERNMENT OF THE REPUBLIC OF ARMENIA

Artak Arzoyan
ACRA CREDIT BUREAU

Sedrak Asatryan
CONCERN-DIALOG LAW FIRM

Inessa Avzhiyan
GLOBAL SPC

Sayad S. Badalyan
INVESTMENT LAW GROUP LLC

Anna Baghdasaryan
TER-TACHATYAN LEGAL AND BUSINESS CONSULTING

Seda Baghdasaryan
GLOBAL SPC

Vardan Bezhanyan
LAW FACULTY, YEREVAN STATE UNIVERSITY

Hovhannes Burmanyan
CORPORATE INTEGRAL SOLUTIONS LLC

Paul Cooper
PRICEWATERHOUSECOOPERS

Kristina Dudukchyan
KPMG

Aikanush Edigaryan
TRANS-ALLIANCE

Samvel Gevorgyan
BSC LLC

Shoghik Gharibyan
KPMG

Hayk Ghazazyan
KPMG

Narek Grigoryan
STATE COMMITTEE OF THE REAL PROPERTY CADASTRE

Sargis Grigoryan
GPARTNERS

Sargis H. Martirosyan
TRANS-ALLIANCE

Armine Hakobyan
GLOBAL SPC

Davit Harutyunyan
PRICEWATERHOUSECOOPERS

Isabella Hovhannisyan
INVESTMENT LAW GROUP LLC

Davit Iskandarian
HSBC BANK ARMENIA CJSC

Paruyr Jangulyan
MINISTRY OF ECONOMY OF ARMENIA

Vahe G. Kakoyan
INVESTMENT LAW GROUP LLC

Ishkhan Karapetyan
SMALL & MEDIUM ENTREPRENURSHIP DEVELOPMENT NATIONAL CENTER OF ARMENIA

Gurgen Migranovich Minasyan
UNION OF BUILDERS OF ARMENIA

Ani Mkrtchian
GLOBAL SPC

Nerses Nersisyan
PRICEWATERHOUSECOOPERS

Marianna Nikoghosyan
GLOBAL SPC

Aram Orbelyan
CONCERN-DIALOG LAW FIRM

Naira Petrosyan
PARADIGMA ARMENIA' CJSC

Vahe Petrosyan
LOGICON DEVELOPMENT LLC

Apetnak Poghosyan
CORPORATE INTEGRAL SOLUTIONS LLC

Aram Poghosyan
GRANT THORNTON LEGAL & TAX LLC

Aida Saribekyan
GLOBAL SPC

Artak Shaboyan
STATE REVENUE COMMITTEE OF THE GOVERNMENT OF THE REPUBLIC OF ARMENIA

Guzh Sinanyan
GLOBAL SPC

Hakob Tadevosyan
GRANT THORNTON LEGAL & TAX LLC

Artur Tunyan
JUDICIAL REFORM PROJECT

Tigran Yedigaryan
CONVERSE BANK CJSC

Liana Yordanyan
TER-TACHATYAN LEGAL AND BUSINESS CONSULTING

Anush Zadoyan
GLOBAL SPC

Samuel Zakarian
GLOBAL SPC

Arman Zargaryan
STATE REVENUE COMMITTEE OF THE GOVERNMENT OF THE REPUBLIC OF ARMENIA

AUSTRALIA

Paul Agnew
MCKAYS SOLICITORS

Elizabeth Allen
PRICEWATERHOUSECOOPERS

Matthew Allison
VEDA ADVANTAGE

Lynda Brumm
PRICEWATERHOUSECOOPERS

David Buda
RBHM COMMERCIAL LAWYERS

Alicia Castillo
ALICIA CASTILLO WEALTHING GROUP

Joe Catanzariti
CLAYTON UTZ, MEMBER OF LEX MUNDI

Gaibrielle Cleary
GOULD RALPH PTY LTD, MEMBER OF RUSSELL BEDFORD INTERNATIONAL

Michael Cooper
GADENS LAWYERS

Tim Cox
PRICEWATERHOUSECOOPERS

Kathryn Dent
GADENS LAWYERS

Lisa Dounis
PRICEWATERHOUSECOOPERS

Ian Farmer
PRICEWATERHOUSECOOPERS

Brett Feltham
PRICEWATERHOUSECOOPERS

Joan Fitzhenry
BAKER & MCKENZIE

Mark Geniale
OFFICE OF STATE REVENUE, NSW TREASURY

Mark Grdovich
BLAKE DAWSON

Benjamin Harris
PRICEWATERHOUSECOOPERS

Jason Henniker
ENERGYAUSTRALIA

Eva Hucker
BAKER & MCKENZIE

Ian Humphreys
BLAKE DAWSON

David Lipworth
PRICEWATERHOUSECOOPERS

John Lobban
BLAKE DAWSON

Tim Manefield
PRICEWATERHOUSECOOPERS

Anna Manthopoulos
CHANG, PISTILLI & SIMMONS

John Martin
THOMSON PLAYFORD

Louise Massey
PRICEWATERHOUSECOOPERS

Christie McGregor
PRICEWATERHOUSECOOPERS

Kylie McPherson
MARQUE LAWYERS

Louise Murphy
MARQUE LAWYERS

Matthew Nelson
PRICEWATERHOUSECOOPERS

Stephanie Newton
PRICEWATERHOUSECOOPERS

Carly Neylan
GADENS LAWYERS

Maja Osterman
BLAKE DAWSON

Kylie Parker
LOGICCA CHARTERED ACCOUNTANTS

Enjel Phoon
MARQUE LAWYERS

Malcolm Pickford
ENERGYAUSTRALIA

Mark Pistilli
CHANG, PISTILLI & SIMMONS

Greg Ralph
GOULD RALPH PTY LTD, MEMBER OF RUSSELL BEDFORD INTERNATIONAL

Bob Ronai
IMPORT-EXPORT SERVICES PTY. LTD.

Claus Schmidt
PANALPINA GULF

Nicholas Sedgwick
MARQUE LAWYERS

Damian Sturzaker
MARQUE LAWYERS

Simon Truskett
CLAYTON UTZ, MEMBER OF LEX MUNDI

David Twigg
ENERGYAUSTRALIA

Nicholas Vesic
MARQUE LAWYERS

Peter Walker
FERRIER HODGSON LIMITED

Andrew Wheeler
PRICEWATERHOUSECOOPERS

Radhika Withana
BAKER & MCKENZIE

Mandi Xu
PRICEWATERHOUSECOOPERS

AUSTRIA

AUSTRIAN REGULATORY AGENCY

Georg Bahn
FRESHFIELDS BRUCKHAUS DERINGER

Georg Brandstetter
BRANDSTETTER PRITZ & PARTNER

Doris Buxbaum
BINDER GRÖSSWANG RECHTSANWÄLTE GMBH

Martin Eckel
E|N|W|C NATLACEN WALDERDORFF CANCOLA RECHTSANWÄLTE GMBH

Agnes Eigner
BRANDSTETTER PRITZ & PARTNER

Tibor Fabian
BINDER GRÖSSWANG RECHTSANWÄLTE GMBH

Julian Feichtinger
CHSH CERHA HEMPEL SPIEGELFELD HLAWATI

Ferdinand Graf
GRAF & PITKOWITZ RECHTSANWÄLTE GMBH

Andreas Hable
BINDER GRÖSSWANG RECHTSANWÄLTE GMBH

Alexander Hofmann
RA DR. ALEXANDER HOFMANN, LL.M.

Lothar Hofmann
HLAW

Helmut Hofmanninger
GRAF & PITKOWITZ RECHTSANWÄLTE GMBH

Sandro Huber
KAMMER DER ARCHITEKTEN UND INGENIEURKONSULENTEN WIEN

Alexander Isola
GRAF & PITKOWITZ RECHTSANWÄLTE GMBH

Susanne Jetschgo
BINDER GRÖSSWANG RECHTSANWÄLTE GMBH

Rudolf Kaindl
KOEHLER, KAINDL, DUERR & PARTNER, CIVIL LAW NOTARIES

Alexander Klauser
BRAUNEIS KLAUSER PRÄNDL RECHTSANWÄLTE GMBH

Florian Kremslehner
DORDA BRUGGER JORDIS

Rudolf Krickl
PRICEWATERHOUSECOOPERS

Ulrike Langwallner
SCHÖNHERR RECHTSANWÄLTE GMBH / ATTORNEYS-AT-LAW

Peter Madl
SCHÖNHERR RECHTSANWÄLTE GMBH / ATTORNEYS-AT-LAW

Wolfgang Messeritsch
NATIONAL BANK OF AUSTRIA

Felix Neuwirther
FRESHFIELDS BRUCKHAUS DERINGER

Ayten Pacariz
KSV 1870

Michael Podesser
PRICEWATERHOUSECOOPERS

Barbara Pogacar
LAW PARTNERS RECHTSANWÄLTE

Friedrich Roedler
PRICEWATERHOUSECOOPERS

Gottfried Schellmann
BRAUNEIS KLAUSER PRÄNDL RECHTSANWÄLTE GMBH

Georg Schima
KUNZ SCHIMA WALLENTIN RECHTSANWÄLTE KEG, MEMBER OF IUS LABORIS

Stephan Schmalzl
GRAF & PITKOWITZ RECHTSANWÄLTE GMBH

Ernst Schmidt
HALPERN & PRINZ

Christian Schuppich
CHSH CERHA HEMPEL SPIEGELFELD HLAWATI

Franz Schwarzinger
REVISIONSTREUHAND, MEMBER OF RUSSELL BEDFORD INTERNATIONAL

Maria Spalt
AUSTRIAN EMBASSY

Benedikt Spiegelfeld
CHSH CERHA HEMPEL SPIEGELFELD HLAWATI

Wolfgang Tichy
SCHÖNHERR RECHTSANWÄLTE GMBH / ATTORNEYS-AT-LAW

Thomas Trettnak
CHSH CERHA HEMPEL SPIEGELFELD HLAWATI

Birgit Vogt-Majarek
KUNZ SCHIMA WALLENTIN RECHTSANWÄLTE KEG, MEMBER OF IUS LABORIS

Gerhard Wagner
KSV 1870

Anton Zeilinger
MINISTRY OF FINANCE

Thomas Zottl
FRESHFIELDS BRUCKHAUS DERINGER

Marcus Zuccato
MINISTRY OF FINANCE

AZERBAIJAN

Ulviyya Abdullayeva
MGB LAW OFFICES

Vagif Ahmadov
SALANS

Shahla Ahmadova
DELOITTE

Aliagha Akhundov
BAKER & MCKENZIE

Gunel Alpman
BAKER & MCKENZIE

Aykhan Asadov
BAKER & MCKENZIE

Ismail Askerov
MGB LAW OFFICES

Natavan Baghirova
BM INTERNATIONAL LLC

Samir Balayev
UNIBANK

Zaur Fati-zadeh
MINISTRY OF TAXES

Fidan Gayibova
BM INTERNATIONAL LLC

Abbas Guliyev
BAKER & MCKENZIE

Arif Guliyev
PRICEWATERHOUSECOOPERS

Elchin Habibov
NATIONAL BANK OF AZERBAIJAN

Samir Hadjiyev
MICHAEL WILSON & PARTNERS LTD.

Nigar Hajieva
BAKER & MCKENZIE

Arzu Hajiyeva
ERNST & YOUNG

Zumrud Ibrahim
BAKER & MCKENZIE

Vagif Karimli
BAKER & MCKENZIE

Nuran Kerimov
DELOITTE

Kamal Mamedzade
SALANS

Javanshir Mammadov
GRATA LAW FIRM

Kamil Mammadov
MAMMADOV & PARTNERS LAW FIRM

Daniel Matthews
BAKER & MCKENZIE

Sabina Mikayilova
DELOITTE

Ruslan Mukhtarov
BM INTERNATIONAL LLC

Rauf Namazov
MINISTRY OF TAXES

Movlan Pashayev
PRICEWATERHOUSECOOPERS

Mustafa Salamov
BM INTERNATIONAL LLC

Vakhid Saparov
GRATA LAW FIRM

Emma Silyayeva
SALANS

Kamil Valiyev
SALANS

Matlab Valiyev
PRICEWATERHOUSECOOPERS

Murad Yahyayev
UNIBANK

Mahmud Yusifli
BAKER & MCKENZIE

BAHAMAS, THE

Kevin Basden
BAHAMAS ELECTRICITY CORPORATION

Erica Culmer-Curry
PRICEWATERHOUSECOOPERS

Makeba Darville
LENNOX PATON

Chaunece M. Ferguson
MACKAY & MOXEY CHAMBERS

Amos J. Ferguson Jr.
FERGUSON ASSOCIATES & PLANNERS

Wendy Forsythe
IMPORT EXPORT BROKERS LTD.

Vann P. Gaitor
HIGGS & JOHNSON

Michael Moss
MINISTRY OF FINANCE BAHAMAS

Castino D. Sands
LENNOX PATON

Kevin Seymour
PRICEWATERHOUSECOOPERS

Burlington Strachan
BAHAMAS ELECTRICITY CORPORATION

BAHRAIN

Khalid Abdulla
TAMEER

Najma AbdulRedha Hassan
MINISTRY OF MUNICIPALITIES & AGRICULTURE AFFAIRS. MUNICIPAL ONE STOP SHOP

Khaled Hassan Ajaji
KINGDOM OF BAHRAIN, MINISTRY OF JUSTICE & ISLAMIC AFFAIRS

Faten Al Haddad
TALAL ABU-GHAZALEH LEGAL (TAG-LEGAL)

Raju Alagarsamy
HASSAN RADHI & ASSOCIATES

Mohamed Al-Ahmadi
BAHRAIN INVESTORS CENTER

Samer Al-Ajjawi
ERNST & YOUNG

Basma AlAlawi
QAYS H. ZU'BI

Ebtihal Al-Hashimi
MINISTRY OF MUNICIPALITIES & AGRICULTURE AFFAIRS. MUNICIPAL ONE STOP SHOP

Haider Alnoaimi
MOHAMED SALAHUDDIN CONSULTING ENGINEERING BUREAU

Shaji Alukkal
PANALPINA WORLD TRANSPORT LLP

Maaria Ashraf
HATIM S. ZU'BI & PARTNERS

Michael Durgavich
ASAR AL RUWAYEH & PARTNERS

Elham Hassan
PRICEWATERHOUSECOOPERS

Seema Isa Al-Thawadi
MINISTRY OF MUNICIPALITIES & AGRICULTURE AFFAIRS. MUNICIPAL ONE STOP SHOP

Noora Janahi
HASSAN RADHI & ASSOCIATES

David Jayaseelan
PRICEWATERHOUSECOOPERS

Ebrahim Karolia
PRICEWATERHOUSECOOPERS

Elie Kassis
AGILITY LOGISTICS

Mohammed Abdul Khaliq
TAMEER

Ming Huey Lim
PRICEWATERHOUSECOOPERS

Mohammed Mirza Abdul Hussain
MINISTRY OF MUNICIPALITIES & AGRICULTURE AFFAIRS. MUNICIPAL ONE STOP SHOP

Abdul-Haq Mohammed
TROWERS & HAMLINS

Hassan Ali Radhi
HASSAN RADHI & ASSOCIATES

Kavi Rajesh
ELECTROTECH

Mohamed Salahuddin
MOHAMED SALAHUDDIN CONSULTING ENGINEERING BUREAU

Thamer Salahuddin
MOHAMED SALAHUDDIN CONSULTING ENGINEERING BUREAU

Esmond Hugh Stokes
HATIM S. ZU'BI & PARTNERS

Baiju Thomas
AGILITY LOGISTICS

Robin Watson
THE BENEFIT COMPANY

BANGLADESH

Zainul Abedin
PRICEWATERHOUSECOOPERS

Tafria Ahmed
DR. KAMAL HOSSAIN & ASSOCIATES

M. Aslam Alam
DIRECTORATE OF LAND RECORDS AND SURVEYS

Md. Shafiul Alam
THE HONGKONG AND SHANGHAI BANKING CORPORATION LTD.

MD. Nurul Amin
DEVELOPMENT CONSTRUCTIONS LTD.

Noorul Azhar
AZHAR & ASSOCIATES

Probir Barua
JUBILEE ENTERPRISE

Sharif Bhuiyan
DR. KAMAL HOSSAIN & ASSOCIATES

Jamilur Reza Choudhury
BRAC UNIVERSITY

Ahmed Zaker Chowdhury
DR. KAMAL HOSSAIN & ASSOCIATES

Badrud Doulah
DOULAH & DOULAH ADVOCATES

Nasirud Doulah
DOULAH & DOULAH ADVOCATES

Shamsud Doulah
DOULAH & DOULAH ADVOCATES

Moin Ghani
DR. KAMAL HOSSAIN & ASSOCIATES

K M A Halim
UPRIGHT TEXTILE SUPPORTS

Abdullah Hasan
DR. KAMAL HOSSAIN & ASSOCIATES

Abdul Hye
BANK OF BANGLADESH

Amir-Ul Islam
AMIR & AMIR LAW ASSOCIATES, member of LEX MUNDI

Sohel Kasem
PRICEWATERHOUSECOOPERS

Asif Khan
PRICEWATERHOUSECOOPERS

Amina Khatoon
DOULAH & DOULAH ADVOCATES

Nabila Rafique
AMIR & AMIR LAW ASSOCIATES, member of LEX MUNDI

Mizanur Rahaman
MINISTRY OF LAW, JUSTICE & PARLIMENTARY AFFAIRS

Ahmedur Rahim
REGISTRAR, JOINT STOCK COMPANIES & FIRMS

Al Amin Rahman
AL AMIN SABRINA & ASSOCIATES

Sajed Sami
FAROOQ AND ASSOCIATES

Mohammad Shahidul Haque
MINISTRY OF LAW, JUSTICE AND PARLIAMENTARY AFFAIRS

Shahriar Syeed
V-TEAC FASHION PVT LTD.

Abdul Wahab
A. WAHAB & CO.

Nurul Wahab
A. WAHAB & CO.

Sabrina Zarin
AL AMIN SABRINA & ASSOCIATES

BELARUS

Amir Al-Haidar
REVERA CONSULTING GROUP

Alexey Anischenko
SORAINEN & PARTNERS FLLC

Aleksandr Anisovitch
PROMAUDIT

Aleksander V. Antushevich
NATIONAL BANK OF THE REPUBLIC OF BELARUS

Dmitry Arkhipenko
REVERA CONSULTING GROUP

Andrey Bartashevich
INSTAR LOGISTICS

Alexander Botian
BOROVTSOV & SALEI LAW OFFICES

Sergey Chistyakov
STEPANOVSKI, PAPAKUL AND PARTNERS LTD.

Aliaksandr Danilevich
DANILEVICH

Aleksey Daryin
REVERA CONSULTING GROUP

Sergei Dubovik
NATIONAL BANK OF THE REPUBLIC OF BELARUS

Andrej Ermolenko
VLASOVA MIKHEL & PARTNERS

Olga Grechko
VLASOVA MIKHEL & PARTNERS

Antonina Ivanova
DICSA AUDIT, LAW & CONSULTING

Marina Kalinovskaya
LAW FIRM JURZNAK, LLC

Michail Aleksandrovich Karpovich
MINSK CABLE (ELECTRICAL) NETWORK

Dmitry Khalimonchyk
LAW FIRM JURZNAK, LLC

Sergey Khostovich
GS PLUS

Alexander Khrapoutski
STEPANOVSKI, PAPAKUL AND PARTNERS LTD.

Alexandre Klenovski
SPARTIS

Nina Knyazeva
BUSINESSCONSULT LAW FIRM

Irina Koikova
DICSA AUDIT, LAW & CONSULTING

Oksana Kotel
REVERA CONSULTING GROUP

Dmitry Kovalchik
STEPANOVSKI, PAPAKUL AND PARTNERS LTD.

Mikhail Kozlov
ASSTRA WEISSRUSSLAND LTD.

Kristina Kriščiūnaitė
PRICEWATERHOUSECOOPERS

Gleb Kripan
*$2)ladimir Kukuruzin
CHSH CERHA HEMPEL SPIEGELFELD HLAWATI*

Elena Kulchitskaya
ASSTRA WEISSRUSSLAND LTD.

Dmitry Kulik
DSV TRANSPORT (BY) LTD.

Valery Schepochkin Kulik
DSV TRANSPORT (BY) LTD.

Egidijus Kundelis
PRICEWATERHOUSECOOPERS

Tatiana Kuvshinova
REVERA CONSULTING GROUP

Oksana Lyakhova
BERNOTAS & DOMINAS GLIMSTEDT

Sergei Makarchuk
CHSH CERHA HEMPEL SPIEGELFELD HLAWATI

Mikalai Markounik
VLASOVA MIKHEL & PARTNERS

Dmitry Matveyev
LAW GROUP ARGUMENT

Konstantin Mikhel
VLASOVA MIKHEL & PARTNERS

Dmitry Montik
DMITRY MONTIK INDIVIDUAL ENTREPRENEUR

Elena Murashko
REVERA CONSULTING GROUP

Valiantsina Neizvestnaya
AUDIT AND CONSULTING LTD., BELARUS

Tatyana Novik
PRIVATE NOTARY

Pavel Patorskij

Olga Pepenina
BERNOTAS & DOMINAS GLIMSTEDT

Ludmila Pichuha
BANK MOSCOW-MINSK

Sergey Pinchuk
SERGEY PINCHUK ANTICRISIS MANAGER

Galina Podrezenok
MINISTRY OF JUSTICE COMPANY REGISTRY

Antonina Raduk
LAW FIRM JURZNAK, LLC

Vassili I. Salei
BOROVTSOV & SALEI LAW OFFICES

Elena Sapego
STEPANOVSKI, PAPAKUL AND PARTNERS LTD.

Sergei Senchuk
STATE COMMITTEE FOR REAL ESTATE REGISTRATION

Alexander Shevko
NATIONAL BANK OF THE REPUBLIC OF BELARUS

Anna Shinkevitch
YUREX LAW FIRM

Dmitry Skorodulin
LAW FIRM JURZNAK, LLC

Anna Skorodulina
LAW FIRM JURZNAK, LLC

Vyacheslav Slabodnik
UNIVEST-M

Lubov Slobodchikova
NATIONAL BANK OF THE REPUBLIC OF BELARUS

Andrey Sviridov
SLONIM TRADE CENTER

Natalia Talai
VLASOVA MIKHEL & PARTNERS

Ivan Timshin
REVERA CONSULTING GROUP

Pavel Tsarev
REVERA CONSULTING GROUP

Pavel Tsarou
REVERA CONSULTING GROUP

Natalya Ulasevich
BERNOTAS & DOMINAS GLIMSTEDT

Sviatlana Valueva
STEPANOVSKI, PAPAKUL AND PARTNERS LTD.

Gregory Verinskij
MINSK CITY CENTER FOR ENGINEERING SERVICES

Igor Verkhovodko
BUSINESSCONSULT LAW FIRM

Khmelnitskiy Vitaliy
REVERA CONSULTING GROUP

Maria Yurieva
SORAINEN & PARTNERS FLLC

Ekaterina Zabello
Vlasova Mikhel & Partners

Darya Zhuk
Bernotas & Dominas Glimstedt

Maxim Znak
Law Firm Jurznak, LLC

BELGIUM

Hubert André-Dumont
McGuire Woods LLP

Jan Bael
Notariskantoor Jan Bael - Ilse De Brauwere

Herlinde Baert
Notariskantoor Jan Bael - Ilse De Brauwere

Erik Bomans
Deminor International SCRL

Charlotte Boumal
Altius

Ellen Carmeliet
Stibbe

Pol Cools
McGuire Woods LLP

Adriaan Dauwe
Altius

Arnaud Dawans
Lucid - Lab for User Cognition and Innovative Design

Kris De Schutter
Loyens & Loeff

Didier De Vliegher
NautaDutilh

Olivier Debray
Claeys & Engels, member of Ius Laboris

Amaury Della Faille
PricewaterhouseCoopers

Jean-Michel Detry
DLA Piper UK LLP

Frank Dierckx
PricewaterhouseCoopers

David DuPont
Ashurst

Aline Etienne
NautaDutilh

Jean Pierre Fierens
Stibbe

Pierrette Fraisse
SPF Finances - AGDP

Conny Grenson
Eubelius Attorneys

Kurt Grillet
Altius

Sandrine Hirsch
Simont Braun

Thibaut Hollanders
DLA Piper UK LLP

Erika Leenknecht
Eubelius Attorneys

Stephan Legein
Federal Public Service Finance

Luc Legon
PricewaterhouseCoopers

Axel Maeterlinck
Simont Braun

Philippe Massart
Sibelga

Dominique Mougenot
Commercial Court Mons

Didier Muraille
National Bank of Belgium

Sabrina Otten
PricewaterhouseCoopers

Tim Roelans
Elegis

Frédéric Souchon
PricewaterhouseCoopers

William Timmermans
Altius

Jan Van Celst
DLA Piper UK LLP

Suzy Vande Wiele
Loyens & Loeff

Sybille Vandenberghe
PricewaterhouseCoopers

Grégory Vandenbussche
AREN, architects and engineers sprl

Marie-Noëlle Vanderhoven
PricewaterhouseCoopers

Tom Vantroyen
Altius

Reinout Vleugels
Squire, Sanders & Dempsey LLP

Johan Vonckers
McGuire Woods LLP

Katrien Vorlat
Stibbe

Bram Vuylsteke
Notary Bram Vuylsteke

Christian Willems
Loyens & Loeff

Dirk Wouters
WVM-Bedrijfsrevisoren BVBA, member of Russell Bedford International

BELIZE

Emil Arguelles
Arguelles & Company LLC

John Avery
Public Utilities Commission

Sherman Ferguson
Belize Electricity Ltd.

Rodolfo Gutierrez
Belize Electricity Ltd.

Russell Longsworth
Caribbean Shipping Agencies Ltd.

Reynaldo F. Magana
Frontier International Business Services Ltd.

Tania Moody
Barrow & Williams

Jose Moreno
Belize Electricity Ltd.

Patricia Rodriguez
Belize Companies Registry Ltd.

Dawn Sampson
Belize Electricity Ltd.

Saidi Vaccaro
Arguelles & Company LLC

Carlton Young
Young's Engineering Consultancy Ltd.

Philip Zuniga
Barrister & Attorney-at-Law

BENIN

Safia Abdoulaye
Cabinet d'Avocats

Diaby Aboubakar
BCEAO

Agathe Affougnon Ago
Cabinet Agathe Affougnon Ago

Saïdou Agbantou
Cabinet d'Avocats

Sybel Akuesson
Cabinet Fiduciaire d'Afrique

Rafikou Alabi
Cabinet Maître Alabi

Dieu-Donné Mamert Assogba
Cabinet Maître Adjai

Jacques Moïse Atchade
Cabinet de Maitre Atchade

Charles Badou
Cabinet d'Avocat Charles Badou

Bienvenu Koffi Bedie
Cabinet d'Avocats

Godefroy Chekete
Societe Beninoise D'Energie Electrique (SBEE)

Alice Codjia-Sohouenou
Attorney-at-Law

Marc Da Costa
Service des Affaires Domaniales

Johannès Dagnon
Groupe Helios Afrique

Aline Dossou-Yovo
Cabinet d'Avocats

Henri Fadonougbo
Tribunal de Premiere Instance de Cotonou

Guy Médard Agbo Fayemi
Cabinet d'Architecture ARCADE International

Carine Hounkponou
Cabinet d'Avocats

Yacouba Konate
France Transfo

Olagnika Salam
Office Notarial Olagnika

Adegbindin Saliou

Hauvy Séka Mathieu
FIDAFRICA / PricewaterhouseCoopers

Nelly Tagnon Gambor
Cabinet Fiduciaire d'Afrique

Dominique Taty
FIDAFRICA / PricewaterhouseCoopers

Jean-Bosco Todjinou
ECOPLAN sarl

Emmanuel Yehouessi
BCEAO

Brice Zinsindohoue
Cabinet d'Avocats

BHUTAN

Tashi Chenzom
Ministry of Labor & Human Resources

Kincho Dorjee
Leko Packers

Ugyen Dorji
Thimphu City Co.

Sonam Gyeltshen
Bhutan Power Corporation Ltd.

Mr Kunzang
Ministry of Finance

Game Tshering
Construction Assocation of Bhutan

Sonam Tshering
Ministry of Finance

Sonam Wangchuk
Ministry of Finance

Tshering Wangchuk
Royal Court of Justice

Sonam P. Wangdi
Ministry of Economic Affairs

Tashi Yezer
Royal Securities Exchange of Bhutan Ltd.

BOLIVIA

Fernando Aguirre
Bufete Aguirre Soc. Civ.

Ignacio Aguirre
Bufete Aguirre Soc. Civ.

Carolina Aguirre Urioste
Bufete Aguirre Soc. Civ.

Christian Amestegui
Asesores Legales CP

Daniela Aragones Cortez
Sanjinés & Asociados Soc. Civ. Abogados

Eduardo Aramayo
PricewaterhouseCoopers

Raúl A. Baldivia
Baldivia Unzaga & Asociados

Adrián Barrenechea
Criales, Urcullo & Antezana

Alexandra Blanco
Guevara & Gutiérrez S.C.

Jose A. Criales
Criales, Urcullo & Antezana

Petronila Gismondi
Consultora "Gismondi" - Contable Tributario

Primitivo Gutiérrez
Guevara & Gutiérrez S.C.

Enrique F. Hurtado
Superintencia de Bancos y Entidades Financieras

Jaime M. Jiménez Alvarez
Medidas Electricas (Jaime Jiménez Alvarez)

Paola Justiniano Arias
Sanjinés & Asociados Soc. Civ. Abogados

Mario Kempff
C.R. & F. Rojas, member of Lex Mundi

Julio César Landívar
Guevara & Gutiérrez S.C.

César Lora Moretto
PricewaterhouseCoopers

Daniel Mariaca
Criales, Urcullo & Antezana

Ariel Morales Vasquez
C.R. & F. Rojas, member of Lex Mundi

Jaime Muñoz-Reyes G.
Corporative Law Bolivia Consultores Asociados

Pablo Ordonez
Ayoroa & Ordonez

Alejandro Peláez Kay
Indacochea & Asociados

Mariana Pereira Nava
Indacochea & Asociados

Oscar Antonio Plaza Ponte
Entidad De Servicios De Información Enserbic S.A.

Julio Quintanilla Quiroga
Quintanilla, Soria & Nishizawa Soc. Civ

Diego Rojas
C.R. & F. Rojas, member of Lex Mundi

Fernando Rojas
C.R. & F. Rojas, member of Lex Mundi

Patricio Rojas
C.R. & F. Rojas, member of Lex Mundi

Esteban Salazar-Machicado
Salazar, Salazar & Asociados, Soc. Civ.

Sergio Salazar-Machicado
Salazar, Salazar & Asociados, Soc. Civ.

Rodolpho Raul Sanjines Elizagoyen
Sanjinés & Asociados Soc. Civ. Abogados

Maria Kim Shin
Würth Kim Costa du Rels

Edmond Tondu
Bolivian Intermodal Container

A. Mauricio Torrico Galindo
Quintanilla, Soria & Nishizawa Soc. Civ

Javier Urcullo
Criales, Urcullo & Antezana

Jaime Urcullo Reyes
Criales, Urcullo & Antezana

Roberto Viscafé
PricewaterhouseCoopers

Mauricio Zambrana Cuéllar
Infocred - Servicio de Informacion Crediticia BIC s.a.

BOSNIA AND HERZEGOVINA

Aida Ajanović
IKRP Rokas & Partners

Dunja Arnaut
Law Office Spaho

Dario Bišćević
DB Schenker

Mubera Brković
PricewaterhouseCoopers

Peter Burnie
PricewaterhouseCoopers

Vianja Dizdarević
Branko Mari Law Office

Dragan Draca
PricewaterhouseCoopers

Ezmana Hadziavdić
Branko Marić Law Office

Senada Havić Hrenovica
LRC Credit Bureau

Merima Hodžić
Law Office Spaho

Ismeta Huremović
Land Registry Office of the Sarajevo Municipal Court

Amra Isic
Branko Marić Law Office

Muhidin Karšić
Law Office of Emir Kovačević

Emmanuel Koenig
PricewaterhouseCoopers

Tom Kyriakopoulos
Kelemenis & Co.

Branko Marić
Branko Marić Law Office

Zoran Micevic

Edisa Peštek
Independent Lawyer

Đorđe Rackovic
Central Bank of Bosnia and Herzegovina

Alma Ramezić
PricewaterhouseCoopers

Adela Rizvić
Lawyers' office Bojana Tkalčić - Djulić, Olodar Prebanić, Adela Rizvić & Arela Jusufbašić - Goloman

Selma Šabanić
IKRP Rokas & Partners

Adina Salkanović

Mehmed Spaho
Law Office Spaho

BOTSWANA

John Carr-Hartley
Armstrongs Attorneys

Ofentse Chifedi
Hoya Removals & Freight

Yvonne K. Chilume
Chilume & Company

Diba M. Diba
Minchin & Kelly

Edward W. Fasholé-Luke II
Luke & Associates

Vincent Galeromeloe
TransUnion ITC

Laknath Jayawickrama
PricewaterhouseCoopers

Akheel Jinabhai
Akheel Jinabhai & Associates

Laurence Khupe
Collins Newman & Co.

Sylvester Lekone
Manica Africa Pty. Ltd.

Finola McMahon
Osei-Ofei Swabi & Co.

Diniar Minwalla
PricewaterhouseCoopers

Mmatshipi Motsepe
Manica Africa Pty. Ltd.

Jack Allan Mutua
Tectura International Botswana

Buhlebenkosi Ncube
Luke & Associates

Kwadwo Osei-Ofei
Osei-Ofei Swabi & Co.

Butler Phirie
PricewaterhouseCoopers

Claudio Rossi
Sharps Electrical (Pty) Ltd.

Daniel Swabi
Osei-Ofei Swabi & Co.

BRAZIL

Antonio Aires
Demarest e Almeida Advogados

Leonardo Gutierrez Alves
Guerra e Batista Advogados

Natalia Alves
Demarest e Almeida Advogados

Antonio Amendola
Felsberg, Pedretti, Mannrich e Aidar Advogados e Consultores Legais

Lucia Aragao
Veirano Advogados Sao Paulo

Mariana Aranha
Machado, Meyer, Sendacz e Opice Advagados

Pedro Vitor Araujo da Costa
Vitor Costa Advogados

Fernanda Azevedo
Rayes, Fagundes & Oliveira Ramos Advogados

Bruno Balduccini
Pinheiro Neto Advogados

Priscyla Barbosa
Veirano Advogados Sao Paulo

Juliana Bastianello Baldin
Machado, Meyer, Sendacz e Opice Advogados

Guilherme Bertolini Fernandes dos Santos
Fleury Malheiros, Gasparini, De Cresci e Nogueira de Lima Advogados

Bernardo Bessa
Felsberg, Pedretti, Mannrich e Aidar Advogados e Consultores Legais

Camila Biral
Demarest e Almeida Advogados

Richard Blanchet
Loeser e Portela Advogados

Adriano Boni De Souza
Noronha Advogados

Adriano Borges
De Vivo, Whitaker, Castro e Gonçalves Advogados

Sergio Bronstein
Veirano Advogados Sao Paulo

Clarissa Abrahão Bruzzi
Noronha Advogados

Júlio César Bueno
Pinheiro Neto Advogados

Paulo Campana
Felsberg, Pedretti, Mannrich e Aidar Advogados e Consultores Legais

Ana Paula Carvalho
Noronha Advogados

Eduardo Castro
Machado Meyer Sendacz e Opice Advogados Advagados

Flávia Coelho Warde
Demarest e Almeida Advogados

Gilberto Deon Corrêa Junior
Veirano Advogados Porto Alegre

Sidinei Corrêa Marques
Banco Central do Brasil

Mirella da Costa Andreola de Almeida
Noronha Advogados

Anderson Bispo da Silva
Guerra e Batista Advogados

Adriana Daiuto
Demarest e Almeida Advogados

Cleber Dar Rovere Peluzo Abreu
Cunha Oricchio Ricca Lopes Advogados

Bruno Henrique de Aguiar
Rayes, Fagundes & Oliveira Ramos Advogados

Anderson Rivas de Almeida
Guerra e Batista Advogados

Sólon de Almeida Cunha
Machado, Meyer, Sendacz e Opice Advogados

Aldo de Cresci Neto
Fleury Malheiros, Gasparini, De Cresci e Nogueira de Lima Advogados

Edilson De Morais
Serasa S.A.

Nadia Demoliner Lacerda
Mesquita Barros Advogados, member of Ius Laboris

Felipe Di Marzo Trezza
Fleury Malheiros, Gasparini, De Cresci e Nogueira de Lima Advogados

Ubajara Arcas Dias
Fleury Malheiros, Gasparini, De Cresci e Nogueira de Lima Advogados

José Ricardo dos Santos Luz Júnior
Duarte Garcia, Caselli Guimarães e Terra Advogados

Joao Paulo F.A. Fagundes
Rayes, Fagundes & Oliveira Ramos Advogados

Vanessa Felício
Veirano Advogados Sao Paulo

Thomas Benes Felsberg
Felsberg, Pedretti, Mannrich e Aidar Advogados e Consultores Legais

Alexsander Fernandes de Andrade
Duarte Garcia, Caselli Guimarães e Terra Advogados

Josney Ferraz
Units Auditores Independentes

Silvia Fiszman
Machado, Meyer, Sendacz e Opice

Álvaro Luis Fleury Malheiros
Fleury Malheiros, Gasparini, De Cresci e Nogueira de Lima Advogados

Susan Christina Forster
Amaral Gurgel Fischer & Forster Advogados

Luís Franciozi
Pinheiro Neto Advogados

Florencia Ortiz Freuler
Machado, Meyer, Sendacz e Opice

Rafael Frota
Vitor Costa Advogados

Rafael Gagliardi
Demarest e Almeida Advogados

Caio Gargione Habice Prado
Machado Meyer Sendacz e Opice Advogados

Thiago Giantomassi Medeiros
Demarest e Almeida Advogados

Michelle Giraldi Lacerda
PricewaterhouseCoopers

Lara Gomes Dias
Machado, Meyer, Sendacz e Opice

Rodrigo Gomes Maia
Noronha Advogados

Adriana Grizante de Almeida
PricewaterhouseCoopers

Eduardo Ferraz Guerra
Guerra e Batista Advogados

Enrique Hadad
Loeser e Portela Advogados

Carlos Alberto Iacia
PricewaterhouseCoopers

Roberta Ibanez
Pinheiro Guimarães Advogados

Marcelo Inglez de Souza
Demarest e Almeida Advogados

Eduardo Takemi Kataoka
Castro, Barros, Sobral, Gomes Advogados

José Paulo Lago Alves Pequeno
Noronha Advogados

Adriana Sforcini Lavrik Esper
Amaral Gurgel Fischer & Forster Advogados

Fernando Loeser
Loeser e Portela Advogados

Marina Maccabelli
Demarest e Almeida Advogados

Newton N.T. Machado
Rayes, Fagundes & Oliveira Ramos Advogados

Pedro Maciel
Veirano Advogados Sao Paulo

Viviane Maria Barbosa da Silva
Machado, Meyer, Sendacz e Opice

André Marques
Pinheiro Neto Advogados

Georges Louis Martens Filho
De Vivo, Whitaker, Castro e Gonçalves Advogados

Fernando Martines Vieira
Noronha Advogados

Thiago Martins
Araújo e Policastro Advogados

Laura Massetto Meyer
Pinheiro Guimarães Advogados

Rodrigo Matos
MBM Brasil Ltda

Eduardo Augusto Mattar
Pinheiro Guimarães Advogados

Felipe Oliveira Mavignier
Fleury Malheiros, Gasparini, De Cresci e Nogueira de Lima Advogados

Thiago Medaglia
Felsberg, Pedretti, Mannrich e Aidar Advogados e Consultores Legais

Denise Medeiros
Noronha Advogados

Marianne Mendes Webber
Noronha Advogados

Cássio Mesquita Barros
Mesquita Barros Advogados, member of Ius Laboris

Gustavo Morel
Veirano Advogados Sao Paulo

Renata Morelli
Rayes, Fagundes & Oliveira Ramos Advogados

Thaís Moretz Sohn Fernandes
APEXBRASIL

Marianna Morselli
Pinheiro Neto Advogados

Luana Murinelli Bastos
Machado, Meyer, Sendacz e Opice

Paulo Nasser
Demarest e Almeida Advogados

Jorge Nemr
Leite, Tosto e Barros

Walter Nimir
De Vivo, Whitaker, Castro e Gonçalves Advogados

Felipe Oliveira
Veirano Advogados Porto Alegre

Andrea Oricchio Kirsh
Cunha Oricchio Ricca Lopes Advogados

Adriana Pallis Romano
Machado, Meyer, Sendacz e Opice

Andre Pan
Consult Group, member of Russell Bedford International

Rafael Passaro
Machado, Meyer, Sendacz e Opice

Fabio Luis Pereira Barboza
Cunha Oricchio Ricca Lopes Advogados

Monica Pinheiro dos Anjos
Planeta Brasil Consultancy

Laércio Pinto
Serasa S.A.

Andréa Pitthan Françolin
De Vivo, Whitaker, Castro e Gonçalves Advogados

Durval Portela
Loeser e Portela Advogados

Rodrigo Eduardo Pricoli
Rayes, Fagundes & Oliveira Ramos Advogados

Daniela Prieto
Veirano Advogados Sao Paulo

Fernanda Rabelo
Pinheiro Guimarães Advogados

Luiz Gustavo Ramos
Rayes, Fagundes & Oliveira Ramos Advogados

Domingos Fernando Refinetti
Machado, Meyer, Sendacz e Opice

Lukas Matthias Rhomberg
De Vivo, Whitaker, Castro e Gonçalves Advogados

Jose Ribeiro do Pardo Junior
Machado, Meyer, Sendacz e Opice

Eliane Ribeiro Gago
Duarte Garcia, Caselli Guimarães e Terra Advogados

Guilherme Rizzo Amaral
Veirano Advogados Porto Alegre

Cezar Roedel
Halley do Brasil

Lia Roston
Rayes, Fagundes & Oliveira Ramos Advogados

José Samurai Saiani
Machado, Meyer, Sendacz e Opice

Bruno Sanchez Belo
Noronha Advogados

Joana Scarpa
Veirano Advogados Sao Paulo

Carolina Schreier
KLA-Koury Lopes Advogados

Ingrid Schwarz R. de Mendonça
Noronha Advogados

Raissa Simões Tavares de Melo
Demarest e Almeida Advogados

Keila Fonseca Soares
Noronha Advogados

Walter Stuber
Walter Stuber Consultoria Juridica

Claudio Taveira
Pinheiro Neto Advogados

Milena Tesser
Rayes, Fagundes & Oliveira Ramos Advogados

Marcos Tiraboschi
Veirano Advogados Sao Paulo

Carlos Tortelli
Consult Group, member of Russell Bedford International

Paulo Trani Mello
Noronha Advogados

Luiz Fernando Valente De Paiva
Pinheiro Neto Advogados

Juliana Vasconcelos
APEXBRASIL

José Wahle
Veirano Advogados Sao Paulo

Eduardo Guimarães Wanderley
Veirano Advogados Sao Paulo

Celso Xavier
Demarest e Almeida Advogados

Marcos Yanaka
MBM Brasil Ltda

BRUNEI DARUSSALAM

Danny Chua
Brunei Transporting Company

Cynthia Kong
Widdows Kong & Associates

Kevin Lee
Wisma Management

Kin Chee Lee
Lee Corporatehouse Associates

Lennon Lee
PricewaterhouseCoopers

Yew Choh Lee
Y.C. Lee & Lee Advocates & Solicitors

Siew Yen Lim
The Judicial Department Brunei

Teck Guan Lim
Ernst & Young

Chris Loh
PricewaterhouseCoopers

Naimah Md Ali
Attorney General's Chambers

Colin Ong
Dr. Colin Ong Legal Services

See Tiat Quek
PricewaterhouseCoopers

David Sandison
PricewaterhouseCoopers

Michelle Sim
Ernst & Young

Martin Sinnung Jr.
Brunei Tansporting Company Kg Kiulap

Shazali Sulaiman
KPMG

Joanita Zain
The Brunei Economic Development Board

BULGARIA

Svetlin Adrianov
Penkov, Markov & Partners

Andrey Aleksandrov
Kambourov & Partners

Borislav Atanasov
Djingov, Gouginski, Kyutchukov & Velichkov

Svetlana Balabanova
TravelInn Ltd.

Lilia Banakieva
Penkov, Markov & Partners

Nikolay Bandakov
Kambourov & Partners

Kalin Bonev
Landwell & Associés - PricewaterhouseCoopers Legal Services

Nikolai Bozhilov
Unimasters Logistics Plc.

Maria Danailova
Wolf Theiss

George Dimitrov
Dimitrov, Petrov & Co.

Kristina Dimitrova
Landwell & Associés - PricewaterhouseCoopers Legal Services

Vesselin Dinkov
Landwell & Associés - PricewaterhouseCoopers Legal Services

Silvia Dulevska
Bulgarian National Bank

Anastas Georgiev
Registry Agency of Bulgaria

Georgy Georgiev
Landwell & Associés - PricewaterhouseCoopers Legal Services

Velislava Georgieva
Economou International Shipping Agency Limited

Marieta Getcheva
PricewaterhouseCoopers

Matea Gospodinova
Djingov, Gouginski, Kyutchukov & Velichkov

Ralitsa Gougleva
Djingov, Gouginski, Kyutchukov & Velichkov

Katerina Gramatikova
Dobrev, Kinkin & Lyutskanov

Angel Kalaidjiev
Kalaidjiev, Georgiev & Minchev

Yavor Kambourov
Kambourov & Partners

Hristina Kirilova
Kambourov & Partners

Lilia Kisseva
Djingov, Gouginski, Kyutchukov & Velichkov

Donko Kolev
Partner Bulgaria Ltd.

Nikolay Kolev
Borislav Boyanov & Co.

Ilya Komarevsky
Tsvetkova, Bebov and Co.

Boika Komsulova
PricewaterhouseCoopers

Stephan Kyutchukov
Djingov, Gouginski, Kyutchukov & Velichkov

Polina Marinova
Landwell & Associés - PricewaterhouseCoopers Legal Services

Ivan Markov
Penkov, Markov & Partners

Vladimir Natchev
Arsov Natchev Ganeva

Yordan Naydenov
Borislav Boyanov & Co.

Neli Nedkova
Wolf Theiss

Darina Oresharova
Experian Bulgaria EAD

Yulia Peeva
Rex Consulting Ltd., member of Russell Bedford International

Lilia Pencheva
Experian Bulgaria EAD

Miglena Peneva
Georgiev, Todorov & Co.

Veselka Petrova
Tsvetkova, Bebov and Co.

Martin Plamenov Stanchev
Dobrev, Kinkin & Lyutskanov

Gergana Popova
Georgiev, Todorov & Co.

Alexander Rangelov
PricewaterhouseCoopers

Elina Ruseva
Penkov, Markov & Partners

Roman Stoyanov
Penkov, Markov & Partners

Margarita Stoyanova
Kambourov & Partners

Laura Thomas
LM Legal Services Ltd.

Kaloyan Todorov
Wolf Theiss

Svilen Todorov
Todorov & Doykova Law Firm

Nona Todorova
Experian Bulgaria EAD

Lily Trifonova
Rex Consulting Ltd., member of Russell Bedford International

Georgi Tzvetkov
Djingov, Gouginski, Kyutchukov & Velichkov

Maria Urmanova
Landwell & Associés - PricewaterhouseCoopers Legal Services

Kamena Valcheva
Tsvetkova, Bebov and Co.

Miroslav Varnaliev
Unimasters Logistics Plc.

Venzi Vassilev
Rex Consulting Ltd, member of Russell Bedford International

Kalina Vitkovska
Economou International Shipping Agency Limited

Vessela Tcherneva Yankova
V Consulting Bulgaria

BURKINA FASO

Diaby Aboubakar
BCEAO

Bernard Bamouni
SINCAT

Fortune Bicaba
Etude de Maitre Fortune Bicaba

Flora Josiane Bila
Cabinet Yaguibou & Yanogo

Aimé Bonkoungou
SONABEL

Dieudonne Bonkoungou
Cabinet Ouedraogo & Bonkoungou

Bobson Coulibaly
Cabinet d'Avocats Barthélemy Kere

Denis Dawende
Office Notarial Me Jean Celestin Zoure

Jean-Claude Gnamien
FIDAFRICA / PricewaterhouseCoopers

Fulgence Habiyaremye
Cabinet d'Avocats Barthélemy Kere

Barthélémy Kere
Cabinet d'Avocats Barthélemy Kere

Gilbert Kibtonre
CEFAC

Clarisse Kienou
Direction générale des impots

Vincent Armand Kobiane
ARDI Architectes Conseils

Eddie Komboïgo
Komboïgo & Associes

Colette Lefebvre
Inspection du Travail

Frédéric O. Lompo
Etude Maître Lompo

N. Henri Ouedraogo
Ministere des Finances et du Budget

Ousmane Honore Ouedraogo
Maison de l'entreprise du Burkina Faso

Pascal Ouedraogo
Cabinet d'Avocats Barthélemy Kere

Alain Serge Paré
Cabinet Yaguibou & Yanogo

Marie Jeanne Saba
Direction Génerale des Impôts

Hermann Lambert Sanon
Groupe Hage

Moussa Sawadogo
Direction du Cadastre

Moussa Sogodogo
Cabinet Ledoux Seina

Hyppolite Tapsoba
Tribunal d'Instance de Ouagadougou

Dominique Taty
FIDAFRICA / PricewaterhouseCoopers

Moussa Traore
Direction générale des impots

Fousséni Traoré
FIDAFRICA / PricewaterhouseCoopers

Yacouba Traoré
Commune de Ouagadougou

Laurent Traore Sy
ONEA

Bouba Yaguibou
SCPA Yaguibou & Yanogo

Emmanuel Yehouessi
BCEAO

Rahmatou Zongo
Cabinet Yaguibou & Yanogo

Ousmane Prosper Zoungrana
Tribunal de Grande Instance de Ouagadougou

Jean Celéstin Zoure
Office Notarial Me Jean Celestin Zoure

BURUNDI

Joseph Bahizi
Banque de la République du Burundi

Sylvestre Banzubaze
Avocat au barreau du Burundi

Jean De Dieu Basabakwinshi
IMATCO

Cyprien Bigirimana
Tribunal de Grande Instance de Gitega

Ange Gakundwakazi
Deloitte

Gerard Handika
Deloitte

Dominik Kohlhagen
Institute of Development Policy and Management (IOB), University of Antwerp

Ildephonse Nahimana
Banque de la République du Burundi

Bonaventure Nicimpaye
Intercontact Services, S.A.

Claver Nigarura
Rubeya & Co - Advocates

Lambert Nigarura
Mkono & Co Advocates

Gustave Niyonzima
Mkono & Co Advocates

Alain Niyubahwe
Financial and Private sectors development Project

Antoine Ntsigana
SODETRA Ltd.

Happy Ntwari
Mkono & Co Advocates

Gilbert L.P. Nyatanyi
Mkono & Co Advocates

Déogratias Nzemba
Attorney-at-Law

Prosper Ringuyeneza
Architecture et Construction (A.C.)

Willy Rubeya
Rubeya & Co - Advocates

Benjamin Rufagari
Deloitte

Fabien Segatwa
Etude Me Segatwa

Gabriel Sinarinzi
Cabinet Me Gabriel Sinarinzi

Audace Sunzu
REGIDESO-Burundi

Egide Uwimana
Tribunal du Travail de Bujumbura

CAMBODIA

Kosal Chan
ACLEDA Bank Plc.

Rithy Chey
B.N.G. - Advocates & Solicitors

Charya Chum
Arbitration Council Foundation

Naryth Hem Hour
B.N.G. - Advocates & Solicitors

Phalla Im
Sciaroni & Associates

Visal Iv
Electricite du Cambodge

Chhorpornpisey Keo
ACLEDA Bank Plc.

Vicheka Lay
B.N.G. - Advocates & Solicitors

Michael Liam Garvey
BNG Legal

Jean Loi
PricewaterhouseCoopers

Alexander May
DFDL Mekong Law Group

Long Mom
RAF International Forwarding (Cambodia) Inc.

Kaing MoniKa
The Garment Manufacturers Association in Cambodia

Phan Phalla
Supreme National Economic Council

Vichet Phang
B.N.G. - Advocates & Solicitors

Ham Phea
Ham Phea Law Office

Thea Pheng
B.N.G. - Advocates & Solicitors

Saray Phomra
B.N.G. - Advocates & Solicitors

Allen Prak
B.N.G. - Advocates & Solicitors

Kuntheapini Saing
Arbitration Council Foundation

Muny Samreth
PricewaterhouseCoopers

Chanthy Sin
Linex

Lor Sok
Arbitration Council Foundation

Suy Sokha
HR Inc. (Cambodia) Co., Ltd.

Sorphea Sou
Arbitration Council Foundation

Vuthy Sreng
PricewaterhouseCoopers

Ousaphea Suos
ACLEDA Bank Plc.

David Symansky
HR Inc. (Cambodia) Co., Ltd.

Michael Tan
RAF International Forwarding (Cambodia) Inc.

Rathvisal Thara
B.N.G. - Advocates & Solicitors

Janvibol Tip
Tip & Partners

Sinath Un
DFDL Mekong Law Group

CAMEROON

Roland Abeng
Cabinet d'Avocats Abeng Roland

Pierre Aloma
Guichet Unique des Operations du Commerce Exterieur-Gie

Gilbert Awah Bongam
Achu and Fon-Ndikum Law Firm

Feh Henry Baaboh
Henry, Samuelson & Co.

Esther Badjeck
Andritz Vatech Hydro

Caroline BARLA
CeB CRéA

Thomas Didier Remy Batoumboug
Cadire

Pierre Bertin Simbafo
BICEC

Isidore Biyiha
Guichet Unique des Opérations du Commerce Extérieur-Gie

Hiol Bonheur
Cabinet SFR

Miafo Bonny Bonn
Bonnybonn Enterprises

David Boyo
Boyo & Patimark LLP

Oscar D'Estaing Deffosso
FIDAFRICA / PricewaterhouseCoopers

Anne Marie Diboundje Njocke
Cabinet Ekobo

Paul Marie Djamen
BICEC

Aurélien Djengue Kotte
Cabinet Ekobo

Laurent Dongmo
Jing & Partners

Régine Dooh Collins

Annette Ebelle
Cadire

Marie Marceline Enganalim
Etude Me Enganalim Marceline

Pascal Enpe

Lucas Florent Essomba
Cabinet Essomba & Associés

Badjeck Esther
Freelance Lawyer

Marie-Claude Etoke

Mbu Etonga
Ngwafor & Partners

Fankam Gaelle Laure
Cabinet SFR

Hervé Guiffo
Damco Cameroun SA

Caroline Idrissou-Belingar
BEAC

Samuel Iyug Iyug
Groupement des Entreprises de Fret et Messagerie du Cameroun

Angoh Angoh Jacob
Legal Power Law Firm

Paul T. Jing
Jing & Partners

Henri Pierre Job
Cabinet d'Avocats Henri Job

Etoke Joël

Serge Jokung
Cabinet Maître Marie Andrée NGWE

Serge Albert Jokung
Cabinet Maître Marie Andrée NGWE

Julienne Kengue Piam
Nimba Conseil SARL

Jean Aime Kounga
Cabinet d'Avocats Abeng Roland

Sarah Limunga
High Court Fako

Jean Michel Mbock Biumla
M & N Law Firm, cabinet d'avocats

Augustin Yves Mbock Keked
Cadire

Rosine Adèle Mekeu Sonfack
Nimba Conseil SARL

Patrick Menyeng Manga
Cabinet d'Avocats Abeng Roland

Ingrid Martinette Mezang Mvom
Nimba Conseil SARL

Jules Minamo
Karvan Finance

A.D. Monkam
Etude de notaire Wo'o

Jacqueline Moussinga Bapes
Etude Me Jacqueline Moussinga

Valerie Moussombo
Cabinet Maître Marie Andrée NGWE

Henri Moutalen
FIDAFRICA / PricewaterhouseCoopers

Jean Jacques Mpanjo Lobe
MCA Audit & Conseil

Aimé Ndock Len
M & N Law Firm, cabinet d'avocats

Marcelin Yoyo Ndoum
Etude de notaire Wo'o

Isidore Baudouin Ndzana
FIDAFRICA/ PricewaterhouseCoopers

Félix Faustin Ngoh
Cabinet d'Avocats Henri Job

Ephraim Ngwafor
Ngwafor & Partners

Marie-Andrée Ngwe
Cabinet Maître Marie Andrée NGWE

Patrice Guy Njoya
Cabinet Maître Marie Andrée NGWE

Jacques Nyemb
Cabinet Nyemb

Olivier Priso
Ville de Douala Communauté Urbaine de Douala

Nisrine Senoussi
FIDAFRICA / PricewaterhouseCoopers

Hakilas Paul Tchagna
FIDAFRICA / PricewaterhouseCoopers

Nadine Tinen Tchangoum
FIDAFRICA / PricewaterhouseCoopers

Duga Titanji
Duga & Co. Law Firm

Chrétien Toudjui
Afrique Audit Conseil Baker Tilly

Eliane Yomsi
Karvan Finance

CANADA

Saad Ahmad
Blake, Cassels & Graydon, member of Lex Mundi

David Bish
Goodmans LLP

Ann Borooah
Toronto City Hall

Cindy Chung
Corporations Canada

Allan Coleman
Osler, Hoskin & Harcourt LLP

John Craig
Heenan Blaikie LLP, member of Ius Laboris

Rod Davidge
Osler, Hoskin & Harcourt LLP

David G. Ellis
CB Richard Ellis d.o.o.

Jeremy Fraiberg
Osler, Hoskin & Harcourt LLP

Bhavin Ganatra
Forwarding Unlimited Inc.

Yoine Goldstein
McMillan LLP

Steven Golick
Osler, Hoskin & Harcourt LLP

John Humphries
Toronto City Council (Building Department)

Pamela S. Hughes
Blake, Cassels & Graydon, member of Lex Mundi

Robert Hughes
Osler, Hoskin & Harcourt LLP

Armando Iannuzzi
Russell Bedford International

Andrew Kent
McMillan LLP

Harris Kligman
Russell Bedford International

Joshua Kochath
Forwarding Unlimited Inc.

George Kotsifas
City of London

Susan Leslie
First Canadian Title

Craig Lockwood
Osler, Hoskin & Harcourt LLP

William McCarthy
First Canadian Title

Artem Miakichev
Osler, Hoskin & Harcourt LLP

Thomas O'Brien
PricewaterhouseCoopers

Alfred Page
Borden Ladner Gervais LLP

Eric Paton
PricewaterhouseCoopers

Saul Plener
PricewaterhouseCoopers

Antonin Pribetic
Steinberg Morton Hope & Israel LLP

Christopher Richter
Woods LLP

Damian Rigolo
Osler, Hoskin & Harcourt LLP

Jenifer Robertson
Electrical Safety Authority

Harris M. Rosen
Fogler Rubinoff

Kelly Russell
PricewaterhouseCoopers

Paul Schabas
Blake, Cassels & Graydon, member of Lex Mundi

Karen Simmons
Toronto City Hall

Shane Todd
Heenan Blaikie LLP, member of Ius Laboris

Sharon Vogel
Borden Ladner Gervais LLP

George Waggott
Lang Michener LLP

CAPE VERDE

Hermínio Afonso
PricewaterhouseCoopers

Bruno Andrade Alves
PricewaterhouseCoopers

Susana Caetano
PricewaterhouseCoopers

Liver Canuto
PricewaterhouseCoopers

Ana Catarina Carnaz
PricewaterhouseCoopers

Ana Raquel Costa
PricewaterhouseCoopers

Ilídio Cruz
Gabinete de Advocacia Consultoria e Procuradoria Juridica

Jorge Lima Delgado Lopes
Núcleo Operacional da Sociedade de Informação

Quilda do Canto
AUDITEC - Auditores & Consultores

Joana Gomes Rosa
Advocacia/Consultoria

Jose Manuel Fausto Lima
Empresa de Electricidade e Agua (Electra)

Luis Pedro Maximiano
Millennium Challenge Account - MCA Cape Verde

Francisco Guimarães Melo
PricewaterhouseCoopers

João M.A. Mendes
AUDITEC - Auditores & Consultores

Ana Pinto Morais
PricewaterhouseCoopers

Catarina Nunes
PricewaterhouseCoopers

José Manuel Pinto Monteiro
Advogados & Jurisconsultos

Miguel Garoupa Puim
PricewaterhouseCoopers

Armando J.F. Rodrigues
PricewaterhouseCoopers

Elisa Rodrigues
Núcleo Operacional da Sociedade de Informação

Aguinaldo Rosario
CIC- Cabo Verde LDA

Tito Lívio Santos Oliveira Ramos
ENGIC

Arnaldo Silva
Arnaldo Silva & Associados

Jose Spinola
FPS

João Carlos Tavares Fidalgo
Banco Central de Cabo Verde

Liza Helena Vaz
PricewaterhouseCoopers

Leendert Verschoor
PricewaterhouseCoopers

CENTRAL AFRICAN REPUBLIC

Jean Christophe Bakossa
L'ordre Centraficain des Architectes

Christiane Doraz-Serefessenet
Cabinet Notaire Doraz-Serefessenet

Emile Doraz-Serefessenet
Cabinet Notaire Doraz-Serefessenet

Marie-Edith Douzima-Lawson
Cabinet Douzima & Ministère de la fonction publique

Dolly Gotilogue
Cabinet Ledoux Seina

Caroline Idrissou-Belingar
BEAC

Groupe Kamach

Jean Paul Maradas Nado
Ministère de l'Urbanisme

Timothee M'beto
TTCI

Serge Médard Missamou
Club OHADA

Jacob Ngaya
Direction Génerale des Impôts

Gina Roosalem
Chambre des Notaires de Centrafrique

Nicolas Tiangaye
Nicolas Tiangaye Law Firm

CHAD

Adoum Daoud Adoum Haroun
S.C.G.A.D.A. et Fils

Ahmat Affono Tchari
Société Tchadienne d'Eau et d'Electricité (STEE)

Amir Allamine
Ministere de la Justice Garde des Sceaux/ Tribunal de Commerce de N'Djamena

Gabriel Nathé Amady
Avocat

Atadet Azarak Mogro
Société Tchadienne d'Eau et d'Electricité (STEE)

Theophile B. Bongoro
Cabinet Notarial Bongoro

Oscar D'Estaing Deffosso
FIDAFRICA / PricewaterhouseCoopers

Thomas Dingamgoto
Cabinet Thomas Dingamgoto

Ernest Djagba Balandi
BEAC - Chad

Alex Djekadom
Ministere des Finances - Direction des grandes entreprises

Amane Rosine Djibergui
Cabinet Notarial Djibergui

Mahamat Ousman Djidda
Cabinet d'Architecture & Urbanisme

N'Doningar Djimasna
Faculté de Droit, Université de N'Djamena

Elysee Eldjimbaye Mbaihoudou
Huissier de Justice/ Chambre Nationale des Huissiers de Justice du Tchad

Mahamat Nour Idriss Haggar
Société Tchadienne d'Eau et d'Electricité (STEE)

Caroline Idrissou-Belingar
BEAC

Delphine K Djiraibe
Avocate à la Cour

Francis Kadjilembaye
Cabinet Thomas Dingamgoto

Béchir Madet
Office Notarial

Moustapha Ali Moustapha
Ministere de la Justice Garde des Sceaux/ Tribunal de Commerce de N'Djamena

Jean Paul Nendigui
N Consulting

Josue Ngadjadoum
Avocat

Issa Ngarmbassa
Etude Me Issa Ngar mbassa

Hissen Ngaro
Huissier de Justice/ Chambre Nationale des Huissiers de Justice du Tchad

Tchoutcha Ousman
Société Tchadienne d'Eau et d'Electricité (STEE)

Nissaouabé Passang
Etude Me Passang

Nisrine Senoussi
FIDAFRICA / PricewaterhouseCoopers

Senoussi Ahmat Senoussi
Cabinet d'Architecture & Urbanisme

Koulamallah Souradj
Chamber of Commerce, Industry, Agriculture, Mine and Crafts of Chad

Amos D. Tatoloum Onde
Societe Africaine d'Architecture et d'Ingenierie

Nadine Tinen Tchangoum
FIDAFRICA / PricewaterhouseCoopers

Issouf Traore
Imperial Tobacco

Sobdibé Zoua
Cabinet Sobdibe Zoua

Patedjore Zoukalne
Direction de l'enregistrement des Domaines, du Timbre et de la Conservation Fonciere

CHILE

Luis Avello
PricewaterhouseCoopers Legal Services

Angeles Barría
Philippi, Yrarrazaval, Pulido & Brunner, Abogados Ltda

Magdalena Barros
Baker & McKenzie

Sandra Benedetto
PricewaterhouseCoopers

José Benitez
PricewaterhouseCoopers Legal Services

Jorge Benitez Urrutia
Urrutia & Cía

Carolina Benito Kelly
Núñez Muñoz y Cia Ltda Abogados

Miguel Capo Valdes
Besalco S.A.

Myriam Caro
PricewaterhouseCoopers

Héctor Carrasco
Superintendencia de Bancos e Instituciones Financieras

Josefina Casals
PricewaterhouseCoopers

Andrés Chirgwin
Chirgwin SpA Abogados

Cristobal Correa Echavarria
Guerrero, Olivos, Novoa y Errázuriz

Camilo Cortés
Guerrero, Olivos, Novoa y Errázuriz

Karla Cortez
PricewaterhouseCoopers Legal Services

Ramon Delpiano
Jaime Guzman E. Fundacion

Eduardo Dorat
Cariola Diez Perez-Copatos & Cia

César Valenzuela Escalona
Chilectra

Claudia Paz Escobar
Chirgwin SpA Abogados

Nicolas Fernandez
Cariola Diez Perez-Copatos & Cia

Pamela Flores
PricewaterhouseCoopers

Pabla Gainza
Cariola Diez Perez-Copatos & Cia

Rodrigo Galleguillos
Núñez Muñoz y Cia Ltda Abogados

Cristian Garcia-Huidobro
Boletin Comercial

Andrés González
NÚÑEZ MUÑOZ Y CIA LTDA ABOGADOS

Juan Pablo Gonzalez M.
GUERRERO, OLIVOS, NOVOA Y ERRÁZURIZ

José Gutiérrez
PRICEWATERHOUSECOOPERS

Christian Hermansen Rebolledo
ACTIC CONSULTORES

Manuel Hinojosa
NÚÑEZ MUÑOZ Y CIA LTDA ABOGADOS

Javier Hurtado
CÁMARA CHILENA DE LA CONSTRUCCIÓN

Fernando Jamarne
ALESSANDRI & COMPAÑÍA

Andrés Jara
GUERRERO, OLIVOS, NOVOA Y ERRÁZURIZ

Marcelo Laport
PRICEWATERHOUSECOOPERS

León Larrain
BAKER & MCKENZIE

Carolina Lastra
PRICEWATERHOUSECOOPERS

Jose Luis Letelier
CARIOLA DIEZ PEREZ-COPATOS & CIA

Luis Maldonado Croquevielle
CONSERVADOR DE BIENES RAÍCES DE SANTIAGO

Pablo Martel
NÚÑEZ MUÑOZ Y CIA LTDA ABOGADOS

Carolina Masihy
CAREY Y CÍA LTDA.

Juan Pablo Matus
CARIOLA DIEZ PEREZ-COPATOS & CIA

Consuelo Maze
NÚÑEZ MUÑOZ Y CIA LTDA ABOGADOS

Raimundo Moreno
CARIOLA DIEZ PEREZ-COPATOS & CIA

Enrique Munita
PHILIPPI, YRARRAZAVAL, PULIDO & BRUNNER, ABOGADOS LTDA

Rodrigo Muñoz
NÚÑEZ MUÑOZ Y CIA LTDA ABOGADOS

Gerardo Ovalle Mahns
YRARRÁZAVAL, RUIZ-TAGLE, GOLDENBERG, LAGOS & SILVA

Luis Parada Hoyl
BAHAMONDEZ, ALVAREZ & ZEGERS

Miguel Pavez
RUSSELL BEDFORD CHILE, MEMBER OF RUSSELL BEDFORD INTERNATIONAL

Maria Fernanda Peters
CARIOLA DIEZ PEREZ-COPATOS & CIA

Alberto Pulido A.
PHILIPPI, YRARRAZAVAL, PULIDO & BRUNNER, ABOGADOS LTDA

Alfonso Reymond Larrain
CHADWICK & ALDUNATE ABOGADOS

Ricardo Riesco
PHILIPPI, YRARRAZAVAL, PULIDO & BRUNNER, ABOGADOS LTDA

Isabel Rios
BAKER & MCKENZIE

Constanza Rodriguez
PHILIPPI, YRARRAZAVAL, PULIDO & BRUNNER, ABOGADOS LTDA

Edmundo Rojas García
CONSERVADOR DE BIENES RAÍCES DE SANTIAGO

Pamela Rubio
NÚÑEZ MUÑOZ Y CIA LTDA ABOGADOS

Bernardita Saez
ALESSANDRI & COMPAÑÍA

Marco Salgado
ALCAÍNO, RODRÍGUEZ & SAHLI LIMITADA

Andrés Sanfuentes
PHILIPPI, YRARRAZAVAL, PULIDO & BRUNNER, ABOGADOS LTDA

Martín Santa María O.
GUERRERO, OLIVOS, NOVOA Y ERRÁZURIZ

Francisco Selamé
PRICEWATERHOUSECOOPERS LEGAL SERVICES

Marcela Silva
PHILIPPI, YRARRAZAVAL, PULIDO & BRUNNER, ABOGADOS LTDA

Luis Fernando Silva Ibañez
YRARRÁZAVAL, RUIZ-TAGLE, GOLDENBERG, LAGOS & SILVA

Cristobal Smythe
BAHAMONDEZ, ALVAREZ & ZEGERS

Alan Spencer
ALESSANDRI & COMPAÑÍA

Charles Spencer
SPENCER GLOBAL CHILE

Cristobal Sumar
PRICEWATERHOUSECOOPERS

Juan Turner
BAHAMONDEZ, ALVAREZ & ZEGERS

Sebastián Valdivieso
YRARRÁZAVAL, RUIZ-TAGLE, GOLDENBERG, LAGOS & SILVA

Luis Felipe Vergara Maldonado
CONSERVADOR DE BIENES RAÍCES DE SANTIAGO

Paula Warnier
PRICEWATERHOUSECOOPERS

Arturo Yrarrázaval Covarrubias
YRARRÁZAVAL, RUIZ-TAGLE, GOLDENBERG, LAGOS & SILVA

Matías Zegers
BAHAMONDEZ, ALVAREZ & ZEGERS

CHINA

May Bai
LOVELLS

Rex Chan
PRICEWATERHOUSECOOPERS

Rico Chan
BAKER & MCKENZIE

Elliott Youchun Chen
JUN ZE JUN LAW OFFICES

Jie Chen
JUN HE LAW OFFICES, MEMBER OF LEX MUNDI

Yixin Chen
DAVIS POLK & WARDWELL

Yw Chung
BAKER BOTTS LLP

Yu Du
MMLC GROUP

Hongtao Fan
JOINWAY LAWFIRM

Grace Fang
PINSENT MASONS

Wei Gao
ZY & PARTNERS

Leo Ge
GLOBAL STAR LOGISTICS CO. LTD.

Alexander Gong
BAKER & MCKENZIE

Scott Guan
JADE & FOUNTAIN LAW OFFICES (PRC)

Lawrence Guo
JADE & FOUNTAIN LAW OFFICES (PRC)

Kian Heong Hew
PINSENT MASONS

Mark Ho
JADE & FOUNTAIN LAW OFFICES (PRC)

Min (Cindy) Huang
O'MELVENY & MYERS LLP

John T. Kuzmik
BAKER BOTTS LLP

Edward E. Lehman
LEHMAN, LEE & XU

Ian Lewis
MAYER BROWN LLP

Clare Li
NORONHA ADVOGADOS

Qing Li
QING

Deng Liang
JUN HE LAW OFFICE, MEMBER OF LEX MUNDI

Derek Liu
LOVELLS

Lucy Lu
KING & WOOD PRC LAWYERS

Matthew Murphy
MMLC GROUP

Jackie Qi
PINSENT MASONS

Gustavo Rabello
NORONHA ADVOGADOS

Stephen Rynhart
JONES LANG LASALLE

Han Shen
DAVIS POLK & WARDWELL

Jack Sun
LOVELLS

Sarah Sun
PRICEWATERHOUSECOOPERS

Lawrence Sussman
O'MELVENY & MYERS LLP

Jessie Tang
GLOBAL STAR LOGISTICS CO. LTD.

Terence Tung
MAYER BROWN LLP

Andy Wang
PINSENT MASONS

Audrey Wang
QINDAO LAW FIRM

Celia Wang
PRICEWATERHOUSECOOPERS

Fenghe Wang
DACHENG LAW OFFICES

Guoqi Wang
HUA-ANDER CPAS, MEMBER OF RUSSELL BEDFORD INTERNATIONAL

Jin Wang
LOVELLS

Kelly Wang
MMLC GROUP

Li Wang
DEHENG LAW OFFICES

William Wang
PRICEWATERHOUSECOOPERS

Anthea Wong
PRICEWATERHOUSECOOPERS

Cassie Wong
PRICEWATERHOUSECOOPERS

Kent Woo
GUANGDA LAW FIRM

Jingjun Wu
DAVIS POLK & WARDWELL

Sarah Xuan
MMLC GROUP

Frank Yang
MAYER BROWN LLP

Bo Yu
PRICEWATERHOUSECOOPERS

Natalie Yu
SHU JIN LAW FIRM

Xia Yu
MMLC GROUP

Laura Yuan
KING & WOOD PRC LAWYERS

Josey Zhang
K&L GATES LLP

Nicholas Zhang
PRICEWATERHOUSECOOPERS

Yi Zhang
KING & WOOD PRC LAWYERS

Johnson Zheng
XIAMEN ALL CARBON CORPORATION

Cevela Zhou
O'MELVENY & MYERS LLP

Judy Zhu
MAYER BROWN LLP

Wang Zichuan
DEHENG LAW OFFICES

COLOMBIA

Carlos Alcala
LLOREDA CAMACHO & CO.

Enrique Alvarez
LLOREDA CAMACHO & CO.

Natalia Angel
BRIGARD & URRUTIA, MEMBER OF LEX MUNDI

Jaime Mauricio Angulo Sanchez
COMPUTEC - DATACRÉDITO

Lorena Arambula
CÁRDENAS & CÁRDENAS

Alexandra Arbelaez
RUSSELL BEDFORD COLOMBIA, MEMBER OF RUSSELL BEDFORD INTERNATIONAL

Manuela Arizmendi
POSSE HERRERA & RUIZ

María Camila Bagés
BRIGARD & URRUTIA, MEMBER OF LEX MUNDI

Marcela Barberena
CAVELIER ABOGADOS

Luis Alfredo Barragán
BRIGARD & URRUTIA, MEMBER OF LEX MUNDI

Claudia Benavides
GÓMEZ-PINZÓN ZULETA ABOGADOS S.A.

Juan Pablo Bonilla
BAKER & MCKENZIE

Gloria María Borrero Restrepo
CORPORACIÓN EXCELENCIA EN LA JUSTICIA

Leonardo Calderón Perdomo
COLEGIO DE REGISTRADORES DE INSTRUMENTOS PÚBLICOS DE COLOMBIA

Ana Maria Calero
CAVELIER ABOGADOS

Carolina Camacho
POSSE HERRERA & RUIZ

Claudia Marcela Camargo
PRICEWATERHOUSECOOPERS

Darío Cárdenas
CÁRDENAS & CÁRDENAS

Daniel Cardoso
PRICEWATERHOUSECOOPERS

Ernesto Cavelier
RODRIGUEZ & CAVELIER

Juan Pablo Cepeda
SOCIEDAD PORTUARIA REGIONAL DE CARTAGENA

Felipe Cuberos
PRIETO & CARRIZOSA S.A.

María Helena Díaz Méndez
PRICEWATERHOUSECOOPERS

Carlos Fradique-Méndez
BRIGARD & URRUTIA, MEMBER OF LEX MUNDI

Liliana Fuentes
RUSSELL BEDFORD COLOMBIA, MEMBER OF RUSSELL BEDFORD INTERNATIONAL

Luis Hernando Gallo Medina
GALLO MEDINA ABOGADOS ASOCIADOS

Isabella Gandini
RODRIGUEZ & CAVELIER

Hermes García
CAVELIER ABOGADOS

Clara Inés Gómez
LLOREDA CAMACHO & CO.

Olga Lucía Guevara
BRIGARD & URRUTIA, MEMBER OF LEX MUNDI

Santiago Gutiérrez
LLOREDA CAMACHO & CO.

Monica Hernandez
ARRIETA BUSTAMANTE

John Herreno
HM & COMPANY LTDA

Jorge Lara-Urbaneja
LARA CONSULTORES

Ernesto López
CÁRDENAS & CÁRDENAS

Gabriela Mancero
CAVELIER ABOGADOS

Luisa Fernanda Mantilla
CAVELIER ABOGADOS

María Nella Marquez
CAVELIER ABOGADOS

Cristina Mejía
POSSE HERRERA & RUIZ

Carlos Mejia Gomez
LLOREDA CAMACHO & CO.

Luis Gabriel Morcillo
BRIGARD & URRUTIA, MEMBER OF LEX MUNDI

Fabian Moreno
LLOREDA CAMACHO & CO.

María Neira Tobón
HOLGUÍN, NEIRA & POMBO ABOGADOS

Luis E. Nieto
NIETO & CHALELA

Mónica Pedroza Garcés
CORPORACIÓN EXCELENCIA EN LA JUSTICIA

Carlos Felipe Pinilla Acevedo
PINILLA GONZÁLEZ & PRIETO ABOGADOS

Carolina Posada
POSSE HERRERA & RUIZ

Raul Quevedo
LLOREDA CAMACHO & CO.

Catalina Reyes
LLOREDA CAMACHO & CO.

Irma Rivera
BRIGARD & URRUTIA, MEMBER OF LEX MUNDI

Luis Carlos Robayo
RUSSELL BEDFORD COLOMBIA, MEMBER OF RUSSELL BEDFORD INTERNATIONAL

Sonia Elizabeth Rojas Izaquita
GALLO MEDINA ABOGADOS ASOCIADOS

Cristina Rueda Londoño
BAKER & MCKENZIE

Angela Salazar Blanco
LLOREDA CAMACHO & CO.

Paula Samper Salazar
GÓMEZ-PINZÓN ZULETA ABOGADOS S.A.

Juan Daniel Sierra
RODRIGUEZ & CAVELIER

Pablo Sierra
POSSE HERRERA & RUIZ

Paola Spada
CORPORACIÓN EXCELENCIA EN LA JUSTICIA

Raúl Alberto Suárez Arcila
INDEPENDENT PRACTITIONER (ATTORNEY-AT-LAW)

Maria Teresa Tamara
LLOREDA CAMACHO & CO.

Gustavo Tamayo Arango
LLOREDA CAMACHO & CO.

Jose Alejandro Torres
POSSE HERRERA & RUIZ

Patricia Vergara
GÓMEZ-PINZÓN ZULETA ABOGADOS S.A.

Carolina Villadiego Burbano
CORPORACIÓN EXCELENCIA EN LA JUSTICIA

Laura Villaveces
BRIGARD & URRUTIA, MEMBER OF LEX MUNDI

Alberto Zuleta
GÓMEZ-PINZÓN ZULETA ABOGADOS S.A.

COMOROS

Hassoumani Assoumani
TRIBUNAL DE PREMIÈRE INSTANCE DE MORONI

Remy Grondin
VITOGAZ COMORES

Haroussi Idrissa
TRIBUNAL DE PREMIÈRE INSTANCE DE MORONI

Ahamada Mahamoudou
CABINET LEDOUX SEINA

Mohamed Maoulida
AUDIT CONSEIL-INTERNATIONAL

CONGO, DEM. REP.

Alphin Babala Mangala
GTS EXPRESS

Jean Adolphe Bitenu
ANAPI

Deo Bukayafwa
MBM CONSEIL

Armand Ciamala
CIAMALA & PARTNERS

Edmond Cibamba Diata
CABINET EMERY MUKENDI WAFWANA & ASSOCIÉS

Victor Créspel Musafiri
CABINET D'AVOCAT JCC & A

Hervé Diakiese
CABINET LEDOUX SEINA

Prosper Djuma Bilali
CABINET MASAMBA

Irénée Falanka
CABINET JEAN BOSCO MUAKA & ASSOCIATES

Patrick Gérenthon
AGETRAF S.A.R.L. - SDV

David Guarnieri
PRICEWATERHOUSECOOPERS LEGAL SERVICES

Amisi Herady
ANAPI

Sandra Kabuya
CABINET JEAN BOSCO MUAKA & ASSOCIATES

Mukaba Kalambayi
SOCIÉTÉ NATIONALE D'ELECTRICITÉ (SNEL)

Pierre Kazadi Tshibanda
CABINET MASAMBA

Arly Khuty
AVOCAT

Eldon Khuty
AGETRAF S.A.R.L. - SDV

Phistian Kubangusu Makiese
CABINET MASAMBA

Pierre-Pépin Kwampuku Latur
CABINET PEPIN KWAMPUKU

Jerome A. Mbuyi Kabeya Laba
CIAMALA & PARTNERS

Jean-Délphin Lokonde Mvulukunda
CABINET MASAMBA

Nobel Lubamba Nguba
CABINET AVOCATS ASSOCIÉS ANDRE ET VINCENT

Serge Mwankana Lulu

Vital Lwanga Bizanbila
CABINET VITAL LWANGA

Crispin Makaya
CABINET JEAN BOSCO MUAKA & ASSOCIATES

Noel Mangala
CABINET CERTAC

Jean Claude Mbaki Siluzaku
CABINET MBAKI ET ASSOCIÉS

Bernard Claude Mbu ne Letang
CABINET DE MAÎTRE MBU NE LETANG

Didier Mopiti
MBM CONSEIL

Louman Mpoy
CABINET MPOY - LOUMAN & ASSOCIÉS

Jean Bosco Muaka
CABINET JEAN BOSCO MUAKA & ASSOCIATES

Emery Mukendi Wafwana
CABINET EMERY MUKENDI WAFWANA & ASSOCIÉS

M. Hilaire Mumvudi Mulangi
MINISTÈRE DE L'URBANISME ET DE L'HABITAT

Jacques Munday
CABINET NTOTO ET NSWAL

Marius Muzembe Mpungu
CABINET KABASELE - MFUMU & ASSOCIÉS

Victorine Bibiche Nsimba Kilembe
BARREAU DE KINSHASA/ MATETE

Laurent Okitonembo
CABINET DJUNGA & RISASI

Jean-Louis Paquet
ATELIER D' ARCHITECTURE

Marc Perazzone
CABINET ARCHITECTE MARC PERAZZONE

Pierre Risasi
CABINET DJUNGA & RISASI

Dominique Taty
FIDAFRICA / PRICEWATERHOUSECOOPERS

Mbuyi Tshibuabua
SOCIÉTÉ NATIONALE D'ELECTRICITÉ (SNEL)

Yoko Yakembe

CONGO, REP.

Jean Francois Apoko
MAIRIE DE BRAZZAVILLE

Jean Roger Bakoulou
BANQUE DES ETATS DE L'AFRIQUE CENTRALE

Felicte Clarisse Batantou
DIRECTION DÉPARTEMENTALE DE LA REFORME FONCIÈRE DU CADASTRE

Prosper Bianga
CONSEIL DU BARREAU DE BRAZZAVILLE

Prosper Bizitou
FIDAFRICA / PricewaterhouseCoopers

Antoine Bokolo Joue
CAP ARCHITECTS

Mroin Boris

Andre Boungou
MINISTERE DE LA CONSTRUCTION, DE L'URBANISME ET DE L'HABITAT

David Bourion
FIDAFRICA / PricewaterhouseCoopers

Claude Coelho
CABINET D'AVOCATS CLAUDE COELHO

J. F. Dathet
SDV

Georges Ebale
TRIBUNAL DE COMMERCE DE BRAZZAVILE

Jean-Philippe Esseau
CABINET ESSEAU

Mathias Essereke
CABINET D'AVOCATS CLAUDE COELHO

Henriette Lucie Arlette Galiba
OFFICE NOTARIAL ME GALIBA

Gaston Gapo
ATELIER D'ARCHITECTURE ET D'URBANISME

A.A. Matondo Goma
COUR D'APPEL DE BRAZZAVILLE CONGO REP.

David Guarnieri
PRICEWATERHOUSECOOPERS LEGAL SERVICES

Caroline Idrissou-Belingar
BEAC

Karelle Koubatika
OFFICE 2K

Sylvert Bérenger Kymbassa Boussi
ETUDE MAITRE BÉATRICE DIANZOLO, HUISSIER DE JUSTICE

Emmanuel Le Bras
FIDAFRICA / PricewaterhouseCoopers

Christian Eric Locko
BRUDEY, ONDZIEL GNELENGA, LOCKO CABINET D'AVOCATS

Salomon Louboula
ETUDE NOTARIALE

Jean Prosper Mabassi
ORDRE NATIONAL DES AVOCATS DU CONGO BARREAU DE BRAZZAVILLE

Guy Remy Makosso
ORDRE NATIONAL DES AVOCATS DU CONGO BARREAU DE BRAZZAVILLE

Felix Makosso Lassi
CABINET NOTARIAL LASSI

Roger Masamba Makela
UNIVERSITE PROTESTANTE AU CONGO

Ado Patricia Marlene Matissa
CABINET NOTARIAL MATISSA

Rose Mavoungou
CENTRE DE FORMALITES ADMINISTRATIVES DES ENTREPRISES

Françoise Mbongo
CABINET MBONGO

Norbert Diétrich M'Foutou
ETUDE DE MAITRES SÉRAPHIN MCAKOSSO-DOUTA ET NORBERT M'FOUTOU

Martial Wildovert Moukoko
SOCIETE NATIONALE DES EAUX

Robert Ngabou
CAP ARCHITECTS

Brigitte Ngolete
MAIRIE DE BRAZZAVILLE

Paulin Ntsouari

Regina Nicole Okandza Yoka
DIRECTION GÉNERALE DES IMPÔTS

Armand Robert Okoko

Brice Ondongo-Ezhet
CAC

Jean Petro
CABINET D'AVOCATS JEAN PETRO

Adrien Pittie
SDV

Chimène Prisca Nina Pongui
ETUDE DE ME CHIMÈNE PRISCA NINA PONGUI

Alexis Sah
POUVOIR JUDICIAIRE

Jean Bertin Sela
CABINET NOTARIAL SELA

Dominique Taty
FIDAFRICA / PricewaterhouseCoopers

Louis Zingat-Makosso
SOCIÉTÉ NATIONALE D'ELECTRICITÉ (SNEL)

COSTA RICA

Aisha Acuña
ANDRÉ TINOCO ABOGADOS

Mariana Alfaro
CORDERO & CORDERO ABOGADOS

Carlos Araya
QUIRÓS & ASOCIADOS CENTRAL LAW

Carlos Barrantes
PRICEWATERHOUSECOOPERS

Alejandro Bettoni Traube
DONINELLI & DONINELLI - ASESORES JURÍDICOS ASOCIADOS

Eduardo Calderón-Odio
BLP ABOGADOS

Bernardo Calvo
GRUPO MEGA DE COSTA RICA BR, S.A

Juan José Carreras
BLP ABOGADOS

Adriana Castro
BLP ABOGADOS

Leonardo Castro
OLLER ABOGADOS

Silvia Chacon
ALFREDO FOURNIER & ASOCIADOS

Daniel Chaves
CINDE

Ricardo Cordero B.
CORDERO & CORDERO ABOGADOS

Hernán Cordero Maduro
CORDERO & CORDERO ABOGADOS

Luis Fernando Escalante J.
GRUPO MEGA DE COSTA RICA BR, S.A

Roberto Esquivel
OLLER ABOGADOS

Freddy Fachler
PACHECO COTO

Marianna Fonseca
BLP ABOGADOS

V. Andrés Gómez
PRICEWATERHOUSECOOPERS

Rolando Gonzalez
CORDERO & CORDERO ABOGADOS

Andrea González
BLP ABOGADOS

Randall González
BLP ABOGADOS

David Gutierrez
BLP ABOGADOS

Carolina Gutiérrez
OLLER ABOGADOS

Paola Gutiérrez Mora
LEX COUNSEL

Mario Gutiérrez Quintero
LEX COUNSEL

Jorge Guzmán
LEX COUNSEL

Roy Guzman Ramirez
COMPAÑÍA NACIONAL DE FUERZA Y LUZ

María del Mar Herrera
BLP ABOGADOS

Milena Hidalgo
TELETEC S.A.

Randall Zamora Hidalgo
COSTA RICA ABC

Vivian Jiménez
OLLER ABOGADOS

Ivannia Méndez Rodríguez
OLLER ABOGADOS

Andres Mercado
OLLER ABOGADOS

Gabriela Miranda
OLLER ABOGADOS

Jorge Montenegro
SCGMT ARQUITECTURA Y DISEÑO

Eduardo Montoya Solano
SUPERINTENDENCIA GENERAL DE ENTIDADES FINANCIERAS

Cecilia Naranjo
LEX COUNSEL

Pedro Oller
OLLER ABOGADOS

Ramón Ortega
PRICEWATERHOUSECOOPERS

Alvaro Quesada Loría
AGUILAR CASTILLO LOVE

Mauricio Quiros
QUIROS & ASOCIADOS, ABOGADOS Y NOTARIOS

Miguel Ruiz Herrera
LEX COUNSEL

Jose Luis Salinas
SCGMT ARQUITECTURA Y DISEÑO

Fernando Sanchez Castillo
RUSSELL BEDFORD COSTA RICA, MEMBER OF RUSSELL BEDFORD INTERNATIONAL

Luis Sibaja
LEX COUNSEL

Miguel Golcher Valverde
COLEGIO DE ENGENIEROS ELECTRICISTAS

Marianela Vargas
PRICEWATERHOUSECOOPERS

Ricardo Vargas
OLLER ABOGADOS

Rocio Vega
GRUPO MEGA DE COSTA RICA BR, S.A

Rodrigo Zapata
LEX COUNSEL

Jafet Zúñiga Salas
SUPERINTENDENCIA GENERAL DE ENTIDADES FINANCIERAS

CÔTE D'IVOIRE

Diaby Aboubakar
BCEAO

Ika Raymond Any-Gbayere
ANY RAY & PARTNERS

César Asman
CABINET N'GOAN, ASMAN & ASSOCIÉS

Jean-Luc Bernard
SDV - SAGA CI

Aminata Cone
SCPA DOGUÉ-ABBÉ YAO & ASSOCIÉS

Issa Diabaté
KOFFI & DIABATÉ

Junior Doukoure
ANY RAY & PARTNERS

Dorothée K. Dreesen
ETUDE MAITRE DREESEN

Bertrand Fleury
SDV - SAGA CI

Jean Claude Gnamien
FIDAFRICA / PRICEWATERHOUSECOOPERS

Barnabe Kabore
NOVELEC SARL

Guillaume Koffi
CONSEIL NATIONAL DE L'ORDRE DES ARCHITECTES

Dogbémin Gérard Kone
SCPA NAMBEYA-DOGBEMIN & ASSOCIES

Kiyobien Kone
SOCIÉTÉ CIVILE PROFESSIONNELLE D'AVOCATS (SCPA) LE PARACLET

Mahoua Kone
ETUDE DE MAÎTRE KONE MAHOUA

Germain Kouame
CIE

Arsène Dablé Kouassi
SCPA DOGUÉ-ABBÉ YAO & ASSOCIÉS

Charlotte-Yolande Mangoua
ETUDE DE MAÎTRE MANGOUA

Adeline Messou
FIDAFRICA / PRICEWATERHOUSECOOPERS

Patricia N'guessan
CABINET JEAN-FRANÇOIS CHAUVEAU

Jacques Otro
CONSEIL NATIONAL DE L'ORDRE DES ARCHITECTES

Athanase Raux
CABINET RAUX, AMIEN & ASSOCIÉS

Dominique Taty
FIDAFRICA / PRICEWATERHOUSECOOPERS

Fatoumata Konaté Touré Bebo
CABINET DE NOTAIRE KONATÉ TOURÉ BEBO

Fousséni Traoré
FIDAFRICA / PRICEWATERHOUSECOOPERS

Jean Christian Turkson
CIE

Emmanuel Yehouessi
BCEAO

Léon Désiré Zalo
MINISTÈRE D'ETAT, MINISTÈRE DE L'AGRICULTURE

Seydou Zerbo
SCPA DOGUÉ-ABBÉ YAO & ASSOCIÉS

CROATIA

Andrea August
FINANCIAL AGENCY - CENTRE FOR HITRO.HR

Zoran Avramović
MINISTRY OF JUSTICE

Ivana Bandov
JURIC AND PARTNERS ATTORNEYS AT LAW

Hrvoje Bardek
CMS ZAGREB

Ivo Bijelić
PRICEWATERHOUSECOOPERS

Marijana Božić
DIVJAK, TOPIĆ & BAHTIJAREVIĆ

Marko Borsky
DIVJAK, TOPIĆ & BAHTIJAREVIĆ

Irena Brezovečki
VIDAN LAW OFFICE

Lana Brlek
PRICEWATERHOUSECOOPERS

Belinda Čačić
ČAČIĆ & PARTNERS

Stefanija Čukman
JURIĆ AND PARTNERS ATTORNEYS AT LAW

Martina Čulap
LEKO & PARTNERS

Saša Divjak
DIVJAK, TOPIĆ & BAHTIJAREVIĆ

Ronald Given
WOLF THEISS ZAGREB

Ivan Gjurgjan
LAW FIRM GJURGJAN & ŠRIBAR RADIĆ

Tom Hadžija
SIKIRIC & HADŽIJA ATTORNEY PARTNERSHIP

Lidija Hanžek
HROK D.O.O.

Anita Heršak Klobučarević
POROBIJA & POROBIJA LAW FIRM

Jana Hitrec
ČAČIĆ & PARTNERS

Branimir Iveković
VIDAN LAW OFFICE

Irina Jelčić
HANŽEKOVIĆ, RADAKOVIĆ & PARTNERS, MEMBER OF LEX MUNDI

Krešimir Jelaković
ŠAVORIĆ & PARTNERS

Sanja Jurkonić
PRICEWATERHOUSECOOPERS

Janos Kelemen
PRICEWATERHOUSECOOPERS

Branko Kirin
ČAČIĆ & PARTNERS

Marija Krizanec
JURIC AND PARTNERS ATTORNEYS AT LAW

Anita Krizmanić
MAČEŠIĆ & PARTNERS, ODVJETNICKO DRUSTVO

Dubravka Lacković
CMS ZAGREB

Miroslav Leko
LEKO & PARTNERS

Krešimir Ljubić
LEKO & PARTNERS

Marko Lovrić
DIVJAK, TOPIĆ & BAHTIJAREVIĆ

Miroljub Mačešić
MAČEŠIĆ & PARTNERS, ODVJETNICKO DRUSTVO

Josip Marohnić
DIVJAK, TOPIĆ & BAHTIJAREVIĆ

Andrej Matijevich
MATIJEVICH LAW OFFICE

Tomislav Pedišić
VUKMIR & ASOCIATES LAW FIRM

Marija Petrović
DIVJAK, TOPIĆ & BAHTIJAREVIĆ

Ivan Podvorec
MBB UWS PROM D.O.O.

Sanja Porobija
POROBIJA & POROBIJA LAW FIRM

Tihana Posavec
DIVJAK, TOPIĆ & BAHTIJAREVIĆ

Gordan Rotkvic
PRICEWATERHOUSECOOPERS

Anita Rubini-Puller
POROBIJA & POROBIJA LAW FIRM

Boris Sarovic
ŠAVORIĆ & PARTNERS

Djuro Sessa
COUNTY COURT IN ZAGREB

Ana Sihtar
SIHTAR ATTORNEYS AT LAW

Dragutin Sikirić
SIKIRIC & HADZIJA ATTORNEY PARTNERSHIP

Manuela Špoljarić
LEKO & PARTNERS

Irena Šribar Radić
LAW FIRM GJURGJAN & ŠRIBAR RADIĆ

Mario Štefanić
TRANSADRIA

POROBIJA & POROBIJA

Zoran Tasić
CMS ZAGREB

Ivan Ćuk
VUKMIR & ASOCIATES LAW FIRM

Ivana Urem
ASSONO LTD. CROATIA

Hrvoje Vidan
VIDAN LAW OFFICE

Zrinka Vrtarić
CMS ZAGREB

Željko Vrban

Eugen Zadravec
EUGEN ZADRAVEC LAW FIRM

CYPRUS

Alexandros Alexandrou
TORNARITIS LAW FIRM

Irene Anastassiou
DR. K. CHRYSOSTOMIDES & CO LLC

Andreas Andreou
CYPRUS GLOBAL LOGISTICS

Anita Boyadjian
INFO CREDIT GROUP

Antonis Charalambous
LIMASSOL MUNICIPALITY

Antonis Christodoulides
PRICEWATERHOUSECOOPERS

Kypros Chrysostomides
DR. K. CHRYSOSTOMIDES & CO LLC

Achilleas Demetriades
LELLOS P DEMETRIADES LAW OFFICE LLC

Alexandros Economou
CHRYSSES DEMETRIADES & CO

Marios Eliades
M.ELIADES & PARTNERS LLC

Haris Fereos
FEREOS & ASSOCIATES

Pavlos Fereos
FEREOS & ASSOCIATES

Stephanos Fereos
FEREOS & ASSOCIATES

Panicos Florides
P.G. ECONOMIDES & CO LIMITED, MEMBER OF RUSSELL BEDFORD INTERNATIONAL

Stefani Gabriel
PRICEWATERHOUSECOOPERS

Iacovos Hadjivarnavas
CYPRUS GENERAL BONDED AND TRANSIT STORES ASSOCIATION

Nasia Hadjivasili
PRICEWATERHOUSECOOPERS

Samantha G. Hellicar
ANTIS TRIANTAFYLLIDES & SONS LLC

Christina Ioannidou
IOANNIDES DEMETRIOU LLC

Demetra Kalogerou
CYPRUS STOCK EXCHANGE

Panicos Kaouris
PRICEWATERHOUSECOOPERS

George Karakannas
*CH.P. KARAKANNAS
ELECTRICAL LTD.*

Thomas Keane
CHRYSSES DEMETRIADES & CO

Harris Kleanthous
DELOITTE

Christina Kotsapa
*ANTIS TRIANTAFYLLIDES &
SONS LLC*

Nicholas Ktenas
*ANDREAS NEOCLEOUS & CO.
LEGAL CONSULTANTS*

George M. Leptos
LEPTOS GROUP

Pieris M. Markou
DELOITTE

Christos Mavrellis
CHRYSSES DEMETRIADES & CO

Alexia Mouskou
IOANNIDES DEMETRIOU LLC

Marios Panagiotou
TORNARITIS LAW FIRM

Themis Panayi
CYPRUS STOCK EXCHANGE

Georgios Papadopoulos
M.ELIADES & PARTNERS LLC

Christina Papakyriakou
Hasikou
*ANTIS TRIANTAFYLLIDES &
SONS LLC*

Marios Pelekanos
*MESARITIS PELEKANOS
ARCHITECTS - ENGINEERS*

Maria Pilikou
*DR. K. CHRYSOSTOMIDES &
CO LLC*

Michael Pistoula
LIMASSOL MUNICIPALITY

Petros Rialas
*P.G. ECONOMIDES & CO
LIMITED, MEMBER OF RUSSELL
BEDFORD INTERNATIONAL*

Criton Tornaritis
TORNARITIS LAW FIRM

Stelios Triantafyllides
*ANTIS TRIANTAFYLLIDES &
SONS LLC*

Panikos Tsiailis
PRICEWATERHOUSECOOPERS

Christodoulos Vassiliades
*CHRISTODOULOS G.
VASSILIADES & CO LLC*

CZECH REPUBLIC

ALLEN & OVERY LLP

Vladimír Ambruz
AMBRUZ & DARK LAW FIRM

Tomas Babacek
AMBRUZ & DARK LAW FIRM

Libor Basl
BAKER & MCKENZIE

Stanislav Bednář
PETERKA & PARTNERS

Stanislav Beran
PETERKA & PARTNERS

Tomáš Běhounek
*BNT - PRAVDA & PARTNER,
V.O.S.*

Tamara Brixiová
PETERKA & PARTNERS

Michal Buchta
AMBRUZ & DARK LAW FIRM

Hana Cekalova
*SQUIRE, SANDERS & DEMPSEY,
V.O.S., ADVOKATNI KANCELAR*

Filip Celadnik
PETERKA & PARTNERS

Jiří Černý
PETERKA & PARTNERS

Pavel Cirek
*ENERGY REGULATOR OFFICE
CZECH REPUBLIC*

Martin Dančišin
GLATZOVÁ & CO.

Dagmar Dubecka
KOCIAN SOLC BALASTIK

Tereza Erényi
*PRK PARTNERS S.R.O.
ADVOKÁTNÍ KANCELÁŘ*

Jitka Ernestová
PETERKA & PARTNERS

Kristýna Fiaerová
PETERKA & PARTNERS

Panicos Florides
*P.G. ECONOMIDES & CO
LIMITED, MEMBER OF RUSSELL
BEDFORD INTERNATIONAL*

Michal Forýtek
LINKLATERS

Martin Froněk
WHITE & CASE

Jakub Hajek
AMBRUZ & DARK LAW FIRM

Michal Hanko
BUBNIK, MYSLIL & PARTNERS

Jarmila Hanzalova
*PRK PARTNERS S.R.O.
ADVOKÁTNÍ KANCELÁŘ*

Jitka Hlavova
*PRK PARTNERS S.R.O.
ADVOKÁTNÍ KANCELÁŘ*

Michal Hrnčíř
AMBRUZ & DARK LAW FIRM

Pavel Jakab
PETERKA & PARTNERS

Ludvik Juřička
AMBRUZ & DARK LAW FIRM

Adela Krbcová
PETERKA & PARTNERS

Martin Krechler
GLATZOVÁ & CO.

Alea Kubá
AMBRUZ & DARK LAW FIRM

Petr Kucera
CCB - CZECH CREDIT BUREAU

Petr Kuhn
WHITE & CASE

Zuzana Luklova
AMBRUZ & DARK LAW FIRM

Ondrej Machala
*NOTARY CHAMBER, CZECH
REPUBLIC*

Petr Měšťánek
KINSTELLAR

Jiří Markvart
AMBRUZ & DARK LAW FIRM

Peter Maysenhölder
*BNT - PRAVDA & PARTNER,
V.O.S.*

Veronika Mistova
*PRK PARTNERS S.R.O.
ADVOKÁTNÍ KANCELÁŘ*

Lenka Mrazova
PRICEWATERHOUSECOOPERS

David Musil
PRICEWATERHOUSECOOPERS

Jarmila Musilova
CZECH NATIONAL BANK

Lenka Navrátilová
AMBRUZ & DARK LAW FIRM

Petr Novotny
AMBRUZ & DARK LAW FIRM

Marketa Penazova
AMBRUZ & DARK LAW FIRM

Jan Petřík
*BRZOBOHATÝ BROŽ & HONSA,
V.O.S.*

Jan Procházka
AMBRUZ & DARK LAW FIRM

Markéta Protivankova
VEJMELKA & WÜNSCH, S.R.O.

Pavla PYikrylová
PETERKA & PARTNERS

Petros Rialas
*P.G. ECONOMIDES & CO
LIMITED, MEMBER OF RUSSELL
BEDFORD INTERNATIONAL*

Zdenek Rosicky
*SQUIRE, SANDERS & DEMPSEY,
V.O.S., ADVOKATNI KANCELAR*

Leona Ševčíková
PANALPINA CZECH S.R.O.

Robert Sgariboldi
PANALPINA CZECH S.R.O.

Dana Sládečková
CZECH NATIONAL BANK

Ladislav Smejkal
WHITE & CASE

Petra Sochorova
*HAVEL & HOLÁSEK S.R.O.,
ADVOKÁTNÍ KANCELÁŘ*

Anna Staňková
*HAVEL & HOLÁSEK S.R.O.,
ADVOKÁTNÍ KANCELÁŘ*

Paul Stewart
PRICEWATERHOUSECOOPERS

Marie Strachotová
PETERKA & PARTNERS

Nina Studentova
*PRK PARTNERS S.R.O.
ADVOKÁTNÍ KANCELÁŘ*

Marek Švehlík
MAREK ŠVEHLÍK

Růžena Trojánková
KINSTELLAR

Klara Valentova
AMBRUZ & DARK LAW FIRM

Ludìk Vrána
VRÁNA & PELIKÁN

Vaclav Zaloudek
WHITE & CASE

DENMARK

Elsebeth Aaes-Jørgensen
*NORRBOM VINDING, MEMBER
OF IUS LABORIS*

Peter Bang
PLESNER

Thomas Bang
LETT LAW FIRM

Thomas Booker
*ACCURA
ADVOKATAKTIESELSKAB*

Ole Borch
BECH-BRUUN LAW FIRM

Katrine Bundgaard
PHILIP LAW FIRM

Peter Burhøj
*KROMANN REUMERT, MEMBER
OF LEX MUNDI*

Jeppe Buskov
*KROMANN REUMERT, MEMBER
OF LEX MUNDI*

Frants Dalgaard-Knudsen
PLESNER

Mogens Ebeling
BRUUN & HJEJLE

Eivind Einersen
PHILIP LAW FIRM

Jakob Eriksen
LETT LAW FIRM

Lars Fogh
*ACCURA
ADVOKATAKTIESELSKAB*

Anne Birgitte Gammeljord
*GORRISSEN FEDERSPIEL
KIERKEGAARD*

Anne Louise Haack Andersen
LETT LAW FIRM

Lita Misozi Hansen
PRICEWATERHOUSECOOPERS

Anders Hjortsholm
*KROMANN REUMERT, MEMBER
OF LEX MUNDI*

Jens Hjortskov
PHILIP LAW FIRM

Peter Honoré
*KROMANN REUMERT, MEMBER
OF LEX MUNDI*

Jens Steen Jensen
*KROMANN REUMERT, MEMBER
OF LEX MUNDI*

Jeppe Jørgensen
BECH-BRUUN LAW FIRM

William Kanta
*KROMANN REUMERT, MEMBER
OF LEX MUNDI*

Lars Kjaer
BECH-BRUUN LAW FIRM

Dorte Kjærgaard
*ACCURA
ADVOKATAKTIESELSKAB*

Aage Krogh
MAGNUSSON

Christine Larsen
PLESNER

Susanne Schjølin Larsen
*KROMANN REUMERT, MEMBER
OF LEX MUNDI*

Alexander M. P. Johannessen
*KROMANN REUMERT, MEMBER
OF LEX MUNDI*

Andreas Nielsen
BRUUN & HJEJLE

Susanne Nørgaard
PRICEWATERHOUSECOOPERS

Jim Øksnebjerg
*ADVOKATAKTIESELSKABET
HORTEN*

Henrik Pedersen
PRICEWATERHOUSECOOPERS

Jette H. Ronøe
BECH-BRUUN LAW FIRM

Louise Krarup Simonsen
*KROMANN REUMERT, MEMBER
OF LEX MUNDI*

Rajvinder Singh
EXPERIAN NORTHERN EUROPE

Martin Sørensen
2M EL-INSTALLATION A/S

Niels Bang Sørensen
*GORRISSEN FEDERSPIEL
KIERKEGAARD*

Kolja Staunstrup
*KROMANN REUMERT, MEMBER
OF LEX MUNDI*

Kim Trenskow
*KROMANN REUMERT, MEMBER
OF LEX MUNDI*

Ulla Trolle
MINISTRY OF TAXATION

Knud Villemoes Hansen
*NATIONAL SURVEY AND
CADASTRE*

DJIBOUTI

Rahma Abdi Abdillahi
*BANQUE CENTRALE DE
DJIBOUTI*

Abdillahi Aidid Farah
AVOCAT À LA COUR

Wabat Daoud
CABINET LEDOUX SEINA

Félix Emok N'Dolo
CHD GROUP

Mourad Farah
NOTARY

Fatouma Mahamoud Hassan
CABINET MAHAMOUD

Mayank Metha
*MAERSK SEALAND LINE
DJIBOUTI*

Ibrahim Mohamed Omar
CABINET CECA

Abdallah Mohammed Kamil
ETUDE NOTARIALE

Mohamed Omar Mohamed
CABINET MEDOMAR

Lantosoa Hurfin Ralaiarinosy
*GROUPEMENT COSMEZZ
DJIBOUTI S.A.*

Aicha Youssouf Abdi
CABINET CECA

DOMINICA

Alix Boyd-Knights
HOUSE OF ASSEMBLY

Kathy Buffong
*ATTORNEY GENERAL'S
CHAMBERS*

Carl Duncan
*INDEPENDENT REGULATORY
COMMISSION*

Marvlyn Estrado
*KPB CHARTERED
ACCOUNTANTS*

Kareem Guiste
*INDEPENDENT REGULATORY
COMMISSION*

F. Adler Hamlet
REALCO COMPANY LIMITED

Foued Issa
ISSA TRADING LTD.

Sandra Julien
COMPANIES AND INTELLECTUAL PROPERTY OFFICE

Alick C. Lawrence
LAWRENCE ALICK C. CHAMBERS

Charlene Mae Magnaye
PRICEWATERHOUSECOOPERS

Richard Peterkin
PRICEWATERHOUSECOOPERS

Joan K.R. Prevost
PREVOST & ROBERTS

Eugene G. Royer
EUGENE G. ROYER CHARTERED ARCHITECT

Leah Shillingford
DOMINICA AMALGAMATED WORKERS UNION

DOMINICAN REPUBLIC

Lilly Acevedo
HEADRICK RIZIK ALVAREZ & FERNÁNDEZ

Cristian Alvarez
RC ADVISORS, MEMBER OF RUSSELL BEDFORD INTERNATIONAL

Caroline Bono
PRICEWATERHOUSECOOPERS

Ana Isabel Caceres
TRONCOSO Y CACERES

Giselle Castillo
SUPERINTENDENCIA DE BANCOS

Laureana Corral
DANNA CONSULTING

Leandro Corral
ESTRELLA & TUPETE

Mariano Corral
DANNA CONSULTING

José Cruz Campillo
JIMÉNEZ CRUZ PEÑA

Robinson Cuello Shanlatte
PROGRAMA DE CONSOLIDACION DE LA JURISDICCION INMOBILIARIA PODER JUDICIAL

Lisa de Freitas
DE FREITAS DE FREITAS AND JOHNSON

Richard De la Cruz
RC ADVISORS, MEMBER OF RUSSELL BEDFORD INTERNATIONAL

Marcos de Leon
SUPERINTENDENCIA DE BANCOS

Sarah de León Perelló
HEADRICK RIZIK ALVAREZ & FERNÁNDEZ

Rosa Díaz
JIMÉNEZ CRUZ PEÑA

Joaquín Guillermo Estrella Ramia
ESTRELLA & TUPETE

Alejandro Fernández de Castro
PRICEWATERHOUSECOOPERS

Mary Fernández Rodríguez
HEADRICK RIZIK ALVAREZ & FERNÁNDEZ

Jose Ernesto Garcia A.
TRANSGLOBAL LOGISTIC

Gloria Gasso
HEADRICK RIZIK ALVAREZ & FERNÁNDEZ

Pablo Gonzalez Tapia
GONZÁLEZ & COISCOU

Luis J. Jiménez
JIMÉNEZ CRUZ PEÑA

José Antonio Logroño Morales
ADAMS GUZMAN & LOGROÑO

José Ramón Logroño Morales
ADAMS GUZMAN & LOGROÑO

Fabiola Medina
MEDINA & RIZEK, ABOGADOS

Laura Medina
JIMÉNEZ CRUZ PEÑA

Ramón Ortega
PRICEWATERHOUSECOOPERS

Andrea Paniagua
PRICEWATERHOUSECOOPERS

Carolina Pichardo
BIAGGI & MESSINA

Sandra Piña
HEADRICK RIZIK ALVAREZ & FERNÁNDEZ

Edward Piña Fernandez
BIAGGI & MESSINA

Hilda Patricia Polanco Morales
SÁNCHEZ RAFUL SICARD & POLANCO ABOGADOS

Maria Portes
CASTILLO Y CASTILLO

Alejandro Miguel Ramirez Suzaña
RAMIREZ SUZAÑA & ASOC.

Aristides Reyes
EDEESTE

Nelson Rodriguez
GAMEI

Katherine Rosa
JIMÉNEZ CRUZ PEÑA

Francisco Sánchez
CEBALLOS & SANCHEZ, INGENIERÍA Y ENERGÍA, C. POR A.

Maricell Silvestre Rodriguez
JIMÉNEZ CRUZ PEÑA

Katherine Stefan
JIMÉNEZ CRUZ PEÑA

Miriam Stern
SÁNCHEZ RAFUL SICARD & POLANCO ABOGADOS

Juan Tejeda
PRICEWATERHOUSECOOPERS

Vilma Verras Terrero
JIMÉNEZ CRUZ PEÑA

Patricia Villar
PANALPINA WORLD TRANSPORT DOMINICAN REPUBLIC SANTO DOMINGO

Chery Zacarías
MEDINA & RIZEK, ABOGADOS

ECUADOR

Pablo Aguirre
PRICEWATERHOUSECOOPERS

Jaime Mauricio Angulo
DATA-CREDITO

Juan Arias
FALCONI PUIG ABOGADOS

Diego Cabezas-Klaere
CABEZAS & CABEZAS-KLAERE

Xavier Andrade Cadena
ANDRADE VELOZ & ASOCIADOS

Silvana Coka G.
GEOTRANSPORT S.A.

Fernando Coral
PANALPINA WORLD TRANSPORT ECUADOR QUITO

Lucía Cordero Ledergerber
FALCONI PUIG ABOGADOS

Renato Coronel
PINTO & GARCES ASOC. CIA LTDA, MEMBER OF RUSSELL BEDFORD INTERNATIONAL

Fernando Del Pozo Contreras
GALLEGOS, VALAREZO & NEIRA

Miguel Falconi-Puig
FALCONI PUIG ABOGADOS

Martin Galarza
PUENTE REYES & GALARZA ATTORNEYS AT LAW CIA. LTDA.

Juan Carlos Gallegos Happle
GALLEGOS, VALAREZO & NIERA

Enrique Gomez
PUENTE REYES & GALARZA ATTORNEYS AT LAW CIA. LTDA.

Leopoldo González R.
PAZ HOROWITZ ABOGADOS

Rodrigo Jijón
PÉREZ, BUSTAMANTE Y PONCE, MEMBER OF LEX MUNDI

Juan Manuel Marchán
PÉREZ, BUSTAMANTE Y PONCE, MEMBER OF LEX MUNDI

Francisco Javier Naranjo Grijalva
PAZ HOROWITZ ABOGADOS

Esteban Ortiz
PÉREZ, BUSTAMANTE Y PONCE, MEMBER OF LEX MUNDI

Jorge Paz Durini
PAZ HOROWITZ ABOGADOS

Bruno Pineda-Cordero
PÉREZ, BUSTAMANTE Y PONCE, MEMBER OF LEX MUNDI

Xavier Amador Pino
ESTUDIO JURIDICO AMADOR

Ramiro Pinto
PINTO & GARCES ASOC. CIA LTDA, MEMBER OF RUSSELL BEDFORD INTERNATIONAL

Patricia Ponce Arteta
BUSTAMANTE Y BUSTAMANTE

Juan Jose Puente
PUENTE REYES & GALARZA ATTORNEYS AT LAW CIA. LTDA.

Angel Alfonso Puente Reyes
PUENTE, GOMEZ & CO LAW FIRM CIA. LTDA.

Falconi Puig
FALCONI PUIG ABOGADOS

Diego Ramírez
FABARA & COMPAÑIA ABOGADOS

Sandra Reed
PÉREZ, BUSTAMANTE Y PONCE, MEMBER OF LEX MUNDI

Gustavo Romero
ROMERO ARTETA PONCE

Myriam Dolores Rosales Garcés
SUPERINTENDENCIA DE BANCOS Y SEGUROS

Montserrat Sánchez
CORONEL Y PÉREZ

Pablo Fernando Sarzosa Játiva
API ECUADOR

Michelle Semanate
FALCONI PUIG ABOGADOS

Leonardo Sempértegui
SEMPÉRTEGUI ONTANEDA

Esmeralda Tipán
EMPRESA ELÉCTRICA "QUITO" SA

Max Torres
PRICEWATERHOUSECOOPERS

Ruth Urbano
SEMPÉRTEGUI ONTANEDA

Felipe Urdaneta
ACREDITA BURÓ DE INFORMACIÓN CREDITICIA S.A

César Vélez Calderón
COVELCAL

EGYPT, ARAB REP.

Abdel Aal Aly
AFIFI WORLD TRANSPORT

Naguib Abadir
NACITA CORPORATION

Amal Abd El Razek
EGYPTIAN TAX AUTHORITY

Sara Abdel Gabbar
TROWERS & HAMLINS

Ibrahim Mustafa Ibrahim Abdel Khalek
GENERAL AUTHORITY FOR INVESTMENT GAFI

Said Abdel Moniem
AAW CONSULTING ENGINEERS

Ahmed Abou Ali
HASSOUNA & ABOU ALI

Gamal Abou Ali
HASSOUNA & ABOU ALI

Ghada Adel
PRICEWATERHOUSECOOPERS

Hazem Ahmed Fathi
HASSOUNA & ABOU ALI

Abd El Wahab Aly Ibrahim
ABD EL WAHAB SONS

Sara Ammar
AL KAMEL LAW OFFICES

Sayed Ammar
AL KAMEL LAW OFFICES

Hanan Arafat
MINISTRY OF HOUSING, UTILITIES & URBAN DEVELOPMENT

Tim Armsby
TROWERS & HAMLINS

Khaled Balbaa
KPMG

Karim Dabbous
SHERIF DABBOUS, AUDITORS & FINANCIAL CONSULTANCIES, MEMBER OF RUSSELL BEDFORD INTERNATIONAL

Sherif Dabbous
SHERIF DABBOUS, AUDITORS & FINANCIAL CONSULTANCIES,

MEMBER OF RUSSELL BEDFORD INTERNATIONAL

Sameh Dahroug
IBRACHY & DERMARKAR LAW FIRM

Said Diab
SHERIF DABBOUS, AUDITORS & FINANCIAL CONSULTANCIES, MEMBER OF RUSSELL BEDFORD INTERNATIONAL

Amany El Bagoury
AL KAMEL LAW OFFICE

Hanan el Dib
AL-AHL FIRM

Hussein El Gebaly
MINISTRY OF HOUSING, UTILITIES & URBAN DEVELOPMENT

Mohamed Refaat El Houshy
THE EGYPTIAN CREDIT BUREAU I-SCORE

Hassan El Maraashly
AAW CONSULTING ENGINEERS

Amr El Monayer
MINISTRY OF FINANCE

Amina El Oteify
EGYPTIAN FINANCIAL SUPERVISORY AUTHORITY

Mai El- Shaarawy
TROWERS & HAMLINS

Emad El Shalakany
SHALAKANY LAW OFFICE, MEMBER OF LEX MUNDI

Khaled El Shalakany
SHALAKANY LAW OFFICE, MEMBER OF LEX MUNDI

Passant El Tabei
PRICEWATERHOUSECOOPERS

Soheir Elbanna
IBRACHY LAW FIRM

Karim Elhelaly
AL-AHL FIRM

Ashraf Elibrachy
IBRACHY LAW FIRM

Mostafa Elshafei
IBRACHY LAW FIRM

Hassan Fahmy
MINISTRY OF INVESTMENT

Ghada Farouk
SHALAKANY LAW OFFICE, MEMBER OF LEX MUNDI

Tarek Gadllah
IBRACHY LAW FIRM

Emad Hassan
MINISTRY OF STATE FOR ADMINISTRATIVE DEVELOPMENT

Tarek Hassib
AL KAMEL LAW OFFICES

Omneia Helmy
EGYPTIAN CENTER FOR ECONOMIC STUDIES

Mohamed Hisham Hassan
MINISTRY OF INVESTMENT

Stephan Jäger
AMERELLER RECHTSANWÄLTE

Mohamed Kamel
AL KAMEL LAW OFFICE

Mohanad Khaled
BDO, KHALED & CO

Shahira Khaled
AL KAMEL LAW OFFICE

Taha Khaled
BDO, Khaled & Co

Minas Khatchadourian
Egypt Legal Desk

Ussama Khattab
Bridges To Business

Adel Kheir
Adel Kheir Law Office

Mustafa Makram
BDO, Khaled & Co

Sherif Mansour
PricewaterhouseCoopers

Mostafa Mostafa
Al Kamel Law Office

Mostafa Mohamed Mostafa
Al Kamel Law Office

Ahmed Refat
Egyptian Tax Authority

Tarek Fouad Riad
Kosheri, Rashed & Riad

Fatma Salah
Ibrachy & Dermarkar Law Firm

Mohamed Serry
Serry Law Office

Ramy Shalash
Abdallah Shalash

Omar Sherif
Shalakany Law Office, member of Lex Mundi

Randa Tharwat
Nacita Corporation

Greiss Youssef
Afifi World Transport

Eman Zakaria
Ministry of Manpower & Migration

Shereen Zaky
Shalakany Law Office, member of Lex Mundi

Mohsen Ziko
Al Kamel Law Office

Mona Zobaa
Ministry of Investment

EL SALVADOR

Ana Margoth Arévalo
Superintendencia del Sistema Financiero

Francisco Armando Arias Rivera
Arias & Muñoz

Irene Arrieta de Díaz Nuila
Arrieta Bustamante

Carlos Castillo
Romero Pineda & Asociados, member of Lex Mundi

Ricardo Cevallos
Consortium Centro América Abogados

Walter Chávez
Gold Service

Maria Marta Delgado
Arias & Muñoz

Porfirio Diaz Fuentes
DLM & Asociados

Laura Duran De Jimemez
Asociación Protectora de Créditos de El Salvador (PROCREDITO)

Alejandro Fernández de Castro
PricewaterhouseCoopers

Roberta Gallardo de Cromeyer
Arias & Muñoz

Carlos Hernán Gil
Lexincorp

Federico Gurdian
García & Bodán

Erwin Alexander Haas Quinteros
Rusconi, Valdez, Medina & Asociados

Carlos Henriquez
Gold Service

Emilio Iraheta
Gold Service

Luis Lievano
Associacion de Ingenieros y Arquitectos

Thelma Dinora Lizama de Osorio
Superintendencia del Sistema Financiero

Jerson Lopez
Gold Service

Fidel Márquez
Arias & Muñoz

Luis Alonso Medina Lopez
Rusconi, Valdez, Medina & Asociados

Astrud María Meléndez
Asociación Protectora de Créditos de El Salvador (PROCREDITO)

Jorge Mendez
Romero Pineda & Asociados, member of Lex Mundi

Edgar Mendoza
PricewaterhouseCoopers

Miriam Eleana Mixco Reyna
Gold Service

Jocelyn Mónico
Aguilar Castillo Love

Jose Navas
All World Cargo, SA de CV

Ramón Ortega
PricewaterhouseCoopers

Susana Palacios
Arias & Muñoz

Jose Antonio Polanco
Lexincorp

Ana Patricia Portillo Reyes
Guandique Segovia Quintanilla

Hector Rios
Consortium Centro América Abogados

Kelly Beatriz Romero
Rusconi, Valdez, Medina & Asociados

Roxana Romero
Romero Pineda & Asociados, member of Lex Mundi

Adonay Rosales
PricewaterhouseCoopers

Mario Enrique Sáenz
Sáenz & Asociados

Ana Guadalupe Sáenz Padilla
Sáenz & Asociados

Flor Sanchez
PricewaterhouseCoopers

Alonso V. Saravia
Asociacion Salvadoreña de Ingenieros y Arquitectos (ASIA)

Juan Tejeda
PricewaterhouseCoopers

Manuel Telles Suvillaga
Lexincorp

Mauricio Antonio Urrutia
Superintendencia del Sistema Financiero

Julio Vargas
García & Bodán

Ligia Villeda
Arrieta Bustamante

EQUATORIAL GUINEA

Caroline Idrissou-Belingar
BEAC

Heidi B. Johansen
GlobalTrans Internacional

Sébastien Lechêne
FIDAFRICA / PricewaterhouseCoopers

Paulino Mbo Obama
Oficina de estudieos - ATEG

Ponciano Mbomio Nvo
Gabinete Juridico

François Münzer
FIDAFRICA / PricewaterhouseCoopers

Dominique Taty
FIDAFRICA / PricewaterhouseCoopers

ERITREA

Rahel Abera
Berhane Gila-Michael Law Firm

Senai Andemariam
University of Asmara

Paulos Bereket
Ministry of Land, Water and Environment

Tesfai Ghebrehiwet
Department of Energy

Biniam Ghebremichael
Eritrean Airlines

Kebreab Habte Michael
Kebreab Habte Michael Legal Consulting

Tekeste Mesghenna
MTD Enterprises PLC

Habtemicael Weldegiorgis
Ministry of Land, Water and Environment

ESTONIA

Risto Agur
Sorainen

Katrin Altmets
Sorainen

Airi Asperk
Konkurentsiamet Estonian Competition Authority

Aet Bergmann
Luiga Mody Hääl Borenius

Mark Butzmann
BNT Attorneys-at-law OÜ

Ülleke Eerik
Estonian Land Board

Indrek Ergma
Sorainen

Valters Gencs
Gencs Valters Law Firm

Helen Ginter
Sorainen

Külli Haab
Konkurentsiamet Estonian Competition Authority

Heili Haabu
Luiga Mody Hääl Borenius

Kristjan Hänni
Kawe Kapital

Pirkko-Liis Harkmaa
Lepik & Luhaäär LAWIN

Triinu Hiob
Lepik & Luhaäär LAWIN

Risto Hübner
Law Office Tark & Co.

Annika Jaanson
Luiga Mody Hääl Borenius

Andres Juss
Estonian Land Board

Meelis Kaps
Eesti Energia Jaotusvõrk OÜ (Distribution Grid)

Kadri-Catre Kasak
Ministry of Justice

Gerli Kilusk
Lepik & Luhaäär LAWIN

Ermo Kosk
Lepik & Luhaäär LAWIN

Villu Kõve
Estonian Supreme Court

Tanja Kriisa
PricewaterhouseCoopers

Paul Künnap
Sorainen

Piret Lappert
Sorainen

Priit Lepasepp
Sorainen

Liina Linsi
Lepik & Luhaäär LAWIN

Kaidi Lippus
Ministry of Justice

Karin Madisson
Sorainen

Margus Magi
Ministry of Justice

Siiri Malmberg
Hansa Law Offices

Johan Maunsbach
MAQS Law Firm

Veiko Meos
Krediidiinfo A.S.

Jaanus Mody
Luiga Mody Hääl Borenius

Margus Mugu
Luiga Mody Hääl Borenius

Liina Naaber-Kivisoo
Lepik & Luhaäär LAWIN

Arne Ots
Raidla Lejins & Norcous

Karl J. Paadam
Sorainen

Karina Paatsi
Luiga Mody Hääl Borenius

Raino Paron
Raidla Lejins & Norcous

Kirsti Pent
Law Office Tark & Co.

Leho Pihkva
Sorainen

Kristiina Puuste
KPMG

Liza Rastorgujeva
MAQS Law Firm

Ants Ratas
CF&S AS

Heidi Rätsep
Centre of Registers & Information Systems

Kaidi Reiljan-Sihvart
Lepik & Luhaäär LAWIN

Dmitri Rozenblat
Lepik & Luhaäär LAWIN

Piret Saartee
Ministry of Justice

Martin Simovart
Lepik & Luhaäär LAWIN

Monika Tamm
Lepik & Luhaäär LAWIN

Marjaa Teder
Luiga Mody Hääl Borenius

Tarvi Thomberg
Eesti Energia Jaotusvõrk OÜ (Distribution Grid)

Holger Tilk
Lepik & Luhaäär LAWIN

Villi Tõntson
PricewaterhouseCoopers

Veikko Toomere
MAQS Law Firm

Karolina Ullman
MAQS Law Firm

Neve Uudelt
Raidla Lejins & Norcous

Ingmar Vali
Registrite ja infosusteemide Keskus

Hannes Vallikivi
Law Office Tark & Co.

Mirjam Vili
bnt Attorneys-at-law OÜ

Ago Vilu
PricewaterhouseCoopers

Andres Vinkel
Hansa Law Offices

Vesse Võhma
Lepik & Luhaäär LAWIN

Urman Volens
Sorainen

Urmas Volens
Sorainen

Joel Zernask
KPMG

ETHIOPIA

Daniel Alemu
Consultant & Attorney-at-Law

Abdella Ali
Abdella Ali Law Office

Fikadu Asfaw
FIKADU LAW OFFICE

Teklu Asqualu
EXPRESS TRANSIT SERVICE ENTERPRISE PLC.

Bekure Assefa
BEKURE ASSEFA LAW OFFICE

Berhanu Yegezu Beyene
GAD CONSTRUCTION PLC

Wossen Teshome Bokan
TESHOME GABRE-MARIAM LAW FIRM

Teferra Demiss
LEGAL AND INSURANCE CONSULTANT AND ATTORNEY

Solomon Desta
NATIONAL BANK OF ETHIOPIA

Bahre Gezahagn
EXPRESS TRANSIT SERVICE ENTERPRISE PLC.

Berhane Ghebray
BERHANE GHEBRAY & ASSOCIATES

Zekarias Keneaa
ADDIS ABABA UNIVERSITY

Taddesse Lencho
ADDIS ABABA UNIVERSITY

Molla Mengistu
ADDIS ABABA UNIVERSITY

Semenh Sisay
LEWA PLC

Eyasu Tequame
JEHOIACHIN TECHNO PVT. LTD. CO.

Amsale Tsehaye
AMSALE TSEHAYE & ASSOCIATES LAW OFFICE

Tameru Wondmagegnehu
TAMERU WONDMAGEGNEHU LAW OFFICES

FIJI

David Aidney
WILLIAMS & GOSLING LTD.

Caroll Sela Ali
CROMPTONS SOLICITORS

Eddielin Almonte
PricewaterhouseCoopers

Jon Apted
MUNRO LEYS

Nehla Basawaiya
MUNRO LEYS

Mahendra Chand
MUNRO LEYS

William Wylie Clarke
HOWARDS LAWYERS

Dilip Jamnadas
JAMNADAS AND ASSOCIATES

Nilesh Prasad
MITCHELL, KEIL & ASSOCIATES

Ramesh Prasad Lal
CARPENTERS SHIPPING

Colin Radford
LARSEN HOLTOM MAYBIN & COMPANY LIMITED, ARCHITECTS & ENGINEERS

Varun Shandil
MUNRO LEYS

Om Dutt Sharma
FIJI ELECTRICITY AUTHORITY

Shelvin Singh
PARSHOTAM & CO.

Narotam Solanki
PricewaterhouseCoopers

Shayne Sorby
MUNRO LEYS

Chirk Yam
PricewaterhouseCoopers

Eddie Yuen
WILLIAMS & GOSLING LTD.

FINLAND

Hanna Ahtikoski
LAW OFFICE ADVOCARE

Ville Ahtola
CASTRÉN & SNELLMAN ATTORNEYS LTD.

Manne Airaksinen
ROSCHIER ATTORNEYS LTD., MEMBER OF LEX MUNDI

Kasper Björkstén
HELEN SÄHKÖVERKKO OY

Claudio Busi
CASTRÉN & SNELLMAN ATTORNEYS LTD.

Mikko Eerola
WASELIUS & WIST

Marja Eskola
PricewaterhouseCoopers

Johannes Frände
ROSCHIER ATTORNEYS LTD., MEMBER OF LEX MUNDI

Esa Halmari
HEDMAN PARTNERS

Johanna Haltia-Tapio
HANNES SNELLMAN LLC

Tuija Hartikainen
PricewaterhouseCoopers

Seppo Havia
DITTMAR & INDRENIUS

Harry Hedman
HEDMAN OSBORNE CLARKE

Heikki Hiltunen
ROSCHIER ATTORNEYS LTD., MEMBER OF LEX MUNDI

Mia Hukkinen
ROSCHIER ATTORNEYS LTD., MEMBER OF LEX MUNDI

Jenni Hupli
CASTRÉN & SNELLMAN ATTORNEYS LTD.

Nina Isokorpi
ROSCHIER ATTORNEYS LTD., MEMBER OF LEX MUNDI

Lauri Jääskeläinen
BUILDING CONTROL DEPARTMENT OF THE CITY OF HELSINKI

Pekka Jaatinen
CASTRÉN & SNELLMAN ATTORNEYS LTD.

Virpi Jalonen
PricewaterhouseCoopers

Nina Järvinen
CARGOWORLD AB/OY

Jukka-Pekka Joensuu
PricewaterhouseCoopers

Juuso Jokela
SUOMEN ASIAKASTIETO OY - FINSKA

Sakari Kauppinen
NATIONAL BOARD OF PATENTS & REGISTRATION

Antti Kivipuro
ENERGY MARKET AUTHORITY FINLAND

Suvi Knaapila
DITTMAR & INDRENIUS

Elina Kumpulainen
PricewaterhouseCoopers LEGAL SERVICES

Mina Lang
CASTRÉN & SNELLMAN ATTORNEYS LTD.

Jouni Lehtinen
HELEN SÄHKÖVERKKO OY

Tiina Leppälahti
HELEN SÄHKÖVERKKO OY

Patrik Lindfors
LINDFORS & CO, ATTORNEYS-AT-LAW LTD.

Patrick Lindgren
LAW OFFICE ADVOCARE

Tuomas Lukkarinen
NATIONAL LAND SURVEY OF FINLAND

Lasse Luukkainen
CASTRÉN & SNELLMAN ATTORNEYS LTD.

Natalia Malgina
HEDMAN OSBORNE CLARKE

Tero Malmivaara
PricewaterhouseCoopers LEGAL SERVICES

Anna-Kaisa Nenonen
CASTRÉN & SNELLMAN ATTORNEYS LTD.

Minna Oksa
PricewaterhouseCoopers LEGAL SERVICES

Ilkka Pesonen
WABUCO OY, MEMBER OF RUSSELL BEDFORD INTERNATIONAL

Markku Pulkkinen
HEDMAN PARTNERS

Mikko Reinikainen
PricewaterhouseCoopers

Veli-Pekka Saajo
ENERGY MARKET AUTHORITY FINLAND

Tatu Simula
ROSCHIER ATTORNEYS LTD., MEMBER OF LEX MUNDI

Petri Taivalkoski
ROSCHIER ATTORNEYS LTD., MEMBER OF LEX MUNDI

Esa Tiainen
NATIONAL LAND SURVEY OF FINLAND

Marko Vuori
KROGERUS ATTORNEYS LTD.

Rauli Werdermann
SCHENKER CORP.

Gunnar Westerlund
ROSCHIER ATTORNEYS LTD., MEMBER OF LEX MUNDI

Kai Wist
PricewaterhouseCoopers

FRANCE

ALLEN & OVERY LLP

Romain Arnaud
VAUGHAN AVOCATS

Antoine Azam-Darley
AZAM-DARLEY & ASSOCIÉS

Nicolas Barberis
ASHURST

Andrew Booth
ANDREW BOOTH ARCHITECT

Franck Buffaud
DELSOL AVOCATS

Laure Canu
MAYER BROWN LLP

Frédérique Chifflot Bourgeois
LAWYER AT THE BAR OF PARIS

Michel Combe
LANDWELL & ASSOCIÉS - PricewaterhouseCoopers LEGAL SERVICES

Stephane Coulaux
COULAUX-MARICOT-GEORGANTA (CMG LEGAL)

Ann Creelman
VATIER & ASSOCIÉS

Raphaëlle de Ruffi de Pontevès
LANDWELL & ASSOCIÉS - PricewaterhouseCoopers LEGAL SERVICES

Anne Delerable
GIDE LOYRETTE NOUEL A.A.R.P.I.

Olivier Everaere
AGENCE EPURE SARL

Benoit Fauvelet
BANQUE DE FRANCE

Sylvie Ghesquiere
BANQUE DE FRANCE

Kevin Grossmann
MAYER BROWN LLP

Christophe Guenard
LANDWELL & ASSOCIÉS - PricewaterhouseCoopers LEGAL SERVICES

Philipe Guibert
FIEEC

Marc Jobert
JOBERT & ASSOCIÉS

Caroline Joly
LANDWELL & ASSOCIÉS - PricewaterhouseCoopers LEGAL SERVICES

Carol Khoury
JONES DAY

Daniel Arthur Laprès
CABINET D'AVOCATS

Magali Lemaistre
CONFÉDÉRATION FRANÇAISE DU COMMERCE INTERENTREPRISES (CGI)

Jean-Louis Martin
JONES DAY

Nicolas Mordaunt-Crook
LANDWELL & ASSOCIÉS - PricewaterhouseCoopers LEGAL SERVICES

Nathalie Morel
MAYER BROWN LLP

Frédéric Roussel
FONTAINE, ROUSSEL & ASSOCIÉS

Hugues Roux
BANQUE DE FRANCE

Virginie Sabag
CONFÉDÉRATION FRANÇAISE DU COMMERCE INTERENTREPRISES (CGI)

Carole Sabbah
MAYER BROWN LLP

Isabelle Smith Monnerville
VAUGHAN AVOCATS

Jean Luc Vallens
COURT OF APPEAL

François Verdot
SALANS

Philippe Xavier-Bender
GIDE LOYRETTE NOUEL A.A.R.P.I.

Claire Zuliani
TRANSPARENCE, MEMBER OF RUSSEL BEDFORD INTERNATIONAL

GABON

Marcellin Massila Akendengue
SEEG, SOCIÉTÉ D'ENERGIE ET D'EAU DU GABON

Marie Carmel Ketty Ayimambenwe
BANQUE INTERNATIONALE POUR LE COMMERCE ET L'INDUSTRIE DU GABON

Benoît Boulikou
SEEG, SOCIÉTÉ D'ENERGIE ET D'EAU DU GABON

Daniel Chevallon
MATELEC

Fabrice Guida
CLUB OHADA GABON

Caroline Idrissou-Belingar
BEAC

Michael Jeannot
MATELEC

Pélagie Massamba Mouckocko
FIDAFRICA / PricewaterhouseCoopers

Mirielle Moundakou Mapicka
CLUB OHADA GABON

Jean Hilaire Moussavou
FUMU TECHNOLOGIE

Célestin Ndelia
ETUDE MAÎTRE NDELIA CÉLESTIN

Joel Ndong
DIRECTION GÉNÉRALE DE L'URBANISME

Ruben Mindonga Ndongo
CABINET MAÎTRE ANGUILER

Lubin Ntoutoume
AVOCAT

Olivier P. N'Zahou
CLUB OHADA GABON

Marie-Jose Ongo Mendou
FFA JURIDIQUE & FISCAL

Nadine Owanga Tetey Logi
CLUB OHADA GABON

Laurent Pommera
FIDAFRICA / PricewaterhouseCoopers

Christ Hermann Pounah
CLUB OHADA GABON

Christophe A. Relongoué
FIDAFRICA / PricewaterhouseCoopers

GAMBIA, THE

Alpha Amadou Barry
Deloitte

Abdul Aziz Bensouda
Amie Bensouda & Co.

Amie N.D. Bensouda
Amie Bensouda & Co.

Lamin Ceesay
Solie Law Chambers

Ida Denise Drameh
Ida D. Drameh & Associates

Cherno Alieu Jallow
Deloitte

Kulo Jatta
Department of Land and Surveys

Lamin S. Jatta
Deloitte

Sulayman M. Joof
S.M. Joof Agency

Nani Juwara
National Water and Electricity Company Ltd.

George Kwatia
PricewaterhouseCoopers

Tijan Mbye
Maj Consult Ltd.

Omar Njie
Law Firm Omar Njie

Pa M. M. N'jie
Trust Bank Ltd.

Maxwell Ntiri
PricewaterhouseCoopers

Kingsley Owusu-Ewli
PricewaterhouseCoopers

Ebrima Sambou
Office of the Chief Justice, Judiciary of The Gambia

Hawa Sisay-Sabally

Raymond Sock
Legal Consultant

Darcy White
PricewaterhouseCoopers

GEORGIA

Zurab Antelidze
Ministry of Finance

Natalia Babakishvili
Mgaloblishvili, Kipiani, Dzidziguri (MKD) Law Firm

Giorgi Begiashvili
Begiashvili & Co. Limited Law Offices

Ketevan Beradze
BGI Legal

Sandro Bibilashvili
BGI Legal

Vladimer Chkhaidze
National Agency of Public Registry

Paul Cooper
PricewaterhouseCoopers

Kakha Damenia
GDC Solutions

Tsitsi Doborjginidze
Caucastransexpress Ltd.

Tsotne Ebralidze
ARCI Architecture & Development

Courtney Fowler
PricewaterhouseCoopers

David Giorgadze
Association for Protection of Landowners Rights (APLR)

Lasha Gogiberidze
BGI Legal

Mamuka Gordeziani
ITM Global Logistics

Levan Gotua
Ministry of Finance

Bela Gutidze
GDC Solutions

Tamuna Gvaramia
BGI Legal

Batu Gvasalia
National Agency of Public Registry

Nino Javakhidze
Chancellery of the Government of Georgia

David Kakabadze
Georgian Legal Partnership

Irakli Kandashvili

Pasha Karim
Globalink Logistics Group

Mari Khardziani
National Agency of Public Registry

Koba Koakhidze
JSC Creditinfo Georgia

David Koberidze
Chancellery of the Government of Georgia

Aieti Kukava
Alliance Group Holding

Vakhtang Lejava
Chancellery of the Government of Georgia

Ekaterine Meskhidze
National Agency of Public Registry

Merab Narmania
Chancellery of the Government of Georgia

Vachtang Okreshidze
Georgia National Energy and Water Supply Regulatory Commission

Vakhtang Paresishvili
DLA Piper Georgia LP

Irakli Pipia
DLA Piper Georgia LP

Tamar Popkhadze
PricewaterhouseCoopers

Joseph Salukvadze
Tbilisi State University

Natia Samushia
Chancellery of the Government of Georgia

Manzoor Shah
Globalink Logistics Group

Manana Shurghulaia
Chancellery of the Government of Georgia

Rusa Sreseli
GDC Solutions

Anna Tabidze
Mgaloblishvili, Kipiani, Dzidziguri (MKD) Law Firm

Giorgi Tavartkiladze
Deloitte

Tato Urjumelashvili
State Procurement Agency

GERMANY

Friedhold E. Andreas
Freiling, Andreas & Partner

Gabriele Apfelbacher
Cleary Gottlieb Steen & Hamilton LLP

Marco Bach
PricewaterhouseCoopers

Henning Berger
White & Case

Astrid Berle
SCHUFA Holding AG

Jennifer Bierly
GSK Stockmann + Kollegen

Joerg Boehmer

Michael Brems
Cleary Gottlieb Steen & Hamilton LLP

Thomas Büssow
PricewaterhouseCoopers

Thomas Buhl
Cleary Gottlieb Steen & Hamilton LLP

Nikolaus Bunting
Institute for Law and Finance Germany

Helge Dammann
PricewaterhouseCoopers Legal Services

Andreas Eckhardt
PricewaterhouseCoopers Legal Services

Dieter Endres
PricewaterhouseCoopers

Peter Fissenewert
Buse Heberer Fromm

Sabine Funke
Cleary Gottlieb Steen & Hamilton LLP

Markus J. Goetzmann
C·B·H Rechtsanwälte

Jana Greiser
PricewaterhouseCoopers Legal Services

Björn Grund
Cleary Gottlieb Steen & Hamilton LLP

Andrea Gruss
Merget + Partner

Klaus Günther
Linklaters Oppenhoff & Rädler

Robert Gutte
Cleary Gottlieb Steen & Hamilton LLP

Rüdiger Harms
Cleary Gottlieb Steen & Hamilton LLP

Ilka Heinemeyer
SJ Berwin LLP

Stefan Heinrich
Cleary Gottlieb Steen & Hamilton LLP

Götz-Sebastian Hök
Dr. Hök Stieglmeier & Partner

Markus Jakoby
Jakoby Rechtsanwälte

Christof Kautzsch
Salans

Johann Klein
Beeh & Happich GmbH Wirtschaftsprüfungs-gesellschaft Steuerberatungsge-sellschaft, member of Russell Bedford International

Jörg Kraffel
White & Case

Peter Limmer
Notare Dr. Limmer & Dr. Friederich

Christoph Lindenau
PricewaterhouseCoopers Legal Services

Frank Lohrmann
Cleary Gottlieb Steen & Hamilton LLP

Cornelia Marquardt
Norton Rose

Susanne Mattern
PricewaterhouseCoopers

Werner Meier
Cleary Gottlieb Steen & Hamilton LLP

Dirk Meyer-Claassen
Senatsverwaltung für Stadtentwicklung Berlin

Eike Najork
C·B·H Rechtsanwälte

Wolfgang Nardi
Kirkland & Ellis LLP

Dirk Otto
Norton Rose

Daniel Panajotow
Cleary Gottlieb Steen & Hamilton LLP

Peter Polke
Cleary Gottlieb Steen & Hamilton LLP

Sebastian Prügel
White & Case

Michael Roemer
Vattenfall Europe Distribution Hamburg GmbH

Christoph Schauenburg
Cleary Gottlieb Steen & Hamilton LLP

Friedrich Tobias Schoene
Hogan & Hartson LLP

Kirstin Schwedt
Linklaters Oppenhoff & Rädler

Ingrid Seitz
Deutsche Bundesbank

Ahmad Soltan
Wimexas Ltd..

Dirk Stiller
PricewaterhouseCoopers Legal Services

Tobias Taetzner
PricewaterhouseCoopers

Holger Thomas
SJ Berwin LLP

Matthias Thorns
BDA | Confederation of German Employers

Valentin Todorow
Hogan & Hartson LLP

Katharina von Rosenstiel
Orrick Hölters & Elsing

Lena Wallenhorst
Cleary Gottlieb Steen & Hamilton LLP

Stephan Werner

Annekatren Werthmann-Feldhues
PricewaterhouseCoopers Legal Services

Thomas Winkler
Domus AG, member of Russell Bedford International

Gerlind Wisskirchen
CMS Hasche Sigle

Boris Witt
Cleary Gottlieb Steen & Hamilton LLP

Uwe Witt
PricewaterhouseCoopers Legal Services

Christian Zeissler
C·B·H Rechtsanwälte

GHANA

George K Acquah
Laryea, Laryea & Co. P.C.

Larry Adjetey
Law Trust Company

Benjamin Agbotse
H & G Architects and Consultants

Godwin Amartey
Andah and Andah

Nene Amegatcher
Sam Okudzeto & Associates

K. B. Andah
Andah and Andah

Wilfred Kwabena Anim-Odame
Land Valuation Board

Ellen Bannerman
Bruce-Lyle Bannerman & Associates

Stella Bentsi-Enchill
Lexconsult and Company

Abed Buabur
Andah and Andah

Emmanuel Dorsu
Town and Country Planning Department

Clifford Fiadjoe
Andah and Andah

Angela Gyasi
Bentsi-Enchill & Letsa, member of Lex Mundi

Farida Karim
Crown Agents Ghana Ltd.

Rosa Kudoadzi
Bentsi-Enchill & Letsa, member of Lex Mundi

George Kwatia
PricewaterhouseCoopers

Samuel Kwofie
Ghana Grid Company

Kenneth D. Laryea
Laryea, Laryea & Co. P.C.

Nortey Miriam
PricewaterhouseCoopers

Sam Okudzeto
Sam Okudzeto & Associates

Kingsley Owusu-Ewli
PRICEWATERHOUSECOOPERS

Stefan Peter
PANALPINA LTD.

Jacob Saah
SAAH & CO.

Julien Tardy
SDV (GHANA) LTD.

Darcy White
PRICEWATERHOUSECOOPERS

GREECE

George Apostolakos
APOSTOLAKOS ARCHITECTS

Ioanna Argyraki
*KYRIAKIDES GEORGOPOULOS &
DANIOLOS ISSAIAS LAW FIRM*

Andreas Bagias
KELEMENIS & CO.

Antonis Bavas
STEPHENSON HARWOOD

Ira Charisiadou
*ELIAS PARASKEVAS ATTORNEYS
1933*

Alkistis - Marina Christofilou
I.K. ROKAS & PARTNERS

Sotiris Constantinou
GRANT THORNTON

Theodora D. Karagiorgou
KOUTALIDIS LAW FIRM

Eleni Dikonimaki
*TEIRESIAS S.A. INTERBANKING
INFORMATION SYSTEMS*

Panagiotis Drakopoulos
DRAKOPOULOS LAW FIRM

Alexandra Economou
DRAKOPOULOS LAW FIRM

Margarita Flerianou
*ECONOMOU INTERNATIONAL
SHIPPING AGENCIES*

Sotiris Gioussios
GRANT THORNTON

Antigoni Gkarla
PRICEWATERHOUSECOOPERS

Yanos Gramatidis
*BAHAS, GRAMATIDIS &
PARTNERS*

Elina Kanataki
DRAKOPOULOS LAW FIRM

Constantinos Kapitsinos
*SPYRIDAKIS TSOUKALA LAW
FIRM (ST LAW FIRM)*

Evangelos Karaindros
*EVANGELOS KARAINDROS LAW
FIRM*

Artemis Karathanassi
PRICEWATERHOUSECOOPERS

Constantine Karydis
*PRICEWATERHOUSECOOPERS
LEGAL SERVICES*

Yannis Kelemenis
KELEMENIS & CO.

Constantinos Klissouras
ANAGNOSTOPOULOS BAZINAS

Alexandra Kondyli
KARATZAS & PARTNERS

Nicholas Kontizas
*ZEPOS & YANNOPOULOS,
MEMBER OF LEX MUNDI*

Panos Koromantzos
*BAHAS, GRAMATIDIS &
PARTNERS*

Olga Koromilia
*PRICEWATERHOUSECOOPERS
LEGAL SERVICES*

Yannis Kourniotis
*M & P BERNITSAS LAW
OFFICES*

Tom Kyriakopoulos
KELEMENIS & CO.

Dimitrios Kremalis
*KREMALIS LAW FIRM, MEMBER
OF IUS LABORIS*

Vassiliki G. Lazarakou
*ZEPOS & YANNOPOULOS,
MEMBER OF LEX MUNDI*

Ioanna Lazaridou -
Elmaloglou
KELEMENIS & CO.

Konstantinos Logaras
*ZEPOS & YANNOPOULOS,
MEMBER OF LEX MUNDI*

Evangelia Martinovits
I.K. ROKAS & PARTNERS

Margarita Matsi
KELEMENIS & CO.

John Mazarakos
*ELIAS PARASKEVAS ATTORNEYS
1933*

Makariou Panagiota
GRANT THORNTON

Panayis Panagiotopoulos
*KREMMYDAS-DORIS &
ASSOCIATES LAW FIRM*

Antonis Pantazis
PRICEWATERHOUSECOOPERS

Elena Papachristou
*ZEPOS & YANNOPOULOS,
MEMBER OF LEX MUNDI*

Konstantinos Papadiamantis
POTAMITISVEKRIS

Constantinos Papadogiannis
*ACRON TECHNICAL
COMMERCIAL LTD.*

Kyriakos Papadogiannis
*ACRON TECHNICAL
COMMERCIAL LTD.*

Athanassia Papantoniou
KELEMENIS & CO.

Alexios Papastavrou
POTAMITISVEKRIS

Dimitris E. Paraskevas
*ELIAS PARASKEVAS ATTORNEYS
1933*

Katerina Politi
*KYRIAKIDES GEORGOPOULOS &
DANIOLOS ISSAIAS LAW FIRM*

Mary Psylla
PRICEWATERHOUSECOOPERS

Vasiliki Salaka
KARATZAS & PARTNERS

Harris Skordakis
*PRICEWATERHOUSECOOPERS
LEGAL SERVICES*

Iro Stamataki
KELEMENIS & CO.

Alexia Stratou
*KREMALIS LAW FIRM, MEMBER
OF IUS LABORIS*

John Tripidakis
*JOHN M. TRIPIDAKIS AND
ASSOCIATES*

Antonios Tsavdaridis
I.K. ROKAS & PARTNERS

Mania Tsoumita
KELEMENIS & CO.

Ioannis Vekris
POTAMITISVEKRIS

Sofia Xanthoulea
*JOHN M. TRIPIDAKIS AND
ASSOCIATES*

Vicky Xourafa
*KYRIAKIDES GEORGOPOULOS &
DANIOLOS ISSAIAS LAW FIRM*

Fredy Yatracou
PRICEWATERHOUSECOOPERS

GRENADA

Raymond Anthony
RAYMOND ANTHONY & CO.

Robert Branch
SUPREME COURT

James Bristol
HENRY, HENRY & BRISTOL

Thaddus Charles
*INLAND REVENUE
DEPARTMENT*

Christopher DeRiggs
*MINISTRY OF FINANCE,
PLANNING, ENERGY, FOREIGN
TRADE & CO-OPERATIVES*

Carlyle Felix
*MINISTRY OF FINANCE,
PLANNING, ENERGY, FOREIGN
TRADE & CO-OPERATIVES*

Jo Francis
MINISTRY OF LEGAL AFFAIRS

Anette Henry
SUPREME COURT

Kelvin Jacobs
CREATIVE DESIGN

Kurt LaBarrie
CREATIVE DESIGN

Niel Noel
*HENRY HUDSON - PHILLIPS
& CO.*

Darshan Ramdhani
MINISTRY OF LEGAL AFFAIRS

Valentino Sawney
TRADSHIP INTERNATIONAL

David Sinclair
*SINCLAIR ENTERPRISES
LIMITED*

Trevor St. Bernard
LEWIS & RENWICK

Lisa Telessord
SUPREME COURT

Shireen Wilkinson
*WILKINSON, WILKINSON &
WILKINSON*

Daniella Williams Mitchell
DANNY WILLIAMS & CO.

GUATEMALA

José Aguilar
MAYORA & MAYORA, S.C.

Pedro Aragón
ARAGÓN & ARAGÓN

Elias Arriaza
*CONSORTIUM LEGAL,
RODRÍGUEZ, ARCHILA,
CASTELLANOS, SOLARES &
AGUILAR*

Anabella Arzú
ACZALAW

Ruby María Asturias Castillo
ACZALAW

María de los Angeles Barillas
Buchhalter
SARAVIA & MUÑOZ

Edgar Baltazar Barquín Durán
*SUPERINTENDENCIA DE
BANCOS*

Jorge Rolando Barrios
*BONILLA, MONTANO,
TORIELLO & BARRIOS*

Neri Benitez
*EMPRESA ELÉCTRICA DE
GUATEMALA, S.A.*

Cecilia Bonilla
AGUILAR CASTILLO LOVE

Maria del Pilar Bonilla
*BONILLA, MONTANO,
TORIELLO & BARRIOS*

Agustín Buezo
ARROW CARGO

Edy Cabrera
PRICEWATERHOUSECOOPERS

Rodrigo Callejas Aquino
CARRILLO & ASOCIADOS

José Alfredo Cándido Durón
*SUPERINTENDENCIA DE
BANCOS*

Juan Pablo Carrasco de
Groote
*DÍAZ-DURÁN & ASOCIADOS
CENTRAL LAW*

Francisco José Castillo
Chacón
AGUILAR CASTILLO LOVE

Juan Carlos Castillo Chacón
AGUILAR CASTILLO LOVE

Paola van der Beek de
Andrino
*CÁMARA GUATEMALTECA DE
LA CONSTRUCCIÓN*

Rolando De Paz Barrientos
*SOLUTIONS OF INFORMATICA
OF CENTRAL AMERICA, INC.*

Luis Diaz
TransUnion GUATEMALA

Hugo Daniel Figueroa Estrada
*SUPERINTENDENCIA DE
BANCOS*

Rodolfo Fuentes
*PROTECTORA DE CRÈDITO
COMERCIAL*

José Gonzalez
PRECON

Raúl Stuardo Juárez Leal
*SUPERINTENDENCIA DE
BANCOS*

María Isabel Luján
Zilbermann
QUIÑONES, IBARGÜEN & LUJÁN

Eduardo Mayora Alvarado
MAYORA & MAYORA, S.C.

Edgar Mendoza
PRICEWATERHOUSECOOPERS

Christian Michelangeli
CARRILLO & ASOCIADOS

Roberto Moreno Rodríguez
Alcalá
*MORENO RUFFINELLI &
ASOCIADOS*

Roberto Ozaeta
*PRICEWATERHOUSECOOPERS
LEGAL SERVICES*

Marco Antonio Palacios
PALACIOS & ASOCIADOS

Rita Pérez
ARAGÓN & ARAGÓN

Melida Pineda
CARRILLO & ASOCIADOS

Evelyn Rebuli
QUIÑONES, IBARGÜEN & LUJÁN

Alfredo Rodríguez Mahuad
*CONSORTIUM LEGAL,
RODRÍGUEZ, ARCHILA,
CASTELLANOS, SOLARES &
AGUILAR*

Rodrigo Salguero
PRICEWATERHOUSECOOPERS

Cynthia Sequeira
PALACIOS & ASOCIADOS

José Augusto Toledo Cruz
ARIAS & MUÑOZ

Elmer Vargas
ACZALAW

Sergio Velásquez
*COMISIÓN NACIONAL DE
ENERGÍA ELÉCTRICA*

Ernesto Viteri Arriola
VITERI & VITERI

GUINEA

Aminata Bah Tall
NIMBA CONSEIL SARL

Boubacar Barry
JURIFIS CONSULT GUINÉE

Mohamed Camara
SOCOPAO - SDV

Oumar Dabo
ARCHI

Ahmadou Diallo
CHAMBRE DES NOTAIRES

Djenabou Diallo
NIMBA CONSEIL SARL

Maimouna Diallo
NIMBA CONSEIL SARL

El Hajj Barry Djoudja
AICHFEET

Abdel Aziz Kaba
NIMBA CONSEIL SARL

Lansana Kaba
CARIG

Nouke Kourouma
*DIRECTION NATIONALE
DE L'HABITAT ET DE LA
CONSTRUCTION*

Mohamed Lahlou
*FIDAFRICA /
PRICEWATERHOUSECOOPERS*

Guy Piam
NIMBA CONSEIL SARL

Raffi Raja
CABINET KOÙMY

Dominique Taty
*FIDAFRICA /
PRICEWATERHOUSECOOPERS*

Abdourahamane Tounkara
GUINÉE CONSULTING

Aboubacar Salimatou Toure
NIMBA CONSEIL SARL

Yansane Fatoumata Yari
Soumah
OFFICE NOTARIAL

GUINEA-BISSAU

Diaby Aboubakar
BCEAO

Marceano Barbosa
REGISTRAR

Jaimentino Có
MINISTÉRIO DO COMÉRCIO

Adelaida Mesa D'Almeida
JURISCONTA SRL

Agostinho Joaquim Gomes
MUNICIPALITY OF BISSAU

Octávio Lopes
OCTÁVIO LOPES ADVOGADOS -
MIRANDA ALLIANCE

Osiris Francisco Pina Ferreira
CONSELHO JUDICIAL DA
MAGISTRADURA

Djunco Suleiman Ture
MUNICIPALITY OF BISSAU

Carlos Vamain
GOMES & VAMAIN
ASSOCIADOS

Emmanuel Yehouessi
BCEAO

GUYANA

Ashton Chase
LAW OFFICE OF ASHTON
CHASE ASSOCIATES

Desmond Correia
CORREIA & CORREIA LTD.

Geoffrey Da Silva
GUYANA OFFICE FOR
INVESTMENT

Lucia Desir
D & J SHIPPING SERVICES

GUYANA POWER & LIGHT INC.

Kashir Khan
ATTORNEY-AT-LAW

Rakesh Latchana
RAM & MCRAE

Carolyn Paul
SUPREME COURT OF
JUDICATURE

R.N. Poonai
POONAI & POONAI

PUBLIC UTILITIES
COMMISSION GUYANA

Christopher Ram
RAM & MCRAE

Vishwamint Ramnarine
PFK BARCELLOS, NARINE
& CO

Reginald Roach
R&D ENGINEERING

Gidel Thomside
NATIONAL SHIPPING
CORPORATION LTD.

Josephine Whitehead
CAMERON & SHEPHERD

Troy Williams
RAM & MCRAE

HAITI

Lionel Allen
ARCHITECT

Martin Camille Cangé
ELECTRICITÉ D'HAÏTI

Jean Gerard Eveillard
CABINET EVEILLARD

Gilbert Giordani
ETUDE BRISSON CASSAGNOL

Robert Laforest
CABINET LAFOREST

Garry Lhérisson
MINISTÈRE DES TRAVAUX
PUBLICS, TRANSPORTS ET
COMMUNICATIONS

Louis Gary Lissade
CABINET LISSADE

Joseph Paillant
ORDRE DES COMPTABLES
PROFESSIONELS AGRÉES
D'HAÏTI

Micosky Pompilus
CABINET D'AVOCATS
CHALMERS

Paul Emile Simon
ARCHITECT

Salim Succar
CABINET LISSADE

HONDURAS

Juan José Alcerro Milla
AGUILAR CASTILLO LOVE

Jose Miguel Alvarez
CONSORTIUM CENTRO
AMERICA ABOGADOS

José Simón Azcona
IABSA

Manuel Betancourth
DYCELEC S DE R.L.

César Cabrera
TRANSUNION

Jose Ernesto Calix
EMPRESA NACIONAL DE
ENERGÍA ELÉCTRICA

Janeth Castañeda de Aquino
GRUPO CROPA PANALPINA

Carmen Chevez
CNBS - COMISION NACIONAL
DE BANCOS Y SEGUROS

Jaime Colindres Rosales
DYCELES S DE R.L.

Ramón Discua
BATRES, DISCUA, MARTINEZ
ABOGADOS

Gilda Espinal Veliz
ASJ - ASOCIACION PARA UNA
SOCIEDAD MAS JUSTA

Angela Figueroa
ASJ - ASOCIACION PARA UNA
SOCIEDAD MAS JUSTA

Lillizeth Garay
CNBS - COMISION NACIONAL
DE BANCOS Y SEGUROS

Jessica Handal
ARIAS & MUÑOZ

Juan Diego Lacayo González
AGUILAR CASTILLO LOVE

Marcela López Carrillo
PRICEWATERHOUSECOOPERS

Dennis Matamoros Batson
ARIAS & MUÑOZ

Ramón E. Morales
PRICEWATERHOUSECOOPERS

Vanessa Oquelí
GARCÍA & BODÁN

Ramón Ortega
PRICEWATERHOUSECOOPERS

Mauricio Quiñónez
PRICEWATERHOUSECOOPERS

Dino Rietti
ARQUITECNIC

José Rafael Rivera Ferrari
CONSORTIUM CENTRO
AMERICA ABOGADOS

Enrique Rodriguez Burchard
AGUILAR CASTILLO LOVE

Fanny Rodríguez del Cid
ARIAS & MUÑOZ

René Serrano
ARIAS & MUÑOZ

Godofredo Siercke
GARCÍA & BODÁN

Cristian Stefan Handal
ZACARÍAS & ASOCIADOS

Roberto Manuel Zacarías
Urrutia
ZACARÍAS & ASOCIADOS

HONG KONG SAR,
CHINA

ALLEN & OVERY LLP

Albert P.C. Chan
THE HONG KONG
POLYTECHNIC UNIVERSITY

Allan Chan
THE LAND REGISTRY OF HONG
KONG

Nicholas Chan
SQUIRE, SANDERS & DEMPSEY

Vashi Ram Chandi
EXCELLENCE INTERNATIONAL

Deborah Y. Cheng
SQUIRE, SANDERS & DEMPSEY
L.L.P.

Candace Chu
ECONOMIC ANALYSIS AND
BUSINESS FACILITATION
UNIT, HONG KONG SAR
GOVERNMENT

Jimmy Chung
RUSSELL BEDFORD HONG
KONG LIMITED, MEMBER
OF RUSSELL BEDFORD
INTERNATIONAL

Keith Man Kei Ho
WILKINSON & GRIST

Rod Houng-Lee
PRICEWATERHOUSECOOPERS

Tam Yuen Hung
GUANGDONG AND HONG KONG
FEEDER ASSOCIATION LTD.

Salina Ko
APL

Howard Lam
LINKLATERS

Lauren Lau
KLC KENNIC LUI & CO

Damon Law
BAKER AND MCKENZIE

Phila Law
ECONOMIC ANALYSIS AND
BUSINESS FACILITATION
UNIT, HONG KONG SAR
GOVERNMENT

Tommy Li
BURKE, FUNG & LI SOLICITORS

Kennic L H Lui
KLC KENNIC LUI & CO

Justin Ma
LINKLATERS

James Ngai
RUSSELL BEDFORD HONG
KONG LIMITED, MEMBER
OF RUSSELL BEDFORD
INTERNATIONAL

Kok Leong Ngan
CLP POWER HONG KONG
LIMITED

Randolph Perry
ORRICK, HERRINGTON &
SUTCLIFFE LLP

Kenneth Poon
THE LAND REGISTRY OF HONG
KONG

Martinal Quan
METOPRO ASSOCIATES
LIMITED

Jude Ryan
ORRICK, HERRINGTON &
SUTCLIFFE LLP

Alex Sahi
TOP IMPETUS

Ervin Tan
ORRICK HERRINGTON &
SUTCLIFFE

Eric Tang
ASIA BUSINESS SERVICE
LIMITED

Sara Tong
TEMPLE CHAMBERS

Laurence Tsong
TRANSUNION HONG KONG

Yeeling Wan
STEPHENSON HARWOOD & LO

Yuen-ho Wan
RUSSELL BEDFORD HONG
KONG LIMITED, MEMBER
OF RUSSELL BEDFORD
INTERNATIONAL

Fergus Wong
PRICEWATERHOUSECOOPERS

Jackson Wong
HONG KONG ECONOMIC &
TRADE OFFICE

Ricky Yiu
BAKER & MCKENZIE

Peter Yu
PRICEWATERHOUSECOOPERS

Frank Yuen
KLC KENNIC LUI & CO

HUNGARY

Mark Balastyai
FUTUREAL GROUP

Péter Bárdos
DR. BÁRDOS ATTORNEY-AT-
LAW

Sándor Békési
PARTOS & NOBLET LOVELLS

Hedi Bozsonyik
SZECSKAY ATTORNEYS AT LAW

Zsuzsanna Cseri
BÁRD, CSERI & PARTNERS
LAW FIRM

Gabriella Erdos
PRICEWATERHOUSECOOPERS

Ágnes Fábry
PRK BELLÁK & PARTNERS

Éva Gargya
NAGY ÉS TRÓCSÁNYI LAW
OFFICE, MEMBER OF LEX
MUNDI

Anna Gáspár
BUILD-ECON LTD.

Dóra Horváth
RÉTI, ANTALL & MADL
LANDWELL LAW FIRM

Norbert Izer
PRICEWATERHOUSECOOPERS

Zsuzsanna Károlyi
PRK BELLÁK & PARTNERS

Petra Lencs
BÁRD, CSERI & PARTNERS
LAW FIRM

Lívia Mihovics
RÉTI, ANTALL & MADL
LANDWELL LAW FIRM

László Mohai
MOHAI LAW OFFICE

Robert Nagy
BISZ CENTRAL CREDIT
INFORMATION PLC.

Sándor Németh
SZECSKAY ATTORNEYS AT LAW

Christopher Noblet
PARTOS & NOBLET LOVELLS

Faith Okpukpan
JONES LANG LASALLE

Örs Pénzes
NAGY ÉS TRÓCSÁNYI LAW
OFFICE, MEMBER OF LEX
MUNDI

Andrea Soós
SOOSLAW OFFICE

Vera Szalkai
KÖZTI ZRT.

András Szecskay
SZECSKAY ATTORNEYS AT LAW

Ágnes Szent-Ivány
SÁNDOR SZEGEDI SZENT-IVÁNY
KOMÁROMI EVERSHEDS

Viktória Szilágyi
NAGY ÉS TRÓCSÁNYI LAW
OFFICE, MEMBER OF LEX
MUNDI

László Szqcs
RÉTI, ANTALL & MADL
LANDWELL LAW FIRM

Adrienn Tar
SZECSKAY ATTORNEYS AT LAW

Ádám Tóth
DR. TÓTH & DR. GÁSPÁR
KÖZJEGYZQI IRODA

Gábor Varga
BISZ CENTRAL CREDIT
INFORMATION PLC.

Vera Várkonyi
NOTARY

Agnes Wolford
BUDAPEST VIII. DISTRICT
MUNICIPALITY

Blanka Zombori
PRICEWATERHOUSECOOPERS

ICELAND

Halla Ýr Albertsdóttir
PRICEWATERHOUSECOOPERS

Elin Arnadottir
PRICEWATERHOUSECOOPERS

Kristján Ásgeirsson
ARKITEKTASTOFAN OG

Þórður Búason
REYKJAVIK CONSTRUCTION
AGENCY

Eymundur Einarsson
ENDURSKODUN OG RÁÐGJÖF
EHF, MEMBER OF RUSSELL
BEDFORD INTERNATIONAL

Ólafur Eiríksson
LOGOS, MEMBER OF LEX MUNDI

Skuli Th. Fjeldsted
FJELDSTED, BLÖNDAL & FJELDSTED

Elísabet Guðbjörnsdóttir
PRICEWATERHOUSECOOPERS

Guðrún Guðmundsdóttir
JÓNAR TRANSPORT

Hjördís Gulla Gylfadóttir
BBA LEGAL

Bryndís Gunnlaugsdóttir
PRICEWATERHOUSECOOPERS

Reynir Haraldsson
JÓNAR TRANSPORT

Margrét Hauksdóttir
THE LAND REGISTRY OF ICELAND

Jón Ingi Ingibergsson
PRICEWATERHOUSECOOPERS

Erlingur E. Jónasson
ISTAK

Jóhanna Áskels Jónsdóttir
PRICEWATERHOUSECOOPERS

Tómas J. Jónsson
LÖGFRÆÐISTOFU REYKJAVÍKUR

Hrafnhildur Kristinsdóttir
LOGOS, MEMBER OF LEX MUNDI

Ásta Kristjánsdóttir
PRICEWATERHOUSECOOPERS

Benedetto Nardini
BBA LEGAL

Dagbjört Oddsdóttir
BBA LEGAL

Kristján Pálsson
JÓNAR TRANSPORT

Eyvindur Sólnes
LVA-LEGAL SERVICES

Jóhannes Stephensen
CREDITINFO ICELAND

Gunnar Sturluson
LOGOS, MEMBER OF LEX MUNDI

Rúnar Svavar Svavarsson
ORKUVEITA REYKJAVÍKUR, DISTRIBUTION-ELECTRICAL SYSTEM

Stefán A. Svensson
JURIS LAW OFFICE

INDIA

Amit Agarwal
PRICEWATERHOUSECOOPERS

Mahima Ahluwalia
TRILEGAL

P. V. Balasubramaniam
BFS LEGAL

Meghalee Barthakur
PRICEWATERHOUSECOOPERS LEGAL SERVICES

Ramanuj Basu
PRICEWATERHOUSECOOPERS LEGAL SERVICES

Piyush Bhandari
PROTEAM CONSULTING PRIVATE LIMITED

Pradeep Bhandari
PROTEAM CONSULTING PRIVATE LIMITED

Vanita Bhargava
KHAITAN & CO

Atul Bhatia
TRILEGAL

Gaurav Bhattacharya
JURIS CHAMBERS

Prabjot Bhullar
KHAITAN & CO

Nidhi Bothra
VINOD KOTHARI & CO., COMPANY SECRETARIES

Bharat Budholia
JURIS CORP

Binoy Chacko
COMPANIESINN.COM INDIA PRIVATE LIMITED

Subhayu Chatterjee
KHAITAN & CO

Jyoti Chaudhari
LEGASIS SERVICES PVT. LTD.

Prashant Chauhan

Vijay Pratap Singh Chauhan
KHAITAN & CO

Daizy Chawla
SINGH & ASSOCIATES ADVOCATES AND SOLICITORS

Manjula Chawla
PHOENIX LEGAL

Sachin Chugh
SINGHI CHUGH & KUMAR, CHARTERED ACCOUNTANTS

Ketan Dalal
PRICEWATERHOUSECOOPERS

Vishwang Desai
DESAI & DIWANJI

Thambi Durai
T. DURAI & CO.

D. Ferdinand
BFS LEGAL

Vir Gandhi
PROFOUND OUTSOURCING SOLUTIONS PVT. LTD.

Rahul Garg
PRICEWATERHOUSECOOPERS

Tanushree Ghildiyal
KNM & PARTNERS, LAW OFFICES

Arindam Ghosh
KHAITAN & CO

Indranil Ghosh
FOX MANDAL

Karanvir Gill
KHAITAN & CO

Vijay Goel
SINGHANIA & CO. LLP

Chandrika Gogia
PRICEWATERHOUSECOOPERS

Sameer Guha
TRILEGAL

Nikhil Gupta
PRICEWATERHOUSECOOPERS

Rikha Gupta
KHAITAN & CO

Akil Hirani
MAJMUDAR & CO.

Joy Jacob
KHAITAN

Rishi Jain
PRICEWATERHOUSECOOPERS LEGAL SERVICES

Ruchi Jain
PRICEWATERHOUSECOOPERS LEGAL SERVICES

Anil Jarial
JURIS CORP

Sunaina Jhingan
SINGH & ASSOCIATES ADVOCATES AND SOLICITORS

Dharmendra Johari
STONEX INC.

Rajat Joneja
KNM & PARTNERS, LAW OFFICES

Nitin Kala
FOX MANDAL

Rajas Kasbekar
LITTLE & CO.

Charandeep Kaur
TRILEGAL

Anuj Keashri
K N J PARTNERS

Amruta Kelkar
JURIS CORP

Anup Khanna
MAJMUDAR & CO.

Bhavna Kohli
PRICEWATERHOUSECOOPERS LEGAL SERVICES

Anuraag Kothari
TRILEGAL

Vinod Kothari
VINOD KOTHARI & CO., COMPANY SECRETARIES

Avinash Kumar
K N J PARTNERS

Hitesh Kumar
SINGHANIA & PARTNERS, SOLICITORS & ADVOCATES

Mukesh Kumar
KNM & PARTNERS, LAW OFFICES

Yashasvini Kumar
TRILEGAL

Manoj Kumar Singh
SINGH & ASSOCIATES ADVOCATES AND SOLICITORS

Sougata Kundu
PRICEWATERHOUSECOOPERS LEGAL SERVICES

Shreedhar Kunte
SHARP AND TANNAN - MEMBER OF RUSSELL BEDFORD

Moin Ladha
KHAITAN & CO

Rozmin Lakhani
JURIS CORP

Debasis Law
FOX MANDAL

Prachi Loona
JURIS CORP

Rajiv Luthra
LUTHRA & LUTHRA

Neha Madan
KESAR DASS B & ASSOCIATES

Manish Madhukar
INFINI JURIDIQUE

Ravi Mahto
TRILEGAL

Shipra Makkar
SINGH & ASSOCIATES ADVOCATES AND SOLICITORS

Jignesh Makwana
SWIFTINDIAINC CORPORATE SERVICES PRIVATE LIMITED

Som Mandal
FOX MANDAL

Vipender Mann
KNM & PARTNERS, LAW OFFICES

Rishabh G Mastaram
DESAI & DIWANJI

Dara Mehta
LITTLE & CO.

Jitesh Mehta
SOURCE INDIA

Preeti G. Mehta
KANGA & CO.

Shishir Mehta
KHAITAN

Sharad Mishra
NEO MULTIMEDIAN

Saurabh Misra
SAURABH MISRA & ASSOCIATES, ADVOCATES (PKA)

Hemal Modi
SHARP AND TANNAN - MEMBER OF RUSSELL BEDFORD

Shyamal Mukherjee
PRICEWATERHOUSECOOPERS

Sudip Mullick
KHAITAN & CO

Rajiv Mundhra
CROWN AGENTS (INDIA) PVT LTD.

Ramaratnam Muralidharan
PRICEWATERHOUSECOOPERS

Vijay Nair
KNM & PARTNERS, LAW OFFICES

Huzefa Nasikwala
JURIS CORP

Chandra Nilesh
PHOENIX LEGAL

G. Pal
LITTLE & CO.

Girija Shankar Pandey
MAX NEW YORK LIFE INSURANCE COMPANY LIMITED

Shreyas Patel
MAJMUDAR & CO.

Sanjay Patil
BDH INDUSTRIES LIMITED

Dhruv Paul
TRILEGAL

Bhadrinath madhusudan Pogul
KALKI INTERNATIONAL

Nitin Potdar
J. SAGAR ASSOCIATES, ADVOCATES & SOLICITORS

Anand Prasad
TRILEGAL

Kaushik Rajan
KHAITAN & CO

Mohan Rajasekharan
PHOENIX LEGAL

Gopalakrishnan Ramachandran
FOX MANDAL

Smrithi Ramesh
BFS LEGAL

Ashok Ramgir
HARSH IMPEX

Harsh Ramgir
HARSH IMPEX

Ami Ranjan
SINGHANIA & PARTNERS, SOLICITORS & ADVOCATES

Dipak Rao
SINGHANIA & PARTNERS, SOLICITORS & ADVOCATES

Rahul Renavikar
PRICEWATERHOUSECOOPERS

Abhishek Saket
INFINI JURIDIQUE

Vandana Sekhri
JURIS CORP

Ramani Seshadri
DPAS GROUPS

Parag Shah
FOX MANDAL

Abhsihek Sharma
KHAITAN & CO

Shweta Sharma
PRICEWATERHOUSECOOPERS LEGAL SERVICES

Vina Sharma
INFINI JURIDIQUE

K.M. Aasim Shehzad
BFS LEGAL

Vikram Shroff
NISHITH DESAI ASSOCIATES

Manjosh K Sidhu

Praveen Singh
FOX MANDAL

Ravinder Pal Singh
INTERNATIONAL SURGICAL INDS.

Mukesh Singhal
KNM & PARTNERS, LAW OFFICES

Ravinder Singhania
SINGHANIA & PARTNERS, SOLICITORS & ADVOCATES

Abhishek Singla
PRICEWATERHOUSECOOPERS LEGAL SERVICES

Harshita Srivastava
NISHITH DESAI ASSOCIATES

Rajesh Tayal
KNM & PARTNERS, LAW OFFICES

Praveen Tiwary
FOX MANDAL

Praveen Kumar Tiwary
FOX MANDAL

Aparna Tripathy
INFINI JURIDIQUE

Suhas Tuljapurkar
LEGASIS SERVICES PVT. LTD.

Suneet Tyagi
SINGHANIA & PARTNERS, SOLICITORS & ADVOCATES

Navratan Uppal
B M METAL CRAFTS

Ratandeep Uppal
B M METAL CRAFTS

Ajay Verma
JURIS CHAMBERS

Ramesh Babu Vishwanathula
VISHWANATH & GLOBAL ATTORNEYS

Rajat Vohra
TRILEGAL

Hoshedar Wadia
JURIS CORP

Amit Yadkikar
DESAI & DIWANJI

INDONESIA

Nafis Adwani
ALI BUDIARDJO, NUGROHO, REKSODIPUTRO, MEMBER OF LEX MUNDI

Almer Apon
PT BUANA MAS CITRA LESTARI

Hamud M. Balfas
ALI BUDIARDJO, NUGROHO, REKSODIPUTRO, MEMBER OF LEX MUNDI

Rick Beckmann
BRIGITTA I. RAHAYOE & PARTNERS

Fabian Buddy Pascoal
HANAFIAH PONGGAWA & PARTNERS

Ita Budhi
PT PRIMA WAHANA CARAKA / PRICEWATERHOUSECOOPERS

Tony Budidjaja
BUDIDJAJA & ASSOCIATES LAW OFFICES

S.H Juni Dani
BUDIDJAJA & ASSOCIATES LAW OFFICES

Melli Darsa
MELLI DARSA & CO.

Utari Dyah Kusuma
BRIGITTA I. RAHAYOE & PARTNERS

Ira A. Eddymurthy
SOEWITO SUHARDIMAN EDDYMURTHY KARDONO

Ayik Gunadi
ALI BUDIARDJO, NUGROHO, REKSODIPUTRO, MEMBER OF LEX MUNDI

Didik S. Hadiwidodo
PT. NASIO KARYA PRATAMA

Michael Hasian Giovanni
BRIGITTA I. RAHAYOE & PARTNERS

Ray Headifen
PT PRIMA WAHANA CARAKA / PRICEWATERHOUSECOOPERS

Erwandi Hendarta
HADIPUTRANTO, HADINOTO & PARTNERS

Mohammad Kamal Hidayat
FURNITURE FIKAMAR

Rahayuningsih Hoed
MAKARIM & TAIRA S.

Brigitta Imam Rahayoe
BRIGITTA I. RAHAYOE & PARTNERS

Adiwidya Imam Rahayu
BRIGITTA I. RAHAYOE & PARTNERS

Mirza Karim
KARIMSYAH LAW FIRM

Herry N. Kurniawan
ALI BUDIARDJO, NUGROHO, REKSODIPUTRO, MEMBER OF LEX MUNDI

Rudy Kusmanto
MAKARIM & TAIRA S.

Winita E. Kusnandar
KUSNANDAR & CO.

Ferry P. Madian
ALI BUDIARDJO, NUGROHO, REKSODIPUTRO, MEMBER OF LEX MUNDI

Ella Melany
HANAFIAH PONGGAWA & PARTNERS

Karen Mills
KARIMSYAH LAW FIRM

Norma Mutalib
MAKARIM & TAIRA S.

Suria Nataadmadja
SURIA NATAADMADJA & ASSOCIATES

Mia Noni Yuniar
BRIGITTA I. RAHAYOE & PARTNERS

Denny Rahmansyah
SOEWITO SUHARDIMAN EDDYMURTHY KARDONO

Ilman Rakhmat
KARIMSYAH LAW FIRM

Muhammad Razikun
MUC CONSULTING GROUP, MEMBER OF RUSSELL BEDFORD INTERNATIONAL

Gatot Sanyoto
KUSNANDAR & CO.

Nur Asyura Anggini Sari
BANK INDONESIA

Indra Setiawan
ALI BUDIARDJO, NUGROHO, REKSODIPUTRO, MEMBER OF LEX MUNDI

Nurul Setyorini
MELLI DARSA & CO.

Kevin Omar Sidharta
ALI BUDIARDJO, NUGROHO, REKSODIPUTRO, MEMBER OF LEX MUNDI

Bambang Soelaksono
THE SMERU RESEARCH INSTITUTE

Galinar R. Kartakusuma
Summitmas
MAKARIM & TAIRA S.

Gatot Triprasetio
WIDYAWAN & PARTNERS

Jono Yeo
BUDIDJAJA & ASSOCIATES LAW OFFICES

IRAN, ISLAMIC REP.

Mohammad Reza Abdi
IRANIAN NATIONAL TAX ADMINISTRATION

Camellia Abdolsamad
INTERNATIONAL LAW OFFICE OF DR. BEHROOZ AKHLAGHI & ASSOCIATES

Hamid Reza Adabi
STATE ORGANIZATION FOR REGISTRATION OF DEEDS &PROPERTIES

Mostafa Agah
AGAH LAW FIRM

Allah Mohammad Aghaee
IRANIAN NATIONAL TAX ADMINISTRATION

Nazem Ahmadian Nasrabadi
STATE ORGANIZATION FOR REGISTRATION OF DEEDS &PROPERTIES

Behrooz Akhlaghi
INTERNATIONAL LAW OFFICE OF DR. BEHROOZ AKHLAGHI & ASSOCIATES

Hamid Alaedini
PORT AND MARITIME ORGANIZATION

Mohammad Alimohammadi
NOVINALLOYS SEMNAN

Ali Amani
DAYARAYAN AUDITING & FINANCIAL SERVICES

Mahdi Amouri
IRANIAN NATIONAL TAX ADMINISTRATION

Mehenoosh Aryanpoor
INTERNATIONAL LAW OFFICE OF DR. BEHROOZ AKHLAGHI & ASSOCIATES

Hassan Badamchi
HAMI LEGAL SERVICES

Mohammad Badamchi
HAMI LEGAL SERVICES

Peyman Barazandeh
GHODS NIROO ENGINEERING COMPANY

Gholamhossein Davani
DAYARAYAN AUDITING & FINANCIAL SERVICES

Morteza Dezfoulian
MORTEZA

Maryam Ebrahimi
TEHRAN STOCK EXCHANGE(TSE)

Mona Ebrahimi
INTERNATIONAL LAW OFFICE OF DR. BEHROOZ AKHLAGHI & ASSOCIATES

Sarah Es,haghi
THE STATE ORGANIZATION FOR REGISTRATION OF DEEDS AND PROPERTIES

Pejman Eshtehardi
IRAN COUNSELORS

Mahmoud Eskandari
IRAN TRADE PROMOTION ORGANIZATION

Shirzad Eslami
OJE LAW OFFICE

Hossein Fahimi
SECURITIES AND EXCHANGE ORGANIZATION OF IRAN

Zahra Farzaliyan
STATE ORGANIZATION FOR REGISTRATION OF DEEDS & PROPERTIES

Behzad Feizi
AGAHAN & CO.

Mashallah Gerami
THE STATE ORGANIZATION FOR REGISTRATION OF DEEDS AND PROPERTIES

Abbas Ali Ghassai
ZARIN IRAN PORCELAIN INDUSTRIES

Mohammad Reza Hajian
CENTRAL BANK OF IRAN

Akbar Hendizadeh
IRAN COUNSELORS

S. Hamid Hosseini
MERAAT INT'L GROUP

Behboud Hosseinpour
PORT AND MARITIME ORGANIZATION

Mohammad Jalili
IRAN CREDIT SCORING

Mehdi Jariani
TEMAD COMPANY

Hossein Kakhki
IRAN CUSTOMS OFFICE

Kiumars Kermanshahi
IRAN TRADE PROMOTION ORGANIZATION

Kheirollah Khadem
IRAN TRADE PROMOTION ORGANIZATION

Alireza Khanjan
IRANIAN NATIONAL TAX ADMINISTRATION

Majid Mahallati
MAHALLATI & CO. CHARTERED ACCOUNTANTS

Shahrzad Majdameli
INTERNATIONAL LAW OFFICE OF DR. BEHROOZ AKHLAGHI & ASSOCIATES

Fatemeh Sadat Mirsharifi
IRAN MINISTRY OF COMMERCE

Younes Gharbali Moghadam
PORT AND MARITIME ORGANIZATION

Mozaffar Mohammadian
TEEMA BAR INTERNATIONAL TRANSPORT

Mohammad Mohammadinejad
NAMAVARAN MOHANDESI INTERNATIONAL INVESTMENT Co

Mehrdad Mostaghimi
GHODS NIROO ENGINEERING COMPANY

Rasoul Nowrouzi
IRAN TRADE PROMOTION ORGANIZATION

Mohammad Reza Pasban
ALLAME TABATABAEI UN.-IRANIAN CENTRAL BAR ASSOCIATION

Farmand Pourkarim
TEHRAN MUNICIPALITY

Yehya Rayegani
FARJAM LAW OFFICE

Kazem Sammak
NAMAVARAN MOHANDESI INTERNATIONAL INVESTMENT Co

Amin Setayesh
STATE ORGANIZATION FOR REGISTRATION OF DEEDS &PROPERTIES OF ISLAMIC REPUBLIC OF

Encyeh Seyed Sadr
INTERNATIONAL LAW OFFICE OF DR. BEHROOZ AKHLAGHI & ASSOCIATES

Farhand Shaafi
NAMAVARAN MOHANDESI INTERNATIONAL INVESTMENT Co

Mir Shahbiz Shafe'e
DR. JAMAL SEIFI & ASSOCIATES

Cyrus Shafizadeh
TAVAKOLI & SHAHABI

Farzan Shirranbeigi
TEHRAN MUNICIPALITY

Arvind Sinha
BUSINESS ADVISORS GROUP

Abdollah Soltani
THE STATE ORGANIZATION FOR REGISTRATION OF DEEDS AND PROPERTIES

Mohammad Soltani
SECURITIES AND EXCHANGE ORGANIZATION OF IRAN

Pedram Soltani
PERSOL CORPORATION

Abbas Taghipour
CENTRAL BANK OF IRAN

Mohammad Reza Talischi
PERSOL CORPORATION

Farhad Yazdi
FARHAD YAZDI

IRAQ

Hadeel Salih Abboud Al-Janabi
MENA ASSOCIATES, MEMBER OF AMERELLER RECHTSANWÄLTE

Faik Abdul Rasool
IRAQI INSTITUTE FOR ECONOMIC REFORM

Ghassan Abdul Sada
MINISTRY OF LABOR & SOCIAL AFFAIRS

Imad Abdul Satar Al Qassab
IMAD AL QASSAB LAW OFFICE

Saad Abdul Wahab A. Qader
IRAQI ENGINEERS UNION

Emad Abdullatif
IRAQI INSTITUTE FOR ECONOMIC REFORM

Mohammad Al Jabouri
TALAL ABU-GHAZALEH LEGAL (TAG-LEGAL)

Hadeel Al Janabi
MENA ASSOCIATES, MEMBER OF AMERELLER RECHTSANWÄLTE

Ahmad Al Jannabi
MENA ASSOCIATES, MEMBER OF AMERELLER RECHTSANWÄLTE

Tariq Al Jibori
AL -WAHDA MUNICIPALITY

Mohamed Al Kawaz
AL RAFAN CO. FOR GENERAL TRADING

Omar Al Nemer
TALAL ABU-GHAZALEH LEGAL (TAG-LEGAL)

Luay Al-Kayssi
IRAQI ASSOCIATION OF SECURITIES DEALERS

Mustafa Alshawi
IRAQI INSTITUTE FOR ECONOMIC REFORM

Munther B. Hamoudi
AL ATTAR REAL- ESTATE OFFICE

Ali Baker
AL-FURAT FOR LEGAL AND BUSINESS CONSULTANCY LLC

Duraid Basil
IRAQI INSTITUTE FOR ECONOMIC REFORM

Majed Butrous

Ahmed Dawood
AL -WAHDA MUNICIPALITY

Hassan Dhiaa
Hassan Dhiaa Law office

Hassan Fouad Munam
Court of First Instance in Al Karada District

Jabar Hamza Lateef

Khalid Haseeb Khalil
Khalid Haseeb Office for Book Keeping

Naem Hassan
Al -Wahda Municipality

Yasir Husam
Al -Wahda Municipality

Ryadh Ibrahim Fadhil
Ministry of Labor & Social Affairs

Stephan Jäger
Amereller Rechtsanwälte

Bilal Jasim
Al Mi'amar Real Estate Office

Kadhum Jawad Aljibori
Al Mansour Law Office

Fakhri Kadhum
Al -Wahda Municipality

Dhia M. Hashim

Ali Mawlawi
Iraq Center for Economic Reform

Jamal Mehdi Shalal
Al Attar Real- Estate Office

Ali Mohamed Aboud Saied
Baghdad Bureau For Real-Estate Investment

Mudher Mohammed Salih
Iraq Central Bank

Mohammad Murad
Al Rafidain Brokers

Ibrahim Musa Qadori Ahmed
Al Rawdha Real-estate Office

Husham Mustafa Ahmed
Al Asfar Co. Commercial agencies

Ammar Naji
Al-Furat for Legal and Business Consultancy LLC

Auday Najim Ali
Ashour International Bank

Riadh Raouf Al Heeti

Talal Sabeeh Shawqy Ameen
Ministry of Labor & Social Affairs

Issam Saied Khalil Al Ani
Issam Al Ani Law Office

Ahmed Salih Al-Janabi
Mena Associates, member of Amereller Rechtsanwälte

Haider Salman
Bait Al Hikma for Legal Services and Consultancy LLC

Hider Salman
Haider Salman Al-Jnabi Law office

Mohamed Shareef Ali
Mohamed Shareef Law Office

Yasir Yahya Al Mana

Khaled Yaseen
Iraqi National Investment Commission

IRELAND

Margaret Austin
Eugene F. Collins Solicitors

Andrew Bates
Dillon Eustace

Roisin Bennett
Reddy Charlton McKnight

Mairead Britton
Matheson Ormsby Prentice

Alan Browning
LK Shields Solicitors, member of Ius Laboris

Aisling Burke
Arthur Cox, member of Lex Mundi

Diarmuid Clancy
Property Registration Authority

Ronan Cotter
Arthur Cox, member of Lex Mundi

Eoin Cunneen
LK Shields Solicitors, member of Ius Laboris

Richard Curran
LK Shields Solicitors, member of Ius Laboris

John Fitzgerald
ByrneWallace

Ciara Garry
FGS Dublin

James Gilhooly
Law Library

Paul Glenfield
Matheson Ormsby Prentice

Micheál Grace
Mason Hayes + Curran

Niamh Hackett
LK Shields Solicitors, member of Ius Laboris

Darren Isaacson
Arthur Cox, member of Lex Mundi

William Johnston
Arthur Cox, member of Lex Mundi

Bruneau Joseph
LK Shields Solicitors, member of Ius Laboris

Colm Kelly
PricewaterhouseCoopers

Damien Keogh
Matheson Ormsby Prentice

Jennifer Malone
ByrneWallace

Peter McLay
Matheson Ormsby Prentice

Julie Murphy O'Connor
Matheson Ormsby Prentice

Regan O' Driscoll
Matheson Ormsby Prentice

Michael O'Connor
Matheson Ormsby Prentice

Niav Ohiggins
Arthur Cox, member of Lex Mundi

Deirdre O'Mahony
Arthur Cox, member of Lex Mundi

Robert O'Shea
Matheson Ormsby Prentice

Richard O'Sullivan
P.J. O'Driscolls, Solicitors

Judith Riordan
Mason Hayes + Curran

Leanne Robson
Matheson Ormsby Prentice

Brendan Sharkey
Reddy Charlton McKnight

Gavin Simons
ByrneWallace

Michael Treacy
Property Registration Authority

Colm Walsh
Irish International Freight Association

Maeve Walsh
Reddy Charlton McKnight

ISRAEL

Paul Baris
Yigal Arnon & Co.

Ofer Bar-On
Shavit Bar-On Gal-On Tzin Nov Yagur, Law Offices

Jeremy Benjamin
Goldfarb Levy Eran Meiri Tzafrir & Co.

Marina Benvenisti
Ruth Cargo

Yitzhak Chikorel
Deloitte

Koby Cohen
PricewaterhouseCoopers

Clifford Davis
S. Horowitz & Co., member of Lex Mundi

Ido Gonen
Goldfarb Levy Eran Meiri Tzafrir & Co.

Roee Hecht
Shavit Bar-On Gal-On Tzin Nov Yagur, Law Offices

Aaron Jaffe
Yigal Arnon & Co.

Yossi Katsav
Ruth Cargo

Zeev Katz
PricewaterhouseCoopers

Vered Kirshner
PricewaterhouseCoopers

Adam Klein
Goldfarb Levy Eran Meiri Tzafrir & Co.

Gideon Koren
Gideon Koren & Co. Law Offices

Orna Kornreich-Cohen
Shavit Bar-On Gal-On Tzin Nov Yagur, Law Offices

Benjamin Leventhal
Gideon Fisher & Co.

Michelle Liberman
S. Horowitz & Co., member of Lex Mundi

Jakob Melcer Adv.
E.S. Shimron, I. Molho, Persky & Co.

Rotem Muntner
Ruth Cargo

Doron Nathaniel
Haim Nathaniel Ltd.

Meir Nussbaum
Deloitte

Danit Rimon
Lipa Meir & Co.

David Rosen
Idiliti Maritime Consulting

Gerry Seligman
PricewaterhouseCoopers

Amir Shani
AMIT Ltd.

Maya Shaton
S. Horowitz & Co., member of Lex Mundi

Yifat Shkedi-Shatz
S. Horowitz & Co., member of Lex Mundi

Daniel Singerman
Business Data Israel + Personal Check

Helena Storm
Russell Bedford International

Daphna Tsarfaty
Goldfarb Levy Eran Meiri Tzafrir & Co.

Eylam Weiss
Weiss- Porat & Co.

ITALY

Allen & Overy LLP

Marianna Abbaticchio
Ristuccia & Tufarelli

Fabrizio Acerbis
PricewaterhouseCoopers

Federico Antich
Studio dell'Avvocato Antich

Gea Arcella

Gaetano Arnò
TLS / PricewaterhouseCoopers Legal Services

Maria Pia Ascenzo
Bank of Italy

Romina Ballanca
PricewaterhouseCoopers

Paola Barazzetta
TLS / PricewaterhouseCoopers Legal Services

Lamberto Barbieri
CRIF S. P. A.

Matteo Bascelli
Orrick, Herrington & Sutcliffe LLP

Giuseppe Battaglia
Portolano Colella Cavallo

Susanna Beltramo
Studio Legale Beltramo

Maria Clementina Binacchi
Studio notarile eliana morandi

Guido Boni
European University Institute

Luigi Brunetti
SDV Logistics Ltd.

Sergio Calderara
Almaviva S.p.a. / G.Matica S.r.l.

Alessandro Cardia
Grieco e Associati

Cecilia Carrara
Legance

Lucia Ceccarelli
Portolano Colella Cavallo

Giorgio Cherubini
Pirola Pennuto Zei & Associati

Sabrina Chibbaro
Studio notarile eliana morandi

Domenico Colella
Portolano Colella Cavallo

Fabrizio Colonna
CBA Studio Legale e Tributario

Mattia Colonnelli de Gasperis
Colonnelli de Gasperis Studio Legale

Gian Franco Condo

Barbara Corsetti
Portolano Colella Cavallo

Filippo Corsini
Chiomenti Studio Legale

Sabrina Costanzo
Cleary Gottlieb Steen & Hamilton LLP

Salvatore Cuzzocrea
PricewaterhouseCoopers

Antonio de Martinis
Spasaro De Martinis Law Firm

Raffaella De Martinis
Spasaro De Martinis Law Firm

Claudio Di Falco
Cleary Gottlieb Steen & Hamilton LLP

Massimo Cremona
Pirola Pennuto Zei & Associati

Emanuele Ferrari
Studio Notarile Ferrari

Paola Flora
Ashurst

Maria Theresa Fontana
Spasaro De Martinis Law Firm

Pier Andrea Fré Torelli Massini
Carabba & Partners

Linda Nicoletta Frigo
Gruppo Pam S.p.a.

Andrea Gangemi
Portolano Colella Cavallo

Vincenzo Fabrizio Giglio
Studio Legale Giglio

Antonio Grieco
Grieco e Associati

Guido Grisi

Paolo Grondona
Norton Rose

Valentino Guarini
*TLS /
PricewaterhouseCoopers
Legal Services*

Federico Guasti
Studio Legale Guasti

Goffredo Guerra
*Studio Legale Tributario
Associato*

Francesco Iodice
*Cleary Gottlieb Steen &
Hamilton LLP*

Giovanni Izzo
*Abbatescianni Studio
Legale e Tributario*

Ignazio la Candia
*Pirola Pennuto Zei &
Associati*

Paolo Lucarini
PricewaterhouseCoopers

Stefano Macchi di Cellere
Jones Day

Chiara Magnante
*Portolano Colella
Cavallo*

Donatella Martinelli
*Alegal International Law
Firm*

Cristiano Martinez
*Orrick, Herrington &
Sutcliffe LLP*

Pietro Masi
*Portolano Colella
Cavallo*

Patrizia Masselli
*Cleary Gottlieb Steen &
Hamilton LLP*

Maria Grazia Medici
*Verusio e Cosmelli Studio
Legale*

Mario Miccoli
Notaio Miccoli

Riccardo Micheli
Ristuccia & Tufarelli

Nunzia Moliterni
Jones Lang LaSalle SpA

Micael Montinari
*Portolano Colella
Cavallo*

Eliana Morandi
*Studio notarile eliana
morandi*

Gianmatteo Nunziante
Nunziante Magrone

Francesco Nuzzolo
PricewaterhouseCoopers

Marcella Panucci
*Confindustria (National
Business Association)*

Paolo Pasqualis
Notary

Giovanni Patti
*Abbatescianni Studio
Legale e Tributario*

Federica Peres
*Portolano Colella
Cavallo*

Martina Pivetti
*TLS /
PricewaterhouseCoopers
Legal Services*

Laura Prosperetti
*Cleary Gottlieb Steen &
Hamilton LLP*

Sharon Reilly
*Toffoletto e Soci Law
Firm, member of Ius Laboris*

Marianna Ristuccia
Ristuccia & Tufarelli

Tommaso Edoardo Romolotti
*Studio Legale Romolotti
Marretta*

Carlo Umberto Rossi
Rossi Budelli Law Firm

Giovanni B. Sandicchi
*Cleary Gottlieb Steen &
Hamilton LLP*

Lamberto Schiona
Studio Legale Schiona

Mario Scofferi
Scofferi Studio legale

Massimiliano Silvetti
Nunziante Magrone

Carlo Sinatra
*Lombardi Molinari e
Associati*

Pierluigi Sodini
Unioncamere

Piervincenzo Spasaro
*Spasaro De Martinis Law
Firm*

Maria Antonietta Tanico
Studio Legale Tanico

Andrea Tedioli
Tedioli Law Firm

Maria Lucia Tizzani
*CBA Studio Legale e
Tributario*

Giacinto Tommasini
*Alegal International Law
Firm*

Luca Tufarelli
Ristuccia & Tufarelli

Rachele Vacca de Dominicis
Grieco e Associati

Mario Valentini
*Pirola Pennuto Zei &
Associati*

Angelo Zambelli
Dewey & LeBoeuf

Filippo Zucchinelli
*TLS /
PricewaterhouseCoopers
Legal Services*

JAMAICA

Theresa Bowen
Lex Caribbean

Michael A. Bryce
*Office of Utilities
Regulation*

Solomon Burchell
*Ministry of Energy and
Mining*

Robert Colley
*Myers, Fletcher & Gordon,
member of Lex Mundi*

Eric Alexander Crawford
PricewaterhouseCoopers

Natalie Farrell-Ross
*Myers, Fletcher & Gordon,
member of Lex Mundi*

Nicole Foga
Foga Daley

Nicole Goodin
*Jamaica Public Service
Company Limited*

Inger Hainsley-Bennett
*Company's Office of
Jamaica*

Michael Hall
PricewaterhouseCoopers

Corrine N. Henry
*Myers, Fletcher & Gordon,
member of Lex Mundi*

Hopeton Heron
*Office of Utilities
Regulation*

Karen Hughes
*Ministry of Justice and
Legal Affairs*

Joan Lawla

Noelle Llewellyn Heron
*Tax Administration
Services Department*

Zia Mian
*Office of Utilities
Regulation*

Viveen Morrison
*PricewaterhouseCoopers-
Duke Street*

Kellie-Ann Murray
*Jamaica Promotions
Corporation (JAMPRO)*

Gina Phillips Black
*Myers, Fletcher & Gordon,
member of Lex Mundi*

Andrea E. Rattray
Rattray Patterson Rattray

Hilary Reid
*Myers, Fletcher & Gordon,
member of Lex Mundi*

Venice Ricketts
*Jamaica Inland Revenue
Department*

Yvonne Riley
*Jamaica National
Insurance Scheme (NIS)
Office*

Heather Rowe
*Jamaica Public Service
Company Limited*

Humprey Taylor
Taylor Construction Ltd.

Densil Thorpe
*Jamaica National
Insurance Scheme (NIS)
Office*

Sophia Williams
National Land Agency

George Wright
*Jamaica's Tax
Administration at the
Ministry of Finance &
Public Service*

JAPAN

Allen & Overy LLP

Fumiko Amano
*Zeirishi-Hojin
PricewaterhouseCoopers*

Miho Arimura
*Hatasawa & Wakai Law
Firm*

Toyoki Emoto
Atsumi & Partners

Mijo Fujita
*Adachi, Henderson,
Miyatake & Fujita*

Osamu Fujiwara
*Orrick, Herrington &
Sutcliffe LLP*

Tastuya Fukui
Atsumi & Partners

Nozomi Fukushima
*Zeirishi-Hojin
PricewaterhouseCoopers*

Mika Haga
Atsumi & Partners

Shigeru Hasegawa
*Zeirishi-Hojin
PricewaterhouseCoopers*

Tamotsu Hatasawa
*Hatasawa & Wakai Law
Firm*

Kan Hayashi
*Zeirishi-Hojin
PricewaterhouseCoopers*

Akiko Hiraoka
Atsumi & Partners

Takashi Hirose
Oh-Ebashi LPC & Partners

Kane Huang
*Orrick, Herrington &
Sutcliffe LLP*

Michiya Iwasaki
Atsumi & Partners

Tomomi Kagawa
*Credit Information Center
Corp.*

Aya Kamimura
Nishimura & Asahi

Yosuke Kanegae
Oh-Ebashi LPC & Partners

Hideki Thurgood Kano
*Anderson Mori &
Tomotsune*

Chie Kasahara
Atsumi & Partners

Kazumoto Kitamura
Atsumi & Partners

Kenichi Kojima
Ushijima & Partners

Yukie Kurosawa
O'Melveny & Myers LLP

Yoji Maeda
O'Melveny & Myers LLP

Yuki Maeda
Nishimura & Asahi

Toshio Miyatake
*Adachi, Henderson,
Miyatake & Fujita*

Tsuyoshi Mizoguchi
*Zeirishi-Hojin
PricewaterhouseCoopers*

Michihiro Mori
Nishimura & Asahi

Naomasa Nakagawa
*Orrick, Herrington &
Sutcliffe LLP*

Miho Niunoya
Atsumi & Partners

*Tokyo Electric Power
Company*

Takefumi Sato
*Anderson Mori &
Tomotsune*

Tetsuro Sato
Baker & McKenzie

Yoshihito Shibata
*Bingham McCutchen
Murase, Sakai & Mimura
Foreign Law Joint
Enterprise*

Hiroaki Shinomiya
Atsumi & Partners

Hisako Shiotani
Atsumi & Partners

Sachiko Sugawara
Atsumi & Partners

Hidetaka Sumomogi
Nishimura & Asahi

Hiroyuki Suzuki
*Zeirishi-Hojin
PricewaterhouseCoopers*

Yuri Suzuki
Atsumi & Partners

Hiroaki Takahashi
Atsumi & Partners

Junichi Tobimatsu
*Mori Hamada &
Matsumoto*

Shuhei Tsudo
*Orrick, Herrington &
Sutcliffe LLP*

Kenji Utsumi
*Nagashima Ohno &
Tsunematsu*

Jun Yamada
*Anderson Mori &
Tomotsune*

Michi Yamagami
*Anderson Mori &
Tomotsune*

Akio Yamamoto
Kajima Corporation

Kazuhiro Yanagida
Nishimura & Asahi

JORDAN

Saleh Abd El-Ati
*Ali Sharif Zu'bi, Advocates
& Legal Consultants,
member of Lex Mundi*

Hayja'a Abu AlHayja'a
*Talal Abu-Ghazaleh
Legal (TAG-Legal) Jordan
Amman*

Anas Abunameh
Law & Arbitration Centre

Ibrahim Abunameh
Law & Arbitration Centre

Bushra Abu-Tayeh
*Ali Sharif Zu'bi, Advocates
& Legal Consultants,
member of Lex Mundi*

Maha Al Abdallat
Central Bank of Jordan

Eman M. Al-Dabbas
*International Business
Legal Associates*

Arafat Alfayoumi
Central Bank of Jordan

Omar Aljazy
*Aljazy & Co.Advocates &
Legal Consultants*

Ali Almashaqba
*Electricity Regulatory
Commission (ERC)*

Zaina Al-Nabulsi
*Ali Sharif Zu'bi, Advocates
& Legal Consultants,
member of Lex Mundi*

Micheal T. Dabit
MICHEAL T. DABIT & ASSOCIATES

Tariq Hammouri
HAMMOURI & PARTNERS

George Hazboun
HAZBOUN & CO. FOR INTERNATIONAL LEGAL BUSINESS CONSULTATIONS

Tayseer Ismail
EAST ECHO CO.

Zeina Jaradat
PRICEWATERHOUSECOOPERS

Youssef S. Khalilieh
RAJAI DAJANI & ASSOCIATES LAW OFFICE

Enad Khirfan
ALI SHARIF ZU'BI, ADVOCATES & LEGAL CONSULTANTS, MEMBER OF LEX MUNDI

Rasha Laswi
ZALLOUM & LASWI LAW FIRM

Emad Majid
PRICEWATERHOUSECOOPERS

Rola Makhadmeh
KHALIFEH & PARTNERS

Firas Malhas
INTERNATIONAL BUSINESS LEGAL ASSOCIATES

Ridha Nasair
LAW GATE ATTORNEYS ORG

Mustafa Nasereddin
TALAL ABU-GHAZALEH LEGAL (TAG-LEGAL) JORDAN AMMAN

Khaldoun Nazer
KHALIFEH & PARTNERS

Mutasem Nsair
KHALIFEH & PARTNERS

Ahmad Quandour
KHALIFEH & PARTNERS

Osama Y. Sabbagh
THE JORDANIAN ELECTRIC POWER CO. LTD. (JEPCO)

Noreen Simonian
CROWN LOGISTICS

Stephan Stephan
PRICEWATERHOUSECOOPERS

Azzam Zalloum
ZALLOUM & LASWI LAW FIRM

Kareem Zureikat
ALI SHARIF ZU'BI, ADVOCATES & LEGAL CONSULTANTS, MEMBER OF LEX MUNDI

Abdelmajeed Zwairi
ODAT & CO

KAZAKHSTAN

Askar Abubakirov
AEQUITAS LAW FIRM

Kirill Afanasyev
KAZAKHSTAN CONSULTING

Zulfiya Akchurina
GRATA LAW FIRM

Aktan Akhmetov
FIRST CREDIT BUREAU

Saida Akhmetova
SALANS

Zhabelov Alim
PANALPINA WORLD TRANSPORT LLP

Ainur Atekeyeva
SALANS

Assel Aubakirova
CHADBOURNE & PARKE LLP

Nailya Azizova
PANALPINA WORLD TRANSPORT LLP

Jypar Beishenalieva
MICHAEL WILSON & PARTNERS LTD.

Assel Bekturganova
GRATA LAW FIRM

Richard Bregonje
PRICEWATERHOUSECOOPERS

Shaimerden Chikanayev
GRATA LAW FIRM

Yulia Demurova
DENTON WILDE SAPTE & CO

Botakoz Dykanbayeva
GRATA LAW FIRM

Ardak Dyussembayeva
AEQUITAS LAW FIRM

Courtney Fowler
PRICEWATERHOUSECOOPERS

Vladimir P. Furman
MCGUIRE WOODS LLP

Togzhan Ibrayeva
SIGNUM LAW FIRM

Semion Issyk
AEQUITAS LAW FIRM

Thomas Johnson
DENTON WILDE SAPTE & CO

Mariyash Kabikenova
REHABILITATION MANAGER

Elena Kaeva
PRICEWATERHOUSECOOPERS

Ramina Kaliyeva
SALANS

Viktoria Katanayeva
GRATA LAW FIRM

Assel Kazbekova
MICHAEL WILSON & PARTNERS LTD.

Tatyana Kim
MARKA AUDIT ACF LLP

Yerbol Konarbayev
GRATA LAW FIRM

Ana Kravchenko
GRATA LAW FIRM

Sholpanai Kudaibergenova
LLP IAC BUISNESS CONSULTING, MEMBER OF RUSSELL BEDFORD INTERNATIONAL

Gulfiya Kurmanova
HALYK BANK KAZAKHSTAN

Irina Latipova
MARKA AUDIT ACF LLP

Assel Makhadiyeva
ORIS LAW FIRM

Aigerim Malikova
PRICEWATERHOUSECOOPERS

Sanju Mani
M&M LOGISTICS

Vsevolod Markov
MCGUIRE WOODS LLP

Bolat Miyatov
GRATA LAW FIRM

Victor Mokrousov
CHADBOURNE & PARKE LLP

Tatiana Muratova
CHADBOURNE & PARKE LLP

Assel Mussina
DENTON WILDE SAPTE & CO

Abylkhair Nakipov
SIGNUM LAW FIRM

Nazira Nurbayeva
PRICEWATERHOUSECOOPERS

Nadezhda Oparina
CHADBOURNE & PARKE LLP

Zhanar Ordabayeva
MCGUIRE WOODS LLP

Yuliya Penzova
AEQUITAS LAW FIRM

Yelena Pestereva
CHADBOURNE & PARKE LLP

Elvis Roberts
CRUZ LOGISTICS

Olga Salimova
ORIS LAW FIRM

Kanat Skakov
SALANS

Myrza Sokurov
PRICEWATERHOUSECOOPERS

Karina Sultanaliyeva
AEQUITAS LAW FIRM

Edil Tunlikbaev
ALMATY URBAN PLANNING AND ARCHITECTURE DEPARTMENT

Amir Tussupkhanov
ORIS LAW FIRM

Yekaterina V. Kim
MICHAEL WILSON & PARTNERS LTD.

Michael Wilson
MICHAEL WILSON & PARTNERS LTD.

Severin Wilson
KAZAKHSTAN CONSULTING

Marina Yudina
PANALPINA WORLD TRANSPORT LLP

Dubek Zhabykenov
BA SERVICES INTERNATIONAL LLC

Danat Zhakenov
ZHAKENOV & PARTNERS

Valerie A. Zhakenov
ZHAKENOV & PARTNERS

Sofiya Zhylkaidarov
SIGNUM LAW FIRM

KENYA

Abdulwahid Aboo
ABDULWAHID ABOO & COMPANY, MEMBER OF RUSSELL BEDFORD INTERNATIONAL

Zulfiquarali Aboo
ABDULWAHID ABOO & COMPANY, MEMBER OF RUSSELL BEDFORD INTERNATIONAL

Jackson Awele
KAPLAN & STRATTON

Vicky Bharij
DALY & FIGGIS ADVOCATES

Oliver Fowler
KAPLAN & STRATTON

Peter Gachuhi
KAPLAN & STRATTON

Francis Gichuhi
PRISM DESIGNS AFRICA

Edmond Gichuru
POST BANK

William Ikutha Maema
ISEME, KAMAU & MAEMA ADVOCATES

James Kamau
ISEME, KAMAU & MAEMA ADVOCATES

Karori Kamau
ISEME, KAMAU & MAEMA ADVOCATES

Patrick Karara
PRICEWATERHOUSECOOPERS

Judith Kavuki
KOKA KOIMBURI & CO.

Hamish Keith
DALY & FIGGIS ADVOCATES

Peter Kiara
PETER KIARA- INDIVIDUAL ARCHITECT

Felix Kioko
B.M. MUSAU & CO. ADVOCATES

Meshack T. Kipturgo
SIGINON FREIGHT LTD.

Owen Koimburi
KOKA KOIMBURI & CO.

Evelyn Masita
KOKA KOIMBURI & CO.

Rosemary Mburu
INSTITUTE OF TRADE DEVELOPMENT

Mansoor A. Mohamed
RUMAN SHIPCONTRACTORS LIMITED

Evelyn Mukhebi
PRICEWATERHOUSECOOPERS

Nkatha Murungi
KAPLAN & STRATTON

Amyn Mussa
ANJARWALLA & KHANNA ADVOCATES

Wachira Ndege
CREDIT REFERENCE BUREAU AFRICA LTD.

Christina Ndiho
KAPLAN & STRATTON

James Ngomeli
THE KENYA POWER AND LIGHTING COMPANY LTD.

Beatrice Bosibori Nyabira
ISEME, KAMAU & MAEMA ADVOCATES

Julia Nyaga
KAPLAN & STRATTON

Conrad Nyukuri
CHUNGA ASSOCIATES

Stephen Okello
PRICEWATERHOUSECOOPERS

Sean Omondi
DALY & FIGGIS ADVOCATES

Sam Omukoko
METROPOL EAST AFRICA LTD.

Esther Omulele
MURIU MUNGAI & CO ADVOCATES

Tom Odhiambo Onyango
OCHIENG, ONYANGO, KIBET & OHAGA

Cephas Osoro
OSORO AND CO, CERTIFIED PUBLIC ACCOUNTANTS

Sonal Sejpal
ANJARWALLA & KHANNA ADVOCATES

Deepen Shah
WALKER KONTOS ADVOCATES

Rajesh Shah
PRICEWATERHOUSECOOPERS

Diana Situma
WALKER KONTOS ADVOCATES

David Tanki
LAN-X AFRICA LTD.

Joseph Taracha
CENTRAL BANK OF KENYA

KIRIBATI

Kenneth Barden
ATTORNEY-AT-LAW

Taake Cama
MINISTRY OF FINANCE

Paul McLaughlin
CA BELLA BETIO CONSTRUCTION

Batitea Tekanito
DEVELOPMENT BANK OF KIRIBATI

KOREA, REP.

Cheolhyo Ahn
YULCHON

Dong-Ook Byun
KOREA CUSTOMS SERVICE

Min-Sook Chae
KOREA CREDIT BUREAU

Hyeong-Tae Cho
SAMIL PRICEWATERHOUSECOOPERS

Min-Jung Cho
KOREA CREDIT BUREAU

Han-Jun Chon
SAMIL PRICEWATERHOUSECOOPERS

Eui Jong Chung
BAE, KIM & LEE LLC

Sang-goo Han
YOON YANG KIM SHIN & YU

C.W. Hyun
KIM & CHANG

James I.S. Jeon
SOJONG PARTNERS

In Bum Jin
CHEON JI ACCOUNTING CORPORATION, MEMBER OF RUSSELL BEDFORD INTERNATIONAL

Hye-Sun Kim
CHAMJON APPAREL

Hyo-Sang Kim
KIM & CHANG

Jung-In Kim
KOREA CREDIT BUREAU

Keunyeop Kim
PANALPINA IAF LTD.

Kyu-Dong Kim
SAMIL PRICEWATERHOUSECOOPERS

Kyung-Jung Kim
PANKO

S.E. Stephan Kim
SOJONG PARTNERS

Se Jin Kim
Hwang Mok Park P.C.

Wonhyung Kim
Yoon Yang Kim Shin & Yu

Yoon Young Kim
Hwang Mok Park P.C.

Joong Hoon Kwak
Lee & Ko

Ki Hyun Kwon
Cheon Ji Accounting Corporation, member of Russell Bedford International

Hye Jeong Lee
Ahnse Law Offices

Jin-Young Lee
Samil PricewaterhouseCoopers

Jong Ho Lee
Sojong Partners

Jung Myung Lee
Hwang Mok Park P.C.

Kyu Wha Lee
Lee & Ko

Myun Ok Lee
Yoon Yang Kim Shin & Yu

Ji Woong Lim
Yulchon

Jung Ha Lim
Hwang Mok Park P.C.

Paul McLaughlin
Ca'Bella Betio Construction

Ho Joon Moon
Lee & Ko

Timothy O'Brien
Kim & Chang

Yon-Kyun Oh
Kim & Chang

Sang Il Park
Hwang Mok Park P.C.

Soo-Hwan Park
Samil PricewaterhouseCoopers

Jeong Seo
Kim & Chang

Yoo Soon Shim
Cheon Ji Accounting Corporation, member of Russell Bedford International

Won-Il Sohn
Yulchon

Jin-Ho Song
Kim & Chang

Kyung Hee Suh
Yulchon

Dong-Suk Wang
Korea Credit Bureau

KOSOVO

Agron E. Beka
Immobilia

Peter Burnie
PricewaterhouseCoopers

Sokol Elmazaj
Boga & Associates

Lorena Gega
PricewaterhouseCoopers

Maliq Gjyshinca
Intereuropa Kosovo Prishtina

Mustafa Hasani
Kosovo Investment Promotion Agency

Menagjer Rarhim Hoxha
ISARS

Albert Islami
Albert Islami & Partners

Bejtush Isufi
Interlex Associates L.L.C.

Agron Krasniqi
Boga & Associates

Isak Mehmeti
Municipality of Prishtina

Arben Mustafa
Intereuropa Kosovo Prishtina

Besim Osmani
Interlex Associates L.L.C.

Mehdi Pllashniku
Kosovo Business Registartion Agency

Laura Qorlaze
PricewaterhouseCoopers

Iliriana Osmani Serreqi
Avokatura Osmani

Bardhyl Shehu
TRUST

Jeton Vokshi
Intereuropa Kosovo Prishtina

Shaha Zylfiu
Central Bank of the Republic of Kosovo

Atdhe Dika
Kalo & Associates

KUWAIT

Ihab Abbas
Deloitte

Labeed Abdal
The Law Firm of Labeed Abdal

Nazih Abdul Hameed
Al Markaz Law Firm

Mahmoud Abdulfattah
The Law Offices of Mishari Al-Ghazali

Waleed Abdulrahim
Abdullah Kh. Al-Ayoub & Associates, member of Lex Mundi

Lina A.K. Adlouni
KIPCO Asset Management Company K.S.C

Abdullah Al-Ayoub
Abdullah Kh. Al-Ayoub & Associates, member of Lex Mundi

Mishari M. Al-Ghazali
The Law Offices of Mishari Al-Ghazali

Reema Ali
Ali & Partners

Akusa Batwala
ASAR-Al Ruwayeh & Partners

Nada Bourahmah
The Law Offices of Mishari Al-Ghazali

Tim Bullock
Deloitte

Mary Carmel Byrne
Al Markaz Law Firm

Paul Day
ASAR-Al Ruwayeh & Partners

Sam Habbas
ASAR-Al Ruwayeh & Partners

Chirine Krayem Moujaes
The Law Offices of Mishari Al-Ghazali

Medhat Mubarak
Al Markaz Law Firm

Amer Nabulsi
DLA Piper

Anupama Nair
Abdullah Kh. Al-Ayoub & Associates, member of Lex Mundi

Mohamed Omar
Al Markaz Law Firm

Mohammed Ramadan
Al Markaz Law Firm

Shafeek Rhaman
AA May International for Global Shipping

Mini Shivadas
The Law Firm of Labeed Abdal

Ahmed Zakaria
ASAR-Al Ruwayeh & Partners

KYRGYZ REPUBLIC

Shuhrat Akhmatakhunov
Kalikova & Associates Law Firm

Niyazbek Aldashev
Lorenz International Law Firm

Nurlan Alymbaev
USAID, Judicial Reform Assistance Project, Kyrgyz Republic, Millennium Challenge Account Threshold Program

Beishenbek Alymkulov
Lorenz International Law Firm

Akjoltoi Elebesova
Credit Information Bureau Ishenim

Aiperi Esengeldieva
Lorenz International Law Firm

Courtney Fowler
PricewaterhouseCoopers

Natalia Galliamova
Third Party Arbitrage Court

Saltanat Ismailova
PricewaterhouseCoopers

Nurbek Ismankulov
M&M Transport Logistic Services

Nurzhan Issatov
PricewaterhouseCoopers

Merim Kachkynbaeva
Kalikova & Associates Law Firm

Elena Kaeva
PricewaterhouseCoopers

Gulnara Kalikova
Kalikova & Associates Law Firm

Tatiana Kim
International Entrepreneurship Fund

Nurdin Kumushbekov
USAID Business Environment Project

Svetlana Lebedeva
Lorenz International Law Firm

Marina Lim
Kalikova & Associates Law Firm

Vyacheslav Vasilievich Lunev

Barno Marazykova
"Partner" Law Firm

Ase Momoshova
Kalikova & Associates Law Firm

Almas Nakipov
PricewaterhouseCoopers

Karlygash Ospankulova
Kalikova & Associates Law Firm

Natalya Pak
"Partner" Law Firm

Magomec Saaduev
Kalikova & Associates Law Firm

Kanat Seidaliev
Grata Law Firm

Mirgul Smanalieva
"Partner" Law Firm

Maksim Smirnov
Kalikova & Associates Law Firm

Aisuluu Sydygalieva
USAID BEI Project

Azamat Talantbek uulu
USAID Business Environment Project

Gulnara Uskenbaeva
Alpha Sheersfield

Ali Ramazanovich Vodyanov
Electrosila

LAO PDR

Sithong Chanthasouk
DFDL Mekong Law Group

Aristotle David
DFDL Mekong Law Group

Daodeuane Duangdara
PricewaterhouseCoopers

Walter Heiser
DFDL Mekong Law Group

Chris Manley
DFDL Mekong Law Group

Varavudh Meesaiyati
PricewaterhouseCoopers

Vongphacnanh Onepaseuth
DFDL Mekong Law Group

Somphone Phasavath
Lao Freight Forwarder Co. Ltd.

Ketsana Phommachanh
Ministry of Justice

Thavorn Rujivanarom
PricewaterhouseCoopers

Vichit Sadettan
Lao Freight Forwarder Co. Ltd.

Senesakoune Sihanouvong
DFDL Mekong Law Group

Darika Soponawat
PricewaterhouseCoopers

Souvanno Sphabmixay
PricewaterhouseCoopers

Kristy Thatcher
DFDL Mekong Law Group

Sengdara Tiamtisack
Lao Freight Forwarder Co. Ltd.

Andrea Wilson
DFDL Mekong Law Group

LATVIA

Ilze Abika
Skudra & Udris Law Offices

Martins Aljens
Raidla Lejins & Norcous

Ilona Bauda
Loze, Grunte & Cers

Elina Bedanova
Raidla Lejins & Norcous

Eva Berlaus-Gulbe
Sorainen

Iveta Berzina
Skudra & Udris Law Offices

Andis Burkevics
Sorainen

Andis Čonka
Latvijas Banka

Zane Džule
Liepa, Skopiņa/ Borenius

Ingrida Dimina
PricewaterhouseCoopers

Valters Diure
Klavins & Slaidins LAWIN

Zlata Elksnina-Zascirinska
PricewaterhouseCoopers

Valters Gencs
Gencs Valters Law Firm

Ilga Gudrenika-Krebs
Klavins & Slaidins LAWIN

Janis Irbe
Latvenergo AS, Sadales Tikls

Sandis Jermuts
Sabiedrisko pakalpojumu regul aanas komisija

Dace Kalnmeiere
Liepa, Skopina/ Borenius

Nikita Koroteckis
LINKORG.EU

Irina Kostina
Klavins & Slaidins LAWIN

Indrikis Liepa
Liepa, Skopina/ Borenius

Janis Loze
Loze, Grunte & Cers

Alexey Melsitov
MTA Maritime Transport & Agencies

Irina Olevska
Liepa, Skopina/ Borenius

Zane Paeglite
Sorainen

Sergejs Rudans
Liepa, Skopina/ Borenius

Lāsma Rugāte
Sorainen

Dace Silava-Tomsone
Raidla Lejins & Norcous

Sarmis Spilbergs
Klavins & Slaidins LAWIN

Zane Štālberga – Markvarte
Markvarte Lexchange Law Office

Marite Straume-Cerbule
RE & RE Ltd.

Maija Tipaine
Raidla Lejins & Norcous

Agate Ziverte
PricewaterhouseCoopers

LEBANON

Hanan Abboud
PricewaterhouseCoopers

Wassim Abou Nader
Mena City Lawyers

Wadih Abou Nasr
PricewaterhouseCoopers

Manal Assir
UNDP

Antoine Baaklini
BAB International

Jean Baroudi
Baroudi & Associates

Tarek Baz
Hyam G. Mallat Law Firm

Melynda BouAoun
Badri and Salim El Meouchi Law Firm, member of Interleges

Najib Choucair
Central Bank of Lebanon

Alice Choueiri
Mena City Lawyers

Sanaa Daakour
Mena City Lawyers

Michel Doueihy
Badri and Salim El Meouchi Law Firm, member of Interleges

Hanadi El Hajj
Mena City Lawyers

Chadia El Meouchi
Badri and Salim El Meouchi Law Firm, member of Interleges

Dania George
PricewaterhouseCoopers

Abdallah Hayek
Hayek Group

Walid Honein
Badri and Salim El Meouchi Law Firm, member of Interleges

Maher Hoteit
Mena City Lawyers

Mahdi Husseini
Badri and Salim El Meouchi Law Firm, member of Interleges

Fady Jamaleddine
Mena City Lawyers

Elie Kachouh
ELC Transport Services SAL

Georges Kadige
Kadige & Kadige Law Firm

Michel Kadige
Kadige & Kadige Law Firm

Claudine Karaki
Ministry of Finance

Najib Khattar
Khattar Associates

Albert Laham
Law Office of Albert Laham

Sader Makram
Association of Banks in Lebanon (ABL)

Georges Mallat
Hyam G. Mallat Law Firm

Nabil Mallat
Hyam G. Mallat Law Firm

Fadi Moghaizel
Moghaizel Law Firm, member of Lex Mundi

Mario Mohanna
Patrimoine Conseil SARL

Mirvat Mostafa
Mena City Lawyers

Rania Mrad
Khattar Associates

Pierre Nehme
Bureau d'Etudes Pierre Nehme

Toufic Nehme
Law Office of Albert Laham

Elias Rammouz
Mena City Lawyers

Mireille Richa
Tyan & Zgheib Law Firm

Jihane Rizk Khattar
Khattar Associates

Jihad Rizkallah
Badri and Salim El Meouchi Law Firm, member of Interleges

Elias A. Saadé
Moghaizel Law Firm, member of Lex Mundi

Rached Sarkis
Rached Sarkis Office

Antoine Sfeir
Badri and Salim El Meouchi Law Firm, member of Interleges

George Tannous
Beirut International Movers

Bassel Tohme
Mena City Lawyers

Hala. Tyan
Moghaizel Law Firm, member of Lex Mundi

Nady Tyan
Tyan & Zgheib Law Firm

Rania Yazbeck
Tyan & Zgheib Law Firm

LESOTHO

Tankiso Hlaoli

Bernice Khoachele
National Environment Secretariat

Selebalo Lekokoto
Lesotho National Development Corporation

Makhala Leteba
Sheeran & Associates

Lebereko Lethobane
Labour Court Lesotho

Qhalehang Letsika
Mei & Mei Attorneys Inc.

Vincent Mabulu
Lesotho Architects, Engineers & Surveyors Association

Realeboha Makamane
High Court

Thabo Makeka
Association of Lesotho Employers and Business

Tseliso Daniel Makhaphela
Ministry of Local Government

Thakane Makume
Lesotho Electricity Company (Pty) Ltd.

Moeketsi Marumo
PowerConsult (Pty) Ltd.

Leoma Matamne
Molepe Quantity Surveyors

Mathias Matshe
Sheeran & Associates

Tony Mcalpine
Moores Rowland

Thandiwe Metsing

Moeletsi Moamohe
Safmarine Maersk

Molomo Mohale
Systematic Architects

Lebenya Moleko
Moleko Electrial Contractors

Denis Molyneaux
Webber Newdigate

Tseliso Monaphathi
High Court

Mamophete Mophethe
Phillips Clearing & Forwarding Agent (Pty) Ltd.

Ebenezer Keneiloe Mopoti
Archiplane Studio Lesotho Ltd.

Theodore Ntlatlapa
DNT Architects

A.R.Thabiso Ramokoena
NedBank Lesotho Ltd.

Duduzile Seamatha
Sheeran & Associates

Tiisetso Sello-Mafatle
Sello-Mafatle Attorneys

Mokhethi Shelile
Lesotho National Development Corporation

Marorisang Thekiso
Sheeran & Associates

Phoka Thene
Sello-Mafatle Attorneys

George Thokoa
Maseru Electro Services Pty Ltd.

Mahlape Tjela
NedBank Lesotho Ltd.

LIBERIA

Christian Allison
Central Bank of Liberia

Amos P. Andrews
Ecobank

Khalil Azar
Beever Company

Christiana Baah
PricewaterhouseCoopers

F. Augustus Caesar, Jr.
Caesar Architects, Inc.

Henry Reed Cooper
Cooper & Togbah Law Firm

Frank Musah Dean
Dean & Associates

S. Peter Doe-Kpar
Monthly and Probate Court

Christine Sonpon Freeman
Cooper & Togbah Law Firm

Paul Greene
Ministry of Finance, Liberia

Winleta Henries Reeves
Dean & Associates

Cyril Jones
Jones & Jones

Abu Kamara
Ministry of Commerce & Industry

George Kwatia
PricewaterhouseCoopers

Martha Lackay
Liberia Electricity Corporation

J. Johnny Momoh
Sherman & Sherman

Sylvanus O' Connor
AEP Consultants Inc.

Kingsley Owusu-Ewli
PricewaterhouseCoopers

Bloh Sayeh
Center for National Documents & Records / National Archives

Amos Siebo
Liberia Reconstruction and Development Committee

Nyenati Tuan
Tuan Wreh Law Firm

Darcy White
PricewaterhouseCoopers

Melvin Yates
Compass Inc., Clearing and Forwarding

Harvy T. Yuan, Sr.
Liberia Electricity Corporation

LITHUANIA

Kęstutis Adamonis
Sorainen

Lina Aleknaite - Van der Molen
Eversheds Saladzius

Gintas Andruaka
Raidla Lejins & Norcous

Petras Baltusevičius
DSV Transport UAB

Donatas Baranauskas
Vilniaus Miesto 14 - Asis Notaru Biuras

Kim Bartholdy
DSV Transport UAB

Šarūnas Basijokas
Bernotas & Dominas Glimstedt

Vilius Bernatonis
Sutkiene, Pilkauskas & Partners

Eglé Jankauskaité
Bernotas & Dominas Glimstedt

Andrius Bogdanovičius
JSC "Creditinfo Lietuva"

Ina Budelinait
Sorainen

Dovil Burgien
Law Firm Lideika, Petrauskas, Valiknas ir partneriai LAWIN, member of Lex Mundi

Sergej Butov
Sorainen

Robertas Čiočys
Law Firm Lideika, Petrauskas, Valiknas ir partneriai LAWIN, member of Lex Mundi

Giedre Dailidenaite
BNT Attorneys APB

Gintaras Daugela
Bank of Lithuania

Vita Dauksaite
Law Firm Lideika, Petrauskas, Valiknas ir partneriai LAWIN, member of Lex Mundi

Goda Deltuvait
Sorainen

Giedre Domkute
AAA Baltic Service Company -Law firm

Antanas Dzinga
Sorainen

Dalia Foigt-Norvaiaien
Regija Borenius

Valters Gencs
Gencs Valters Law Firm

Simas Gudynas
Law Firm Lideika, Petrauskas, Valiknas ir partneriai LAWIN, member of Lex Mundi

Frank Heemann
BNT Attorneys APB

Egl Jankauskait
Bernotas & Dominas Glimstedt

Agne Jonaityt
Sorainen

Povilas Junevičius
Law Firm Lideika, Petrauskas, Valiknas ir partneriai LAWIN, member of Lex Mundi

Aurimas Kačinskas
JSC "Creditinfo Lietuva"

Romas Karaliunas
Bank of Lithuania

Povilas Karlonas
Sorainen

Romualdas Kasperavičius
State Enterprise Centre of Registers

Jonas Kiauleikis
Regija Borenius

Jurate Kraujalyte
AMERINDE CONSOLIDATED,
INC LITHUANIA VILNIUS

Kristina Kriščiūnaitė
PRICEWATERHOUSECOOPERS

Ronaldas Kubilius
PRICEWATERHOUSECOOPERS

Egidijus Kundelis
PRICEWATERHOUSECOOPERS

Žilvinas Kvietkus
RAIDLA LEJINS & NORCOUS

Valdis Leikus
ERNST & YOUNG BALTIC UAB

Giedr Liaugminait
KPMG

Viktorija Ma iulien
SORAINEN

Asta Macijauskiene
BERNOTAS & DOMINAS
GLIMSTEDT

Gytis Malinauskas
SORAINEN

Linas Margevicius
LEGAL BUREAU OF LINAS
MARGEVICIUS

Marius Matiukas
SUTKIENE, PILKAUSKAS &
PARTNERS

Rkta Matonien
VILNIUS CITY MUNICIPALITY

Vaidotas Melynavicius
AAA BALTIC SERVICE
COMPANY -LAW FIRM

Tomas Mieliauskas
LAW FIRM FORESTA

Bronislovas Mikkta
STATE ENTERPRISE CENTRE OF
REGISTERS

Tadas Milasius
SORAINEN

Indr Minkuvien
ERNST & YOUNG BALTIC UAB

Asta Misiukiene
MINISTRY OF ECONOMY OF
THE REPUBLIC OF LITHUANIA

Simona Oliakevi ikt -Cic nien
LAW FIRM LIDEIKA,
PETRAUSKAS, VALIKNAS IR
PARTNERIAI LAWIN, MEMBER
OF LEX MUNDI

Žygimantas Pacevičius
REGIJA BORENIUS

Rytis Paukat
LAW FIRM LIDEIKA,
PETRAUSKAS, VALIKNAS IR
PARTNERIAI LAWIN, MEMBER
OF LEX MUNDI

Mindaugas Peicius
BANK OF LITHUANIA

Algirdas Pekays
SORAINEN

Mantas Petkevičius
SORAINEN

Angelija Petrauskien
VILNIUS CITY MUNICIPALITY

Aidas Petrosius
STATE ENTERPRISE CENTRE OF
REGISTERS

Marius Rindinas
LAW FIRM ZABIELA,
ZABIELAITE & PARTNERS

Milda Ručinskaitė
MINISTRY OF ECONOMY OF
THE REPUBLIC OF LITHUANIA

Dalia Sidagiene
MINISTRY OF ECONOMY OF
THE REPUBLIC OF LITHUANIA

Rimantas Simaitis
RAIDLA LEJINS & NORCOUS

Alius Stamkauskas
UAB ELMONTA

Jonas Stamkauskas
UAB ELMONTA

Rimantas Vaicenavicius
BANK OF LITHUANIA

Vilija Vaitkut Pavan
LAW FIRM LIDEIKA,
PETRAUSKAS, VALIKNAS IR
PARTNERIAI LAWIN, MEMBER
OF LEX MUNDI

Rolandas Valiknas
LAW FIRM LIDEIKA,
PETRAUSKAS, VALIKNAS IR
PARTNERIAI LAWIN, MEMBER
OF LEX MUNDI

Egle Valiuliene
LAW FIRM LIDEIKA,
PETRAUSKAS, VALIKNAS IR
PARTNERIAI LAWIN, MEMBER
OF LEX MUNDI

Lina Vosylien
KPMG

Darius Zabiela
LAW FIRM ZABIELA,
ZABIELAITE & PARTNERS

Indre Zakalskyte
ERNST & YOUNG BALTIC UAB

Giedre Zalpyte
BNT ATTORNEYS APB

Jkrat Zarankien
ERNST & YOUNG BALTIC UAB

Audrius Žvybas
BERNOTAS & DOMINAS
GLIMSTEDT

LUXEMBOURG

ALLEN & OVERY LLP

Eleonora Broman
LOYENS & LOEFF

Guy Castegnaro
CASTEGNARO CABINET
D'AVOCATS, MEMBER OF IUS
LABORIS

Christel Dumont
OOSTVOGELS

Thomas Ecker
VILLE DE LUXEMBOURG -
SERVICE DE L'ÉLECTRICITÉ

Gérard Eischen
CHAMBER OF COMMERCE
OF THE GRAND-DUCHY OF
LUXEMBOURG

Martine Gerber Lemaire
OOSTVOGELS

François Kremer
ARENDT & MEDERNACH

Tom Loesch
LINKLATERS

Nuria Martin
LOYENS & LOEFF

Peter Moons
LOYENS & LOEFF

Elisabeth Omes
BONN SCHMITT STEICHEN,
MEMBER OF LEX MUNDI

Françoise Pfeiffer
PFEIFFER & SAGNARD

Judith Raijmakers
LOYENS & LOEFF

Geoffrey Scardoni
LOYENS & LOEFF

Jean-Luc Schaus
LOYENS & LOEFF

Roger Schintgen
PAUL WURTH S.A

Alex Schmitt
BONN SCHMITT STEICHEN,
MEMBER OF LEX MUNDI

Elodie Simonian
OOSTVOGELS

Alessandro Sorcinelli
LINKLATERS

MACEDONIA, FYR

Natasa Andreeva
NATIONAL BANK OF THE
REPUBLIC OF MACEDONIA

Svetlana Andreovska
MONEVSKI LAW FIRM

Zlatko Antevski
LAWYERS ANTEVSKI

Aleksandra Arsoska
IKRP ROKAS & PARTNERS

Benita Beleskova
IKRP ROKAS & PARTNERS

Dragan Blažev
TIMELPROJECT ENGINEERING

Eli Bocevska
PRICEWATERHOUSECOOPERS

Vladimir Bocevski
MENS LEGIS CAKMAKOVA
ADVOCATES

Biljana Čakmakova
MENS LEGIS CAKMAKOVA
ADVOCATES

Tanja Cenova-Mitrovska
KATASTAR

Ljupco Georgievski
KATASTAR

Theodoros Giannitsakis
IKRP ROKAS & PARTNERS

Pavlinka Golejski
MENS LEGIS CAKMAKOVA
ADVOCATES

Ana Hadzieva
POLENAK LAW FIRM

Vesna Hristova
LAW OFFICE NIKOLOVSKI

Natasha Hroneska

Biljana Ickovska
LAW OFFICE NIKOLOVSKI

Aleksandar Ickovski
PRICEWATERHOUSECOOPERS

Nena Ivanovska
JUDICIAL REFORM
IMPLEMENTATION PROJECT

Maja Jakimovska
MENS LEGIS CAKMAKOVA
ADVOCATES

Aneta Jovanoska - Trajanovska
LAWYERS ANTEVSKI

Valentina Jovanovska Vasileva
IKRP ROKAS & PARTNERS

Sam Juncker
MACEDONIAN COURT
MODERNIZATION PROJECT

Dejan Knezović
LAW OFFICE KNEZOVIC &
ASSOCIATES

Zlatko T. Kolevski
KOLEVSKI LAW OFFICE

Lidija Krstevska
EU HARMONIZATION UNIT

Miroslav Marchev
PRICEWATERHOUSECOOPERS

Irena Mitkovska
LAWYERS ANTEVSKI

Biljana Mladenovska
LAWYERS ANTEVSKI

Valerjan Monevski
MONEVSKI LAW FIRM

Svetlana Neceva
LAW OFFICE PEPELJUGOSKI

Goran Nikolovski
LAW OFFICE NIKOLOVSKI

Zlatko Nikolovski
NOTARY CHAMBER OF R. OF
MACEDONIA

Kiril Papazoski
MONEVSKI LAW FIRM

Vasko Pejkov
REPUBLIC OF MACEDONIA
SECURITIES AND EXCHANGE
COMMISSION

Ljubica Ruben
MENS LEGIS LAW FIRM

Lidija Sarafimova Danevska
NATIONAL BANK OF THE
REPUBLIC OF MACEDONIA

Biljana Saraginova
MONEVSKI LAW FIRM

Zdravko Stefanovski
TOPLIFIKACIJA ENGEENRING

Ljupka Stojanovska
LAW OFFICE NIKOLOVSKI

Biljana Tanevska
LAWYERS ANTEVSKI

Slavica Trckova
LAW OFFICE TRCKOVA

Vladimir Vasilevski
BETASPED INTERNATIONAL
FREIGHT FORWARDING

Eva Veljanovska
MENS LEGIS CAKMAKOVA
ADVOCATES

Sanja Veljanovska
MENS LEGIS LAW FIRM

Metodija Velkov
POLENAK LAW FIRM

MADAGASCAR

Rakotondrazaka Aina
MADAGASCAR CONSEIL
INTERNATIONAL

Eric Robson Andriamihaja
ECONOMIC DEVELOPMENT
BOARD OF MADAGASCAR

Tsiry Nambinina
Andriamisamanana
MADAGASCAR CONSEIL
INTERNATIONAL

Josoa Lucien Andrianelinjaka
BANQUE CENTRALE DE
MADAGASCAR

Andriamanalina Andrianjaka
OFFICE NOTARIAL DE
TAMATAVE

Philippe Antoine
Harilalanorohanitra
MADAGASCAR LAW OFFICES

Raphaël Jakoba
MADAGASCAR CONSEIL
INTERNATIONAL

Hanna Keyserlingk
CABINET HK JURIFISC.

Pascaline R. Rasamoeliarisoa
DELOITTE

Sahondra Rabenarivo
MADAGASCAR LAW OFFICES

Serge Lucien Rajoelina
JIRO SY RANO MALAGASY
(JIRAMA)

Lanto Tiana Ralison
FIDAFRICA /
PRICEWATERHOUSECOOPERS

Laingoniaina
Ramarimbahoaka
MADAGASCAR CONSEIL
INTERNATIONAL

Michel Ramboa
MADAGASCAR LAW OFFICES

Fanja Randriamanantena
FIDAFRICA /
PRICEWATERHOUSECOOPERS

Rivolalaina Randrianarisoa
FIDAFRICA /
PRICEWATERHOUSECOOPERS

William Randrianarivelo
FIDAFRICA /
PRICEWATERHOUSECOOPERS

Michael Ratrimo
MADAGASCAR INTERNATIONAL
CONTAINER TERMINAL
SERVICES LTD.

Mialy Ratsimba
FIDAFRICA /
PRICEWATERHOUSECOOPERS

Théodore Raveloarison
JARY - BUREAU D'ETUDES
ARCHITECTURE INGENIERIE

Andriamisa Ravelomanana
FIDAFRICA /
PRICEWATERHOUSECOOPERS

Jean Marcel Razafimahenina
DELOITTE

Rivolala Razanatsimba
JIRO SY RANO MALAGASY
(JIRAMA)

Njiva Razanatsoa
BANQUE CENTRALE DE
MADAGASCAR

Louis Sagot
CABINET D'AVOCAT LOUIS
SAGOT

Ida Soamiliarimana
MADAGASCAR CONSEIL
INTERNATIONAL

Dominique Taty
FIDAFRICA /
PRICEWATERHOUSECOOPERS

MALAWI

Sylvia Ali
KNIGHT FRANK

Johann Boshoff
PRICEWATERHOUSECOOPERS

Kevin M. Carpenter
PRICEWATERHOUSECOOPERS

Joseph Chavula
SDV LOGISTICS LTD.

Marshal Chilenga
TF & PARTNERS

Aamir Rashid Jakhura
FARGO GROUP OF COMPANIES

Wiseman Kabwazi
ESCOM

Omar Paison Kaisi
4TH ARCHITECTURAL DIMENSION

Chimwemwe Kalua
GOLDEN & LAW

Cyprian Kambili
IFC MALAWI

Kalekeni Kaphale
KALEKENI KAPHALE

Alfred Majamanda
MBENDERA & NKHONO ASSOCIATES

Misheck Msiska
PRICEWATERHOUSECOOPERS

Charles Mvula
DUMA ELECTRICS - CONTROL SYSTEMS AND ENERGY MANAGEMENT

Mtchuka Mwale
NICHOLLS & BROOKES

Grant Nyirongo
ELEMECH DESIGNS

Dinker A. Raval
WILSON & MORGAN

Duncan Singano
SAVJANI & CO.

MALAYSIA

Jamil A. Hamid
ARKITEK KITAS SDN BHD

Nor Azimah Abdul Aziz
COMPANIES COMMISSION OF MALAYSIA

Dato' Hasmah BT. Abdullah
INLAND REVENE BOARD OF MALAYSIA

Sonia Abraham
AZMAN, DAVIDSON & CO.

Wan Ahmad Iskandar Wan Adnan
MINISTRY OF INTERNATIONAL TRADE AND INDUSTRY

Ar Saifuddin Ahmad
SNO ARCHITECT SDN BHD

Alwizah Al-Yafii Ahmad Kamal
ZAID IBRAHIM & CO

Dato' Abdul Halim Ain
ADMINISTRATIVE AND DIPLOMATIC SERVICE, MALAYSIA

Dato' Sh. Yahya bin Sh. Mohamed Almurisi
MINISTRY OF HUMAN RESOURCES

Mohd Azlan B. Mohd Radzi
LAND & MINES OFFICE

Shamsuddin Bardan
MALAYSIAN EMPLOYERS FEDERATION

Azryain Borhan
COMPANIES COMMISSION OF MALAYSIA

Hong Yun Chang
TAY & PARTNERS

Ar Teoh Chee Wui
ARCHICENTRE SDN BHD

Ruban Chelliah
STANCO AND RUCHE CONSULTING

Yuan Yuan Cheng
SKRINE, MEMBER OF LEX MUNDI

Andrew Ean Vooi Chiew
LEE HISHAMMUDDIN ALLEN & GELDHILL

Meng Sim Chuah
RUSSELL BEDFORD LC & COMPANY, MEMBER OF RUSSELL BEDFORD INTERNATIONAL

Tze Keong Chung
CTOS SDN BHD

Mukhriz Hamzah
MINISTRY OF INTERNATIONAL TRADE AND INDUSTRY

Hasnah Binti Dato' Mohammed Hashim
FEDERAL COURT OF MALAYSIA

Sien Yian Hee
PRICEWATERHOUSECOOPERS

Hj. Hasim Hj. Ismail
LAND & MINES OFFICE

Hung Hoong
SHEARN DELAMORE & CO.

Mohd Razali Hussain
MALAYSIA PRODUCTIVITY CORPORATION

Nazariah Ibrahim
TENAGA NASIONAL BERHAD

Subkiah Binti Jamaludin
INLAND REVENE BOARD OF MALAYSIA

Kumar Kanagasabai
SKRINE, MEMBER OF LEX MUNDI

Kumar Kanagasingam
LEE HISHAMMUDDIN ALLEN & GELDHILL

Mohammad Sanusi Abdul Karim
MINISTRY OF INTERNATIONAL TRADE AND INDUSTRY

Kesavan Karuppiah
MINISTRY OF HUMAN RESOURCES

Dato' Azemi Kasim
ADMINISTRATIVE AND DIPLOMATIC SERVICE, MALAYSIA

Abdul Kadir Bin Kassim
KADIR, ANDRI & PARTNERS

Geeta Kaur
SDV SDN BHD MALAYSIA

Ng Swee Kee
SHEARN DELAMORE & CO.

Chuan Keat Khoo
PRICEWATERHOUSECOOPERS

Christopher Lee
CHRISTOPHER LEE & CO.

Mai Yeen Leong
PROFESSIONAL INNOVATORS SDN. BHD.

Bernard Lim
PHK MANAGEMENT SERVICES SDN BHD

Koon Huan Lim
SKRINE, MEMBER OF LEX MUNDI

Lay Sim Lim
RUSSELL BEDFORD LC & COMPANY, MEMBER OF RUSSELL BEDFORD INTERNATIONAL

Theresa Lim
PRICEWATERHOUSECOOPERS

Kok Leong Loh
RUSSELL BEDFORD LC & COMPANY, MEMBER OF RUSSELL BEDFORD INTERNATIONAL

Caesar Loong
RASLAN - LOONG

Nurliyana Md Zukri
AZMI & ASSOCIATES

Suhara Mohamad Sidik
AZMI & ASSOCIATES

Azmi Mohd Ali
AZMI & ASSOCIATES

Aminuddin Mohd Khalil
ARKITEK KITAS SDN BHD

Zuhaidi Mohd Shahari
AZMI & ASSOCIATES

Oy Moon Ng
CTOS SDN BHD

Aminah BT Abd. Rahman
MINISTRY OF HOUSING AND LOCAL GOVERNMENT MALAYSIA

N Ravi
MITSUI O.S.K LINES (M) SDN BHD

Norhaslinda Salleh
COMPANIES COMMISSION OF MALAYSIA

Sharizan Sarif
AZMI & ASSOCIATES

Andy Seo
FEDERATION OF MALAYSIAN MANUFACTURERS

Hui Shan Siah
WONG & PARTNERS

S Parameswaran Shanmughanathan
TENAGA NASIONAL BERHAD

Noeline Chanan Singh
MALAYSIA PRODUCTIVITY CORPORATION

Veerinderjeet Singh
MALAYSIAN INSTITUTE OF TAXATION

Visu Sinnadurai

Yong Hsian Siong
WONG & PARTNERS

Muhendaran Suppiah
MUHENDARAN SRI

Francis Tan
AZMAN, DAVIDSON & CO.

Kenneth Tiong
THE ASSOCIATED CHINESE CHAMBERS OF COMMERCE AND INDUSTRY OF MALAYSIA (ACCCIM)

Hock Chai Toh
BANK NEGARA MALAYSIA

Sugumaran Vairavappillai
MINISTRY OF HUMAN RESOURCE MALAYSIA

Heng Choon Wan
PRICEWATERHOUSECOOPERS

Ah Sah Wee
SELANGOR FREIGHT FORWARDERS AND LOGISTICS ASSOCIATION

Peter Wee
PRICEWATERHOUSECOOPERS

Mun Yi
SHEARN DELAMORE & CO.

Melina Yong
RASLAN - LOONG

Mohamad Ridzwan Zainal Abidin
SNO ARCHITECT SDN BHD

Nur Ishqi Hayati Zakaria
COMPANIES COMMISSION OF MALAYSIA

Shezlina Zakaria
MALAYSIA PRODUCTIVITY CORPORATION

Mohd Yazid Zamr
SNO ARCHITECT SDN BHD

Ar Mohd Zulhemlee An
W AND W ARCHITECTS

MALDIVES

Mifzal Ahmad
MINISTRY OF ECONOMIC DEVELOPMENT

Jatindra Bhattray
PRICEWATERHOUSECOOPERS

Asma Chan-Rahim
SHAH, HUSSAIN & CO. BARRISTERS & ATTORNEYS

Mohamed Hameed
ANTRAC PVT. LTD.

Dheena Hussain
SHAH, HUSSAIN & CO. BARRISTERS & ATTORNEYS

Yudhishtran Kanagasabai
PRICEWATERHOUSECOOPERS

Ahmed Murad
BANK OF MALDIVES PLC.

Aishath Samah
BANK OF MALDIVES PLC.

Shuaib M. Shah
SHAH, HUSSAIN & CO. BARRISTERS & ATTORNEYS

Ahmed Shibau
CUBE X COMPANY PVT LTD.

Mariyam Sunaina
BANK OF MALDIVES PLC.

MALI

Imirane Abdoulaye
DIRECTION NATIONALE DE L'URBANISME ET DE L'HABITAT

Diaby Aboubakar
BCEAO

Faradji Baba
COUR D'APPEL DE BAMAKO

Amadou Camara
SCP CAMARA TRAORÉ

Céline Camara Sib
ETUDE ME CELINE CAMARA SIB

Mahamane I. Cisse
CABINET LEXIS CONSEILS

Boubacar Coulibaly
MATRANS MALI SARL

Sekou Dembele
ETUDE DE MAÎTRE SEKOU DEMBELE

Abou Diallo
API MALI

Fatimata Dicko Zouboye

Mohamed Abdoulaye Diop
SDV

Djénéba Diop Sidibe
SCP D'AVOCAT DIOP-DIALLO

Mahamane Djiteye
JURIFIS CONSULT

Yacouba Guindo
AD

Gaoussou Haîdara
ETUDE GAOUSSOU HAIDARA

Maiga Seydou Ibrahim
CABINET D'AVOCATS SEYDOU IBRAHIM MAIGA

Adama Kane
SCAE

Yacouba Massama Keïta

Mamadou Ismaïla Konate
JURIFIS CONSULT

Gaoussou A. G. Konaté
CABINET D'ARCHITECTURE - ETUDES TECHNIQUES

Arbonkana Maiga
LOBOU CONSEILS

Soumana Makadji
GMI - AUDIT

Maiga Mamadou
KAFO JIGINEW

Fata Mariko
DAMCO

Adeline Messou
FIDAFRICA / PRICEWATERHOUSECOOPERS

Bérenger Y. Meuke
JURIFIS CONSULT

Keita Zeïnabou Sacko
API MALI

Alassane T. Sangaré

Nouhoum Sidibe
DIRECTION NATIONALE DE L'URBANISME ET DE L'HABITAT

Malick Badara Sow
ATELIER D'ARCHITECTURE ET D'URBANISME

Mamadou Moustapha Sow
CABINET SOW & ASSOCIÉS

Abdoul Kader Sylla
DAMCO

Perignama Sylla
ARCHITECT DE/AU

Salif Tall
ETUDE DE MAÎTRE AHMADOU TOURE

Dominique Taty
FIDAFRICA / PRICEWATERHOUSECOOPERS

Alhousseini Touré
ARCADE SARL

Mahamadou Traore

Alassane Traoré
ICON SARL

Fousséni Traoré
FIDAFRICA / PRICEWATERHOUSECOOPERS

Amidou Wague
SDV

Emmanuel Yehouessi
BCEAO

MARSHALL ISLANDS

Kenneth Barden
ATTORNEY-AT-LAW

Mary Sheryl Jane Profeta
MARSHALL ISLANDS SOCIAL SECURITY ADMINISTRATION

Phillip Welch
MICRONESIAN SHIPPING AGENCIES INC.

MAURITANIA

Ishagh Ahmed Miske
CABINET ISHAGH MISKE

Rodolphe Kadoukpe Akoto
MAERSK MAURITANIA NOUADHIBOU BRANCH

Esteit Mohamedou Amane
MAURITANIENNE DE CONSTRUCTION ET d'EQUIPEMENTS (MCE)

Tidiane Bal
BSD & ASSOCIÉS

Fatoumata Diarra
BSD & ASSOCIÉS

Mine Ould Abdoullah
PRIVATE PRACTICE

Abdallahi Ould Ahmed Baba
ATELIER d'ARCHITECTURE ET DESIGN

Ahmed Salem Ould Bouhoubeyni
CABINET BOUHOUBEYNI

Brahim Ould Daddah
CABINET DADDAH CONSEILS

Aliou Sall
ASSURIM CONSULTING

Ndeye Khar Sarr
BSD & ASSOCIÉS

Dominique Taty
FIDAFRICA / PRICEWATERHOUSECOOPERS

MAURITIUS

Jean-François Boisvenu
BLC CHAMBERS

André Bonieux
PRICEWATERHOUSECOOPERS

Urmila Boolell
BANYMANDHUB BOOLELL CHAMBERS

Beche Bruno
KROSS BORDER TRUST SERVICES LTD., MEMBER OF RUSSELL BEDFORD INTERNATIONAL

Jean Phillipe Chan See
MAERSK LTD.

D.P. Chinien
REGISTRAR OF COMPANIES AND BUSINESSES, OFFICE OF THE REGISTRAR OF COMPANIES

Vincent Chong Leung
JURISTCONSULT CHAMBERS

Sandy Chuong
GLOVER & GLOVER CHAMBERS

Sootam Chutoori
DAGON INGENIEUR CONSEIL LTÉE

Roland Constantin
ETUDE CONSTANTIN

Rajendra Dassyne
CHAMBERS OF NOTARIES OF MAURITIUS

Catherine de Rosnay
LEGIS & PARTNERS

Ujoodha Dhanun
KROSS BORDER TRUST SERVICES LTD., MEMBER OF RUSSELL BEDFORD INTERNATIONAL

Shalinee Dreepaul-Halkhoree
JURISTCONSULT CHAMBERS

Robert Ferrat
LEGIS & PARTNERS

Yannick Fok
GLOVER & GLOVER CHAMBERS

Gavin Glover
GLOVER & GLOVER CHAMBERS

J. Gilbert Gnany
MAURITIUS COMMERCIAL BANK LTD.

Yandraduth Googoolye
BANK OF MAURITIUS

Darmalingum Goorriah
ETUDE ME DARMALINGUM GOORRIAH

Arvin Halkhoree
CITILAW

Mikash Hassamal
GLOVER & GLOVER CHAMBERS

Marc Hein
JURISTCONSULT CHAMBERS

Nitish Hurnaum
GLOVER & GLOVER CHAMBERS

Jane Jouanis
JURISTCONSULT CHAMBERS

Thierry Koenig
DE COMARMOND & KOENIG

Anthony Leung Shing
PRICEWATERHOUSECOOPERS

Stephen John Mendes
CUSTOMS AND EXCISE DEPARTMENT

Ramdas Mootanah
ARCHITECTURE & DESIGN LTD.

Loganayagan Munian
ARTISCO INTERNATIONAL

Jingree Neeshal
KROSS BORDER TRUST SERVICES LTD., MEMBER OF RUSSELL BEDFORD INTERNATIONAL

Daniel Ng Cheong Hin
MAURITIUS CARGO COMMUNITY SERVICES LTD.

Marie Cristelle Joanna Parsooramen
BANYMANDHUB BOOLELL CHAMBERS

Priscilla Pattoo-Mungur
JURISTCONSULT CHAMBERS

Siv Potayya
JURISTCONSULT INTERNATIONAL & Co LTD.

Iqbal Rajahbalee
BLC CHAMBERS

André Robert
ATTORNEY-AT-LAW

Anjali Roy
ETUDE GUY RIVALLAND

Shailesh Seebaruth
GLOVER & GLOVER CHAMBERS

Gilbert Seeyave
BDO DE CHAZAL DU MEE

Gaetan Siew
L&S ARCHITECTS

Deviantee Sobarun
MINISTRY OF FINANCE

Parikshat Teeluck
DAMCO LOGISTICS (MAURITIUS)

Shamina Toofanee
PRICEWATERHOUSECOOPERS

Natasha Towokul-Jiagoo
JURISTCONSULT INTERNATIONAL & Co LTD.

Cindy Upiah
BANYMANDHUB BOOLELL CHAMBERS

Muhammad R.C. Uteem
UTEEM CHAMBERS

MEXICO

Gabriel Aguilar
PRICEWATERHOUSECOOPERS

Jesus Alvarado Nieto
BAKER & MCKENZIE

Francisco Samuel Arias González
NOTARY PUBLIC 28

Jose Garcia Bautista
DELOITTE

Carlos Cano
PRICEWATERHOUSECOOPERS

Oscar O. Cano
ADEATH LOGISTICS S.A DE C.V.

Josue Cantu

Pedro Flores Carrillo
MOORE STEPHENS OROZCO MEDINA S.C.

María Casas López
BAKER & MCKENZIE

Tania Castellanos
PRICEWATERHOUSECOOPER

Hector Castro
PRICEWATERHOUSECOOPERS

Rodrigo Conesa
RITCH MUELLER, S. C.

Fabio Corominas de la Pera
BAKER & MCKENZIE

Eduardo Corzo Ramos
HOLLAND & KNIGHT-GALLÁSTEGUI Y LOZANO, S.C.

Jose Covarrubias-Azuela
SOLORZANO, CARVAJAL, GONZALEZ Y PEREZ-CORREA, S.C.

Raul de la Sierra Cauley
BARRERA, SIQUEIROS Y TORRES LANDA

Oscar de La Vega
BASHAM, RINGE Y CORREA, MEMBER OF IUS LABORIS

Frederico de Noriega Olea
BARRERA, SIQUEIROS Y TORRES LANDA

Felipe Dominguez
MOORE STEPHENS OROZCO MEDINA S.C.

Dolores Enriquez
PRICEWATERHOUSECOOPERS

Pablo Escalante
DELOITTE

Luis Miguel Esparza
PRICEWATERHOUSECOOPER

Salvador Esquivel
PRICEWATERHOUSECOOPERS

Roberto Fagoaga
SÁNCHEZ-DEVANNY ESEVERRI, S.C.

Julio Flores Luna
GOODRICH, RIQUELME Y ASOCIADOS

Salvador Fonseca
CHADBOURNE & PARKE MEXICO

Carlos Frias
PRICEWATERHOUSECOOPERS

Manuel Galicia
GALICIA Y ROBLES, S.C.

Hans Goebel
JÁUREGUI, NAVARRETE Y NADER, S.C.

Dalia Goldsmit
PRICEWATERHOUSECOOPERS

Daniel Gómez Alba
CAAAREM

Teresa de Lourdes Gómez Neri
GOODRICH, RIQUELME Y ASOCIADOS

César Gonzalez
PRICEWATERHOUSECOOPERS

Alvaro Gonzalez-Schiaffino
PRICEWATERHOUSECOOPERS

Luis Enrique Graham
CHADBOURNE & PARKE MEXICO

Carlos R. Grimm
BAKER & MCKENZIE

Yves Hayaux-du-Tilly
JÁUREGUI, NAVARRETE Y NADER, S.C.

Eduardo Heftye
LOPEZ VELARDE, HEFTYE Y SORIA

Jorge Jimenez
LOPEZ VELARDE, HEFTYE Y SORIA

Jorge Jiménez
RUSSELL BEDFORD MEXICO, MEMBER OF RUSSELL BEDFORD INTERNATIONAL

Alejandro Ledesma
PRICEWATERHOUSECOOPERS

Josue Lee
INAKI ECHEVERRIA ARQUITECTOS

Ricardo León-Santacruz
SÁNCHEZ-DEVANNY ESEVERRI, S.C.

Gerardo Lozano Alarcón
HOLLAND & KNIGHT-GALLÁSTEGUI Y LOZANO, S.C.

Lucia Manzo
GALICIA Y ROBLES, S.C.

José Antonio Marquez González
NOTARY PUBLIC 28

Renato Martínes Quezada
BAKER & MCKENZIE

Carlos Manuel Martinez
PRICEWATERHOUSECOOPERS

Edgar Francisco Martínez Herrasti
GOODRICH, RIQUELME Y ASOCIADOS

Bernardo Martínez Negrete
GALICIA Y ROBLES, S.C.

Carla E. Mendoza Pérez
BAKER & MCKENZIE

María del Carmen Monforte Larrañaga
PRICEWATERHOUSECOOPERS

Carlos E. Montemayor
PRICEWATERHOUSECOOPERS

Rocío Montes
PRICEWATERHOUSECOOPERS

Humberto Morales- Barron
SÁNCHEZ-DEVANNY ESEVERRI, S.C.

José de Jesús Moreno Ruíz
CFE-DVMS (FEDERAL ELECTRICITY COMMISSION)

Jaime Israel Moreno-Treviño
SÁNCHEZ-DEVANNY ESEVERRI, S.C.

Eloy F. Muñoz M.
IMEYEL SOLUCIONES INTEGRALES, S.A

Omar Nieto
PRICEWATERHOUSECOOPER

Boris Otto
CHADBOURNE & PARKE MEXICO

Lázaro Peña
PRICEWATERHOUSECOOPERS

Arturo Perdomo
GALICIA Y ROBLES, S.C.

Pablo Perezalonso Eguía
RITCH MUELLER, S. C.

Eduardo Perez Armienta
MOORE STEPHENS OROZCO MEDINA S.C.

Fernando Perez-Correa
SOLORZANO, CARVAJAL, GONZALEZ Y PEREZ-CORREA, S.C.

Guillermo Piecarchic
PMC ASOCIADOS

Gerardo Prado-Hernandez
SÁNCHEZ-DEVANNY ESEVERRI, S.C.

David Puente-Tostado
SÁNCHEZ-DEVANNY ESEVERRI, S.C.

Samer Qudah
AL TAMIMI & COMPANY ADVOCATES & LEGAL CONSULTANTS

Alvaro Quintana
ALVARO QUINTANA SC

Mariel Rebollo
JÁUREGUI, NAVARRETE Y NADER, S.C.

Hector Reyes Freaner
BAKER & MCKENZIE

Claudia Ríos
PRICEWATERHOUSECOOPERS

Sergio Rodriguez
CHADBOURNE & PARKE MEXICO

Cecilia Rojas
GALICIA Y ROBLES, S.C.

Jose Rodriguez Sanchez
RUSSELL BEDFORD MEXICO, MEMBER OF RUSSELL BEDFORD INTERNATIONAL

Cristina Sánchez-Urtiz
MIRANDA & ESTAVILLO, S.C.

Francisco Santoyo
*Comisión Federal de
Electricidad*

Monica Schiaffino Pérez
*Basham, Ringe y Correa,
member of Ius Laboris*

Raúl Uribe Garcia
Uribe Engenieros S.A.

Juan Francisco Torres Landa
Ruffo
*Barrera, Siqueiros y Torres
Landa*

Laura Astrid Treviño-Perez
*Sánchez-DeVanny Eseverri,
S.C.*

Maribel Trigo Aja
*Goodrich, Riquelme y
Asociados*

G. Roberto Quintana Vargas
*Instalaciones Quintana
Vargas*

Layla Vargas Muga
*Goodrich, Riquelme y
Asociados*

Carlos Vela
PricewaterhouseCoopers

Claudio Villavicencio
Fernández
Deloitte

Rafael Villamar-Ramos
*Sánchez-DeVanny Eseverri,
S.C.*

Humberto Zapien
Deloitte

Ernesto Zarate Leon
Thorsa

MICRONESIA, FED. STS.

Kenneth Barden
Attorney-at-Law

Patrick Mackenzie
Bank of FSM

Silberio S. Mathias
Micropc

Ronald Pangelinan
A&P Enterprises, Inc.

Kevin Pelep
*Office of the Registrar of
Corporations*

Salomon Saimon
*Micronesia legal services
corporation*

Joe Vitt
*Pohnpei Transfer &
Storage, Inc.*

MOLDOVA

Nicolae Botan
Business Research Company

Robert Beto Brunn
DAI

Victor Burac
Victor Burac Law Firm

Andrei Caciurenco
ACI Partners Law Office

Andrian Candu
*PricewaterhouseCoopers
Legal Services*

Octavian Cazac
Turcan & Turcan

Svetlana Ceban
PricewaterhouseCoopers

Marin Chicu
Turcan & Turcan

Vitalie Ciofu
Gladei & Partners

Alla Cotos
PricewaterhouseCoopers

Anna Cusnir
Schonherr

Igor Domente
S.C. "Luvitan Grup" SRL

Sergiu Dumitrasco
PricewaterhouseCoopers

Serghei Filatov
ACI Partners Law Office

Iulia Furtuna
Turcan & Turcan

Roger Gladei
Gladei & Partners

Oxana Gutu
*Mobiasbanca Groupe
Societe Generale*

Adrian Guzun
Schonherr

Vladimir Iurkovsky
Schonherr

Roman Ivanov
Vernon David & associates

Remy Kormos
DAI

Mihaela Mitroi
PricewaterhouseCoopers

Igor Odobescu
ACI Partners Law Office

Aelita Orhei
Gladei & Partners

Carolina Parcalab
Turcan & Turcan

Tatiana Stefanet
Gladei & Partners

Mariana Stratan
Turcan & Turcan

Alexander Turcan
Turcan & Turcan

Irina Verhovetchi
ACI Partners Law Office

Marina Zanoga
Turcan & Turcan

MONGOLIA

Badarch Bayarmaa
Lynch & Mahoney

Batzaya Bodikhuu
*Anand & Batzaya
Advocates Law Firm*

Richard Bregonje
PricewaterhouseCoopers

David C. Buxbaum
Anderson & Anderson

Batbayar Byamba
GTs Advocates LLC

Ts. Dagvadorj
Gobi Corporation

Khatanbat Dashdarjaa
Arlex Consulting Services

Byambatseren Dorjpurev
Arlex Consulting Services

Courtney Fowler
PricewaterhouseCoopers

Odmaa Khurelbold
Anderson & Anderson

Maygmarsuren Lkhagvasuren
Anderson & Anderson

Daniel Mahoney
Lynch & Mahoney

Sebastian Merriman
PricewaterhouseCoopers

Odonhuu Muuzee
Tsets Law Firm

Tsogt Tsend
*Administrative Court of
Capital City*

Jane Wang
PricewaterhouseCoopers

MONTENEGRO

Aleksandar Adamovic
Pacorini Montenegro

Bojana Andrić
Čelebić

Veselin Anđušić
Čelebić

Safeta Babačić
FinancePlus

Bojana Bošković
Ministry of Finance

Vasilije Bošković
Law Firm Bošković

Peter Burnie
PricewaterhouseCoopers

Marija Crnogorac
KN Karanović& Nikolić

Savo Djurović
Adriatic Marinas doo

Vuk Drašković
*Bojovic Dasic Kojovic
Attorneys at Law*

Dragan Draca
PricewaterhouseCoopers

Vesko Dragičević
*Chamber of Economy of
Montenegro, Association
of Small Enterprises and
Entrepreneurs*

Rina Ivančević
Municipality of Podgorica

Marko Ivković
KN Karanović & Nikolić

Tanja Janović
Law Office Vujačić

Maja Jokanović
Ministry of Economy

Srđan Kalezić
*Tax Authority
Montenegro*

Stevan Karadaglić
*Chamber of Economy of
Montenegro, Sector for
Associations and Economic
Development*

Radoš-Lolo Kastratović
Advokatska Kancelarija

Marija Klikovac
Law Office Vujačić

Ivana Kojić
KN Karanović & Nikolić

Darko Konjević
CEED

Ana Krsmanović
Ministry of Finance

Mirjana Ljumović
*Government of
the Republic of*

*Montenegro Real Estate
Administration*

Nikola Martinović
Advokatska Kancelarija

Željko Mijović
Zetatrans

Momir Milička
*Tax Authority
Montenegro*

Djordje Nikolić
*Nikolić Kokanović
Otašević Law Office*

Mićo Orlandić
*Government of
the Republic of
Montenegro Real Estate
Administration*

Djuro Otašević
*Nikolić Kokanović
Otašević Law Office*

Mirjana Pešalj
*Government of the
Republic of Montenegro*

Novica Pešić
Law Office Vujačić

Nikola Perović
Plantaže

Dragan Prelević
Prelević Law Firm

Slobodan Raščanin
UNHCR

Dragana Radević
CEED

Ana Radivojević
PricewaterhouseCoopers

Radmila Radoičić
Law Office Vujačić

Novo Radović
*Tax Authority
Montenegro*

Slavko Radović
Cijevna Komerc

Dražen Raičković
FinancePlus

Slađana Raičković
FinancePlus

Dragan Rakočević
*Commercial Court of
Podgorica*

Admir Rebronja
FinancePlus

Tijana Saveljic
Prelevi Law Firm

Slaven Šćepanović

Lidija Šećković
*Tax Authority
Montenegro*

Velimir Strugar
EPCG AD Nikšić

Goran Tuponja
*German Technical
Cooperation*

Duško Vojinović
*Government of
the Republic of
Montenegro Real Estate
Administration*

Saša Vujačić
Law Office Vujačić

Jelena Vujisić
Law Office Vujačić

Predrag Vujović
Zetatrans

Veselin Vuković
*Central Bank of
Montenegro*

MOROCCO

Samir Agoumi
Dar Alkhibra

Lamya Alami

Younes Anibar
Cabinet Younes Anibar

Linda Oumama Benali
Cabinet Notaire

Khalid Boumichi
Tecnomar

Richard Cantin
*Juristructures - Project
Management & Legal
Advisory Services LLP*

Sylvain Da Fonseca
Alleance advisory Maroc

Mohssin El Makoudi
Dar Alkhibra

Nadia Fajr

Fatima Zohra Gouttaya
Etude de notariat moderne

Nicolas Granier
Alleance advisory Maroc

Amin Hajji
*Amin Hajji & Associés
Association d'Avocats*

Zohra Hasnaoui
Hasnaoui Law Firm

Ahmad Hussein
*Talal Abu-Ghazaleh Legal
(TAG-Legal)*

Bahya Ibn Khaldoun
Université Mohamed V

Naoual Jellouli
*Ministère de l'économie et
des finances*

Mehdi Kettani
Kettani & Associés

Nadia Kettani
Kettani & Associés

Karine Lasne
*Landwell & Associés -
PricewaterhouseCoopers
Legal Services*

Wilfried Le Bihan
*CMS Bureau Francis
Lefebvre*

Medhi Lebady
*Cabinet d'Architecture
Lebady*

Anis Mahfoud
*Abouakil & Benjelloun
Avocats - AB AVOCATS*

Abdelaziz Messaoudi
*Ministère de l'économie et
des finances*

Aboulfadl Najat
Etude de notariat moderne

Hicham Oughza
Dar Alkhibra

Jamal Rahal
Experian

Nesrine Roudane
Nero Boutique Law Firm

Mehdi Salmouni-Zerhouni
Salmouni-Zerhouni Law Firm

Houcine Sefrioui
Etude de notariat moderne

Abdeselam Tazi
Area sarl

Marc Veuillot
Alleance advisory Maroc

Chigar Zineb
Etude de notariat moderne

MOZAMBIQUE

Calu Abubacar
Electrovisao Lda

Sheila Ali
MGA Advogados & Consultores

Mark Badenhorst
PricewaterhouseCoopers

Carolina Balate
PricewaterhouseCoopers

Loren Benjamin
PricewaterhouseCoopers

António Baltazar Bungallah
Sal & Caldeira - Advogados e Consultores, Lda

Eduardo Calú
Sal & Caldeira - Advogados e Consultores, Lda

Neide Chande
Pimenta, Dionísio e Associados

Dipak Chandulal
MGA Advogados & Consultores

António Chicachama
Direcção Nacional de Energia Eléctrica

Pedro Couto
H. Gamito, Couto, Gonçalves Pereira e Castelo Branco & Associados

Avelar Da Silva
Intertek International Ltd.

Thera Dai
Furtado, Bhikha, Loforte, Popat & Associados, Advogados

Paul De Chalain
PricewaterhouseCoopers

Carlos de Sousa e Brito
Carlos de Sousa & Brito & Associados

Rita Furtado
H. Gamito, Couto, Gonçalves Pereira e Castelo Branco & Associados

Jorge Graça
MGA Advogados & Consultores

Soraia Issufo
Sal & Caldeira - Advogados e Consultores, Lda

Ássma Omar Nordine Jeque
Sal & Caldeira - Advogados e Consultores, Lda

Rui Laforte
Furtado, Bhikha, Loforte, Popat & Associados, Advogados

Pedro Lemos
Sal & Caldeira - Advogados e Consultores, Lda

Marla Mandlate
Sal & Caldeira - Advogados e Consultores, Lda

Joao Martins
PricewaterhouseCoopers

Lara Narcy
H. Gamito, Couto, Gonçalves Pereira e Castelo Branco & Associados

Auxílio Eugénio Nhabanga
FBLP - R.Furtado, N. Bhikha, R.Loforte, M. Popat & Associados, Advogados, Lda

Paulo Pimenta
Pimenta, Dionísio e Associados

Álvaro Pinto Basto
MGA Advogados & Consultores

Malaika Ribeiro
PricewaterhouseCoopers

Luís Filipe Rodrigues
Sal & Caldeira - Advogados e Consultores, Lda

Firza Sadek
Pimenta, Dionísio e Associados

Leonardo Uamusse
Electricidade de Moçambique

NAMIBIA

Joos Agenbach
Koep & Partners

Ronnie Beukes
City of Windhoek Electricity Department

Benita Blume
H.D. Bossau & Co.

Hanno D. Bossau
H.D. Bossau & Co.

Chris Brandt
Chris Brandt & Associates

Andy Chase
Stauch+Partners Architects

Dirk Hendrik Conradie
Conradie & Damaseb

Ferdinand Diener
City of Windhoek Electricity Department

Hans-Bruno Gerdes
Engling, Stritter & Partners

Ismeralda Hangue
Deeds Office

Sakaria Kadhila Amoomo
Pereira Fishing (Pty) Ltd.

Herman Charl Kinghorn
HC Kinghorn Legal Practitioner

Frank Köpplinger
G.F. Köpplinger Legal Practitioners

Richard Traugott Diethelm Mueller
Koep & Partners

Axel Stritter
Engling, Stritter & Partners

Marius van Breda
TransUnion Namibia

Meyer Van den Berg
Koep & Partners

Paul A. E. Wolff
Manica Africa Pty. Ltd. Namibia

NEPAL

Lalit Aryal
LA & Associates Chartered Accountants

Tulasi Bhatta
Unity Law Firm & Consultancy

Tankahari Dahal
Niraula Law Chamber & Co.

Prakash Kafle
Agni Cement Industries P. Ltd.

Gourish K. Kharel
KTO Inc.

Mohan Krishna Kharel
KTO Inc.

Ashok Man Kapali
Shangri-La Freight Pvt. Ltd.

Bijaya Mishra
Pradhan & Associates

Matrika Niraula
Niraula Law Chamber & Co.

Rajan Niraula
Niraula Law Chamber & Co.

Dev Raj Paudyal
Ministry of Land Reform and Management

Devendra Pradhan
Pradhan & Associates

Anup Raj Upreti
Pioneer Law Associates

Chiranjivi Sharma
Nepal Electricity Authority

Madan Sharma
PricewaterhouseCoopers

Ramji Shrestha
Pradhan & Associates

Ram Chandra Subedi
Apex Law Chamber

L.R. Tamang
Hyonjan Electrical Engineering Fabricator P. Ltd.

Mahesh Kumar Thapa
Sinha - Verma Law Concern

Sajjan B.S. Thapa
Legal Research Associates

NETHERLANDS

Joost Achterberg
Kennedy Van der Laan

Dirk-Jan Berkenbosch
PricewaterhouseCoopers

Karin W.M. Bodewes
Baker & McKenzie

Mark Bodt
PricewaterhouseCoopers

Sytso Boonstra
PricewaterhouseCoopers

Roland Brandsma
PricewaterhouseCoopers

Martin Brink
Van Benthem & Keulen NV

Stephan de Baan
Berkman Forwarding B.V.

Margriet de Boer
De Brauw Blackstone Westbroek

Hans J.H. de Wilde
KAB Auditors & Tax Advisers, member of Russell Bedford International

Henriette Derks
Liander

Myrna Dop
Royal Netherlands Notarial Organization

Arjan Enneman
Expatax BV

Ruud Horak
Elektrotechniek Boermans BV

Kitty Hutten
PricewaterhouseCoopers

Marcel Kettenis
PricewaterhouseCoopers

Christian Koedam
PricewaterhouseCoopers

Andrej Kwitowski
DHV B.V.

Stefan Leening
PricewaterhouseCoopers

Hugo Oppelaar
Houthoff Buruma Coöperatief U.A.

Peter Plug
Office of Energy Regulation

Mark G. Rebergen
De Brauw Blackstone Westbroek

Helena Redons Schaatsberen
Municipality of Amsterdam

Hugo Reumkens
Van Doorne N.V.

Jan Willem Schenk
Baker & McKenzie

Françoise Schoordijk
DLA Piper Nederland N.V.

Salima Seamari
De Brauw Blackstone Westbroek

Stéphanie Spoelder
Baker & McKenzie

Fedor Tanke
Baker & McKenzie

Maarten Tinnemans
De Brauw Blackstone Westbroek

Helene van Bommel
PricewaterhouseCoopers

Paul van der Molen
Cadastre, Land Registry and Mapping Agency

Marije Van der Veer
De Brauw Blackstone Westbroek

Gert-Jan van Gijs
VAT Logistics (Ocean Freight) BV

Sjaak van Leeuwen
Stichting Bureau Krediet Registratie

Jan van Oorschot
Liander

Petra van Raad
PricewaterhouseCoopers

Marcel Willems
Kennedy Van der Laan

Christiaan Zijderveld
Simmons & Simmons

NEW ZEALAND

Matthew Allison
Veda Advantage

Jania Baigent
Simpson Grierson, member of Lex Mundi

Kevin Best
PricewaterhouseCoopers

Geoff Bevan
Chapman Tripp

Shelley Cave
Simpson Grierson, member of Lex Mundi

Philip Coombe
Panalpina World Transport New Zealand Auckland

Phil Creagh
Anderson Creagh Lai

John Cuthbertson
PricewaterhouseCoopers

Daniel De Vries
Veda Advantage

William Fotherby
Bell Gully

Koustabh Gadgil
Investment New Zealand (a division of New Zealand Trade and Enterprise)

David Harte
Insolvency and Trustee Services

Matt Kersey
Russell McVeagh

Greg King
Jackson Russell

Jeffrey Lai
Anderson Creagh Lai

Mahesh Lala
Jackson Russell

Kate Lane
Minter Ellison Rudd Watts

Leroy Langeveld
Simpson Grierson, member of Lex Mundi

John Lawrence
Auckland City Council

Thomas Leslie
Bell Gully

Andrew Minturn
QUALTECH INTERNATIONAL LTD.

Nicholas Moffatt
BELL GULLY

Robert Muir
LAND INFORMATION NEW ZEALAND

Catherine Otten
NEW ZEALAND COMPANIES OFFICE

Ian Page
BRANZ

Mihai Pascariu
MINTER ELLISON RUDD WATTS

John Powell
RUSSELL McVEAGH

David Quigg
QUIGG PARTNERS

Jim Roberts
HESKETH HENRY LAWYERS

Catherine Rowe
PRICEWATERHOUSECOOPERS

Michael Slyuzberg
INLAND REVENUE DEPARTMENT

Neill Sullivan
LAND INFORMATION NEW ZEALAND

Murray Tingey
BELL GULLY

Michael McLean Toepfer
WANAKA OFFICE AWS LEGAL

Ben Upton
SIMPSON GRIERSON, MEMBER OF LEX MUNDI

Richard Wilson
JACKSON RUSSELL

NICARAGUA

Adriana Acuña
MUNICIPALIDAD DE MANAGUA

Bertha Argüello de Rizo
ARIAS & MUÑOZ

Favio Josué Batres
ALVARADO Y ASOCIADOS, MEMBER OF LEX MUNDI

Minerva Adriana Bellorín Rodríguez
ACZALAW

María José Bendaña Guerrero
BENDAÑA & BENDAÑA

Carlos Alberto Bonilla López
SUPERINTENDENCIA DE BANCOS

Blanca Buitrago
GARCÍA & BODÁN

Ramón Castro
ARIAS & MUÑOZ

Sergio David Corrales Montenegro
GARCÍA & BODÁN

Juan Carlos Cortes Espinoza
PRICEWATERHOUSECOOPERS

Zayda Cubas
ALVARADO Y ASOCIADOS, MEMBER OF LEX MUNDI

Gloria Maria de Alvarado
ALVARADO Y ASOCIADOS, MEMBER OF LEX MUNDI

Maricarmen Espinosa de Molina
MOLINA & ASOCIADOS CENTRAL LAW

Melvin Estrada
GARCÍA & BODÁN

Terencio Garcia Montenegro
GARCÍA & BODÁN

Engelsberth Gómez
PRO NICARAGUA

Claudia Guevara
AGUILAR CASTILLO LOVE

Eduardo Jose Gutierrez Rueda
CONSORTIUM TABOADA Y ASOCIADOS

Gerardo Hernandez
CONSORTIUM TABOADA Y ASOCIADOS

Ruth Huete
PRICEWATERHOUSECOOPERS

Rodrigo Ibarra Rodney
ARIAS & MUÑOZ

Leonardo Icaza
MUNICIPALIDAD DE MANAGUA

María Fernanda Jarquín
ARIAS & MUÑOZ

Fabiola Martinez
VENTANILLA UNICA DE INVERSIONES

Alvaro Molina
MOLINA & ASOCIADOS CENTRAL LAW

Roberto Montes
ARIAS & MUÑOZ

Soraya Montoya Herrera
MOLINA & ASOCIADOS CENTRAL LAW

Michael Navas
PRO NICARAGUA

Ramón Ortega
PRICEWATERHOUSECOOPERS

Mazziel Rivera
ACZALAW

Ana Teresa Rizo Briseño
ARIAS & MUÑOZ

Erwin Rodriguez
ACZALAW

Felipe Sánchez
ACZALAW

Alfonso José Sandino Granera
CONSORTIUM TABOADA Y ASOCIADOS

Julio E. Sequeira
EVENOR VALDIVIA P. & ASOCIADOS

Arnulfo Somarriba
TransUnion

Denis González Torres
G.E. ELECTROMECÁNICA & CIA LTDA.

Rodrigo Taboada
CONSORTIUM TABOADA Y ASOCIADOS

Manuel Ignacio Tefel Cuadra
PRICEWATERHOUSECOOPERS

Carlos Tellez
GARCÍA & BODÁN

Daysi Ivette Torres Bosques
DAYSI IVETTE

Juana Vargas
DAYSI IVETTE

NIGER

Mamane Badamassi Annou
MILLENNIUM CHALLENGE ACCOUNT - NIGER

Mamoudou Aoula
PROJET DE DÉVELOPPEMENT DES INFRASTRUCTURES LOCALES-PDIL-BUREAU NATIONAL DE COOR

Sidi Sanoussi Baba Sidi
CABINET D'AVOCATS SOUNA-COULIBALY

Boniface Combary
DIRECTION DE L'URBANISME ET DE L'HABITAT

Moussa Coulibaly
CABINET D'AVOCATS SOUNA-COULIBALY

Jonathan Darboux
BCEAO

Abdou Djando
EMTEF

Aïssatou Djibo
ETUDE DE MAÎTRE DJIBO AÏSSATOU

Jean-Claude Gnamien
FIDAFRICA / PRICEWATERHOUSECOOPERS

Sani Halilou
MAERSK S.A.

Issoufou Harouna
S.C.P.A. MANDELA

Ali Idrissa Sounna
TOUTELEC NIGER SA

Bernar-Oliver Kouaovi
CABINET KOUAOVI

Diallo Rayanatou Loutou
CABINET LOUTOU - ARCHITECTES

Issaka Manzo
EGTC

Ibrahim Mounouni
BUREAU D'ETUDES BALA & HIMO

Achimi M. Riliwanou
ETUDE DE MAÎTRE ACHIMI RILIWANOU

Daouda Samna
S.C.P.A. MANDELA

Maman Sani Kanta
MILLENNIUM CHALLENGE ACCOUNT - NIGER

Ali Seyni
MILLENNIUM CHALLENGE ACCOUNT - NIGER

Dominique Taty
FIDAFRICA / PRICEWATERHOUSECOOPERS

Idrissa Tchernaka
ETUDE D'AVOCATS MARC LE BIHAN & COLLABORATEURS

Fousséni Traoré
FIDAFRICA / PRICEWATERHOUSECOOPERS

Ramatou Wankoye
OFFICE NOTARIAL ETUDE WANKOYE

NIGERIA

Olusegun Abijo
FNA ARCHITECTS LTD.

Oluseyi Abiodun Akinwunmi
AKINWUNMI & BUSARI, LEGAL PRACTIONERS (A & B)

Diaby Aboubakar
BCEAO

Olaleye Adebiyi
WTS ADEBIYI & ASSOCIATES

Folaranmi Adetunji Adegbite
F.A. ADEGBITE & ASSOCIATES

Kunle Adegbite
ADEGBITE - STEVENS & Co

Steve Adehi
STEVE ADEHI AND Co

Olufunke Adekoya
AELEX, LEGAL PRACTITIONERS & ARBITRATORS

Taiwo Adeshina
JACKSON, ETTI & EDU

Francis Adewale
VISTA BRIDGE GLOBAL RESOURCES LIMITED

Oloruntobi Adewale
VISTA BRIDGE GLOBAL RESOURCES LIMITED

Duro Adeyele
BAYO OJO & Co.

Olusola Adun
NOUVEAU ASSOCIATES

Adesegun Agbebiyi
ALUKO & OYEBODE

Oluwatomi Agbola
OLANIWUN AJAYI LP

Daniel Agbor
UDO UDOMA & BELO-OSAGIE

Izinegbe Aibangbee
PRICEWATERHOUSECOOPERS

Kenneth Aitken
PRICEWATERHOUSECOOPERS

Tolulola Akintimehin
NOUVEAU ASSOCIATES

Dafe Akpeneye
PRICEWATERHOUSECOOPERS

Segun Aluko
ALUKO & OYEBODE

Tracy Amadigwe
ALKINGSHOLA CHAMBERS

Linda Arifayan
WTS ADEBIYI & ASSOCIATES

Esther Atoyebi
OKONJO, ODIAWA & EBIE

Akinshola Babatunde
ALKINGSHOLA CHAMBERS

Olalekan Bakare
PERCHSTONE & GRAEYS

Yetunde Bamidele
AKINWUNMI & BUSARI, LEGAL PRACTIONERS (A & B)

Rabi Bawa
PERCHSTONE & GRAEYS

Barr. N.U. Chianakwalam
LEGAL STANDARD CONSULTING

Weyinmi Edodo
IPDC LIMITED

Emmanuel Egwuagu
OBLA & Co.

Nnenna Ejekam
NNENNA EJEKAM ASSOCIATES

0 Ekar
JACKSON, ETTI & EDU

Ebele Enedah
PUNUKA ATTORNEYS & SOLICITORS

Samuel Etuk
1ST ATTORNEYS

Anse Agu Ezetah
CHIEF LAW AGU EZETAH & Co.

Babatunde Fagbohunlu
ALUKO & OYEBODE

Olubunmi Fayokun
ALUKO & OYEBODE

Adejoke A. Gbenro
ADEBANKE ADEOLA &Co.

Justice Idehen-Nathaniel
PERCHSTONE & GRAEYS

Oluwaseyi Ikuewumi
PRICEWATERHOUSECOOPERS

Stanley Ikwendu
AELEX, LEGAL PRACTITIONERS & ARBITRATORS

Margaret Ivowi
PRICEWATERHOUSECOOPERS

Okorie Kalu
PUNUKA ATTORNEYS & SOLICITORS

Tomisin Lagundoye
UDO UDOMA & BELO-OSAGIE

Adenike laoye
ECOBANK

Ibrahim Eddy Mark
NIGERIAN BAR ASSOCIATION

Egwuagu Emmanuel Nomso
OBLA & Co.

Chidnma Nwaogu
PUNUKA ATTORNEYS & SOLICITORS

Victor Obaro
LIBRA LAW OFFICE

Oluwakemi Oduntan
JADE & STONE SOLICITORS

Nelson Ogbuanya
NOCS CONSULTS

Godson Ogheneochuko
UDO UDOMA & BELO-OSAGIE

Ozofu Ogiemudia
UDO UDOMA & BELO-OSAGIE

Alayo Ogunbiyi
ABDULAI, TAIWO & Co.

Ayokunle Ogundipe
PERCHSTONE & GRAEYS

Oghenetekevwe Okobiah
JACKSON, ETTI & EDU

Christine Okokon
UDO UDOMA & BELO-OSAGIE

Patrick Okonjo
OKONJO, ODIAWA & EBIE

Dozie Okwuosah
CENTRAL BANK OF NIGERIA

Stephen Ola Jagun
JAGUN ASSOCIATES

Adefunke Oladosu
AKINWUNMI & BUSARI, LEGAL PRACTIONERS (A & B)

Banke Olanikpekun
WTS ADEBIYI & ASSOCIATES

Ayotunde Ologe
SYNERGY LEGAL PRACTITIONERS AND PROPERTY CONSULTANTS

Bimbola Olowe
JACKSON, ETTI & EDU

Babatunde Olubando
BABATUNDE OLUBANDO & Co

Tolulope Omidiji
PRICEWATERHOUSECOOPERS

Jennifer Omozuwa
PERCHSTONE & GRAEYS

Fred Onuobia
*G. ELIAS & CO. SOLICITORS
AND ADVOCATES*

Ijeoma Onweluzo
OLANIWUN AJAYI LP

Donald Orji
JACKSON, ETTI & EDU

Christian Oronsaye
ALUKO & OYEBODE

Tunde Osasona
*WHITESTONE WORLDWIDE
LTD.*

Kola Osholeye
ELEKTRINT (NIGERIA) LIMITED

Olufunilayo Otsemebor
ALUKO & OYEBODE

Abraham Oyakhilome
*FIRST & FIRST INTERNATIONAL
AGENCIES*

Gbenga Oyebode
ALUKO & OYEBODE

Taiwo Oyedele
PRICEWATERHOUSECOOPERS

Bukola Oyinlola
PERCHSTONE & GRAEYS

Titilola Rotifa
OKONJO, ODIAWA & EBIE

Konyin Ajayi San
OLANIWUN AJAYI LP

Yewande Senbore
OLANIWUN AJAYI LP

Serifat Solebo
LAND SERVICES DIRECTORATE

Alabi Sule
ELEKTRINT (NIGERIA) LIMITED

Adeola Sunmola
UDO UDOMA & BELO-OSAGIE

Nneamaka Udekwe
PRICEWATERHOUSECOOPERS

Reginald Udom
ALUKO & OYEBODE

Aniekan Ukpanah
UDO UDOMA & BELO-OSAGIE

Adamu M. Usman
F.O. AKINRELE & CO.

Emmanuel Yehouessi
BCEAO

NORWAY

Anders Aasland Kittelsen
*ADVOKATFIRMAET SCHJØDT
DA*

Jan L. Backer
WIKBORG, REIN & CO.

Kristian Berentsen
*ADVOKATFIRMA DLA PIPER
NORWAY DA*

Stig Berge
THOMMESSEN AS

Trine Bjerke Welhaven
*HOMBLE OLSBY
advokatfirma AS*

Eirik Brønner
KVALE ADVOKATFIRMA DA

Einard Brunes
RAEDER ADVOKATFIRMA

Lars Davidsen
HAFSLUND

Lars Ekeland
*ADVOKATFIRMAET HJORT DA,
MEMBER OF IUS LABORIS*

Knut Ekern
PRICEWATERHOUSECOOPERS

Simen Aasen Engebretsen
DELOITTE

Stein Fagerhaug
DALAN ADVOKATFIRMA DA

Line Foss Hals
WIKBORG, REIN & CO.

Amund Fougner
*ADVOKATFIRMAET HJORT DA,
MEMBER OF IUS LABORIS*

Christian Friestad
*ADVOKATFIRMAET
PRICEWATERHOUSECOOPERS
AS*

Line Granhol
*ADVOKATFIRMA DLA PIPER
NORWAY DA*

Andreas Hanssen
*ADVOKATFIRMA DLA PIPER
NORWAY DA*

Pål Hasner
PRICEWATERHOUSECOOPERS

Olav Hermansen
NorStella FOUNDATION

Heidi Holmelin
ADVOKATFIRMAET SELMER DA

Therese Høyer Grimstad
*ADVOKATFIRMAET HJORT DA,
MEMBER OF IUS LABORIS*

Odd Hylland
PRICEWATERHOUSECOOPERS

Hanne Karlsen
RAEDER ADVOKATFIRMA

Per Einar Lunde
PRICEWATERHOUSECOOPERS

Joakim Marstrander
*ADVOKATFIRMA VOGT &
WIIG AS*

Knut Martinsen
THOMMESSEN AS

Karl Erik Nedregotten
PRICEWATERHOUSECOOPERS

Halfdan Nitter
*NITTER AS, MEMBER
OF RUSSELL BEDFORD
INTERNATIONAL*

Thomas Nordgård
*ADVOKATFIRMA VOGT &
WIIG AS*

Ole Kristian Olsby
*HOMBLE OLSBY
advokatfirma AS*

Helge Onsrud
*NORWEGIAN MAPPING
AUTHORITY, CADASTRE AND
LAND REGISTRY, CENTRE
FOR PROPERTY RIGHTS AND
DEVELOPMENT*

Johan Ratvik
*ADVOKATFIRMA DLA PIPER
NORWAY DA*

Ståle Skutle Arneson
*ADVOKATFIRMA VOGT &
WIIG AS*

Christel Spannow
PRICEWATERHOUSECOOPERS

Svein Sulland
ADVOKATFIRMAET SELMER DA

Stine Bryn Sverdrup
PRICEWATERHOUSECOOPERS

Espen Trædal
*ADVOKATFIRMAET
PRICEWATERHOUSECOOPERS
AS*

Marita Vidvei Bjelland
PRICEWATERHOUSECOOPERS

Joakim Zahl Fjell
PRICEWATERHOUSECOOPERS

OMAN

Hamad Al Abri
*MUSCAT ELECTRICITY
DISTRIBUTION COMPANY*

Zahir Abdulla Al Abri
*MUSCAT ELECTRICITY
DISTRIBUTION COMPANY*

Zubaida Fakir Mohamed Al
Balushi
CENTRAL BANK OF OMAN

Ahmed Al Barwani
DENTON WILDE SAPTE & Co

Salman Ali Al Hattali
*MUSCAT ELECTRICITY
DISTRIBUTION COMPANY*

Said bin Saad Al Shahry
SAID AL SHAHRY LAW OFFICE

Zuhaira Al Sulaimani
*AL BUSAIDY, MANSOOR JAMAL
& CO.*

Majid Al Toky
TROWERS & HAMLINS

Hussain Al Zadjali
BANK MUSCAT

Khalid Khamis Al-Hashmi
MUSCAT MUNICIPALITY

Leyan Al-Mawali
TROWERS & HAMLINS

Hilal Almayahi
MUSCAT MUNICIPALITY

Ahmed al-Mukhaini
SAID AL SHAHRY LAW OFFICE

Mohamed Alrashdi
MUSCAT MUNICIPALITY

Russell Aycock
PRICEWATERHOUSECOOPERS

David Ball
SAID AL SHAHRY LAW OFFICE

Richard L. Baltimore III
SAID AL SHAHRY LAW OFFICE

Mahmoud Bilal
SAID AL SHAHRY LAW OFFICE

Francis D'Souza
BDO JAWAD HABIB

Precilla D'Souza
*AL TAMIMI & COMPANY
ADVOCATES & LEGAL
CONSULTANTS*

Mehreen B. Elahi
*AL BUSAIDY, MANSOOR JAMAL
& CO.*

Zareen George
*AL BUSAIDY, MANSOOR JAMAL
& CO.*

Hind Hadi
*AL BUSAIDY, MANSOOR JAMAL
& CO.*

Justine Harding
DENTON WILDE SAPTE & Co

Robert Kenedy
*CURTIS MALLET - PREVOST,
COLT & MOSLE LLP*

Salim Khairulla
OMAN FLOUR MILLS

Ziad Khattab
*TALAL ABU-GHAZALEH LEGAL
(TAG-Legal)*

P.E. Lalachen MJ
INDEPENDENT CONSULTANT

Jose Madukakuzhy
KHIMJI RAMDAS

Pushpa Malani
PRICEWATERHOUSECOOPERS

Mansoor Jamal Malik
*AL BUSAIDY, MANSOOR JAMAL
& CO.*

Tufol Mehdi
MUSCAT MUNICIPALITY

Yashpal Mehta
BDO JAWAD HABIB

Subha Mohan
*CURTIS MALLET - PREVOST,
COLT & MOSLE LLP*

Ahmed Naveed Farooqui
*OMAN CABLES INDUSTRY
(SAOG)*

Bruce Palmer
*CURTIS MALLET - PREVOST,
COLT & MOSLE LLP*

Raghavendra Pangala
SEMAC & PARTNERS LLC

Dali Rahmattala Habboub
DENTON WILDE SAPTE & Co

Paul Sheridan
DENTON WILDE SAPTE & Co

Rajshekhar Singh
BANK MUSCAT

Ganesan Sridhar
BANK MUSCAT

Sridhar Sridharan
ERNST & YOUNG

Paul Suddaby
PRICEWATERHOUSECOOPERS

Yasser Taqi
*CURTIS MALLET - PREVOST,
COLT & MOSLE LLP*

Mathai Thomas
TROWERS & HAMLINS

PAKISTAN

Adeel Abbas
*MAXIM INTERNATIONAL LAW
FIRM*

Ali Jafar Abidi
STATE BANK OF PAKISTAN

Masooma Afzal
HASEEB LAW ASSOCIATES

Owais Ahmad
UNITED LAW ASSOCIATES

Taqi Ahmad
PRICEWATERHOUSECOOPERS

Waheed Ahmad
*MAXIM INTERNATIONAL LAW
FIRM*

Jawad Ahmed
*MUHAMMAD FAROOQ & CO.
CHARTERED ACCOUNTANTS*

Zaki Ahmed
ABRAHAM & SARWANA

Ahmad Syed Akhter
*PYRAMID TRANSPORTATION
GROUP*

Ali Javed Bajwa
HASEEB LAW ASSOCIATES

Major Javed Bashir
GREENFIELDS INTERNATIONAL

Faisal Daudpota
KHALID DAUDPOTA & CO.

Junaid Daudpota
KHALID DAUDPOTA & CO.

Zaki Ejaz
*ZAKI & ZAKI (ADVOCATES
AND SOLICITORS)*

Kausar Fecto
*KAUSAR FECTO & CO.
CHARTERED ACCOUNTANTS*

Khalid Habibullah
ABRAHAM & SARWANA

Irfan Haider
*PYRAMID TRANSPORTATION
GROUP*

Irfan Mir Halepota
*LAW FIRM IRFAN M.
HALEPOTA*

Asim Hameed Khan
*IVON TRADING COMPANY
PVT. LTD.*

Asma Hameed Khan
SURRIDGE & BEECHENO

Rashid Ibrahim
A.F. FERGUSON & CO.

Fiza Islam
*LEGIS INN (ATTORNEYS &
CORPORATE CONSULTANTS)*

Muzaffar Islam
*LEGIS INN (ATTORNEYS &
CORPORATE CONSULTANTS)*

Masooma Jaffer
ABRAHAM & SARWANA

Rubina Javed
TEXPERTS (PRIVATE) LIMITED

M Javed Hassan
TEXPERTS (PRIVATE) LIMITED

Aftab Ahmed Khan
SURRIDGE & BEECHENO

Fiza Islam
*LEGIS INN (ATTORNEYS &
CORPORATE CONSULTANTS)*

Nasir Mehmood Ahmed
BUNKER LOGISTICS

Rashid Rahman Mir
*RAHMAN SARFARAZ RAHIM
IQBAL RAFIQ CHARTERED
ACCOUNTANTS, MEMBER
OF RUSSELL BEDFORD
INTERNATIONAL*

Faiza Muzaffar
*LEGIS INN (ATTORNEYS &
CORPORATE CONSULTANTS)*

Abdul Rahman
QAMAR ABBAS & CO.

Zaki Rahman
*EBRAHIM HOSAIN, ADVOCATES
AND CORPORATE COUNSEL*

Tariq Saeed Rana
SURRIDGE & BEECHENO

Abdur Razzaq
QAMAR ABBAS & CO.

Mudassir Rizwan
PRICEWATERHOUSECOOPERS

Qamar Sajjad
Maxim International Law Firm

Abdul Salam
Legis Inn (Attorneys & Corporate Consultants)

Hamza Saleem
Mohsin Tayebaly & Co., Corporate Legal Consultants, Barristers and Advocates

Jawad A. Sarwana
Abraham & Sarwana

Shahid Sattar
Apex Power Solutions (Pvt.) Ltd.

Muhammad Siddique
Securities and Exchange Commission of Pakistan

Mirza Taqi Ud-Din Ahmad
PricewaterhouseCoopers

Mian Haseeb ul Hassan
Haseeb Law Associates

Chaudhary Usman
Ebrahim Hosain, Advocates and Corporate Counsel

Saleem uz Zaman
Hayat Noorwala and Zaman

Ali Yasir Virk
Haseeb Law Associates

Sana Waheed
Zafar & Associates LLP

Muhammad Yousuf
Haider Shamsi & Co., Chartered Accountants

Ilyas Zafar
Zafar & Associates LLP

Abdul Salam Zahed
AISA

Akhtar Zaidi
Zain Consulting

Asf Ali Zaidi
Pyramid Transportation Group

PALAU

Kenneth Barden
Attorney-at-Law

Cristina Castro
Western Caroline Trading Co.

Yukiwo P. Dengokl
Dengokl & Parkinson

Kevin N. Kirk
The Law Office of Kirk and Shadel

Rose Ongalibang
Palau Supreme Court

William L. Ridpath
William L. Ridpath, Attorney at Law

David Shadel
The Law Office of Kirk and Shadel

Peter C. Tsao
Western Caroline Trading Co.

PANAMA

Amanda Barraza de Wong
PricewaterhouseCoopers

Francisco A. Barrios G.
PricewaterhouseCoopers

Gustavo Adolfo Bernal
Sociedad Panameña de Ingenieros y Arquitectos

Carlos Klaus Bieberach
PricewaterhouseCoopers

Jose A. Bozzo
Garrido & Garrido

Luis Chalhoub
Icaza, Gonzalez-Ruiz & Aleman

Aurelia Chen
Mossack Fonseca & Co.

Rigoberto Coronado
Mossack Fonseca & Co.

Jeanina Aileen Diaz
PricewaterhouseCoopers

Marisol Ellis
Icaza, Gonzalez-Ruiz & Aleman

Michael Fernandez
CAPAC (Cámara Panameña de la Construcción)

Jorge R. González Byrne
Arias, Alemán & Mora

Khiet Le Trinh
Sucre, Arias & Reyes

Ricardo Madrid
PricewaterhouseCoopers

Ana Lucia Márquez
Arosemena Noriega & Contreras

Ivette Elisa Martínez Saenz
Patton, Moreno & Asvat

Erick Rogelio Muñoz
Sucre, Arias & Reyes

José Miguel Navarrete
Arosemena Noriega & Contreras

Ramón Ortega
PricewaterhouseCoopers

Sebastian Perez
Union Fenosa - EDEMET – EDECHI

Jorge Quijano
Arosemena Noriega & Contreras

Luz María Salamina
Asociación Panameña de Crédito

Veronica Sinisterra
Arosemena Noriega & Contreras

Valentín Ureña
Arosemena Noriega & Contreras

Ramón Varela
Morgan & Morgan

PAPUA NEW GUINEA

Paul Barker
Consultative Implementation & Monitoring Council

David Caradus
PricewaterhouseCoopers

Dave Conn
POM Chamber of Commerce and Industry

Alois Daton
IRC Internal Revenue Commission

Richard Flynn
Blake Dawson

Gary Jufa
IRC Internal Revenue Commission

Ignatius Kadiko
Department of Commerce and Industry

Ambeng Kandakasi
Supreme Court of Justice

Sarah Kuman
Allens Arthur Robinson

John Leahy
Peter Allan Lowing Lawyers

Bruce Mackinlay
Credit & Data Bureau Limited

Angela Mageto
NCDC -Municipality

Antonia Nohou
PricewaterhouseCoopers

John Numapo
Magisterial Services District Office

Ivan Pomaleu
IPA

Lawrence Stocks
Stocks & Partners

Thomas Taberia
Peter Allan Lowing Lawyers

PARAGUAY

Perla Alderete
Vouga & Olmedo Abogados

Manuel Arias
Vouga & Olmedo Abogados

Florinda Benitez
Notary public

Ligia Benitez
Ligia Benitez Escribania

Hugo T. Berkemeyer
Berkemeyer, Attorneys & Counselors

Luis Alberto Breuer
Berkemeyer, Attorneys & Counselors

Esteban Burt
Peroni, Sosa, Tellechea, Burt & Narvaja, member of Lex Mundi

Lorena Dolsa
Berkemeyer, Attorneys & Counselors

Estefanía Elicetche
Peroni, Sosa, Tellechea, Burt & Narvaja, member of Lex Mundi

Natalia Enciso Benitez
Notary public

Ana Franco
BDO Rubinsztein & Guillén

Néstor Gamarra
Servimex SACI

Jorge Guillermo Gomez
PricewaterhouseCoopers

Nadia Gorostiaga
PricewaterhouseCoopers

Carl Thomas Gwynn
Gwynn & Gwynn - Legal Counselling and Translations

María Antonia Gwynn
Berkemeyer, Attorneys & Counselors

Norman Gwynn
Gwynn & Gwynn - Legal Counselling and Translations

Carlos R. Gwynn S.
Gwynn & Gwynn - Legal Counselling and Translations

Carmelo Insfran
Administración Nacional de Electricidad

Jorge Jimenez Rey
Banco Central del Paraguay

Nestor Loizaga
Ferrere Attorneys

Rocío Penayo
Moreno Ruffinelli & Asociados

Yolanda Pereira
Berkemeyer, Attorneys & Counselors

Juan Pablo Pesce
Vivion S.A.

Beatriz Pisano
Ferrere Attorneys

Enrique Riera
Estudio Jurídico Riera Abogados

Armindo Riquelme
Fiorio, Cardozo & Alvarado

Natalio Rubinsztein
BDO Rubinsztein & Guillén

María Inés Segura
Moreno Ruffinelli & Asociados

Federico Silva
Ferrere Attorneys

Ruben Taboada
PricewaterhouseCoopers

Maria Gloria Triguis Gonzalez
Berkemeyer, Attorneys & Counselors

PERU

Daniel Abramovich
Payet, Rey, Cauvi Abogados

Walter Aguirre
PricewaterhouseCoopers

Jose Alarcon
Colegio de Notarios

Marco Antonio Alarcón Piana
Estudio Echecopar

Milagros Alfageme Navarro
PricewaterhouseCoopers

Humberto Allemant
PricewaterhouseCoopers

Pamela Arce
Rebaza, Alcazar & De Las Casas Abogados Financieros

Guilhermo Auler
Avendaño, Forsyth & Arbe Abogados

Juan Luis Avendaño Cisneros
Miranda & Amado Abogados

Sergio Barboza
Pizarro, Botto & Escobar Abogados

Milagros A. Barrera
Barrios Fuentes Gallo Abogados

Raul Barrios
Barrios Fuentes Gallo Abogados

Vanessa Barzola
PricewaterhouseCoopers Legal Services

Maritza Barzola Vilchez
Barzola & Asociados s.c., member of Russell Bedford International

Rocio Barzola Vilchez
Barzola & Asociados s.c., member of Russell Bedford International

Cesar Bazan Naveda
Colegio de Notarios

Carol Flores Bernal
ONUDFI

Vanessa Calderon Barcelo
Municipalidad de San Isidro

Fernando Castro Kahn
Muñiz, Ramírez, Peréz-Taiman & Luna Victoria Attorneys at Law

Sandro Cogorno
Avendaño, Forsyth & Arbe Abogados

Anahi Com
Rebaza, Alcazar & De Las Casas Abogados Financieros

Talí Cordero
PricewaterhouseCoopers

Joanna Dawson
Estudio Olaechea, member of Lex Mundi

Alfonso De Los Heros Pérez Albela
Estudio Echecopar

Paula Devescovi
Barrios Fuentes Gallo Abogados

Ana María Diez
Estudio Olaechea, member of Lex Mundi

Juan Carlos Durand Grahammer
Durand Abogados

Luis Fernando Edwards
Barrios Fuentes Gallo Abogados

Luis Felipe Espinosa
Rebaza, Alcazar & De Las Casas Abogados Financieros

Arturo Ferrari
Muñiz, Ramírez, Peréz-Taiman & Luna Victoria Attorneys at Law

Guillermo Ferrero
Estudio Ferrero Abogados

Inés Flores-Araoz
Barzola & Asociados s.c., member of Russell Bedford International

Luis Enrique Narro Forno
SUNAT

Maria Frassinetti
TAX ADMINISTRATION OF PERU

Carol Fuentes
CONUDFI

Jorge Fuentes
ESTUDIO RUBIO, LEGUÍA, NORMAND Y ASOCIADOS

Carlos Gallardo Torres
GENERAL AGENCY OF FOREIGN ECONOMIC MATTERS, COMPETITION AND PRIVATE INVESTMENT

Viviana García
DELMAR UGARTE ABOGADOS

Juan García Montúfar
ESTUDIO RUBIO, LEGUÍA, NORMAND Y ASOCIADOS

Antonio Guarniz
ESTUDIO FERRERO ABOGADOS

Marco Tulio Gutierrez
ESTUDIO JURIDICO MARCO TULIO GUTIERREZ S CIVIL RL

Cecilia Guzman-Barron
BARRIOS FUENTES GALLO ABOGADOS

Oscar J. Hernandez
GAMMA CARGO S.A.C.

Ronald Hidalgo
NISSAN MAQUINARIAS SA

Alfonso Higueras Suarez
EQUIFAX PERU S.A.

Jose A. Honda
ESTUDIO OLAECHEA, MEMBER OF LEX MUNDI

Diego Huertas del Pino
BARRIOS FUENTES GALLO ABOGADOS

Rafael Junco
CAMARA PERUANA DE LA CONSTRUCCION

Juan Carlos Leon
ADEX

Lilly Llanos Sanchodavila
COLEGIO DE NOTARIOS

José Llosa
CREDITEX

German Lora
PAYET, REY, CAUVI ABOGADOS

Milagros Maravi Sumar
ESTUDIO RUBIO, LEGUÍA, NORMAND Y ASOCIADOS

Carlos Martinez Ebell
ESTUDIO RUBIO, LEGUÍA, NORMAND Y ASOCIADOS

Jesús Matos
ESTUDIO OLAECHEA, MEMBER OF LEX MUNDI

Cecilia Mercado
GAMMA CARGO S.A.C.

Jorge Mogrovejo
SUPERINTENDENTCY OF BANKING

Claudio Mundaca
BARRIOS FUENTES GALLO ABOGADOS

Franco Muschi Loayza
PAYET, REY, CAUVI ABOGADOS

Gabriel Musso Canepa
ESTUDIO RUBIO, LEGUÍA, NORMAND Y ASOCIADOS

Augusto Palma
PRICEWATERHOUSECOOPERS

Danilo Peláez
SWISSOTEL

Lucianna Polar
ESTUDIO OLAECHEA, MEMBER OF LEX MUNDI

Nelly Poquis
MUNICIPALIDAD DE SAN ISIDRO

Bruno Marchese Quintana
ESTUDIO RUBIO, LEGUÍA, NORMAND Y ASOCIADOS

Carlos Javier Rabanal Sobrino
DURAND ABOGADOS

Fernando M. Ramos
BARRIOS FUENTES GALLO ABOGADOS

Alberto Rebaza
REBAZA, ALCAZAR & DE LAS CASAS ABOGADOS FINANCIEROS

Sonia L. Rengifo
BARRIOS FUENTES GALLO ABOGADOS

Alonso Rey Bustamante
PAYET, REY, CAUVI ABOGADOS

Emil Ruppert
ESTUDIO RUBIO, LEGUÍA, NORMAND Y ASOCIADOS

Carolina Sáenz Llanos
ESTUDIO RUBIO, LEGUÍA, NORMAND Y ASOCIADOS

Pío Salazar
BARRIOS FUENTES GALLO ABOGADOS

Adolfo Sanabria Mercado
MUÑIZ, RAMÍREZ, PERÉZ-TAIMAN & LUNA VICTORIA ATTORNEYS AT LAW

Arturo Ruiz Sanchez
ESTUDIO RUBIO, LEGUÍA, NORMAND Y ASOCIADOS

Martin Serkovic
ESTUDIO OLAECHEA, MEMBER OF LEX MUNDI

Claudia Sevillano
PIZARRO, BOTTO & ESCOBAR ABOGADOS

Hugo Silva
RODRIGO, ELÍAS, MEDRANO ABOGADOS

Liliana Tsuboyama
ESTUDIO ECHECOPAR

Manuel A. Ugarte
DELMAR UGARTE ABOGADOS

Daniel Ulloa
REBAZA, ALCAZAR & DE LAS CASAS ABOGADOS FINANCIEROS

Rodrigo Urrutia
REBAZA, ALCAZAR & DE LAS CASAS ABOGADOS FINANCIEROS

Jack Vainstein
VAINSTEIN & INGENIEROS S.A.

Erick Valderrama Villalobos
PRICEWATERHOUSECOOPERS

José Antonio Valdez
ESTUDIO OLAECHEA, MEMBER OF LEX MUNDI

Manuel Villa-García
ESTUDIO OLAECHEA, MEMBER OF LEX MUNDI

Agustín Yrigoyen
ESTUDIO AURELIO GARCÍA SAYÁN- ABOGADOS

PHILIPPINES

Myla Gloria Amboy
JIMENEZ GONZALES BELLO VALDEZ CALUYA & FERNANDEZ

Manuel Batallones
BAP CREDIT BUREAU

Anna Bianca Torres
PJS LAW

Alexander Cabrera
PRICEWATERHOUSECOOPERS / ISLA LIPANA & CO.

Ernesto Caluya Jr
JIMENEZ GONZALES BELLO VALDEZ CALUYA & FERNANDEZ

Cecile M.E. Caro
SYCIP SALAZAR HERNANDEZ & GATMAITAN

Sandhya Marie Castro
ROMULO, MABANTA, BUENAVENTURA, SAYOC & DE LOS ANGELES, MEMBER OF LEX MUNDI

Kenneth Chua
QUISUMBING TORRES, MEMBER FIRM OF BAKER & MCKENZIE INTERNATIONAL

Barbara Jil Clara
SYCIP SALAZAR HERNANDEZ & GATMAITAN

Emerico O. de Guzman
ANGARA ABELLO CONCEPCION REGALA & CRUZ LAW OFFICES (ACCRALAW)

Jaime Raphael Feliciano
ROMULO, MABANTA, BUENAVENTURA, SAYOC & DE LOS ANGELES, MEMBER OF LEX MUNDI

Anthony Fernandes
FIRST BALFOUR, INC

Rachel Follosco
FOLLOSCO MORALLOS & HERCE

Catherine Franco
QUISUMBING TORRES, MEMBER FIRM OF BAKER & MCKENZIE INTERNATIONAL

Geraldine Garcia
FOLLOSCO MORALLOS & HERCE

Andres Gatmaitan
SYCIP SALAZAR HERNANDEZ & GATMAITAN

Gwen Grecia-de Vera
PJS LAW

Kathlyn Joy Guanzon
JIMENEZ GONZALES BELLO VALDEZ CALUYA & FERNANDEZ

Tadeo F. Hilado
ANGARA ABELLO CONCEPCION REGALA & CRUZ LAW OFFICES (ACCRALAW)

Karen Jimeno
BAKER & MCKENZIE

Rafael Khan
SIGUION REYNA MONTECILLO & ONGSIAKO

Victoria Limkico
JIMENEZ GONZALES BELLO VALDEZ CALUYA & FERNANDEZ

Recio Marichelle
ANGARA ABELLO CONCEPCION REGALA & CRUZ LAW OFFICES (ACCRALAW)

Lory Anne McMullin
JIMENEZ GONZALES BELLO VALDEZ CALUYA & FERNANDEZ

Cheryll Grace Montealegre
PRICEWATERHOUSECOOPERS / ISLA LIPANA & CO.

Jesusito G. Morallos
FOLLOSCO MORALLOS & HERCE

Freddie Naagas
SCM CREATIVE CONCEPTS INC.

Alan Ortiz
FOLLOSCO MORALLOS & HERCE

Carla Ortiz
ROMULO, MABANTA, BUENAVENTURA, SAYOC & DE LOS ANGELES, MEMBER OF LEX MUNDI

Emmanuel C. Paras
SYCIP SALAZAR HERNANDEZ & GATMAITAN

Lianne Ivy Pascua-Medina
QUASHA ANCHETA PENA & NOLASCO

Zayber John Protacio
PRICEWATERHOUSECOOPERS / ISLA LIPANA & CO.

Kristine Quimpo
JIMENEZ GONZALES BELLO VALDEZ CALUYA & FERNANDEZ

Senen Quizon
PUNONGBAYAN & ARAULLO

Janice Kae Ramirez
QUASHA ANCHETA PENA & NOLASCO

Judy Alice Repol
ANGARA ABELLO CONCEPCION REGALA & CRUZ LAW OFFICES (ACCRALAW)

Roderick Reyes
JIMENEZ GONZALES BELLO VALDEZ CALUYA & FERNANDEZ

Ricardo J. Romulo
ROMULO, MABANTA, BUENAVENTURA, SAYOC & DE LOS ANGELES, MEMBER OF LEX MUNDI

Neptali Salvanera
ANGARA ABELLO CONCEPCION REGALA & CRUZ LAW OFFICES (ACCRALAW)

Felix Sy
BAKER & MCKENZIE

Sheryl Tanquilut
ROMULO, MABANTA, BUENAVENTURA, SAYOC & DE LOS ANGELES, MEMBER OF LEX MUNDI

Angelo Tapales
QUISUMBING TORRES, MEMBER FIRM OF BAKER & MCKENZIE INTERNATIONAL

Ma. Melva Valdez
JIMENEZ GONZALES BELLO VALDEZ CALUYA & FERNANDEZ

Maria Winda Ysibido
PRICEWATERHOUSECOOPERS

Redentor C. Zapata
QUASHA ANCHETA PENA & NOLASCO

Gil Roberto Zerrudo
QUISUMBING TORRES, MEMBER FIRM OF BAKER & MCKENZIE INTERNATIONAL

POLAND

ALLEN & OVERY LLP

Ewa Aachowska - Brol
WIERZBOWSKI EVERSHEDS, MEMBER OF EVERSHEDS INTERNATIONAL LTD.

Bruno Andrade Alves
PRICEWATERHOUSECOOPERS

Piotr Andrzejak
SOBTYSIDSKI KAWECKI & SZL ZAK

Michal BarBowski
WARDYDSKI & PARTNERS, MEMBER OF LEX MUNDI

Barbara Berckmoes
PRICEWATERHOUSECOOPERS

Aleksander Borowicz
BIURO INFORMACJI KREDYTOWEJ S.A.

Ana Catarina Carnaz
PRICEWATERHOUSECOOPERS

PaweB Chrupek
PKF TAX SP. Z O.O.

Krzysztof Ciepliński
GIDE LOYRETTE NOUEL, MEMBER OF LEX MUNDI

Bo|ena Ciosek
WIERZBOWSKI EVERSHEDS, MEMBER OF EVERSHEDS INTERNATIONAL LTD.

Ana Raquel Costa
PRICEWATERHOUSECOOPERS

Jaroslaw Czech
WARDYDSKI & PARTNERS, MEMBER OF LEX MUNDI

Edyta Dubikowska
SQUIRE SANDERS ŚWIĘCICKI KRZEŚNIAK SP. K.

John Duggan
PRICEWATERHOUSECOOPERS

Rafal Dziedzic
GIDE LOYRETTE NOUEL, MEMBER OF LEX MUNDI

Jaime Esteves
PRICEWATERHOUSECOOPERS

Paweł Grześkowiak
GIDE LOYRETTE NOUEL, MEMBER OF LEX MUNDI

Jakub Guzik
SOBTYSIDSKI KAWECKI & SZL ZAK

Tomasz Kański
SOŁTYSIŃSKI KAWECKI & SZLĘZAK

Piotr Kaim
PRICEWATERHOUSECOOPERS

Iwona Karasek
JAGIELLONIAN UNIVERSITY KRAKOW

Katarzyna Konstanty
NIKIEL I ZACHARZEWSKI
ADWOKACI I RADCOWIE
PRAWNI

Zbigniew Korba
PricewaterhouseCoopers

Olga Koszewska
Chadbourne & Parke LLP

Jan Kucicki
Ministry of Infrastructure

Agnieszka Lisiecka
WardyDski & Partners

Monika Majewska
Ministry of Infrastructure

Monika Makosa
PricewaterhouseCoopers

Mateusz Medyński
WardyŃski & Partners,
member of Lex Mundi

Francisco Guimarães Melo
PricewaterhouseCoopers

Aleksandra Minkowicz-Flanek
PricewaterhouseCoopers

Ana Pinto Morais
PricewaterhouseCoopers

Michal Niemirowicz-Szczytt
BNT Neupert Zamorska &
Partnerzy s.c.

Catarina Nunes
PricewaterhouseCoopers

Jacek PawBowski
PricewaterhouseCoopers

Krzysztof Pawlak
SoBtysiDski Kawecki &
Szl zak

Weronika Pelc
WardyDski & Partners,
member of Lex Mundi

BartBomiej Raczkowski
BartBomiej Raczkowski
Kancelaria Prawa Pracy

Manuel Raposo
PricewaterhouseCoopers

Anna Ratajczyk-Salamacha
Gide Loyrette Nouel,
member of Lex Mundi

Piotr Sadownik
Gide Loyrette Nouel,
member of Lex Mundi

Katarzyna Sarek
BartBomiej Raczkowski
Kancelaria Prawa Pracy

Zbigniew SkórczyDski
Chadbourne & Parke LLP

Dariusz Smiechowski
Union of Polish Architects

Iwona Smith
PricewaterhouseCoopers

Luís Filipe Sousa
PricewaterhouseCoopers

Agnieszka Stenzel-Rosa
WardyDski & Partners,
member of Lex Mundi

Ewelina Stobiecka
E/N/W/C Rechtsanwalte
E.Stobiecka Kancelaria
prawna sp.k.

Aukasz Szegda
WardyDski & Partners,
member of Lex Mundi

Ewa Szurminska-Jaworska
PricewaterhouseCoopers

Dariusz Tokarczuk
Gide Loyrette Nouel,
member of Lex Mundi

Otylia Trzaskalska-Stroinska
Ministry of Economy
Poland

Liza Helena Vaz
PricewaterhouseCoopers

Dominika Wagrodzka
BNT Neupert Zamorska &
Partnerzy s.c.

Tomasz WardyDski
WardyDski & Partners,
member of Lex Mundi

Radoslaw Waszkiewicz
SoBtysiDski Kawecki &
Szl zak

Robert Windmill
Windmill G siewski &
Roman Law Office

Steven Wood
Blackstones

Tomasz Zabost

Malgorzata Zamorska
BNT Neupert Zamorska &
Partnerzy s.c.

Tomasz Zasacki
WardyDski & Partners,
member of Lex Mundi

Cezary Żelaźnicki
PricewaterhouseCoopers

PORTUGAL

Victor Abrantes
Victor Abrantes -
International Sales Agent

Hermínio Afonso
PricewaterhouseCoopers

Alc-Servicos ao Domicilio

Paula Alegria Martins
Mouteira Guerreiro, Rosa
Amaral & Associados -
Sociedade de Advogados
R.L.

Bruno Andrade Alves
PricewaterhouseCoopers

Carlos Andrade
Direcção Municipal de
Gestão Urbanística

Filipa Arantes Pedroso
Morais Leitão, Galvão
Teles, Soares da Silva &
Associados, Member of Lex
Mundi

Miguel Azevedo
J & A Garrigues, S.L.

Manuel P. Barrocas
Barrocas Sarmento Neves

Barbara Berckmoes
PricewaterhouseCoopers

Marco Bicó da Costa
Credinformações/ Equifax

Diana Borges
CGM Gonçalo Capitão,
Gali Macedo e associados

Ana Catarina Carnaz
PricewaterhouseCoopers

Tiago Castanheira Marques
Abreu Advogados

Gabriel Cordeiro
Direcção Municipal de
Gestão Urbanística

Marcelo Correia Alves
Barrocas Sarmento Neves

Ana Raquel Costa
PricewaterhouseCoopers

Duarte de Athayde
Abreu Advogados

Miguel de Avillez Pereira
Abreu Advogados

João Cadete de Matos
Banco de Portugal

Carlos de Sousa e Brito
Carlos de Sousa & Brito &
Associados

John Duggan
PricewaterhouseCoopers

Jaime Esteves
PricewaterhouseCoopers

Bruno Ferreira
J & A Garrigues, S.L.

Jorge Figueiredo
PricewaterhouseCoopers

Ana Freitas
Direcção Municipal de
Gestão Urbanística

Bruno Garcia Borragine
Noronha Advogados

Paulo Henriques
University of Coimbra

Miguel Inácio Castro
Mouteira Guerreiro, Rosa
Amaral & Associados -
Sociedade de Advogados
R.L.

Maria João Ricou
Cuatrecasas, Gonçalves
Pereira & Associados

Andreia Junior
CGM Gonçalo Capitão,
Gali Macedo e associados

Patric Lamarca
Noronha Advogados

Caetano Leitão
Barros, Sobral, G. Gomes &
Associados

Maria Manuel Leitão Marques
Secretary of State
for Administrative
Modernisation

Tiago Lemos
PLEN - Sociedade de
Advogados, RL

Tiago Gali Macedo
CGM Gonçalo Capitão,
Gali Macedo e associados

Ana Margarida Maia
Miranda Correia
Amendoeira & Associados

Miguel Marques dos Santos
J & A Garrigues, S.L.

Isabel Martínez de Salas
J & A Garrigues, S.L.

Francisco Guimarães Melo
PricewaterhouseCoopers

Susana Melo
Grant Thornton
Consultores, Lda.

Joaquim Luis Mendes
Grant Thornton
Consultores, Lda.

Luis Mendes de Almeida
Abreu Advogados

Marianne Mendes Webber
Noronha Advogados

José Monteiro
JMSROC, lda, member
of Russell Bedford
International

Leonor Monteiro
Abreu Advogados

Ana Pinto Morais
PricewaterhouseCoopers

António Mouteira Guerreiro
Mouteira Guerreiro, Rosa
Amaral & Associados -
Sociedade de Advogados
R.L.

Rita Nogueira Neto
J & A Garrigues, S.L.

Catarina Nunes
PricewaterhouseCoopers

Ema Palma
JMSROC, lda, member
of Russell Bedford
International

Rui Peixoto Duarte
Abreu Advogados

Pedro Pereira Coutinho
J & A Garrigues, S.L.

António Luís Pereira
Figueiredo
Instituto Dos Registos e
Do Notario

Raquel Pereira Santos
Morais Leitão, Galvão
Teles, Soares da Silva &
Associados, Member of Lex
Mundi

Acácio Pita Negrão
PLEN - Sociedade de
Advogados, RL

Margarida Ramalho
Associação de Empresas
de Construção, Obras
Públicas e Serviços

Carla Ramos
Barros, Sobral, G. Gomes &
Associados

Manuel Raposo
PricewaterhouseCoopers

Armando J.F. Rodrigues
PricewaterhouseCoopers

Filomena Rosa
Instituto Dos Registos e
Do Notario

César Sá Esteves
SRS Advogados

David Salgado Areias
Areias Advogados

Francisco Salgueiro
Neville de Rougemont &
Associados

Pedro Santos
Grant Thornton
Consultores, Lda.

Filipe Santos Barata
Cuatrecasas, Gonçalves
Pereira

Alexandra Santos Dias
Mouteira Guerreiro, Rosa
Amaral & Associados -
Sociedade de Advogados
R.L.

Inês Saraiva de Aguilar
António Frutuoso de Melo
e Associados - Sociedade de
Advogados, R.L.

Manuel Silveira Botelho
António Frutuoso de Melo
e Associados - Sociedade de
Advogados, R.L.

Isa Simones de Carvalho
Noronha Advogados

Ricardo Soares Domingos
Noronha Advogados

Luís Filipe Sousa
PricewaterhouseCoopers

Carmo Sousa Machado
Abreu Advogados

João Paulo Teixeira de Matos
J & A Garrigues, S.L.

Nuno Telleria
Barros, Sobral, G. Gomes &
Associados

Maria Valente
SRS Advogados

Liza Helena Vaz
PricewaterhouseCoopers

Leendert Verschoor
PricewaterhouseCoopers

PUERTO RICO

Alfredo Alvarez-Ibañez
O'Neill & Borges

Juan Aquino
O'Neill & Borges

James A. Arroyo
TransUnion De Puerto
Rico

Hermann Bauer
O'Neill & Borges

Giancarlo Bracamonte
Ransa

Stephany Bravo de Rueda Arce
Ransa

Nikos Buxeda Ferrer
Adsuar Muñiz Goyco Seda
& Pérez-Ochoa, P.S.C

Jorge Capó Matos
O'Neill & Borges

Samuel Céspedes Jr
McConnell Valdés LLC

Walter F. Chow
O'Neill & Borges

Andrés Colberg
William Estrella Law
Offices

Shylene De Jesus
O'Neill & Borges

Myrtelena Díaz Pedora
Adsuar Muñiz Goyco Seda
& Pérez-Ochoa, P.S.C

Alberto G. Estrella
William Estrella Law
Offices

Ubaldo Fernandez
O'Neill & Borges

Dagmar Fernández
Quiñones & Sánchez, PSC

David Freedman
O'Neill & Borges

Carla Garcia
O'Neill & Borges

Virginia Gomez
Puerto Rico Electric
Power Authority

Gerardo Hernandez
William Estrella Law
Offices

Sary Iglesias
PricewaterhouseCoopers

Grisselle Lebron
PricewaterhouseCoopers

Frederick B. Martínez
Martínez Odell & Calabria

Oscar O Meléndez - Sauri
Coto Malley & Tamargo, LLP

Luis Mongil-Casasnovas
Martinez Odell & Calabria

Carlos Nieves
Quiñones & Sánchez, PSC

Keila Ortega
Ralph Vallone Jr., Law Offices

Rafael Pérez-Villarini
FPV & Galindez CPAs, PSC, member of Russell Bedford International

Edwin Quiñones
Quiñones & Sánchez, PSC

Thelma Rivera
Goldman Antonetti & Córdova P.S.C

Victor Rodriguez
Multitransport & Marine Co.

Edgardo Rosa
FPV & Galindez CPAs, PSC, member of Russell Bedford International

Jorge M. Ruiz Montilla
McConnell Valdés LLC

Carlos Sagardía
O'Neill & Borges

Patricia Salichs
O'Neill & Borges

Antonio Santos
Pietrantoni Méndez & Alvarez LLP

Eduardo Tamargo
Coto Malley & Tamargo, LLP

Yasmin Umpierre-Chaar
O'Neill & Borges

Carlos Valldejuly
O'Neill & Borges

Travis Wheatley
O'Neill & Borges

QATAR

Abdelmoniem Abutiffa
Qatar International Law Firm

Ahmad Anani
Al Tamimi & Company Advocates & Legal Consultants

Nisrine Boutros
International Legal Consultants LLC

Ian Clay
PricewaterhouseCoopers

Michel Daillet
International Legal Consultants LLC

Hasan El Shafiey
Nadoury & Nahas Law Offices

Dalal K. Farhat
Arab Engineering Bureau

Mohamed Fouad
Sultan Al-Abdulla & Partners

Samar A. Ismail
Khatib & Alami

Milan Joshi
Bin Yousef Cargo Express W.L.L

Upuli Kasturiarachchi
PricewaterhouseCoopers

Sajid Khan
PricewaterhouseCoopers

Sujani Nisansala
PricewaterhouseCoopers

Fadi Sabsabi
Al Tamimi & Company Advocates & Legal Consultants

David Salt
Clyde & Co. Legal Consultants

Aarij Wasti
Denton Wilde Sapte & Co

Terence G.C. Witzmann
HSBC

ROMANIA

Allen & Overy LLP

Adriana Almasan
Stoica & Asociatii Attorneys-at-Law

Lungu Ana-Maria
D&B David si Baias SCA - Romania

Cosmin Anghel
Badea Asociatii in Association with Clifford Chance

Andrei Badiu
3B Expert Audit, member of Russell Bedford International

Cristopher Berlew
Salans

Monica Biciusca
Anghel Stabb & Partners

Emanuel Băncilă
D&B David si Baias SCA

Lucian Catrinoiu
Stoica & Asociatii Attorneys-at-Law

Mara Ciju
Lina & Guia S.C.A

Victor Ciocîltan
Oancea Ciocîltan & Asociatii

Marinela Cioroab
Savescu si Asociatii

Anamaria Corbescu
Salans

Dorin Coza
Sulica Protopopescu Vonica

Tiberiu Csaki
Salans

Anca Danilescu
Zamfirescu Racoci Predoiu Law Partnership

Peter De Ruiter
PricewaterhouseCoopers

Luminita Dima
Nestor Nestor Diculescu Kingston Petersen

Adriana Dobre
D & B David si Baias S.C.A.

Emilia Dragu
Taxhouse SRL

Ion Dragulin
National Bank of Romania

Laura Adina Duca
Nestor Nestor Diculescu Kingston Petersen

Serban Epure
Biroul de Credit

Corneliu Frunzescu
D & B David si Baias S.C.A.

Adriana Gaspar
Nestor Nestor Diculescu Kingston Petersen

Monica Georgiadis
Marian Dinu Law Office

Gina Gheorghe
Tanasescu, Leaua, Cadar & Asociatii

Georgiana Ghitu
Marian Dinu Law Office

Florentina Golisteanu
Salans

Florina Gradeanu
Gradeanu & Partners

Mihai Grigoriu
Gradeanu & Partners

Andreea Grigorescu
PricewaterhouseCoopers

Mihai Guia
Lina & Guia S.C.A

Iulian Iosif
Muşat & Asociaţii

Diana Emanuela Ispas
Nestor Nestor Diculescu Kingston Petersen

Stanciulescu Iulia Cristina
D&B David si Baias SCA - Romania

Vasile Iulian
Conelectro

Crenguta Leaua
Tanasescu, Leaua, Cadar & Asociatii

Cristian Lina
Lina & Guia S.C.A

Amalia Lincaru
Salans

Edita Lovin
Retired Judge of Romanian Supreme Court of Justice

Dumitru Viorel Manescu
National Union of Civil Law Notaries of Romania

Oana Manuceanu
D&B David si Baias SCA

Gelu Titus Maravela
Muşat & Asociaţii

Carmen Medar
D & B David si Baias S.C.A.

Rodica Miu
D&B David si Baias SCA

Dominic Morega
Muşat & Asociaţii

Adriana Neagoe
National Bank of Romania

Manuela Marina Nestor
Nestor Nestor Diculescu Kingston Petersen

Madalin Niculeasa
Nestor Nestor Diculescu Kingston Petersen

Tudor Oancea
Oancea Ciocîltan & Asociatii

Delia Paceagiu
Nestor Nestor Diculescu Kingston Petersen

Cosmin Petru-Bonea
Salans

Alina Popescu
Muşat & Asociaţii

Mariana Popescu
National Bank of Romania

Cristian Predan
Gebrueder Weiss srl

Irina Preoteasa
D&B David si Baias SCA

Monica Preotescu
Nestor Nestor Diculescu Kingston Petersen

Radu Protopopescu
Sulica Protopopescu Vonica

Marius Pătrăşcanu
Muşat & Asociaţii

Adriana Puscas
Sulica Protopopescu Vonica

Raluca Radu
Salans

Cristian Radulescu
Taxhouse SRL

Angela Rosca
Taxhouse SRL

Laura Sarghiuta
Sarghiuta Laura Law Office

Romana Schuster
PricewaterhouseCoopers

Alexandru Slujitoru
D & B David si Baias S.C.A.

David Stabb
Anghel Stabb & Partners

Sorin Corneliu Stratula
Stratula Mocanu & Asociatii

Andrei Săvescu
Săvescu si Asociatii

Laura Tiuca
Salans

Anda Todor
Salans

Madalina Trifan
Salans

Lorena Tudor
PricewaterhouseCoopers

Anca Vatasoiu
Salans

Mihai Vintu
D&B David si Baias SCA

Cristina Virtopeanu
Nestor Nestor Diculescu Kingston Petersen

Roxana Vorniceanu
Nestor Nestor Diculescu Kingston Petersen

Alina Zarzu
Taxhouse SRL

RUSSIAN FEDERATION

Allen & Overy LLP

Marat Agabalyan
Herbert Smith CIS LLP

Alexey Almazov
Prosperity Project Management

Maxim Anisimov
Prosperity Project Management

Ekaterina Avilova
PricewaterhouseCoopers Legal Services

Fedor Bogatyrev
Law Firm ALRUD

Maria Bykovskaya
Gide Loyrette Nouel Vostok

Andrey Demusenko
Russia Consulting

Valery Fedoreev
Baker & McKenzie

Maria Gorban
Gide Loyrette Nouel Vostok

Igor Gorchakov
Baker & McKenzie

Evgeniy Gouk
PricewaterhouseCooper

Dina Gracheva
Law Firm ALRUD

Bill Henry
PricewaterhouseCoopers

Anton Kalanov
Interexpertiza LLC

Pavel Karpunin
Capital Legal Services LLC

Maria Kosova
Orrick, Herrington & Sutcliffe LLP

Alyona Kozyreva
Macleod Dixon

Irina Kultina
Russell Bedford International

Stepan Lubavsky
Hannes Snellman LLC

Dmitry Lyakhov
Russin & Vecchi, LLC.

Ilya Murzinov
Baker & McKenzie

Sergey Naumkin

Igor Nevsky
Russell Bedford International

Andrey Odabashian
PricewaterhouseCooper

Gennady Odarich
PricewaterhouseCoopers Legal Services

Olga Sirodoeva
Orrick, Herrington & Sutcliffe LLP

Rainer Stawinoga
Russia Consulting

Ivetta Tchistiakova-Berd
Gide Loyrette Nouel Vostok

Pavel Timofeev
Hannes Snellman LLC

Vladislav Zabrodin
Capital Legal Services LLC

Evgeny Zavarzin
Orrick (CIS) LLC

Andrey Zelenin
Lidings Law Firm

Alexei Zhuk
Hannes Snellman LLC

RWANDA

Emmanuel Abijuru
Cabinet d'Expertise en Droit des Affaires

Nippur Aranibar
National Bank of Rwanda

Purushothaman Balakrishnan
Swift Freight International (Rwanda)

Alberto Basomingera
Cabinet d'Avocats Mhayimana

Guillermo Bolaños
National Bank of Rwanda

Pierre Célestin Bumbakare
Rwanda Revenue Authority

Claudine Gasarabwe
Gasarabwe Claudine & Associes

Jean Havugimana
Rwanda Revenue Authority

Désiré Kamanzi
Kamanzi, Ntaganira & Associates

Angélique Kantengwa
National Bank of Rwanda

Theophile Kazaneza
Kigali Bar Association

Rodolphe Kembukuswa
SDV Logistics Ltd.

Isaïe Mhayimana
Cabinet d'Avocats Mhayimana

Joseph Mpunga
Kigali City Construction One Stop Centre

Alexandre Mugenzangabo
Mucyo & Associés

Richard Mugisha
Trust Law Chambers

Virginie Mukashema

Léopold Munderere
Avocat

Pothin Muvara
Office of the Registrar of Land Titles

Ernest Mwiza
Ernest Mwiza

Andre Ndejuru
Mr Andre Ndejuru

Martin Nkurunziza
Deloitte

Abel Nsengiyumva
Cabinet Abel Nsengiyumva

Jean Claude Nsengiyumva
Tribunal de Commerce de Musanze

Paul Pavlidis
Credit Reference Bureau Africa Limited

Sandrali Sebakara
Bureau d'Etudes CAEDEC

Ravi Vadgama
Credit Reference Bureau Africa Limited, Kenya

SAMOA

Mike Betham
Transam Ltd.

Lawrie Burich
Quantum Contrax Ltd.

Murray Drake
Drake & Co.

Ruby Drake
Drake & Co.

Graham Hogarth
Transam Ltd.

George Latu
Latu Ey Lawyers

Vitaoa Pele Fuata'i
Ministry of Natural Resources & Environment

John Ryan
Transam Ltd.

Patea Malo Setefano
Ministry of Natural Resources & Environment

Tanya Toailoa
To'ailoa Law Office

Toleafoa RS Toailoa
To'ailoa Law Office

SÃO TOMÉ AND PRINCIPE

António de Barros A. Aguiar
SOCOGESTA

André Aureliano Aragão
André Aureliano Aragão Jurisconsulta & Advogado

Edmar Carvalho
Miranda Correia Amendoeira & Associados

Abreu Conceição
Soares Da Costa

Celiza Deus Lima
JPALMS Advogados

Saul Fonseca
Miranda Correia Amendoeira & Associados

Raul Mota Cerveira
Miranda Correia Amendoeira & Associados

Cláudia Santos
Miranda Correia Amendoeira & Associados

SAUDI ARABIA

Asad Abedi
The Allaince of Abbas F. Ghazzawi & Co. and Hammad, Al-Mehdar & Co.

Danya Aboalola
Bafakih & Nassief

Anas Akel
Bafakih & Nassief

Naïm Al Chami
Talal Abu-Ghazaleh Legal (TAG-Legal)

Ahmed Al Jaber
EMDAD Arriyadh

Fayez Aldebs
Al Juraid & Company / PricewaterhouseCoopers

Ali. R. Al-Edrees
Al-Bassam

Nasser Alfaraj
Baker & McKenzie Bahrain Manama

Nader Alharbi
Al-Jadaan & Partners Law Firm

Abdullah Al-Hashim
Al-Jadaan & Partners Law Firm

Hesham Al-Homoud
The Law Firm of Dr. Hesham Al-Homoud

Abdulrahman Al-Ibrahim
Electricity & Co-Generation Regulatory Authority

Ahmed Aljabr
Advanced Elements Est

Mohammed Al-Jadaan
Al-Jadaan & Partners Law Firm

Nabil Abdullah Al-Mubarak
Saudi Credit Bureau - SIMAH

Fayez Al-Nemer
Talal Bin Naif Al-Harbi Law Firm

Ayedh Al-Otaibi
Saudi Arabian General Investment Authority

Mohammed Al-Soaib
Al-Soaib Law Firm

Wicki Andersen
Baker Botts LLP

Abdul Moeen Arnous
Law Office of Hassan Mahassni

Khalid Asitani
EMDAD Arriyadh

Wael Bafakieh
Bafakih & Nassief

Mahmoud Yahya Fallatah
National Water Company

Majed Mohammed Garoub
Law Firm of Majed M. Garoub

Imad El-Dine Ghazi
Law Office of Hassan Mahassni

Rahu Goswami
Law Office of Hassan Mahassni

Shadi Haroon
Law Office of Mohanned Bin Saud Al-Rasheed in association with Baker Botts LLP

Jochen Hundt
Al-Soaib Law Firm

Zaid Mahayni
Law Office of Hassan Mahassni

Ahmed Mekkawy
Bafakih & Nassief

Abdulrahman M. Al Mohizai
Electricity & Co-Generation Regulatory Authority

Fadi Obaidat
Talal Abu Gazaleh Legal (TAG-Legal)

Mustafa Saleh
EMDAD Arriyadh

Firas` Sawaf
Law Office of Hassan Mahassni

George Sayen
Baker & McKenzie Bahrain Manama

Abdul Shakoor
Globe Marine Services Co.

Wisam Sindi
The Allaince of Abbas F. Ghazzawi & Co. and Hammad, Al-Mehdar & Co.

Peter Stansfield
Al-Jadaan & Partners Law Firm

Sameh M. Toban
Toban, Attorneys at law & Legal Advisors

Natasha Zahid
Baker Botts LLP

Abdul Aziz Zaibag
Alzaibag Consultants

Soudki Zawaydeh
Al Juraid & Company / PricewaterhouseCoopers

SENEGAL

Khaled Abou El Houda
Cabinet Kanjo Koita

Diaby Aboubakar
BCEAO

M. Cissé
Construction Metallique Africaine

Rita Da Costa Fall
APIX -Agence chargée de la Promotion de l'Investissement et des Grands Travaux

Amadou Diouldé Diallo
Ministère de l'Urbanisme,de l'Habitat, de la Construction et de l' Hydraulique

Fidèle Dieme
SENELEC

Issa Dione
SENELEC

Alassane Diop
DP World

Fodé Diop
Art Ingegierie Afrique

Khadijatou Fary Diop Thiombane
Cabinet Jurafrik Conseil en Affaires (JCA)

Amadou Drame
Cabinet d'Avocat

Cheikh Fall
Cabinet d'Avocat

Hamza Fall
SCP Mame Adama Gueye & Associés

Balla Gningue
SCP Mame Adama Gueye & Associés

Khaled A. Houda
Cabinet Ledoux Seina

Matthias Hubert
FIDAFRICA / PricewaterhouseCoopers

Alioune Ka
Etude Notariale Ka

Papa Ismaél Ka
Etude Notariale Ka

Oumy Kalsoum Gaye
Chambre de Commerce d'Industrie et d'Agriculture de Dakar

Sidy Kanoute
Cabinet Ledoux Seina

Mouhamed Kebe
SCP GENI, SANKALE & KEBE

Ousseynou Lagnane
BDS

Patricia Lake Diop
Etude Me Patricia Lake Diop

Moussa Mbacke
Etude notariale Moussa Mbacke

Mamadou Mbaye
SCP Mame Adama Gueye & Associés

Ibrahima Mbodj
Cabinet Ledoux Seina

Adeline Messou
FIDAFRICA / PricewaterhouseCoopers

Pierre Michaux
FIDAFRICA / PricewaterhouseCoopers

Aly Mar NDIAYE
Commission de Régulation du Secteur de l'Electricité

Cheikh Tidiane Ndiaye
Secom-Afrique

Pape M. Ndiaye
Damco Senegal Dakar

Ablaye N'Diaye
Service Régional de l'Urba de Dakar D.A.U

Joséphine Ngom
FIDAFRICA / PricewaterhouseCoopers

Bara Sady
Port Autonome de Dakar

Mbacké Sene
SENELEC

Daniel-Sedar Senghor
Etude Notariale

Allé Sine
Direction Générale des Impôts et Domaines - DGID

Codou Sow-Seck
SCP GENI, SANKALE & KEBE

Mor Talla Tandian
Etude Ba & Tandian

Dominique Taty
FIDAFRICA / PricewaterhouseCoopers

Ousmane Thiam
Maersk Logistics Senegal Dakar

Ibra Thiombane
Cabinet Jurafrik Conseil en Affaires (JCA)

Emmanuel Yehouessi
BCEAO

SERBIA

Milos Andjelković
WOLF THEISS

Bojana Babić
BOJOVIĆ DAŠIĆ KOJOVIĆ

Dragan Bando
LEGAL ADVISORY GROUP

Marija Bojović
BOJOVIĆ DAŠIĆ KOJOVIĆ

Milan Brković
ASSOCIATION OF SERBIAN BANKS

Branko Bukvić
ŽIVKOVIĆ & SAMARDŽIĆ LAW OFFICE

Peter Burnie
PRICEWATERHOUSECOOPERS

Ana Čalić
PRICA & PARTNERS LAW OFFICE

Jovan Cirković
HARRISON SOLICITORS

Nataša Cvetičanin
LAW OFFICES JANKOVIĆ, POPOVIĆ & MITIĆ

Vladimir Dabić
THE INTERNATIONAL CENTER FOR FINANCIAL MARKET DEVELOPMENT

Lidija Djerić
LAW OFFICES POPOVIĆ, POPOVIĆ, SAMARDŽIJA & POPOVIĆ

Uroš Djordjević
ŽIVKOVIĆ & SAMARDŽIĆ LAW OFFICE

Bojana Djurović
WOLF THEISS

François d'Ornano
GIDE LOYRETTE NOUEL, MEMBER OF LEX MUNDI

Dragan Draca
PRICEWATERHOUSECOOPERS

Danica Gligorijević
PRICA & PARTNERS LAW OFFICE

Petar Kojdić
MORAVČEVIC, VOJNOVIĆ & ZDRAVKOVIĆ O.A.D. U SARADNJI SA SCHÖNHERR

Čedomir Kokanović
NIKOLIĆ KOKANOVIĆ OTASEVIĆ LAW OFFICE

Dubravka Kosić
LAW OFFICE KOSIĆ

Marija Kostić
LAW OFFICES JANKOVIĆ, POPOVIĆ & MITIĆ

Vidak Kovačević
WOLF THEISS

Marija Krizanec
JURIC AND PARTNERS ATTORNEYS AT LAW

Zach Kuvizić
KUVIZIĆ LAW OFFICE

Marc Lassman
BOOZ ALLEN HAMILTON SERBIA BELGRADE

Miladin Maglov
SERBIAN BUSINESS REGISTERS AGENCY

Marijana Malidzan
REGULATORY REVIEW UNIT

Aleksandar Mančev
PRICA & PARTNERS LAW OFFICE

Milena Manojlović
GIDE LOYRETTE NOUEL, MEMBER OF LEX MUNDI

Vladimir Milić
PRICEWATERHOUSECOOPERS

Vladimir Milošević
JOKSOVIĆ, STOJANOVIĆ AND PARTNERS

Marko Mrvić
LAW OFFICE KOSIĆ

Djordje Nikolić
NIKOLIĆ KOKANOVIĆ OTASEVIĆ LAW OFFICE

Lidija Obrenović
BOJOVIĆ DAŠIĆ KOJOVIĆ

Darija Ognjenović
PRICA & PARTNERS LAW OFFICE

Igor Oljačić
LAW OFFICE KOSI

Djuro Otasević
NIKOLIĆ KOKANOVIĆ OTASEVIĆ LAW OFFICE

Vladimir Perić
PRICA & PARTNERS LAW OFFICE

Vukasin Petković
PRICA & PARTNERS LAW OFFICE

Mihajlo Prica
PRICA & PARTNERS LAW OFFICE

Branko Radulović
REGULATORY REVIEW UNIT

Nebojša Savičević
TRIMO INZENJERING D.O.O.

Ana Stanković
MORAVČEVIC, VOJNOVIĆ & ZDRAVKOVIĆ O.A.D. U SARADNJI SA SCHÖNHERR

Milan Stefanović
REGULATORY REVIEW UNIT

Milo Stevanovich
BOOZ ALLEN HAMILTON SERBIA BELGRADE

Jovana Stevović
NIKOLIĆ KOKANOVIĆ OTASEVIĆ LAW OFFICE

Petar Stojanović
JOKSOVIĆ, STOJANOVIĆ AND PARTNERS

Milena Tasić
NIKOLIĆ KOKANOVIĆ OTASEVIĆ LAW OFFICE

Lidija Tomasović
LAW OFFICES POPOVIĆ, POPOVIĆ, SAMARDŽIJA & POPOVIĆ

Ana Tomić
JOKSOVIĆ, STOJANOVIĆ AND PARTNERS

Jovana Tomić
ŽIVKOVIĆ & SAMARDŽIĆ LAW OFFICE

Snežana Tosić
SERBIAN BUSINESS REGISTERS AGENCY

Tanja Vasić
BOJOVIĆ DAŠIĆ KOJOVIĆ

Miloš Vulić
PRICA & PARTNERS LAW OFFICE

Milenko Vucaj
ELEKTRODISTRIBUCIJA BEOGRAD D.O.O.

Bojan Zepinić
BSD ADVISORS TAX & FINANCE

Miloš Živković
ŽIVKOVIĆ & SAMARDŽIĆ LAW OFFICE

SEYCHELLES

Laura. A. Alcindor Valabhji
STERLING OFFSHORE LIMITED

France Gonzalves Bonte
BARRISTERS NOTARY PUBLIC

Bobby Brantley Jr.
STERLING OFFSHORE LIMITED

Francis Chang-Sam
LAW CHAMBERS OF FRANCIS CHANG-SAM

Lucienne Charlette
SEYCHELLES REGISTRAR GENERAL

Andre D. Ciseau
SEYCHELLES PORTS AUTHORITY

Antony Derjacques
DERJACQUES & ELIZABETH CHAMBERS

Alex Ellenberger
LOCUS ARCHITECTURE PTY. LTD.

Gerard Esparon
SEYCHELLES MINISTRY OF NATIONAL DEVELOPMENT

Conrad Lablache
PARDIWALLA TWOMEY LABLACHE

Roy Labrosse
ELECTRICAL SOLUTIONS

Margaret Nourice
STAMP DUTY COMMISSION

Unice Romain
SEYCHELLES PORTS AUTHORITY

Serge Rouillon
ATTORNEY-AT-LAW

Divino Sabino
PARDIWALLA TWOMEY LABLACHE

Kieran B. Shah
BARRISTER & ATTORNEY-AT-LAW

Rupert Simeon
SEYCHELLES MINISTRY OF FINANCE

Harry Tirant
TIRANT & ASSOCIATES

Melchior Vidot
SUPREME COURT OF SEYCHELLES

SIERRA LEONE

Desmond D. Beckley
DALTTECH / DESMI ENTERPRISES

Evelyn Bening
PRICEWATERHOUSECOOPERS

Roy Chalkley
SHIPPING AGENCIES LTD. (BOLLORÉ AFRICA LOGISTICS)

Leslie Theophilus Clarkson
AHMRY SERVICES

Michaela Kadijatu Conteh
WRIGHT & CO.

Mariama Dumbuya
RENNER THOMAS & CO., ADELE CHAMBERS

William L. Farmer
MINISTRY OF LANDS, COUNTRY PLANNING AND THE ENVIRONMENT

Eke Ahmed Halloway
HALLOWAY & PARTNERS

Millicent Hamilton-Hazeley
CLAS LEGAL

Francis Kaifala
WRIGHT & CO.

Mariama Kallay
GOVERNMENT OF SIERRA LEONE

Samuel Kargbo
CLAS LEGAL

Shiaka Kawa
EDRA CONSULTANCY

George Kwatia
PRICEWATERHOUSECOOPERS

Thelma Kelechi Osili
WRIGHT & CO.

Kingsley Owusu-Ewli
PRICEWATERHOUSECOOPERS

Christopher J. Peacock
SERPICO TRADING ENTERPRISES

Fatmata Sorie
WRIGHT & CO.

Eddinia Swallow
WRIGHT & CO.

Alhaji Timbo
NATIONAL POWER AUTHORITY

Darcy White
PRICEWATERHOUSECOOPERS

Rowland Wright
WRIGHT & CO.

SINGAPORE

Malcolm BH Tan
INSOLVENCY & PUBLIC TRUSTEE'S OFFICE

Hooi Yen Chin
GATEWAY LAW CORPORATION

Paerin Choa
TSMP LAW CORPORATION

Douglas Chow
MINISTRY OF TRADE & INDUSTRY

Kit Min Chye
TAN PENG CHIN LLC

Paula Eastwood
PRICEWATERHOUSECOOPERS

Aaron Goh
PRICEWATERHOUSECOOPERS

May Ching Ida Han
DONALDSON & BURKINSHAW

Sheau Peng Hoo
SUBORDINATE COURTS

Janet Koh
ACCOUNTING & CORPORATE REGULATORY AUTHORITY, ACRA

Ashok Kumar
ALLEN & GLEDHILL LLP

K. Latha
ACCOUNTING & CORPORATE REGULATORY AUTHORITY, ACRA

Yvonne Lay
MINISTRY OF FINANCE

Eng Beng Lee
RAJAH & TANN LLP

Jonathan Lee
RAJAH & TANN LLP

Kwok Ting Lee
PARTNERS GROUP PTE LTD. (SINGAPORE)

Laura Liew
LEGIS POINT LLC

Yik Wee Liew
WONGPARTNERSHIP LLP

Kexin Lim
PRICEWATERHOUSECOOPERS

William Lim
CREDIT BUREAU SINGAPORE PTE LTD.

Chris Loh
PRICEWATERHOUSECOOPERS

Mei Xin Loh
WONG TAN & MOLLY LIM LLC

Hwei Min Ng
MINISTRY OF MANPOWER

Max Ng
GATEWAY LAW CORPORATION

Sheikh Babu Nooruddin
AL NOOR INTERNATIONAL (SINGAPORE) PTE. LTD.

Beng Hong Ong
WONG TAN & MOLLY LIM LLC

Terrence Ong
ACCOUNTING & CORPORATE REGULATORY AUTHORITY, ACRA

Tan Peng Chin
TAN PENG CHIN LLC

See Tiat Quek
PRICEWATERHOUSECOOPERS

Shari Rasanayagam
KINETICA PTE. LTD. (THE CORPORATE SERVICES ARM ASSOCIATED WITH KELVIN CHIA PARTNERSHIP)

David Sandison
PRICEWATERHOUSECOOPERS

Disa Sim
RAJAH & TANN LLP

Douglas Tan
STEVEN TAN PAC, MEMBER OF RUSSELL BEDFORD INTERNATIONAL

Roy Tan
SINGAPORE CUSTOMS

Winston Tay
SINGAPORE CUSTOMS

Siu Ing Teng
SINGAPORE LAND AUTHORITY

Jennifer Yeo
YEO-LEONG & PEH LLC

Stefanie Yuen Thio
TSMP LAW CORPORATION

SLOVAK REPUBLIC

ALLEN & OVERY LLP

Zuzana Amrichová
PRICEWATERHOUSECOOPERS

Martina Behuliaková
GEODESY, CARTOGRAPHY AND
CADASTRE AUTHORITY OF THE
SLOVAK REPUBLIC

Jana Borská
ČECHOVÁ & PARTNERS,
MEMBER OF LEX MUNDI

Margareta Boskova
PRICEWATERHOUSECOOPERS

Todd Bradshaw
PRICEWATERHOUSECOOPERS

Ján Budinský
SLOVAK CREDIT BUREAU, S.R.O.

Peter Cavojsky
CLSERVICES, S.R.O.

Katarína Čechová
ČECHOVÁ & PARTNERS,
MEMBER OF LEX MUNDI

Kristina Cermakova
PETERKA & PARTNERS

Jana Fabianova
ČECHOVÁ & PARTNERS,
MEMBER OF LEX MUNDI

Peter Formela
ABONEX, S.R.O.

Miroslava Terem Greatiaková
PRICEWATERHOUSECOOPERS

Simona Halakova
ČECHOVÁ & PARTNERS,
MEMBER OF LEX MUNDI

Radoslava Hoglová
ZUKALOVÁ - ADVOKÁTSKA
KANCELÁRIA S.R.O.

Miroslav Jalec
ZAPADOSLOVENSKA
ENERGETIKA, A.S.

Michaela Jurková
ČECHOVÁ & PARTNERS,
MEMBER OF LEX MUNDI

Tomáa Kamenec
DEDÁK & PARTNERS

Veronika Keszeliova
ČECHOVÁ & PARTNERS,
MEMBER OF LEX MUNDI

Roman Konrad
PROFINAM, S.R.O.

Soňa Kročková
PRICEWATERHOUSECOOPERS

Lubomir Lesko
PETERKA & PARTNERS

Marek Lovas
PRICEWATERHOUSECOOPERS

Lucia Magova
PRICEWATERHOUSECOOPERS

Přemysl Marek
PETERKA & PARTNERS

Jaroslav Niznansky
MN LEGAL S.R.O.

Ladislav Pompura
MONAREX AUDIT CONSULTING

Gerta Sámelová-Flassiková
ALIANCIAADVOKÁTOV AK,
S.R.O.

Michal Simunic
ČECHOVÁ & PARTNERS,
MEMBER OF LEX MUNDI

Jaroslav Škubal
PRK PARTNERS S.R.O.
ADVOKÁTNÍ KANCELÁŘ

Lubica Suhajova
PRICEWATERHOUSECOOPERS

Maria SvidroHová
MONAREX AUDIT CONSULTING

Michal Toman
PRICEWATERHOUSECOOPERS

Roman Turok-Hetes
NATIONAL BANK OF SLOVAKIA

Peter Varga
PRK PARTNERS S.R.O.
ADVOKÁTNÍ KANCELÁŘ

Martin Vavrinčík
ČECHOVÁ & PARTNERS,
MEMBER OF LEX MUNDI

Zuzana Wallova
NATIONAL BANK OF SLOVAKIA

Dagmar Zukalová
ZUKALOVÁ - ADVOKÁTSKA
KANCELÁRIA S.R.O.

SLOVENIA

Marjan Babi
AGENCY OF THE REPUBLIC
OF SLOVENIA FOR PUBLIC
LEGAL RECORDS AND RELATED
SERVICES

Barbara Balanti
ODVETNIKI ŠELIH &
PARTNERJI

Teja Batagelj
AGENCY OF THE REPUBLIC
OF SLOVENIA FOR PUBLIC
LEGAL RECORDS AND RELATED
SERVICES

Ana Berce
ODVETNIKI ŠELIH &
PARTNERJI

Nataša Božović
BANK OF SLOVENIA

Erika Braniselj

Egon Breitenberger
ADMINISTRATION UNIT
LJUBLJANA

Mitja Černe
BDO EOS SVETOVANJE D.O.O.

Vid Čibej
PRICEWATERHOUSECOOPERS

Andrej Cvar
CITY STUDIO

ENERGY AGENCY OF THE
REPUBLIC OF SLOVENIA

Luka Fabiani
FILIPOV, PETROVIČ, JERAJ
IN PARTNERJI O.P., D.O.O.
IN COOPERATION WITH
SCHÖNHERR

Ana Filipov
FILIPOV, PETROVIČ, JERAJ
IN PARTNERJI O.P., D.O.O.
IN COOPERATION WITH
SCHÖNHERR

Ana Grabnar
ROJS, PELJHAN, PRELESNIK &
PARTNERJI, O.P., D.O.O.

Barbara Guzina
DELOITTE

Andrej Jarkovič
LAW FIRM JANEŽIČ &
JARKOVIČ LTD.

Jernej Jeraj
FILIPOV, PETROVIČ, JERAJ
IN PARTNERJI O.P., D.O.O.
IN COOPERATION WITH
SCHÖNHERR

Živa Južnič
ODVETNIKI ŠELIH &
PARTNERJI

Mia Kalaš
ODVETNIKI ŠELIH &
PARTNERJI

Janos Kelemen
PRICEWATERHOUSECOOPERS

Miro Koaak

Vid Kobe
FILIPOV, PETROVIČ, JERAJ
IN PARTNERJI O.P., D.O.O.
IN COOPERATION WITH
SCHÖNHERR

Marijan Kocbek
DLA PIPER PRAGUE LLP

Rok Kokalj
ROJS, PELJHAN, PRELESNIK &
PARTNERJI, O.P., D.O.O.

Vita Korinaek
CITY STUDIO

Vida Kovše
ODVETNIKI ŠELIH &
PARTNERJI

Nevenka Kržan
KPMG SLOVENIA LJUBLJANA

Nada Kumar

Alea Lunder
CMS REICH-ROHRWIG HAINZ
D.O.O

Marjan Mahni
KPMG SLOVENIA LJUBLJANA

Nina Mlakar

Eva Možina
MIRO SENICA IN ODVETNIKI

Clare Moger
PRICEWATERHOUSECOOPERS

Lojze Mrhar
VIATOR & VEKTOR

Matjaz Nahtigal
ODVETNIKI ŠELIH &
PARTNERJI

Siniaa Niaavi
DATA D.O.O

Jure Nikoli
CARGO-PARTNER

Matic Novak
ROJS, PELJHAN, PRELESNIK &
PARTNERJI, O.P., D.O.O.

Sonja Omerza
PRICEWATERHOUSECOOPERS

Grega Peljhan
ROJS, PELJHAN, PRELESNIK &
PARTNERJI, O.P., D.O.O.

Pavle Pensa
LAW OFFICE JADEK & PENSA
D.N.O. - O.P.

Bostjan Petauer
BDO EOS SVETOVANJE D.O.O.

Tomaž Petek
SURVEYING & MAPPING
AUTHORITY

Tomaž Petrovič
SCHÖNHERR RECHTSANWÄLTE
GMBH / ATTORNEYS-AT-LAW

Natasa Pipan Nahtigal
ODVETNIKI ŠELIH &
PARTNERJI

Petra Plevnik
MIRO SENICA IN ODVETNIKI

Igor Podbelšek
ELEKTRO LJUBLJANA D.D

Bojan Podgoraek
NOTARIAT

Andrej Poglajen
CHAMBER OF CRAFT AND
SMALL BUSINESS OF SLOVENIA

Aleksander Rajh
VIATOR & VEKTOR

Marjana Ristevski
PRICEWATERHOUSECOOPERS

Bostjan Sedmak
SCHÖNHERR RECHTSANWÄLTE
GMBH / ATTORNEYS-AT-LAW

Nina Šelih
ODVETNIKI ŠELIH &
PARTNERJI

Melita Trop
MIRO SENICA IN ODVETNIKI

Lea Volovec
LAW OFFICE JADEK & PENSA
D.N.O. - O.P.

Matthias Wahl
SCHÖNHERR RECHTSANWÄLTE
GMBH / ATTORNEYS-AT-LAW

Katja Wostner
BDO EOS SVETOVANJE D.O.O.

Anka Zagar
CARGO-PARTNER

Tina Žvanut Mioč
LAW OFFICE JADEK & PENSA
D.N.O. - O.P.

James Apaniai
JAMES APANIAI LAWYERS

SOLOMON ISLANDS

Ruth Liloqula
MINISTRY OF JUSTICE AND
LEGAL AFFAIRS

Haelo Pelu
MINISTRY OF JUSTICE AND
LEGAL AFFAIRS

Roselle R. Rosales
PACIFIC ARCHITECTS LTD.

Gregory Joseph Sojnocki
MORRIS & SOJNOCKI
CHARTERED ACCOUNTANTS

Pamela Wilde
MINISTRY FOR JUSTICE AND
LEGAL AFFAIRS

SOUTH AFRICA

Ann Aitken
BAKER & MCKENZIE

Ross Alcock
EDWARD NATHAN
SONNENBERGS INC.

Mark Badenhorst
PRICEWATERHOUSECOOPERS

Loren Benjamin
PRICEWATERHOUSECOOPERS

Kobus Blignaut
EDWARD NATHAN
SONNENBERGS INC.

Matthew Bonner
BAKER & MCKENZIE

Johan Botes
CLIFFE DEKKER HOFMEYR INC.

Beric Croome
EDWARD NATHAN
SONNENBERGS INC.

Haydn Davies
WEBBER WENTZEL

Paul De Chalain
PRICEWATERHOUSECOOPERS
ZAMBIA LUSAKA

Gretchen de Smit
EDWARD NATHAN
SONNENBERGS INC.

Daniel Francois Fyfer
CLIFFE DEKKER HOFMEYR INC.

Elise Gibson
GROSSKOPFF LOMBART
HUYBERECHTS & ASS

Tim Gordon-Grant
BOWMAN GILFILLAN, MEMBER
OF LEX MUNDI

Kim Goss
BOWMAN GILFILLAN, MEMBER
OF LEX MUNDI

Igno Gouws
WEBBER WENTZEL

Danie Hattingh
MULTI FREIGHT SERVICES

Simone Immelman
CLIFFE DEKKER HOFMEYR INC.

Unathi Kondile
BOWMAN GILFILLAN, MEMBER
OF LEX MUNDI

Ryan Kraut
BDO SPENCER STEWARD
SOUTHERN AFRICAN
CO-ORDINATION (PTY)
LIMITED

Matthew Kruger
WEBBER WENTZEL

Njah Martins
UNIVERSITY OF STELLENBOSCH

Gabriel Meyer
DENEYS REITZ INC./ AFRICA
LEGAL

Kacey Moses
AFRICAN SEAS FREIGHT
FORWARDERS

Sizwe Msimang
BOWMAN GILFILLAN, MEMBER
OF LEX MUNDI

Kemp Munnik
BDO SPENCER STEWARD
SOUTHERN AFRICAN
CO-ORDINATION (PTY)
LIMITED

Dave Oshry
FORDHAM & OSHRY INC.,
MEMBER OF RUSSELL BEDFORD
INTERNATIONAL

Bradleigh Scott
TRANSUNION

Andres Sepp
OFFICE OF THE CHIEF
REGISTRAR OF DEEDS

Richard Shein
BOWMAN GILFILLAN, MEMBER
OF LEX MUNDI

Arvind Sinha
BUSINESS ADVISORS GROUP

Johann Spies
WEBBER WENTZEL

Jane Strydom
TRANSUNION

Claire van Zuylen
BOWMAN GILFILLAN, MEMBER
OF LEX MUNDI

St Elmo Wilken
MERVYN TABACK
INCORPORATED

Andrew Wood
GROSSKOPFF LOMBART
HUYBERECHTS & ASS

SPAIN

ALLEN & OVERY LLP

Basilio Aguirre
REGISTRO DE LA PROPIEDAD
DE ESPAÑA

Nuria Armas
BANCO DE ESPAÑA

Ana Armijo
ASHURST

Jacobo Baltar
BAKER & McKENZIE

Santiago Barrenechea
LANDWELL,
PRICEWATERHOUSECOOPERS
LEGAL SERVICES

Vicente Bootello
J & A GARRIGUES, S.L.

Agustín Bou
JAUSAS

Héctor Bouzo Cortejosa
SOLCAISUR S.L.

Antonio Bravo
EVERSHEDS LUPICINIO

Laura Camarero
BAKER & McKENZIE

Lorenzo Clemente Naranjo
J & A GARRIGUES, S.L.

Francisco Conde Viñuelas
CUATRECASAS, GONÇALVES
PEREIRA

Jaume Cornudella i Marquès
LANDWELL, ABOGADOS Y
ASESORES FISCALES

Sara Crespo
J & A GARRIGUES, S.L.

Patricia de Anduaga
ECHECOPAR ABOGADOS LAW
FIRM

Almudena del Río Galán
COLEGIO DE REGISTRADORES
DE LA PROPIEDAD Y
MERCANTILES DE ESPAÑA

Agustín Del Río Galeote
GÓMEZ-ACEBO & POMBO
ABOGADOS

Anselmo Diaz Fernández
BANK OF SPAIN

Yune Dirube Rubio
ECHECOPAR ABOGADOS LAW
FIRM

Rossanna D'Onza
BAKER & McKENZIE

Antonio Fernández
J & A GARRIGUES, S.L.

Valentín García González
CUATRECASAS, GONÇALVES
PEREIRA

Borja García-Alamán
J & A GARRIGUES, S.L.

Cristina Gomendio
J & A GARRIGUES, S.L.

Juan Ignacio Gomeza Villa
NOTARIO DE BILBAO

Joaquín Rodriguez Hernández
COLEGIO DE REGISTRADORES

Igor Kokorev
PÉREZ - LLORCA

Jaime Llopis
CUATRECASAS, GONÇALVES
PEREIRA

Daniel Marín
GÓMEZ-ACEBO & POMBO
ABOGADOS

Ana Martín
J & A GARRIGUES, S.L.

Jorge Martín - Fernández
CLIFFORD CHANCE

Gabriel Martínez
MARTINEZ, OJEDA Y
ASOCIADOS, MEMBER
OF RUSSELL BEDFORD
INTERNATIONAL

José Manuel Mateo
J & A GARRIGUES, S.L.

Nicolás Nogueroles Peiró
COLEGIO DE REGISTRADORES
DE LA PROPIEDAD Y
MERCANTILES DE ESPAÑA

Ana Novoa
BAKER & McKENZIE

Jose Palacios
J & A GARRIGUES, S.L.

Daniel Parejo Ballesteros
J & A GARRIGUES, S.L.

Guillermo Rodrigo
CLIFFORD CHANCE

Déborah Rodríguez
CLIFFORD CHANCE

Eduardo Rodríguez-Rovira
URÍA & MENÉNDEZ, MEMBER
OF LEX MUNDI

Iñigo Sagardoy
SAGARDOY ABOGADOS,
MEMBER OF IUS LABORIS

Eduardo Santamaría Moral
J & A GARRIGUES, S.L.

Ramón Santillán
BANCO DE ESPAÑA

Catalina Santos
J & A GARRIGUES, S.L.

Pablo Santos
GÓMEZ-ACEBO & POMBO
ABOGADOS

Cristina Soler
GÓMEZ-ACEBO & POMBO
ABOGADOS

Angel Suárez-Barcena

Francisco Téllez
J & A GARRIGUES, S.L.

Adrián Thery
J & A GARRIGUES, S.L.

Alejandro Valls
BAKER & McKENZIE

Ricardo Veloso
VMP - VELOSO, MENDES, PATO
E ASSOCIADOS - SOCIEDADE DE

Juan Verdugo
J & A GARRIGUES, S.L.

Carlos Vérgez Muñoz
CLIFFORD CHANCE

SRI LANKA

Shanaka Amarasinghe
JULIUS & CREASY

Savantha De Saram
D.L. & F. DE SARAM

Sharmela de Silva
TIRUCHELVAM ASSOCIATES

Sadhini Edirisinghe
F.J. & G. DE SARAM, MEMBER
OF LEX MUNDI

Chamindi Ekanayake
NITHYA PARTNERS

Amila Fernando
JULIUS & CREASY

Jivan Goonetilleke
D.L. & F. DE SARAM

Naomal Goonewardena
NITHYA PARTNERS

Merinka Gunawardane
SUDATH PERERA ASSOCIATES

Sean Henricus
TIRUCHELVAM ASSOCIATES

Dharshika Herath Gunarathna
SUDATH PERERA ASSOCIATES

Sonali Jayasuriya
D.L. & F. DE SARAM

Tudor Jayasuriya
F.J. & G. DE SARAM, MEMBER
OF LEX MUNDI

Inoka Jayawardhana
F.J. & G. DE SARAM, MEMBER
OF LEX MUNDI

Mahes Jeyadevan
PRICEWATERHOUSECOOPERS

Yudhishtran Kanagasabai
PRICEWATERHOUSECOOPERS

Janaka Lakmal
CREDIT INFORMATION BUREAU
LTD.

Poorna Mendis
F.J. & G. DE SARAM, MEMBER
OF LEX MUNDI

Fathima Mohamed
SUDATH PERERA ASSOCIATES

Fathima Amra Mohamed
SUDATH PERERA ASSOCIATES

Thilanka Ratnayaka
TIRUCHELVAM ASSOCIATES

Hiranthi Ratnayake
PRICEWATERHOUSECOOPERS

Perera Sanjeevani
NITHYA PARTNERS

Shane Silva
JULIUS & CREASY

Priya Sivagananathan
JULIUS & CREASY

Malarmathy Tharmaratnam
TIRUCHELVAM ASSOCIATES

Sithie Tiruchelvam
TIRUCHELVAM ASSOCIATES

Charmalie Weerasekera
SUDATH PERERA ASSOCIATES

Shashi Weththasinghe
JULIUS & CREASY

ST. KITTS AND NEVIS

Michella Adrien
MICHELLA ADRIEN LAW
OFFICE

Rublin Audain
AUDAIN & ASSOCIATES

Georid Belle
CUSTOMS & EXCISE
DEPARTMENT

Nicholas Brisbane
N. BRISBANE & ASSOCIATES

Idris Fidela Clarke
FINANCIAL SERVICES
DEPARTMENT

Neil Coates
PRICEWATERHOUSECOOPERS

Joanna Collins
INLAND REVENUE AUTHORITY

Tamara Daniel
HENDERSON LEGAL CHAMBERS

Jan Dash
LIBURD AND DASH

Peter Davids
P.W.DAVIDS & ASSOCIATES

Kennedy de Silva
CUSTOMS AND EXCISE
DEPARTMENT

Terence Decosta
MINISTRY OF SUSTAINABLE
DEVELOPMENT

H. Grant
CARIBBEAN ASSOCIATED
ATTORNEYS

Barbara L. Hardtman
HARDTMAN & ASSOCIATES

K. Gregory Hardtman
HARDTMAN & ASSOCIATES

Marsha T. Henderson
HENDERSON LEGAL CHAMBERS

Dollrita Jack-Cato
WEBSTER DYRUD MITCHELL

Stanley Jacobs
SKIPA

Peter Jenkins
JENKINS & ASSOCIATES

Dahlia Joseph
DANIEL BRANTLEY &
ASSOCIATES

Damian E. S. Kelsick
KELSICK, WILKIN AND
FERDINAND

Elizabeth A. Kelsick
KELSICK, WILKIN AND
FERDINAND

Herman Liburd
LIBURD AND DASH

Marcella Liburd
BRYANT & LIBURD

Tamara Malcolm
LIBURD AND DASH

Adeola Moore
INLAND REVENUE AUTHORITY

Jeoffrey Nisbett
JEFFREY & NISBETTS

Miselle O'Brien
DUBLIN AND JOHNSON

Sandrine Powell-Huggins
HENDERSON LEGAL CHAMBERS

Randy Prentice
FRANK B. ARMSTRONG LTD.

Nervin Rawlins
INLAND REVENUE AUTHORITY

Larkland M. Richards
LARKLAND M. RICHARDS &
ASSOCIATES

Arlene Ross-Daisley
WEBSTER DYRUD MITCHELL

Anastacia Saunders
FRANK B. ARMSTRONG LTD.

Warren Thompson
CONSTSVCS

Vernon S. Veira
VERNON S. VEIRA &
ASSOCIATES

Charles Walwyn
PRICEWATERHOUSECOOPERS

Deidre N. Williams
WALWYNLAW

ST. LUCIA

Clive Antoine
MINISTRY OF
COMMUNICATIONS WORKS
TRANSPORT AND PUBLIC
UTILITIES

Thaddeus M. Antoine
FRANCIS & ANTOINE

Candace Cadasse
NICHOLAS JOHN & CO.

Peter I. Foster
PETER I. FOSTER &
ASSOCIATES

Peterson D. Francis
PETERSON D. FRANCIS
WORLDWIDE SHIPPING &
CUSTOMS SERVICES LTD.

Trevor Louisy
ST. LUCIA ELECTRICITY
SERVICES LTD.

Charlene Mae Magnaye
PRICEWATERHOUSECOOPERS

Duane C. Marquis
NLBA ARCHITECTS

Bradley Paul
BRADLEY PAUL ASSOCIATES

Richard Peterkin
PRICEWATERHOUSECOOPERS

Leandra Gabrielle Verneuil
CHAMBERS OF JENNIFER REMY
& ASSOCIATES

Andie A. Wilkie
GORDON & GORDON CO.

ST. VINCENT AND THE GRENADINES

Kay R.A. Bacchus-Browne
KAY BACCHUS - BROWNE
CHAMBERS

Aurin Bennett
AURIN BENNETT ARCHITECTS

Graham Bollers
REGAL CHAMBERS

Rickie Burnett
HIGH COURT

Parnel R. Campbell
CAMPBELL'S CHAMBERS

Mira E. Commissiong
EQUITY CHAMBERS

Natalie Creese
NATIONAL COMMERCIAL BANK
(SVG) LTD. (NCB (SVG) LTD.)

Gillian DaSilva
NATIONAL COMMERCIAL BANK
(SVG) LTD. (NCB (SVG) LTD.)

Theona R. Elizee-Stapleton
COMMERCE & INTELLECTUAL
PROPERTY OFFICE (CIPO)

Tamara Gibson-Marks
HIGH COURT REGISTRARY

Sean Joachim
CARIBTRANS

Robin John
KPMG

Stanley John
ELIZABETH LAW CHAMBERS

Brenan B. King
EQUINOX MARINE SURVEYING & CONSULTING

Roxann Knights
KNIGHTS CHAMBERS

Serge L'Africain
SCOTIABANK

Errol E. Layne
ERROL E. LAYNE CHAMBERS

Charlene Mae Magnaye
PRICEWATERHOUSECOOPERS

Moulton Mayers
MOULTON MAYERS ARCHITECTS

Sabrina Neehall
SCOTIABANK

Floyd A. Patterson
INTERNATIONAL LIAISON PARTNER BDO EASTERN CARIBBEAN

Richard Peterkin
PRICEWATERHOUSECOOPERS

Pamella Phillips
ST. VINCENT PORT AUTHORITY

Irwina Phills
ST. VINCENT CUSTOMS AUTHORITY

Kalvin Pompey
INLAND REVENUE AUTHORITY

Patrice Roberts-Samuel
LABOUR DEPARTMENT

Shelford Stowe
PHYSICAL PLANNING AND CONTROL DEP.

Arthur F. Williams
WILLIAMS & WILLIAMS

L.A. Douglas Williams
LAW FIRM OF PHILLIPS & WILLIAMS

SUDAN

Abdullah Abozaid
LAW OFFICE OF ABDULLAH A. ABOZAID

Abdalla Abuzeid
LAW OFFICE OF ABDALLA A. ABUZEID

Mohamed Ibrahim Adam
DR. ADAM & ASSOCIATES

Eihab Babiker
EIHAB BABIKER & ASSOCIATES - ADVOCATES

Elmugtaba Bannaga
ELKARIB AND MEDANI

Tagwa Bashir
SDV TRANSINTRA SUDAN

Amani Ejami
EL KARIB & MEDANI ADVOCATES

Tariq Mohmoud Elsheikh Omer
MAHMOUD ELSHEIKH OMER & ASSOCIATES ADVOCATES

Ahmed Mahdi
MAHMOUD ELSHEIKH OMER & ASSOCIATES ADVOCATES

Amel M. Sharif
MAHMOUD ELSHEIKH OMER & ASSOCIATES ADVOCATES

Abdel Gadir Warsama
DR. ABDEL GADIR WARSAMA GHALIB & ASSOCIATES LEGAL FIRM

SURINAME

Marcel K. Eyndhoven
N.V. ENERGIEBEDRIJVEN SURINAME

Stanley Marica
ADVOKATENKANTOOR MARICA LAW FIRM

Anouschka Nabibaks
BDO ABRAHAMSRAIJMANN & PARTNERS

Nannan Panday J.C.P.
NANNAN PANDAY LAWYERS

Rita Ramdat - Thakoer
CHAMBER OF COMMERCE & INDUSTRY

Angèle J. Ramsaransing-Karg
BDO ABRAHAMSRAIJMANN & PARTNERS

Adiel Sakoer
N.V. GLOBAL EXPEDITION

Inder Sardjoe
N.V. EASY ELECTRIC

Martha P. Schaap
HAKRINBANK N.V.

Albert D. Soedamah
LAWFIRM SOEDAMAH & ASSOCIATES

Radjen A. Soerdjbalie
NOTARIAAT R.A. SOERDJBALIE

Jennifer van Dijk-Silos
LAW FIRM VAN DIJK-SILOS

Rene van Essen
VERENIGING SURINAAMS BEDRIJFSLEVEN, SURINAME TRADE & INDUSTRY ASSOCIATION

Carel van Hest

Dayenne Wielingen - Verwey
VERENIGING SURINAAMS BEDRIJFSLEVEN, SURINAME TRADE & INDUSTRY ASSOCIATION

SWAZILAND

Veli Dlamini
INTERFREIGHT PTY. LTD. SWAZILAND

Vincent Galeromeloe
TRANSUNION ITC

Phumlile Tina Khoza
MUNICIPAL COUNCIL OF MANZINI

Paul Lewis
PRICEWATERHOUSECOOPERS

Andrew Linsey
PRICEWATERHOUSECOOPERS

Mangaliso Magagula
MAGAGULA & HLOPHE

Naledi Makhubu
TRANSUNION ITC

Sabelo Masuku
MAPHANGA HOWE MASUKU NSIBANDE

Caroline Mlambo
STANDARD BANK

Kenneth J. Motsa
ROBINSON BERTRAM

Bongani Mtshali
FEDERATION OF SWAZILAND EMPLOYERS AND CHAMBER OF COMMERCE

Nozizwa Mulela
STANDARD BANK

José Rodrigues
RODRIGUES & ASSOCIATES

P.M. Shilubane
P.M. SHILUBANE & ASSOCIATES

Bob Sigwane
SIGWANE AND PARTNERS

Pieter Smoor
BUILDING DESIGN GROUP

Bradford Mark Walker
BRAD WALKER ARCHITECTS

Patricia Zwane
TRANSUNION ITC

SWEDEN

Nicklas Anth
PANALPINA AB

Martin Bergander
GÄRDE WESSLAU ADVOKATBYRÅ

Mats Berter
MAQS LAW FIRM

Alexander Broch
BROCHS REDOVISNINGSBYRAA KB

Linda Broström-Cabrera
PRICEWATERHOUSECOOPERS

Pernilla Carring
ADVOKATFIRMAN LINDAHL

Jenny Dangre
ADVOKATFIRMAN VINGE KB, MEMBER OF LEX MUNDI

Roger Gavelin
PRICEWATERHOUSECOOPERS

Lars Hartzell
ELMZELL ADVOKATBYRÅ AB, MEMBER OF IUS LABORIS

Emil Hedberg
ADVOKATFIRMAN VINGE KB, MEMBER OF LEX MUNDI

Petter Holm
GÄRDE WESSLAU ADVOKATBYRÅ

Carl-Axel Holmberg
ELMZELL ADVOKATBYRÅ AB, MEMBER OF IUS LABORIS

Mats Holmlund
VATTENFALL ELDISTRIBUTION AB

Bengt Kjellson
LANTMÄTERIET

Niklas Körling
SETTERWALLS ADVOKATBYRÅ

Johan Lannering
MAQS LAW FIRM

Johan Lindberg
ADVOKATFIRMAN LINDAHL

Christoffer Monell
MANNHEIMER SWARTLING ADVOKATBYRÅ

Dain Nevonen
ADVOKATFIRMAN VINGE KB, MEMBER OF LEX MUNDI

Karl-Arne Olsson
GÄRDE WESSLAU ADVOKATBYRÅ

Mattias Örnulf
HÖKERBERG & SÖDERQVIST ADVOKATBYRÅ KB

Carl Östring
MAGNUSSON

Jesper Schönbeck
ADVOKATFIRMAN VINGE KB, MEMBER OF LEX MUNDI

SWITZERLAND

Amr Abdel Aziz
CMS VON ERLACH HENRICI AG

Rashid Bahar
BÄR & KARRER AG

Beat M. Barthold
FRORIEP RENGGLI

Christian Berger
PRICEWATERHOUSECOOPERS

Marc Bernheim
STAIGER, SCHWALD & PARTNER LTD.

Sébastien Bettschart
ABELS AVOCATS

Bernhard G. Burkard
NOTARIAT BERNHARD BURKARD

Andrea Cesare Canonica
SWISS CUSTOMS

Maxime Chollet
TAVERNIER TSCHANZ

Damien Conus
TAVERNIER TSCHANZ

Robert P. Desax
PRICEWATERHOUSECOOPERS

Suzanne Eckert
WENGER PLATTNER

Gaudenz Geiger
STAIGER, SCHWALD & PARTNER LTD.

Mark W. Hippenmeyer
ALTENBURGER LTD. LEGAL+TAX

Jakob Hoehn
PESTALOZZI, MEMBER OF LEX MUNDI

Ueli Huber
HOMBURGER

Urs Klöti
PESTALOZZI, MEMBER OF LEX MUNDI

Armin Marti
PRICEWATERHOUSECOOPERS

MIGROS-GENOSSENSCHAFTS-BUND

Georg Naegeli
HOMBURGER

Patrick Niklaus
PRICEWATERHOUSECOOPERS

Sara Rousselle-Ruffieux
TAVERNIER TSCHANZ

Daniel Schmitz
PRICEWATERHOUSECOOPERS

Andreas Staubli
PRICEWATERHOUSECOOPERS

Daniel Steudler
SWISSTOPO, DIRECTORATE FOR CADASTRAL SURVEYING

Edmond Tavernier
TAVERNIER TSCHANZ

Stephane Valat
ORRICK, HERRINGTON & SUTCLIFFE LLP

Beatrice Vetsch
PRICEWATERHOUSECOOPERS

Flurin von Planta
PLANTA & PLANTA

Patrick Weber
EKZ ELEKTRIZITÄTSWERKE DES KANTONS ZÜRICH

Marc Widmer
FRORIEP RENGGLI

Pascal Wirth
PRICEWATERHOUSECOOPER

SYRIAN ARAB REPUBLIC

Boulos Al Ashhab
AUDITING CONSULTING ACCOUNTING CENTER

Mouazza Al Ashhab
AUDITING CONSULTING ACCOUNTING CENTER

Rawaa Al Midani
MINISTRY OF TRADE & ECONOMY

Bisher Al-Houssami
AL-ISRAA INT'L FREIGHT FORWARDER

Abdul Raouf Hamwi
CIVIL ENGINEERING OFFICE

Bashir Haza
DIRECTOR: DIRECTORATE OF INTERNAL TRADE. MINISTRY OF TRADE & ECONOMY

Yaser Hmedan
YASER I. HMEDAN'S LAW FIRM

Mazen Ibrahim
IBRAHIM & ALOUSY LAW FIRM

Fadi Kardous
KARDOUS LAW OFFICE

Mazen N. Khaddour
INTERNATIONAL LEGAL BUREAU

Loubna Khoury
AUDITING CONSULTING ACCOUNTING CENTER

Saad Kurdy
ELSAAD PHARMA

Zena Nahat
KARDOUS LAW OFFICE

Gabriel Oussi
OUSSI LAW FIRM

Housam Safadi
SAFADI BUREAU

TAIWAN, CHINA

Vera Chang
LCS & PARTNERS

Victor Chang
LCS & PARTNERS

Yu-Chien Chang
PRICEWATERHOUSECOOPERS

Christine Chen
WINKLER PARTNERS

Edgar Y. Chen
TSAR & TSAI LAW FIRM, MEMBER OF LEX MUNDI

Eve Chen
EIGER LAW

Hui-ling Chen
WINKLER PARTNERS

Yo-Yi Chen
FORMOSA TRANSNATIONAL

Chun-Yih Cheng
FORMOSA TRANSNATIONAL

Yu-Chung Chiu
MINISTRY OF THE INTERIOR

Peter Dernbach
WINKLER PARTNERS

John Eastwood
EIGER LAW

Steven Go
PRICEWATERHOUSECOOPERS

Ainsley Hsieh
EIGER LAW

Sophia Hsieh
*TSAR & TSAI LAW FIRM,
MEMBER OF LEX MUNDI*

Barbara Hsu
SDV LOGISTICS LTD.

Robert Hsu
SDV LOGISTICS LTD.

Tony Hsu
PAMIR LAW GROUP

Margaret Huang
LCS & PARTNERS

Nelson Huang
YANGMING PARTNERS

T.C. Huang
HUANG & PARTNERS

Charles Hwang
YANGMING PARTNERS

James J.M. Hwang
*TSAR & TSAI LAW FIRM,
MEMBER OF LEX MUNDI*

Joan Jing
PRICEWATERHOUSECOOPERS

Nathan Kaiser
EIGER LAW

Chih-Shan Lee
WINKLER PARTNERS

Yu-Hsun Li
PRICEWATERHOUSECOOPERS

Justin Liang
BAKER & MCKENZIE

Chuh Ru Lin
*JOINT CREDIT INFORMATION
CENTER*

Emily Lin
PAMIR LAW GROUP

Frank Lin
REXMED INDUSTRIES CO., LTD.

Jennifer C. Lin
*TSAR & TSAI LAW FIRM,
MEMBER OF LEX MUNDI*

Ming-Yen Lin
*DEEP & FAR, ATTORNEYS-
AT-LAW*

Nelson J Lin
HUANG & PARTNERS

Rich Lin
LCS & PARTNERS

Yishian Lin
PRICEWATERHOUSECOOPERS

Catherine Liu
SDV LOGISTICS LTD.

Julia Liu
SDV LOGISTICS LTD.

Violet Lo
PRICEWATERHOUSECOOPERS

Joseph Ni
GOOD EARTH CPA

Lawrence S. Ong
PRICEWATERHOUSECOOPERS

J. F. Pun
CHEN, SHYUU & PUN

Lloyd G. Roberts III
WINKLER PARTNERS

Michael Schreiber
YANGMING PARTNERS

Tanya Y. Teng
HUANG & PARTNERS

Bee Leay Teo
BAKER & MCKENZIE

C.F. Tsai
*DEEP & FAR, ATTORNEYS-
AT-LAW*

Eric Tsai
PRICEWATERHOUSECOOPERS

Rita Tsai
APL

Joe Tseng
LCS & PARTNERS

Chao-Yu Wang
YANGMING PARTNERS

Chien-jui Wang
CEPD

Shih-Ming You
MINISTRY OF THE INTERIOR

TAJIKISTAN

Bakhtiyor Abdulhamidov
*AKHMEDOV, AZIZOV &
ABDULHAMIDOV ATTORNEYS*

Rasul Abdullaev
*REPRESENTATIVE
OF "GAZPROM
ZARUBEJNEFTEGAZ" IN RT*

Sherzod Abdurakhmanov
USAID/BEI, PRAGMA CORP

Zarrina Adham
HUMO

Shavkat Akhmedov
*AKHMEDOV, AZIZOV &
ABDULHAMIDOV ATTORNEYS*

Najib Ashraf
KN IBRAKOM FZCO.

Gulshan Ashurbekova
USAID/BEI, PRAGMA CORP

Farhad Azizov
*AKHMEDOV, AZIZOV &
ABDULHAMIDOV ATTORNEYS*

Jienshoh Bukhoriev
USAID/BEI, PRAGMA CORP

Firuz Bulbulov
*THE COLLEGIUM OF AUDITORS
OF TAJIKISTAN*

Courtney Fowler
PRICEWATERHOUSECOOPERS

Sobir Abduvaliyevich Haitov
AGROINVESTBANK

Ashraf Sharifovich Ikromov
LLC "MOVAROUNNAHR"

Elena Kaeva
PRICEWATERHOUSECOOPERS

Parviz Kamoliddinov
*TSG - USAID REGIONAL
TRADE LIBERALISATION AND
CUSTOMS PROJECT (RTLC)*

Manuchehr Kasimov
GLOBALINK LOGISTICS GROUP

Assel Khamzina
PRICEWATERHOUSECOOPERS

Valeriy Kim

Umar Muhammadkarim
GLOBALINK LOGISTICS GROUP

Takhir Nabiev
AITEN CONSULTING GROUP

Sharif Rahimzoda
*NATIONAL BANK OF
TAJIKISTAN*

Jamshed Rahmonberdiev
SOMON CAPITAL JSC

Faizali Rajabov
TECHNOINVEST

Ravshan Rashidov
LAW FIRM LEX

Bakhtiyor Rustamov
*ASIAN BUSINESS GROUP,
MEMBER OF RUSSELL BEDFORD
INTERNATIONAL*

Firdavs Sadikov
SOMON CAPITAL JSC

Emin Sanginov
*MINISTRY OF LABOR
TAJIKISTAN*

Marina Shamilova
LEGAL CONSULTING GROUP

Takdir Sharifov
*ASSOCIATION OF ANTI CRISIS
MANAGERS TAJIKISTAN*

Nurali Shukurov
USAID/BEI, PRAGMA CORP

Elena Simonova
KONSULTANT AUDIT

Habibullo Sulaymonov
*STROY SERVICE
CONSTRUCTION ASSOCIATION*

Mahmadyusuf Tashrifov
*NATIONAL BANK OF
TAJIKISTAN*

Aliya Utegaliyeva
PRICEWATERHOUSECOOPERS

Jamshed Yusufiyon
*NATIONAL BANK OF
TAJIKISTAN*

TANZANIA

Patrick Ache
MKONO & CO ADVOCATES

Krista Bates van Winkelhof
AKO LAW

Moses Dancan
GAPCS

Theresia Dominic
*UNIVERSITY OF DAR ES
SALAAM*

Nasra Hassan
MKONO & CO ADVOCATES

Johnson Jasson
*JOHNSON JASSON &
ASSOCIATES ADVOCATES*

Wilbert B. Kapinga
MKONO & CO ADVOCATES

Rehema Khalid-Saria
MKONO & CO ADVOCATES

Daniel Krips
MKONO & CO ADVOCATES

Victoria Makani
CRB ATTORNEYS

Lotus Menezes
MKONO & CO ADVOCATES

Vincent Mhina
AKO LAW

Nimrod Mkono
MKONO & CO ADVOCATES

Angela Mndolwa
AKO LAW

Jean Bosco Mugemana
INFO CONSULTANCY LIMITED

Exaud Mushi
*NORPLAN TANZANIA
LIMITED*

Octavian Mushukuma
CRB ATTORNEYS

Cheggy Mziray
CRB ATTORNEYS

Alex Thomas Nguluma
REX ATTORNEYS

Charles R.B. Rwechungura
CRB ATTORNEYS

Eric Rwelamira
ADEPT CHAMBERS

Emmy Salewi
*NORPLAN TANZANIA
LIMITED*

Rishit Shah
PRICEWATERHOUSECOOPERS

Geoffrey Sikira
CRB ATTORNEYS

Eve Hawa Sinare
REX ATTORNEYS

Richard Sisa
GAPCS

Mohamed H. Sumar
SUMAR VARMA ASSOCIATES

David Tarimo
PRICEWATERHOUSECOOPERS

Mustafa Tharoo
ADEPT CHAMBERS

Sinare Zaharan
REX ATTORNEYS

THAILAND

ALLEN & OVERY LLP

Janist Aphornratana
PRICEWATERHOUSECOOPERS

Chanakarn Boonyasith
SIAM CITY LAW OFFICES LTD.

Phadet Charoensivakorn
*NATIONAL CREDIT BUREAU
CO. LTD.*

Thunyaporn Chartisathian
*ALLENS ARTHUR ROBINSON /
SIAM PREMIER INTERNATIONAL
LAW OFFICE LIMITED*

Chinnavat Chinsangaram
*WEERAWONG, CHINNAVAT &
PEANGPANOR LTD.*

EEC LINCOLNE SCOTT CO LTD.

Muncharee Ittipalin
APL

Tayvee Kanokjote
*THAILAND LAND TITLING
PROJECT OFFICE*

Yingyong Karnchanapayap
*TILLEKE & GIBBINS
INTERNATIONAL LTD.*

Chaiwat Keratisuthisathorn
*TILLEKE & GIBBINS
INTERNATIONAL LTD.*

Suwat Kerdphon
DEPARTMENT OF LANDS

Chanida Leelanuntakul
SIAM CITY LAW OFFICES LTD.

William Lehane
*ALLENS ARTHUR ROBINSON /
SIAM PREMIER INTERNATIONAL
LAW OFFICE LIMITED*

Sakchai Limsiripothong
*WEERAWONG, CHINNAVAT &
PEANGPANOR LTD.*

Pratchayapa Mahamontree
SIAM CITY LAW OFFICES LTD.

Angsuma Montienkasem
PRICEWATERHOUSECOOPERS

Sally Mouhim
*TILLEKE & GIBBINS
INTERNATIONAL LTD.*

Felchesmi Mramba
*TANZANIA ELECTRIC SUPPLY
COMPANY LIMITED – TANESCO*

Anuwat Ngamprasertkul
PRICEWATERHOUSECOOPERS

Tanadee Pantumkomol
CHANDLER & THONG-EK

Ratana Poonsombudlert
CHANDLER & THONG-EK

Supan Poshyananda
*SECURITIES AND EXCHANGE
COMMISSION*

Chitchai Punsan
*TILLEKE & GIBBINS
INTERNATIONAL LTD.*

Sudthana Puntheeranurak
*NATIONAL CREDIT BUREAU
CO. LTD.*

*RATCHABURI ELECTRICITY
GENERATING HOLDING PCL.*

Sutatip Raktiprakorn
SIAM CITY LAW OFFICES LTD.

Piyanuj Ratprasatporn
*TILLEKE & GIBBINS
INTERNATIONAL LTD.*

Anake Rattanajitbanjong
*TILLEKE & GIBBINS
INTERNATIONAL LTD.*

Vunnipa Ruamrangsri
PRICEWATERHOUSECOOPERS

Thavorn Rujivanarom
PRICEWATERHOUSECOOPERS

Sawat Sangkavisit
*ALLENS ARTHUR ROBINSON /
SIAM PREMIER INTERNATIONAL
LAW OFFICE LIMITED*

Somchai Sathiramongkolkul
PRICEWATERHOUSECOOPERS

Jeffrey Sok
*ALLENS ARTHUR ROBINSON /
SIAM PREMIER INTERNATIONAL
LAW OFFICE LIMITED*

Kowit Somwaiya
LAWPLUS LTD.

Pornchai Srisawang
*TILLEKE & GIBBINS
INTERNATIONAL LTD.*

Picharn Sukparangsee
SIAM CITY LAW OFFICES LTD.

Siripong Supakijjanusorn
PRICEWATERHOUSECOOPERS

Hunt Talmage
CHANDLER & THONG-EK

Pattara Vasinwatanapong
VICKERY & WORACHAI LTD.

Harold K. Vickery Jr.
VICKERY & WORACHAI LTD.

Patcharaporn Vinitnuntarat
SIAM CITY LAW OFFICES LTD.

Pimvimol Vipamaneerut
*TILLEKE & GIBBINS
INTERNATIONAL LTD.*

Nopporn Vongsrivong
PricewaterhouseCoopers

Kamol Watcharamanee
PricewaterhouseCoopers

Auradee Wongsaroj
Chandler & Thong-ek

TIMOR-LESTE

Jose Pedro Camoes
Asosiasaun Advogado

David Dyer
DAI

Jofino Ronuel Fernandes Reci
Credit Registry Information System BPA

Renato Guerra de Almeida
Miranda Correia Amendoeira & Associados Timor-Leste Dili

Eusebio Guterres
UNIDO Business Regulatory consultant

Alzira Lay
SDV Logistics Ltd.

Aderito LCA de Araujo
Archtimor Engineering Consultant

Rafael Ribeiro
SDV Logistics Ltd.

Tjia Soh Siang
Tjia & Tchai Associates

TOGO

Diaby Aboubakar
BCEAO

Jean-Marie Adenka
Cabinet Adenka

Kokou Gadémon Agbessi
Cabinet Lucratif

Kafoui Agboyibor
Cabinet Me Yawovi Agboyibor

Martial Akakpo
SCP Martial Akakpo

Adzewoda Ametsiagbe
Direction Générale de l'Urbanisme et de l'Habitat

Coffi Alexis Aquereburu
Aquereburu and Partners Cabinet d'Avocats

Cecile Assogbavi
Etude Notariale

Sylvanus Dodzi Awutey
Cabinet Lucratif

Romain Dansou
Agence EPAUC nouvelle

Foli Doe-Bruce
A.U.D.E.P. International

Compagnie Energie Electrique du Togo (La CEET)

Koffi Joseph Dogbevi
Cabinet Lucratif

Akouvi Thèrese Donu
SCP Martial Akakpo

Messan Raphael Ekoue Hagbonon
Centre d'etudes d'architecture et d'urbanisme

Sonhaye Gbati
Fondation Heinrich Klose

Komlan Cyrille Houssin
SCP Martial Akakpo

Kodjo John Kokou
Cabinet d'Avocats John Kokou

Atchroe Leonard Johnson
SCP Aquereburu & Partners

Akpénè Amito Kpégba
SCP Martial Akakpo

Comlan Eli-Eli N'soukpoé
SCP Martial Akakpo

Theophile Komla Nyaku
Autorite de Reglemengtation du Secteur de L'Electricite

Olivier Pedanou
Cabinet Lucratif

Hauvy Séka Mathieu
FIDAFRICA / PricewaterhouseCoopers

Galolo Soedjede
Cabinet Ledoux Seina

Dominique Taty
FIDAFRICA / PricewaterhouseCoopers

Inès Mazalo Tekpa
Cabinet Lucreatif

Emmanuel Yehouessi
BCEAO

Edem Amétéfé Zotchi
SCP Martial Akakpo

TONGA

Inoke Afu
Dateline Transam Shipping

Christopher Andrew Hartwell
IFC Tonga

Ashleigh Matheson
Westpac Bank of Tonga

Tapu Panuve
Electricity Commission

Sipiloni Raas
Jaimi Associates - Architects

Dana Stephenson
Law Office

Fine Tohi
Dateline Transam Shipping

Jone Vuli
Westpac Bank of Tonga

TRINIDAD AND TOBAGO

Israiell Ali
Trinidad & Tobago Electricity Commission

Nigel Bobb
Trinidad & Tobago Electricity Commission

Stephanie Bonaparte-Primus
S. I. Primus & Sons Ltd.

Tiffanny Castillo
M. Hamel-Smith & Co., member of Lex Mundi

Colvin Chen
Gillespiie & Steel Ltd.

Terry Curtis
TransUnion

Stacy Lee Daniell
M. Hamel-Smith & Co., member of Lex Mundi

Gerard Emmanuel-Rodriguez
Regulated Industries Commission

Nadia Henriques
M. Hamel-Smith & Co., member of Lex Mundi

Peter Inglefield
PricewaterhouseCoopers

Terence Inniss
Lex Caribbean

Rehanna La Borde
PricewaterhouseCoopers

Colin Laird
Colin Laird Associates

Marcia Leonard
The Fast Freight Group

Keomi Lourenco
M. Hamel-Smith & Co., member of Lex Mundi

Wendell Mayers
Trinidad & Tobago Electricity Commission

Marjorie Nunez
Lex Caribbean

Gregory Pantin
Hamel-Smith & Co.

John Phillip
Government Electrical Inspectorate

Fanta Punch
M. Hamel-Smith & Co., member of Lex Mundi

Kelvin Ramsook
Trinidad & Tobago Electricity Commission

Myrna Robinson-Walters
M. Hamel-Smith & Co., member of Lex Mundi

Stephen A. Singh
Johnson, Camacho & Singh

Jonathan Walker
M. Hamel-Smith & Co., member of Lex Mundi

Allyson West
PricewaterhouseCoopers

Grantley Wiltshire
M. Hamel-Smith & Co., member of Lex Mundi

TUNISIA

Abdelmonêm Achour
Cabinet Achour

Mohamed Moncef Barouni
ACR

Adly Bellagha
Adly Bellagha & Associates

Hend Ben Achour
Adly Bellagha & Associates

Olfa Ben Aicha-Saidi
PricewaterhouseCoopers Legal Services

Othman Ben Arfa
Société Tunisienne de l'Elecricité et du Gaz (STEG)

Ismail Ben Farhat
Adly Bellagha & Associates

Wassim Ben Mahmoud
Architect

Miriam Ben Rejeb
PricewaterhouseCoopers Legal Services

Abdelfetah Benahji
Ferchiou & Associés

Manel Bondi
PricewaterhouseCoopers

Elyes Chafter
Chafter Raouadi Law Firm

Zine el Abidine Chafter
Chafter Raouadi Law Firm

Kmar Chaïbi
Banque Centrale de Tunisie

Faouzi Cheikh
Banque Centrale de Tunisie

Abdelmalek Dahmani
Dahmani Transit International

Mohamed Derbel
BDO Tunisie

Mohamed Lotfi El Ajeri
Avocat a la Cour et mediateur agree par le B.B.MC

Yassine El Hafi
Adly Bellagha & Associates

Abderrahmen Fendri
PricewaterhouseCoopers

Yessine Ferah
F & A Law Firm

Amel Ferchichi
Gide Loyrette Nouel, member of Lex Mundi

Noureddine Ferchiou
Ferchiou & Associés

Slim Gargouri
CPA

Anis Jabnoun
Gide Loyrette Nouel, member of Lex Mundi

Badis Jedidi
Gide Loyrette Nouel, member of Lex Mundi

Sami Kallel
Kallel & Associates

Amina Larbi
Gide Loyrette Nouel, member of Lex Mundi

Mabrouk Maalaoui
PricewaterhouseCoopers

Dina Magroun
Avocat a la Cour et mediateur agree par le B.B.MC

Mohamed Ali Masmoudi
PricewaterhouseCoopers Legal Services

Sarah Mebazaa
Comete Engineering

Radhi Meddeb
Comete Engineering

Faouzi Mili
Mili and Associates

Ben Afia Mohamed Salah
Orga Audit, member of Russell Bedford International

Mohamed Taieb Mrabet
Banque Centrale de Tunisie

Imen Nouira
Conservation Foncière Tunisia

Habiba Raouadi
Chafter Raouadi Law Firm

Rachid Tmar
PricewaterhouseCoopers Legal Services

TURKEY

İhsan Akar
Ernst & Young

Emre Akarkarasu
PricewaterhouseCoopers

Cansu Akgün
SDEO Attorneys at Law

Sami Aksoy
Tiryakioglu & Partners

Seza Ceren Aktaş
PricewaterhouseCoopers

Kenan Alpdündar
Central Bank of the Republic of Turkey

Mustafa Alper
YASED - International Investors Association

Arda Alposkay
Devres Law office

Melsa Ararat
Corporate Governance Forum of Turkey, Sabanci University

Ozgur Asik
INLAWCO Law Firm

Melis Atasagun
Pekin & Bayar Law Firm

Ugur Ates
Serap Zuvin Law Offices

Erdem Atilla
Pekin & Pekin

Derya Baksı Pekyalçın
Tarlan & Pekyalçın Law Office

Gokce Balcioglu
Özel & Özel Attorneys At Law

Tuba Baltacı
ADMD Law Firm

Hatice Bas
INLAWCO Law Firm

Binnaz Basaran
Abu-Ghazaleh Intellectual Property

Arzu Basmaci
Mehmet Gün & Partners

Ayça Bayburan
ADMD Law Firm

Pelin Baysal
Mehmet Gün & Partners

Yildirim Bozbiyik
Ministry of Finance

Burcu Çakalli
KPMG

Erdal Calikoglu
Ernst & Young

Esin Çamlıbel
Turunç Law Office

Mustafa Çamlica
Ernst & Young

Maria Lianides Çelebi
Bener Law Office, member of Ius Laboris

M. Fadlullah Cerrahoğlu
CERRAHOĞLU LAW FIRM

Fikret Çetinkaya
KPMG

Orçun Çetinkaya
MEHMET GÜN & PARTNERS

Dilek Çolakel
PRICEWATERHOUSECOOPERS

Niyazi Çömez
DELOITTE

Yavuz Dayıoğlu
PRICEWATERHOUSECOOPERS

Maria de la Colina
*PRICEWATERHOUSECOOPERS
LEGAL SERVICES*

Rüçhan Derici
3E DANIŞMANLIK LTD. ŞTI.

Kazim Derman
KREDIT KAYIT BUREAU

Emine Devres
DEVRES LAW OFFICE

Ebru Dicle
*TURKISH INDUSTRIALISTS' AND
BUSINESSMEN'S ASSOCIATION
(TUSIAD)*

Başak Diclehan
KPMG

Murat Volkan Dülger
DÜLGER LAW FIRM

Çisil Durgun
CERRAHOĞLU LAW FIRM

Cemal Dursun
SDEO ATTORNEYS AT LAW

Murat Emirhanoğlu
KPMG

Sedat Eratalar
DELOITTE

Gökben Erdem Dirican
PEKIN & PEKIN

Sadik Ferik
ERNST & YOUNG

Umurcan Gago
PRICEWATERHOUSECOOPERS

Zeynephan Gemicioğlu
CERRAHOĞLU LAW FIRM

Arman Gezer
DELOITTE

Caglar Gezer
PRICEWATERHOUSECOOPERS

Osman Nuri Gönenç
*CENTRAL BANK OF THE
REPUBLIC OF TURKEY*

Sait Gözüm
DELOITTE

Sezin Güner
PEKIN & PEKIN

A. Feridun Güngör
ERNST & YOUNG

Ahmet Güran
TURUNÇ LAW OFFICE

Ayşegül Gürsoy
CERRAHOĞLU LAW FIRM

Riza Gumbusoglu
MEHMET GÜN & PARTNERS

Salih Zeki Hakli
TOBB

Aydin Bugra Ilter
*TANRIOVER ATTORNEYS AT
LAW*

Gül Incesulu
ÇAKMAK AVUKATLIK BÜROSU

Şebnem Işık
MEHMET GÜN & PARTNERS

Özlem Kizil
ÇAKMAK AVUKATLIK BÜROSU

Melis Saliha Kiziltay
ADMD LAW FIRM

Ozgur Kahraman
ERNST & YOUNG

Ibrahim Kara
KREDIT KAYIT BUREAU

Ali Ozan Karaduman
MEHMET GÜN & PARTNERS

Aslan Kaya
*DMF SYSTEM INTERNATIONAL
INDEPENDENT AUDITING,
CONSULTING & CERTIFIED
PUBLIC ACCOUNTING CO.,
MEMBER OF RUSSELL BEDFORD
INTERNATIONAL*

Gözde Kayacik
PEKIN & BAYAR LAW FIRM

Betül Kencebay
*YASED - INTERNATIONAL
INVESTORS ASSOCIATION*

Burak Kepkep
*AKDOGAN USLAS ATTORNEYS
AT LAW*

Çiğdem Koğar
*CENTRAL BANK OF THE
REPUBLIC OF TURKEY*

Tuncay Köroglu
CERRAHOĞLU LAW FIRM

Nergis Kundakçioğlu
CERRAHOĞLU LAW FIRM

Zeki Kurtçu
DELOITTE

Orhan Yavuz Mavioğlu
ADMD LAW FIRM

Didem Meray
SERAP ZUVIN LAW OFFICES

Banu Mert
CERRAHOĞLU LAW FIRM

Sila Muratoğlu
*BAYIRLI & MURATOĞLU LAW
FIRM*

Diğdem Muslu
BAŞARAN NAS YMM A.S.

Lerzan Nalbantoğlu
TURUNÇ LAW OFFICE

Adnan Nas
PRICEWATERHOUSECOOPERS

Şebnem Önder
ÇAKMAK AVUKATLIK BÜROSU

Mert Oner
KPMG

Hakan Orhan
ERNST & YOUNG

Çağlayan Orhaner Dündar
ORHANER LAW OFFICE

Zeynephan Oğuz
CERRAHOĞLU LAW FIRM

Özlem Ouzlar
TURUNÇ LAW OFFICE

Fatih Özşahin
DELOITTE

Ayse Ozcan
*ACACIA INTERNATIONAL
LAWYERS*

Dursun Ozcan
ERNST & YOUNG

Selin Ozdamar
*ÖZEL & ÖZEL ATTORNEYS
AT LAW*

Caner Özen
*ÖZEL & ÖZEL ATTORNEYS
AT LAW*

Mert Özerden
ADMD LAW FIRM

Saziye Saadet Ozfirat
SDEO ATTORNEYS AT LAW

Ekin Kavukçuoğlu Özgülsen
DELOITTE

Pinar Ozhan
TIRYAKIOGLU & PARTNERS

Tuba Özsezen
*YASED - INTERNATIONAL
INVESTORS ASSOCIATION*

Neva Ozturk
ANKARA UNIVERSITY

Yasemin Pamuk
*ACACIA INTERNATIONAL
LAWYERS*

Serkan Pamukkale
BIRSEL LAW OFFICES

Ahmed Pekin
PEKIN & PEKIN

Ferhat Pekin
PEKIN & BAYAR LAW FIRM

Suzet Rodikli
PRICEWATERHOUSECOOPERS

Çağıl Şahin Biber
PRICEWATERHOUSECOOPERS

Batuhan Şahmay
*BENER LAW OFFICE, MEMBER
OF IUS LABORIS*

Bilge Saltan
DÜLGER LAW FIRM

Hasan Sariçiçek
KPMG

Sinan Sariaslan
*DMF SYSTEM INTERNATIONAL
INDEPENDENT AUDITING,
CONSULTING & CERTIFIED
PUBLIC ACCOUNTING CO.,
MEMBER OF RUSSELL BEDFORD
INTERNATIONAL*

Duygu Şeftalici
CERRAHOĞLU LAW FIRM

Ömer Kayhan Seyhun
*CENTRAL BANK OF THE
REPUBLIC OF TURKEY*

Burcu Sezgin
INLAWCO LAW FIRM

Defne Zeynep Sirakaya
CERRAHOĞLU LAW FIRM

M. Ufuk Söğütlüoğlu
DELOITTE

Esin Taboglu
*CORPORATE GOVERNANCE
FORUM OF TURKEY, SABANCI
UNIVERSITY*

Aylin Tarlan Tüzemen
*TARLAN & PEKYALÇIN LAW
OFFICE*

Baris Teksoy
TIRYAKIOGLU & PARTNERS

Muge Temel
*ÖZEL & ÖZEL ATTORNEYS
AT LAW*

Elif Tezcan Bayirli
*BAYIRLI & MURATOĞLU LAW
FIRM*

Bilgin Tiryakioglu
TIRYAKIOGLU & PARTNERS

Güzel Toker
PRICEWATERHOUSECOOPERS

Berna Toksoy
*TURKISH INDUSTRIALISTS' AND
BUSINESSMEN'S ASSOCIATION
(TUSIAD)*

Noyan Turunç
TURUNÇ LAW OFFICE

Ibrahim Tutar
*PENETRA CONSULTING AND
AUDITING*

Ebru Tuygun
DELOITTE

N.Kerem Üler
*ÖZEL & ÖZEL ATTORNEYS
AT LAW*

Hilal Ünal
GOKSER MACHINE LTD.

Yegan Üreyen
MEHMET GÜN & PARTNERS

Serdar Unver
*ACACIA INTERNATIONAL
LAWYERS*

Hülya Yılmaz
DELOITTE

H.Barış Yalçın
PRICEWATERHOUSECOOPERS

Selcen Yalçın
MEHMET GÜN & PARTNERS

Ayşegül Yalçınmani Merler
CERRAHOĞLU LAW FIRM

Begüm Yavuzdoğan
MEHMET GÜN & PARTNERS

Beril Yayla
MEHMET GÜN & PARTNERS

Hande Yemisci
LAW

Aylin Yontar
CERRAHOĞLU LAW FIRM

Filiz Yüksel
CERRAHOĞLU LAW FIRM

Murat Yülek
*PGLOBAL GLOBAL ADVISORY
AND TRAINING SERVICES LTD.*

Serap Zuvin
SERAP ZUVIN LAW OFFICES

UGANDA

Bernard Baingana
PRICEWATERHOUSECOOPERS

Michael Balimukuubo
MMAKS ADVOCATES

Bernard Bamwine
*KWESIGABO, BAMWINE &
WALUBIRI ADVOCATES*

Nicholas Ecimu
*SEBALU & LULE ADVOCATES
AND LEGAL CONSULTANTS*

Matovu Emmy
MARMA TECHNICAL SERVICES

Sarfaraz Jiwani
SEYANI BROS. & CO.

Charles Kalu Kalumiya
*KAMPALA ASSOCIATED
ADVOCATES*

Oscar Kambona
*KAMPALA ASSOCIATED
ADVOCATES*

Francis Kamulegeya
PRICEWATERHOUSECOOPERS

Didymus Byenkya Kato
*ATACO FREIGHT SERVICES
LTD.*

Peter Kauma
*KIWANUKA & KARUGIRE
ADVOCATES*

Andrew Kibaya
*SHONUBI, MUSOKE & CO.
ADVOCATES*

Muzamiru Kibeedi
KIBEEDI & CO.

Paul Kibuuka
KIBUUKA CONSULTING GROUP

Robert Kiggundu
ARCH FORUM LTD.

Geoffrey Kiryabwire
*COMMERCIAL DIVISION, HIGH
COURT OF UGANDA*

Kiryowa Kiwanuka
*KIWANUKA & KARUGIRE
ADVOCATES*

Robert Komakec
ARCH FORUM LTD.

Kitugwanidde Krespo
MARMA TECHNICAL SERVICES

James Kyazze
*SHONUBI, MUSOKE & CO.
ADVOCATES*

Timothy Kyepa
*SHONUBI, MUSOKE & CO.
ADVOCATES*

Hakim Lugemwa
*UGANDA ENTREPRENEURS
BUSINESS FOUNDATION*

Joseph Luswata
*SEBALU & LULE ADVOCATES
AND LEGAL CONSULTANTS*

Robinah Lutaaya
PRICEWATERHOUSECOOPERS

Michael Malan
COMPUSCAN CRB LTD.

Cornelius Mukiibi
*C.MUKIIBI.SENTAMU & CO.
ADVOCATES*

Andrew Munanura Kamuteera
*SEBALU & LULE ADVOCATES
AND LEGAL CONSULTANTS*

Peters Musoke
*SHONUBI, MUSOKE & CO.
ADVOCATES*

Rachel Mwanje Musoke
MMAKS ADVOCATES

Noah Mwesigwa
*SHONUBI, MUSOKE & CO.
ADVOCATES*

Diana Ninsiima
MMAKS ADVOCATES

Eddie Nsamba-Gayiya
*CONSULTANT SURVEYORS AND
PLANNERS*

Julius Ojok
*SEBALU & LULE ADVOCATES
AND LEGAL CONSULTANTS*

Godwin Othieno
KAMPALA CITY COUNCIL

Alex Rezida
*NANGWALA, REZIDA & CO.
ADVOCATES*

Harriet Wandira Rumanyika
SDV Transami (U) Ltd.

Ruth Sebatindira
Ligomarc Advocates

Monica Kisubi Senjako
SDV Transami (U) Ltd.

Alan Shonubi
*Shonubi, Musoke & Co.
Advocates*

Manish Siyani
*Seyani Brothers & Co. (U)
Ltd.*

Isaac Walukagga
MMAKS Advocates

Godfrey Zziwa
*Muwanguzi, Zziwa & Musisi
Advocates*

UKRAINE

Oleg Y. Alyoshin
Vasil Kisil & Partners

Andrey Astapov
*Astapov Lawyers
International Law Group*

Roman Badalis
BNT & partners

Ron J. Barden
PricewaterhouseCoopers

Olena Basanska
*CMS Cameron McKenna
Ukraine*

Anastasiya Bolkhovitinova
DLA Piper Ukraine LLC

Timur Bondaryev
*Arzinger & Partners
International Law Firm*

Alexander Borisov
*Grant Thornton Ukraine
Kiev*

Maksym Borodchuk
Chadbourne & Parke LLP

Olena Brodovska
*CMS Cameron McKenna
Ukraine*

Anna Bukvych
Baker & McKenzie

Maryna Bychkova
DLA Piper Ukraine LLC

Serhiy Chorny
Baker & McKenzie

Aleksandr Deputat
Elit Group

Anna Deshko
Damco

Maxim Dikiy
HLB Ukraine

Tetyana Dovgan
Chadbourne & Parke LLP

Michael Eritspokhov
*Panalpina World
Transport Ukraine Kiev*

Anna Gebeleva
LF - INYURPOLIS Law Firm

Sergiy Gryshko
*CMS Cameron McKenna
Ukraine*

Ivanna Honina
Grischenko & Partners

Vitaliy Kazakov
*Grant Thornton Ukraine
Kiev*

Michael Kharenko
Sayenko Kharenko

Oleksii Kharitonov
LF - INYURPOLIS Law Firm

Natalya Kim
Chadbourne & Parke LLP

Andriy Kirmach
Chadbourne & Parke LLP

Arno Klijbroek
*AJK Trade & Investment
Consultancy*

Sergei Konnov
Konnov & Sozanovsky

Maxim Kopeychykov
Ilyashev & Partners

Evgeniy Kornievskiy
Konnov & Sozanovsky

Ivan Korotkov
KPMG

Tatyana Kuzmenko
*Astapov Lawyers
International Law Group*

Tatiana Lizogub
*Panalpina World
Transport Ukraine Kiev*

Borys Lobovyk
Konnov & Sozanovsky

Yulia Logunova
DLA Piper Ukraine LLC

Olga Mikheieva
*CMS Cameron McKenna
Ukraine*

Arsenyy Milyutin
Magisters

Vladyslava V. Motrenko
Vasil Kisil & Partners

Svitlana Musienko
DLA Piper Ukraine LLC

Adam Mycyk
*CMS Cameron McKenna
Ukraine*

Iryna Mykolayenko
IBCH

Yuliya Nogovitsyna
KPMG

Oleksandr Padalka
Asters

Magdalena Patrzyk
PricewaterhouseCoopers

Iryna Pidlisna
Salans Ukraine Kiev

Sava Poliakov
Grischenko & Partners

Vitaliy Pravdyuk
Konnov & Sozanovsky

Maria Prysyazhnyuk
PricewaterhouseCoopers

Dmitry Pyatachenko
IFC

Yuliana Revyuk
KPMG

Oleksandr Rudenko
*Astapov Lawyers
International Law Group*

Vladimir Sayenko
Sayenko Kharenko

Olga Serbul
*Law Firm IP & C. Consult,
LLC*

Mykhailo Shchitka
Vasil Kisil & Partners

Oleg Shevchuk
Proxen & Partners

Hanna Shtepa
Baker & McKenzie

Anzhelika Shtukaturova
Salans Ukraine Kiev

Roman Shulyar
Chadbourne & Parke LLP

Markian B. Silecky
Salans Ukraine Kiev

Anna Sisetska
Vasil Kisil & Partners

Svitlana Teush
*Arzinger & Partners
International Law Firm*

Nataliya Tkachenko
DLA Piper Ukraine LLC

Zakhar Tropin
Proxen & Partners

Oleksandr Vygovskyy
Asters

Zeeshan Wani
*Globalink Transportation
& Logistics Worldwide LLP*

Olexiy Yanov
*Law Firm IP & C. Consult,
LLC*

Yulia Yashenkova
*Astapov Lawyers
International Law Group*

Tatiana Zamorska
KPMG

Marina V. Zarina
Private Notary

Anton Zinchuk
LF - INYURPOLIS Law Firm

UNITED ARAB
EMIRATES

Karim Abaza
*Shalakany Law Office,
member of Lex Mundi*

Moutaz Abddullat
*Talal Abu-Ghazaleh Legal
(TAG-Legal)*

Yakub Ahmed
Orchid Paper Trading

Obaid Saif Atiq Al Falasi
*Dubai Electricity and
Water Authority*

Alya Hussain Al Hammadi
Dubai Trade

Essam Al Tamimi
*Al Tamimi & Company
Advocates & Legal
Consultants*

Mahmood Albastaki
Dubai Trade

Saeed Al-Hamiz
Central Bank of the UAE

Wicki Andersen
Baker Botts LLP

Wicki Andersen
Baker Botts LLP

T Sureh Babu
Landmark group

Piyush Bhandari
*Proteam Consulting
Private Limited*

Prakash Bhanushali
*Alsahm Al Saree Transport
& Clearing*

Hiten Bhatia
*Silver Line Shipping &
Clearing*

Jennifer Bibbings
Trowers & Hamlins

Mazen Boustany
Habib Al Mulla & Co.

R Chandran
Sea Bridge Shipping Co. LLC

Lisa Dale
*Al Tamimi & Company
Advocates & Legal
Consultants*

Indira Deepa
PricewaterhouseCoopers

Mohammad A. El-Ghul
Habib Al Mulla & Co.

Gorashi Elsheikh
Dubai Municipality

Anthea Fernandes
*Shalakany Law Office,
member of Lex Mundi*

Laëtitia Fernandes
*Helene Mathieu Legal
Consultants*

Laetitia Fernandez
*Helene Mathieu Legal
Consultants*

Rohit Ghai
Al Jabha Group

Mona Hammadi
Baker Botts LLP

Samer Hamzeh
Trowers & Hamlins

Omar Hegazy
*Shalakany Law Office,
member of Lex Mundi*

Sydene Helwick
*Al Tamimi & Company
Advocates & Legal
Consultants*

Ashiq Hussain
Dubai Trade

Zaid Kamhawi
Emcredit

Salim Ahmed Khan
Dubai Trade

Shahid M. Khan
*Busit Al Roken &
Associates*

Vipul Kothari
*Kothari Auditors &
Accountants*

B.S. Krishna Moorthy
Landmark group

Ravi Kumar
Dubai Trade

Senthil Kumar
GLG Shipping

Charles S. Laubach
*Afridi & Angell, member of
Lex Mundi*

Gagan Malhotra
Dubai Trade

Helene Mathieu
*Helene Mathieu Legal
Consultants*

Ravi Nandi
BASF Chemicals

Yasser Omar
*Shalakany Law Office,
member of Lex Mundi*

Vijendra Vikram Singh Paul
*Talal Abu-Ghazaleh Legal
(TAG-Legal)*

V. Prakash
Al Tajir Glass Industries

Yusuf Rafiudeen
*Dubai Electricity and
Water Authority*

Dorai Raj
Goldline Worldwide Inc.

Dean Rolfe
PricewaterhouseCoopers

Shoeb Saher
Habib Al Mulla & Co.

Khalid Mohamed Saleh
Dubai Municipality

Mohammed Ahmed Saleh
Dubai Municipality

Herbert Schroder
Emcredit

M. Vivekanand Shetty
Eros Group

Surendar Singh
IAL Logistics Emirates LLC

Arvind Sinha
Business Advisors Group

Sreekumar Sivasankaran
*Globelink West Star
Shipping L.L.C.*

Douglas Smith
Habib Al Mulla & Co.

Rachel Storr
*Gates Engineering &
Services*

Mohammed Thani
Dubai Land Department

Raju V. Varghese
Al Yousuf L.L.C

Robyn Waller
Trowers & Hamlins

Gary Watts
*Al Tamimi & Company
Advocates & Legal
Consultants*

Rania Yousseph
Habib Al Mulla & Co.

Natasha Zahid
Baker Botts LLP

UNITED KINGDOM

Allen & Overy LLP

Varsha Aithala
Simmons & Simmons

Tim Andrews
Stephenson Harwood

Kwame Asamoah
Macintyre Hudson LLP

Jon Atkey
*Her Majesty's Land
Registry*

Graham Bartlett
SITPRO Ltd.

Nick Benwell
Simmons & Simmons

Jim Bligh
*CBI - The Confederation of
British Industry*

Georgie Blyth
*PricewaterhouseCoopers
Legal Services*

Katy Byatt
Weil, Gotshal & Manges LLP

Joy Chen
Simmons & Simmons

Stephanie Chiu
Simmons & Simmons

Mark Corby
Jabil Global Services

Vera Dantas Innes
Noronha Advogados

Paul de Bernier
Mayer Brown LLP

Ben Digby
CBI - The Confederation of British Industry

Darryl Evans
PricewaterhouseCoopers Legal Services

Nick Francis
PricewaterhouseCoopers

Paul Gilbert

Ursula Goniszewska
Simmons & Simmons

Helen Hall
DLA Piper UK LLP

Jonathan Harries
PricewaterhouseCoopers Legal Services

Katie Harrison
Simmons & Simmons

Lynn Hiestand
Skadden, Arps, Slate, Meagher & Flom LLP

Neville Howlett
PricewaterhouseCoopers

Stephen Hubner
Shepherd & Wedderburn

Simon Jay
Cleary Gottlieb Steen & Hamilton LLP

Emily Jee
DLA Piper UK LLP

Magnus Jones
Cleary Gottlieb Steen & Hamilton LLP

Esther Kelly
Cleary Gottlieb Steen & Hamilton LLP

Gillian Key-Vice
Experian Ltd.

Shahriar Khan
Crown Agents

Susan Knowles
Her Majesty's Land Registry

Jessica Lloyd
PricewaterhouseCoopers

Mushtak Macci
Lubbock Fine, member of Russell Bedford International

James Macdonald
Noronha Advogados

Christopher Mallon
Skadden, Arps, Slate, Meagher & Flom LLP

Andrew Maple
Approved Inspector Services Limited

Barry Marshall
PricewaterhouseCoopers

Charles Mayo
Simmons & Simmons

Hannah Morley
Simmons & Simmons

Roya Motalleb-Zadeh
Cleary Gottlieb Steen & Hamilton LLP

Alison Murrin
Ashurst

Annemarie Payne
Mayer Brown LLP

David Pickstone
PricewaterhouseCoopers Legal Services

Steve Pocock
Crown Agents

Alex Rogan
Skadden, Arps, Slate, Meagher & Flom LLP

Andrew Shutter
Cleary Gottlieb Steen & Hamilton LLP

Caroline Stakim
Shepherd & Wedderburn

Sharmin Takin
Cleary Gottlieb Steen & Hamilton LLP

Lance Terry
Glanvilles Solicitors

Paul Timmins
Approved Inspector Services Limited

Mark Waddington
Crown Agents

Nicola Walker
CBI - The Confederation of British Industry

Carmel Weitzmann
PricewaterhouseCoopers Legal Services

Geoffrey Wilkinson
MLM Building Control

Sally Willcock
Weil, Gotshal & Manges LLP

Andrew Wilson
Andrew Wilson & Co

Dermot Winters
Freeth Cartwright LLP

UNITED STATES

Stephen Anderson
PricewaterhouseCoopers

Pamy Arora
Cornell Group, Inc

Luke A. Barefoot
Cleary Gottlieb Steen & Hamilton LLP

Eli Best
Cleary Gottlieb Steen & Hamilton LLP

Courtney Brown
Cleary Gottlieb Steen & Hamilton LLP

Victor Chiu
Cleary Gottlieb Steen & Hamilton LLP

Richard Conza, Esq.
Cleary Gottlieb Steen & Hamilton LLP

Margaret Cowan
Cleary Gottlieb Steen & Hamilton LLP

James Denn
New York State Public Service Commission

Joshua L. Ditelberg
Seyfarth Shaw LLP

Lindsay Dunn
Cleary Gottlieb Steen & Hamilton LLP

Patrick Fuller Fuller, Esq.
Cleary Gottlieb Steen & Hamilton LLP

Benjamin E. Gehrt
Seyfarth Shaw LLP

Boris Grosman
L & B electrical international

Sonya H.S. Lee
Cleary Gottlieb Steen & Hamilton LLP

Adam Heintz
Morrison and Foerster

Steven Horowitz
Cleary Gottlieb Steen & Hamilton LLP

James Hough
Morrison and Foerster

Neil Jacobs
NI Jacobs & Associates

Charles L. Kerr
Morrison and Foerster

Joshua Kochath
Forwarding Unlimited Inc.

Arthur Kohn
Cleary Gottlieb Steen & Hamilton LLP

Walter Krauklis
Jarvis International Freight, Inc

Michael Lazerwitz, Esq.
Cleary Gottlieb Steen & Hamilton LLP

Jay Lee
Cleary Gottlieb Steen & Hamilton LLP

Bradford L. Livingston
Seyfarth Shaw LLP

Tom McNamara
Davis Graham & Stubbs LLP

Howard Miller
Girardi Keese

Randy Moes
Office of Secretary State of Texas

Robert Morris
PricewaterhouseCoopers

Kelly J. Murray
PricewaterhouseCoopers

David Newberg
Collier, Halpern, Newberg, Nolletti, & Bock

Samuel Nolen
Richards, Layton & Finger, P.A., member of Lex Mundi

Sean O'Neal
Cleary Gottlieb Steen & Hamilton LLP

Jeffrey Penn
Cleary Gottlieb Steen & Hamilton LLP

Igor Putilov
Link Lines Logistics Inc

Stephen Raslavich
United States Bankruptcy Court

Rolando Rocha
Global Link Network

Sandra Rocks
Cleary Gottlieb Steen & Hamilton LLP

Barbara Roth
Hogan & Hartson LLP

David Snyder
Snyder & Snyder, LLP

Frederick Turner
Snyder & Snyder, LLP

David Wilson
Holme Robert & Owen

Clemens Ziegler
Cleary Gottlieb Steen & Hamilton LLP

URUGUAY

Juan Achugar
Banco Central del Uruguay

Martin S. Acosta
Galante & Martins

Eduardo Ameglio
Guyer & Regules, member of Lex Mundi

Fernando Bado
Estudio Dr. Mezzera

Alicia Barral
PricewaterhouseCoopers

Carlos Brandes
Guyer & Regules, member of Lex Mundi

Virginia Brause
Jiménez de Aréchaga, Viana & Brause

Luz Calvo de Gross
Calvo-Lopardo-Prats & Asociados

Martín Colombo
Ferrere Internacional

Nicolas Constantinidi
Jiménez de Aréchaga, Viana & Brause

Leonardo Couto
Jose Maria Facal & Co.

Jorge De Vita
Jorge de Vita Studio

Javier Dominguez
Guyer & Regules, member of Lex Mundi

María Durán
Hughes & Hughes

Noelia Eiras
Hughes & Hughes

Gabriel Ejgenberg
Estudio Bergstein

Agustín Etcheverry Reyes
Estudio Blanco & Etcheverry

Agustina Fernández Giambruno
Fernandez Secco & Asociados

Javier Fernández Zerbino
Bado, Kuster, Zerbino & Rachetti

Juan Federico Fischer
Fischer & Schickendantz

Federico Florin
Guyer & Regules, member of Lex Mundi

Federico Formento
Fischer & Schickendantz

Sergio Franco
PricewaterhouseCoopers

Diego Galante
Galante & Martins

Pablo Galmarini
Galmarini

Enrique Garcia Pini
Administración Nacional de Usinas y Transmisión Eléctrica (UTE)

Andres Hessdorfer Rozen
Olivera & Delpiazzo

Ariel Imken
Superintendencia de Instituciones de Intermediación Financiera - Banco Central del Uruguay

Alfredo Inciarte Blanco
Estudio Pérez del Castillo, Inciarte, Gari Abogados

Cecilia Larrosa
Guyer & Regules, member of Lex Mundi

Ricardo Mezzera
Estudio Dr. Mezzera

Matilde Milicevic Santana
Equifax - Clearing de Informes

Alejandro Miller Artola
Guyer & Regules, member of Lex Mundi

Pablo Moyal
Stavros Moyal y Asociados, member of Russell Bedford International

Alfredo H. Navarro
Navarro Abogados

Juan Martín Olivera
Olivera & Delpiazzo

María Concepción Olivera
Olivera & Delpiazzo

Ricardo Olivera-García
Olivera & Delpiazzo

María Cecilia Orlando
Guyer & Regules, member of Lex Mundi

Juan Orticochea
Guyer & Regules, member of Lex Mundi

Ismael Pignatta Sánchez
Guyer & Regules, member of Lex Mundi

María José Poey
Guyer & Regules, member of Lex Mundi

Nathalie Polak
Guyer & Regules, member of Lex Mundi

Carlos Rodríguez Capurro
Estudio Blanco & Etcheverry

Fabian Roizen
Guyer & Regules, member of Lex Mundi

Lucia Salaverry
Fernandez Secco & Asociados

Eliana Sartori
PRICEWATERHOUSECOOPERS

Enrique Schickendantz
FISCHER & SCHICKENDANTZ

Leonardo Slinger
GUYER & REGULES, MEMBER OF LEX MUNDI

Alvaro Tarabal
GUYER & REGULES, MEMBER OF LEX MUNDI

Ana Inés Terra
ESTUDIO BERGSTEIN

Augusto Tricotti
ERT

Juan Ignacio Troccoli
FISCHER & SCHICKENDANTZ

Horacio Viana
JIMENEZ DE ARÉCHAGA VIANA & BRAUSE

Gerardo Viñoles
VIÑOLES ARQUITECT STUDIO

Mónica Vitovich
STAVROS MOYAL Y ASOCIADOS, MEMBER OF RUSSELL BEDFORD INTERNATIONAL

UZBEKISTAN

Askar K. Abdusagatov
OOO "PROGRESS-DEVELOPMENT"

Ravshan Adilov
DENTON WILDE SAPTE & CO

Mels Akhmedov
BAS

Natalya Apukhtina
DENTON WILDE SAPTE & CO

Umid Aripdjanov
GRATA LAW FIRM

Sevil Bekirova
GLOBALINK LOGISTICS GROUP

Khalid Farooq
GLOBALINK LOGISTICS GROUP

Irina Gosteva
DENTON WILDE SAPTE & CO

Larissa Grigoryevna
TASHKENT COMMERCIAL COURT

Nodir B. Hakimov
EUROPEAN ELITE CONSTRUCTION

Nail Hassanov
LAW FIRM LEGES ADVOKAT

Mouborak Kambarova
DENTON WILDE SAPTE & CO

Pasha Karim
GLOBALINK LOGISTICS GROUP

Alisher T. Kasimov
EUROPEAN ELITE CONSTRUCTION

Nurali Eshibaevich Khalmuratov
NATIONAL INSTITUTE OF CREDIT INFORMATION OF CENTRAL BANK OF THE REPUBLIC OF UZBEKISTAN

Olga Kim
GRATA LAW FIRM

Marina Kondratova
MARIKON AUDIT LLC, MEMBER OF RUSSELL BEDFORD INTERNATIONAL

Laziza Rakhimova
GRATA LAW FIRM

Mouzaffar Salomov
BANKLARARO KREDIT BYUROSI

Valeria Samborskaya
NATIONAL CENTRE OF GEODESY & CARTOGRAPHY

Alexander Samborsky
NATIONAL CENTRE OF GEODESY & CARTOGRAPHY

Nizomiddin Shakhabutdinov
LAW FIRM LEGES ADVOKAT

Sofia Shakhrazieva
GRATA LAW FIRM

Alisher Shaykhov
CHAMBER OF COMMERCE AND INDUSTRY OF UZBEKISTAN

Judge Tadjiev
TASHKENT COMMERCIAL COURT

Petros Tsakanyan
AZIZOV & PARTNERS

Laziza Walter
GRATA LAW FIRM

Nodir Yuldashev
GRATA LAW FIRM

VANUATU

Christopher Dawson
DAWSON BUILDERS

Paul de Montgolfier
CABINET AJC

David Hudson
HUDSON & SUGDEN

Chris Kernot
FR8 LOGISTICS LTD.

John Malcolm
GEOFFREY GEE & PARTNERS

Jean-Marc Pierre
DEPARTMENT OF LANDS, SURVEYS & RECORDS

Mark Stafford
BARRETT & PARTNERS

VENEZUELA, RB

Jorge Acedo-Prato
HOET PELAEZ CASTILLO & DUQUE

Yanet Aguiar
MACLEOD DIXON

Juan Enrique Aigster
HOET PELAEZ CASTILLO & DUQUE

Servio T. Altuve Jr.
SERVIO T. ALTUVE R. & ASOCIADOS

Andrea Ignacia Alvarado
HOET PELAEZ CASTILLO & DUQUE

Ramon Alvins
MACLEOD DIXON

Carlos Bachrich Nagy
DE SOLA PATE & BROWN, ABOGADOS - CONSULTORES

Edgar Berroteran
HOET PELAEZ CASTILLO & DUQUE

Claudia Bustamante
PRICEWATERHOUSECOOPERS

Sergio Casinelli
MACLEOD DIXON

Diego Castagnino
HOET PELAEZ CASTILLO & DUQUE

Arturo De Sola Lander
DE SOLA PATE & BROWN, ABOGADOS - CONSULTORES

Carlos Domínguez Hernández
HOET PELAEZ CASTILLO & DUQUE

Jose Fereira
RODRIGUEZ & MENDOZA

Francisco Gámez Arcaya
GÁMEZ & VERA ABOGADOS

Antulio Giménez
HOTEL MELIÀ CARACAS

Alejandro Giolito
PRICEWATERHOUSECOOPERS

Diego Gonzalez Crespo
CASAS RINCON GONZALEZ RUBIO & ASOCIADOS

Carlos Gouveia
ARKI ELÉCTRICA CA

Vanessa Hernández
PRICEWATERHOUSECOOPERS

Alfredo Hurtado
HURTADO ESTEBAN & ASOCIADOS, MEMBER OF RUSSELL BEDFORD INTERNATIONAL

Maigualida Ifill
PRICEWATERHOUSECOOPERS

Ana Lugo
HOET PELAEZ CASTILLO & DUQUE

Lorena Mingarelli Lozzi
DE SOLA PATE & BROWN, ABOGADOS - CONSULTORES

Fernando Miranda
PRICEWATERHOUSECOOPERS

John R. Pate
DE SOLA PATE & BROWN, ABOGADOS - CONSULTORES

Thomas J. Pate Páez
DE SOLA PATE & BROWN, ABOGADOS - CONSULTORES

Eduardo Porcarelli
CONAPRI

Juan Carlos Pró-Rísquez
MACLEOD DIXON

Melissa Puga Santaella
CONAPRI

Daniel Rosas
MACLEOD DIXON

Pedro Saghy
MACLEOD DIXON

Anatoliy Sattarov

Laura Silva Aparicio
HOET PELAEZ CASTILLO & DUQUE

John Tucker
HOET PELAEZ CASTILLO & DUQUE

Ricardo Useche
ELECTRIFICACIONES GUAYANA CA

UZBEKENERGO

Carlos Velandia Sanchez
ASOCIACIÓN VENEZOLANA DE DERECHO REGISTRAL "AVEDER"

Anhelisa Villarroel
CONAPRI

Olga Vinogradova
GLOBALINK LOGISTICS GROUP

VIETNAM

Minh Hong Bui
LDV LAWYERS

Giles Thomas Cooper
DUANE MORRIS LLC

Nguyen Dang Viet
BIZCONSULT LAW FIRM

My Linh Dao
BAKER & MCKENZIE

François d'Hautefeuille
GIDE LOYRETTE NOUEL A.A.R.P.I.

Van Dinh Thi Quynh
PRICEWATERHOUSECOOPERS

Ngoan Doan
GRANT THORNTON VIETNAM

Dang The Duc
INDOCHINE COUNSEL

David Fitzgerald
PRICEWATERHOUSECOOPERS

Albert Franceskinj
DS AVOCATS

Giang Ha Thi Phuong
PRICEWATERHOUSECOOPERS

Franz Hepp De Sevelinges
GIDE LOYRETTE NOUEL A.A.R.P.I.

Nguyen Hoang Kim Oanh
BAKER & MCKENZIE

Le Hong Phong
BIZCONSULT LAW FIRM

Kim Ngoan Huynh
GIDE LOYRETTE NOUEL A.A.R.P.I.

Tuong Long Huynh
GIDE LOYRETTE NOUEL A.A.R.P.I.

Anh Tuan Le
CREDIT INFORMATION CENTRE - STATE BANK OF VIETNAM

Phuc Le Hong
LUATVIET - ADVOCATES & SOLICITORS

Thuy Le Nguyen Huy
INDOCHINE COUNSEL

Nguyen Phan Manh Long
HUNG & PARTNERS

Ho Phuong Luan
INDOCHINE COUNSEL

Hoang Ha Luu
LDV LAWYERS

Tien Ngoc Luu
VISION & ASSOCIATES

Hoang Minh Duc
DUANE MORRIS LLC

Duy Minh Ngo
DC LAW

Dao Nguyen
MAYER BROWN LLP

Hai Thao Nguyen
BAKER & MCKENZIE

Linh Chi Nguyen
BAKER & MCKENZIE

Minh Tuan Nguyen
QUANG MINH NAM LAW FIRM LTD.

Van Anh Nguyen
VIETBID LAW FIRM

Tram Nguyen - Huyen
GIDE LOYRETTE NOUEL A.A.R.P.I.

Ronald Parks
GRANT THORNTON VIETNAM

Viet D. Phan
TRAN H.N. & ASSOCIATES

Vu Anh Phan
INDOCHINE COUNSEL

Mai Phan Thi
DUANE MORRIS LLC

Yee Chung Seck
BAKER & MCKENZIE

Dinh The Phuc
ELECTRICITY REGULATORY AUTHORITY OF VIETNAM

Nguyen Thi Thu Hong
GIDE LOYRETTE NOUEL A.A.R.P.I.

Nguyen Thi Thu Huyen
GIDE LOYRETTE NOUEL A.A.R.P.I.

Nhung Thieu Hong
PRICEWATERHOUSECOOPERS

Ngo Quang Thuy
NT TRADE LAW LLC

Tan Heng Thye
CHEN SHAN & PARTNERS

Antoine Toussaint
GIDE LOYRETTE NOUEL A.A.R.P.I.

V.N. Trinh
PANALPINA WORLD TRANSPORT VIETNAM HO CHI MINH CITY

Nguyen Anh Tuan
DP CONSULTING LTD.

Tuyêt Hanh VM Thi
CHEN SHAN & PARTNERS

Nguyen Thu Thuy Vo
SDV LOGISTICS LTD.

Dzung Vu
YKVN LAWYERS

Andrea Wilson
DFDL MEKONG LAW GROUP

WEST BANK AND GAZA

Hani Sobhi Abd Jildeh
JERUSALEM DISTRICT ELECTRICITY COMPANY (JDECO)

Ata Al Biary
JERUSALEM DISTRICT ELECTRICITY COMPANY (JDECO)

Sharhabeel Al-Zaeem
SHARHABEEL AL-ZAEEM AND ASSOCIATES

Haytham L. Al-Zu'bi
AL-ZU'BI LAW OFFICE, ADVOCATES & LEGAL CONSULTANTS

Mohammed Amarneh
THE DEMOCRACY AND WORKERS RIGHTS CENTER

Moayad Amouri
PRICEWATERHOUSECOOPERS

Nada Atrash
ARCHITECTURE & DESIGN

Ali Faroun
PALESTINIAN MONETARY AUTHORITY

Samir Huleileh
PADICO

Hiba I. Husseini
Husseini & Husseini

Nabil Isifan
Netham, DPK Consulting, a Division of ARD

Fadi Kattan
Transjordanian Engineering Ltd.

Mohamed Khader
Lausanne Trading Consultants

Michael F. Orfaly
PricewaterhouseCoopers

Wael Sa'adi
PricewaterhouseCoopers

Samir Sahhar
Office of Samir Sahhar

Maysa Sirhan
Palestinian Monetary Authority

YEMEN, REP.

Tariq Abdullah
Law Offices of Sheikh Tariq Abdullah

Khaled Al Buraihi
Khaled Al Buraihi for Advocacy & Legal Services

Yaser Al-Adimi
Abdul Gabar A. Al-Adimi for Construction & Trade

Adel Aldhahab
Alsanabani & Aldhahab Law Office

Mohamed Taha Hamood Al-Hashimi
Mohamed Taha Hamood & Co.

Abdulkadir AL-Hebshi
ALCO - Advocacy and Legal Consultatians Office

Rashad Khalid Al-Howiadi
Central Bank of Yemen

Ismail Ahmed Alwazir
Alwazir Consultants, Advocates & Legal Research

Randall Cameron
KPMG

Abdulla Farouk Luqman
Luqman Legal Advocates & Legal Consultants

Nowar M. Mejanni
KPMG

Esam Nadeesh
ALCO - Advocacy and Ligal Consultatians Office

Khaled Mohammed Salem Ali
Luqman Legal Advocates & Legal Consultants

ZAMBIA

Anessie Banda Bobo
Patents and Companies Registration Office (PACRO)

Gyavira Bwalya
ZESCO Ltd

Bonaventure Chibamba Mutale
Ellis & Co.

Mwelwa Chibesakunda
Chibesakunda & Company (part of DLA Piper Group)

Sydney Chisenga
Corpus Legal Practitioners

Eddie Musonda Chunga
Ministry of Land

Arshad A Dudhia
Musa Dudhia & Company

Robin Durairajah
Chibesakunda & Company (part of DLA Piper Group)

Grant Henderson
Chibesakunda & Company (part of DLA Piper Group)

Mubanga Kangwa
Chibesakunda & Company (part of DLA Piper Group)

Liywalii Kanyimba
PricewaterhouseCoopers

Chance Kaonga
National Council for Construction

Mutale Kasonde
Chibesakunda & Company (part of DLA Piper Group)

Kirstie Krige
Chibesakunda&Co

Bonaventure Mbewe
Barclays Bank

Jyoti Mistry
PricewaterhouseCoopers

Gerald Mkandawire
SDV

Paul Frobisher Mugambwa
PricewaterhouseCoopers

Henry Musonda
Kiran & Musonda Associates

Francis Mwape
National Council for Construction

Kanti Patel
Christopher, Russell Cook & Co.

Solly Patel
Christopher, Russell Cook & Co.

Aleksandar Perunicic
SDV

Mabvuto Sakala
Corpus Legal Practitioners

Valerie Sesia
Customized Clearing And Forwarding Ltd.

Anderson Zikonda
High Court Judge

ZIMBABWE

Richard Beattie
The Stone/ Beattie Studio

Peter Cawood
PricewaterhouseCoopers

Innocent Chagonda
Atherstone & Cook

Eliab T. Chikwenhere
Zesa Holdings Limited

Beloved Dhlakama
Byron Venturas & Partners

Paul Fraser
Lofty & Fraser

Obert Chaurura Gutu
Gutu & Chikowero

Patrick Jonhera
Gutu & Chikowero

R.T. Katsande
Zimbabwe Electricity Transmission & Distribution Company

Peter Lloyd
Gill, Godlonton & Gerrans

Manuel Lopes
PricewaterhouseCoopers

Rita Makarau
High Court Zimbabwe

Trust Salpisio Manjengwah
Wintertons Law Firm

Rumbidzai Matambo
Dube, Manikai and Hwacha Legal Practitioners

Lloyd Mhishi
Dube, Manikai and Hwacha Legal Practitioners

Honour P. Mkushi
Sawyer & Mkushi

Sternford Moyo
Scanlen & Holderness

Benjamin Mukandi
Freight World (Pvt) Ltd

T. Muringani
Speartec

Canicious Mushavi
CNMIG

Ostern Mutero
Sawyer & Mkushi

Maxwell Ngorima
BDO Kudenga & Company

Vanani Nyangulu
V.S. Nyangulu & Associates

Ben Rafemoyo
Zesa Holdings Limited

C.M. Ruzengwe
HLB Ruzengwe & Company

Rex Shana
High Court Zimbabwe

Chris Venturas
Byron Venturas & Partners